WILSON:

The New Freedom

WILSON

THE

NEW FREEDOM

By ARTHUR S. LINK

PRINCETON, NEW JERSEY

PRINCETON UNIVERSITY PRESS

1956

Printed in the United States of America

FOR

RICHARD W. LEOPOLD

THE organization of the central themes of this second volume in my life of Woodrow Wilson—the major stages in Wilson's own personal and political growth and the development of his most important domestic and foreign policies from November 1912 to November 1914 —took shape in an obvious way, for the most part chronologically. On the other hand, there were some matters—the contributions and policies of the members of the Wilson circle and American policies in the Central American and Caribbean regions—that did not fit well into the chronological pattern because they spanned the entire period of Wilson's first administration. In order to effect a fair division of labor in this series, I have included accounts of the policies of the Cabinet members and of relations with the Central American republics in the present volume and have reserved an account of American policies in the Caribbean for the third volume.

My method in what I hope is this nearly definitive biography has been to focus the story as much as possible upon Wilson and upon the men and events that intimately affected the President and his policies. At the same time, I have not ignored those currents of thought and action at home and abroad which helped to shape the domestic and foreign policies of the Wilson administration. The result is a considerable admixture of history with biography. Because there had to be some limits to what might otherwise have been an endless undertaking, I decided not to include any detailed discussion of affairs with which Wilson had nothing to do or which affected him only slightly, such as local and state developments unrelated to the mainstream of national politics. It seemed equally apparent that I should not discuss such matters as cultural and intellectual developments in which Wilson took no interest and which are ordinarily not dealt with in political biography.

I have given some indication of the sources for this volume in the footnotes and bibliography. However, students who desire a more extended bibliography and an evaluation of the various printed and manuscript sources for the period 1910-1917 should consult the bibliographical essay in my *Woodrow Wilson and the Progressive Era*, published by Harper & Brothers in the New American Nation Series in 1954.

The research for this volume and the writing of it have spanned many years, and I have accumulated an extraordinary burden of indebtedness to institutions and individuals during this long interval. The Princeton University Research Committee and the Institute for Advanced Study helped me begin my research by making several grants from 1946 to 1949. The John Simon Guggenheim Memorial Foundation, the College of Liberal Arts of Northwestern University, and the Northwestern University Research Committee enabled me to do extensive research in 1950 and 1951. The Institute for Advanced Study and the College of Liberal Arts of Northwestern joined hands to make it possible for me to have a year's leave of absence in 1954 and 1955, during which I wrote a large part of this volume. Finally, the Northwestern University Research Committee provided generous assistance for the last details of checking and proofreading. It is literally true that I could not have done the research for this book or have written it without this substantial support.

Friends throughout the country have been equally unsparing in their assistance. I thank the hundreds of men and women in libraries from Chapel Hill to Cambridge and from Cambridge to Evanston, especially those pre-eminent friends of Wilson scholars, Miss Katharine E. Brand, formerly of the Library of Congress, and President-Emeritus Charles Seymour of Yale University, Curator of the Papers of Edward M. House, for facilitating my research. I am indebted to the chairman of my Department, Professor Gray C. Boyce, to the Dean of my College, Simeon E. Leland, and to my friends, the late Professor Edward M. Earle and Dr. J. Robert Oppenheimer, Director of the Institute for Advanced Study, for their encouragement and patience over the years. I could not begin to describe the debt that I owe to my long-suffering friends who read this volume in manuscript form—Professors Richard W. Leopold and J. Lyndon Shanley of Northwestern, Professor John M. Blum of the Massachusetts Institute of Technology, and Miss Jean MacLachlan of Princeton, New Jersey. Their criticisms and suggestions were so extensive and invaluable as to give them a claim to the authorship, but not to the defects, of this book. I thank Mr. Herbert S. Bailey, Jr., and Miss Miriam Brokaw of the Princeton University Press for their many kindnesses in the past and for their assistance while this book was being published; my old friend and neighbor, Mr. P. J. Conkwright, for his inspired design; Mrs. Marion G. Hartz of the Institute for Advanced Study for typing the second draft of the manuscript; my students, Mr. Naaman J. Woodland, Jr., for his help in checking and proofreading, and Mr. David W. Hirst, for his assistance in obtaining illustrations; and Dr. Thomas H. Spence, Jr., director of the Historical Foundation of the Presbyterian and Reformed Churches, Montreat, North Carolina, for his hospitality while I worked in his library. The dedication expresses inadequately the gratitude that I owe to my colleague and collaborator, Professor Richard W. Leopold, for his friendship and help at all times and in all circumstances. To my wife, Margaret Douglas Link, I continue to owe thanks that cannot be expressed in words. She continues to be my best critic.

It is a fortuitous but a happy circumstance that this volume should be published on the centenary of the birth of Woodrow Wilson. I hope that it does honor to the memory of a great man.

A.S.L.

Evanston, Illinois
March 25, 1956

CONTENTS

W|ILLUSTRATIONS|W

Following page 90

CHAPTER I

The Aftermath of Victory

IT WAS cloudy and unseasonably warm in Princeton on November 6, 1912, the day after the election that had given control of the federal government to Woodrow Wilson and his fellow Democrats.[1] By the time Wilson rose at nine o'clock, "a little sleepy" after the tumultuous demonstration of the night before, the first callers had already arrived at his house on Cleveland Lane. All morning they came—students at the university, enjoying an unexpected holiday, neighbors and friends, and of course the old companions in combat, the professors who had supported Wilson in many bitter battles over university policies. Somehow the President-elect found time to compose a message to the country, which he gave to the newspapermen at noon. It was a reassurance to "honest and enlightened business men" and a promise of government "released from all selfish and private influences, devoted to justice and progress."[2]

Then the procession of politicians began. Henry Morgenthau, Frederick C. Penfield, Abram I. Elkus, and Rolla Wells, all from the national Democratic headquarters in New York, stayed for an early lunch. They were followed at one o'clock by the Democratic national chairman, William F. McCombs, who came to offer Cabinet suggestions and to press the claims of the deserving. After posing with McCombs for the photographers, Wilson led his bodyguard, Captain Bill McDonald, an old Texas Ranger, on a hike through the campus to Lake Carnegie. "I am through with statements," he told reporters after he returned to Cleveland Lane. "I am now going to do some hard thinking."[3]

But how could a man think amid the confusion of the days that followed? "Our little house was a terrible mess and mother, for the first and only time in her life, walked through rooms pretending that

---

[1] For the election of 1912 and events immediately preceding the beginning of this volume, see Arthur S. Link, *Wilson: The Road to the White House*, pp. 467-528; hereinafter cited as Link, *Wilson*, I.

[2] *Newark Evening News*, November 6, 1912.

[3] New York *World*, November 7, 1912.

she didn't see the confusion and disorder," Wilson's daughter remembered. "Even the tables and shelves in the studio were piled high and the easel was pushed aside to make room for efficient young women and their typewriters."[4] Some fifteen thousand letters of congratulation, supplication, and advice poured into Princeton; old friends and new thronged to Cleveland Lane, some urging this appointment, others telling, for example, that the proud citizens of Columbia, South Carolina, had purchased Wilson's boyhood home in their city and would restore it for his use in winter.[5] Nor did the customary social obligations abate.

The worst distraction, however, was the constant public din about Cabinet appointments, an extra session of Congress, and future Democratic policies. Wilson tried to quiet the speculation by issuing a stern warning on November 7: "No announcement will have the least authority unless made over my own signature. These are matters which must be determined by very deliberate counsel and not by gossip."[6] A futile gesture, it only stimulated a new round of rumors and increased the demand for an early extra session, which most Democratic congressmen wanted in order to begin revision of the tariff.

Wilson needed rest and a time to think, not the confusion of conferences and crowds. "I find myself, after two years of continuous strain, rather completely fagged out," he explained. ". . . I want to get my head cleared for what is to follow before I ask for final counsel or form any judgments of my own aside from the big essentials."[7] Inevitably his thoughts turned toward Bermuda, the refuge to which he had often fled before. "As soon as I knew that I had been sentenced to four years of hard labor, I thought of a rest in Bermuda," he declared.[8] On November 16, 1912, he sailed from New York aboard the

[4] Eleanor Wilson McAdoo, *The Woodrow Wilsons*, p. 182; quoted by permission of Mrs. Eleanor Wilson McAdoo.

[5] Wilson soon discovered that he had scant time for winter vacations, but the suggestion that he return to Columbia evoked poignant memories of a happy boyhood. "When I was a half-grown boy," he told reporters on November 12, 1912, after talking with the delegation from South Carolina, "my father built a house in Columbia, which my mother altogether planned. . . . In that little Southern home I had perhaps the largest number of my boyhood associations. Of course I expect to have my same old room when I return to the old homestead." *Newark Evening News*, November 12, 1912.

[6] New York *World*, November 8, 1912.

[7] W. W. to W. J. Bryan, c. November 13, 1912, Swem Notebooks, in the Ray Stannard Baker Collection, Library of Congress; hereinafter cited as the Baker Collection.

[8] Address in Hamilton, Bermuda, November 18, 1912, *Newark Evening News*, November 19, 1912.

Bermudian with his wife Ellen, their daughters Jessie and Eleanor, and only one secretary. Before he left, he issued a statement saying he would call Congress into special session before April 15, 1913.

The voyage was a tonic, an "escape from the turmoil." The reporters on board were unobtrusive, and Wilson found relaxation in long walks on deck, in sleep, and in regaling fellow passengers with stories from his inexhaustible fund. As the ship docked at Hamilton, Bermuda's capital, on November 18, crowds lined the streets and wharves, and the mayor welcomed the distinguished guest. But the ceremonies were brief, and the Wilsons were soon settled at Glen Cove Cottage, which looked out over Salt Kettle Creek and commanded a sweeping view of beautiful Hamilton Harbor.

Within a week Wilson had completed his main task, that of answering a mountain of letters. On December 2 he visited Bermuda's colonial parliament and afterward scanned and wrote a preface for the manuscript of *The New Freedom*, which William Bayard Hale had compiled from Wilson's campaign addresses and brought to Bermuda for his approval. It was, moreover, impossible to escape political cares, as Colonel Edward M. House, Wilson's new adviser, and Joseph P. Tumulty, his secretary, sent frequent reports and advice on national and New Jersey politics, while "letters by the score" came in from people Wilson had never heard of. And of course there were the social engagements that a President-elect and his family could not ignore: a state dinner and tea at the Governor's "palace," a dinner party at the home of a Princeton friend, and a dinner given by the American consul.

For the most part, however, there were few obligations in this "lotus land," where one grew "content with doing nothing"; and the month was a time of pleasant leisure such as Wilson would not know again until he had laid down the burdens of the presidency. He followed no routine but came and went at will, now rowing across the bay to Hamilton for a saunter through the town, now cycling or riding through the island with Ellen. "We were enthralled by the spell of the place," Eleanor Wilson writes. "It was another world—a world moving in a slower tempo—charming, leisurely and permeated with the fragrance of tropical flowers and luxurious vegetation. . . . Father knew it well and showed us all his favorite views and the hidden beauties he had discovered on his previous visits."[9] Best of all was the

[9] Eleanor W. McAdoo, *The Woodrow Wilsons*, p. 186; quoted by permission of Mrs. Eleanor Wilson McAdoo.

way in which the reporters let Wilson forget that he was the President-elect of the United States. Only once did an audacious photographer violate Wilson's privacy, and his angry warning—"You are no gentleman. If you want a good thrashing, keep that up"[10]—maintained the other newspapermen at a respectful distance.

"We all feel ready for anything," Wilson told reporters as the *Bermudian* berthed at New York on December 16, 1912. Important tasks lay ahead. New Jersey affairs, for example, remained a pressing concern, for Wilson had resolved to retain the governorship until the legislature, which would meet in January 1913, had completed his reform program for the state. There was the task of preparing the American people for the coming change of national government and of planning a legislative program with the Democratic leaders in Congress. And there was the problem of building a new administration, from local officeholders to Cabinet members and Ambassadors, out of materials virtually unknown. This was the most difficult requirement of all, for the Democrats, deprived of national power for sixteen years, had fragmentized, quarreled incessantly, and grown unaccustomed to governing a great nation, while Wilson had as yet neither wide acquaintance nor real standing in the party.

Wilson's difficulties were, moreover, compounded by a fierce struggle for position between the two leaders of the national Democratic organization, William F. McCombs, and his chief assistant in the New York headquarters, William G. McAdoo.[11] Their rivalry had nearly disrupted the Democratic organization during the presidential campaign; it now threatened to spread to the ranks of the party workers on the lower levels.

McAdoo, however, had emerged on top by election day. He had been the driving force in the campaign and had been admitted to the intimacy of the Wilson family circle. In contrast, McCombs had sunk progressively in the Wilsonian favor since the early days of the pre-nomination campaign. Although he had given his time and money in the effort for Wilson's nomination, he had never won Wilson's confidence or affection, chiefly because he was too friendly with organization politicians and gave advice too freely.[12] Wilson had made Mc-

[10] *Newark Evening News*, November 22, 1912.

[11] Link, *Wilson*, I, 481-486.

[12] A large collection of letters written to Wilson during 1911 and 1912 have recently been deposited in the New Jersey State Library at Trenton. Included in the

Combs national chairman in July 1912 only to avoid confirming the rumors that he was an ingrate.

All the while, however, McCombs was pathetically unaware of his fall from grace. On election day he talked, "in a wild and crazy way," with Colonel House in New York. He expected Wilson to offer him the Secretaryship of State, House recorded, and "thought he might refuse it and take nothing as he could make a million dollars in four years at his practice of law."[13]

On November 6, 1912, the day following his conference with House, McCombs went to Princeton to help the President-elect make plans for the future. According to McCombs' recollection, it was a cold and hostile meeting. "Before we proceed," Wilson allegedly began, "I wish it clearly understood that I owe you nothing," adding in a second breath, "Remember that God *ordained that I should be the next President of the United States*." McCombs reminded Wilson that he and others had helped and said that he wished to submit names for the Cabinet and other posts. "I reserve the privilege of naming whom I please for my official family," the national chairman remembered Wilson replying. It was "the briefest interview" he ever had with Wilson, McCombs writes.[14] As we will see, it marked his demise as a political leader of any consequence.

Wilson's deep antagonism toward McCombs intensified the President-elect's normal repugnance at Cabinet-making and reinforced his determination to circumvent the National Committee. Above all, because he disliked McCombs, he turned to personal friends he could trust—to Tumulty and especially to Colonel House, a Texan with a comfortable income and considerable experience in the politics of his state who had come into the Wilson organization in a quiet way in 1911.

Wilson and House began serious Cabinet discussions in House's apartment in New York on November 2, 1912, and continued them on November 16, the day Wilson sailed for Bermuda. After his holiday,

---

collection are a number of letters from McCombs which well illustrate his inability to handle the sensitive New Jersey Governor.

[13] The Diary of Edward M. House, Yale University Library, November 5, 1912; hereinafter cited as the House Diary.

[14] William F. McCombs, *Making Woodrow Wilson President*, pp. 207-209. Scholars might well disagree as to the credibility of McCombs' account. This writer believes that it is essentially accurate, if exaggerated. Wilson could be cold and arrogant toward a person he did not like. By this time, his dislike of McCombs had turned into such neurotic revulsion that he was incapable of dealing with the National Chairman in a normal way.

he and House corresponded and conferred frequently until the final Cabinet choice was made. In addition, Wilson consulted often with Tumulty in the Secretary's office in the State House in Trenton.

It was a difficult business at best, but the burden was made almost intolerable for the new Democratic leader by reporters who would not let him think in peace, and by a host of would-be advisers with candidates for nearly every office. The curiosity and gossip of the reporters infuriated Wilson. Making the Cabinet was his own affair, and he countered questions with plain intimations that the newspapermen should mind their own business.

For example, to stop the rumor—which was true—that he had offered the first post in his Cabinet to William Jennings Bryan during a conference on December 21, 1912, Wilson told reporters that Bryan had not been mentioned at the meeting as a "candidate for a cabinet post." "You gentlemen," he said solemnly, "must learn sooner or later that you must take me at my word. I have told you repeatedly that I have reached no decisions, and I object very much to questions which put my word in doubt."[15] But the rumors about Bryan and other Cabinet appointees would not down, and Wilson lost his temper when a reporter queried him again on February 4, 1913. "I'm not here to amuse the newspapers," he declared. ". . . If the newspapers expect me to do [so], . . . I'll be damned if I will." His face flushed, and he brought his hand down hard on his desk. Then, smiling, he added: "Pardon me for blowing up. These stories about Cabinet appointments are all false. I have told you men here in Trenton that I have made no selections for the Cabinet, and to keep on questioning me about it is to doubt my veracity."[16] The reporters continued to speculate, but they asked the President-elect no more leading questions. And when the Cabinet list was finally published, it included the names of three men who had never been publicly mentioned during the pre-inaugural period.

Since he made a pretense of seeking advice, Wilson could not shut out the party leaders who came to recommend, but he held off the office seekers with somber warnings. "I have a general principle," he announced on one occasion, "that those who apply are the least likely to be appointed."[17] And when a reporter at Trenton asked him if anyone had applied for a Cabinet position, he replied grimly, "No one

15 New York *World*, December 22, 1912.
16 *Newark Evening Star*, February 4, 1913.
17 New York *World*, December 22, 1912.

has yet committed that indiscretion." Consequently, Wilson's friends soon learned that their only hope for preferment lay in assiduously avowing that they did not want the offices they had set their hearts upon.

The New York *American,* for example, once printed a story saying that Dudley Field Malone, a New York Democrat, would be named Collector of the Port of New York. Malone took the first train to Trenton and hastened to the State House to assure Wilson that he had had nothing to do with that "infernal lie." Then he rounded up the reporters and said:

> You fellows are all friends of mine; we've been all over the country together, and I think you like me and wouldn't like to see me lose out on anything. . . . And now, fellows, about this damn story in the American, will you print the following in your papers to-morrow? Just say this:
> "Mr. Malone, when seen today, said there was no truth in the story. He is not a candidate for any office. Not only has none been tendered him, but no intimation has been given from any source that he is being considered. Mr. Malone has no expectations of giving up his present work."
> And when you've printed that, boys, will you be kind to a poor down-trodden Irishman and leave my name out altogether?[18]

In his Cabinet discussions, Wilson confronted first the unpleasant problem posed by William J. Bryan, the Nebraska Commoner who had led the Democratic party from 1896 to 1912. House and all other Democratic leaders except McCombs agreed that Bryan must have the premier post. "If I am elected, what in the world am I going to do with W. J. Bryan?" Wilson asked Albert S. Burleson of Texas in October 1912. "Make him Secretary of State," Burleson replied,[19] and Democratic politicians and editors throughout the country confirmed the necessity in letters and editorials.

Actually, Wilson knew from the beginning that he had no alternative. The sagacious Mr. Dooley stated the situation better than most political writers of the day: Bryan is "a gr-reat statesman, that is thrue, an' he might make a mistake anny day an' take the big chair at th' head iv th's boord. But that wudden't be me principal raison

---

[18] Charles Willis Thompson to William Powell, April 4, 1913, the Papers of Charles Willis Thompson, Princeton University Library; hereinafter cited as the Thompson Papers.
[19] R. S. Baker, interview with A. S. Burleson, March 17-19, 1927, Baker Collection.

f'r invitin' him to th's fam'ly circle. It wud be that, beyond all his other charms, with a brick in his hand he's as expert as a rifleman. An' I'd rather have him close to me bosom thin on me back."[20]

Conservative spokesmen might protest that Bryan's appointment would "seriously alarm the entire business community"; that Bryan was more an agitator than a statesman; and that Wilson could not appoint Bryan without being "defiled" by Bryanism, "the worst example of demagogy assailing the National credit known to our history."[21] Mrs. Wilson might protest that a Bryan-Wilson rupture was inevitable and that having the Nebraskan in the Cabinet was "unnecessarily inviting trouble."[22] The hard fact remained, however, that Bryan still commanded the loyalty of millions of Democrats and the support of many congressmen. Not to have appointed him might have caused a party rupture with catastrophic consequences for the new administration.

For the most part Wilson accepted the inevitable gracefully, but he had little respect for Bryan's judgment, dreaded the prospect of potential disagreements over party policies, and in his quandary wondered if there were some way out. Perhaps the Commoner would accept the ambassadorship to England; perhaps he would agree to go to Russia to repair relations with that Empire.[23] But Wilson knew this was only wishful thinking; and he took the plunge and invited the Nebraskan to a conference in Trenton.

· Bryan came to the State House at ten o'clock in the morning of December 21, 1912. "Why, Mr. Bryan, I'm so glad to see you," Wilson said with apparent conviction. "Hello, Governor, I'm glad to find you looking so well," Bryan replied. For nearly three hours and a half the two men talked about Cabinet appointments, platform pledges, and party policies. Wilson offered the Secretaryship of State, and Bryan accepted. "I told him," Bryan later recalled, "that there was one thing about which I felt concerned and that was whether he would regard the exclusion of intoxicating liquors from our table as an insurmountable objection to my assuming the duties of the office.

[20] Finley Peter Dunne, in the *New York Times*, February 2, 1913.

[21] John R. Dunlap to W. W., January 21, 1913, the Papers of Woodrow Wilson, Library of Congress; hereinafter cited as the Wilson Papers; New York *Nation*, xcvi (February 13, 1913), 144; *New York Times*, February 1, 1913.

[22] James Kerney, *The Political Education of Woodrow Wilson*, pp. 287-288.

[23] House Diary, November 16 and December 18 and 19, 1912. The latter suggestion came from House.

He promptly responded that it was a matter upon which we could feel perfectly free to follow our own wishes."[24]

All during the months until the inauguration, Bryan remained unobtrusive and confined his offers of assistance to minor matters. When House visited Bryan in Miami in late January 1913 for a conference on Cabinet and diplomatic appointments, for example, he found the Commoner was in "a delightful humor," "as pleased with his new place as a child with a new toy," and eager to help without interfering.[25] Wilson gladly reciprocated his good will. When the newspapers predicted dissension between the two Democratic leaders, Wilson sent Bryan a few lines "merely by impulse from the heart." "How contemptible the efforts of the papers are, the last few days, to make trouble for us and between us," he wrote, "—and how delightful it is —to me, as I hope it is to you—to know, all the while, how perfect an understanding exists between us!"[26]

Infinitely more difficult than the task of beguiling the genial Bryan was the problem of handling McCombs and of favoring McAdoo without driving the former into open rebellion. Soon after the election, Wilson and House decided to make McAdoo Secretary of the Treasury[27] and to get rid of McCombs, as Wilson put it, by giving him a first-class ambassadorship.[28]

McCombs of course did not know these plans, was still determined to have a Cabinet appointment, and was growing angrier every day at his exclusion from the discussions of the Democratic high command. At Colonel House's apartment on December 14, 1912, for example, he was in a threatening mood. "He says he is no longer a boy," House wrote, "and will not be treated as one, that the Governor has shown him no consideration since last March and that he will stand it no longer. . . . He now states that he will remain as Chairman of the National Committee and will show what he can do towards block-

---

[24] *Newark Evening News*, December 21, 1912; New York *World*, December 22, 1912; William J. and Mary B. Bryan, *The Memoirs of William Jennings Bryan*, pp. 187-188; quoted by permission of the John C. Winston Company, publishers; W. J. Bryan to Harry Walker, January 20, 1915, the Papers of William Jennings Bryan, Library of Congress; hereinafter cited as the Bryan Papers, Library of Congress.

[25] Charles Seymour (ed.), *The Intimate Papers of Colonel House* (4 vols.), I, 104-106.

[26] W. W. to W. J. Bryan, February 23, 1913, Bryan Papers, Library of Congress.

[27] Wilson extended the invitation to McAdoo in person in New York on February 1, 1913. W. G. McAdoo, *Crowded Years, The Reminiscences of William G. McAdoo*, pp. 177-178.

[28] House Diary, November 16, 1912.

ing legislation etc."[29] And in subsequent conferences with House, Mc-Combs complained bitterly of Wilson's snubbing and warned that above all McAdoo must not go into the Cabinet.[30]

The more McCombs talked, however, the greater became Wilson's determination to be rid of him, even if it meant, as House warned, an open break. Wilson told House on February 21, 1913, for example, that "he never got anywhere with McCombs; that he was weak and vain; that he had no suggestions of value to make. . . . He said it was becoming unbearable; that he had made a mistake while President of Princeton in trying to reconcile that kind of people, and that he did not intend to make such a mistake again."[31]

The showdown came on February 28, 1913, when Wilson and House conferred until after midnight with McCombs in House's apartment in New York. McCombs learned finally that he could not have a Cabinet appointment and that his archenemy, McAdoo, would be Secretary of the Treasury.[32] He must have learned then, also, that Wilson wanted him to accept the ambassadorship to France, an offer that was formally tendered a few days later. But Wilson's objective— to exile McCombs and thus compel him to resign as national chairman—was too obvious. Although he was tempted and several times agreed to accept, in the end McCombs decided to remain at his post in order to do what he could to obtain patronage for the men who had been in the forefront of the movement to nominate Wilson. "There is this great gain: if you had accepted the post at Paris, we should have lost your services as Chairman of the National Committee," Wilson wrote, with superb irony, for publication after McCombs had finally made his decision. "We could ill afford to do that. The party will certainly gain by what in this case the administration has lost."[33]

Another crucial controversy during the pre-inaugural period involved the appointment of an Attorney General. No appointment, not even that of the Secretary of the Treasury, was so important, and none would so clearly reveal the intentions of the incoming President; for the long battle to bring the large corporations and allied financial interests under public control seemed near culmination in late 1912.

[29] *ibid.*, December 14, 1912.

[30] *ibid.*, December 23, 1912, and February 19, 1913.

[31] *ibid.*, February 21, 1913.

[32] W. F. McCombs, *Making Woodrow Wilson President*, pp. 216-218, contains an accurate account of this meeting.

[33] W. W. to W. F. McCombs, August 6, 1913, Wilson Papers.

Wilson thought almost instinctively of Louis D. Brandeis of Boston, who had emerged as the most trenchant critic of industrial monopoly and had been Wilson's only really important adviser during the campaign of 1912.[34] Here, surely, was such a man as Wilson had in mind when he told House, "I've got to have men in the cabinet who have passed the acid test of honesty. Men who are brave. Men who are efficient. Men who have imagination."[35]

Moreover, independents, progressives, and champions of social justice made it clear that they would consider Brandeis' appointment a test of Wilson's own progressivism. As Felix Frankfurter put it, Brandeis was the inspiration of most young reformers; he had given "definite directions" for the realization of their dreams of social and economic justice.[36] "I do not know that a better man can be found," Bryan advised. "He has a standing among reformers and I am quite sure that all progressives would be pleased." Senator Robert M. La Follette of Wisconsin sent word that Brandeis, more than anyone else in Washington, could "pull together the progressives—whether La Follette, Democratic or Bull Mooser—and harmonize progressive legislation."[37]

Yet Brandeis was also perhaps the best-hated man in the United States. Big businessmen and their lawyers regarded him as a harebrained radical bent upon wrecking American prosperity. The financial leaders of Boston and their allies feared him all the more because he had led the fight against the acquisition of the Boston & Maine Railroad by the New York, New Haven, & Hartford Railroad—the climax of J. P. Morgan's campaign to monopolize the transportation facilities of New England—and because as Attorney General Brandeis might prosecute the directors of the New Haven for violating the Sherman Antitrust Act. As one Boston newspaper observed, "Nowadays in almost any well regulated trust office in the East the suggestion

[34] Link, *Wilson*, 1, 488-493.

[35] Honoré Willsie, "How the Cabinet Was Made," unpublished MS. in the Papers of Edward M. House, Yale University Library; hereinafter cited as the House Papers.

[36] Felix Frankfurter to Norman Hapgood, February 12, 1913, Wilson Papers. No man mentioned for appointment, not even Bryan, had such wide support from all elements in the progressive movement. See, for example, Clarence N. Goodwin to W. W., November 9, 1912; John Brisben Walker to W. W., December 3, 1912; Ben B. Lindsey to W. W., December 20, 1912; Edward A. Filene to W. W., December 21, 1912; Henry Moskowitz to N. Hapgood, February 11, 1913; Hamilton Holt to W. W., February 28, 1913, and hundreds of other letters in the Wilson Papers.

[37] W. J. Bryan to W. W., December 25, 1912, *ibid.*; Charles R. Crane to W. W., February 10, 1913, *ibid.*

that Brandeis has been formally picked for the position of attorney general is enough to cause a general collapse."[38]

Even before Wilson began serious Cabinet discussions, therefore, the "best" people of Boston opened a heavy campaign to discredit Brandeis and thus prevent his appointment as Attorney General. "An ugly report, which came to me several days ago from a man who ought to know," a Washington correspondent wrote to Brandeis, "is to the effect that a number of strong Boston men are opposing you strenuously."[39] The report was accurate. Immediately after the election, for example, A. Lawrence Lowell, president of Harvard University, warned Wilson that Brandeis did not "stand very high in the opinion of the best judges in Massachusetts,"[40] while Henry L. Higginson, investment banker of Boston, spurred his friends to protest: "We must stop the chance of his being taken."[41] So vehement was the opposition that as early as November 16, 1912, Wilson and House temporarily eliminated Brandeis from consideration, "because he was not thought to be entirely above suspicion and it would not do to put him in such a place."[42]

However, Wilson wavered after the publication of a report that Brandeis would be appointed Attorney General had evoked a flood of commendatory letters that revealed his strength among progressives. On December 21, 1912, Wilson told Bryan that he was still considering Brandeis. Shortly afterward, he asked a Boston friend to get "all the disinterested opinion" he could collect, adding, "Of course I

[38] *Boston Journal*, November 21, 1912.

[39] Raymond W. Pullman to L. D. Brandeis, December 23, 1912, the Papers of Louis D. Brandeis, Law Library of the University of Louisville; hereinafter cited as the Brandeis Papers.

[40] W. W. to A. L. Lowell, c. November 15, 1912, paraphrasing Lowell's letter, in Swem Notebooks, Baker Collection. See also Edward R. Warren to W. W., November 18, 1912; and James Ford Rhodes to W. W., December 19, 1912, both in Wilson Papers.

[41] H.. L. Higginson to Richard Olney, November 12, 1912, the Papers of Richard Olney, Library of Congress; hereinafter cited as the Olney Papers.

In addition, Higginson persuaded his friend Cleveland H. Dodge of New York, a classmate and intimate friend of Wilson, to convey charges against Brandeis to the President-elect. James Kerney tells the story: "Dodge was a somewhat unconscious figure in the situation. His purpose was rather to prevent Wilson from making grave blunders than to influence the appointment of anyone to office. . . . Higginson . . . was the medium who filtered the onslaughts through Dodge to Wilson." *The Political Education of Woodrow Wilson*, p. 285; quoted by permission of Appleton-Century-Crofts, Inc., publishers.

[42] House Diary, November 16, 1912.

know how some of the best men in Boston hate him, but I think I know the reason for that feeling."[43] At the same time, he was in frequent correspondence with Norman Hapgood, former editor of *Collier's* and one of Brandeis' best friends, regarding the numerous impeachments of Brandeis' integrity and professional behavior.

Gradually, however, Wilson yielded to House and Brandeis' other opponents. House and Wilson discussed the Attorney Generalship on December 18, 1912. "I told him," House recorded, "that it was with much regret that I had to advise him, that I liked . . . [Brandeis] personally but he was not fit for that place."[44] And when Senators Charles A. Culberson of Texas and James A. O'Gorman of New York confirmed House's judgment in a conference with Wilson on January 19, 1913, the President-elect finally gave in. A few days later, moreover, he agreed with House that it would be unwise even to make Brandeis Solicitor General.[45]

But where could Wilson find an Attorney General who was a champion of the people among a profession closely identified with the special interests? Representative A. Mitchell Palmer, a leader of the young progressives in Pennsylvania, was an avowed aspirant, but Bryan was strongly opposed to his appointment. There was Bryan's own candidate, former Governor Joseph W. Folk of Missouri, but he was allegedly too radical and was unacceptable to the dominant Democratic faction in his state.

By late January 1913, Wilson was wondering where to turn: "I find no search quite so difficult as that for an Attorney-General, because I want a man of experience and balance and yet a man thoroughly on the people's side."[46] In the end, he yielded to House's persistent counsel and appointed James C. McReynolds, a Tennessee Democrat practicing law in New York. Wilson met McReynolds in House's apartment on February 15, 1913, and offered him the post as head of the Justice Department a week later.

Yet Wilson continued to hope that he might find some way to bring Brandeis into his official circle. There was an alternative, one that Norman Hapgood had suggested, to make the Boston lawyer Secretary of Commerce and Labor, or Secretary of Commerce if Congress created separate departments. In a long conference with Hapgood on

[43] W. W. to A. W. Tedcastle, January 3, 1913, Accessions to the Wilson Papers, Library of Congress; hereinafter cited as Accessions to the Wilson Papers.

[44] House Diary, December 18, 1912.

[45] *ibid.*, January 10, 17, and 24, 1913.

[46] W. W. to W. J. Bryan, January 22, 1913, Baker Collection.

about January 28, 1913, the President-elect admitted that he had been "somewhat impressed" by the charges against Brandeis.[47] But Hapgood offered a convincing refutation,[48] and Wilson resolved to have an end to the controversy. On February 13 he brushed aside Colonel House's objection that a large part of the "reputable" people of New England thought that Brandeis was "dishonest." "He said he had investigated Brandeis' record and he could not bring himself to believe that he had done anything to cause criticism. . . . The President-elect spoke ardently in his favor and criticized Brandeis' critics." House knew the time for silence had come: "We dropped the matter for a while and took it up later and I reluctantly acquiesced in his appointment to the Bureau of Commerce."[49]

Even as Wilson spoke, however, a new anti-Brandeis movement was forming in Boston among the Democratic leaders who were closely allied with the financial interests and feared that Brandeis' appointment would mean the end of their influence in patronage matters.[50] When the *Boston Post* announced authoritatively on February 18, 1913, that Brandeis would be the next Secretary of Commerce and Labor, practically all the party leaders of Massachusetts, bluestocking and Irish alike, rose in rebellion. Thomas P. Riley, Democratic state chairman, and Humphrey O'Sullivan, a party leader in Lowell, visited Wilson in Trenton on February 26, 1913. More impressive than their arguments were the letters of protest that they brought from Governor Eugene N. Foss, Mayor John F. Fitzgerald of Boston, Richard Olney, Colonel William A. Gaston, Henry L. Higginson, Charles F. Choate, Sherman L. Whipple, and Clarence W. Barron— practically the entire Democratic leadership in Massachusetts.[51]

Coming as it did to confirm the advice of men whom Wilson trusted most, like Colonel House and Cleveland H. Dodge, the opposition of the Massachusetts Democrats to Brandeis' appointment was decisive. We do not know precisely when Wilson gave in, but the reporters knew the truth by March 1, 1913. The following day the newspapers announced that Wilson had turned for his Secretary of Commerce to

---

[47] N. Hapgood to L. D. Brandeis, January 28, 1913, Brandeis Papers.

[48] N. Hapgood to W. W., January 30, 1913, Wilson Papers.

[49] House Diary, February 13, 1913, account of a conference at Princeton.

[50] *Springfield* (Massachusetts) *Republican*, February 8, 1913; *Springfield* (Massachusetts) *Union*, February 16, 1913.

[51] *New York Times*, February 27, 1913; New York *World*, February 27, 1913; but especially *Boston Post*, March 2 and 3, 1913.

William C. Redfield, an anti-Tammany congressman from Brooklyn who had made a small reputation as a manufacturer favoring low tariffs.

"You little know how much gratification is felt about the 'street' over the success of eliminating Brandeis from the Cabinet," an investment banker wrote after reading the official Cabinet list on March 4, 1913.[52] In contrast, progressives everywhere were downcast and dismayed. "Brandeis turn down breaks all our hearts," wrote Senator La Follette.[53] "I am pretty blue about the cabinet matter," Hapgood wrote to Brandeis. ". . . A long article in the Philadelphia North American yesterday said it was a clear line-up of two forces—the progressives everywhere for you, the interests everywhere against, and the country will think W. showed the white feather."[54] "It is still a greater disappointment that the kind of influence, financial and otherwise, that was used against you should have been apparently successful," another friend said.[55] However, the victory of the allied financial and political interests in this struggle was to be less impressive than it seemed at the time.

Meanwhile, Wilson and House had been at work filling the other, less controversial Cabinet posts. It was in part a pleasant task, an opportunity for Wilson to honor men he admired. From the outset of the discussions, for example, there was never any doubt that Josephus Daniels, editor of the Raleigh *News and Observer* and director of publicity in the New York Democratic headquarters during the campaign of 1912, would be in the Cabinet. "You may be sure that what you say about Josephus Daniels appeals to my heart as well as to my head," Wilson wrote from Bermuda to a North Carolinian. "I have known him long enough to love him."[56] Wilson first thought of Daniels for the Postmaster Generalship but agreed with House that he needed a more aggressive man, with larger influence in Congress, for that post. On February 23, 1913, therefore, he offered Daniels the Secretaryship of the Navy. "I know of no one I trust more entirely

---

[52] William A. Tucker to E. M. House, March 4, 1913, House Papers.

[53] R. M. La Follette to Josephine La Follette Siebecker, March 6, 1913, in Belle Case and Fola La Follette, *Robert M. La Follette* (2 vols.), I, 462.

[54] N. Hapgood to L. D. Brandeis, March 4, 1913, Brandeis Papers.

[55] Charles Warren to L. D. Brandeis, March 4, 1913, *ibid.*

[56] W. W. to Thomas Dixon, c. December 10, 1912, Swem Notebooks, Baker Collection.

or affectionately," he wrote. ". . . I cannot spare you from my council table."[57]

Moreover, Wilson recognized the necessity of honoring the large group of Texas progressive Democrats, who had made the largest contribution to the success of his campaign for the presidential nomination. Above all others, Wilson wanted House among his official advisers and, on January 8, 1913, offered him his choice of Cabinet posts, except for the Secretaryship of State. But House refused, saying he preferred to remain an unofficial adviser,[58] and worked instead for the appointment of Albert S. Burleson, veteran congressman and chairman of the Democratic caucus in the House, as Postmaster General.

It was an uphill struggle, for Burleson had been too active in his own behalf, while Bryan was doubtful of his progressivism. On January 8, 1913, Wilson told House that he was determined not to go into Congress for Cabinet material; perhaps it was his way of telling House he would not choose Burleson.[59] Wilson soon changed his mind, however, after receiving an urgent letter from Oscar W. Underwood of Alabama, chairman of the ways and means committee and perhaps the most influential Democrat in the House of Representatives. There must be someone in the Cabinet, Underwood wrote, who had the "implicit confidence and esteem" of the House Democrats; Burleson was their choice.[60] The Alabaman's intervention was probably decisive. "I am writing to ask if you will accept the post of Post Master General in my Cabinet," Wilson wrote a month later to Burleson. "If I wrote a thousand lines I could not say more of my confidence in you or of my desire to have the best men at my side."[61]

No appointment, unless it was the Attorney Generalship, was potentially so explosive as that of a Secretary of the Interior, who would play a key role in determining the new administration's conservation policies. Following the election of 1912 there were many evidences that

[57] Wilson's letter and Daniels' affectionate reply, dated February 25, 1913, are in the Papers of Josephus Daniels, Library of Congress (hereinafter cited as the Daniels Papers) and are reproduced in Josephus Daniels, *The Wilson Era, Years of Peace—1910-1917*, between pp. 112-113.

[58] House Diary, January 8, 1913; E. M. House to W. W., January 9, 1913, Wilson Papers; E. M. House to S. E. Mezes, January 13 and 24, 1913, House Papers.

[59] It is significant that House omitted Burleson's name from a "slate to ponder over" which he sent to Wilson on January 9, 1913, and included only one Texan, Thomas H. Ball of Houston, in his list of reserve possibilities.

[60] O. W. Underwood to W. W., January 13, 1913, Wilson Papers.

[61] W. W. to A. S. Burleson, February 23, 1913, the Papers of Albert S. Burleson, Library of Congress; hereinafter cited as the Burleson Papers.

private interests, with the aid of Democratic politicians in the western states, were ready to launch an all-out raid upon the water power resources and timber, grazing, and mineral lands in the public domain. "The public domain thieves are whetting their knives to carve up and divide the remainder of the public assets," a leading conservationist warned. "I could go over in detail the campaigns of some Democratic Congressmen from Western States and show how they have been firing the . . . grafters . . . with the idea that good days are coming when the bars will be let down."[62] The greatest danger, as Gifford Pinchot, the leader of the conservation group, pointed out, was that a state-rights President and party would surrender to the powerful western demands that the federal government turn the public domain over to the states.[63]

President William Howard Taft had helped to wreck his administration and party in 1909 by defying the conservationists in their fight against his Secretary of the Interior, Richard A. Ballinger. Would Wilson make the same kind of mistake, by yielding to what was obviously the majority western sentiment and appointing a Secretary of the Interior to preside over the dissolution of the public domain?

The conservation leaders feared that the President-elect might act unknowingly or expediently. "President Wilson's administration will be wrecked from the start . . . unless he sees to it that the man at the head of the Interior Department is of a sort to stand out against the reaction which is confidently expected by the Southern reactionaries and by the turkey buzzards that are now resting on the fence," one of them warned.[64] "Any let-down in the control of the public assets, whether in the name of 'States' rights' or more 'liberal' policies, will force the issue at once, and no patriotic citizen can bear to think of another administration being Ballingerized. The danger is imminent, as you would know if you could hear the talk of the Southern and Western representatives of the grafters."[65]

Soon after Wilson's return from Bermuda, western Democrats began a persistent campaign to bring him to their point of view and to com-

[62] William Kent to W. G. McAdoo, December 6, 1912, the Papers of William Kent, Yale University Library; hereinafter cited as the Kent Papers.

[63] G. Pinchot to N. Hapgood, November 7, 1912, Wilson Papers; also Amos Pinchot to N. Hapgood, November 7, 1912, *ibid.*

[64] William Kent to W. G. McAdoo, December 6, 1912, Kent Papers.

[65] W. Kent to L. D. Brandeis, December 12, 1912, Brandeis Papers; also W. Kent to J. P. Tumulty, January 27, 1913, Wilson Papers; W. Kent to W. W., January 28, 1913, Kent Papers.

pel the naming of a Westerner as head of the Interior Department. All during late December 1912 and early January 1913 they came to Trenton and Princeton to press the claims of their respective candidates; and in late January Democratic senators from five western states banded together to support any one of five candidates, chief among whom were former Governor Alva Adams of Colorado and former Governor Edwin L. Norris of Montana.[66]

But the more the Westerners persisted, the more Wilson determined to name his own man. There were few men in the country whom he admired as much as Newton D. Baker, Mayor of Cleveland and one of the young Democrats who had led the Wilson movement before the Baltimore convention. Soon after the election Wilson told Baker, perhaps in a general way, that he wanted him by his side in Washington.[67] Then, at a conference at House's apartment in New York on February 18, 1913, the President-elect urged Baker to accept the post as head of the Interior Department. But, as before, Baker refused, saying that his place was in Cleveland, in the front lines of the progressive movement.[68] Wilson then turned to Franklin K. Lane of California, a member of the Interstate Commerce Commission, who was both a Westerner and enough of a conservationist to avoid arousing the wrath of the eastern element. Wilson, incidentally, took Lane entirely upon House's recommendation and met him for the first time only on inauguration day.

For Secretary of Agriculture, Wilson and House apparently thought seriously only of David F. Houston, Chancellor of Washington University and House's intimate friend, and of Walter H. Page, editor of *World's Work* and one of Wilson's oldest friends. Both men were North Carolinians and leaders in the movement to bring the South culturally and economically abreast with the other sections. House preferred Houston and urged his appointment from the outset of the Cabinet discussions, and Page generously supported him. "Would you be kind enough to sound H[ouston] . . . on the Secretaryship of Agriculture for me?" Wilson wrote to House on February 7, 1913. "On that case I am clear and my choice is made." It was quickly done.

There yet remained only the appointment of a Secretary of War and a Secretary of Labor, after Congress, in the closing days of the Taft

[66] *New York Times*, January 1, 1913; New York *World*, January 1, 3, and 23, 1913.
[67] N. D. Baker to W. W., November 15, 1912, Wilson Papers, implies the gist of Wilson's letter, a copy of which is not among the Papers.
[68] Charles Seymour (ed.), *The Intimate Papers of Colonel House*, I, 108-109.

administration, approved a measure to create a separate Department of Labor. There was only one choice the President-elect could make to head the new department. He was William B. Wilson, former secretary-treasurer of the United Mine Workers, Democratic congressman from Pennsylvania from 1907 to 1913, and chairman of the House labor committee during his last term in Congress. Samuel Gompers, venerable president of the American Federation of Labor, came to Trenton on February 24, 1913, to urge William B. Wilson's appointment. We can be sure that he won a cordial promise from the President-elect.[69]

Finding a Secretary of War, however, was more difficult, because Wilson and House failed to consider the matter seriously until a month before the inaugural. On about February 18, 1913, they agreed to move Lane from the Interior to the War Department and to make Walter Page Secretary of the Interior; but the plan went awry when congressional leaders pointed out that Page, a North Carolinian, could not be head of the Interior Department because tradition commanded that no Southerner should have control of the department that dispensed pensions to Union veterans.

In desperation, Wilson next turned, on February 21 or 22, to A. Mitchell Palmer. Although bitterly disappointed, because he wanted to be Attorney General instead,[70] Palmer offered to accept the Treasury post if McAdoo would become Secretary of War.[71] When Wilson promptly vetoed the proposed shift, Palmer declined the appointment as Secretary of War on the ground that he was a Quaker. Many generations of his people had borne strong testimony against "war and the preparation for war," he wrote on February 24. ". . . As a Quaker War Secretary I should consider myself a living illustration of a horrible incongruity."[72]

It was now only a week until the inauguration, and a Secretary of War was not even in sight. Wilson turned to Tumulty for help on March 1, 1913. "I then went to the library in my home in New Jersey,"

---

[69] Neither the Woodrow Wilson Papers nor the Papers of William B. Wilson, Pennsylvania Historical Society (hereinafter cited as the W. B. Wilson Papers), contain any materials relating to William B. Wilson's appointment.

[70] "Mitchell Palmer came at ten o'clock. The Governor offered him the War Portfolio. Palmer was visibly disappointed and will probably not accept it. . . . He wants to be Attorney General to advance his own fortunes as he thinks it would be possible for him to obtain a lucrative practice after four years of service under the Government." House Diary, February 22, 1913.

[71] *ibid.*, February 23, 1913.

[72] A. M. Palmer to W. W., February 24, 1913, Accessions to the Wilson Papers.

Tumulty recalled, "and in looking over the *Lawyers' Diary* I ran across the name of Lindley Garrison, who at the time was vice-chancellor of the state of New Jersey. . . . I telephoned the President-elect that night and suggested the name of Lindley Garrison, whose reputation as a distinguished judge of the Chancery Court was known to the President-elect."[73] At Wilson's invitation, Garrison came to Trenton the next day, thinking Wilson meant to promote him to the Chancellorship. Stunned by the invitation to become Secretary of War, Garrison replied that he knew nothing of the army, was a lawyer by training, and was temperamentally unfit for political life. But Wilson insisted, and Garrison accepted the following day.[74]

Meanwhile, Wilson had gone through perhaps the hardest personal struggle of all—the selection of a Secretary to be his intimate adviser and liaison with the press in Washington. Joe Tumulty, who had served as the New Jersey Governor's Secretary with dog-like devotion since January 1911, was the obvious choice and was pathetically eager to serve.

Tumulty, however, was a Roman Catholic, and the report that he might go to Washington provoked frenzied protest from the virulent anti-Catholic element and an influential minority of the Protestant leadership. "I cannot close without saying that you should not have a Catholic for a Private Secretary," a Georgian advised the President-elect, "for the secrets of state will always be made known by him to his Priest and thence to the Papal Delegate."[75] If Tumulty stood at Wilson's side, another anti-Roman watchman warned, "riots would follow and the results might become more serious than we would like to suggest or think."[76]

Wilson, certainly, was not oblivious to this deep current of anti-Catholic sentiment, and his wife was deeply disturbed.[77] On the other hand, the President-elect was more susceptible to the insinuations, discreetly spread by McCombs and his friends, that Tumulty was personally unfit to speak for the President of the United States because

[73] J. P. Tumulty, *Woodrow Wilson As I Know Him*, p. 138.

[74] R. S. Baker, interview with L. M. Garrison, November 30, 1928, Baker Collection; James Kerney, *The Political Education of Woodrow Wilson*, pp. 304-305.

[75] William H. All to W. W., November 26, 1912, Wilson Papers.

[76] Louisville *Pentecostal Herald*, xxv (February 5, 1913), 1. For more moderate Protestant protests, see the New York *Christian Advocate*, lxxxvii (February 13, 1913), 213-214; and the *Lutheran Observer*, lxxxi (February 21, 1913), 228-229.

[77] See the account of her conversation with Colonel House, in the House Diary, January 15, 1913.

he was too much the Irish ward-type of politician, lacking in breeding and social grace. "The trouble with Tumulty," Wilson told House on December 18, 1912, "is that he cannot see beyond Hudson County, his vision is so narrow." Tumulty had nearly all the necessary qualifications, Wilson added three weeks later, but he had "others that would not fit him for the Washington atmosphere in such a place as that contemplated." He had decided, therefore, to offer him "a collectorship or something better," instead of the secretaryship.[78] On February 3, 1913, however, Wilson yielded to House's quiet pleading in Tumulty's behalf, chiefly because he had no alternative now that his first choice, Newton D. Baker, was unavailable.

Informally announced on March 4, 1913, the list of Cabinet appointments evoked restrained approval from all sections and segments of opinion, conservative and progressive. Conservatives admitted that Bryan's appointment had been a political necessity and hoped that responsibility would sober the Commoner and stop him from "that persistent and mischievous meddling with Congress and with party policies that has made him such a disturbing influence."[79] Daniels' appointment, the *New York Times* said on March 6, 1913, had "the look of a noble reward for service rendered." But for the most part observers agreed that Wilson had done remarkably well, considering the paucity of statesmanship in the Democratic party and the obvious necessity of building an administration that was broadly representative and could work with Congress.

Most important, all commentators agreed that it was Wilson's own Cabinet. As the New York *World* correctly put it, "Whether strong or weak in its various elements, this is no Cabinet of political trade and barter. It was fashioned by no political boss. It was fashioned for no political boss. It was fashioned to placate neither sordid political interests nor sordid financial interests. Every member stands on his own merits."[80]

A second major pre-inaugural task confronting Wilson upon his

[78] *ibid.*, December 18, 1912, and January 8, 1913.

[79] *New York Times*, March 6, 1913; also George Harvey, in *Harper's Weekly*, LVII (March 15, 1913), 3-4; and W. H. Taft to H. D. Taft, March 8, 1913, the Papers of William Howard Taft, Library of Congress; hereinafter cited as the Taft Papers.

[80] New York *World*, March 4, 1913. For representative progressive comment, see also Albert Shaw to W. W., April 2, 1913, Wilson Papers; New York *Nation*, XCVI (March 13, 1913), 248; *The Survey*, XXIX (March 15, 1913), 840-841; R. M. La Follette, "The New Cabinet," *La Follette's Weekly Magazine*, V (March 15, 1913), 1.

return from Bermuda was that of establishing his leadership among the Democratic veterans in Congress and planning with them for the special session that would meet in April 1913. Colonel House went to Washington in late November 1912, just before the lame duck session opened, in order to get "the lay of the land." He found all of Wilson's friends confident and eager to embark upon an ambitious reform program. For example, Carter Glass of Virginia, who would be the new chairman of the House banking committee, was "ready to cooperate . . . to the fullest extent" in the preparation of a banking and currency bill that Wilson could approve.[81]

Upon House's advice, Wilson in Bermuda wrote cordially to the Democratic leaders, inviting them to confer with him soon after his return.[82] Bryan came first, on December 21, 1912. Then came Bryan's implacable foe, Champ Clark, for an apparently pleasant conference at the State House on Christmas Eve. Confined to his bed in Princeton with a heavy cold, Wilson discussed banking reform with Carter Glass on December 27. Four days later he met Oscar W. Underwood for a long talk about tariff legislation in the special session. And so it went until the end of February 1913. For the most part, the President-elect talked only about the need for teamwork and courage and refused to be drawn into specific discussions or into party controversies.

One issue, however, Wilson could not ignore, for his own leadership was involved in its outcome. It was the strong movement then on foot for a constitutional amendment to limit the President to a single term.

Having championed a single term amendment since the 1890's, on the ground that the President would be able to "serve the people with singleness of purpose unembarrassed by any selfish interest" if he knew he could not succeed himself, Bryan had incorporated a plank approving the change into the Democratic platform of 1912. Few persons took the matter seriously, until President Taft and conservative Republicans joined with the Democrats in the Senate on February 1, 1913, to win the approval of an amendment limiting the Chief Executive to a single six-year term. Taft and his friends obviously wanted to close the door of the White House to Theodore Roosevelt; Bryan's

---

[81] E. M. House to W. W., November 28, 1912, Wilson Papers.

[82] e.g., W. W. to W. J. Bryan, November 23, 1912, printed in Ray S. Baker, *Woodrow Wilson: Life and Letters* (8 vols.), III, 418; and W. W. to Champ Clark, c. December 10, 1912, Swem Notebooks, Baker Collection.

critics charged that he sought to ensure his own nomination in 1916 by barring Wilson from a second term.[83]

The Senate's action and the receipt of a letter from A. Mitchell Palmer on February 4, 1913, seeking his opinion, spurred Wilson into immediate action. He replied on February 5 with a passionate defense of the right of the people to determine the presidential succession: "We singularly belie our own principles by seeking to determine by fixed constitutional provision what the people shall determine for themselves and are perfectly competent to determine for themselves. We cast a doubt upon the whole theory of popular government. I believe that we should fatally embarrass ourselves if we made the constitutional change proposed."[84]

What Wilson's friends feared most was a quarrel with Bryan over the proposed amendment and the possibility of a second term for Wilson. Actually, there was never any such danger. Wilson had House show Bryan a copy of his letter on the single term amendment before House delivered it in person to Palmer,[85] and Bryan reciprocated by approving a change in the proposed amendment to defer its application until March 5, 1921,[86] and by raising no protest when the House judiciary committee quietly buried the resolution.[87]

Wilson's final task before the inauguration was to rally the American people to moral dedication, in preparation for the coming battles to destroy overweening privilege and to liberate the nation's economic energies. In a series of four pre-inaugural addresses he spoke eloquently of simple things—of service, the public good, and the splendid opportunities ahead. When he had finished, no man could doubt that he stood on the threshold of the presidency fired with a determination to govern wisely and well.

[83] e.g., New York *World*, February 23, 1913.

[84] W. W. to A. M. Palmer, February 5, 1913, Ray S. Baker and William E. Dodd (eds.), *The Public Papers of Woodrow Wilson, The New Democracy* (2 vols.), I, 25; hereinafter cited as *The New Democracy*.

[85] W. W. to E. M. House, February 5, 1913, Baker Collection.

[86] W. J. Bryan to H. D. Clayton, February 25, 1913, Wilson Papers.

[87] The single term amendment dropped out of sight until early in 1916, when it seemed Bryan might oppose Wilson's renomination on the ground that it would violate the Democratic platform of 1912. Wilson, thereupon, gave his letter to Palmer to the press, which published it on January 10 and 11, 1916. At the same time, Wilson's friends warned that they would publish Bryan's letter to Henry D. Clayton, cited above, favoring exempting Wilson from the operation of the proposed amendment, if the Nebraskan raised any objection to Wilson's renomination. *New York Times*, February 17, 1916.

Wilson opened his campaign in a fighting mood, with an address before the Southern Society of New York on December 17, 1912, the day after his return from Bermuda. He spoke from the heart, without notes, not merely to fellow Southerners but to the business community of America as well. "Men have got to stand up now and be counted, and put their names down on this side or on that," he declared. ". . . I want to appeal to you, gentlemen, to conceive of yourselves as trustees of those interests of the nation with which your personal interests have nothing to do."

There had been much recent talk of panic, he went on; perhaps certain financial leaders planned to create one in order to stop the progress of reform. If any man dared execute such a plan, he warned, "I promise him, not for myself but for my countrymen, a gibbet as high as Haman —not a literal gibbet, because that is not painful after it has been used, but a figurative gibbet, upon which the soul quivers so long as there are persons belonging to the family who can feel ashamed."[88]

Ten days later, on December 27, 1912, Wilson went to Staunton, Virginia, for a birthday celebration in his natal town. Still suffering from the cold that had sent him to bed on Christmas Day, he traveled against the advice of his physician. "I must go," he said. "The people of Virginia would be sadly disappointed if I should fail."

Virginia welcomed her distinguished son with crowds and bonfires all along the route of the Chesapeake & Ohio Railroad from Washington to Staunton, while five thousand men with torchlights followed the automobile from the station to the Presbyterian manse, in which Wilson had been born fifty-six years before.

It was a warm and memorable homecoming. "My, my, Marster Tommie, is this really you?" exclaimed an old Negro, who had cared for Wilson when he was a baby. Eleanor Wilson tells a good story: "One afternoon he slipped off to visit an old aunt whom he had not seen since he was a boy. She was very old and deaf, and used a long black ear-trumpet. After a few minutes of rather difficult conversation, she asked kindly, 'Well, Tommy, what are you doing now?' Father said modestly, 'I've been elected President, Aunt Janie.' 'What?' 'President.' 'Well, well,' said the old lady querulously, 'president of what?' Father seized the trumpet desperately and roared into its black depths, 'Presi-

---

[88] *Twenty-seventh Annual Dinner of the New York Southern Society* (n.p., n.d.), pamphlet in the Woodrow Wilson Collection, Princeton University Library; New York *World*, December 18, 1912.

dent of the United States,' whereupon she smiled skeptically and dismissed him."[89]

On the day following his arrival, Wilson received the Governor of Virginia and a host of other officials at an informal reception at the manse, reviewed a parade at noon, and greeted the townspeople in an address at the Mary Baldwin Seminary. He had just begun to speak when Mrs. Wilson walked to his side and asked him to put on his hat. Hundreds of voices took up the request, "Put on your hat, Governor!" "I thank you for the suggestion," he said, complying. "That was a suggestion in front and a command from behind."[90]

He talked lovingly of Virginia and of his memories of student days at the University of Virginia, and how he had often visited five cousins at Mary Baldwin—though he did not mention that he had fallen desperately in love with one of them, who had broken his heart by refusing his proposal of marriage. Then, in a more serious mood, he talked about the tasks ahead and about the need for new ideals of service to replace the old materialism. "Do you suppose that gives a man a very light-hearted Christmas?" he asked. "I could pick out some gentlemen, not confined to one state, some gentlemen likely to be associated with the government of the United States, who have not yet had it dawn upon their intelligence what it is that government is set up to do. There are men who will have to be mastered in order that they shall be made the instruments of justice and of mercy. This is not a rose-water affair. This is an office in which a man must put on his war paint. Fortunately, I am not of such a visage as to mind marring it. . . . There must be some good hard fighting, not only in the next four years, but in the next generation in order that we may achieve the things that we have set out to achieve."[91]

Wilson fired his parting shot during the evening of December 28, at a banquet at the Staunton Military Academy given by the Governor and the Democratic leaders of the Commonwealth. It was a light-hearted affair, with a round of generous toasts, until the President-elect spoke. "Some Virginia people are troubled with inability to believe the Virginia Bill of Rights," he declared with asperity. "Some people were afraid of me. In Virginia, for instance, there was no enthusiasm for my nomination. One of these men at least is possibly

[89] Eleanor W. McAdoo, *The Woodrow Wilsons*, p. 195; quoted by permission of Mrs. Eleanor Wilson McAdoo.

[90] New York *World*, December 29, 1912.

[91] Transcription of the address from the Swem Notebooks, Baker Collection.

here to-night." This was an undisguised reference to Representative Henry D. Flood and the conservative Democratic state leaders who had fought to prevent his nomination.[92] Some observers thought Wilson meant to hearten the Virginia progressives in their war against the reactionary state machine.[93]

Wilson carried his campaign for moral rededication next to the Middle West, with an address before the Commercial Club of Chicago on January 11, 1913. Before an audience that included J. Ogden Armour, Cyrus H. McCormick, and scores of leaders in business, industry, and finance, he lashed out at men who had restricted credit and conspired to establish monopoly. "I cannot deal with you until you make the general public understand your motives, because their belief that you are not acting upon high motives is the fundamental, underlying, governing belief of the way they vote," he warned. "You have got to clear yourselves before the general jury."[94]

The climax of this pre-inaugural series came on January 13, 1913, with an extemporaneous address before the New Jersey electors in Trenton, in which the President-elect spoke movingly of the tasks ahead. Men's minds and consciences were yielding to the new spirit of service, he began. "That spirit is now beginning to thrill the whole body. Men are finding that they will be bigger men and bigger business men if they will spend some of their brains on something that has nothing to do with themselves. . . . Now we have . . . set forward on this journey that is ahead of us. We have found the old road and we are going to follow it, and anybody is welcome to come along with us that wants to, and we are not going to remember whether he tried to find other roads or not, provided he comes along. . . . I feel myself no bitterness about anything that has happened. There are some gentlemen who, I fear, think that I have entertained bitter feeling toward them, whom I would love to see and grasp hands with at the end of the journey."[95]

Yet to thousands of businessmen and bankers the road in front seemed hazardous indeed. Already disturbed by widespread evidences of popular discontent, many of them were driven deeper into fear by Wilson's forthright utterances. Did his talk about a gibbet as high as

[92] Richmond *Times-Dispatch*, December 29, 1912.

[93] New York *World*, December 30, 1912; *Richmond News Leader*, December 30, 1912; R. H. Dabney to W. W., January 26, 1913, Wilson Papers.

[94] *New York Times*, January 13, 1913.

[95] *ibid.*, January 14, 1913.

Haman, for example, signify the beginning of the general popular assault upon property they had so long dreaded? Many feared that it did and spoke ominously of impending troubles.[96]

With Wilson's approval, Colonel House conferred with the leaders of Wall Street on February 26, 1913, in order to quiet the alarm and "steady financial conditions."[97] To Henry C. Frick, Henry P. Davison, Otto Kahn, and others, House had words of assurance. "I told them that *they* were responsible for the unhappy financial feeling and *not* Governor Wilson; that he had said nothing directly or indirectly that would warrant any belief that he was going to make an attack upon business. I said, his utterances while idealistic were intended to raise the moral stamina of the nation, and were not for the purpose of writing such sentiment into law, . . . that while he was a progressive, at the same time there would be no measure enacted into law, over his signature, which was in the least degree demagogic." The tycoons, House observed, were "like a lot of children whose fears must be quieted. They must be told that there are no bears around to hurt them."[98]

In contrast to the fears of the business leaders was the overwhelming response of the large majority of thoughtful Americans to Wilson's call for courage and rededication. "The Woodrow Wilson who has stood up to shake his fist in the face of stock market manipulators is not the Woodrow Wilson we thought he was in the campaign," Frank Munsey's Progressive organ admitted after the gibbet speech. "He is a bigger and better Woodrow Wilson than the American people knew in the contest for the Presidency."[99] "Nothing could please me more than that speech of yours in New York the other day," a leading western Bull Mooser wrote to Wilson.[100]

But it remained for Frank Cobb to give the authoritative answer to Wilson's critics: "Did Wall Street think Woodrow Wilson was . . . a political confidence man engaged in buncoing the American people? . . . There can be only one interpretation of this criticism. Either Wall Street thought Woodrow Wilson was a coward who could be scared, or a demagogue who could be dealt with, or a snob who could be flattered, or a corruptionist who would traffic for the favor of Big

---

[96] New York *World*, January 15 and 16, 1913.
[97] E. M. House to T. W. House, February 27, 1913, House Papers.
[98] House Diary, February 26, 1913.
[99] *New York Press*, December 19, 1912.
[100] Ben B. Lindsey to W. W., December 20, 1912, Wilson Papers.

Business, or a traitor to the principles of government which he advocated throughout the campaign."[101]

Such charges and countercharges, however, were soon forgotten as the nation turned its eyes toward the inauguration and the impending change of government. Before we describe the events of March 4, 1913, and afterward, however, we must turn back to New Jersey and relate the story of Wilson's last struggles in that state.

[101] New York *World*, January 15, 1913; see also *La Follette's Weekly Magazine*, v (February 1, 1913), 1.

Farewell to New Jersey

"I WILL stay on the job at Trenton until we put through the reforms that we have promised," Wilson announced on November 7, 1912. "I will get together with the party leaders and speak for them as well as for myself."[1] All the superficial signs pointed toward a triumphal climax to Wilson's New Jersey career and an easy fulfillment of the state Democratic campaign pledges of 1912—antitrust legislation, jury reform, and the convoking of a convention to rewrite New Jersey's antiquated constitution. The Republican rupture had enabled the Democrats to capture control of both houses of the legislature by overwhelming majorities.[2] Even more gratifying to Wilson was the fact that his old antagonist, James Smith, Jr., of Newark, had retired from politics after suffering an ignominious defeat in the Democratic senatorial primary on September 24, 1912.[3]

Indeed, so reassuring did the prospect seem that Wilson virtually abdicated leadership in New Jersey politics during the weeks following the election of 1912. He met the incoming Democratic legislators at the State House on November 12, 1912, for example, but failed to use the opportunity to plan for the impending session. More important, by going to Bermuda he left his forces without effective leadership in a critical party struggle that preceded the meeting of the legislature. It was a contest for the speakership of the Assembly, which unexpectedly developed into a test of strength between the Wilson forces and the Newark Democratic organization now headed by James R. Nugent, the nephew of James Smith, Jr.

There were two candidates for the speakership—Charles O'Connor Hennessy of Bergen County, a radical Wilsonian, and Leon R. Taylor of Monmouth County, a quondam Wilson follower with an eye on

---

[1] *Newark Evening News*, November 7, 1912. I have transposed these sentences.

[2] The political complexion of the One Hundred and Thirty-seventh Legislature, which met in January 1913, was as follows: twelve Democrats and nine Republicans in the Senate, and fifty-one Democrats and eight Republicans in the Assembly.

[3] Representative William Hughes of Paterson defeated Smith by a vote of 62,532 to 33,490.

the main political chance. Wilson should either have stayed at home and marshaled his forces behind Hennessy or else have remained out of the controversy altogether. Instead, he did neither. Declaring that he had no candidate, he gave charge of state affairs to Tumulty and went to Bermuda confident of Hennessy's election. "I hope sincerely that Hennessy may be selected as you expect. Any other solution would make the session very difficult for me," he wrote to Tumulty near the end of November 1912. "I should be very much mortified to lose in that contest," he added a few days later.[4]

The records do not reveal whether Tumulty bungled or whether the situation got out of his control. In any event, the caucus of House Democrats that met in Trenton on December 3, 1912, chose Taylor over Hennessy by a vote of twenty-six to twenty-two, in part because Nugent delivered the twelve Essex County assemblymen to Taylor after Tumulty had refused to approve Nugent's friend, Thomas F. Martin of Jersey City, as majority leader of the House.[5] The decisive issue in the contest, however, was not loyalty to Wilson but local option,[6] for in the same caucus Tumulty won the election of a Wilson supporter, Charles M. Egan of Jersey City, as House majority leader over Martin.

Smarting from Hennessy's defeat, Wilson returned from Bermuda in a fighting mood. At the State House on December 17, 1912, he learned firsthand that Nugent was working quietly to regain control of the Democratic party in New Jersey after March 4, 1913. In words that recalled the audacious leader who had seized control of the state organization in 1910 and 1911, Wilson renewed his war upon the Nugent machine.

"I have been surprised by numerous inquiries as to whether I would continue to 'take interest' in the political affairs of the state after assuming my duties as President, and yet I realize the significance of these inquiries," he declared in a statement to the people of New Jersey. "Last summer I warned the voters of the state very explicitly that the men who formerly controlled and discredited our politics were awaiting their opportunity to recover their control, and were expecting to find it. What I then said has been abundantly verified by what has

[4] W. W. to J. P. Tumulty, two undated letters in the Swem Notebooks, Baker Collection.

[5] *Newark Evening News*, December 3, 1912.

[6] As Hennessy was a local optionist with the open support of the Anti-Saloon League, the brewery lobby threw its support to Taylor and made his victory possible. *ibid.*, November 20 and 30, 1912; Jersey City *Jersey Journal*, December 18, 1912.

happened in the interval. I am keenly aware of the fact that these men have so little respect for the voters of New Jersey that they think all they have to do is to wait to come back into power.

"They will be sorely disappointed. They cannot again impose upon the voters of New Jersey. If they should in some evil moment recover control of the party machinery they will only ruin the party and put it permanently out of power. Every step they take, therefore, to re-establish their power should be at once exposed and stopped. The people of the state need not fear that I will become indifferent so long as their confidence encourages me to believe that they wish my aid and counsel. I shall in the future use every proper and legitimate power I have and every influence at my disposal to support and assist the new forces which have regenerated our life during the past two years. I shall not go back in this business, for I understand my duty to be to stand back of the progressive forces in the Democratic party every-where and at every juncture, and I feel that in those matters I am under particular obligations of conscience and gratitude to the people of New Jersey."[7]

Twice again during the same day, to a delegation of Georgians who had come to Trenton to offer him a winter home in Augusta, and later to the Southern Society of New York, Wilson reiterated his pledge of continued assistance to New Jersey progressives. "The situation is that a final choice has to be made whether or not New Jersey is to remain progressive," he told the delegation from Augusta. "I enlisted in the fight on such terms that I cannot even seem to separate myself from the state and the fight." "I came here in a downcast mood," he told the Southern Society. "They say you can only judge the strength of the stream by swimming against it. I have been swimming against the stream in New Jersey all day. Yes, we have straightened things out in New Jersey, but the trouble is they will not stay straight forever. There are men over there who are now glorying in the fact that they can count the days until they get rid of me. That's the reason I told them to-day that they are not going to get rid of me."[8]

During the two weeks between his return from Bermuda and the opening of the legislature, Wilson maneuvered to recover control over state affairs. In a long conference with Leon R. Taylor on December 19, 1912, for example, the Governor assured the next Speaker that he bore

[7] New York *World*, December 18, 1912.
[8] *ibid.; Newark Evening News*, December 18, 1912.

him no ill will. "He said . . . that he had not authorized any fight against me, nor had he wanted Mr. Hennessy because he didn't want me," Taylor afterward reported. "Concluding our conversation on this subject, he told me that he was satisfied with my election."[9] The following day, December 20, Wilson discussed revision of New Jersey's corporation laws with his advisers. At the same time, he was hard at work on his last annual message to the legislature.

The Governor's chief concern during this Christmas season, however, was an impending struggle over the state treasurership, which by the end of the year had developed into a clear test of strength between the Wilson forces and the Nugent machine. Wilson's candidate was Edward E. Grosscup of Gloucester County, Democratic state chairman, who had helped depose Nugent from the party's leadership in 1911. In an effort to punish Grosscup and weaken Wilson's influence in Hudson County, Nugent supported Edward I. Edwards, state comptroller, a popular Jersey City banker with large influence in county politics.

Battle lines were drawn on January 3, 1913, after an angry exchange between Wilson and Edwards at the State House. Wilson told Edwards he could not have the treasurership. Edwards accused the Governor of using the patronage against him and afterward declared that Wilson had "cowardly" refused to admit that he, Edwards, had always been a loyal Wilson man. "Even if he has got the whole county back of him, I'll beat him," he told reporters.[10]

Wilson retaliated swiftly. In a public statement on January 6, 1913, he announced his opposition to Edwards' candidacy, declaring, "I feel very strongly indeed that it is unwise and inexpedient that a banker should be elected to the post of treasurer. . . . I sincerely hope that Mr. Grosscup will be chosen." At the same time, he summoned the Democratic members of the legislature to the State House and conferred with them the next day. "I feel perfectly sure of the result," he told reporters as he left for Princeton that night. "In fact, I have not the slightest doubt as to the outcome."[11]

Actually, there had never been much doubt about the result, but Wilson's intervention turned defeat into a rout for the Nugent forces. The joint Democratic caucus approved Grosscup over Edwards by a vote of forty-two to five on January 15, 1913, and a joint session of the legislature confirmed the selection thirteen days later.

[9] *Newark Evening News*, December 20, 1912.
[10] *ibid.*, January 3 and 4, 1913.   [11] *ibid.*, January 6, 7, and 8, 1913.

Meanwhile, the legislature had assembled on January 14, 1913, and heard Wilson's last annual message. After a "personal note," in which he proudly recounted the reforms of the past two years, the Governor outlined a program to bring the progressive movement in New Jersey to fruition: reform of the state's corporation laws, which encouraged monopoly, stock-watering, and the issuance of fraudulent securities; revision of the state's jury system, which was "notoriously subject to political influence and control"; the calling of a constitutional convention, "in which the new forces of our day may speak and have a chance to establish their ascendancy over the rule of machines and bosses"; and a number of lesser reforms.

"I look back with the greatest admiration," Wilson concluded, "to that fine group of men in the Houses whose names all the State knows and honors, who set the pace in the days when the State was to be redeemed. It is men like these who have rendered the policies and reforms of the last two years possible. It is men like these who will carry them forward, and the people of the State will sustain them. . . . The future is with those who serve, and who serve without secret or selfish purpose. A free people has come to know its own mind and its own friends."[12]

During the next few weeks, Wilson and his friends set zealously to their main task, that of antitrust reform, as if they meant to destroy the industrial oligarchy that had its legal domicile in New Jersey. How this situation had come about can be briefly told.

In the 1870's and 1880's a number of producers, notably in petroleum, cotton-seed oil, lead, sugar refining, and whisky, had pooled their properties under a common management known as a trust, in order to achieve a monopoly of their respective branches of industry. However, various state authorities retaliated by forcing the dissolution of the trusts, on the ground that they violated the common-law rules against restraint of trade. New Jersey then took the lead in providing a body of state law that afforded a "legal" means of effecting consolidations, by revising her corporation code to permit one corporation to hold stock in other concerns. First written into the New Jersey code in 1888, the holding company form was refined and clarified in 1889, 1893, and 1896 and soon became the legal structure of practically all the giant corporations. The outlawed Standard Oil Trust, for example, simply reincorporated as the Standard Oil Company of New Jersey; and when J. P. Morgan

---

[12] *Journal of the Sixty-ninth Senate of the State of New Jersey*, pp. 7-17. The quotation is from p. 17.

arranged a consolidation of 60 per cent of the steel industry in 1901, he established a holding company, the United States Steel Corporation, under New Jersey law. Little wonder it was, therefore, that New Jersey soon earned the title of "the mother of the trusts," for the state did a thriving business in charters and grew rich on corporation taxes.

Wilson had raised the issue of antitrust reform during his campaign for the governorship in 1910, but the matter had sunk out of sight during the legislative sessions of 1911 and 1912. And when he had revived the antitrust issue during the campaign of 1912 by making destruction of monopoly the cornerstone of the New Freedom, Roosevelt had replied with the taunt that Wilson as Governor had done nothing to revise New Jersey's notorious corporation laws.

Stung by Roosevelt's attack, Wilson was determined to satisfy his critics after the Democratic victory in November 1912. Ignorant of the law and uninterested in the details of proposed legislation, he asked Edwin R. Walker, head of the Chancery Court of New Jersey, and Bennett Van Syckel, a retired justice of the state Supreme Court, to prepare measures of reform. The results of their labor were seven bills, known as the "Seven Sisters," which were presented to the press by Chancellor Walker on January 20, 1913, and introduced in the upper house the following day by the Democratic majority leader, Senator J. Warren Davis.

Four of the "Seven Sisters" outlawed in specific language all attempts to create monopoly or suppress competition, made corporation officials personally liable for infractions, and sought to prevent stock-watering. Two others compelled corporation directors to obtain the written approval of the state Board of Public Utility Commissioners for any proposed merger of noncompeting firms and stipulated the method of financing such mergers. But the heart of Wilson's program was the bill that became Chapter 18 of the Acts of the Legislature of 1913. For the future it forbade the formation of new industrial holding companies.[13]

In spite of rumors of a plot by the large corporate interests to prevent the passage of the "Seven Sisters," serious opposition to the bills never materialized. First, because most of them simply embodied what the Supreme Court of the United States had already said while elaborating the Sherman Act of 1890, the federal antitrust statute; and no corporate spokesman could protest without seeming to defend monopoly and

[13] *Acts of the One Hundred and Thirty-seventh Legislature of the State of New Jersey*, Chapters 13-19, pp. 25-34.

cutthroat competition. And second, because the key bill relating to holding companies specifically legalized all holding companies chartered under previous law. As Wilson observed, it was drawn "with a view to keeping within the constitutional requirements" and did not

Putting Teeth in It
Macauley in the New York *World*

"illegally interfere with vested rights."[14] Officials of existing supercorporations could scarcely object, while all would-be consolidators could go to more hospitable states for charters in the future.

The Senate judiciary committee held brief hearings on the "Seven

---

[14] Jersey City *Jersey Journal*, January 22, 1913.

Sisters" early in February and heard mild criticisms directed at a few details. Slightly amended, the bills passed the Senate on February 13 and the House on February 18 and became law with Wilson's signature on February 19, 1913. "Honest business and honest men have nothing to fear from these acts," the Governor declared in a statement issued soon afterward. "Those who would engage in the heartless practice of ruining rivals and filching from the pockets of the people more than they ought reasonably to demand are the only ones who will have cause to regret their enactment. I predict that under them the people of New Jersey will enter upon a new era of prosperity."[15]

Many contemporaries hailed the "Seven Sisters" as "the new declaration of independence written by us for our children," as one editor put it,[16] and most historians have echoed their praise. But while the measures revealed Wilson's determination to strike at monopoly, they also revealed his willingness to accept easy solutions, his naïveté concerning methods of effecting antitrust reform, and, in the words of George L. Record, a New Jersey progressive leader, his "most colossal ignorance of economics."[17] For the most part, the "Seven Sisters" merely reaffirmed old common-law doctrines against restraint of trade, and the one important measure, forbidding the chartering of new holding companies, neither disturbed the existing industrial complex nor provided a means of preventing future corporate oligarchy. By striking blindly at an indispensable but often perverted corporate form, it revealed a common progressive tendency to shadowbox with the issue of corporation control.

In any event, the people of New Jersey soon lost their Wilsonian virtue when corporations moved to friendlier states like Delaware and filing fees and corporation taxes declined precipitously after 1913. The legislature began the process of amendment in 1915 and repealed the "Seven Sisters" altogether in 1920.

Meanwhile, with the help of his stalwarts in the legislature, Wilson won approval of other parts of his final program: ratification of amendments providing for a federal income tax and the direct election of United States senators;[18] adoption of a measure empowering the Board

[15] *ibid.*, February 20, 1913.

[16] *Newark Evening News*, January 25, 1913.

[17] George L. Record to R. S. Baker, c. August 20, 1928, Baker Collection.

[18] Joint Resolutions Nos. 1 and 3, *Acts of the One Hundred and Thirty-seventh Legislature*, pp. 793-795.

of Public Utility Commissioners to compel railroads to eliminate dangerous grade crossings;[19] and approval of a bill requiring railroads to use full crews on trains running in New Jersey.[20] However, on the two crucial issues of a constitutional convention and jury reform, Wilson met with frustration and humiliating defeat. Overshadowed by more spectacular events in Washington, this denouement of Wilson's career in New Jersey has been largely forgotten. And yet it, particularly the jury reform controversy, clearly revealed some of the weaknesses of his leadership—his greater concern for getting things done than for the nature of the achievement itself, and his inability to work with men whom he disliked and distrusted.

Constitutional reform had long been a prime objective of the New Jersey progressives, for the state was governed under a constitution that gave control of the Senate to the sparsely populated rural counties, denied the northern urban counties representation in the House proportionate to their numbers, made the Governor a figurehead except in appointments, permitted the legislature to interfere in municipal affairs, and made the amending process so difficult that only two amendments had been approved since the constitution's adoption in 1844. Although constitutional reform was not a partisan issue, the election of an overwhelmingly Democratic legislature in 1912 upon a platform squarely demanding the calling of a convention gave Wilson and the Democrats the opportunity to achieve an important progressive objective.

Drafted with Wilson's approval by the two leaders in the fight for constitutional reform, Charles O'Connor Hennessy and George L. Record, and introduced by Hennessy in the Assembly on January 15, 1913, the Governor's bill provided for the election of a convention of sixty delegates, apportioned in the same manner as the membership of the Assembly. The convention should meet on September 3, 1913, and submit a new constitution for the approval of the voters on May 19, 1914. Wilson was especially pleased by the provision for the election of delegates on a nonpartisan basis by preferential ballot.

With the strong support of political leaders of all stripes from the urban counties and of the leading city newspapers, the Hennessy bill passed the House on March 20, 1913, by the thumping majority of forty to seventeen. It was a different story, however, in the Senate, where party lines were shattered by the refusal of the rural senators to yield their privileged position. Personal appeals by the Governor

[19] Chapter 57, *ibid.*, pp. 91-93. [20] Chapter 190, *ibid.*, pp. 342-345.

could not budge the rural majority; they defeated the Hennessy bill on March 26 by a vote of fourteen to four. The only support for the measure in the Senate came from the urban counties of Essex, Bergen, Morris, and Passaic.[21]

This controversy was merely a prelude to the last and greatest battle of Wilson's New Jersey career, his fight for jury reform. Under the system prevailing in New Jersey in 1913, sheriffs drew grand and petit juries for the county courts unrestrained by any political or judicial agency. It was a system that made corruption and the perversion of justice almost inevitable. Sheriffs in the urban counties were usually lieutenants of the local machine; in turn the machine often sold protection against indictment to saloon keepers, brewers, public utilities, criminals, and corrupt business interests. Moreover, the boss who controlled the sheriff enjoyed virtual sovereignty over the electoral process, because no pliant grand jury would indict for election frauds.

In some counties, consequently, the corruption of the jury system was an integral part of government. "I know I am going to my political doom when I say what I am going to say," Representative Joseph W. Salus, Republican from Atlantic City, declared in the House during the debate on jury reform. ". . . I have served on grand juries, and I have been the foreman of a grand jury, and I was picked by the sheriff because he knew what I would do. He knew how I was going to vote on certain lines. He knew I would never vote to indict a saloonkeeper for selling liquor on Sunday."[22] "It was easier to indict an innocent man under some of the grand juries than to indict a murderer," testified former Common Pleas Judge Robert Carey of Jersey City, who went on to tell how grand juries had ignored overwhelming evidence and refused to indict stuffers of ballot boxes and members of the underworld allied with corrupt politicians.[23]

By the end of 1912, however, it seemed that the time was ripe for reform. Both parties stood committed; the public and the newspapers were aroused; and a special legislative Commission on Jury Reform was at work on a remedy. Wilson sounded the keynote in his annual message of January 14, 1913. "The drawing of grand juries, and even upon occasion the drawing of petit juries, is notoriously subject to political influence and control in this State," he told the legislators.

[21] *Newark Evening News*, March 26 and 27, 1913; *Journal of the Sixty-ninth Senate*, p. 799.
[22] *Newark Evening News*, April 3, 1913.
[23] Jersey City *Jersey Journal*, May 15, 1913.

"This can and should be remedied. You can not neglect it without seeming indifferent to justice and fair play."[24] Then, on January 20, 1913, the Jury Commission pointed the way to reform by recommending legislation to entrust the selection of jurors to bipartisan two-man commissions in each county appointed by the judges of the state Circuit Court.[25]

Although a powerful anti-jury reform coalition, consisting of the Nugent machine, the liquor dealers and saloon keepers, and the sheriffs, was forming by the time the commission issued its report, there were few signs of any open opposition. Wilson called a caucus of the Democratic legislators at the State House on January 29, 1913, and pleaded eloquently for the redemption of platform pledges. Without serious opposition, the caucus voted, thirty-four to fifteen, in favor of legislation that would deprive sheriffs of all control over the selection of juries.[26]

Yet the anti-jury reform forces, led by Nugent's friend, Thomas F. Martin of Jersey City, were already hard at work on counterstrategy. In private conference, Wilson had told Martin that he thought the appointment of jury commissions by the Governor, which someone had suggested, would be even worse than the selection of juries by the sheriffs. At two meetings of the Democratic caucus on February 17 and 19, 1913, Martin sprang the trap he had been carefully laying. At the first caucus, the Democratic legislators rejected Wilson's bill, already introduced by Representative John W. Zisgen of Bergen County, to entrust the appointment of jury commissions to justices of the state Supreme Court. At the second meeting, the Democrats voted to vest appointment of the jury commissions in the Governor.[27]

No doubt Wilson understood Martin's strategy, which was to lure the Governor into a position in which he would seem to be opposing jury reform. But in his eagerness to get some kind of legislation before he went to Washington, Wilson told the caucus that he would yield to the majority and support the new proposal. It was a tactical error of the first magnitude. The plan for jury commissions appointed by the Governor was a direct violation of the Democratic platform pledge of a nonpolitical jury system. Worse still, Wilson confused his own supporters and prevented the formation of a bipartisan reform coalition by his hasty abandonment of principle.

[24] *Journal of the Sixty-ninth Senate*, p. 10.
[25] The commission's report is printed in *ibid.*, pp. 43-48.
[26] Jersey City *Jersey Journal*, January 29, 1913.
[27] *ibid.*, February 18 and 20, 1913; *Newark Evening Star*, February 19, 1913.

Events following hard on the heels of the second Democratic caucus revealed the extreme weakness of Wilson's position. Representative Zisgen introduced a revised bill embodying the plan for jury commissions appointed by the Governor on February 19, 1913. It evoked little enthusiasm from Wilson's friends and stirred the opposition of the Republican minority and renewed obstruction by Wilson's Democratic foes.

For example, Sheriff N. Peter Wedin, a Democratic leader in Hudson County, led a large delegation of sheriffs to the State House in a powerful assault upon the revised Zisgen bill. "It is a bill which, if passed, will make it impossible for the people of Hudson County to elect a single Democrat to office next fall," Wedin warned. "It would practically kill the party in Hudson."[28] The editorial spokesman of the Nugent organization in Essex County, which had opposed the plan for judge-made jury commissions on the ground that it would lead to "judicial usurpation,"[29] now came out in violent opposition to the revised Zisgen bill. "The question thus raised," it alleged, ". . . involves the principle of home rule, popular control, personal liberty and class distinction, as well as the fitness of the people to choose an elective officer, which the Assembly bill flatly denies."[30]

Worse still for Wilson, the labor leaders of northern New Jersey flocked to Trenton to oppose the Zisgen bill during the House judiciary committee's hearings on the measure. "We are in favor of electing our sheriff and of having him select the jurors as now," Henry F. Hilfers of the Essex Trades Council declared. "If you have got to have jury commissions at all, let them be elected by the people. I don't know what the next bill will be; it may be one to have the Governor appoint the sheriffs."[31]

The tide was obviously turning against the Zisgen bill even before the judiciary committee reported it to the House. To recover some measure of control over the confused legislative situation, Wilson sent an urgent message to the legislature on February 25, 1913. "I speak with absolute confidence when I say that I know the public opinion of this State now cries out and demands reform of no hesitating or doubtful character," he stated. "Redeem the expectations which have been formed of us and . . . bring this matter to a conclusion so definite and speedy that no man's purpose can be called in question. Those

---

[28] Jersey City *Jersey Journal*, February 27, 1913.
[29] *Newark Evening Star*, January 16, 1913.
[30] *ibid.*, February 25, 1913.   [31] *ibid.*

who hesitate in this matter will be under a very grave responsibility."[32]

However, Martin and the anti-Wilson forces in the Assembly replied with renewed obstruction instead of "definite and speedy" action. When Zisgen reported his measure to the House on February 26, 1913, Martin countered with an amendment providing that the bill should not go into effect in any county until the voters of the county had approved it in referendum. It was a clever move. By delaying consideration of the measure until Wilson had gone to Washington and by throwing the issue into an uncertain political arena, Martin and Nugent obviously hoped they could defeat jury reform altogether. Yet Wilson could not oppose a referendum without repudiating his faith in the basic democratic process. "All right," he replied, when an assistant informed him about the Martin amendment. "I believe in the referendum. If the people don't want this measure I don't want it."[33]

Even so, this denial of an objective upon which Wilson had set his heart was a bitter blow, and he lashed out at his enemies and told the people of the state that he would return to fight: "I want to say again [that] while the opposition of the sheriffs to the bill is perfectly natural, I know very well the character of the rest of the lobby that is now arrayed against the bill. This lobby consists very largely of men representing interests which they know will be in danger if they do not control the selection of the grand and petit juries. I am in this fight to stay, the traveling facilities between Washington and New Jersey being excellent. . . . The people of New Jersey demand jury reform and they will get it. The longer it takes to get it, the worse it will be for the gentlemen that oppose it."[34]

The days of the governorship were now drawing to a close. On February 25, 1913, Wilson wrote out by hand a brief message of his resignation, and Tumulty delivered it to the two houses. Then, in an appropriate ceremony at the State House at noon on March 1, 1913, Chief Justice William S. Gummere administered the oath to the new Governor, James F. Fielder, President of the Senate. The Senate majority leader, J. Warren Davis, spoke feelingly of Wilson's leaving, and Wilson replied with his valedictory.

"I cannot pretend that I am not moved by very deep emotions today,"

[32] *Minutes of Votes and Proceedings of the One Hundred and Thirty-seventh General Assembly*, p. 590; hereinafter cited as *Minutes of the General Assembly, 1913*.

[33] Jersey City *Jersey Journal*, February 26, 1913.

[34] *ibid.*, February 27, 1913.

he began. "I had not expected to say anything. It would, indeed, have been my preference not to say anything because there are some feelings that are too deep for words and that seem to be cheapened by being put into words.

"I already loved the State of New Jersey when I became its Governor, but that love has been deepened and intensified during these last two and a half years. I now feel a sense of identification with the people of this State and the interests of this State which have seemed to enlarge my own personality and which has been the greatest privilege of my life.

"Therefore, in handing the seal of the State to the new Governor, I want to utter a few words of poignant regret that I cannot serve this great State directly any longer."[35]

Fielder replied graciously, hailing the man who had been "given for the glory and the uplift of these United States." Friends wished him godspeed in his new tasks, while the newspapers remembered how he had redeemed the state and given the people a vision of unselfish service. But it was not yet farewell to New Jersey for Woodrow Wilson. He knew word had gone out that the free and easy days of irresponsible corruption would return once he was safely in the White House; and he kept an anxious eye on events in Trenton during the weeks following his inauguration as President.

With Jim Nugent in command, the Assembly passed the revised Zisgen bill[36] on March 13, 1913, with a new referendum amendment offered by Martin. It was a measure to make any jury reform impossible, for the referendum amendment stipulated that the Zisgen bill should go into effect only after the voters had approved it in referendums in each county, that such referendums should not be held unless 10 per cent of the voters so petitioned, and that the Zisgen bill must be approved by a number of voters equal to 30 per cent of the total votes cast for members of the General Assembly in the preceding general election.[37] As the *Jersey Journal* observed, the House Democrats had given the people a new lesson in how to use a progressive device to block reform.[38]

Martin's betrayal of his pledge of an "honest" referendum was, how-

[35] *Newark Evening News*, March 1, 1913.

[36] That is, the bill providing for the appointment of jury commissions by the Governor.

[37] The text of the Martin amendment is printed in *Minutes of the General Assembly, 1913*, pp. 800-801.

[38] Jersey City *Jersey Journal*, March 15, 1913.

ever, a godsend to Wilson and his followers. By earlier approving the referendum proposal, Wilson had embarrassed his friends who demanded unencumbered legislation. Now, because of Martin's blunder, Wilson was able to repudiate the referendum principle altogether. "I feel very strongly our party's unequivocal commitment to jury reform and that the terms of [the] referendum in the present bill are a virtual nullification of the reform," he advised Governor Fielder and Senator Davis in a public telegram on March 17, 1913. "Can we not give the people what they demand without qualification?"[39]

At the same time, the President appealed to Mayor H. Otto Wittpenn of Jersey City to abandon support of the referendum principle and to help swing the Hudson County delegation in the Assembly into line behind the unamended Zisgen bill. "The President fears that the effort to tack on a referendum will be construed, in the present circumstances, as a way of nullifying and perhaps defeating the measure," the command from the White House read. "The President's feeling is therefore altered. Our party's obligation is plain, and the President hopes very earnestly that you will join with the advocates of the original measure."[40]

Events in Trenton developed rapidly following Wilson's intervention. On March 18, 1913, the Senate unanimously approved the Zisgen bill without the referendum, while Fielder and Wittpenn joined forces in a drive to push the Senate bill through the Assembly.[41] In the showdown, however, Martin rallied to stave off overwhelming defeat in the lower house. With the support of all the Essex County assemblymen but one, most of the Republican minority, and three Democrats from Hudson County, he won approval of a referendum amendment to the Senate bill by a vote of twenty-seven to twenty-six. But he gained the victory only by conceding an "honest" referendum, that is, one providing that the Zisgen bill would go into effect when a majority of the persons voting in the county referendums approved it. The Assembly then adopted the Senate bill with the referendum amendment by a vote of forty-two to twelve.[42]

Wilson could now have jury reform subject only to the "honest" kind of referendum he had earlier said he could not oppose. However,

---

[39] W. W. to J. F. Fielder and J. W. Davis, March 17, 1913, Wilson Papers; printed in the *New York Times*, March 18, 1913.
[40] W. W. to H. O. Wittpenn, March 18, 1913, Wilson Papers.
[41] *Newark Evening News*, March 19, 1913.
[42] *Minutes of the General Assembly, 1913*, pp. 939-940.

in conference with Governor Fielder, State Chairman Grosscup, Senator Davis, United States Senator William Hughes, and Tumulty in Washington on March 21, 1913, the President agreed to jettison altogether the Zisgen bill providing for the appointment of jury commissions by the Governor and to go back to the original plan for appointment by Supreme Court or Circuit Court judges.[43] It was risky strategy, but it at least gave the Wilson forces a proposal they could in conscience support, and it might win the crucial help of the Republican minority.

The Wilson leaders executed their new plans soon after the Washington conference. When the Senate-House conference committee met on March 27, 1913, Senator Davis proposed approval of the measure sponsored by William T. Read, chairman of the Jury Reform Commission and Republican leader in the Senate, providing for the appointment of jury commissions by the Circuit Court judges.[44] At the same time, the President sent a public appeal and a warning. "We are watching with the deepest interest down here the course of business at Trenton," he wrote to Governor Fielder on March 27. "The feeling grows upon me every day that it is absolutely necessary for the prestige of the party not only, but for the vindication of the reforms we all stand for, that the Jury Reform bill should be put through in its integrity. . . . I feel these things so deeply that I think it would be fatal to submit to any kind of defeat." If the legislature would not approve jury reform at this session, Wilson continued, Fielder should call a special session; and he, Wilson, would come back to New Jersey "and make at least one address to the people."[45] His fighting blood was aroused, Wilson told reporters the following day; he was ready for a final battle with "the same old gang."[46] "I think the whole state will be aroused about the matter before we get through with it; and it is something that is worth rousing it about," he added on March 30.[47]

The battle did indeed come off, but not in the way that Wilson and his friends had planned. The conference committee submitted a divided report on April 1, 1913. The minority, Senators Davis and John

[43] *Newark Evening News*, March 21 and 22, 1913.

[44] *ibid.*, March 28, 1913.

[45] W. W. to J. F. Fielder, March 27, 1913, Wilson Papers; printed in the *Newark Evening News*, March 28, 1913.

[46] *Newark Evening News*, March 28, 1913.

[47] W. W. to J. F. Fielder, March 30, 1913, Wilson Papers, in reply to J. F. Fielder to W. W., March 28, 1913, *ibid.*, promising to call a special session if the legislature refused to approve the Read bill.

W. Slocum of Monmouth County, urged the approval of the Read bill. The majority, led by Representative Martin, countered with a new plan for a state-wide referendum in which the people would decide between two methods of jury reform—selection of juries by the sheriffs under strict court supervision, or selection by commissions appointed by Circuit Court judges. Embodied in a measure introduced by Representative Walter L. McDermott of Jersey City, the majority's proposal passed the Assembly on April 2, 1913.

Although the McDermott bill permitted the people to choose between two methods of thoroughgoing reform, Wilson would accept no compromise at the hands of men he hated and despised. He would fight blindly and, as it turned out, ineffectively, rather than yield initiative and control. Governor Fielder wavered and intimated on April 2 that he might accept the McDermott bill.[48] But the President or Tumulty must have whipped Fielder into line, for the following day he declared that he would not sign any bill with a referendum attached.[49] The result was that the legislature adjourned on April 4, 1913, with the impasse unbroken and the prospects for any kind of jury legislation clouded. One wag in the Assembly voiced the popular disgust:

> Hickory, dickory, dock,
> Referendum rot.
> A straight bill knocked,
> Reform is blocked.
> Hickory, dickory, dock.

Governor Fielder's call, issued on April 14, 1913, for a special session to meet early in May, stirred Wilson's friends in New Jersey into renewed action, but they worked against insuperable odds in this, the final phase of the fight. Wilson's earlier gyrations on the details of jury reform legislation had been embarrassing enough, but now he insisted upon retaining leadership in the struggle without leading. Time and again progressive leaders warned that they faced defeat unless the President came out wholeheartedly in favor of a specific jury reform plan as an alternative to the McDermott bill.[50] Yet this was

---

[48] *Newark Evening News*, April 2, 1913.   [49] *ibid.*, April 3, 1913.

[50] Charles O'Connor Hennessy put the matter bluntly: "The President must contend, without reservation, for a commission appointed by the supreme court judge or by the circuit court judge, if we are not to surrender our whole case to the enemy. There seems to be no alternative. If he does not do this he will greatly weaken the position of Governor Fielder and the other men, like myself, who have endeavored consist-

precisely what Wilson now refused to do. "There are some difficulties about advocating a particular form of jury bill in detail, which I will mention to you when I see you," he wrote in response to Governor Fielder's plea that he support a specific measure.[51]

Wilson, on the other hand, had meanwhile agreed to return to New Jersey to renew the struggle for jury reform on the eve of the special session. He opened his campaign in Nugent's stronghold on May 1, 1913, with evening speeches in Newark and Elizabeth. Beginning with moving words about coming home to fight for the people, he went on to excoriate Nugent in terms stronger than he had ever used before and denounced sheriff-made juries as a "disgrace to the judicial system of the state." But when he came to the specific method of reform he fumbled, told how he had yielded his own judgment and supported the plan for jury commissions appointed by the Governor, and moved quickly to a new subject.[52]

Progressive leaders in New Jersey were plainly disappointed by the President's refusal to stand boldly for a specific plan. The Newark speech was "provokingly evasive," declared the *Jersey Journal* of Jersey City, heretofore one of Wilson's strongest editorial champions in the state. "He did not come within a mile of hitting the nail on the head. . . . Mr. Wilson should tell the people of New Jersey what it is that he wants. If he fails to do so, what earthly purpose will his present visit to his home State to advocate reforms serve?"[53]

The President only compounded the confusion the following day, May 2, 1913, when he met most of the Democratic legislators in a conference at the Carteret Club in Jersey City. Wilson talked in generalities, until Representative McDermott interrupted to ask him to tell the conferees what plan of jury reform he preferred. He had his private views, Wilson replied, but he would not attempt to dictate a specific solution. The conference proceeded in confusion and broke up without agreement.[54]

---

ently and constantly to represent the Wilson view of the situation." C. O'C. Hennessy to J. P. Tumulty, April 20, 1913, Wilson Papers. For strong expressions of the same sentiments, see Nelson B. Gaskill to W. W., April 15, 1913; James Kerney to J. P. Tumulty, April 19, 1913; and Winston Paul to J. P. Tumulty, April 23, 1913, all in *ibid*.

[51] W. W. to J. F. Fielder, April 30, 1913, *ibid*.

[52] The *Newark Evening News*, May 2, 1913, prints the most reliable texts of Wilson's Newark and Elizabeth speeches.

[53] Jersey City *Jersey Journal*, May 2, 1913.

[54] *ibid*., May 3, 1913; *Newark Evening News*, May 3, 1913; *New York Times*, May 3, 1913.

During the evening of the same day, Wilson returned to Jersey City for the concluding address of his brief tour. He was haggard, worn, and short-tempered. "Your very generous reception of me to-night makes me feel very much more comfortable than I did this forenoon, for example, in another part of the city," he began in a barbed reference to McDermott, "where the tender sensibilities of one of the Assemblymen from this county led me to conclude that he considered it an affront to his personal dignity that I should, without his invitation, have come into the county over which his influence so beneficently presided." In the remainder of his speech, however, the President avoided any exposition of a specific jury reform measure and ended with a new blast at the Nugent organization.[55]

In spite of his refusal to stand for a plan, Wilson's campaign served one important purpose: it confirmed the conviction of most party leaders that the jury reform controversy must end before it ruined the party and ensured a Republican victory in the impending gubernatorial and legislative campaigns. At a conference with the President at the Carteret Club during the afternoon of May 2, 1913, Governor Fielder, Mayor Wittpenn, Senator Davis, State Chairman Grosscup, and other Wilson leaders struggled to find a solution. In the end they approved a new plan for county jury commissions composed of the sheriff and another member appointed by the Chancellor, or head of the Chancery Court of New Jersey. Moreover, they agreed, as a last resort, to permit the people to vote upon the plan in a state-wide referendum, if that were necessary to obtain a legislative majority for the measure.[56]

When the special session convened on May 6, 1913, however, the Wilson leaders at first worked hard to force the adoption of the Chancellor-sheriff plan, which was embodied in a bill introduced by the House majority leader, Charles M. Egan of Jersey City, without any provision for a referendum. For a time it seemed they would succeed, especially after they won approval of the Egan bill by the Democratic caucus on May 6 and defeated Martin in two test votes in the Assembly on the following day. But in the crucial struggle in the lower house on May 9, 1913, the Wilson managers failed either to obtain a majority for the Egan bill without a referendum or to prevent Martin from introducing a substitute measure.

A few intransigent progressives urged the President to go down fighting rather than concede victory to Martin and Nugent on the

---

[55] *New York Times*, May 3, 1913.
[56] *Newark Evening News*, May 3, 1913; Jersey City *Jersey Journal*, May 3, 1913.

referendum issue.[57] By now, however, most Democratic leaders were, as Governor Fielder put it, "sick of the whole jury reform fracas"[58] and willing to accept the referendum, if that would bring peace to the shattered party. They thus agreed in a conference following the hectic Assembly session of May 9; Tumulty gave the President's assent the next day; and Speaker Taylor, who had not become personally involved in the controversy, volunteered to try to win a majority for the Egan bill with a referendum amendment.[59]

It was quickly done. When the Assembly convened on May 12, 1913, Martin withdrew his substitute measure and the Egan bill, with a referendum amendment attached, was approved by a vote of thirty-nine to fifteen. Only the Republicans and a few irreconcilable Wilsonians were in opposition.[60] Then, on May 26, the Senate approved the revised Egan bill, and the long fight was over. At the same time, the legislature approved a special jury reform bill offered by the Governor. Under its terms, which went into effect immediately and would be nullified only if the people approved the Egan bill in the November election, the sheriff would prepare jury lists and draw the names of jurors under the strict surveillance of the justices of the state Supreme Court.[61] The Fielder bill was not long in operation, however, for the voters approved the Egan Act by a majority of 30,000 on November 4, 1913.

By the end of the jury reform ordeal Wilson was involved in momentous national questions and serious diplomatic crises, sick of New Jersey politics, and eager to abandon his promises to lead the progressive forces of his state. For example, when Matthew C. Ely, editor of the Hoboken *Hudson Observer*, appealed to him to come out against Frank Hague, the Nugent leader in Jersey City, who had won nomination for the city commission, Wilson refused. "I see little points of irritation already," he wrote on June 4, 1913, "which convince me that my intervention in the matter of the pending elections in Jersey City

[57] George M. LaMonte to J. P. Tumulty, May 13, 1913, Wilson Papers; Simon P. Northrup to J. P. Tumulty, May 13, 1913, *ibid.*

[58] *New York Times*, May 10, 1913.

[59] Taylor told the story of these maneuvers in a statement printed in the *Newark Evening News*, May 19, 1913.

[60] *Minutes of the General Assembly, 1913*, pp. 1988-1990.

[61] The Egan Act is Chapter 20 of the Acts of the special session; the Fielder Act is Chapter 1. They are printed in *Acts of the One Hundred and Thirty-seventh Legislature*, pp. 803-806, 828-834.

might be much more harmful than beneficial."[62] As he had indicated earlier, he did not wish "even to seem to assume the role of leadership, which has naturally passed to others."[63]

As much as he would have now liked to withdraw, Wilson could not ignore the most important question facing the New Jersey party leaders in the spring of 1913—the succession to the governorship. A veteran Democrat, Frank S. Katzenbach of Trenton, had entered the race in December 1912 with the support of the Nugent machine; but as Nugent soon shifted his support, Katzenbach never had a chance. The real contenders were Governor Fielder and Mayor Wittpenn of Jersey City, the leader of progressive Democrats in Hudson County. Although he was the strongest candidate at the outset, Wittpenn rapidly lost strength during the spring when his enemy in Jersey City, Frank Hague, joined forces with Nugent in support of Fielder. It was Hague's way of destroying Wittpenn's power and making himself master of the Hudson County Democracy. At the same time that he profited from the Hague-Nugent vendetta against Wittpenn, Fielder gained strong support among the Wilsonians in consequence of his unflinching loyalty to the President during the jury reform fight.

What the Wilson leaders feared the most was an open fight between Wittpenn and Fielder and a rupture in the progressive ranks. When neither Wittpenn nor Fielder would withdraw, Tumulty took charge in June and July 1913. Through conference and correspondence he found that most New Jersey Wilsonians agreed that the President must support Fielder and persuade the Jersey City Mayor to withdraw. "Political matters in the Democratic party have reached a point where it is absolutely necessary that something be done if the progressive Democracy is to be solidified and preserved," warned the editor of the *Elizabeth Evening Times*. "There must be some arrangement that will bring most of the followers of Fielder and Wittpenn together."[64] Only Wilson had sufficient prestige to force such a union, the state highway commissioner declared.[65]

It was not pleasant to have to choose between loyal supporters, but the choice was inevitable, especially after Fielder promised to maintain the fight against the Nugent machine and to carry on the Wilson

[62] M. C. Ely to W. W., May 19, 1913, Wilson Papers; W. W. to M. C. Ely, May 27 and June 4, 1913, *ibid.*

[63] W. W. to W. F. Sadler, Jr., May 23, 1913, *ibid.*

[64] L. T. Russell to J. P. Tumulty, July 19, 1913, *ibid.*

[65] E. A. Stevens to W. W., July 3, 1913, *ibid.*

policies.[66] "It has given me a great deal of concern that, in view of your having been generous enough to consult me with regard to the advisability of your becoming a candidate for the nomination for Governor at the primaries, it was clearly incumbent upon me to form and express an opinion," Wilson wrote in a public letter to Wittpenn on July 23, 1913. "I felt, as I explained to you at the time you requested my opinion, that your desire to know my judgment forced me to make a practical political choice as between friends, friends who had been of great service to me personally as well as to the public in the political contests of the past two years. But there is nothing else for it, and I yesterday told Mr. Grosscup, as had been agreed, what my judgment was. It is that we ought to support Mr. Fielder's candidacy. . . ."[67] Wittpenn withdrew gracefully on July 25, 1913.[68]

With the support of the Wilsonians and the Nugent machine,[69] Fielder defeated Katzenbach in the Democratic gubernatorial primary on September 23, 1913, by more than 45,000 votes. His nomination assured, Fielder then declared his independence of the Essex organization and tried to read Nugent and his followers out of the party at the Democratic state convention in Trenton on September 30, 1913.

Wilson had had serious misgivings about the quality of Fielder's progressivism, but he now hastened to give his blessing. "I want to express my warm admiration for the stand you have taken with regard to the men who are not sincerely serving the Democratic party," the President wrote in public commendation the day after Fielder repudiated Nugent's support. "It will straighten the lines of attack at every point and I feel confident that the people of the state will rally to your support in such fashion as once again to emphasize their allegiance to the things that are right and which look forward to a future of increasing justice and righteous achievement in the field of government." "I cannot refrain from giving myself the opportunity to say to you that you have begun your fight along exactly the right lines," Wilson added a week later. ". . . I believe that you never did any-

---

[66] Redmond F. Kernan to J. P. Tumulty, June 11, 1913, *ibid.*

[67] W. W. to H. O. Wittpenn, July 23, 1913, *ibid.*; printed in the *New York Times*, July 27, 1913.

[68] H. O. Wittpenn to W. W., July 25, 1913, Wilson Papers.

[69] "Every anti-Wilson man that I have met in the State of New Jersey is in a jubilant frame of mind," wrote one of Wittpenn's friends after his withdrawal. "For instance, I know that Mr. Smith [James Smith, Jr.] has expressed great satisfaction because the one thing that he wished to accomplish was the elimination of Mr. Wittpenn." G. M. LaMonte to W. W., July 30, 1913, *ibid.*

thing to set your cause and ours forward more distinctly than to come out at the very beginning as you did in direct avowal of the facts. Along this line lies victory; along any other may lie defeat. The people of the State supported me in these things, and they will support you, for New Jersey is for clean, decent government."[70]

Fielder's blast at Nugent set the Newark machine hard to work for the Republican candidate, Edward C. Stokes, and raised the specter of a Republican victory in a contest which the entire nation regarded as a crucial test for the President.[71] Thus Wilson's friends begged him to come back and take charge of the campaign. "You and President Wilson have got to win this fight," one of them wrote to Tumulty, "and you might just as well make up your mind to do that or we are doomed to defeat."[72] But Wilson refused to be drawn into the campaign, except to give his approval to Fielder by public letters and to send Bryan and other Democratic leaders into the state. Actually, the outcome was never in doubt, in spite of the panic of the Wilson men. Because of the continued disruption of the G.O.P., Fielder won the governorship by a plurality of nearly 33,000, while the Democrats again carried both houses of the legislature.

On the surface, it seemed that the results in New Jersey were an emphatic mandate for the continuation of the Wilson policies. "I am sure that no small part of it [the victory]," Wilson wrote in congratulation to the Governor, "was due to the conviction,—which must be stronger now than ever, after the splendid campaign you have conducted,—that you are able to set the State forward in her course of honest and well-considered reform."[73]

The truth was, however, that the election of 1913 marked a turning point in the twentieth-century political history of New Jersey: a reversion from Democratic insurgency toward a traditional pattern in state politics. While Fielder won the governorship, Nugent remained master of the Essex County machine and Hague extended his control over Hudson County. Hereafter, the Hague-Nugent combination would grow in power until it had won mastery of the Democratic party in New Jersey by 1917.

The extent to which Fielder and the Wilson Democrats had lost

[70] W. W. to J. F. Fielder, October 1 and 8, 1913, *ibid.*

[71] W. C. Gebhardt to J. P. Tumulty, October 1, 1913, *ibid.*; William McTague to J. P. Tumulty, October 3, 1913, *ibid.*; A. B. Cosey to J. P. Tumulty, October 13, 1913, *ibid.*

[72] L. T. Russell to J. P. Tumulty, October 1, 1913, *ibid.*

[73] W. W. to J. F. Fielder, November 7, 1913, *ibid.*

control of the state was amply demonstrated when the legislature convened in January 1914. "I have been up against some difficult legislative situations during my experience at Trenton," Fielder wrote at the end of the session, "but this is the worst that I ever encountered. There are several factions of Democrats and at least two of the Republicans with outside influences constantly at work on each and beside the Democratic Assemblymen, for the most part, are the most unreliable lot of men we ever had to deal with. One never knows upon whom he can count to assist in legislation. This Legislature will adjourn with practically all of our Party promises unfulfilled."[74]

By the spring of 1914 Wilson had lost all personal interest in New Jersey affairs and had given charge of the federal patronage in the state to Tumulty and Postmaster General Burleson. More concerned with winning a Democratic majority in the congressional elections of 1914 than with building progressive strength, Tumulty and Burleson called off Wilson's war against the New Jersey bosses and set about supporting the strongest county factions, regardless of their political character, even though this policy compelled recognition of men whom Wilson had once scourged and also implied the betrayal of loyal Wilsonians.

The case that marked the beginning of this shift in policy was the appointment of J. J. O'Hanlon, a Nugent lieutenant and one of Wilson's bitterest foes in Essex County, as postmaster of South Orange in May 1914, in order to ensure the re-election of Congressman Edward W. Townsend of Montclair. The progressive Democrats in Essex County, who had risked their political lives by trying to wrest control of the county organization from Nugent, were stunned.

The appointment "will have malevolent effects throughout the whole of Essex," the president of the Democratic Club of South Orange wrote in protest, "and is taken as a definite note of an understanding with the underworld of politics—a blow at the first causes for Wilson as a political power and a principle. It is virtually a Notice to Quit to those who have held principle and Wilsonism above Bossism and party manipulation for personal ends. It is a confession of surrender to the Old Gang, . . . a statement that principles enunciated at Trenton find no echo at Washington."[75] "Cases of this kind are developing every day in New Jersey," Wittpenn observed.[76]

[74] J. F. Fielder to J. P. Tumulty, March 26, 1914, *ibid.*
[75] James F. McGrath to Senator J. E. Martine, May 16, 1914, *ibid.*
[76] H. O. Wittpenn to J. P. Tumulty, May 7, 1914, *ibid.*

But the Washington administration persevered in the new policy, although the Republicans captured the legislature in 1914 and the governorship in 1916. By 1916 the Wilson war against "the same old gang" was over, and during the following years the President's feeling toward his former enemies mellowed. "Nugent is a strange fellow, and while we had some powerful disagreements I always had a sneaking feeling of regard for him," Wilson later told a friend. For his part, "Nugent, in the later years, had come to regard the Wilson leadership of the party as providential, although disagreeing with what he termed the surrender on woman-suffrage and other advanced ideas. It was the Nugent organization in Essex County that gave Wilson his best latter-day support in New Jersey."[77]

This was the way in which the old Hudson-Essex axis regained control of the Democratic party in New Jersey, with the active support of the man who had once said that he was "under particular obligations of conscience and gratitude" to persevere in the fight for clean and forward-looking government. Meanwhile, the disinherited progressives had retired to wage a rearguard action that would not again develop into a frontal assault until the years following the Second World War.

[77] James Kerney, *The Political Education of Woodrow Wilson*, pp. 471-472; quoted by permission of Appleton-Century-Crofts, Inc., publishers.

CHAPTER III

The President of the United States

IT WAS hard for Wilson to leave Princeton, the village of his youth and manhood. There were memories too intimate to be told, chords of friendship and hatred that bound him to the place. "We are not as light-hearted as we might be," he wrote a few days before going to Washington. "Much as we have suffered in Princeton, deep as are the wounds our hearts have received here, it goes hard with us to leave it."[1]

It would have been easier not to say good-by, but students, friends, and townspeople would not let him go without a last farewell. On Saturday night, March 1, 1913, some fifteen hundred of them gathered in front of the house on Cleveland Lane, while a local spokesman made a brief speech and handed Wilson a silver loving cup from "the Citizens of Princeton."

"I feel very deeply complimented that you should have gathered here tonight to say good-bye to me and to bid me godspeed," he replied. "I have felt a very intimate identification with this town. . . . I am turning away from this place in body but not in spirit, and I am doing it with genuine sadness. The real trials of life are the connections you break, and when a man has lived in one place as long as I have lived in Princeton . . . he knows what it means to change his residence and to go into strange environments and surroundings.

"I have never been inside of the White House, and I shall feel very strange when I get inside of it. I shall think of this little house behind me and remember how much more familiar it is to me than that is, and how much more intimate a sense of possession there must be in the one case than in the other.

"One cannot be neighbor to the whole United States. I shall miss my neighbors. I shall miss the daily contact with the men I know and by whom I am known, and one of the happiest things in my thoughts will be that your good wishes go with me. . . . With your confidence and

[1] W. W. to Mary A. Hulbert, February 23, 1913, printed in R. S. Baker, *Woodrow Wilson*, IV, 3.

the confidence of men like you, the task that lies before me will be gracious and agreeable."[2]

There was a last farewell on the day of leaving, Monday, March 3, 1913. "With motor cars standing in line, a crowd around the house and Secret Service men waiting on the doorstep," Eleanor Wilson recalled, "father and mother suddenly rebelled and, leaving us to follow, walked alone to the station where the special train was waiting."[3] We can only wonder what they said to each other as they walked down Library Place, past the home they had built and loved. We can only guess what memories filled Wilson's mind as they went through the campus of the university in which the battles of the Wilson era still reverberated. Those memories must have been sad and bitter. The special train filled with students, with a private car for the Wilsons, was ready for them at the station. "We stood on the back platform when the train pulled out and, although father and mother were smiling and waving, I thought they both looked very wistful as the lovely classic towers of Princeton faded in the distance."[4]

Ellen never saw Princeton again. Wilson returned to vote in the Democratic primary on September 23, 1913, and stayed for three hours. "All my old feeling about the place surged over me, a mixture of affection and tragedy," he wrote soon afterward. He met his former intimate and successor as president of the university, John Grier Hibben, and his mortal foe, Dean Andrew F. West. "I was not obliged to speak to West," he said, "but I met Hibben face to face and had to force myself to behave as I knew I should, not cordially (that was spiritually impossible) but politely."[5]

Wilson came back a second time for a reunion of his class of 1879 on June 13, 1914. "I . . . must admit that it cost me a great deal to be there myself," he confided afterward to a friend. "Fortunately, the thing was so arranged as not to bring me into contact with men whom it would be embarrassing for me to meet, and the day went off as delightful as it could."[6]

Afterward, the President came to Princeton only to vote and returned to Washington as quickly as possible; and as the months and years passed, the bitter memories crowded out the happy ones, and love

[2] *New York Times*, March 2, 1913.
[3] Eleanor W. McAdoo, *The Woodrow Wilsons*, p. 199; quoted by permission of Eleanor Wilson McAdoo.
[4] *ibid.*
[5] W. W. to X, September 28, 1913.
[6] W. W. to X, June 17, 1914, Wilson Papers.

for his alma mater turned to scorn. Toward the end of his life he could say: "Princeton was sold two or three times under my nose. . . . If I had a son, I wouldn't know where to send him for a liberal education in America; Princeton is exactly what they say of it, a fine country club, where many of the alumni make snobs of their boys."[7]

The Wilsons arrived in Washington in the mid-afternoon of March 3, 1913, and went straight to the Shoreham Hotel virtually unnoticed, for the city was full of rejoicing Democrats and absorbed in a mammoth suffrage parade. At six o'clock they paid a brief ceremonial call at the White House, and then, after a family dinner, the President-elect went to the New Willard Hotel for a pre-inaugural celebration with some eight hundred Princeton alumni. "Fellows, I hadn't expected to say anything to-night, because the only appropriate thing to say I can't say, for the reason that there are no words for it," Wilson declared. "There are some emotions that are very much deeper than a man's vocabulary can reach, and I have a feeling to-night that moves me very much indeed."[8]

Tuesday, March 4, 1913, opened with friendly skies—a good omen, some men thought, for the first Democratic inaugural in twenty years.[9] Wilson rose at eight o'clock. An hour later he conferred with Bryan and McCombs and soon afterward left for the White House with the incoming Vice President, Thomas R. Marshall, and a committee of congressmen and senators. Shortly after ten o'clock the inaugural party left the presidential mansion for the Capitol. After brief ceremonies, they entered the Senate chamber, where Marshall took the oath as Vice President. Taft walked ponderously to his seat in the front of the secretary's desk. Wilson moved more quickly, glancing at the ornate ambassadorial uniforms, the cluster of dark-robed justices, and the assembled congressmen and senators; he looked serious and a bit perplexed.

The climactic ceremonies began after Marshall's brief speech. Escorted by the congressional committee, Taft and Wilson walked to the stands outside the east façade of the Capitol and confronted a cheering throng of fifty thousand onlookers. Then, amid even louder cheers, came Bryan, the other new Cabinet members, leaders from the two houses of Congress, and Mrs. Wilson and her party. Almost before

[7] James Kerney, *The Political Education of Woodrow Wilson*, p. 481; quoted by permission of Appleton-Century-Crofts, Inc., publishers.

[8] *New York Times*, March 4, 1913.

[9] I have relied mainly upon Louis Seibold's moving account in the New York *World*, March 5, 1913, for the following description of the events of March 4, 1913.

the onlookers knew it, Wilson was standing before the Chief Justice, Edward D. White, taking the oath of office. The sun burst through the clouds as he kissed the Bible upon which he had taken the oath as Governor of New Jersey. His lips touched the 119th Psalm, at the verses:

> And take not the word of truth utterly out of my mouth;
>   for I have hoped in thy judgments.
> So shall I keep thy law continually for ever and ever.
> And I will walk at liberty: for I seek thy precepts.
> I will speak of thy testimonies also before kings, and
>   will not be ashamed.
> And I will delight myself in thy commandments, which I
>   have loved.
> My hands also will I lift up unto thy commandments,
>   which I have loved; and I will meditate in thy
>   statutes.

Turning to the crowd, Wilson noticed that the police had cleared a large area in front of the inaugural stand. "Let the people come forward," he commanded. Then, when the commotion had ended, he began his inaugural address with the simple declaration: "My fellow-citizens: There has been a change of government. It began two years ago, when the House of Representatives became Democratic by a decisive majority. It has now been completed."

The change of government, he continued, meant that the nation had taken stock of material gains accomplished at the cost of "lives snuffed out, of energies overtaxed and broken, the fearful physical and spiritual cost to the men and women and children upon whom the dead weight and burden of it all has fallen pitilessly the years through." The nation had come to a sober second thought and resolved to begin anew— to reform the tariff laws and an antiquated banking and currency system and to put government at the service of humanity. It was a task of slow restoration, not of destruction, he went on, concluding with a memorable peroration:

"This is not a day of triumph; it is a day of dedication. Here muster, not the forces of party, but the forces of humanity. Men's hearts wait upon us; men's lives hang in the balance; men's hopes call upon us to say what we will do. Who shall live up to the great trust? Who dares fail to try? I summon all honest men, all patriotic, forward-look-

The New Freedom
Macauley in the New York *World*

ing men, to my side. God helping me, I will not fail them, if they
will but counsel and sustain me!"[10]

His solemn duty over, Wilson relaxed, smiled at the cheering crowd,
and laughed as Taft, Bryan, and other friends shook his hand. It was a
scene that moved the onlookers. There was Taft, the symbol of the
great party that had ruled for sixteen years and was now repudiated

[10] R. S. Baker and W. E. Dodd (eds.), *The New Democracy*, I, 1-6.

by the American people. There stood the Nebraskan, three times rejected, whose cup ran over on this day of vindication. And there was of course the new President, strong in dedication but as yet untested in the great Washington arena.

After the inaugural ceremonies, Wilson and Taft drove to the White House for lunch. The Tafts said good-by and left for the station, while the President and his wife took their places in the reviewing stand in front of the White House to greet the people of the United States. All afternoon they marched up Pennsylvania Avenue, some 300,000 of them. There were units from the armed services and the state militia. There were cowboys and Indians in warpaint, Tammany Braves in top hats and gray gloves, Southerners with the rebel yell and bands blaring "Dixie," and the victorious Democratic hosts from Boston to San Francisco. The celebration ended that night with a fireworks display at the Washington Monument but without the traditional inaugural ball. It had been canceled earlier at Wilson's request, because Ellen Wilson objected to the social ostentation that accompanied such affairs.

It was an auspicious beginning for the new administration. Wall Street accepted the transfer of power without panic or a break in stock prices.[11] Conservatives could not quarrel with Wilson's broad indictment of materialism and his promise of careful reform,[12] while his call for a new dedication evoked a warm response from social reformers, idealists, and religious leaders. "We hope and believe that your inauguration marks the dawning of the day of the new freedom for which we have looked and longed" and "It was a voice out of high heaven and will go forth unto everlasting"[13] were typical comments in the thousands of letters that Wilson received.

The most generous comment of all, however, came from the editorial spokesman of Theodore Roosevelt. "President Wilson's inaugural is the call of a prophet to a Nation to repent of its sins and return, not to the methods but to the spirit of the Fathers . . . ," the *Outlook* declared. "In this appeal *to* the Nation President Wilson speaks *for* the Nation. He interprets the vision of the Nation. He addresses not a sleeping but an awakened conscience."[14] No man could tell what the

[11] *Financial World*, xxvii (March 8 and 15, 1913), 393, 449.

[12] e.g., see George Harvey's comment in *Harper's Weekly*, lvii (March 8, 1913), 4.

[13] T. E. Gibbon to W. W., March 5, 1913, Wilson Papers; E. O. Lovett to W. W., March 7, 1913, *ibid.*

[14] New York *Outlook*, ciii (March 15, 1913), 573-574. For similar comment, see the

future held, but all observers could agree, as one editor put it, that "The results . . . will be of absorbing interest to study. They are certain to be big with political change; they may mean the beginning of a wholly new epoch."[15]

What was he like, this man to whom had been entrusted the leadership of the American people during the next four fateful years? Whence did he derive his ideals and purposes? To what degree was he a creature of the intellect; to what degree was he governed by his prejudices and passions? How did he operate in the world of men struggling for place and power?

The man who stood before the Chief Justice and took the oath of office as President on that March morning had changed little physically from the early days of his presidency of Princeton, except that the lines in his face were deeper and his hair was grayer. He was of average build and height, about five feet eleven inches in his shoes, but he possessed an extraordinary physiognomy. A perceptive reporter has described it as follows:

"Woodrow Wilson's face is narrow and curiously geometrical. It is a rectangle, one might say, the lines are so regular. His forehead is high and his iron gray hair retreats from it somewhat, which adds to this effect. His face is refined, a face that shows breeding and family in every line, but it is heavy boned. The cheek bones are rather high and the jaw thrusts forward in a challenging way. The mouth is small, sensitive, with full lips, a mouth almost too well shaped for a man, and a woman might envy the arched eyebrows. But the almost brutal strength of the general bony structure of the face, and that aggressive jaw promise an active, iron willed, fighting man. His eyes, blue-gray they looked in that light behind his nose glasses, are very penetrating. They have a way of narrowing when he talks that gives him a stern, almost grim expression."[16]

This look of sternness when he set his jaw was perhaps the most notable feature of Wilson's aspect. There is a portrait of him hanging in the Faculty Room in Nassau Hall at Princeton, which well displays the grimness of character that his long and often somber face could reveal. In this remarkable painting, his eyes flash through the glasses,

---

following editorials in the religious press: *America*, VIII (March 8, 1913), 518; *The Presbyterian*, LXXXIII (March 5, 1913), 8; *Congregationalist and Christian World*, XCVIII (March 13, 1913), 361; and Nashville *Christian Advocate*, LXXIV (March 14, 1913), 323-324.

[15] New York *Nation*, XCVI (March 6, 1913), 223.

[16] W. S. Couch, in the New York *World*, December 18, 1910.

his lips are tightly compressed, and his jaw juts forward, as if in defiance.

But for all his appearance of resolution and personal strength, there was a frailness in Wilson's physique that proved a serious impediment throughout his adult career and ultimately a disaster. Like Theodore Roosevelt, Wilson had been a frail and sickly child; unlike his great contemporary, Wilson never mastered his physical weaknesses or conditioned his body for the severe strains he put upon it. Driving too hard at Princeton, he had narrowly escaped a breakdown in 1906. He conserved his strength more carefully after that warning, and he contrived to carry the burdens of a strenuous political career and of the presidency until 1919. But he survived only by refusing to allow himself to become exhausted, and this fact goes far toward explaining many of his deficiencies as administrator, intellectual, and friend.

It is easier to describe Wilson's physical characteristics than to analyze his intellectual interests and processes, for he fits into no simple classification. We might begin by pointing out that he was a person of limited interests and narrow reading. He had little command of foreign languages and almost no interest in political developments abroad before he entered the White House; he was indifferent to the great scientific developments that were transforming the philosophy and technology of his age; he knew virtually nothing about serious art and music. His reading in the field of literature, moreover, was desultory, spasmodic, and erratic. He was passionately fond of Keats, Wordsworth, Browning, Swinburne, Shelley, Tennyson, and Arnold, among the English poets; of Jane Austen, Sir Walter Scott, Stanley Weyman, and Mary N. Murfree, among the novelists; and of Lamb, Bagehot, and G. K. Chesterton among the essayists. Yet he never read widely among these few authors; and he was generally ignorant of much of the world's great literature.[17]

Indeed, even in his own specialties of political science, constitutional law, and English and American history, Wilson was surprisingly poorly read. Two of his early scholarly books, *The State* (1889) and *Division and Reunion* (1893), gave evidence of intensive scholarship in comparative government and American history. However, they marked the zenith of his career as a scholar; and afterward, during the 1890's, he

[17] Stockton Axson, notes on various parts of R. S. Baker's MS., in the Baker Collection; R. S. Baker, memorandum of conversations with Stockton Axson, February 8, 10, and 11, 1925, *ibid.*; Gamaliel Bradford, "Brains Win and Lose," *Atlantic Monthly*, cxlvii (February 1931), 155.

turned more and more toward the works of a few great historical masters—Macaulay, Green, and Turner, for example—and toward writing
in the field of essays and popular history and biography. Then, after
he assumed the presidency of Princeton in 1902, his serious reading
virtually ceased. Indeed, he told a reporter in 1916, "I haven't read a
serious book through for fourteen years,"[18] and there is no evidence to
contradict his assertion. It is little wonder, therefore, that he was often
ignorant of the currents of economic, political, and social thought that
were revolutionizing scholarship in the social sciences after the 1890's,
and that he derived such knowledge as he had of these developments
secondhand.

There were, besides, curious limitations in Wilson's intellectual processes. This was true, primarily, because he was interested in ideas chiefly
to the degree to which they could be put to practical use and hardly at
all for their own sake. Thus because his thinking was pragmatic rather
than philosophical, he had little interest in pure speculation and tended
to judge public men, both historical and contemporary, not by their
thought but by their actions; he was rarely an original thinker.

Yet if Wilson was not an intellectual in the ordinary sense of that
word, he was most assuredly a creature of brains, as one of his most
understanding friends has put it. What saved him from pedantry was
the enormous activity of his mind—the constant play of his imagination
and his absorption in ideas that could be put to use in the world of
practical affairs, whether in reconstructing the social life of under-
graduates at Princeton or in devising a new political order for the
world.[19]

There were, in addition, two other resources of strength in the Wilsonian intellect. One was Wilson's ability to absorb ideas and to as-
similate and synthesize them rapidly, which revealed a high degree
of intelligence. The other was closely related—his ability to cut through
verbiage or a maze of detail and to go to the essentials of any problem.
As his brother-in-law observed from long acquaintance, Wilson had a
swift and intuitive comprehension that led him straight to the heart
of a subject.[20] Or, as another friendly contemporary has put it:

"I have never talked with any other public man who gave me such
an impression of being at every moment in complete command of his

[18] Ida M. Tarbell, "A Talk with the President of the United States," *Collier's*, LVIII
(October 28, 1916), 37.

[19] Gamaliel Bradford, "Brains Win and Lose," *loc.cit.*, pp. 153-161.

[20] R. S. Baker, memorandum of conversations with Stockton Axson, March 15-16,
1927, Baker Collection.

entire intellectual equipment, such an impression of alertness, aware-
ness. His face mirrors that eagerness. A new fact, a new aspect of an
old situation, a felicitous statement of current opinion, brings to his
intent eyes an expression of keen intellectual appetite. He pounces
upon ideas half conveyed and consumes them before they are well out
of one's mind; and his pounce is sure and accurate. He gets swiftly to
your point of view, passes upon the facts that you bring him, and in
a few minutes' time has stripped the whole situation to the bare bones
of its fundamental aspects, and has rested his conclusions and decisions
upon a few simple and elemental principles—and all with an incomparable clearness of statement."[21]

Woodrow Wilson was not only a man of ideas; he was, even more
importantly, a citizen of another invisible world, the world of the
spirit in which a sovereign God reigned in justice and in love. One
cannot understand Wilson without taking into account the religious
bases of his life and motivation. Born the son of a Presbyterian minister
and a devout mother and reared in the southern Presbyterian church,
he absorbed completely his father's and his denomination's belief in the
omnipotence of God, the morality of the universe, a system of rewards
and punishments, and the supreme revelation of Jesus Christ. Mankind, he felt, lived not only by the providence of God but also under
His immutable decrees; and nations as well as men transgressed the
divine ordinances at their peril. He shared the Calvinistic belief, held
in his day mainly by southern Presbyterians and members of the Reformed churches in Europe, in predestination—the absolute conviction
that God had ordered the universe from the beginning, the faith that
God used men for His own purposes. From such beliefs came a sure
sense of destiny and a feeling of intimate connection with the sources
of power.

It was almost as if Wilson had been born with these convictions. He
apparently never went through that period of doubt which often se-
cures the faith of intellectuals. He was a loyal member and elder in his
church; he read the Scriptures daily; and he found strength and guidance in prayer. "*My* life would not be worth living," he told a friend,
"if it were not for the driving power of religion, for *faith*, pure and
simple. I have seen all my life the arguments against it without ever
having been moved by them. . . . There are people who *believe* only so
far as they *understand*—that seems to me presumptuous and sets their

[21] R. S. Baker, "Wilson," *Collier's*, LVIII (October 7, 1916), 6.

understanding as the standard of the universe. . . . I am sorry for such people."[22]

Faith in God and submission to the Christian ethic underlay most of Wilson's political assumptions and fired his ambition to serve the Almighty by serving his fellow men. "The way to success in America," he once declared, "is to show you are not afraid of anybody except God and His judgment. If I did not believe that I would not believe in democracy. . . . If I did not believe that the moral judgment would be the last and final judgment in the minds of men, as well as at the tribunal of God, I could not believe in popular government."[23]

"There are great problems . . . before the American people," Wilson said on another occasion. "There are problems which will need purity of spirit and an integrity of purpose such as has never been called for before in the history of this country. I should be afraid to go forward if I did not believe that there lay at the foundation of all our schooling and of all our thought this incomparable and unimpeachable Word of God. If we cannot derive our strength thence, there is no source from which we can derive it, and so I would bid you go from this place, if I may, inspired once more with the feeling that the providence of God is the foundation of affairs, and that only those can guide, and only those can follow, who take this providence of God from the sources where it is authentically interpreted. . . . He alone can rule his own spirit who puts himself under the command of the spirit of God, revealed in His Son, Jesus Christ, our Savior. He is the captain of our souls; he is the man from whose suggestions and from whose life comes the light that guideth every man that ever came into the world."[24]

Wilson's high integrity, his sense of justice, his devotion to duty, and much of his general motivation stemmed in large measure from his spiritual resources. As president of Princeton University, for example, he refused to demean the university's academic integrity in order to win favor with the alumni or potential donors. As President of the United States, he refused to accept expensive gifts, even those offered by persons unknown to him.[25] He refused to allow Harper & Brothers to sell movie rights to his books—"a rather cheap exploitation," he

[22] Mrs. Crawford H. Toy, "Second Visit to the White House," diary entry dated January 3, 1915, MS. in the Baker Collection.

[23] Speech at Philadelphia, July 4, 1914, *New York Times*, July 5, 1914.

[24] Speech before the Sunday School workers and pupils of Trenton, New Jersey, October 1, 1911, *Trenton True American*, October 2, 1911.

[25] e.g., W. W. to J. B. Phinney, February 3, 1915, Wilson Papers.

called it.[26] He stood firm against nepotism when his brother sought the post of Secretary of the Senate in 1913. He intervened personally to protect persons in the public service from "malicious injustice."[27] He set a moral tone that permeated his entire administration and enabled it to survive a war and demobilization without a single really important scandal. His sense of duty alone carried him through dark days and made him ready to risk his life for what he thought were noble causes. But his most striking personal attribute was his certain sense of destiny and his conviction that the right cause would ultimately triumph.

As a husband, father, and friend, Wilson had many warm and winning qualities. In his family circle he was unquestionably the lord and master, but he was uncommonly tender and assumed responsibilities far surpassing the ordinary. For example, he spent a good part of his income before 1913 in helping to educate numerous relatives on both sides of the family; for years he supported uncomplainingly an indigent sister and her family. Among his family and friends, Wilson was generous, understanding, and intensely loyal, so long as he thought his friends were loyal to him. Discarding his austere official manner in the intimate group, he could be uproariously funny as a story-teller or mimic, or quickly moved by demonstrations of affection.

Another significant aspect of Wilson's personality was his inheritance of many of his attitudes and especially the romantic quality of his thought from his rearing in the South and his close association with southern people. He was a Southerner not merely in the superficial sense—in the soft inflections in his speech, his normal courtesy toward friends and associates, and his liking for fried chicken, rice, and sweet potatoes[28]—but in more essential ways. For one thing, he was southern in his deification of women and his strong urge to protect them, and in his belief that women should govern their own sphere and not soil themselves by participation in practical affairs. He inherited and retained the upper-class southern affection for the Negro and the belief that the black man should remain segregated and not aspire toward so-called social equality with the whites. He was southern, above all,

---

[26] W. W. to F. A. Duneka, August 2, 1915, *ibid.*

[27] e.g., W. W. to W. J. Bryan, December 29, 1913, *ibid.*

[28] "Governor Wilson since his marriage has lived on Southern cooking," Ellen Wilson told a reporter in the autumn of 1912. "You see, we have always had cooks from the South or those who were Southern born, and they know how to cook chicken better than anybody in the world, the Governor thinks. . . .

"The Governor's idea of a fine dinner includes chicken Southern style, rice and candied sweet potatoes, with beans and corn, fruit and a salad. Never do we have a meal without rice." *Trenton Evening True American*, October 30, 1912.

in his deep love of community and the land and in his personal identification with the living generations of the dead.[29]

These were some of the sources of Wilson's personal greatness, and all of them had an important impact upon his career as a public man. Superb intelligence and power of penetration, religious conviction and a sense of destiny, integrity, warmth among intimates, and love of community and nation combined with boldness and resolution to make Wilson at times a strong and successful political leader.

But there was a less happy side of Wilson's personality and character. It is not pleasant or easy to describe his personal weaknesses, and yet we cannot know the whole man or understand the ultimately tragic nature of his career if we ignore his unlovely qualities, for they always affected and sometimes controlled his personal and political attitudes and relationships.

To begin with, there is revelation in the nature of his friendships. Few public men have ever craved or needed affection more than did Woodrow Wilson; and in his own way and upon his own terms, he returned the love that he received. Yet he demanded, not forthrightness and a masculine type of give-and-take in his friendships, but a loyalty that never questioned, always understood, and inevitably yielded to his own will. In view of his terms of friendship, it was little wonder that he had few intimates and broke sooner or later with most of them, and that his most enduring friends were admiring, uncritical women, both within and without his household, who always understood and comforted and never questioned.

Other weaknesses were Wilson's egotism and his tendency to exalt intuition over reason. Robert Lansing, Secretary of State from 1915 to 1920, analyzed these defects sharply:

"When one comes to consider Mr. Wilson's mental processes, there is the feeling that intuition rather than reason played the chief part in the way in which he reached conclusions and judgments. In fact, arguments, however soundly reasoned, did not appeal to him if they were opposed to his feeling of what was the right thing to do. Even established facts were ignored if they did not fit in with this intuitive sense, this semi-divine power to select the right. Such an attitude of mind is essentially feminine. In the case of Mr. Wilson, it explains many things in his public career, which are otherwise very perplexing.

"In the first place it gave a superior place to his own judgment.

With him it was a matter of conviction formed without weighing evidence and without going through the process of rational deduction. His judgments were always right in his own mind, because he knew that they were right. How did he know that they were right? Why he *knew* it, and that was the best reason in the world. No other was necessary. It sounds very much like the 'because,' which is popularly termed 'a woman's reason.'

"In consequence to the high place which Mr. Wilson gave to his own judgment, he was less susceptible than other men to the force of argument. When reason clashed with his intuition, reason had to give way."[30]

Numerous contemporaries have confirmed Lansing's judgment concerning the importance of Wilson's egotism. Wilson's "over powering self esteem left no place for common counsel of which he talked so much and in which he did not indulge at all," Lindley M. Garrison, Secretary of War from 1913 to 1916, wrote, for example.[31] "This was his great weakness," William Kent said, "a total inability to rely upon others."[32]

Wilson's supreme confidence in his own judgment came out in blunt assertions of his superior wisdom and virtue. "Wilson was the most self-assured, the most egotistical, and the vainest man I ever knew ...," an unfriendly Princeton contemporary has written. "He once said to me, 'I am so sorry for those who disagree with me.' When I asked why, he replied, 'Because I know that they are wrong.' "[33] To cite a second example, there was the time when he fell into a hot argument with a professor at the Princeton Theological Seminary. In order to end the disagreement, the theological professor said, "Well, Dr. Wilson, there are two sides to every question." "Yes," Wilson shot back, "a right side and a wrong side!"[34]

Wilson had another unfortunate quality that Lansing knew first-hand but did not attempt to describe. The President possessed a turbulent emotional make-up, which was all the more charged because he usually kept it under severe control. As he once candidly said, "If I

[30] "The Mentality of Woodrow Wilson," the Diary of Robert Lansing, November 20, 1921, Library of Congress; hereinafter cited as the Lansing Diary.

[31] L. M. Garrison to William E. Brooks, July 30, 1929, the Papers of William E. Brooks, Library of Congress; hereinafter cited as the Brooks Papers.

[32] W. Kent to R. S. Baker, May 25, 1925, Baker Collection.

[33] Harold C. Syrett (ed.), *The Gentleman and the Tiger, The Autobiography of George B. McClellan, Jr.*, p. 314.

[34] William S. Myers (ed.), *Woodrow Wilson, Some Princeton Memories*, p. 43.

were to interpret myself, I would say that my constant embarrassment is to restrain the emotions that are inside of me. You may not believe it, but I sometimes feel like a fire from a far from extinct volcano, and if the lava does not seem to spill over it is because you are not high enough to see into the basin and see the caldron boil."[35]

Thus Wilson could hate as fiercely as he loved, and over the years he accumulated an astounding array of prejudices—against his old foes at Princeton, for example, or against Republicans who he thought opposed him out of spite and lack of character. As George LaMonte, one of Wilson's associates in New Jersey put it, "Wilson's mind could not work under opposition, for he felt all opposition to be merely irritation, and that if he needed any human associations they must be with people who either lauded him and made it their business to agree with him on everything, or else with people who were comfortable because they didn't understand what he was talking about or were not particularly interested. This accounted for his fondness for women's society."[36]

The President's few intimate friends have left revealing testimony concerning the depths of his prejudices and personal hatreds. Colonel House advised a British friend on the best method of handling Wilson: "Never begin by arguing. Discover a common hate, exploit it, get the President warmed up and then start on your business."[37] "He likes a few [people] and is very loyal to them," the Colonel observed of the President in 1915, "but his prejudices are many and often unjust. He finds great difficulty in conferring with men against whom, for some reason, he has a prejudice and in whom he can find nothing good."[38] Dr. Cary T. Grayson, the White House physician, thought that Wilson was a "man of unusually narrow prejudices" and "intolerant of advice"; and, he added, "If one urges Wilson to do something contrary to his own conviction, he ceases to have any liking for that person."[39]

This tendency to equate political opposition with personal antagonism and to doubt the integrity of any man who disagreed was relatively unimportant so long as Wilson controlled secure majorities in Congress. It was a fatal weakness after the Republicans won control of

[35] Speech before the National Press Club, March 20, 1914, *New York Times,* March 21, 1914.

[36] George LaMonte, quoted in William Kent to R. S. Baker, May 25, 1925, Baker Collection.

[37] Sir Arthur Willert, *The Road to Safety, A Study in Anglo-American Relations,* p. 63.

[38] House Diary, November 22, 1915.   [39] *ibid.,* April 2, 1916.

Congress in 1918, especially during the momentous controversy over the ratification of the Versailles Treaty. It was a weakness, moreover, that put a heavy strain upon Wilson's talents as an administrator. Because he often equated loyalty with agreement and welcomed flattery instead of hardheaded frankness, he was sometimes a poor judge of men. As Senator John Sharp Williams of Mississippi once wrote, "He was the best judge of measures and the poorest of men I ever knew."[40] Because he resented criticism, his advisers usually either told him what they thought he wanted to hear or else remained discreetly silent.

Wilson's exaltation of intuition, his egotism, and his indulgence in personal prejudice were at the same time sources of strength and of weakness. Perhaps they help to explain why the American people admired his boldness and thrilled to his noble visions and the cadence of his oratory and yet did not love him as an individual as they loved Lincoln for his compassion and the two Roosevelts for their personal warmth. How can we reconcile the curious contradictions in Woodrow Wilson—his craving for affection and his refusal to give on equal terms, his love of the people en masse and his ordinary disdain for individuals, the warm idealism of his speeches and the coolness of many of his official relationships, the bigness of his political visions and the pettiness of his hatreds? Being neither mind reader nor psychiatrist, the biographer can only agree with Colonel House that Wilson was "one of the most contradictory characters in history" and hope that the man will reveal himself in the pages that follow.

The White House was like a wonderful new world. After a family dinner following the inaugural parade, the Wilsons "found a little time to inspect their new quarters. There was a continual running through the house from one room to another, a shrill voice screaming to someone else as a new place was discovered. Relatives from the hotels going in and out, visitors and acquaintances seeking admission but added to the turmoil. . . . Along toward midnight the day was considered closed. One by one the family and guests wended their way to their rooms. It was not long after the President had gone upstairs that he rang several bells in the house, not knowing at the time which was which. One of the doorkeepers answered the call and when the President appeared he was clothed in his underwear only. He asked for his trunk, which had gone astray and unfortunately contained his night clothes. Immediate search was made and it was located at the sta-

---

[40] R. S. Baker, interview with J. S. Williams, March 11, 1927, Baker Collection.

tion where an automobile was sent for it; but it did not get to the White House until one o'clock in the morning after the President had already retired."[41]

It was fun to wake up in the White House, to roam through the great rooms and corridors, to eat in the big dining doom, which was beautiful in spite of the animal heads placed on the walls by Theodore Roosevelt. It was exciting to have a corps of servants, to be able to buy the clothes one wanted for the first time without worrying about the cost, to be always the guest of honor at parties, to have automobiles after going for years without one. How grand it all seemed to Eleanor Wilson as she looked back upon those first days in the presidential mansion![42]

There were, of course, new social duties and irritations. There were the traditional state dinners for the Cabinet, the Supreme Court, and the diplomatic corps. There was the inevitable loss of privacy and control over personal movement. There were constant crowds streaming into the White House. There was, for Wilson, the anguish of having to yield to a valet and give up his old gray sack suits for dress becoming a President of the United States.

And yet the remarkable thing is how little personal life changed for the Wilsons. The efficient household staff they had inherited from the Roosevelts and Tafts ran the White House with a minimum of worry. Characteristically, Ellen Wilson spurned the company of Washington's social elite and used her free time for humanitarian work. "I wonder how anyone who reaches middle age can bear it," she once remarked, "if she cannot feel, on looking back, that whatever mistakes she may have made, she has on the whole lived for others and not for herself." It was the way she lived in Washington. She visited the crowded alley slums, often with food and clothing in hand, and worked quietly among congressmen for the enactment of a measure to provide decent housing for Negroes. She toured the governmental departments and had rest rooms for women workers installed where there were none. And one might have found her any day at a meeting of social workers, as a member of the Board of Associated Charities, listening patiently to a case worker describe the misfortunes of a needy family.[43] Withal,

[41] Irwin H. Hoover, *Forty-two Years in the White House*, pp. 58-59; quoted by permission of the Houghton Mifflin Company, publishers.

[42] Eleanor W. McAdoo, *The Woodrow Wilsons*, pp. 212-227.

[43] McGregor (A. J. McKelway), "The Social Activities of the White House," *Harper's Weekly*, LVIII (April 25, 1914), 26-27; Mrs. Ernest P. Bicknell, "The Home-Maker of the White House," *The Survey*, XXXIII (October 3, 1914), 19-22.

she found time to receive delegations and preside at innumerable teas at the White House. Bearing her imprint, they were simple affairs, where one talked about good works, art, music, or books.

Wilson's personal life of course changed after March 4, 1913, but not his ingrained habit of living and doing business according to a nearly inflexible routine. He rose every morning at eight, had breakfast —usually two raw eggs in orange juice, oatmeal, and coffee—at eight-thirty, and arrived at his office at nine. He read his mail and dictated replies to his stenographer. Then, exactly at ten o'clock, he began receiving callers.

No man, not even a Cabinet member, got the President's ear except by an appointment approved by Tumulty; and the late visitor to the Executive Offices, whether congressman or senator, went away without seeing Wilson. Except in unusual circumstances, interviews were limited to ten or fifteen minutes. Wilson listened, sometimes nodded or said a few words, and then rose to tell his visitor good-by. In spite of his unvarying courtesy, it was obvious that he resented the needless demands that some of his callers made upon his energies and time.

On the rare occasions when he was ahead of schedule, the President might walk into the outer office and greet the crowd waiting for a glimpse of him. Theodore Roosevelt had always had a warm, special greeting for such strangers; Taft had often stopped to repeat their names and make a joke. In contrast, Wilson would walk briskly down the line shaking the outstretched hands mechanically and silently. One old fellow, however, broke the routine. "Mr. Wilson," he said, "I've known all the Presidents in my time, and I want to say right here that you're the greatest and best of them since Lincoln!" When this compliment failed to elicit any response, the old man went on: "And when I add that I'm a high-church Presbyterian like yourself, you'll know I'm not lying." Near the end of the line, Wilson turned and shot back, "Whether we are Presbyterians or not, sir, we ought all to speak the truth!"

The appointments were invariably over by one o'clock, when the President went to lunch with his family. He returned to his office at two or two-thirty for more appointments until four, when he left for the balance of the afternoon. During late afternoons and weekends he often played golf with Dr. Grayson, the White House physician, a quiet and gentlemanly Virginian, whom Wilson had inherited from Taft.

Although the President took up golf at Grayson's suggestion for exercise, he soon became a virtual addict. They played at all the courses about Washington except the Chevy Chase Club, in which Wilson refused membership because of its social exclusiveness. "He would play at all hours, sometimes as early as five in the morning and sometimes late in the afternoon. Good or bad weather was just the same to him. When there was snow on the ground, he would have the balls painted red and find amusement in driving them around on the ice and snow."[44]

Dinner in the White House was at seven o'clock. In contrast to Theodore Roosevelt, who gathered writers, politicians, explorers, and persons from all walks of life at his table, the Wilsons usually dined *en famille* or with relatives and a few intimate friends. After Ellen's death in 1914 and Wilson's marriage to Edith Bolling Galt in 1915, social life at the White House quickened, but Ellen had neither energy for nor interest in extensive entertaining. To forget the cares of state, the President often went with his family to the theater and to vaudeville shows. It mattered little whether the plays or the performances were good or bad; Wilson enjoyed them all. During times of crisis Wilson might work in his study late into the night; on the other hand, there were many quiet evenings, when he relaxed with family and friends. George McLean Harper, professor of English literature at Princeton, remembered one of those evenings:

"When we got back to the White House, Mr. Wilson had returned and was evidently very glad to be at home again and at his ease in the midst of his family. We had a quiet familiar hour at dinner, with no other guests and no interruptions. It was just like the old times in Princeton. After dinner we drew up our chairs around a blazing wood fire in the drawing room and talked about books. Mr. Wilson stretched himself out on the hearth rug and recited poetry, as we have often heard him do. . . . Like a happy boy home from school for a holiday the President of the United States rocked back and forth in the firelight, with his knees clasped between his hands, declaiming sonnets, while his face glowed with affection."[45]

[44] I. H. Hoover, *Forty-two Years in the White House*, p. 61; quoted by permission of the Houghton Mifflin Company, publishers.

[45] George M. Harper to R. S. Baker, February 11, 1929, Baker Collection. The foregoing account of Wilson's daily routine is based upon R. S. Baker, interview with C. L. Swem, July 16, 1925, *ibid.*; William B. Hale, "Watching President Wilson at Work," *World's Work*, xxvi (May 1913), 71-72; Francis E. Leupp, "The President—and Mr. Wilson," *The Independent*, lxxvi (November 27, 1913), 392-393; An Onlooker, "Woodrow Wilson the Man," *Harper's Weekly*, lviii (January 10, 1914), 25-26.

There was another side to the life of the new President, however, during the months following the inauguration. There were, among others, the problems of working out a method of doing business with the Cabinet members and of running a great government without becoming overwhelmed by the burden of ordinary administrative routine. In solving these tasks of administration, Wilson further revealed his methods and character as President.

The President and his Cabinet met first informally on March 5, 1913, in the Cabinet Room in the Executive Offices, to "come together and talk about getting started," as Wilson said. They met thereafter on Tuesdays and Fridays until about November 1, 1913, when the President eliminated the Friday meetings and substituted a system of individual conferences.

One member has described Wilson's method in these Cabinet meetings: "As President Wilson took his seat at the head of the table, he looked the moderator, fitting into place and power. His plan from the first was to present some matter or matters about which he desired what he was fond of calling 'common counsel,' and after he had received the reaction of Cabinet members, his practice was to call on each member to present any question that concerned departmental policies, for debate and exchange of news. At one Cabinet meeting he would begin with the Secretary of State, and at the next the Secretary of Labor would be called upon first. . . . He never took a vote, pursuing a course, as he often said, more like a Quaker meeting, in which after full discussion the President would say, 'It seems to me the sense of the meeting is so and so,' and the policy thus ascertained would be the program of the administration."[46]

Wilson's advisers responded with enthusiasm befitting fellow workers in a noble cause. "It is impossible to meet any member of the Cabinet and talk with him five minutes," one observer wrote soon after the inaugural, "without becoming impressed with the fact that the members of the Cabinet believe in one another and believe in their chief, and feel already the exhilaration of taking part in the bringing about of better days."[47] "The President is the most charming man imaginable to work with," one Cabinet member said. ". . . If we can't make this

[46] Josephus Daniels, *The Wilson Era, Years of Peace—1910-1917*, p. 137; quoted by permission of the University of North Carolina Press, publishers.

[47] Ernest H. Abbott, "The New Administration: An Impression," New York *Outlook*, CIII (April 5, 1913), 760.

thing a success, the Democratic Party is absolutely gone, and entirely useless."[48]

Slowly, perhaps inevitably, the original ardor cooled as quarrels and controversies arose. But the development that turned the Cabinet from a genuinely deliberative body into an inconsequential forum was Wilson's discovery that news of the discussions was leaking to reporters. The member responsible was Franklin K. Lane, Secretary of the Interior. Lane was so fond of conversation and so much a gossip that he could not resist the temptation to drop broad hints to his newspaper friends.[49] Precisely when Wilson learned of Lane's weakness, we do not know. In any event, in early September 1913, at the height of one of the recurrent Mexican crises, the President virtually stopped discussing any important question at Cabinet meetings because, as he told his friends, he simply could not trust Lane to keep the secrets of state. The result was that the meetings became for the most part, in Garrison's words, an interesting waste of time.[50]

One unfortunate effect of Wilson's policy of saying nothing important during the Cabinet meetings was the resentment that the Cabinet members consequently felt. "McReynolds added his complaint to that of the other cabinet officials about the President's reticence with them," Colonel House recorded in his Diary in September 1913. "As far as I can gather, he confers with none of them excepting in matters concerning their particular departments. Not one of them has been able to tell me a single thing regarding what the President has in mind for Mexico, or about anything else not connected with their own departments. I can readily see how embarrassing this is to them, and how it hurts their self esteem."[51] Two months later McAdoo "said the Cabinet were complaining that the President did not consult with them regarding Mexico and there was a general feeling among them that he would like to eliminate Cabinet meetings entirely."[52]

As the months passed and, after 1914, the nation entered a period of

[48] F. K. Lane to W. H. Page, March 12, 1913, Anne W. Lane and Louise H. Wall (eds.), *The Letters of Franklin K. Lane, Personal and Political*, pp. 133-134.

[49] R. S. Baker and A. H. Meneely, interview with N. D. Baker, April 6, 1928, Baker Collection; R. S. Baker, interview with T. W. Gregory, March 14-15, 1927, *ibid.*; R. S. Baker, interview with D. F. Houston, December 1, 1928, *ibid.*; R. S. Baker, interview with W. B. Wilson, January 12-13, 1928, *ibid.*; and W. G. McAdoo, *Crowded Years*, pp. 193-194, all attest to the accuracy of this statement.

[50] R. S. Baker, interview with L. M. Garrison, November 30, 1928, Baker Collection.

[51] House Diary, September 6, 1913.　　　　[52] *ibid.*, November 4, 1913.

uncertain neutrality vis-à-vis the European war, Wilson grew increasingly secretive and the Cabinet members almost rebellious. The President, House observed, "never seems to want to discuss things with anyone, as far as I know, excepting me. Even the Cabinet bore him with their importunities, and he often complains of them."[53] In the midst of a crisis that threatened to erupt into war with Germany, House could write: "His immediate entourage, from the Secretary of State down, are having an unhappy time just now. He is consulting none of them and they are as ignorant of his intention as the man in the street."[54] And a few months later McAdoo could remark that his chief had no confidence in the judgment of any of his official advisers,[55] while Walter Page noted the impact of their loss of morale: "The members of the Cabinet do not seem to have the habit of frankness with one another. Each lives and works in a water-tight compartment."[56]

To stop at this point in describing Wilson's relations with his Cabinet, however, would be to draw an incomplete and unfair picture of the President as administrator. Wilson conferred with his advisers frequently, usually by correspondence, about matters relating to their own departments. In personal conference he was invariably courteous and generous. "He was the most satisfactory person to confer with I ever knew," Thomas W. Gregory, Attorney General from 1914 to 1919, testified. "He was always deferential and sympathetic, but he never failed to express himself and to throw light upon and give help in dealing with, the matter under discussion."[57] "To me and with me he was patient, considerate, approachable, sympathetic and amazingly helpful," Newton D. Baker said. "I took my problems to him and always came away with the feeling that he had sought and considered my views and then exercised his clear and powerful mind to the utmost to help me in their solution."[58]

Wilson's method of running the executive branch was to give virtually complete freedom to his Cabinet members in all routine matters and in the formulation of many important policies, so long as those policies did not conflict with his broad objectives or imperil the ad-

---

[53] *ibid.*, November 14, 1914.   [54] *ibid.*, April 2, 1916.
[55] *ibid.*, August 27, 1916.
[56] The Diary of Walter H. Page, c. September 1, 1916, Harvard University Library; hereinafter cited as the Page Diary.
[57] T. W. Gregory to Josephus Daniels, February 19, 1924, the Papers of Thomas Watt Gregory, Library of Congress.
[58] Quoted in George Barton, "Woodrow Wilson: His Human Side," *Current History*, xxii (April 1925), 2.

ministration's standing before Congress and the country. For example, he approved when McAdoo launched the Treasury upon bold financial measures; followed Houston in opposing a bill for the establishment of a federal rural credits system; allowed several Cabinet members to institute segregation and defended them when their action provoked the impassioned opposition of northern humanitarians; and supported Garrison in a Philippine policy that partially repudiated Democratic platform pledges. Only in important foreign policies, in issues involving his leadership of Congress, and in the disposition of the patronage did he take a personal interest.

A minor case that arose in the early spring of 1914 illustrated his administrative methods and ideals. He had promised Bryan to appoint one Summervell to a certain post and subsequently discovered that the appointment rested legally with the Secretary of War, who wanted another man. "I could obtain the appointment of Mr. Summervell," Wilson wrote, "only through the courtesy of the Secretary of War in yielding his judgment to my insistence in the matter. I do not feel justified in acting in that way. I have never felt justified in coercing the judgment of a Cabinet colleague."[59] It was true. He rarely overruled a Cabinet member, and when he did the matter was so serious that the member's resignation had to follow.[60]

In contrast to the usually genial mediator of the Cabinet was the forbidding commander in chief, who dealt sternly with his military and naval advisers when he thought their words or actions raised a threat to civilian supremacy over the military establishment. Wilson's attitude toward the professional military class was conditioned by the fact that, like most other Americans of his time, he had no interest in military and naval strategy, little understanding of the role that force plays in the relations of great powers, and a near contempt for *Realpolitik* and the men who made it. Military men, he thought, should speak only when they were spoken to; and the suggestion that his military advisers might know more about important strategic matters than he was enough to evoke suspicions of a sinister attempt to undermine civilian control.

Some generals like Leonard Wood and admirals like Bradley A. Fiske were unwilling to acknowledge the President's omniscience and fell into official disfavor in consequence. Others, like the sometime

[59] W. W. to W. J. Bryan, March 25, 1914, Wilson Papers.
[60] As in the case of Bryan and Garrison.

Chief of Staff, Major General Hugh L. Scott, were more fortunate because they submitted to the necessity of getting on with the commander in chief.

Scott explained his method in a revealing letter. "Your letter of yesterday received, in which you ask me to urge upon the President the appointment of [Robert] Bacon as Secretary of War," he wrote to a friend soon after Secretary Garrison's resignation. "I know Bacon well and am very fond of him indeed, but I feel that my advocacy of his case would not do him any good as the President would resent my talking to him about any political matter; I have never done so on any occasion as I felt that any such attempt would get me a request to mind my own business."[61]

There was one early incident that further illuminated Wilson's attitude toward the professional military class. The Washington "corral" of the Military Order of the Caraboa,[62] numbering about one hundred army, naval, and marine officers and including a major general and a rear admiral, held its annual dinner on December 11, 1913. These veterans of the Philippine campaign made merry by singing "Damn, Damn, Damn the Insurrectos, Cross-Eyed Kakiack Ladrones" and roared at skits that poked fun at the administration's Philippine policy and at Bryan for drinking grape juice and speaking on the Chautauqua circuit.[63]

It is not difficult to imagine that Wilson's face flushed with anger and that his jaw hardened as he read the newspaper accounts of these hilarities on December 13, 1913. Two days later he ordered Garrison and Daniels to determine whether a court-martial should be held. When the two secretaries recommended a severe reprimand instead, the President replied with a humiliating public rebuke of the officers involved.

"Allow me to thank you for your report on the action of certain officers of the army and navy at the recent dinner of the 'Military Order of the Caraboa,'" Wilson wrote. "The officers who were responsible for the programme of the evening are certainly deserving of a very serious reprimand, which I hereby request be administered; and I cannot rid myself of a feeling of great disappointment that the general

[61] H. L. Scott to Edward S. Farrow, February 12, 1916, the Papers of Hugh L. Scott, Library of Congress; hereinafter cited as the Scott Papers.

[62] The Military Order of the Caraboa was organized in Manila in 1902 and included officers who had served in suppressing the Philippine Insurrection from 1898 to 1902.

[63] New York *World*, December 16, 1913.

body of officers assembled at the dinner should have greeted the carrying out of such a programme with apparent indifference to the fact that it violated some of the most dignified and sacred traditions of the service.

"I have been told that the songs and other amusements of the evening were intended and regarded as 'fun.' What are we to think of officers of the army and navy of the United States who think it 'fun' to bring their official superiors into ridicule and the policies of the government which they are sworn to serve with unquestioning loyalty into contempt? If this is their idea of fun, what is their ideal of duty? If they do not hold their loyalty above all silly effervescences of childish wit, what about their profession do they hold sacred?"[64]

Few presidents in American history have better understood the importance of good press relations and failed more miserably to get on with newspapermen than Woodrow Wilson. An advocate of "pitiless publicity" as Governor of New Jersey, he had talked much about taking reporters into his confidence and had used the newspapers for frequent direct appeals to the people of his state. And he knew that a friendly press, both in New Jersey and throughout the nation, had been a decisive factor in his rise to national leadership.

One of Wilson's first acts as President, therefore, was to institute a semiweekly news conference in order to regularize his relations with the Washington correspondents. "I sent for you . . . ," he told them at the first press conference on March 15, 1913, "to ask that you go into partnership with me, that you lend me your assistance as nobody else can . . . [in telling people in Washington what the country thinks]. I did want you to feel that I was depending upon you, and from what I can learn of you, I think I have a reason to depend with confidence on you to do this thing, not for me, but for the United States, for the people of the United States, and so bring about a day which will be a little better than the days that have gone before us."[65]

No doubt Wilson meant what he said about welcoming the reporters as partners in the task of running the government. None the less, the press conferences, which were unpleasant enough at the beginning, became so intolerable that the President met them only irregularly

[64] W. W. to the Secretaries of War and of the Navy, December 22, 1913, Wilson Papers.

[65] Printed in L. Ames Brown, "President Wilson and Publicity," *Harper's Weekly*, LVIII (November 1, 1913), 20.

during 1914 and abandoned them altogether in June 1915. In spite of all his professions of comradeship, Wilson simply did not like most reporters. They were, he thought, busybodies, who would not leave him or his family alone, and muckrakers, whose chief objectives were to steal state secrets, distort the truth, and make sensational headlines.

"When he came down here I attended the first conference he had with the Washington correspondents," one of his few friends among the newspapermen recalled. "It was appalling. He came into the room, suspicious, reserved, a little resentful—no thought of frankness and open door and cordiality and that sort of thing. In the first place, he was embarrassed. There were about two hundred of the correspondents and it was in the East Room of the White House. It was a silly thing to do. It was a conference with two hundred newspapermen. He could not be as frank as he could have been with one; and he was embarrassed and had this rankling feeling and he utterly failed to get across to those men anything except that this was very distasteful to him; and they, on their part, resented it very, very seriously. They came out of that conference almost cursing, indignant."[66]

Wilson's method in the press conferences was to tell reporters as little as possible about important matters. "The President gave the impression that he was matching his wits against ours," wrote the correspondent for the *New York Times*, "as a sort of mental practice with the object of being able to make responses which seemed to answer the questions, but which imparted little or nothing in the way of information."[67] Wilson, said Arthur Krock, "is the most inaccessible executive of recent times and the weekly conferences with him develop no news whatever as he simply parries all questions."[68]

Because he liked to give the impression of frankness, however, Wilson often resorted to evasion by giving answers that were technically true but actually false—a habit that House once called "grazing the truth." "For this reason, it was impossible to rely on anything he said," one of the best reporters of the time has written. "I do not mean that he lied. I mean that he took such an intellectual pleasure in stating a thing so as to give an opposite impression to the fact, though he kept

---

[66] R. S. Baker, interview with Oliver P. Newman, January 13, 1928, Baker Collection.

[67] R. V. Oulahan to R. S. Baker, March 15, 1929, *ibid.*

[68] A. Krock to Henry Watterson, April 23, 1915, the Papers of Henry Watterson, Library of Congress; hereinafter cited as the Watterson Papers.

strictly to the truth, that one had to be constantly on the alert to keep from being misled."[69]

Many examples of this method of "grazing the truth" might be cited, but one must suffice. In June 1913, Attorney General McReynolds submitted to the Cabinet a plan to hobble the components of the former "Tobacco Trust" by a punitive tax, and Wilson advised him to discuss the matter with the Senate leaders. When correspondents asked the President what he thought of McReynolds' "tobacco tax plan," he replied that, as far as he knew, McReynolds had no "tobacco tax plan." Afterward, Wilson explained that he had regarded McReynolds' proposal as a "suggestion" and not a "plan."[70]

Of course there was often little difference between the half-truth and the lie, and sometimes Wilson resorted to outright prevarication when he thought the public interests demanded dissimulation. "When we reached the apartment and were munching our sandwiches before retiring," House recorded in his Diary on February 14, 1913, "we fell to talking about various matters. The Governor said he thought that lying was justified in some instances, particularly where it involved the honor of a woman. I agreed to this. He thought it was also justified where it related to matters of public policy." Or again, House wrote in his Diary on November 6, 1914, that the President said he felt entirely justified in lying to reporters when they asked questions about foreign policy. House added that he remained silent, for Wilson knew that he disagreed, and they had discussed the question many times.

These tactics deceived no one and did Wilson immense harm among the newspapermen. Wilson's "failure to give the correspondents that measure of confidence and help that had been usual with previous Administrations," James Kerney writes, "was doubtless very influential in setting the tides of sentiment against him at the time when he needed support most."[71] The President's tactics also help to explain the cold contempt that men like Theodore Roosevelt, Henry Cabot Lodge,

---

[69] Charles Willis Thompson, *Presidents I've Known and Two Near Presidents*, p. 297; quoted by permission of the Bobbs-Merrill Company, publishers.

[70] L. Ames Brown, "President Wilson and Publicity," *Harper's Weekly*, LVIII (November 1, 1913), 19-20.

[71] James Kerney, *The Political Education of Woodrow Wilson*, p. 345; quoted by permission of Appleton-Century-Crofts, Inc., publishers. Oliver P. Newman declared that nine tenths of the correspondents disliked Wilson in a journalistic sense. Their hostility did not perhaps matter so long as Wilson had control of the political situation, Newman added; but Wilson needed their support after 1918 and did not get it. R. S. Baker, interview with O. P. Newman, January 13, 1928, Baker Collection.

Elihu Root, and William H. Taft felt toward him. Lodge, for example, fell victim to one of Wilson's half-truths during the campaign of 1916 and ever afterward was convinced that his earlier doubts as to the Democratic leader's honesty were valid. Taft, who was the least virulent of Wilson's critics, made the most charitable comment: "Perhaps it is too rigorous a view to take that a man in his position should not have to lie at times, but what I object to is his unnecessary lying."[72]

There were times when Wilson's resentment at the reporters flared into open anger. When the correspondent for the *New York Herald* reported in late August 1915 that Wilson had broken with House over Mexican policy, for example, the President wrote to the editor of the *Herald*, denouncing the story as "an invention out of the whole cloth" and demanding that he withdraw the reporter from service in Washington.[73] But Wilson reserved his warmest anger for those newspapermen who would not leave his family alone. At a news conference on March 19, 1914, he finally exploded:

"Gentlemen, I want to say something this afternoon. In the first place, I want to say that I know that in saying this I am dealing here in this room with a group of men who respect and observe the honorable limitations of their own function, but there are some men connected with the newspapers who do not. I am a public character for the time being, but the ladies of my household are not servants of the Government and they are not public characters. I deeply resent the treatment they are receiving at the hands of the newspapers at this time. I am going to be perfectly frank with you. Take the case of my oldest daughter. It is a violation of my own impulses even to speak of these things, but my oldest daughter is constantly represented as being engaged to this, that, or the other man in different parts of the country, in some instances to men she has never even met in her life. It is a constant and intolerable annoyance. . . .

"Now, I feel this way, gentlemen: Ever since I can remember I have been taught that the deepest obligation that rested upon me was to defend the women of my household from annoyance. Now I intend to do it, and the only way I can think of is this. It is a way which will impose the penalty in a certain sense upon those whom I believe to be innocent, but I do not see why I should permit representatives of

---

[72] W. H. Taft to Gus J. Karger, April 8, 1915, Taft Papers.

[73] W. W. to the Editor of the *New York Herald*, September 2, 1915, Wilson Papers. Tumulty saved the reporter from his punishment. See John M. Blum, *Joe Tumulty and the Wilson Era*, pp. 63-64.

papers who treat the ladies of my household in this way to have personal interviews. . . . My daughters have no brother whom they can depend upon. I am President of the United States; I cannot act altogether as an individual while I occupy this office. But I must do something. The thing is intolerable. Every day I pick up the paper and see some flat lie, some entire invention, things represented as having happened to my daughters where they were not present, and all sorts of insinuations. . . .

"Now, if you have ever been in a position like that yourselves—and I hope to God you never will be—you know how I feel, and I must ask you gentlemen to make confidential representations to the several papers which you represent about this matter. . . . Now, put yourselves in my place and give me the best cooperation in this that you can, and then we can dismiss a painful subject and go to our afternoon's business."[74]

Wilson's dislike for reporters must have stemmed in part from his disdain of newspapers as agents both of opinion and of news. How were one's friends to know the simple fact of what was happening to him? he asked. "They certainly cannot know from the newspapers. A few, like the New York World, for example, or the Springfield Republican, give the real facts, in their editorials if not in their news columns; but the rest are a tissue of inventions and speculations and of versions of what they would like to believe to be true. I never imagined anything like it. And most of the newspapers are owned or controlled by men who fear and would discredit the present administration."[75] Or again: "The real trouble is that the newspapers get the real facts but do not find them to their taste and do not use them as given them, and in some of the newspaper offices news is deliberately invented. Since I came here I have wondered how it ever happened that the public got a right impression regarding public affairs, particularly foreign affairs."[76]

Actually, Wilson's opinion of the press was intuitive rather than reasonable, because he read few newspapers in the White House. It was his habit at breakfast to glance through, but not to read thoroughly, the New York *World*, the *Springfield Republican*, and occasionally a

[74] "CONFIDENTIAL—NOT TO BE PUBLISHED, Newspaper Interview, March 19, 1914," MS. in the Wilson Papers.

[75] W. W. to X, July 12, 1914.

[76] W. W. to C. W. Eliot, June 1, 1914, printed in R. S. Baker, *Woodrow Wilson*, IV, 234-235.

few other friendly newspapers; and he would sometimes read the editorials that Tumulty clipped and pasted on long yellow sheets. On the whole, however, he ignored the press, particularly the opposition newspapers, and ascertained public opinion in other ways—through his advisers and leaders in Congress and, above all, by the tremendous volume of organized opinion, expressed in letters, petitions, resolutions, and telegrams, which poured daily into the White House.

Yet Tumulty, who had actual charge of the administration's press relations, managed to salvage some measure of journalistic good will. In contrast to Wilson, Tumulty was warmly affectionate in his relations with newspapermen; they in turn "responded with favorable accounts of Wilson, his program, and his purposes."[77] It was Tumulty who prompted Wilson to send flowers when the wife of the *New York Times* correspondent died, or to write appreciative letters to friendly editors and publishers.[78] It was Tumulty, finally, who persuaded the President, before 1917, to give intimate interviews to a few trusted correspondents, Samuel G. Blythe, Ray Stannard Baker, and Ida M. Tarbell.

These three distinguished writers drew warm and winning word portraits of the President as he desperately wanted the American people to know him. Wilson, Blythe wrote, was "social, sociable, and sagacious," "a person of convictions who has the courage of them," "affable and agreeable," "entirely democratic and unassuming,"[79] "one of the most kindly, courteous, considerate, genial and companionable of men," "whose passion is the people—the real people," personally lonely but sustained by the love of his fellow men.[80]

Baker portrayed the man of intellect and the calm leader in time of crisis. "Here at the center of things where the spirit of the nation ques-

[77] J. M. Blum, *Joe Tumulty and the Wilson Era*, p. 64.

[78] "Let me say that every day I open the editorial page of the World expecting to find what I do, a real vision of things as they are," Wilson wrote, for example, to the publisher of the New York *World*. W. W. to Ralph Pulitzer, March 2, 1914, Wilson Papers. See also W. W. to Wallace M. Scudder (*Newark Evening News*), January 5, 1914; W. W. to Solomon B. Griffin (*Springfield*, Massachusetts, *Republican*), January 5, 1914; W. W. to William Allen White (*Emporia*, Kansas, *Gazette*), May 15, 1914; W. W. to E. S. Wilson (Columbus *Ohio State Journal*), May 22, 1914; W. W. to Oswald G. Villard (*New York Evening Post*), August 24, 1914; and W. W. to Frank I. Cobb (New York *World*), March 4, 1915, all in *ibid.*, for other examples.

[79] S. G. Blythe, "Our New President," *Saturday Evening Post*, CLXXXV (March 1, 1913), 49.

[80] S. G. Blythe, "A Talk With the President," *ibid.*, CLXXXVII (January 9, 1915), 3, 37.

tioned itself," Baker wrote after a visit to the White House in 1916, "was a great quietude, steadiness, confidence. . . . It all came to me that night—the undisturbed home, the peaceful surroundings, the thoughtful man at his desk—curiously but deeply as a symbol of immense strength."[81]

Miss Tarbell described the "gentleman, who, having invited you to his table, treats you as a fellow human being." "The sight of him moving so quietly yet energetically through his exacting daily program," she continued, "treating the grave matters which so dominate him gravely, yet able to turn gayly and with full sense of human values to the lighter matters which are equally a part of his business, humanizes and endears him."[82]

Blythe, Baker, and Miss Tarbell made the best case possible, but they did not convince the reporters who knew the other Wilson. Nor did they convince the American people. To them the President remained a leader they might trust and admire, but they rarely loved him.

Wilson's letters to his friends during the first year of his presidency are a far better revelation of his daily life and intimate thoughts than the biographer could ever contrive. He wrote, for example, of his need for the understanding and spiritual support of his friends:

"And *what* a comfort it is to think of all the old, established things, particularly of the friendships which can never alter or fail. They are so deliciously familiar, so dear to the taste and habit of our hearts. As the pressure of life increases, as the rush and hurly-burly grow more and more bewildering, old friends are not swallowed up and lost in the confusion: they stand out more distinct and lovely than ever; they are the solace of our souls. I think I should lose heart if it were not for them."[83]

"Do you really want to know what the present President of the United States lacks and *must* have, if he is to serve his country as he should and give the best that is in him to his tasks? He needs *pleasure* and the unaffected human touch! He cannot live on duty. He cannot feed his heart on 'great questions.' He must have the constant tonic

[81] R. S. Baker, "Wilson," *Collier's*, LVIII (October 7, 1916), 5. I have transposed these sentences.

[82] I. M. Tarbell, "A Talk with the President of the United States," *ibid.* (October 28, 1916), p. 5.

[83] W. W. to Mary A. Hulbert, February 23, 1913, printed in R. S. Baker, *Woodrow Wilson*, IV, 6.

of personal friendships, old and sweet and tested, that have nothing to do with him as a politician, have no relation to his, or any, career, but touch him only as a man, ante-date his public responsibilities and will outlive them,—that *belong* to him, are part of his private and essential life!"[84]

"You see it's this way: we live distracting days. You are witness of that. We are at the beck and call of others (how many, many others!) and almost never have a chance to order our days as we wish to order them, or to follow our own thoughts and devices. The life we lead is one of infinite distraction, confusion,—fragmentary, broken in upon and athwart in every conceivable way; and I, for one, need fixed points upon which to base my . . . actions from hour to hour. My friends are those fixed points. My intercourse with them helps me restore my identity from time to time, to get the confusion out of my nervous system and feel like the real Woodrow Wilson, a fellow of fixed connections, loyal to long established, deep-rooted friendships and associations, living through his heart and his affections, his tastes and all that runs in him independent of circumstance and occupation and momentary tasks. You may judge my uneasiness, therefore, and how my daily confusions are worse confounded if my best friends are themselves eluding my imagination for days together and preventing me from following them; playing hide and seek with my mind; avoiding my company!"[85]

"It is not as cool and refreshing down here as it is at Nantucket. We have no sight of the sea from our windows. There is no fine curve of a free shore line to make us conscious of the edges of the world and of a hot continent standing away from us at far arm's length. The people about us are not naive rustic neighbours whose characters and conduct remind us of the great body of Americans whose affections and opinions make up the life of a great nation, but a sophisticated miscellany of officials and of men and women who know what they want to get from the government and from society about it and spend night and day in search of it. . . . Our ears wait from morning till night for the voices that remind us of friends who have nothing to seek, whose affections sustain us, whose thought does not a little to guide us, that keeps us fresh with the touch of the outside world. . . . You have seen with what distraction our days are spent. Imagine what it would mean to you, in the midst of some such day, to be handed a

[84] W. W. to X, March 23, 1913.

[85] W. W. to Mary A. Hulbert, June 1, 1913, printed in part in R. S. Baker, *Woodrow Wilson*, IV, 154-155.

letter, a long, chatty letter, full of free and intimate talk, from some one who could touch your mind with a familiar and subtle knowledge of all its tastes and ways of thinking, and to drop down in a corner by yourself and devour it. What a rest and relief it would be! How it would swing your mind back into old, delightful channels! You would turn back to your occupations with a sense of having been cheered and made normal again, and with a warm glow at your heart which nobody had known how to impart to it the day through."[86]

"How is a man to get through with days of unbroken anxiety and continuous responsibility of the heaviest kind if he does not have constant evidence that his loyal and loving friends are thinking about him, —thinking such thoughts as ought to make any man strong and confident and happy? What is to keep his spirits from sinking and the blue devils from getting him? Is he to be left helpless and defenceless from them? The President of the United States is not, at any rate in this year of grace, made of steel or whipcord or leather. He is more utterly dependent on his friends, on their sympathy and belief in him, than any man he has ever known or read about. . . . Does he not have to determine what is to be done in Mexico, how that murderous Castro is to be choked off and kept in cold storage, how California is to be restrained from embarrassing us with most of the nations of the world, how the currency is to be reformed and the nations of the world kept at peace with the United States? And how, do you suppose, he is going to do all these things or any important part of them, if his friends do not stand close about him, do not keep in touch with him, do not constantly whisper in his ear the things that will cheer him and keep him in confidence and steadiness of heart? . . . He has many counsellors, but few loving friends. The fire of life burns in him only as his heart is kept warm."[87]

At other times Wilson wrote about life in Washington:

"The week has been a very interesting one with us. The meeting with the two Houses in joint session went off famously. . . . On Thursday I went to the opening game of the base-ball season and tossed out the ball to start the game. Last night I dined with the Gridiron Club (where public men are periodically grilled) and received my first public discipline as President, responsible to all who look on. . . . And so, step by step, am I being more and more thoroughly inducted into the office."[88]

"I suppose,—I fervently hope,—that you do not know how hot this

[86] W. W. to X, June 9, 1913.   [87] W. W. to X, August 3, 1913.
[88] W. W. to X, April 13, 1913.

huge continent has been during the past week. A little life and fresh-
ness has come into the air again now, within the last twenty-four hours
and we breathe freely again, but it was a fierce trial while we were
in it. It was hard to keep one's head cool, and one's temper! You would
have smiled to see me at church this morning. All alone I sat there,
a secret service man directly behind me; and when the service was
over the whole congregation waited till I walked out, trying to look
unself-conscious and at ease, but feeling very miserable indeed. All day
long I have been fighting against the weakness and silliness of feeling
sorry for myself. I feel more than ever like a prisoner, like a sort of
special slave, beguiled by the respect and deference of those about me,
but in fact in durance vile and splendid."[89]

On July 5, 1913, the President joined his family in Cornish, New
Hampshire, at Harlakenden House, which he had leased for two years
as a summer home from Winston Churchill, the novelist. After his
return to Washington, he wrote about life alone in the White House:

"The eight days I spent in New Hampshire with that happy, adorable
family up there did me a lot of good. I had grown stale down here.
Washington is, I should judge, the worst place in America to keep
normal. One's perspective goes wrong along with one's nerves, and
there are a lot of people here who get on your nerves! Since I got
back I have worked off the physical strength I got up there on the golf
links and on the open country roads and in the still pine woods with
their perfume of peace, but I have not worked off the refreshment of
mind. The visit brought the United States back into my consciousness,
with its plain folks and all its normal everyday life, and I am a better
President for it!"[90]

"I work hard, of course (the amount of work a president is expected
to do is preposterous), but it is not that that tells on a fellow. It's the
anxiety attending the handling of . . . affairs in which you seem to be
touching quicksilver,—matters [for] which your own judgments and
principles furnish no standards, and with regard to which you can only
frame conjectures and entertain hopes. I play golf every afternoon, because while you are playing golf you *cannot* worry and be preoccupied
with affairs. Each stroke requires your whole attention and seems the
most important thing in life. I can by that means get perfect diversion
of my thoughts for an hour or so at the same time that I am breathing
the pure out-of-doors. And I take Saturdays off, as nearly as may be
when a telegram or a piece of news may waylay you and hold you up

[89] W. W. to X, June 29, 1913.　　　[90] W. W. to X, July 20, 1913.

at any moment. Even Sundays are not safe. On the whole, however, I have myself well in hand. I find that I am often cooler in my mind than some of those about me. And I of course find a real zest in it all. Hard as it is to nurse Congress along and stand ready to play a part of guidance in anything that turns up, great or small, it is all part of something infinitely great and worth while, and I am content to labour at it to the finish. I keep perfectly well. My young aide looks after me as a mother would look after a child, and is with me practically all the time."[91]

"I am very well. . . . I play ten or eleven holes of golf almost every day, heat or no heat, and on as hilly and sporty a course as one could wish, for beauty or fun, and twice every week I go to the theatre, clad in white and looking, I would fain believe, as cool and care free as I often am on those occasions."[92]

"I have been to church in a dear old-fashioned church such as I used to go to when I was a boy, amidst a congregation of simple and genuine people to whom it is a matter of utter indifference whether there is a season or not, either in New York (or Washington) or Bermuda, or anywhere else between the ends of the earth. On Sundays only my faithful aide and companion, Dr. Grayson, is with me. . . . I do not get out of bed on Sundays until about ten o'clock, just in time to get a little breakfast and get to church; and after my letters are written in the afternoon the doctor and I go off for a little drive in the motor,—unless, as this afternoon, a thunder storm comes up out of mere exasperation that there should have been so sultry a day. It seems to come up after such a day exactly as if in a bad humour, to drive the maddening airs away, chasing them with its great angry breath and growling the while like a wild beast in the chase. The Sunday afternoon letter writing gives me a delightful renewal of the normal thoughts and feelings that belong to me . . . as a friend and home-loving companion, who is never so deeply content as when talking to those whom I love and respect, whom I understand and who understand me,—without explanations of any kind!"[93]

"Every now and again, just to keep my hand in and feel natural, I break a precedent. I broke one to-day, feeling a little stale and dull. I went to church in a white linen suit. It was simply so hot that I

[91] W. W. to Edith G. Reid, August 15, 1913, Accessions to the Wilson Papers, printed in R. S. Baker, *Woodrow Wilson*, iv, 176-177.

[92] W. W. to Mary A. Hulbert, August 3, 1913, printed in *ibid.*, p. 271.

[93] W. W. to Mary A. Hulbert, August 10, 1913, printed in *ibid.*, pp. 271-272.

could not stand any other kind. I created a mild sensation as I entered the church, as I could see by the way the people looked at me; but that of course is what every public man wishes to do, at church or anywhere else, and it did not in the least interfere with my own state of mind during the service."[94]

"I have been a bit under the weather myself for a few days,—perhaps a week; though getting better all the while and now practically well again. I have been under a terrible strain, if the truth must be told, and am still under it, and my little spell of indigestion (for that is what it was) was due, undoubtedly, to my being worn out and unable to run both my stomach and the government. I realize when I stop to think about it all that I never before knew such a strain as I have undergone ever since Congress convened in April. . . . I take the best care I can of myself. The doctor, who is one of my regularly appointed staff, is with me practically at all times of the day, and this summer, while the family has been away, has lived in the house with me, being very watchful and very competent, and I shall fare very well; but I was a bit bored this past week to find myself so 'poorly' that I almost lost interest in golf itself and lay down to rest instead of going out to play. When I did play I hardly had spunk enough to drive the ball a hundred yards. But that is all gone by now. For one thing the weather has changed, . . . and I am feeling very different,—all my spunk comes back."[95]

The family returned soon afterward, and life in the White House resumed its accustomed round. On December 9, 1913, the President came down with a heavy cold. Two weeks later he and his family left Washington for a rest at Pass Christian, on the Gulf Coast of Mississippi. "Here we are esconced in a very comfortable house where they take care of us delightfully," Wilson wrote soon after his arrival. "When we first got here it was intensely cold, but no cold spell can last long here and already the sun is softening the air wonderfully. It will presently be just what we came down to enjoy. My mind is freer from strain than it has been, I believe, since I was chosen Governor of New Jersey, so that I am sure I shall have a fine rest."[96]

There were also festive times in the White House, when Jessie married Francis B. Sayre of Williams College on November 25, 1913, and Eleanor married William G. McAdoo on May 7, 1914. Wilson reacted

[94] W. W. to Mary A. Hulbert, September 7, 1913, printed in *ibid.*, pp. 178-179.
[95] W. W. to Mary A. Hulbert, October 12, 1913, printed in *ibid.*, pp. 189-190.
[96] W. W. to X, December 27, 1913, Wilson Papers.

like the typical loving father. "Jessie and Frank came back from across the water last week: to-day they started for their home in Williamstown," he wrote on February 1, 1914. "The pang of it is still deep in my heart. When they went off on their wedding journey the thing somehow did not seem to me final: they would be back after the honeymoon! But now! This going to make a permanent home for themselves comes on me like a new realization, or—rather—a first realization of what has happened, and I feel bereaved."[97]

But the pain of losing his youngest daughter, whom he loved most of all, was sharper than that which he felt when Jessie married. "Ah! How desperately my heart aches that she is gone," he wrote soon after Eleanor's wedding. "She was simply part of me, the only delightful part; and I feel the loneliness more than I dare admit even to myself. The wedding was as simple and beautiful as any I ever saw or imagined and she has married a noble man, who I feel sure will make her happy and proud, too. But just now I can realize, in my selfishness, only that I have lost her, for good and all."[98] It was a natural jealousy, which quickly subsided.

From the time of Eleanor's wedding until early August 1914, a dark shadow—an illness from which Ellen Wilson could not seem to recover—hung over the White House and cast a pall upon the President's mind and heart. This story will be told in due time; meanwhile, we must turn to the larger political scene and describe the men in the Wilson circle and the problems that were already fast developing at home and abroad.

[97] W. W. to Mary A. Hulbert, February 1, 1914, printed in R. S. Baker, *Woodrow Wilson*, IV, 305.
[98] W. W. to Mary A. Hulbert, May 10, 1914, printed in *ibid.*, p. 342.

CHAPTER IV

The Wilson Circle: Personalities, Problems, and Policies

THE men who moved in the Wilson circle during the years before the First World War were an incongruous group of progressives and conservatives, professional politicians and amateurs, idealists and men trained in the school of reality, but in varying degree they all contributed to the successes and failures of the New Freedom.

The most important member of the Wilson circle, next to the President himself, was Colonel Edward M. House. The friendship between Wilson and the Texan had ripened into intimacy by the end of the campaign of 1912, although the two men had known each other less than a year. As the months and years passed, their friendship deepened, and until 1919 House remained the one person to whom the President felt he could turn in absolute trust.

There was no matter so intimate that it could not be discussed between them; to this "dearest friend," as to no other man, Wilson bared his secret thoughts and troubles. "You are the only person in the world with whom I can discuss everything," Wilson wrote to House after Ellen's death. "There are some I can tell one thing and others another, but you are the only one to whom I can make an entire clearance of mind."[1] The President expressed his feelings toward House again, in a typical letter: "Your praise of anything that I do or say is always very sweet to me. . . . I would rather have your judgment than that of anybody I know."[2]

"Mr. House is my second personality. He is my independent self," Wilson once said of the relationship between them. "His thoughts and mine are one. If I were in his place I would do just as he suggested. . . . If any one thinks he [House] is reflecting my opinion by whatever action he takes, they are welcome to the conclusion."[3]

House described the friendship in even more revealing words:

[1] Charles Seymour (ed.), *The Intimate Papers of Colonel House*, I, 116.
[2] W. W. to E. M. House, January 11, 1915, Wilson Papers.
[3] Quoted in Charles Seymour (ed.), *The Intimate Papers of Colonel House*, I, 114.

"Almost from the first our association was intimate; almost from the first, our minds vibrated in unison. When we had exchanged thoughts with one another he translated our conclusions into action without delay. Nine times out of ten we reached the same conclusions. When we did, neither he nor I felt it necessary to counsel with the other. . . . My physical handicaps and my temperament make it necessary for me to work through other men. I was like a disembodied spirit seeking a corporeal form. I found my opportunity in Woodrow Wilson. But I did not, in the long course of our friendship, attempt to superimpose my personality upon his. Somehow our two souls merged, yet I always remained what I was, and he always remained Woodrow Wilson."[4]

It was one of the most important friendships in history but not the strangest, as George Sylvester Viereck has called it. It was a friendship based upon Wilson's need and House's peculiar capacities. Like most other men of state, Wilson needed a friend above the struggle for place and power, to whom he could turn for advice and spiritual support. Indeed, without such friendship the President was emotionally bereft. Endowed with unusual intelligence and moral strength, House was almost perfectly equipped to meet Wilson's need. He understood the Wilsonian temperament better than any other man. He knew when to speak and when to remain silent. He never argued. But in dealing with the President, House never yielded his own integrity, judgment, or critical capacities.

As his massive Diary reveals, House's supreme ambition was to win power during his lifetime and a large position in the history of his time. He refused official position, not because he was unambitious, but because he sought a larger goal—a share in the presidential power. He scrupulously avoided publicity, not because he was modest, but because he knew he could hold the President's confidence only as a silent partner.

House's chief function in the Wilson circle throughout the period from 1913 to 1919 was to act as the President's confidant and adviser and as his spokesman and liaison with the outside world. He talked with practically everyone prominent in the Democratic party in state and nation. Most of the Wilson entourage turned to him, as the man closest to the throne, for support in the unending struggle for preferment. Furthermore, House was Wilson's chief link with the leaders

---

[4] E. M. House, "Memoirs of Colonel House," unpublished MS. in the Papers of George Sylvester Viereck, Yale University Library.

of the business and banking communities and, after the First World War began, the President's only really important adviser on policy relating to the belligerents.

It was all a fascinating and wonderful experience to this unobtrusive Texan. In personal conversation he radiated warmth, friendship, and understanding; and not knowing that this was his method, every man thought he was on his side. Josephus Daniels, for example, lived a long life thinking House had been his friend, unaware that House had once participated in a cabal to drive him from office. As Daniels' son has said, the Colonel "was an intimate man even when he was cutting a throat."[5]

In contrast to House, who moved in the Wilson circle on many levels, was Louis D. Brandeis, who maintained an Olympian aloofness from the group and yet wielded a large influence in the formulation of domestic policies because he was one of the few persons in the country whose judgment on economic questions the President respected. Brandeis did not impair his standing at the White House by joining his friends in bitter recrimination when the President failed to appoint him to the Cabinet. In April 1913 Wilson offered the Boston lawyer the chairmanship of the Commission on Industrial Relations, recently established by Congress to investigate the causes of industrial unrest.[6] Brandeis refused, but in such a way as to increase the President's trust in his integrity and judgment. As a consequence, Brandeis later had a decisive hand in shaping the Federal Reserve bill and almost single-handedly persuaded the President to adopt an antitrust program that ran counter to Wilson's original plan.

Of the men around Wilson, none made a greater contribution to the success of the New Freedom program and provoked more caustic criticism than did the Secretary of State, William J. Bryan. Appointed to the premier post in order to fulfill a political debt and to ensure party harmony, Bryan moved among the Wilson circle during two of the most critical years of American history. Few men left a deeper imprint upon domestic and foreign policies and few have been so misunderstood as he.

In 1913 there was no happier Democrat in Washington. What a joy it was to ride in the inaugural parade and receive the plaudits of the

[5] Jonathan Daniels, *The End of Innocence*, p. 89.
[6] W. W. to L. D. Brandeis, April 24, 1913, Brandeis Papers.

crowd, to see the Democracy, "undaunted, militant, courageous, never faltering," at last in power, and to play an important part in bringing dreams of two decades to fruition! Bryan expressed his feelings frankly at the outset of his Cabinet career:

"Sometimes I have had over-sanguine friends express regret that I did not reach the presidency. I have had them say that they were sorry that after being connected with these reforms I should not have been given the highest place in the nation. But I have had an answer ready for them. I have told them that they need not weep for me; that I am not an object of sympathy; that two or three hundred years ago they hung men like me; now, they just defeat them for office. And, looking back over the past I am not prepared to say that my defeats were not good for the country. Not that I want to take back anything I have said, or any position that I have taken, but the people were not ready then for the reforms that are now accomplished, and had I been elected at any of the numerous times that I gave the people an opportunity to elect me—had I been elected—I would have had a very difficult task. . . .

"Today we have the people ripe for reform—and I am not sure that our president may not be able to do what I might not have been able to do had I been elected instead of him. But it is not a question that we need discuss, and one that does not concern me, for I have been so much more interested in the securing of the things for which we have been fighting than I have been in the name of the man who held the office, that I am happy in the thought that this government, through these reforms, will be made so good that a citizen will not miss a little thing like the presidency."[7]

The fact that the Nebraskan was able to work in harness after leading the Democratic party for sixteen years was a tribute both to Bryan's generosity and to Wilson's finesse and determination to avoid a fatal rupture. For two years, until disagreement over the proper response to the German submarine challenge drove them apart, the two men worked in perfect harmony and apparent friendship. This was possible, first of all, because Bryan meant what he said about suppressing his own political ambitions in the interest of Democratic achievement, because he fought loyally and effectively for the President, yielded minor points, and was able in the end to help shape the course of legislation. It was possible as well because the President often valued

[7] Address before the Union League of Chicago, April 1913, printed in *The Commoner*, XIII (April 11, 1913), 6.

Bryan's advice and gave him a free hand in several areas of foreign policy and a large share in formulating some of his most important foreign policies.

The two men conferred frequently in person but more often by letters and memoranda, and the thousands of notes in the Wilson Papers and the State Department archives yield revealing testimony to the truth of Bryan's assertion: "No two officials ever got along more amicably. I was in charge of the department and the President and I never differed on a matter of policy until the controversy over American citizens riding on belligerent ships. He did not take a matter out of my hands; he consulted me on every proposition and our correspondence will show that he gave weight to my views."[8]

In fact, the more the two men worked together, the stronger Bryan's friendship for the President grew, while Wilson made a valiant effort to preserve good relations. When hostile editors lampooned the Nebraskan for neglecting his duties and for alleged social gaucheries, Wilson hastened publicly to defend the Secretary's "character, his justice, his sincerity, his transparent integrity, his Christian principle."[9] On another occasion, the following typical exchange occurred: "I have learned not only to value you as a friend and counsellor, but, if you will let me say so, I have found a very strong affection for you growing in my heart," Wilson wrote. "It is a genuine satisfaction to be associated, personally and officially, with one who sees so clearly the fundamental distinctions between democracy and aristocracy, and so bravely stands for the rights and interests of the masses," Bryan replied.[10] It was the highest praise that either could give.

The first task confronting the President and his Secretary was the reorganization of the State Department and the Foreign Service. In personnel the Department was no larger than the foreign office of most second-rate powers, and Wilson and Bryan divided the few available appointments. Actually, it was the President who made the most important appointments to the departmental staff.[11] He named his

---

[8] W. J. Bryan to George Derby, August 1, 1924, copy in the Baker Collection.

[9] W. W. to William L. Marbury, February 5, 1914, Wilson Papers; printed in the *New York Times*, February 7, 1914.

[10] W. W. to W. J. Bryan, March 18, 1915; and W. J. Bryan to W. W., March 19, 1915, both in the Wilson Papers.

[11] Bryan appointed John E. Osborne, a former Governor of Wyoming, as Assistant Secretary of State; Ben G. Davis, as Chief Clerk; and Joseph W. Folk of Missouri, first, and then Cone Johnson of Texas, as Solicitor of the Department. These were positions then considered available as political appointments. Except to appoint Boaz W. Long,

friend, Dudley Field Malone, as Third Assistant Secretary in charge of personnel, and then gave the post to House's young friend, William Phillips, when Malone resigned in November 1913 to become Collector of the Port of New York. For the most important office in the Department under the Secretary, that of Counselor, the President was determined to have the eminent authority on international law, Professor John Bassett Moore of Columbia University. In spite of misgivings about working with Bryan, Moore finally yielded to Wilson's pleading. When he resigned on February 2, 1914, newspapermen assumed that friction with Bryan had been the cause of his unhappiness;[12] the truth probably was that he could no longer abide Wilson's Mexican policy, which he had strongly opposed from the beginning. As Moore's successor, the President named Robert Lansing, a son-in-law of former Secretary of State John W. Foster and a distinguished international lawyer, who became Secretary of State after Bryan's resignation in 1915. Lansing's greatest service lies beyond the scope of this volume, but it should be said that he was one of the leaders of real distinction in the Wilson circle from the outset.

The appointment of Ambassadors and leading Ministers fell by right to the President, and he embarked upon his search determined to break the custom of rewarding rich contributors to party funds and worn-out politicians with posts abroad.

Wilson began early, in January 1913, by urging former President Charles W. Eliot of Harvard to go as Minister to China. When Eliot refused, much to Bryan's relief, because Eliot was a Unitarian and Bryan thought only an orthodox Christian should be sent to such an important missionary field, Wilson turned next to John R. Mott, a leader in the international Y.M.C.A. movement. But Mott also refused, in spite of Wilson's persuasive entreaty. "Mott's decision was a great blow to me," he wrote. "I don't know when I have been so disappointed. This is a difficult road I am traveling in trying to get the finest men in the country to serve me at foreign posts."[13] Finally, he appointed Professor Paul S. Reinsch, a Far Eastern authority at the University of Wisconsin.

---

a friend of Vice President Marshall, as Chief of the Division of Latin American Affairs, and Albert H. Putney, Dean of the Illinois College of Law, as head of the Division of Near Eastern Affairs, however, Bryan left the permanent staff largely undisturbed.

[12] *New York Times*, March 5, 1914; "The President and the Department of State," *The Independent*, LXXVII (March 16, 1914), 365.

[13] W. W. to C. H. Dodge, April 5, 1913, Wilson Papers.

The President-Elect and Mrs. Wilson Leaving Princeton for Washington

Wilson Taking the Oath of Office as President in 1913

The President Demands Tariff Reform

Wilson Speaking at a Flag Day Celebration in Washington, 1913

From left to right: William J. Bryan, Josephus Daniels, the President, Henry Breckinridge, William Phillips, Franklin D. Roosevelt

The Wilsons at Harlakenden, New Hampshire, 1913. From left to right: Margaret, Mrs. Wilson, Eleanor, Jessie, Dr. Wilson

The President and His Cabinet, 1913

From left to right: the President, W. G. McAdoo, J. C. McReynolds, J. Daniels, D. F. Houston, W. B. Wilson, W. C. Redfield, F. K. Lane, A. S. Burleson, L. M. Garrison, W. J. Bryan

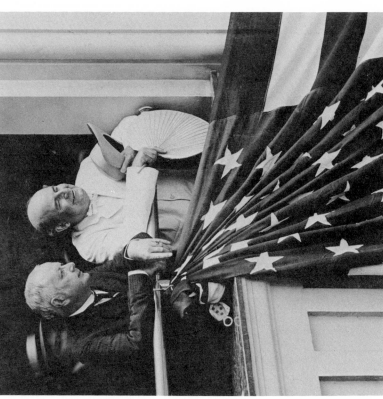

The Secretary of State Is Amused

Wilson Votes in Princeton, 1914

Two Leaders in the Fight for Banking Reform

From left to right: Carter Glass, W. G. McAdoo

Colonel Edward M. House

Finding the right man as Ambassador to Great Britain was the hardest task of all. There were many wealthy Democrats who would have paid handsomely for this choice post, but the President appealed instead to Dr. Eliot, who again refused, and then to Richard Olney of Boston, Secretary of State in Cleveland's Cabinet. "You are the only man Mr. Bryan and I have had in our thoughts who would ideally satisfy the requirements of the post," Wilson urged.[14] When Olney refused, Wilson yielded to the advice of House and McAdoo and turned to his old friend, Walter Page, who accepted eagerly and soon became one of the outstanding members of the Wilson circle.

Page was not only the President's most important diplomatic representative; he was the only one with whom Wilson had intimate personal relations. The two men can best tell the story of their friendship before the early months of 1915, when sharp differences over American neutrality began to drive them apart.

"I called again on the President to ask his instructions," Page related in his Diary soon after his appointment. "He had none. He knew no more about the task that awaited me than I knew. . . . [He] seemed to have in mind only this idea—that he wanted somebody in London whom he knew & upon whose judgment he could rely."[15]

"I not only appreciate your letters but I profit by them, profit very much," the President wrote in appreciation to Page. ". . . I feel after I have read one of your letters as if I had been in London and seen the people you are dealing with and received the same impressions that you, yourself, have received from what they do and say."[16] "I have known Page for many years and I have never known anyone more compelling on paper," Wilson told the Counselor of the Embassy in London in the spring of 1914. "Whenever people have wanted me to do something I might be disinclined to do they would try to get Page to write to me about it. I never could resist him."[17]

A short time later, when one of Page's speeches had provoked the Anglophobes at home, Wilson hastened to send assurances to London. "You may be sure that none of us who knew you or read the speech felt anything but admiration for it . . . ," he wrote. "Mr. Bryan read your speech yesterday to the Cabinet, who greatly enjoyed it."[18] "Please do not distress yourself about that speech . . . ," the President added

[14] W. W. to R. Olney, March 11, 1913, *ibid.*
[15] Page Diary, n.d.
[16] W. W. to W. H. Page, February 24, 1914, Wilson Papers.
[17] Irwin B. Laughlin to R. S. Baker, June 29, 1935, Baker Collection.
[18] W. W. to W. H. Page, March 25, 1914, Wilson Papers.

soon afterward, rejecting Page's offer to resign. "I would be willing to subscribe to every bit of it myself, and there can be no rational objection to it."[19]

The deepest revelation of Wilson's friendship for Page occurred soon afterward and illustrated the near-impossibility of getting and retaining the "right" men as Ambassadors. They were expected not merely to live upon their annual salaries of $17,500, but also to maintain pretentious homes and to entertain in a manner befitting a great and wealthy power. In contrast, the British Ambassador to the United States received a salary of $50,000 a year and a generous living allowance besides. The result of congressional penury was obvious: poor men simply could not afford to be Ambassadors.

Under no illusions about his future when he agreed to go to London, Page planned to spend some $25,000 of his own savings during the first year and then to come home. He explained the situation frankly to Colonel House and the President, saying that he would have to resign unless additional money could somehow be found.[20] By action perhaps unprecedented in American history, Wilson found a solution.

"Something you once, in your great generosity, offered to do for me when I wanted Harry Fine to accept the post of Ambassador to Germany, emboldens me to turn to you in a great difficulty with which I find myself brought face to face," the President wrote to his old friend, Cleveland H. Dodge, in July 1914. "Walter Page is obliged to spend twenty-five thousand a year more than the government allows him or he has to spend. He must come home unless I can find the money for him from some source that will put him under no obligation which will in any way touch him in the performance of his duties. He has learned his job,—learned it admirably: speaks my mind and my point of view to the ministers over there as I am sure no one else could speak them; has got a real hold, socially *and* politically; is, if I know one when I see him, for the present at any rate, an indispensable man in the right management of our foreign relations. I would not know what to do if I were obliged to part with him. My relations with him are intimate, and he has furnished me with more light on difficult foreign matters than all my other informants and advisers put together. I have, therefore, bidden him engage his present house for another year and count on me to do something to help him.

[19] W. W. to W. H. Page, April 2, 1914, *ibid.*

[20] W. H. Page to E. M. House, January 30, 1914, House Papers; W. H. Page to W. W., April 7, 1914, Wilson Papers.

"Will you forgive me and understand me, if I turn to you? I know that you will, and that you will come to my aid if you can. I know of no other friend like you, and of no other friend to whom I could afford to turn in such a matter and with such a request. You will tell me if you cannot do it; and if you can, it will be help that I can afford, in honour and with unmeasured confidence, to accept. Thank God that it is so, and that there is room somewhere for perfect trust!"[21]

Dodge replied that Wilson's "beautiful letter" was "well worth the whole price of admission" and that, since he fortunately no longer had any financial commitments to Princeton, he could easily supply the entire $25,000 annually as long as Page stayed in London.[22] A system of payment was worked out—Dodge sent money to House, who passed it on to Arthur W. Page, the Ambassador's son—so that Page probably never knew who his benefactor was. It is ironic that within two years Wilson had completely lost confidence in Page and was trying to persuade Dodge himself to go as Ambassador to the Court of St. James.

Page's financial plight illustrated Wilson's chief difficulty in staffing the ambassadorial posts. He wanted, for example, to appoint Professor Henry B. Fine, a mathematics professor at Princeton, as Ambassador to Germany; and Dodge offered to give Fine $25,000 a year for four years in order to enable him to live.[23] But Fine refused, in part because he would not accept money even from a dear friend.[24] "It is a great pity that the country has to ask such sacrifices of those who are invited to serve it abroad—a service which every year becomes more exacting and more important," the President declared in exasperation in a public statement on March 23, 1913. "The sacrifice of time, of means, and of opportunity at home is very serious for any but men of large means and leisure, and the diplomatic service is unnecessarily hampered."[25]

In the end, therefore, Wilson had to yield his high ambitions and give ambassadorships, as he earlier had told House he would not do, "to the merely rich who were clamoring for them."[26] For example, he had stated that "under no circumstances" would he give an appointment to James W. Gerard, a wealthy Tammany judge who had contributed heavily to the Democratic war chest in 1912.[27] But the pres-

[21] W. W. to C. H. Dodge, July 12, 1914, printed in R. S. Baker, *Woodrow Wilson*, IV, 33.
[22] C. H. Dodge to W. W., July 13, 1914, Baker Collection.
[23] House Diary, February 13, 1913.
[24] H. B. Fine to W. W., March 29, 1913, Wilson Papers.
[25] *New York Times*, March 24, 1913.   [26] House Diary, January 17, 1913.
[27] Henry White told Edith Bolling Wilson that Gerard gave some $120,000 to the

sure from Gerard's friend, Senator James A. O'Gorman of New York, was so great that the President finally submitted and, as it turned out, sent an incompetent representative to one of the two most important American diplomatic stations. In order to appease Virginia's two powerful senators, he sent Thomas Nelson Page, a second-rate novelist, to Rome and Joseph E. Willard, a wealthy Virginia politician, to Madrid. He rewarded two of his heaviest financial supporters, Frederick C. Penfield and Henry Morgenthau, with the ambassadorships to Austria-Hungary and the Ottoman Empire, respectively. He favored Ohio Democrats with the appointment of William G. Sharp, a wealthy former congressman, as Ambassador to France; and he rewarded the progressive Democratic leaders in Pennsylvania with the appointment of Roland S. Morris and then George W. Guthrie as Ambassador to the Japanese Empire.

One embarrassing episode in connection with the ambassadorial appointments became a near-scandal. Largely at the urging of Senator J. Hamilton Lewis of Illinois, Wilson and Bryan agreed to appoint Henry M. Pindell, an editor from Peoria and the "original Wilson man" in his state, as Ambassador to Russia. It was a seemingly routine matter, until a disgruntled clerk in Lewis' office stole the letters relating to the appointment and sold them to the press. It then came out that the President and Secretary had agreed to appoint Pindell upon the condition that he resign on October 1, 1914. The senator, moreover, had urged Pindell to accept, assuring him that the position would be a sinecure. "There will be no treaties to adjudicate, and no political affairs to bother with, for the Administration will see to that for a year," Lewis had written, "and you would not be tied to St. Petersburg, but would have trips to Berlin and Vienna and the other capitals of Europe, and also Stockholm, and perhaps Copenhagen, and all the attendant delights that go with such trips."[28]

Democratic campaign fund of 1912, most of which was sent to local leaders without being officially reported. Henry White to Mrs. Woodrow Wilson, February 22, 1925, Baker Collection.

[28] J. H. Lewis to H. M. Pindell, September 5, 1913, printed in "The Case of Brother Pindell," *North American Review*, cxcviii (December 1913), 754.

At this time the President was trying to persuade Charles R. Crane of Chicago, a benefactor of many progressive and humanitarian causes, to accept the ambassadorship. "I simply cannot adjust my mind to giving up the idea of having you represent us at the Court of Russia," Wilson wrote, urging Crane not to decline finally. "We are making a temporary appointment in the person of Mr. Pindell of Peoria, who is very glad to consent to the arrangement proposed that he later give place to yourself." W. W. to C. R. Crane, October 3, 1913, Wilson Papers.

Pindell accepted eagerly, and the Senate confirmed his nomination. But the Russian Foreign Minister was so outraged by the way in which the appointment had been arranged that he informed the Secretary of the American Embassy in St. Petersburg that the Imperial authorities would publicly refuse to accept Pindell if the President insisted upon sending him.[29] Pindell of course withdrew, and almost a year passed before Wilson found a man both willing to go to St. Petersburg and acceptable to the Czarist authorities.[30]

There was nothing new about the way Wilson appointed his Ambassadors or the reasons why they were chosen,[31] and on the whole they served their country as well as their Republican counterparts had done. But in the naming of Ministers, Bryan played an active role with consequences sometimes catastrophic. The Commoner was an out-and-out spoilsman, imbued with the Jacksonian conviction that honesty, native intelligence, and party service were sufficient qualifications for public service in any field. The opportunity of rewarding old friends and followers was for him one of the chief joys of holding office; besides, he knew what the pressures were and how the game had to be played.

"We have plenty of friends who have not yet been taken care of," he wrote to the President in August 1913, for example, about the appointment of Ministers. "I am especially anxious to get something for Arkansas. We have not done anything for that state so far and it is one of our most reliable states."[32] "My own disposition, as you know," he further explained, "is to use our prominent Democrats, not only as a reward for what they have been, but because distinction puts them in a position to do something in the future. We have been quite short of prefixes. While Republicans have been able to introduce Secretary so-and-so; Ambassador so-and-so, and Minister so-and-so, not to speak

[29] C. S. Wilson to the Secretary of State, December 7, 1913, *ibid.*

[30] Charles R. Crane refused finally on May 18, 1914. Wilson and Bryan considered appointing former Representative William G. Sharp of Ohio but drew back when the Russian Ambassador in Washington hinted that his government would not welcome Sharp, because he had been a member of the House foreign affairs committee which in 1911 had recommended the denunciation of the Russian-American Commercial Treaty. Finally, on June 20, 1914, the President appointed George T. Marye, a Democratic leader from California and a friend of Bryan, who was acceptable to the Imperial government. Marye was succeeded by David R. Francis, former Governor of Missouri, in early 1916.

[31] As the New York *Nation*, xcvii (November 13, 1913), 450, lamented.

[32] W. J. Bryan to W. W., August 16, 1913, Wilson Papers.

The Employment Agent
Kirby in the New York *World*

of the smaller officials, we have usually had to confine ourselves [to] 'Mister' or 'Honorable.' "[33]

It mattered not whether the positions were political or professional, unimportant or important. It mattered only that they were jobs to be filled by Democrats, whose virtue and ability were measured chiefly by their devotion to the party. For example, in selecting a man to serve as a director of the national bank and national railway of Nicaragua, Bryan chose a former congressman who had fought for Wilson in the preconvention campaign in his state.[34] "Now that you

[33] W. J. Bryan to W. W., June 22, 1914, *ibid.*
[34] W. J. Bryan to W. W., January 15, 1914, *ibid.*

have arrived and are acquainting yourself with the situation," he wrote to the newly appointed Receiver-General of the Dominican customs, to cite another example, "can you let me know what positions you have at your disposal with which to reward deserving Democrats? . . . You have had enough experience in politics to know how valuable workers are when the campaign is on and how difficult it is to find suitable rewards for all the deserving."[35]

Bryan wanted a clean sweep of the Foreign Service, not merely because he was a spoilsman, but also because he believed that the officers in the American diplomatic corps were either incompetent Republicans or else members of a snobbish professional elite fast developing into an aristocracy. To a large extent, Wilson shared these beliefs. The President explained the problem of conducting foreign relations with a body of men which, as one contemporary observed, had become "something resembling a caste, class, or order,"[36] in the following way:

"We find that those who have been occupying the legations and embassies have been habituated to a point of view which is very different, indeed, from the point of view of the present administration. They have had the material interests of individuals in the United States very much more in mind than the moral and public considerations which it seems to us ought to control. They have been so bred in a different school that we have found, in several instances, that it was difficult for them to comprehend our point of view and purpose."[37]

Because he essentially agreed with Bryan that diplomatic appointments on the upper level were political in nature,[38] the President joined

[35] W. J. Bryan to W. W. Vick, August 20, 1913, printed in the *North American Review*, cci (February 1915), 285. When the publication of this letter evoked a storm of protest, Bryan calmly replied: "I am glad to have the public know that I appreciate the services of those who work in politics and feel an interest in seeing them rewarded. I think that is the only charge that can be based on that letter, and, as Mr. Vick received his appointment as a reward for political work, I thought he was a good man to address in expressing my opinion on the subject." *New York Times*, January 16, 1915.

[36] J. Kendrick Kinney, "A Scholar's View of Mr. Bryan," *North American Review*, cxcix (February 1914), 224.

[37] W. W. to C. W. Eliot, September 17, 1913, Wilson Papers.

[38] It should be pointed out in fairness to Bryan that Wilson was also willing to use diplomatic appointments for political purposes. "I wonder if you have communicated with Uruguay about the appointment of Mr. C. C. Smith of New Hampshire," he wrote, for example, to the Secretary of State in August 1913. "We are trying to help out in the pending bye-election [sic] in Maine as much as we can and Senator Hollis [of New Hampshire] was kind enough to intimate that he would be willing to forego Mr. Smith's appointment in order that we might appoint a man from

his Secretary in making a nearly clean sweep of Ministers. Many of Wilson's own appointments in the ministerial category were "the peers, if not indeed the superiors, of their predecessors," as one editor put it,[39] but it was a different story when Bryan and the politicians had free rein.

During the McKinley administration, Secretary of State John Hay had begun the practice of building a professional diplomatic corps, particularly in Latin America, by promoting efficient staff officers to the rank of Minister. Secretaries Elihu Root and Philander C. Knox, under Roosevelt and Taft, had matured the policy, with the result that a large part of the Foreign Service had been professionalized by the time Wilson was inaugurated. This situation was to Bryan both a challenge and an opportunity; and in the greatest debauchery of the Foreign Service in the twentieth century he dismissed all the Ministers who had earned their posts by merit and training and installed an aggregation of friends and party hacks.[40] George Harvey summarized the record as it related to Bryan's Latin American appointments:

"The average experience of the former Ministers to these South and Central American republics was fifteen and one-third years, and their average age at the time of their expulsion was forty-seven. All spoke the language of the countries to which they were accredited. The average age of the new Ministers is fifty-four and one-half, five being past sixty; no one of them, we believe, understands Spanish; and none, of

---

Maine, as that would be serviceable in the present circumstances." W. W. to W. J. Bryan, August 15, 1913, *ibid.*

[39] Paul S. Reinsch, Minister to China; Henry Van Dyke, Minister to the Netherlands; Brand Whitlock, Minister to Belgium; and Ira Nelson Morris, Minister to Sweden, all appointed personally by the President, were men fully representative of the best traditions of the Foreign Service.

[40] A few cases must suffice to illustrate the generalization. As Minister to Costa Rica, Bryan dismissed Lewis Einstein, a brilliant young officer who had served in Paris, Constantinople, and Peking since 1903, and appointed Edward J. Hale, aged editor of the Fayetteville, North Carolina, *Observer*, who had supported Wilson for the presidential nomination. Charles D. White, Minister to Honduras, who had served in many posts since 1904, was replaced by John Ewing, a Wilson supporter of New Orleans. Robert S. R. Hitt, Minister to Guatemala, who had served successively since 1901 as Third Secretary at Paris, Second Secretary at Berlin, Minister to Panama, and Minister to Venezuela, was replaced by William Hayne Leavell, a Presbyterian minister from Texas and Mississippi. As Minister to Rumania, Bryan dismissed John B. Jackson, who had entered the Foreign Service in 1900, and appointed Charles J. Vopicka, a Chicago brewer, who allegedly neither drank his own beer nor allowed it in his home.

course, has had diplomatic experience. In other words, twelve trained and capable representatives, several of whom entered the service under competitive examination and all of whom had long since forsaken partisanship, are superseded by mere party hacks whose ages clearly disqualify them for continuance in office for sufficient time to equip themselves for proper performances of their duties."[41]

Bryan, meanwhile, was also fighting hard to win what was potentially the richest prize of all—control of appointments in the large Consular Service, which had developed into a highly efficient professional body since Theodore Roosevelt removed it from the spoils system in 1906 and established a system of appointment by competitive examination and promotion for merit. Although the Nebraskan argued "strongly and eloquently" that the numerous consular posts should go to deserving Democrats,[42] Wilson stood firm against any further raids. He not only insisted upon appointing consuls from the civil service list[43] but also continued Roosevelt's and Taft's practice of appointing secretaries in the diplomatic corps on a basis of merit.[44]

Most of Bryan's ministerial appointees were mere incompetents, not scoundrels. The one big exception was James M. Sullivan, whose appointment as Minister to the Dominican Republic became one of the most embarrassing scandals of the Wilson administration. A former prize-fight promoter and a New York lawyer intimate with underworld and gambling interests, Sullivan was prominent in Irish ward politics in the Northeast and won the endorsement of Tumulty, Senator O'Gorman, Governor Simeon E. Baldwin of Connecticut, and other reputable Democrats.[45] "So far as I can see," Bryan concluded, "Sullivan is all

[41] George Harvey, "The Diplomats of Democracy," *North American Review*, cxcix (February 1914), 171-172; see also the survey in the *New York Times*, July 9, 1913.

[42] House Diary, April 18, 1913; *New York Times*, July 9, 1913.

[43] Wilson made his first consular appointments, thirty in number, in September 1913. Twenty-eight of the appointees had been promoted; the remaining two had passed examinations for appointment to consular positions. The President, moreover, steadfastly refused to violate the merit system in appointing consuls, even in allegedly exceptional cases. See, e.g., W. W. to W. J. Bryan, August 8, 1913, Wilson Papers: and W. W. to T. W. Hardwick, September 11, 1913, *ibid*. As House advised one Texan, "The only way one can get into the Consular Service is to take the regular civil service examination and then be appointed to the lower grades and work up." E. M. House to W. H. Callaway, October 21, 1913, House Papers.

[44] See W. W. to W. J. Bryan, May 21, 1913, Wilson Papers.

[45] J. M. Blum, *Joe Tumulty and the Wilson Era*, p. 111; W. J. Bryan to W. W., June 9, 1913, Wilson Papers; S. E. Baldwin to W. W., May 24, 1913; H. S. Cummings to W. W., May 20, 1913; and W. Saulsbury to W. W., June 12, 1913, all in *ibid*.

right, and there are a number of reasons why it would be desirable to appoint him, but I have explained to Senator O'Gorman that we cannot afford to have any afterclap."[46] For a time Bryan hesitated; but the pressure from the White House, particularly from Tumulty, became so strong that he dismissed the Minister to the Dominican Republic, William W. Russell, who had been in the Foreign Service since 1895, and appointed Sullivan in late July 1913.

Bryan did not know it then, but the truth, which was later revealed by the New York *World* and a presidential commission of inquiry,[47] was that the man who engineered Sullivan's appointment was William C. Beer of New York, a lobbyist and agent for Samuel M. Jarvis and his *Banco Nacional* of Santo Domingo, who sought control of the deposits of the American Receiver-General of the Dominican customs. Jarvis supported Sullivan's candidacy in return for Sullivan's promise to help get the deposits transferred from S. Michelana & Company of Santo Domingo, an affiliate of the Guaranty Trust Company of New York, to the *Banco Nacional*. Sullivan arranged the transfer after he arrived in the Caribbean republic, but the Receiver-General and the Bureau of Insular Affairs of the War Department, which had charge of the collection of the Dominican customs, soon concluded that the *Banco Nacional* was utterly unreliable and returned the funds to S. Michelana & Company.[48]

The development that led to a public scandal was Sullivan's behavior in the Dominican capital, where he revealed unusual incompetence as a diplomat and worked hand in glove with the then President of the republic, José Bordas Valdés, the *Banco Nacional*, and as many corrupt concessionaires as would cooperate. The newspapers printed intimations of Sullivan's corruption as early as December 1913;[49] but Sullivan denied the charges, and Bryan gave him a clean bill of health.[50] However, conditions in the American legation grew so disgraceful that the Receiver-General of the customs, Walker W. Vick, laid the facts before the Secretary of State in March and April of

[46] W. J. Bryan to W. W., June 9, 1913, *ibid*.

[47] New York *World*, December 7, 8, 9, 10, 11, 13, 1914, and the *New York Times*, January 13, 14, 15, 16, 17, 19, 20, 21, 22, 23, 26, 27, 28 and 29, February 10, and July 27, 1915, for the investigation and report of the special commission.

[48] See W. W. Vick to Frank McIntyre, February 19, 1914; J. M. Sullivan to the Secretary of State, May 25, 1914; L. M. Garrison to W. J. Bryan, June 4, 1914; and F. McIntyre to W. J. Bryan, June 10, 1914, all in the Papers of the Department of State, the National Archives; hereinafter cited as the State Department Papers.

[49] *New York Times*, December 10, 1913.

[50] *ibid*., December 12, 1913.

1914.[51] Although Vick's indictment was confirmed by prominent Americans in Santo Domingo,[52] and although Vick carried his charges to Colonel House and directly to the President,[53] Wilson and Bryan stubbornly refused either to investigate or to recall Sullivan. In desperation, because he believed the nation's honor was involved and that the administration would continue to whitewash Sullivan, Vick took his story to the New York *World*,[54] which conducted its own investigation and began publication of a series on December 7, 1914, that blew the lid off the scandal.

It was now no longer possible for Wilson to refuse to act. On December 8, 1914, he instructed Secretary of War Garrison, Vick's superior, to investigate; and when Garrison replied that Sullivan, not Vick, was the alleged culprit, Wilson asked Bryan to undertake a thorough investigation. "Mr. Vick evidently feels, at any rate he asserts, that the State Department has taken and will take his charges very lightly," the President wrote to Bryan on December 10, 1914. "He is violently prejudiced and, therefore, I suggest that you arrange to have this matter put in the hands of someone who heretofore has not been in touch with it at all and who will be so evidently removed from intimate relationship either with yourself or with me as to be clearly a detached and impartial,—I mean clearly to the public, upon whom Vick is trying to make an impression."[55]

Soon afterward, Bryan appointed James D. Phelan, a friendly Democratic senator-elect from California, to hear the charges against Sullivan and his friends. The hearings that proceeded during January and early February 1915 were a prolonged embarrassment for the administration, as Tumulty, among other leading Democrats, was deeply involved as a friend of Sullivan, and Vick gave out Bryan's "deserving

---

[51] W. W. Vick to W. J. Bryan, March 14, 1914, adverted to in W. W. to W. J. Bryan, March 30, 1914, Wilson Papers; W. W. Vick to W. J. Bryan, April 14, 1914, the Papers of William Jennings Bryan, National Archives (hereinafter cited as the Bryan Papers, National Archives), summarizing Vick's conversation with Bryan on April 13, 1914.

[52] e.g., John J. Moore to W. J. Bryan, April 25, 1914; S. A. Agnew to W. J. Bryan, May 14, 1914; and J. H. Stabler, memorandum entitled "Conditions in Santo Domingo," dated May 22, 1914, all in the State Department Papers.

[53] W. W. Vick to E. M. House, April 22 and September 17, 1914, House Papers; W. W. Vick to W. W., September 7, 1914, Wilson Papers; and W. W. Vick to W. W., December 1, 1914, summarized in L. M. Garrison to W. W., December 8, 1914, *ibid*.

[54] W. W. Vick, "Statement of Walker W. Vick to the Leaders of the Democratic Party," dated February 22, 1915, copy in *ibid*.

[55] W. W. to L. M. Garrison, December 8, 1914; L. M. Garrison to W. W., December 8, 1914; and W. W. to W. J. Bryan, December 10, 1914, all in *ibid*.

Democrats" letter for publication. In his report, presented to Bryan in May and published on July 27, 1915, after the New York *World* had intimated that the administration was suppressing it, Phelan confirmed many of Vick's and the *World's* charges, administered a severe rebuke to the State Department, and recommended that Sullivan be removed at once from his post.[56]

To the end of the episode, Wilson contended that Sullivan had been "very foolish rather than anything worse," but Bryan had no illusions about Sullivan's character or the harm the scandal had done. "Sullivan impressed me as a man of rugged strength and honesty and I gave considerable weight to the fact that he is a Catholic, feeling that because of our intimate relationship with Santo Domingo it would be best to have someone religiously in sympathy with the people," he wrote in a revealing post-mortem on the affair. ". . . I am satisfied, from the testimony, that we were deceived as to the interests which supported Mr. Sullivan's candidacy."[57]

Bryan was nothing if not the most controversial member of the Wilson circle during his tenure as Secretary of State. He drew the censure of the National Civil Service Reform League and leading editors for demoralizing the Foreign Service.[58] He was the object of the scorn of virtually the entire American press, except for the loyal Democratic journals, after the publication of his "deserving Democrats" letter to Vick.[59] He engaged in numerous quarrels with newspapermen, whom he accused of prying and stealing governmental secrets.[60] Finally, he

[56] Sullivan was allowed to resign on July 8, 1915. "I [would] think that to publish the report before giving Mr. Sullivan an opportunity to resign," Wilson advised Acting Secretary of State Robert Lansing on June 22, 1915 (Wilson Papers), "would probably put him in a more disadvantageous and trying position than to give him that opportunity before the report is published. I would suggest, therefore, that he be kindly offered the opportunity to resign and be told the character of the report and its conclusions and the necessity this department feels under to publish it, in view of the publicity given to the whole investigation."

[57] W. J. Bryan to W. W., May 19, 1915, Wilson Papers. For Wilson's opinion, quoted above, see W. W. to R. Lansing, June 22, 1915, *ibid.*

[58] New York *Nation*, xcvii (December 18, 1913), 582; *New York Times*, May 14, 1914; George Harvey, "The Diplomats of Democracy," *North American Review*, cxcix (February 1914), 161-174; New York *Outlook*, cvi (March 7, 1914), 523-525; An American Diplomat, "The Diplomatic Service," *ibid.*, pp. 533-538.

[59] For an excellent review, see "Santo Domingo and Secretary Bryan," New York *Outlook*, cix (February 3, 1915), 267-270; and *Literary Digest*, L (January 30, 1915), 179-180.

[60] W. J. Bryan to W. W., July 30, 1913, Wilson Papers; David Lawrence to W. W., March 24, 1915, *ibid.*, relating the reporters' difficulties with the Secretary of State.

provoked ridicule and eventually widespread demands for his resignation by refusing to serve alcoholic beverages at state dinners and by insisting upon lecturing for profit while Secretary of State.

Bryan inaugurated his so-called "grape-juice diplomacy" at a dinner which he and Mrs. Bryan gave in honor of the retiring British Ambassador, James Bryce, at the New Willard Hotel on April 21, 1913. Mrs. Bryan tells the story:

"When the guests were all seated, Will rose at his place, looking decidedly pale . . . and asked the guests' indulgence for a few moments. He then told them how when President Wilson had asked him to be Secretary of State, he had asked him whether taking the office would necessitate the serving of liquors, and had been given permission to use his own judgment. He told them that we had always been teetotalers, that our fathers were both teetotalers, and that we could not depart from this custom without contradicting all our past. He hoped we might show our hospitality in other ways and that they would pardon us if we omitted wines."[61]

This simple act evoked profuse applause from the religious press,[62] a raising of eyebrows among the social elite, and, as Josephus Daniels has observed, almost as much discussion in the newspapers as if Bryan had resigned from the Cabinet. But it remained for the British press to make the most biting criticisms. "Official life in Washington under the Wilson-Bryan regime holds out little prospect of gaiety," remarked one London editor,[63] while another observed: "W. J. Bryan not only suffers for his principles and mortifies his flesh, as he has every right to do, but he insists that others should suffer and be mortified. This would be well enough if Mr. Bryan were a private citizen, but he is a minister of State, his guests are the diplomats of foreign embassies, and official invitations must be accepted lest continued refusal involve some suspicion of international discourtesy."[64]

The furor over "grape-juice diplomacy," however, was a mere tempest in a teapot as compared with the storm that raged in 1913 and 1914 over Bryan's lecturing for pay. The controversy developed when the Secretary went on the Chautauqua circuit during the summer of

[61] W. J. and M. B. Bryan, *The Memoirs of William Jennings Bryan*, p. 351, quoted by permission of the John C. Winston Company, publishers; see also Bryan's statement, printed in the *New York Times*, April 25, 1913.

[62] e.g., *Congregationalist and Christian World*, xcviii (May 1, 1913), 589; and Nashville *Christian Advocate*, lxxiv (May 2, 1913), 548.

[63] *Pall Mall Gazette*, April 24, 1913.

[64] London *Daily Express*, April 25, 1913.

1913 and explained, in response to newspaper criticism, that he had to lecture in order to meet his insurance premiums and his obligations to church, charity, and education, which totaled nearly $7,000 a year; that he had made large financial sacrifices in order to go into the Cabinet; and that he saw no reason to be ashamed of speaking before the American people.[65]

Bryan's soft answer, however, only fired his critics' wrath. They accused him of neglecting his duties and of demeaning his office by sharing the stage with Swiss girl yodelers, the "Neapolitan Troubadours," or "Sears, the Taffy man";[66] and the New York *World*, "mindful of . . . the dignity of the American Government," offered to pay the Secretary of State $8,000 annually if he would devote his full time to official duties and refrain from lecturing for profit.[67]

The one criticism that cut Bryan deeply was the oft-repeated charge that he was lazy, neglected his duties, and did not know what was going on in the State Department. "As Secretary of State he is ignorant and he will not learn," wrote Frank Cobb in a typical editorial. "He would rather argue than work. . . . A great Secretary of State in these times would be at his desk twelve hours a day. Mr. Bryan would rather be in State Prison. He does not know what is going on in the State Department. He does not know what ought to be going on there."[68] And as the World War increased the perils of the nation and multiplied the burdens of the State Department, an increasing number of critics called upon Bryan to resign. "For the extraordinary tasks of the great war," declared the Olympian *New Republic*, "he is a disaster, a humiliation to himself and to the whole American people. He has disproved the old maxim that crises produce great men. . . . Mr. Bryan is an unnecessary peril injected into a situation that is already perilous enough."[69]

Although he made a valiant effort to think well of his Secretary of

---

[65] Statements printed in the *New York Times*, July 14 and 16, 1913; and *The Commoner*, XIII (August 1913), 5.

[66] New York *Nation*, XCVII (July 24, 1913), 67; "The Bryan Scandal," *ibid.*, September 18, 1913, pp. 256-257; George Harvey, "Mr. Bryan Rides Behind," *North American Review*, CXCIX (March 1914), 321-334.

[67] "The World to Mr. Bryan," New York *World*, September 17, 1913. Bryan's reply was characteristic. "No man should enter public life if he objects to criticism," he said, "and he cannot stay in public life if he permits criticism to turn him from doing what he thinks is right. He must decide his duty for himself, answerable to the public for any mistakes he makes." *ibid.*, September 21, 1913.

[68] *ibid.*, December 2, 1914.

[69] *New Republic*, II (March 13, 1915), 140.

State, Wilson was not unconscious of Bryan's alleged faults and was conducting much important foreign business behind Bryan's back by the end of 1914. More important, the President had joined the large company who wished fervently for the Nebraskan's resignation. On December 3, 1914, House recorded in his Diary, Wilson "spoke with extreme regret of Mr. Bryan's unsuitability for the office of Secretary of State, but did not know what could be done. He intimated that it might be well to let him leave the Cabinet in the event he desired to do so because of some policy with which he might disagree."[70] "If I run again for the Presidency," Wilson told a friend soon afterward, "it will be only to keep Bryan out. I feel like a pig when I sit in my chair and look at him and think, I mustn't let *him* be President. For he would make a very bad President: he would be ruinous to the country, ruinous to his own reputation. He always wants to think the best of everybody but he's the worst judge of character I ever knew, a spoilsman to the core and a determined enemy to civil service reform."[71]

Contemporary and historical judgments have in general supported Wilson's opinion of Bryan's record as Secretary of State. But is the verdict fair?

Bryan's record was marred by faults that should perhaps be charged more to the American political system and to the spirit of his time than to him personally. He was unprepared by training and experience to direct the foreign relations of a great power; he was a spoilsman; and he was endowed with such an excess of virtue that he found it difficult to recognize evil in other men.

On the other hand, a large part of the indictment against the Nebraskan was not only inaccurate but also grossly unfair. Contrary to all the contemporary slurs, Bryan was an indefatigable worker[72] who played a large role in shaping important foreign policies. Yet his greatest achievement as Secretary of State was the way in which he subordinated personal ambition to assure the success of Wilson's domestic program. Even the New York *World* had to admit, grudgingly, "There has been no instance since he became Secretary of State in which his political influence, which the East used to regard as a menace to the Republic itself, has not been used to promote the common good."[73]

[70] House Diary, December 3, 1914.
[71] Mrs. Crawford H. Toy, "Second Visit to the White House," from Mrs. Toy's diary, January 3, 1915, MS. in the Baker Collection.
[72] As an examination of his personal papers and the records of the State Department reveals.
[73] New York *World*, December 2, 1914.

As it often did, the *New Republic* made the most penetrating and the fairest commentary:

"If ever there was anyone who has good reason to complain that virtue is not its own reward, that one is Mr. Bryan. Excess of virtue has brought him to his present plight. By virtue we do not mean the simplicity which makes him a really good soul, the grape juice, the ploughshares made of old sabres, nor even his abiding affection for the boys of '96. We mean literally his virtue, his self-sacrifice and his good faith. The noblest act of his public life was the acceptance of office under Woodrow Wilson. For that Mr. Bryan has paid a bitter price. In a real sense he has ruined himself to insure the unity of the Democratic party and to make possible the President's legislative successes. There is no exaggeration in saying that but for Mr. Bryan's presence in the Cabinet the Democrats could never have passed the best piece of constructive legislation in their history—the Federal Reserve act.

"Criticism of him has been incessant and humiliating. He has had to suffer for his kindness, for his foibles, and all because he took an office which required of him the surrender of his deepest ambitions. Mr. Bryan was not a man whose prestige could be increased by taking office. In a worldly sense he could only lose by it. . . . By genius an agitator and evangelist, he placed himself in a position where inevitably he who had been accustomed to lead the attack became the object of it. He laid his whole reputation at the service of his party."[74]

Another key figure in Wilson's official family was William Gibbs McAdoo, Secretary of the Treasury from 1913 to the end of 1918. Born in Marietta, Georgia, on October 31, 1863, McAdoo had practiced law for a time in Tennessee. Seeking wider opportunities, he moved to New York City in 1892 and won considerable reputation in the early 1900's by organizing a company that built the tubes under the Hudson River between New York and Jersey City. An acquaintance of William F. McCombs, McAdoo joined the Wilson movement in 1911 and, as we have seen in the first volume of this biography, emerged as one of the men Wilson trusted most by the end of the campaign of 1912. The bond of mutual affection grew stronger after McAdoo, a widower, married Eleanor Wilson in 1914.

McAdoo was one of the ablest of the men who were close to Wilson and perhaps the most interesting. Unencumbered by economic and political theories, his mind was agile, bold, and resourceful. But his

[74] *New Republic*, II (March 13, 1915), 139.

dominant trait was a drive for power. "McAdoo," said Newton D. Baker, "had the greatest lust for power I ever saw."[75] It came out in many ways—in McAdoo's tendency to invade the jurisdiction of other Cabinet officers, in his constant efforts to win control of the New York patronage, or in his boast that the so-called masters of Wall Street were eating out of his hand.[76]

Above all, McAdoo's drive for power manifested itself in his persistent desire and unflagging efforts to gain the presidency. He first openly revealed his ambition to Wilson and Colonel House during the autumn of 1914, when it seemed unlikely that the President would run for a second term.[77] Denied the succession in 1916, because Wilson had changed his mind, McAdoo worked hard for the presidential nomination in 1920 and 1924, but the goal remained always elusive.

As Secretary of the Treasury, McAdoo was one of the few advanced progressives in the Wilson circle. His supreme objective was to transfer control over the money supply and interest rates from the private bankers, especially those in Wall Street, to the Treasury Department. Whether this desire arose from genuine conviction concerning the proper role of government, or because McAdoo happened to be head of the Treasury Department, is a moot question.

McAdoo's ambition to establish public control over the money markets came out most significantly during the epic struggle over the writing of the Federal Reserve bill, which will be discussed in a subsequent chapter. It came out, also, in the way in which he used federal funds to accomplish his purpose. He narrowly averted a monetary shortage in June 1913, for example, by offering to issue up to $500,000,000 worth of emergency currency under authority of the Aldrich-Vreeland Act of 1908.[78] He deposited millions of federal funds in national banks in the South and West in the autumns of 1913 and 1914 to assist in crop moving; and he publicly harassed banks that hoarded funds and charged usurious rates.[79] It was not the first time that a Secretary of

[75] R. S. Baker and A. H. Meneely, interview with N. D. Baker, April 6, 1928, Baker Collection.

[76] House Diary, November 4, 1913.

[77] *ibid.*, October 20 and 27, November 4, 1914.

[78] This measure authorized the Treasury to issue short-term currency to so-called national currency associations, formed by national banks, against United States bonds and high-grade commercial securities.

[79] For McAdoo's offer to issue emergency currency in 1913, see the *New York Times*, June 12, 1913; New York *World*, June 13, 1913; and W. G. McAdoo to E. M. House, June 18, 1913, House Papers. For his use of federal funds to relieve financial stringencies in the South and West, see the *New York Times*, August 1, 2, 8, 1913,

the Treasury had intervened in the money markets, but never had one acted so boldly before.

Brandeis' evaluation of McAdoo's record was not far from the mark: "I rate him very highly, and cannot recall any Secretary of the Treasury, since I have been actively interested in public matters, who can compare with him. He is far-seeing, courageous, inventive, effective. He has shown that he not only understands the financial power, but is able to grapple with it; and I do not know of any department of his work in which he has failed to exhibit the qualities of a master."[80]

"In the position of Attorney General I simply could not appoint a radical—that is I could not appoint a known radical," Wilson once declared, in explaining why he had appointed James C. McReynolds instead of Brandeis to head the Justice Department. "The people must have confidence in the Department of Justice—they must have confidence in the Attorney General. He can not be a person of the crusader type in public life."[81] It can be said with some confidence that McReynolds was neither a crusader nor a distinguished public figure when he took office in March 1913.

Born in Elkton, Kentucky, in 1862, McReynolds was graduated from Vanderbilt University in 1882 and the University of Virginia Law School in 1884, practiced law in Nashville, and taught at the Vanderbilt University Law School from 1900 to 1903. He was appointed Assistant Attorney General by President Roosevelt in 1903 and served in that office until 1907. He came back to Washington in 1910 to assist the Attorney General in the antitrust prosecution of the American Tobacco Company and resigned in 1911 when his chief approved a dissolution decree that left control of the reorganized tobacco industry in the hands of the former owners of the so-called "Tobacco Trust."[82] Wilson appointed him to head the Justice Department on House's

---

and June 30 and July 27, 1914; W. G. McAdoo to E. M. House, August 5, 1913, House Papers; John Skelton Williams to W. W., August 23, 1913, Wilson Papers; *Financial Age*, xxviii (August 16, 1913), 241; *Bankers Magazine*, lxxxvii (September 1913), 235-236. For his campaign against hoarders and usurers, see the *Washington Post*, September 24, 1914; *New York Times*, September 25, 26, 27, 29, 30, October 1 and 7, 1914; W. G. McAdoo to E. M. House, October 12, 1914, House Papers.

[80] L. D. Brandeis to Norman Hapgood, July 14, 1916, Brandeis Papers.

[81] David Lawrence, *The True Story of Woodrow Wilson*, p. 75.

[82] "J. C. McReynolds, the New Preceptor for the Trusts," *New York Times Magazine*, March 9, 1913; McGregor (A. J. McKelway), "The Attorney-General for the United States," *Harper's Weekly*, lviii (February 7, 1914), 15.

recommendation, knowing only that he had the reputation of a bitter foe of monopoly.

McReynolds was personally the least popular member of the Wilson circle and the most inscrutable. Proud, sensitive, and aloof, he mixed little with his colleagues; they in turn had no warm affection for him. In spite of his reputation as a radical in 1913, he was at heart an extreme conservative with a narrow view of the proper role that government should play in economic affairs.[83] Even so, he left a deep impression on administration policies during his seventeen months as head of the Justice Department, for he largely mapped out the direction that the President would follow in antitrust prosecutions.

The new Attorney General, however, was nearly ruined by scandal before he could begin. Early in 1913, two Californians, Drew Caminetti and Maury I. Diggs, were indicted for violating the Mann Act, which prohibited the transportation of women across state boundaries for immoral purposes. Soon afterward, Secretary William B. Wilson appointed young Caminetti's father, Anthony E., a Democratic leader from San Francisco, as head of the Immigration Service in the new Department of Labor. About the middle of June 1913, Anthony E. Caminetti asked his chief for a leave of absence to enable him to go to California to assist in his son's defense. As Caminetti's absence would have impeded the organization of the Immigration Service, Secretary Wilson asked McReynolds to postpone the Caminetti-Diggs trial until autumn. McReynolds agreed.[84]

There was nothing sinister or even unusual about the Attorney General's action, but the federal district attorney in San Francisco, John L. McNab, suspected the worst. He resigned by public telegram to the President on June 20, 1913, charging that "attempts have been made to corrupt the Government witnesses, and friends of the defendants are publicly boasting that the wealth and political pre-eminence of the defendants' relatives will procure my hand to be stayed

[83] As a member of the Supreme Court during the constitutional crisis of the 1930's, for example, he worked valiantly with other extreme conservatives to turn back the tide of New Deal progressivism.

It should be emphasized, however, that there was no necessary inconsistency between McReynolds' conservative views and his undoubted antagonism toward monopoly and efforts to restrain competition during the time that he was Attorney General. Indeed, most conservatives believed strongly in competition as the overriding natural economic law and the perfect governor of economic activity.

[84] These are the facts as they were presented in J. C. McReynolds to W. W., June 24, 1913; and W. B. Wilson to J. C. McReynolds, June 24, 1913, both in the Wilson Papers; and in W. B. Wilson to Charles S. Logan, July 3, 1913, William B. Wilson Papers.

at Washington"; moreover, he accused McReynolds of "yielding to influence."[85]

At once Republicans demanded a congressional investigation, and the nation's leading Democratic journal exclaimed that the Attorney General could best serve the administration by resigning.[86] The President, in contrast, moved serenely. While admitting privately that McReynolds and Secretary Wilson had made a serious mistake,[87] he publicly defended the Attorney General's "sound and impartial judgment" and "clear instinct for what was right and fair." In the same breath, however, the President ordered McReynolds to press the Caminetti-Diggs trial "with the utmost diligence and energy."[88] As a leading progressive organ accurately observed, "What the Ballinger case was to the Taft Administration the Caminetti case might easily have become to the Wilson Administration—and worse—if it had not been for President Wilson's prompt and vigorous action."[89]

The furor soon subsided, and McReynolds turned to more important business, the carrying forward of antitrust prosecutions inherited from the Taft administration and the beginning of new ones, which will be discussed in detail in a subsequent chapter.[90] He survived other at-

[85] J. L. McNab to W. W., June 20, 1913, printed in the *New York Times*, June 22, 1913.

[86] New York *World*, June 28, 1913; also New York *Nation*, xcvi (June 26, 1913), 631-632.

[87] W. W. to E. T. Brown, July 22, 1913, Wilson Papers.

[88] W. W. to J. C. McReynolds, June 24, 1913, *ibid*.

[89] New York *Outlook*, civ (July 5, 1913), 489. Caminetti and Diggs were eventually convicted of violating the so-called White Slave Act. There were extenuating circumstances—the two young men had been guilty only of private immorality, not of transporting the women for use in the White Slave trade—and ten of the jurors, a number of prominent Democratic senators, the bench and bar of San Francisco, and, finally, young Caminetti's mother appealed to Wilson to grant a pardon. Key Pittman to W. W., February 17, 1917; James E. Martine to W. W., March 9, 1917; James D. Phelan to W. W., March 10, 1917; and Mark A. Smith to W. W., March 16, 1917, all in the Wilson Papers.

The President, however, would not risk another scandal, although he put his refusal to grant a pardon on other grounds. "It tears my heart to have to say to you that I cannot see my way clear to pardon your son," he wrote to Mrs. Caminetti on March 22, 1917 (*ibid*.), after a tearful interview at the White House. "If I followed the dictates of my heart or allowed myself to be influenced by my genuine friendship for yourself and your husband, I would of course do it; but in matters of this sort it seems to be my imperative duty to leave personal feelings and connections out of the question entirely and look at the matter from the public point of view with regard to the influence it would have upon other cases. When I look at the case of your son from this point of view, it seems to me clearly my duty to withhold pardon."

[90] See below, pp. 417-423.

tacks, which were powerful and apparently sinister, because the President believed he was "formidable, dangerously formidable, to the men who wish to act without sanction of law."[91] It must have been a genuine conviction, for Wilson elevated McReynolds to the Supreme Court in July 1914.

Lindley M. Garrison, Secretary of War from 1913 to 1916, vied with McAdoo for the reputation of being the ablest member of the Cabinet and with McReynolds for being the most austere. Born in Camden, New Jersey, on November 28, 1864, the son of an Episcopal minister, Garrison went briefly to Harvard and then learned his law in the offices of a Philadelphia firm. Practicing law in Philadelphia, Camden, and Jersey City from 1886 to 1904, he rose by dint of hard work to a leading position in the New Jersey bar and was appointed to the Chancery Court of New Jersey in 1904, from which Wilson, at Tumulty's suggestion, drew him into the Cabinet. Garrison was a competent if unimaginative Secretary of War—methodical and efficient, judicial and impartial. He approached the business of running the army as he had the dispensing of justice from the bench; he steadfastly resisted all political pressures and considerations, even necessary ones, and pursued his course regardless of the consequences.

Garrison once wrote an importuning senator a description of his administrative method:

"I have made it a rule ever since I have been in the Department, not to interfere in any way with the ordinary disposition, location of duty, etc., of officers of the Army. Whenever the commanding officer needs service to be done in a certain place, he, as a matter of routine, selects the proper command to perform the duty, and I of course would know nothing whatever about such matters. . . . Each officer is now subject to exactly equal treatment, stands on his own merits, and does whatever duty comes his way. This of course is the only proper way that Army discipline can be maintained and that equity and justice can have sway in the Army."[92]

So closely did Garrison work with the professional army men and follow their lead in matters of policy that many antimilitarists believed that he was virtually a tool of the military class. "I firmly believe the Secretary has fallen entirely under the influence of the Chief of Staff

---

[91] W. W. to W. J. Bryan, September 5, 1913, Wilson Papers.
[92] L. M. Garrison to Ollie M. James, November 17, 1915, the Papers of Lindley M. Garrison, Princeton University Library; hereinafter cited as the Garrison Papers.

[General Leonard Wood]," a pacifist congressman wrote as early as April 1913.[93] "Secretary Garrison has frankly torn off all disguise, disclosing the real purpose which is in his mind, that of placing the United States for the first time under complete military control," another congressman wrote later, during a controversy over army expansion.[94] Or, to cite a final example, the leading single tax organ in the United States was convinced that Garrison was a militarist and an imperialist whose "malign influence" was largely responsible for the reactionary tendencies in the Wilson administration.[95]

In contrast was the near-veneration with which the army leaders regarded their civilian superior. It was expressed in two moving letters by the sometime Chief of Staff, General Hugh L. Scott.

"I find service here with this Secretary very delightful," Scott wrote late in 1914. "He has been a judge on the bench, which has trained him wonderfully for prompt decisions. He is a man of remarkable talent for seeing the truth. He has a kindly heart, and is one of the most forceful and just persons I have ever known. . . . I believe he is the greatest Secretary we have ever had. We certainly have never had one who would keep the politicians out of the War Department the way this one does; they are as scarce around here as hen's teeth."[96]

"Most of the heads of departments have been in here this morning to mingle our tears and commiserate with each other on the loss of our best friends," Scott wrote soon after Garrison had resigned as Secretary of War, "and there was a consensus of opinion that you have been the wisest, most just, most fearless, kindly and courteous man that we have ever had the honor of serving with. You have set the highest mark that has ever been set for the ethics of the War Department."[97]

Actually, the chief reason for Garrison's failure as Secretary of War, if indeed "failure" is the right word, was his excess of virtue—his inflexibility, his refusal ever to compromise, his insistence upon doing the "right" instead of the "political" thing. As an administrator fighting off persistent political attempts to demoralize the service, he was superb;

---

[93] James L. Slayden to O. G. Villard, April 16, 1913, the Papers of Oswald Garrison Villard, Harvard University Library; hereinafter cited as the Villard Papers.

[94] W. W. Bailey to Mrs. Etta Blum, January 4, 1916, the Papers of Warren Worth Bailey, Princeon University Library; hereinafter cited as the Bailey Papers.

[95] *The Public*, xix (February 18, 1916), 145.

[96] H. L. Scott to H. J. Slocum, November 24, 1914, Scott Papers.

[97] H. L. Scott to L. M. Garrison, February 11, 1916, *ibid.*

as a political leader whose chief duty was to guide the President in formulating a military policy acceptable to the legislative branch, he was a failure. And he broke with the President because Wilson did the necessary instead of the heroic thing in a time of crisis, that is, because he compromised on an issue that Garrison considered a simple question of right or wrong.[98]

Although, as will become apparent, Wilson permitted Garrison to determine some important policies, relations between the two men were only formally correct and never cordial. This was true, one might surmise, because each considered himself superior to the other in knowledge and character. Wilson thought that Garrison was an "able fellow" who had become "thoroughly spoiled by adulation heaped upon him by newspapers," and "a great nuisance in Cabinet meetings because he not only talked so much, but tried to inject his opinions into every department."[99] Garrison reciprocated with opinions equally severe. "I once heard a description," he wrote years later, "which as nearly fits the case of President Wilson as any other I know: In describing someone it was said, 'He was a man of high ideals but no principles.' Perhaps I am too little of a politician to understand the ways of those who seek political preference, but I must admit a preference for those who hold fast over those who run fast."[100]

The President must have realized and resented the fact that his Secretary of War understood his faults better than almost any other member of his circle. When Wilson told his Cabinet, "We must forget personalities" and then proceeded relentlessly to discuss them, for example, there was Garrison, sitting in judgment.[101] When Wilson tried to abandon his support of the military reorganization plan he had earlier endorsed, there was Garrison, calling upon him to show his "sincerity and good faith by declining to admit the possibility of compromise with respect to . . . essential fundamental principle."[102] It was usually Wilson who did the talking about sincerity and fundamental principle. He did not beg Garrison to remain in the Cabinet when the Secretary of War offered his resignation in February 1916; on the

[98] R. S. Baker, interview with L. M. Garrison, November 30, 1928, Baker Collection.
[99] House Diary, June 24, 1915.
[100] L. M. Garrison to William E. Brooks, February 24, 1929, Brooks Papers.
[101] R. S. Baker, interview with L. M. Garrison, November 30, 1928, Baker Collection.
[102] L. M. Garrison to W. W., January 14, 1916, printed in the *New York Times*, February 11, 1916.

contrary, Wilson had decided as early as June 1915 to let Garrison go at the first opportunity.[103]

Josephus Daniels, Secretary of the Navy from 1913 to 1921, was, next to Bryan, the most controversial member of the group around Wilson. Born in Washington, North Carolina, on May 18, 1862, Daniels, as editor of the Raleigh *News and Observer*, had been in the forefront of the progressive movement in his state, one of Bryan's chief supporters and advisers in 1896 and afterward, and the chief manager of the Wilson movement in North Carolina in 1911 and 1912. He was a leader of many causes, especially prohibition, and a pillar of the Methodist Episcopal Church, South; his cherubic face radiated an affection for humanity and concealed considerable shrewdness and intelligence.

Because Daniels had managed to survive politically in a state dominated by a conservative Democratic clique, his enemies declared that he never let his progressivism stand in the way of his own preferment. The accusation had some validity, but this very ambivalence made Daniels one of the most important and useful members of the Wilson administration. Because of his intimacy with Bryan, he was able to prevent the Nebraskan's break with the President in 1915 from flaring into open rebellion. As one of the liaisons between advanced progressives and the President, Daniels helped impel his chief along the road toward progressivism in the name of social justice in 1916. Yet he was also on intimate terms with the conservative Democratic leaders in the Senate and used this friendship to help win vital conservative support for several of the most crucial administration policies.

Contemporaries and historians have largely ignored Daniels' significant political contributions and have concentrated upon the more dramatic aspects of his career as Secretary of the Navy. Daniels had fewer defenders and, because of his longer tenure, was abused more frequently than Bryan; comments like "I think Daniels is proving to be more kinds of an ass than any other member of the Cabinet"[104] abound in the correspondence of contemporaries, both Republican and Democratic.

Daniels met with criticism as much because of what he was and what he tried to accomplish as because of his alleged blunders. To begin with, he scandalized the professionals who ran the navy and their

---

[103] House Diary, June 24, 1915.
[104] W. H. Taft to G. J. Karger, December 18, 1913, Taft Papers.

friends because he was a proud plebeian and they thought that God had ordained men for certain ranks and classes. To Daniels, the idea that officers were socially better than enlisted men was incomprehensible, and he set to work to make the navy a training school for democracy by such means as instituting an elaborate basic educational and technical training program for enlisted men in the navy and Marine Corps,[105] and by opening the doors of the Naval Academy to a significant extent to enlisted men. Everywhere, he made a proud display of his social democracy.

Old-line officers were aghast at such leveling. "May I make a friendly suggestion?" Admiral William F. Fullham, for example, asked the Secretary after he had finished making a speech to some recruits. "Today in your address to the enlisted men you called them 'Young gentlemen.' I would advise you to use some other term, as it might be misunderstood. It has never before been done in the Navy."[106]

Daniels' crowning humiliation of the naval officer corps was his General Order, issued on June 1, 1914, prohibiting the use of any alcoholic beverages aboard naval vessels and in navy yards and stations. McKinley's Secretary of the Navy had forbidden the use of spirits by enlisted men in 1899, and Daniels had strong support from the Surgeon General for extending the ban to officers. But the officers fretted in sullen indignation; the Aid for Operations, Admiral Bradley A. Fiske, warned that depriving officers of wine and beer would drive them to the use of whisky and drugs;[107] and the newspapers had a field day denouncing the Secretary or lampooning him as a Gilbertian type. "It is revolutionary," the New York *World* exclaimed. "It is a shameful reflection upon a noble profession. We send our officers to sea chaperoned like school-girls. . . . This use of military discipline as a cloak for sumptuary despotism is so intolerable that Secretary Daniels should be allowed no time in sobering up after his temperance debauch."

Tension over "democracy" in the navy and irritants like the wine mess order exacerbated other points of friction between Daniels and his professional advisers. Unlike Garrison, the North Carolinian was obsessed with a determination to maintain civilian supremacy and seemed inherently suspicious of professional advice. When admirals

---

[105] Josephus Daniels, "Training Our Bluejackets for Peace," *The Independent*, LXXVI (December 11, 1913), 490-492; Josephus Daniels, *The Wilson Era, Years of Peace—1910-1917*, pp. 253-257.

[106] Josephus Daniels, *The Wilson Era, Years of Peace—1910-1917*, p. 273; quoted by permission of the University of North Carolina Press, publishers.

[107] B. A. Fiske to J. Daniels, May 27, 1914, Daniels Papers.

like Fiske asserted that only naval officers could know what was best for the navy, the Secretary would bluntly remind them that it was their business to follow orders. As a consequence, Daniels and his advisers quarreled incessantly and publicly over questions of administration, training, discipline, and the over-all efficiency of the service.

Finally, Daniels added many businessmen and conservatives to the ranks of his enemies by pursuing a relentless war against the manufacturers of armor plate, gun forgings, and other steel products that the navy had to purchase. It began in 1913, when the Bethlehem, United States, and Midvale Steel companies submitted identical bids for armor plate and the presidents of these corporations admitted that they all charged an inflated price because past Secretaries had accepted the lowest bid and then compelled each of them to manufacture one third of the order at the lowest price.[108] Daniels won lower prices by threatening to buy armor plate in England and to ask Congress to build an armor plate factory. It is little wonder that the editorial spokesmen of the steel interests, like Colonel George Harvey, were among his bitterest critics.

All during the period from 1913 to 1916 Daniels' foes maintained a steady fire aimed at driving him from office.[109] But this campaign entered a really serious phase when Colonel House and Edith Bolling Wilson, whom the President had married after Ellen's death, concluded that the North Carolinian was a heavy political liability and must go. "Mrs. Wilson and I . . . decided that the most helpful thing that could be done for the President at this time, would be the elimination of good Josephus Daniels and Joseph Tumulty," House recorded in his Diary on April 6, 1916. "She undertakes to eliminate Tumulty if I can manage the Daniels change."[110]

It was a delicate business, and House worked so quietly that we know little about his machinations. He enlisted Bernard M. Baruch, a stockbroker of New York, who had the courage to tell Wilson that he should dismiss Daniels.[111] The Colonel also tried, unsuccessfully, to persuade Vance C. McCormick of Pennsylvania, soon afterward elected

[108] *New York Times*, May 22, 1913.

[109] e.g., see George Harvey, "Preparedness a Political Issue," *North American Review*, cciii (April 1916), 481-492; Gilson Gardner, "Congress Quit," *Everybody's Magazine*, xxxiv (April 1916), 413-417; and Burton J. Hendrick, "The Case of Josephus Daniels," *World's Work*, xxxii (July 1916), 281-296.

[110] House Diary, April 6, 1916.

[111] E. M. House, memorandum of a conversation with B. M. Baruch, dated June 23, 1916, MS. in the House Papers.

Democratic national chairman, to discuss the matter with the President and suggested that McCormick might become the next Secretary of the Navy.[112] But we do not know whether House ever showed his hand to Wilson.

Daniels survived these and all other such attacks and, ironically, outlasted House and most of his other detractors in the Wilson circle. He did so, in part, because the President knew that Daniels was politically invaluable as his chief liaison with the large Bryan element after the Commoner had resigned, but above all because Daniels was willing to give friendship on Wilson's terms. There was nothing calculated about the North Carolinian's devotion and loyalty; he simply loved the President and supported him without question.

Wilson returned Daniels' love and trust with an affection equally warm. "Thank you with all my heart for your letter of Christmas greetings, handed me yesterday," the President wrote him near the end of 1914. "It helped not a little to keep the cloud from descending on me which threatened me all day. . . . You are . . . of the sort that make life and friendship worth while. It is fine to have a colleague whom one can absolutely trust; how much finer to have one whom one can love! That is a real underpinning for the soul!"[113]

And the more Daniels' critics raged, the stronger Wilson's affection grew. A visitor to the White House in January 1915 tells a revealing story. She repeated one of the anti-Daniels jibes then current, that the Secretary had decreed that the British war song, "Tipperary," should not be sung in the navy. "I have never seen the President angry before," she says of the scene. "I never want to see him angry again. His fist came down on the table: 'Daniels did *not* give the order that Tipperary should not be sung in the navy. He is surrounded by a network of conspiracy and lies. His enemies are determined to ruin him. I can't be sure who they are yet, but when I do get them—God help them.' "[114] There is no reason to believe that Wilson's opinion or loyalty ever changed.

The center of several hard Cabinet fights over conservation policies was Franklin K. Lane, Secretary of the Interior from 1913 to 1920. Born in Canada in 1864, he grew up in California, was prominent in

[112] Jonathan Daniels, *The End of Innocence*, p. 192.

[113] W. W. to J. Daniels, December 26, 1914, Baker Collection.

[114] Mrs. Crawford H. Toy, "Second Visit to the White House," diary entry dated January 5, 1915, MS. in *ibid.*

reform politics in San Francisco around the turn of the century, and served with distinction on the Interstate Commerce Commission from 1906 to 1913. Lane was one of the most charming and convivial members of the Wilson circle. "As a plump, well-fed and well-groomed man with a large white face and bald head," one contemporary has described him, "Lane reminded me immediately of Humpty-Dumpty. He had a jolly look and loved to go to parties."[115] As we have seen, Lane was also the most garrulous member of the Cabinet.

As Secretary of the Interior during the high tide of the progressive movement, Lane enjoyed unusual opportunities for constructive achievement. He was privileged, for example, to help devise programs for the development of Alaska, to open the public domain to fruitful exploitation, and to facilitate the harnessing of the enormous hydroelectric resources of the American continent. But the difficulties confronting him were as great as the opportunities.

To begin with, he had to steer a middle course between the extreme conservationists and an anti-conservation coalition of Westerners and spokesmen of private interests. Armed with the support of the eastern press and eastern political leaders in both parties, the conservationists were one of the most vocal and powerful minorities in the country. Organized in the National Conservation Congress and led by Gifford Pinchot and William Kent, they had helped to save vast reaches of the public domain for future generations. At the same time, they were suspicious and intolerant and more concerned with guarding national resources from the plunderers than with formulating a rational program of use and development. Having helped to destroy the Taft administration during the Ballinger controversy, they were no less watchful and belligerent after 1913 than before.

At the other extreme stood the agents of powerful oil, timber, cattle, and hydroelectric interests, who sought to plunder the public domain, and most of the political leaders of the Rocky Mountain and Pacific Coast states, who demanded that the federal government either open the reserved lands in the public domain to private development or, better still, give the states title to the public domain.[116]

[115] Jonathan Daniels, *The End of Innocence*, pp. 167-168, paraphrasing W. G. McAdoo, *Crowded Years*, p. 182.

[116] See, e.g., the resolution adopted by the legislature of Colorado, cited in the New York *Outlook*, CIV (May 3, 1913), 9, and the resolution adopted by the conference of western governors, cited in *La Follette's Weekly*, V (June 14, 1913), 9-10, for typical expressions of this point of view; and Roy M. Robbins, *Our Landed Heritage: The Public Domain, 1776-1936*, pp. 380-382, for a summary of the western attitude.

The difficulties ahead were not apparent, however, as Secretary Lane turned to his first task in 1913, the preparation of legislation for the development of Alaska. Like many of his contemporaries, Lane thought of this territory as America's new frontier and dreamed of developing a rich young commonwealth. The first step toward fulfillment of the dream, he said, was the construction of a railroad to tap the territory's abundant coal resources; and he and the President threw their weight behind a much controverted measure for a federally owned and operated Alaskan railway. "Whoever owns the railroads of a country determines very largely the future of that country, the character of its population . . . ," Lane remarked. "The policy of governmental ownership of railroads in Alaska seems to me to be the one that will make most certainly for her lasting welfare."[117] Only a few conservatives protested when Congress adopted and the President, on March 12, 1914, approved a measure authorizing the expenditure of $35,000,000 for the construction of a line from Seward to the Bering and Matanuska coal fields and beyond to Fairbanks. It was, Wilson and Lane said, an act of "real helpfulness and brotherhood" and "hope . . . to the heart of the waiting Alaskan."[118]

Lane was not responsible for the terms of a second measure for Alaska, a coal leasing bill for the territory, but he supported the progressives on the House public lands committee who fought successfully to prevent the validation of the claims of the Morgan-Guggenheim

---

The western demand for a "liberal" conservation policy increased as the Wilson administration matured plans for general leasing and water power development bills during 1914 and 1915 and was voiced in the Senate especially by Senators Charles S. Thomas and John F. Shafroth of Colorado. See C. S. Thomas to J. P. Tumulty, April 21, 1915, Wilson Papers, and J. F. Shafroth to W. W., November 15, 1915, *ibid.*, enclosing copies of resolutions adopted by the Colorado legislature opposing the general leasing and water power bills and a copy of a resolution adopted by the Western States Water Power Conference at Portland, Oregon, September 23, 1915, demanding state control over navigable rivers.

It should be added that both Wilson and Lane stood firm in support of the principle of national ownership and control, in spite of numerous warnings that the Democratic party would lose the western states in 1916 unless the administration capitulated to the demand for denationalization. See W. W. to W. J. Bryan, December 29, 1914; W. W. to W. G. McAdoo, November 12, 1915; F. K. Lane to W. W., December 2, 1915; and W. W. to F. K. Lane, December 6, 1915, all in *ibid.*

[117] Honoré Willsie, "Mr. Lane and the Public Domain," *Harper's Weekly*, LVIII (August 23, 1913), 8; see also F. K. Lane, "Annual Report of the Secretary of the Interior," *Reports of the Department of the Interior*, 1913, pp. 10-11.

[118] *New York Times*, March 13, 1914; F. K. Lane, "Report of the Secretary of the Interior," *Reports of the Department of the Interior*, 1914, p. 12.

syndicate—the so-called Cunningham Claims—and to guarantee equal opportunities for small operators.[119] "This is the end of an eight-year struggle," the Secretary exulted after Congress had adopted the leasing bill in October 1914 that progressives demanded. "Eight years ago these coal lands in Alaska were locked up. . . . Now her coal is to be opened to the world under conditions that will prevent monopoly and I trust insure development."[120]

These were measures upon which most progressives could agree, but Lane and his colleagues in the Interior Department were caught in a cross fire in their attempt to formulate a policy for the best use of western grazing lands in the public domain. Conservationists like William Kent and most large stockmen worked for a measure to permit cattlemen to lease enough land to support profitable ranching, while small farmers and ranchers and most congressmen demanded the division of the remaining public range lands into small homesteads to support thousands of families instead of a few large operators. In the end, Wilson and Lane surrendered to the heaviest pressure and let Congress enact the Stock-Raising Homestead Act, approved December 29, 1916, which provided for 640-acre homesteads on lands heretofore designated by the Secretary of the Interior as "chiefly valuable for grazing and raising forage crops." Experience soon proved that it was an unwise measure, one that made proper use of the range impossible and led inevitably to fraud and disappointment.[121]

One of the longest and most crucial domestic struggles of the Wilson era revolved around the formulation of a policy for the private development of hydroelectric power on navigable rivers and on streams in the public domain. By the time Wilson was inaugurated, the infant electric power industry was well on its way toward rivaling the railroads in importance, both in terms of function and of capital invested;[122] and promoters and the agents of the private utilities industry urged adoption of a generous federal policy to encourage the rapid exploita-

[119] *ibid.*, pp. 13-14; I. L. Lenroot to William Kent, October 10, 1914, Kent Papers; "Lenroot's Good Work," *La Follette's Weekly*, VI (October 24, 1914), 4; *Harper's Weekly*, LIX (October 24, 1914), 404.

[120] Quoted in *La Follette's Magazine*, VI (November 1914), 7.

[121] "Report of the Commissioner of the General Land Office," *Reports of the Department of the Interior*, 1917, pp. 177-179; William Kent to R. S. Baker, May 25, 1925, Baker Collection.

[122] From 1902 to 1912 the production of electric power in the United States increased from about six billion kilowatt hours to nearly twenty-five billion, and the capital invested in the electric utilities industry, from $403,000,000 in 1900 to over $2,000,000,000 in 1912.

tion of water power. They were joined by many congressmen and senators from the South and West who, in their desire for the rapid industrialization of their sections, argued that existing legislation severely impeded development.[123] How to encourage further private investment and unlock this great storehouse of energy—estimated at 30,000,000 horsepower in potential hydroelectric installations in the public domain alone—and yet safeguard the interests of the people was one of the most perplexing problems confronting the Wilson administration.

Secretary Garrison made the first move, by preparing a bill in January 1914 that empowered the Secretary of War to license the building of dams on navigable rivers, provided the states in which the dam sites were located had established adequate machinery to regulate electric power rates.[124] Introduced by William C. Adamson of Georgia, chairman of the House interstate commerce committee, and subsequently called the Adamson bill, Garrison's measure at once drew the fire of conservationists because its vague language seemed to make possible the granting of virtually perpetual leases. "I consider the Adamson bill the worst piece of legislation that has come before the House," one conservationist warned the President.[125]

Meanwhile, in consultation with the conservationist group and Scott Ferris of Oklahoma, chairman of the House public lands committee, Secretary Lane had drafted a measure to control the construction of hydroelectric projects in the public domain and in the national forests. Because it provided for definite fifty-year leases and the right of the government to purchase the property at net cost at the expiration of the lease, Lane's measure, known as the Ferris bill, was strong precisely where the Adamson bill was weak.

Soon the rivalry between Garrison and Adamson on the one side and Lane and Ferris on the other had developed into an intense undersurface struggle for control of the administration's water power policy. As-

[123] In 1913, the General Dam Act of 1906 controlled the construction of dams on navigable rivers. This measure required congressional approval for all proposed projects, which had become nearly impossible to obtain in important cases, as progressives objected to the absence in the law of any provision for public control of the utilities companies involved. The construction of dams in the public domain and national forests was impeded, moreover, by the fact that the Secretaries of the Interior and of Agriculture could issue only revocable permits that denied to private interests the security they thought they needed.

[124] L. M. Garrison to W. W., January 30 and February 2, 1914, Wilson Papers; New York *World*, February 20, 1914.

[125] William Kent to W. W., June 27, 1914, Wilson Papers.

suring the conservationists that their fears were groundless, Wilson took firm control. After a conference among Garrison, Lane, Adamson, and Ferris had failed to bring agreement on June 29, 1914, the President called them to the White House on July 2 and shortly afterward helped prepare amendments to the Adamson bill that met the conservationists' demands regarding the length of lease and the right of recapture.[126] "I cannot tell you how much pleasure it gave me to be serviceable in a matter in which I am so deeply interested," Wilson wrote to Ferris, after the conferees had agreed upon a common policy. "I congratulate you and Judge Adamson most heartily on the outcome."[127]

The revised Adamson bill passed the House of Representatives by a large majority early in August 1914, but all the private and public pressure that Wilson could apply failed to bring Senate approval. In fact, the chief lobbyist for the power interests, Rome G. Brown, working with Secretary Garrison and a southern-western coalition headed by Senator James K. Shields of Tennessee, countered in January 1915 with a measure known as the Shields bill. It gave the power companies virtually a free hand and perpetual leases for the development of hydroelectric projects.[128]

There was little discussion of water power legislation during 1915, but a controversy of large dimensions arose when the House approved an administration measure for the development of hydroelectric resources in the public domain, known as the Ferris bill, on January 8, 1916; the Senate public lands committee reported the Ferris bill in mutilated form in February; and the Senate approved the Shields bill on March 8, 1916. Progressives and conservationists countered with a report by the Secretary of Agriculture, which revealed that eighteen companies controlled more than one half the developed hydroelectric facilities of the country and that the trend toward monopoly was increasing;[129] they fought successfully in Congress to neutralize the power

---

[126] The foregoing paragraph is based upon W. W. to W. Kent, June 29, 1914; W. C. Adamson to W. W., June 29, 1914; F. K. Lane to W. W., July 1, 1914; L. M. Garrison, memorandum of White House conference on water power policy, dated July 2, 1914; W. C. Adamson to L. M. Garrison, July 2, 1914; W. Kent to W. W., July 2, 1914; W. W. to F. K. Lane, July 9, 1914; W. W. to L. M. Garrison, July 9 and 10, 1914; L. M. Garrison to F. K. Lane, July 10, 1914; F. K. Lane to W. W., July 11, 1914; and S. Ferris to W. W., July 16, 1914, all in *ibid.*

[127] W. W. to S. Ferris, July 20, 1914, *ibid.*

[128] See particularly *Harper's Weekly*, LX (January 16 and 23 and February 6, 1915), 49, 74, 123.

[129] The report is Department of Agriculture, *Electric Power Development in the United States* (3 vols.), Senate Document No. 316, 64th Cong., 1st sess.

lobby;[130] and they roused the public to the alleged designs of the power interests by frequent and sometimes violent appeals in the press.[131]

Wilson and Lane kept in the background during the controversy, but at all critical times they stood forthrightly for the Adamson and Ferris bills. When William Kent warned that "the water power crowd are the shrewdest and most dangerous people that we have to fight in the country today,"[132] the President replied that it was "better to let the water power run to waste than to settle the question of the use of it in the wrong way."[133] When the Senate public lands committee weakened the provisions in the Ferris bill safeguarding the public interest, Wilson came out in unequivocal support of the original measure.[134] And when Congress refused to act on water power legislation during the spring of 1916, the President appealed personally, urging congressional leaders to expedite the Adamson and Ferris bills.[135]

His effort, however, was in vain. In fact, when Congress reconvened in December 1916 the Senate promptly re-enacted the Shields bill, and Wilson pleaded again unsuccessfully during the early months of 1917, before the adoption of the war resolution diverted his and the nation's attention to more urgent problems.[136] Not until 1920, with the passage of the Water Power Act, which marked the first beginning of

[130] The leaders of the progressive group in the Senate in this struggle were Thomas J. Walsh, Democrat of Montana, and George W. Norris, Republican of Nebraska. For the story of the fight in the upper house, see T. J. Walsh to N. Hapgood, February 19, 1916, the Papers of Thomas J. Walsh, Library of Congress; hereinafter cited as the Walsh Papers; W. Kent to W. W., March 7, 1916, Wilson Papers; T. J. Walsh to W. W., March 14 and 16, 1916, *ibid.*; Gifford Pinchot to H. Watterson, April 10, 1916, Watterson Papers.

[131] See, e.g., Norman Hapgood, "The Shields Bill," *Harper's Weekly*, LXII (March 25, 1916), 295; N. Hapgood, "Water Power in Congress," *ibid.*, April 15, 1916, p. 391; Gifford Pinchot, open letter to the President, *The Public*, XIX (February 11, 1916), 130-131; G. Pinchot, letter printed in *ibid.*, March 3, 1916, p. 200; W. Kent, letter to the President, *ibid.*, March 24, 1916, p. 275; R. F. Pettigrew, "Congress Should Stop Giving Away the People's Property," *ibid.*, December 8, 1916, pp. 1167-1168; "Conservation in Peril," *New Republic*, VII (May 13, 1916), 32-33; "Dangerous Legislation," *Living Church*, LIV (March 4, 1916), 624-625; *Congregationalist and Christian World*, CI (March 23, 1916), 400; *Everybody's Magazine*, XXXIV (June 1916), 781-782.

[132] W. Kent to W. W., March 7, 1916, Wilson Papers.

[133] W. W. to W. Kent, March 9, 1916, *ibid.*

[134] W. W. to T. J. Walsh, March 15, 1916; and W. W. to W. J. Stone, March 24, 1916, both in *ibid.* The House had approved the Ferris bill in 1915.

[135] W. W. to J. W. Kern, April 21, 1916, *ibid.*; W. W. to M. D. Foster, July 3, 1916, *ibid.*

[136] W. W. to A. W. Vernon, December 11, 1916; F. K. Lane to W. W., January 8, 1917; T. J. Walsh to W. W., January 18, 1917; W. W. to T. J. Walsh, January 24, 1917; and W. W. to J. H. Bankhead, January 26, 1917, all in *ibid.*

comprehensive development under federal-state regulation, did the administration finally achieve the progressive solution it had so long been seeking.[137]

In all the controversies that have thus far been discussed, Lane won the praise of progressives and conservationists for his defense of the public interest. And yet when he resigned in 1920 to accept the vice-presidency of Edward L. Doheny's Pan-American Petroleum Company, at a reputed salary of $50,000 a year, many of his erstwhile friends charged that Lane had betrayed their cause during his years in office; and the accusation has persisted. To understand the reasons for this deflation of Lane's reputation we must review the struggle over another major conservation measure, the so-called general mineral leasing bill, and relate the way in which it provoked one of the bitterest controversies of the era.

There was never any disagreement among progressives about the desirability of legislation to enable private interests to exploit oil and mineral resources in the public domain, subject to proper control and payment of ordinary royalties to the United States. Progressives agreed, moreover, that the laws controlling the use of mineral lands in the public' domain in 1913 were obsolete and gave their approval when Lane drafted a measure in 1914 to open oil, phosphate, and potash lands under a general leasing system.[138] There was little discussion of the Lane bill during 1914 and 1915, as Congress postponed action in favor of more urgent legislation. Then, early in 1916, when it seemed that Congress would finally act, a bitter controversy involving the claims of certain parties to oil lands in the naval reserve suddenly developed.

[137] A word might be said about the background of this important measure. During the first week of December 1916, Secretary Lane, Secretary of Agriculture Houston, and the new Secretary of War, Newton D. Baker, drafted a new water power bill to combine the Adamson and Ferris bills. It created a federal Water Power Commission composed of the three Secretaries and empowered to grant fifty-year leases for hydroelectric development on navigable rivers and in the public domain and the national forests. Such projects would be subject to regulation by the Commission and by state regulatory agencies. For the writing of this measure, which eventually became the Water Power Act of 1920, see F. K. Lane to W. W., December 9, 1916, Wilson Papers; and D. F. Houston to C. W. Eliot, December 9, 1916, the Papers of David F. Houston, Harvard University Library; hereinafter cited as the Houston Papers.

[138] There was no general leasing system regulating mining operations in the public domain in 1913. Instead, Congress had applied the so-called placer mining law to oil lands, which allowed individuals to withdraw twenty acres of land and corporations 160 acres. Moreover, Congress had made no proper provision for the development of potash and phosphate lands.

In 1909 and 1910 President Taft had withdrawn some 3,000,000 acres of oil lands from the public domain and had set two reserves aside in California in 1912—Reserve No. 1 in the Elk Hills and Reserve No. 2 in the Buena Vista Hills—for future exploitation by the navy.[139] There had been earlier claims filed for land in the two reserves, mainly in Reserve No. 2, which Congress had validated; there were, besides, a number of claims made after 1909, which attorneys for the Navy Department said were either improper or fraudulent. The most important among the allegedly improper claims were those of the Honolulu Oil Company to land in the heart of Reserve No. 2.

Controversy first developed early in 1916 when Secretary Lane announced that he was convinced that most of the claims of the Honolulu Oil Company were valid and when Secretary Daniels and Attorney General Thomas W. Gregory persuaded the President to ask Lane not to validate the claims until he, the President, had reviewed the matter. The Lane-Daniels quarrel next came into public view when the House approved a mineral leasing bill on January 8, 1916, that provided relief for oil operators who had made claims improperly but in good faith and were already producing oil in the California naval reserves;[140] when the Senate public lands committee, in May 1916, amended the House bill to provide even larger relief for the claimants than the House measure had offered; and when Daniels fought openly to prevent any consideration for operators in the naval reserves who did not have uncontested titles. Finally, the quarrel degenerated into a vendetta when Gifford Pinchot publicly accused Lane of lying and of betraying the cause of conservation[141] and reporters close to the Navy and Justice departments wrote a series of articles for the *New York Herald* attempting to prove that Lane was acting in collusion with the oil operators.

The strain on Lane's good humor was too great. In a long letter to the President, he hit back, charging that Daniels had attempted to involve him in a scandal, had inspired the *New York Herald's* attacks, and had alone been responsible for blocking passage of the mineral

---

[139] In 1915 President Wilson added a third—the area in Wyoming known as Teapot Dome, which contained 9,481 acres.

[140] Most of these claims arose from the fact that many operators, having been advised by their attorneys that Taft's withdrawal of the oil lands in 1909 was illegal, had proceeded to file claims and to drill for oil in the naval reserves. However, Congress, in the so-called Pickett Act of 1910, confirmed the withdrawal; and the Supreme Court, in the so-called Mid-West decision in 1915, affirmed that Taft's withdrawal in 1909 had been legal.

[141] *New York Times*, July 1 and August 14, 1916.

leasing bill by the Senate.[142] Staunch conservationists in Congress were also indignant. "It is to my mind singularly unfortunate that after Secretary Lane has so richly earned the confidence of the country, heretofore so unstintedly extended to him," Senator Thomas J. Walsh of Montana complained to the President, "suspicion should be aroused at this exceedingly critical juncture."[143]

Tempers cooled when Daniels and Gregory disavowed any responsibility for the *Herald* articles,[144] and Lane and the Senate leaders subsequently proposed a compromise by which the holders of dubious patents on land in the naval reserves who had already sunk wells would obtain leases and pay back and future royalties on all oil produced.[145] But Daniels and his friends in Congress refused to compromise and blocked all mineral leasing legislation until 1920. As one authority has written, "During these years, the question of relief for operators on withdrawn lands was always the rock on which legislative proposals were wrecked. . . . Daniels was always at loggerheads with Secretary Lane. . . . In every session of Congress for several years, when the oil and gas bill was brought up, the California operators would demand relief; Secretary Lane would second the motion, and Daniels would promptly refuse to have anything to do with the proposal. In that way the entire bill would be defeated."[146]

Daniels finally gave in after the First World War, however, when the addition of new provisions favorable to the public land states had won the overwhelming support of western senators for the measure.[147] The Mineral Leasing Act, approved February 25, 1920, not only established such a leasing system as Lane had proposed in 1914; it also allowed claimants on lands in the naval reserves to obtain leases on producing wells, as Lane had suggested in 1916.[148]

Fairness to Lane's reputation compels us to add a final word of evaluation concerning his accomplishments as Secretary of the Interior. His important contributions toward the maturing of progressive policies for

---

[142] F. K. Lane to W. W., June 1, 1916, Wilson Papers.

[143] T. J. Walsh to W. W., June 20, 1916, *ibid.*

[144] W. W. to J. D. Phelan, June 8, 1916, *ibid.*; W. W. to T. J. Walsh, June 26, 1916, *ibid.*

[145] F. K. Lane to W. W., December 9, 1916, *ibid.*

[146] John Ise, *The United States Oil Policy*, pp. 332, 334-335; quoted by permission of Yale University Press, publishers.

[147] These provisions awarded 90 per cent of the income from leases to the Reclamation Fund and to the states in which the mineral land being leased was located.

[148] John Ise, *The United States Oil Policy*, pp. 351-352, gives a good summary of the Leasing Act of 1920.

Alaska, water power, and western resources in general have often been ignored. At the same time, some historians, echoing Gifford Pinchot's accusations, have impeached Lane's integrity because he thought the government should deal generously with the California oil men. "A fair argument," one historian has written of Lane, "might be built up to show that he was one of the most dangerous men that have ever held the office of Secretary of the Interior, because, while he was working persistently to promote the ends of exploiting interests, he was writing articles on conservation, and in general preserving an attitude of impenetrable sincerity and respectability."[149] Or again, Josephus Daniels has accused Lane of trying to open the naval oil reserves generally to private operators.[150]

The indictment falls for lack of evidence, and we must conclude that Pinchot and other conservationists believed that Lane was a scoundrel because he did not always agree with them. Looking at Lane's entire record, the historian can only say that the Secretary's contributions to the cause of wise conservation were sizable indeed.

The chief dispenser of patronage in the Wilson administration, otherwise known as the Postmaster General, was Albert Sidney Burleson. Born in San Marcos, Texas, in 1863, the descendant of one of the founders of the Texas Republic, Burleson practiced law in Austin in the 1880's and 1890's and served in the lower house of Congress from 1899 to 1913. Although he was personally a conservative, Burleson was so much the professional politician that he seldom allowed devotion to principle alone to govern his course of action. During the heyday of Bryanism, he was a strong supporter of the Nebraskan. By 1910, when progressive Democrats were obviously rising in Texas, he called himself a progressive and played an important part in helping to swing Texas into the Wilson column before the Baltimore convention. And yet he won the postmaster generalship, not only because his intimate friend, Colonel House, championed his cause, but, more importantly, because the conservative Democratic leaders in the House knew that Burleson would protect their patronage interests and insisted that Wilson appoint him to the post.

Burleson was one of the more idiosyncratic members of the Wilson Cabinet. Although well-educated and widely read, he cultivated by his dress the appearance of a country lawyer. He was blunt, cocky,

[149] *ibid.*, p. 336; quoted by permission of Yale University Press, publishers.
[150] Josephus Daniels, *The Wilson Era, Years of Peace—1910-1917*, p. 378.

and almost pompous, and Wilson called him "the Cardinal" because he strutted. "Burleson is about the only man I know that can make a speech to an audience of one with undiminished enthusiasm," David F. Houston wrote in 1914. ". . . He does everything just as if he were killing snakes, and there is really only one way to deal with him, as I told him, and that is to give him what he wants or to kill him."[151]

Burleson's method with Wilson was always to say what he thought and then to accept the President's decisions without argument or complaint. The Texan's loyalty enabled him to survive to the end of the second administration. "As I look back," he said of Wilson, "I consider him the finest man I ever had to work with. In personal contacts and relationships, he was always the soul of courtesy. When he asked me to do something for him, he would often say, 'Burleson, I hope I haven't disturbed you,' or 'If you don't mind doing it,' or 'If it is not too much trouble to you.' He was always the gentleman."[152]

In the following chapter we will see how Burleson persuaded the President to abandon idealistic plans to transform the Democratic party and how he used the patronage to build support for the administration in Congress and the country. This was contribution enough, and it is no derogation to say that Burleson was more concerned with implementing than with originating administration policies. There was one significant exception, however—the Postmaster General's plan for governmental ownership and operation of the telephone and telegraph facilities of the country.

A brief inquiry from the President in April 1913[153] stimulated the first discussions and a closely guarded investigation by the Post Office Department and by Representative David J. Lewis of Maryland, long an advocate of nationalization of the wire services, during the summer and autumn of 1913.[154] Rumors that the administration contemplated action caused the stock of the American Telephone & Telegraph Company, the leading communications holding company, to decline from 131 3/8 a share on September 29, 1913, to 119 5/8 a share on October 14, 1913.[155] Then, in his first annual report, submitted to Congress in mid-

[151] D. F. Houston to E. M. House, March 19, 1914, Houston Papers.

[152] R. S. Baker, interview with A. S. Burleson, March 17-19, 1927, Baker Collection.

[153] "For a long time I have thought that the government ought to own the telegraph lines of the country and combine the telegraph with the post office. How have you been thinking in this matter?" W. W. to A. S. Burleson, April 4, 1913, Wilson Papers.

[154] *New York Times*, October 2 and 3, 1913.

[155] Albert W. Atwood, "Telephone Securities and Government Ownership," *Harper's Weekly*, LVIII (November 8, 1913), 29-31.

December 1913, Burleson came out publicly in support of governmental ownership of all telephone and telegraph facilities.[156]
It seemed intermittently that the administration might support the project. When the Senate asked for information, for example, a commission in the Post Office Department headed by the First Assistant Postmaster General, Daniel C. Roper of South Carolina, replied on January 31, 1914, with an exhaustive report urging a gradual nationalization, beginning with federal ownership of all telephone systems except rural exchanges.[157] Burleson renewed the discussion in his second annual report, submitted in December 1914, by recommending nationalization of communication services in the territories as a first step toward comprehensive federal operation; and Representative Lewis introduced a bill for complete nationalization by mid-1916 on December 31, 1914.[158] The project was subsequently revived, but Burleson's one *démarche* into the realm of broad policy never had any chance of success, as the President was always halfhearted in his support and conservative criticism early drove him to a virtual disavowal of administration endorsement of the proposal.

David F. Houston, Secretary of Agriculture from 1913 to 1920, and Secretary of the Treasury from 1920 to 1921, was personally less flamboyant than Burleson and politically less controversial than Lane. Born in Monroe, North Carolina, in 1866 and trained in economics at the University of South Carolina and Harvard University, Houston was subsequently president of the Agricultural and Mechanical College of Texas and the University of Texas and chancellor of Washington University in St. Louis. He won his seat in the Wilson Cabinet, not because he was widely known as an authority on farm problems, but because he had the strong support of his old friend, Colonel House.
An unimaginative classical economist who opposed direct federal assistance to underprivileged groups, Houston was something of a misfit in a progressive administration. As we will see, he opposed a measure to establish a long-term federal rural credits system and helped prevent its passage before 1916. When the cotton market collapsed after the outbreak of the First World War, he successfully resisted the demands of southern farmers for federal support of cotton prices. Even so, like Wilson, Houston often found it safer to yield than to fight

[156] *New York Times*, December 14, 1913.
[157] The text of this report is printed in *ibid.*, February 1, 1914.
[158] New York *World*, December 14, 1914; *New York Times*, December 31, 1914.

during a time when the demands of farm groups for a larger program of federal aid were enlarging and gaining irresistibly in power.

Thus, often in spite of himself, Houston made sizable contributions to the success of the Wilsonian program. Gracefully accepting the passage of the rural credits bill in 1916, he subsequently supervised the establishment of a federal farm loan system. Working with A. F. Lever of South Carolina, chairman of the House agricultural committee, and other farm leaders and spokesmen, Houston helped draft a series of measures that vastly enlarged the rural services of the federal government: the Smith-Lever, or Agricultural Educational Extension, Act of 1914, which provided federal funds for agricultural extension work through the land-grant colleges; the Smith-Hughes Act of 1917, providing federal assistance for agricultural and vocational instruction in the public schools; the Cotton Futures Act of 1914 and the Grain Standards Act of 1916, which established national standards for cotton and grains on the produce exchanges; the Warehouse Act of 1916, which established a system of national licensing and inspection of agricultural warehouses and the issuance of warehouse receipts acceptable in the Federal Reserve System as collateral for loans to farmers; and the Federal Aid Road Act of 1916, which marked the beginning of large-scale federal participation in the construction of a national system of modern highways. Houston left his stamp on all these measures by insisting upon the establishment and maintenance of strict federal standards in all programs of grant-in-aid to the states.

Finally, Houston made another important if less spectacular contribution by his enlargement and reorganization of the administrative structure of the Department of Agriculture. Houston's predecessor as Secretary of Agriculture for sixteen years, James Wilson, had been concerned mainly with the production of farm commodities. Following the trails blazed by Theodore Roosevelt's Country Life Commission of 1908 and 1909 and by pioneer agricultural economists, Houston gave greater consideration to the broader social and economic aspects of agriculture. Thus he created a new Cooperative Extension Service, an Office of Information, and an Office of Markets and drew many of the best experts into the service of the Department.[159]

Throughout his long stay in Washington, Houston enjoyed cordial

[159] The foregoing paragraphs are based upon David F. Houston, *Eight Years with Wilson's Cabinet* (2 vols.), I, 199-210; John M. Gaus, *et al., Public Administration and the United States Department of Agriculture*, pp. 30-47; and Harold U. Faulkner, *The Decline of Laissez-Faire, 1897-1917*, pp. 347-348.

official relations with the President. He sincerely admired Wilson's intellectual ability and found him a congenial superior.[160] In turn, Wilson trusted Houston and gave him almost complete control over agricultural policies. And yet Houston was one of the loneliest members of the Wilson circle. Cold and uncommunicative by nature, he had no intimates among the Cabinet, never engaged the President's affection, and secretly resented what he regarded as Wilson's social coolness. But he kept his unhappiness well-concealed and remained seemingly imperturbable—the model expert administrator in the Wilson Cabinet.

William C. Redfield, Secretary of Commerce from 1913 to 1919, and William B. Wilson, Secretary of Labor during the whole Wilson period, were on the periphery of the circle. Neither man enjoyed the President's intimacy; neither initiated any important new policies.

Born in Albany, New York, in 1858, Redfield was an iron and steel manufacturer of Brooklyn who entered politics as an anti-Bryan Democrat in 1896, was elected to Congress during the Democratic landslide of 1910, and gained slight distinction in the Sixty-second Congress as a free trader and an enemy of Tammany Hall. As Secretary of Commerce he was a zealous champion of American business enterprise; but he was not overburdened by an excess of intelligence or of discretion, and his verbosity often strained the patience of the President. Perhaps his chief claim to fame was the fact that he was the last man in American public life to wear side whiskers, "ruddy in hue and sedate in pattern." "He seemed the very image of cautious mercantilism, safe investments, and industrial peace," McAdoo remembered. ". . . Redfield looked somewhat as George F. Baker, the great financier, must have looked in his younger days."[161]

Like Redfield, William B. Wilson was a self-made man; but while Redfield orated and bustled, Wilson moved quietly, said little, and did much. Born in Scotland in 1862, Wilson migrated with his family to Pennsylvania in 1870, went to work as a coal miner at the age of nine, and soon demonstrated qualities of leadership and courage as a pioneer in the struggle for unionization. Black-listed, evicted from his home, and even imprisoned because of his devotion to labor's cause, Wilson never lost faith in God or allowed his radical idealism to become dimmed by cynicism and despair. "I learned years ago," he once wrote, "that he who undertakes to use the faculties which God has given him

---

[160] R. S. Baker, interview with D. F. Houston, December 1, 1928, Baker Collection.
[161] W. G. McAdoo, *Crowded Years*, p. 183.

to make life better for the downtrodden and oppressed must expect to be the victim of the venomous attacks of selfish interests. It has not prevented me in the past, and it will not prevent me now, from working with all my energy for the betterment of mankind."[162] With a strong and active faith, Wilson went on to become secretary-treasurer of the United Mine Workers of America from 1900 to 1908, labor's chief spokesman in Congress from 1907 to 1913, and the sponsor of the most comprehensive program of federal labor legislation in the nation's history before 1933.

As Secretary of Labor, Wilson's chief tasks were to reorganize the Labor Department as an independent entity and to win approval of its work from a hostile conservative press and business leadership. He succeeded in the first task with the help of a superb assistant, Louis F. Post, a single-tax progressive. He succeeded, on the whole, in the second without compromising his support of the trade union movement and by staying in the background and emphasizing mediation and conciliation as a substitute for industrial warfare.

No account of the Wilson circle would be complete without some note of Joseph P. Tumulty, Wilson's secretary from 1911 to 1921. Born in Jersey City in 1879, the son of an enterprising Irish-American businessman, Tumulty was educated in parochial schools and at a Jesuit college, studied law, and served an apprenticeship in local Democratic ward politics in his natal city. Elected to the New Jersey legislature in 1906, he soon emerged as a leader of the insurgent Democratic minority who were fighting for political reform and social and economic justice. As Wilson's secretary and chief adviser on New Jersey affairs from 1911 to 1913, Tumulty rendered indispensable service during the Governor's own apprenticeship. As one of the strategists of the preconvention campaign, he also helped Wilson win the presidential nomination in 1912.

As Secretary to the President from 1913 to 1921, Tumulty was burdened with more numerous tasks than any other man near Wilson. He had charge of the Executive Offices and the routine business of the White House. More important, he was Wilson's chief liaison with the politicians and newspapermen. As his biographer has put it, "Tumulty alone enjoyed free access to his chief. . . . All callers had to reach him through Tumulty. The red rug in Tumulty's office was worn thin by the thousands who carried their hopes and their troubles to the highest

[162] W. B. Wilson to E. W. Whittaker, July 9, 1913, William B. Wilson Papers.

authority in the land. . . . Only when he could not solve their problems himself did he refer them to his chief."[163]

But Tumulty's unofficial duties were even more arduous. Without public opinion polls to guide him, he pored over newspapers, kept the President informed of the drift of press sentiment on leading issues, and frequently added his own personal advice. Most important, he worked closely with the professionals in the Democratic national committee in planning campaigns and had a decisive voice in patronage matters, chiefly in the Northeast. To state the matter briefly, Tumulty was the one totally political functionary in the Wilson group.

Fortunately for the President, his Secretary had abundant political talents. Impulsively generous and sympathetic, he brought warmth to the White House and helped repair the damage done by Wilson's aloofness. And yet Tumulty suffered persistent and severe attacks throughout the period and in the end was caught in a net of intrigue against him.

To begin with, as a Roman Catholic Tumulty was under constant fire from extreme Protestant elements fearful of alleged Catholic ambitions and aggressions in the United States. The President's files bulged with letters and petitions denouncing, as one of them put it, "this monstrous and fiendish political plunderbund, and enemy of mankind" in general and Tumulty in particular. He was accused of complicity in an alleged plot to establish the Roman Catholic Church in the United States, of favoring Catholics in appointments, and of withholding letters from the President's eyes.[164]

From the outset, Wilson was disturbed by "the whole absurd business,"[165] and in time he spoke out strongly in Tumulty's defense. "I beg leave to assure you," he wrote in a public letter early in 1914, "that the impression that any part of my correspondence is withheld from me by my Secretary on account of religious predilections on his part is absurdly and utterly false. I venture to say that no President ever had more frank and satisfactory relations with his Secretary than I

---

[163] J. M. Blum, *Joe Tumulty and the Wilson Era*, p. 59; quoted by permission of the Houghton Mifflin Company, publishers.

[164] There are three boxes (Series VI, Boxes 89-91) in the Wilson Papers packed with anti-Catholic letters, petitions, and literature, most of them from Illinois, Iowa, Missouri, Kansas, and other midwestern states. The virulence and filth of this outpouring rather stagger the reader. Much more moderate were the organs and spokesmen of the large Protestant denominations; but they, too, maintained a steady propaganda to counter alleged Catholic designs.

[165] W. W. to J. S. Williams, February 5, 1914, Wilson Papers.

have with mine."[166] "I never was associated with a man more carefully free from sectarian bias in public affairs than Mr. Tumulty," he wrote again in 1915. ". . . I can say to you with the utmost candor that no attempt that I am aware of has been made to bring improper pressure to bear upon my administration in favor of the communicants of any one church. A great many of the most active public men of the country are Catholics. Their prominence is due to their own personal efforts and to their success in public life, but there is nothing subterranean or sinister about it, and I venture to say that they would hesitate to attempt any improper influence even if they were inclined to do so, knowing as they must know my character and disposition in public affairs."[167] Yet the anti-Catholic attacks persisted and were eventually a powerful weapon in the armory of Tumulty's enemies within the administration.

Tumulty, unfortunately, was more vulnerable on other scores. As an adviser to the President, he was often rash and foolish; if Wilson had heeded his suggestions, for example, the United States might possibly have been at war with Mexico, Germany, and Great Britain all at the same time. He embittered progressives in the administration by his type of politics, which were reminiscent of the ward system, his familiarity with characters in the underworld of the Democracy like James M. Sullivan, and the way in which he worked with reactionary machine elements. He was overweening and intensely jealous of colleagues who were close to the President. But most important was the fact that many leaders in the administration came to believe that he was personally indiscreet and lacked sufficient social grace to represent the President of the United States.

Colonel House has left the fullest record of the development of this antagonism. In early 1913 House had been Tumulty's strongest advocate before Wilson. Yet less than a year later the Colonel wrote in his Diary: "Tumulty talks too much. I find evidences of it on every hand. Stories come to me every day of his indiscretions in this direction. I feel somewhat humiliated when I think of my warm advocacy of Tumulty for Private Secretary. The President desired a man of refinement and discretion and of broad vision. He has instead just the opposite and almost wholly at my insistence."[168]

House's conviction that Tumulty was unfit grew during 1914 and

[166] W. W. to W. W. Prescott, January 19, 1914, *ibid.*
[167] W. W. to J. W. Henry, March 1, 1915, *ibid.*
[168] House Diary, single entry dated December 18, 19, and 20, 1913.

1915 and finally led him to undertake a campaign aimed at forcing the Secretary from office. On September 24, 1915, House urged Wilson to accept Tumulty's resignation if he offered it.[169] Encouraged by the President's apparent concurrence, the Colonel redoubled his pressure on Wilson and proceeded to draw Mrs. Wilson, Vance McCormick, Lansing, and perhaps other leaders in the administration into an anti-Tumulty cabal. Moreover, when the extreme anti-Catholic elements made Tumulty's religion an issue during the campaign of 1916, House was able to drive home the argument that the President should not retain his Secretary because so many Protestants believed that Tumulty was an agent of his church.[170] Wilson was reluctant to yield, but on about November 15, 1916, after a conference with his wife and Colonel House, he finally told Tumulty that he must resign and accept appointment to the Board of General Appraisers of the Customs.

It was a humiliating blow, and Tumulty fought back desperately. First, on November 18, 1916, he sent a pathetic letter to the President in effect refusing to resign and telling Wilson that he would have to dismiss him. "After deep reflection . . . ," Tumulty wrote, "I have decided that I cannot accept the appraisership; nor do I feel that I should embarrass you by accepting any other office. I had hoped with all my heart that I might remain in close association with you; that I might be permitted to continue as your Secretary, a position which gave me the fullest opportunity to serve you and the country. To think of leaving you at this time when the fruits of our long fight have been realized wounds me more deeply than I can tell you. . . . You can not know what this means to me and to mine. I am grateful for having been associated so closely with so great a man. I am heart-sick that the end should be like this."[171]

The day after writing this letter, Tumulty conferred with David Lawrence, a newspaperman close to Wilson, and other intimates and planned the counterblow. Lawrence executed it by going straight to the White House and personally confronting the President. "For three-quarters of an hour we talked," Lawrence afterward wrote. "It was a dramatic conversation only because the author felt that in such a case vehemence was essential in order to impress Mr. Wilson with the ingratitude that would be his if he listened to the enemies of his private

---

[169] *ibid.*, September 24, 1915.

[170] *ibid.*, April 6, May 24, October 22 and 23, November 15, 1916.

[171] J. P. Tumulty to W. W., November 18, 1916, Wilson Papers; also printed in J. M. Blum, *Joe Tumulty and the Wilson Era*, p. 121.

secretary and gratified their wishes. Nobody would understand, the author told the President, how one who had rendered as faithful service to him as had Secretary Tumulty could be asked to retire. None of the newspaper men who knew what had been accomplished by Secretary Tumulty for Woodrow Wilson would understand and the old taunt of New Jersey days—ingratitude—would arise once more. Mr. Wilson seemed to realize that he had wounded his faithful friend —the man who had fought his battles day and night—and he sent word through the author to his private secretary not to be disturbed."[172]

Thus Wilson relented, but, as Tumulty's biographer has observed, he "never again trusted Tumulty as he had before their troubles began. . . . Both men . . . had sacrificed self-respect in agreeing to continue a relationship which had been strained almost beyond endurance."[173]

This ends our description of the men around the President and of their problems and the way in which they contributed to the successes and failures of the New Freedom. In subsequent chapters we will examine their impact upon the administration's important domestic and foreign policies even more specifically than in the present account.

[172] David Lawrence, *The True Story of Woodrow Wilson*, p. 334; copyright 1924 by Doubleday & Company, Inc.

[173] J. M. Blum, *Joe Tumulty and the Wilson Era*, p. 122; quoted by permission of the Houghton Mifflin Company, publishers.

CHAPTER V

The President, Congress, and the Democratic Party

FEW MEN have come to the presidency with bolder schemes of leadership or made greater contributions to the development of effective national government in the United States than Woodrow Wilson. Unusual circumstances for a time enabled him to demonstrate conclusively that the President has it within his power not only to be the chief spokesman of the American people, but also to destroy the wall between the executive and legislative branches in the formulation and adoption of legislative programs. He accomplished this feat, not accidentally, but because he willed to be a strong leader and used his opportunities wisely; and historians a century hence will probably rate his expansion and perfection of the powers of the presidency as his most lasting contribution.

The key to a knowledge of Wilson's contributions lies, first of all, in an understanding of his philosophy of leadership. Since his undergraduate days at Princeton he had been engrossed in the study of politics, which he interpreted largely in terms of the behavior of great men. Immersed in the development of Anglo-American democracy and imbued with Christian beliefs, he had concluded that the ideal leader was the man strong in character, determined in purpose, and bold in vision who could lead the people forward along the road of political progress. "In what, then, does political leadership consist?" he asked in what was perhaps his most self-revealing address. "It is leadership in conduct, and leadership in conduct must discern and strengthen the tendencies that make for development. . . . I do not believe that any man can lead who does not act, whether it be consciously or unconsciously, under the impulse of a profound sympathy with those whom he leads. . . . Such men incarnate the consciences of the men whom they rule . . . [and are] quick to know and to do the things that the hour and . . . [the] nation need."[1]

Such was the ideal leader, but how could he function best in the

[1] Woodrow Wilson, *Leaders of Men*, pp. 43, 53-54, 60.

arena of national politics in a democracy like the United States? This was the question to which Wilson addressed his main attention between the late 1870's and the early 1900's, and the answer at which he arrived was conditioned by his admiration of British political leaders and the parliamentary system, and by the extraordinary dearth of leadership in American national politics between Lincoln and Theodore Roosevelt.

The 1880's and 1890's were a time of almost absolute congressional supremacy and of Presidents who were the captives of congressional and party machines. It was perhaps inevitable that the young Wilson should have dreamed of finding personal opportunities for leadership in the Senate, not in the White House; and that the young scholar in his early writings and addresses, particularly in his most famous essay, *Congressional Government in the United States*, should have written off the President as a useless fifth wheel and called for the adoption of the British Cabinet system, which concentrated leadership and responsibility in an executive agency responsible to the legislature. Even as late as 1913 we find him writing that the President at some time "must be made answerable to opinion in a somewhat more informal and intimate fashion—answerable, it may be, to the Houses whom he seeks to lead, either personally or through a Cabinet, as well as to the people for whom they speak."[2]

Although Wilson never did abandon the belief that the parliamentary system provided the best vehicle for responsible leadership in a democracy, the important point is that his views on the possibility of strong leadership in the presidential-congressional system changed fundamentally during the early 1900's in response to the most significant political development of the time. That development was the revivification of the presidency by Theodore Roosevelt, who demonstrated the potential powers of the Chief Executive by asserting a national leadership through control of public opinion.[3] As a consequence of Roosevelt's success in marshaling public opinion and bludgeoning Congress into action, Wilson had come to view the presidency in a new light by the time he delivered his last scholarly lectures, a series given at Columbia University in 1907 and published under the title of *Constitutional Government in the United States* in 1908. Wilson now

[2] W. W. to A. M. Palmer, February 5, 1913, R. S. Baker and W. E. Dodd (eds.), *The New Democracy*, I, 24.

[3] For significant comment on this point, see Edward S. Corwin in William S. Myers (ed.), *Woodrow Wilson, Some Princeton Memories*, pp. 27-28.

saw the President as a national leader and spokesman, "the only national voice in affairs," who could be irresistible in dealing with Congress so long as he understood and led public opinion.

Events between 1907 and 1913, notably Roosevelt's continued success and Taft's failure as a popular leader, only strengthened Wilson's new view of the presidency. The President, he wrote early in 1913, "is expected by the Nation to be the leader of his party as well as the Chief Executive officer of the Government, and the country will take no excuses from him. He must play the part and play it successfully or lose the country's confidence. He must be prime minister, as much concerned with the guidance of legislation as with the just and orderly execution of law, and he is the spokesman of the Nation in everything, even in the most momentous and most delicate dealings of the Government with foreign nations."[4]

Even before he was inaugurated Wilson let it be clearly understood that he would put his new views of presidential leadership into practice. "He is not without party sympathies and not insensible to party obligations," one reporter wrote after an interview with the President-elect in January 1913, "but he is the president; and in the end it is his judgment that will prevail, as he intends to make it, in the settlement of all matters that come before him for consideration. . . . He has readily assumed all responsibility that has been given him. He feels himself capable. He has faith in himself. And he looks upon himself as an instrument for bringing about certain reforms and for ameliorating certain conditions. The predestined idea is not remote from his thought and conclusion."[5]

Wilson came to the presidency not only equipped in theory but also experienced in leadership as president of Princeton University and Governor of New Jersey. In fact, during his apprenticeship from 1902 to 1913 he had worked out and applied all the methods of leadership that he would use so successfully in Washington.

But his success depended not only upon his methods, but also upon the extraordinary political circumstances prevailing from 1910 to about 1916. To begin with, the reform impulses and movements that had shattered party alignments in the 1890's and disrupted the Republican

[4] W. W. to A. M. Palmer, February 5, 1913, printed in R. S. Baker and W. E. Dodd (eds.), *The New Democracy*, I, 23-24.

[5] Samuel G. Blythe, "Our New President," *Saturday Evening Post*, CLXXXV (March 1, 1913), 4.

party during Taft's administration grew stronger than ever during the years of Wilson's first administration. The majority public opinion, Republican as well as Democratic, demanded tariff, tax, and currency reform, a program aimed at establishing national control in the banking and industrial fields, and increased federal assistance to farmers, workers, and underprivileged groups. Thus, unlike Roosevelt or Bryan, Wilson did not have to help to create the progressive movement during the period of his leadership. His chief task was the relatively easy one of crystallizing and giving direction to an already aroused public opinion.

Wilson's task was further lightened by the peculiar situation that prevailed in Congress during his first term. To begin with, there was no powerful rival leader in Congress. In 1910 a group of young rebels, led by Representative George W. Norris of Nebraska, had sheared the Speaker of the House, Joseph G. Cannon of Illinois, of his power by adopting new rules depriving the Speaker of control over the routing of bills and committee appointments. The effect of this revolution was to destroy one of the most effective counterpoises to presidential power and to create a vacuum in leadership which Wilson speedily filled.

In addition, because of the disruption of the Republican party from 1910 to 1916 the Democrats enjoyed large majorities in the House of Representatives and workable majorities in the Senate, strengthened by insurgent Republican support. But even more important was the character of the Democratic membership of Congress. In the first place, one hundred and fourteen of the two hundred and ninety Democratic members of the House in 1913 had been elected for the first time the year before. Eager to please, because their future careers depended in large measure upon patronage and the administration's success, they were like putty in the President's hands. Secondly, the veteran Southerners in both houses knew that the fate of their party depended upon their success in satisfying the national demand for reform, and they, too, willingly accepted the President's leadership. Thirdly, probably a majority of the senators in both parties were advanced progressives, many of them in closer touch with progressive sentiment than Wilson himself. In these circumstances, it was comparatively simple for Wilson to be the most effective of all leaders in the American constitutional system—the spokesman and mediator of a cooperative congressional majority.

Wilson's least obvious but in a sense most important advantage was the fact that he was a newcomer in national politics and the leader of the Democratic party during a time when it was consciously attempting to transform itself from a sectional, agrarian party into a truly national organization representative of all sections and classes. Unlike Bryan, Wilson was relatively free from personal obligations. Unlike Roosevelt, he was not bound by party commitments made over a long period of years.

It is no derogation of Wilson's contribution to emphasize the circumstances that made strong leadership possible from 1913 to 1917, for his contribution in techniques was of enormous importance. The first of these techniques of leadership was to assert the position of the President as the spokesman of the people and to use public opinion as a spur on Congress. Theodore Roosevelt had demonstrated the usefulness of this method, but Wilson used it to fullest advantage and made it inevitable that any future President would be powerful only in so far as he established communication with the people and spoke effectively for them.

His chief instruments in achieving a position as national spokesman were of course oratory and public messages, by means of which he gave voice to the highest aspirations, first, of the American people, and then, during the war and afterward, of the people of the world. He was a virtuoso and a spellbinder during a period when the American people admired oratory above all other political skills. But as a spellbinder he appealed chiefly to men's minds and spirits, and only infrequently to their passions; and it is doubtful if any leader in American history since Lincoln has succeeded so well in communicating the ideals that the American people have in their better moments tried to live by.

A measure of Wilson's success lay in the fact that he was a romantic moralist who, using the poet's hyperbole to express political truth, raised every issue and conflict to a high stage upon which the human drama was being played out. Were the citizens of Trenton about to vote upon the adoption of commission government? Then they were confronted with an opportunity to show the world whether Americans were capable of enlightened self-government! Were the American people about to enter a world war? Then they were privileged to give their blood and treasure to make the world safe for democracy and to extend the dominion of righteousness throughout the earth!

There were times when the spellbinder was so exhilarated that he said things he did not mean or when his verbiage obscured the ideas that he sought to express. There were also times, during flights of fancy mainly in extemporaneous speeches, when his oratory was like a symphony, meant to be heard and experienced emotionally but not to be logically understood. The following passage, taken from an address on jury reform which Wilson delivered at Elizabeth, New Jersey, on May 1, 1913, illustrates this quality:

"We are going to get jury reform. Don't be nervous about that. We do not need to get it through these gentlemen. There are other gentlemen through whom we can get it. These gentlemen are moths around the candle. All public men are moths around the candle. (I am trying my best to keep my wings out of the flames.) These are incidents in a great communal life which knows no bounds, like the sea itself, and which like the sea itself is ever renewed and ever refreshed and always old and yet always young. It will carry what fleets and navies it pleases, it will move under the winds of the heavens as God commands. These gentlemen may sink or swim, as the chances go, but the mills of the gods will grind on, and they will grind out justice, they will grind out righteousness, they will see that purity is again enthroned in public affairs; and those little hosts of devoted men and women throughout the United States, who have set their faces like the faces of those lifted to the light, to see to it that the suffering, the distressed, the down trodden, the toiling, are served by the laws and policies and constitutions of our time, are a gathering and multiplying army whose songs are not halted by any of the harsh discords of the age, but are going on with a battle song that more and more drowns every note that competes with it; until we begin to see peeping over the hills the light which will eventually spread and broaden upon a great host of brothers loving one another, serving one another, understanding one another, and united in order to lift the human race to the final levels of achievement."[6]

Certain dangers existed in such excesses of nobility and moral vision. There was always the temptation to idealize unpleasant situations and necessities—a temptation to which Wilson sometimes succumbed. It led him to romanticize objectives and to refuse to confront harsh realities. The faults and dangers of his oratory were well described by Herbert Croly:

"Mr. Wilson seems to be one of those people who shuffle off their mortal coil as soon as they take pen in hand. They become tremen-

[6] *Newark Evening News,* May 2, 1913.

dously noble. They write as the monuments of great men might write. They write only upon brass, and for nothing shorter than a millennium. They utter nothing which might sound trivial at the Last Judgment, or embarrass them in the most august company.

"It is the quality of Mr. Wilson's thinking to make even the most concrete things seem like abstractions. Technically he is perfectly aware that ideals are good for what they are good for, in the real world of moving men; actually he conveys only the most remote view of that world. His mind is like a light which destroys the outlines of what it plays upon; there is much illumination, but you see very little."[7]

And yet the conviction remains that at his best Wilson was nearly incomparable as an orator, that he was a political poet who not only intuitively absorbed national ideals but was also able to translate them into words so lofty and inspiring that they perhaps helped to change the course of human history. Certainly the man who could say "This is not a day of triumph; it is a day of dedication. Here muster, not the forces of party, but the forces of humanity. Men's hearts wait upon us; men's lives hang in the balance; men's hopes call upon us to say what we will do," or "The right is more precious than peace, and we shall fight for the things which we have always carried nearest our hearts,— for democracy, for the right of those who submit to authority to have a voice in their own Governments, for the rights and liberties of small nations, for a universal dominion of right by such a concert of free peoples as shall bring peace and safety to all nations and make the world itself at last free"—surely the man who could say these things could speak with the tongue of an angel to recall the visions lost in rivalries for wealth and power.

In addition to oratory and formal public messages, Wilson used frequent informal appeals and statements in the press to maintain an intimate relationship with the people. During the controversy over tariff reform in 1913, for example, he destroyed a powerful lobby simply by denouncing it. He neutralized the opposition of the financial interests to his plan for banking and currency reform by forthright appeals to the people. For a time he even tried to conduct diplomacy through the newspapers.

On the other hand, a word of qualification should be added about the way that the President used this method of public leadership. So firmly did Wilson control Congress from 1913 to 1917 that only upon one important occasion, the debate over military and naval expansion in

---

[7] "The Other-Worldliness of Wilson," *New Republic*, II (March 27, 1915), 194-195.

1916, did he appeal to the people over the head of Congress. During these years his public appeals were almost always directed at building popular support for his party and program against the assaults of private interests and the Republican opposition.

Wilson made his most significant contribution to the development of the presidency, not through exploitation of national leadership—for in this regard he merely perfected a method already highly developed by Theodore Roosevelt—but rather in the way in which he asserted and established leadership of Congress, achieved an absolute mastery of the Democratic party, and in the end fused the powers of the executive and legislative branches in his own person.

He began soon after his inauguration. On March 9, 1913, White House spokesmen announced that the President would help frame important legislation; ten days later these same spokesmen added that Wilson would confer frequently with Democratic leaders in the President's Room in the Capitol.[8] But his most vivid assertion of leadership came soon afterward, when he delivered his message on tariff reform in person before the two houses on April 8, 1913.

It is difficult for a generation accustomed to seeing the President appear frequently before the Congress to understand the symbolic significance of Wilson's act. Thomas Jefferson had abandoned the custom of appearing before Congress on the ground that it resembled too much the King's speech from the throne; and Jefferson's precedent had become an unwritten law during the following century. The White House's announcement on April 6, 1913, that Wilson would deliver his tariff message in person, therefore, provoked shocked indignation among the legislators, especially among Democrats who revered the Jeffersonian model. "I for one very much regret the President's course," exclaimed Senator John Sharp Williams of Mississippi on April 7. ". . . I am sorry to see revived the old Federalistic custom of speeches from the throne. . . . I regret all this cheap and tawdry imitation of English royalty."[9]

Going before Congress, however, was Wilson's way of telling the country that he meant to destroy the mythical wall that had so long divided the executive from the legislative branch.[10] "I think that this

---

[8] New York *World*, March 10 and 20, 1913.

[9] *New York Times*, April 8, 1913.

[10] Apparently it was Oliver P. Newman, a newspaper reporter, who first suggested that Wilson should deliver his message in person. See R. S. Baker, interview with

is the only dignified way for the President to address Congress at the opening of a session, instead of sending the address to be read perfunctorily in the clerk's familiar tone of voice," he explained in a public reply to his critics. "I thought that the dignified and natural thing was to read it."[11] And when he appeared before the joint session the following day, he added:

"I am very glad indeed to have this opportunity to address the two Houses directly and to verify for myself the impression that the President of the United States is a person, not a mere department of the Government hailing Congress from some isolated island of jealous power, sending messages, not speaking naturally and with his own voice —that he is a human being trying to co-operate with other human beings in a common service."

Less obvious and well known were the methods that Wilson used to establish control over the Democratic membership of Congress. Even before he was inaugurated, he had to choose between leadership of a Democratic-insurgent Republican coalition of progressives or leadership as a partisan working exclusively through the Democratic membership and congressional machinery. There were signs during the months before his inauguration that he would attempt to construct a new coalition, but for a number of reasons Wilson decided to remain what he always thought the President should be—a prime minister, the leader of his party, the responsible spokesman for a legislative program. He was able to effect such leadership, incidentally, without wholly alienating the insurgents and independents; and when he reconstructed the Democratic program in 1916, he was able to draw most of the independents into the Democratic ranks.

He took party leadership simply by asserting it boldly. In Trenton, before his inauguration, he took control by conferring in person and by correspondence with committee chairmen and Democratic leaders over the general structure of a legislative program. In Washington, he gave assiduous attention to the minutiae of legislation, conferred frequently at the Capitol and the White House, brought congressional and Cabinet leaders together, mediated when it seemed fundamental differences might disrupt the Democratic ranks, and, when necessary, cracked the patronage whip and used the House and Senate Democratic caucuses to force rebels into line.

O. P. Newman, January 13, 1928, Baker Collection; and David Lawrence, *The True Story of Woodrow Wilson*, pp. 82-83.

[11] *New York Times*, April 8, 1913.

He won control through the sheer force of personality and by using all the inherent powers of the party leader. "I claim no superior attributes of mind or decision over you or over any man in my party," he would tell a protesting congressman; "but you overlook the fact that I have been designated by the people to hold this office and be the official head of this nation. I am simply the instrument of the people for carrying out their desires as I understand them. It is my best judgment that this thing should be done in this way, and you should acquiesce in that judgment; for I must bear the burden of the responsibility to the people, and not you; and I have no desire to divide that responsibility or shift it. I have given this matter careful consideration. This procedure seems right to me. I ask you to adopt my plan. If you do not I am perfectly willing to submit both my plan and yours to the people and abide by their decision; but until the people relieve me of my responsibilities those responsibilities are paramount, and I must insist on my own conception of my duty."[12]

Although he could threaten and use the patronage as ruthlessly as any President in American history to compel obedience, Wilson preferred to win the support of congressmen by appealing to their reason and their sense of national duty. "We always come away feeling that we have been convinced, not by Mr. Wilson—certainly not driven or bossed by him—but with the feeling that we are all—President, Congress, and people—in the presence of an irresistible situation," a congressman friendly to Wilson explained. "Here are the facts, he says; here are the principles, here are our obligations as Democrats. What are we going to do about it? He has a curious way of making one feel that he, along with all of us, is perfectly helpless before the facts in the case."[13]

In one sense this description of Wilson's method is accurate. On numerous critical occasions he willingly compromised important points to gain a larger goal and won his objectives by leading instead of by driving. And yet the conclusion cannot be escaped that he was also, in the showdown, the master, determined and able to bend Congress and his party to his personal will, able even to effect sudden and violent shifts in policy without the previous knowledge and consent of party leaders in Congress.

One observer stated the matter shrewdly: "He is agreeable, mild-

[12] S. G. Blythe, "Wilson in Washington," *Saturday Evening Post*, CLXXXVI (November 8, 1913), 8.

[13] Ray S. Baker, "Wilson," *Collier's*, LVIII (October 7, 1916), 6.

mannered, pleasant, even solicitous about it all; but . . . he is firmly and entirely the leader, and insists upon complete recognition as such. He smiles when he tells a man to do a thing, but that smile does not decrease or soften the imperativeness of the order. He is a polite but not an easy boss. . . . He is the top, the middle and the bottom of it [all]. There is not an atom of divided responsibility. He has accepted every issue as his, has formulated every policy as his, and is insisting —and with success—on strict adherence to his plans. The Democratic party revolves round him. He is the center of it; the biggest Democrat in the country—the leader and the chief."[14]

This method worked, among other reasons, because few congressmen and senators dared to challenge him. Because there was no congressional machine capable of resistance, congressmen and senators stood alone in opposition to the man who had completely fused the powers of the presidency and of the party leader. As a perceptive English observer noted, they were, besides, "conscious of an intellectual inferiority, of a narrower point of view, of the limitations in their knowledge, of less elevated purposes and motives, of an almost entire ignorance as to how things will strike him."[15] So complete was his control, in fact, that he remained the master of his party even when the country had turned against him and when he insisted upon policies that most Democrats thought were catastrophic.

The more Wilson led, the more his critics, friendly as well as hostile, accused him of harboring dictatorial ambitions. "Is the National Legislature to be held *in terrorem* in order to justify the self-assumed role of the All-Wise Teacher of the White House?" one prominent financial journal asked,[16] for example, while an English analyst wrote approvingly about Wilson's "new bossism."[17]

Wilson resented such attacks but never answered them publicly. "Do not believe anything you read in the newspapers," he wrote to a friend. ". . . Their lying is shameless and colossal! Editorially the papers which are friendly (and some which are not) represent me, in the most foolish way, as master of the situation here, bending Congress to my indomitable individual will. That is, of course, silly. Congress is made up of thinking men who want the party to succeed as much

[14] S. G. Blythe, "Wilson in Washington," *loc.cit.*, p. 8.
[15] Sydney Brooks, in the London *Daily Chronicle*, March 4, 1914.
[16] *Financial World*, xx (April 12, 1913), 3.
[17] A. Maurice Low, " 'The New Bossism,' " *Harper's Weekly*, lvii (April 19, 1913), 8.

as I do, and who wish to serve the country effectively and intelligently. They have found out that I am honest and that I have no personal purpose of my own to serve (except that 'If it be a sin to covet honour, then am I the most offending soul alive!') and accept my guidance because they see that I am attempting only to mediate their own thoughts and purposes. I do not know how to wield a big stick, but I do know how to put my mind at the service of others for the accomplishment of a common purpose. They are using me; I am not driving them."[18]

Whether he achieved results by leading or by driving is at this point irrelevant. The important fact is that Woodrow Wilson had substantially transformed the American presidency by the end of his rule. When Franklin D. Roosevelt later recovered the full powers of national and party leadership for the presidency, many critics charged that he was acting in a unique and revolutionary way in order to subvert the Constitution and establish a personal dictatorship. Actually, he was only following the example of the President under whom he had served for eight years.

It might be well to conclude this brief introduction to Wilson as a national political leader with the words of his own wise contemporaries. "Under Mr. Wilson," the authoritative voice of American progressivism declared, "the prestige of the Presidency has been fully restored. He has not only expressly acknowledged and acted on this obligation of leadership, as did Mr. Roosevelt, but he has sought to embody it in constitutional form."[19] "Aside from definite legislative achievements . . . ," Walter Page's journal stated, "Mr. Wilson has introduced one definite idea into American political life. Because of his career, American politics can never be precisely the same thing that it was before. This one idea is that of party leadership. . . . This, then, is President Wilson's great contribution to our political philosophy and practice. . . . He has given the office [of President] a new and high dignity; he has shown that it possesses greater power for usefulness than we had imagined; and certainly no President can have succeeded more completely than that."[20]

[18] W. W. to Mary A. Hulbert, September 21, 1913, printed in R. S. Baker, *Woodrow Wilson*, IV, 183.

[19] *New Republic*, I (December 5, 1914), 11-12.

[20] *World's Work*, XXIX (March 1915), 489. For additional contemporary comment on Wilson as leader, see "Two Years of Wilson," New York *World*, March 4, 1915; "Mr. Wilson's First Two Years," *New York Times*, March 5, 1915; Sydney Brooks, unsigned, "A Premiere-President," London *Nation*, XIII (May 17, 1913), 259-260; S. Brooks, editorials in the London *Times*, September 13 and October 4, 1913; S. Brooks,

Wilson led the Democratic party in part because he controlled it. He controlled it not merely by strong postures and a bold voicing of public opinion but also by using the immense patronage at his command as an instrument of effective government. Confronted by no entrenched national party organization and no body of officeholders loyal to another man, he was able to build from the ground up and to weld the widely scattered and disparate Democratic forces into nearly as effective a political organization as one can build in the United States. And yet in achieving this position of partisan leadership he confronted a dilemma that has faced all Presidents intent upon reform. He had to choose between working through the men in power in the Democratic party in Congress and in the state and city organizations, many of whom had opposed the things for which he stood, or risking the defeat of his legislative program by supporting only his progressive friends.

There could be no doubt during the period of post-election dedication and idealism and the first months of the new administration that Wilson meant to regenerate the Democratic party by giving initiative and control to its progressive element. Time and again in speeches and public statements during the pre-inaugural period he voiced this intention. "I have no liberty in the matter," he declared, for example, in an address before the New Jersey electors in Trenton on January 13, 1913. "I have given bonds. My sacred honor is involved, and nothing more could be involved. Therefore, I shall not be acting as a partisan when I pick out progressives, and only progressives. I shall be acting as a representative of the people of this great country."[21]

To Wilson, as to most progressives of his time, progressivism meant a general attitude and a method of approach more than a finely spun ideology. It meant, in brief, the combining of a fundamental demo-

---

unsigned, "President Wilson's Record," London *Nation*, XVI (March 6, 1915), 709-710; S. Brooks, "President Wilson," London *Outlook*, XXXV (March 6, 1915), 299; "The President and Legislation," New York *Nation*, XCVI (April 10, 1913), 350; "Wilson and Legislation," *ibid.*, XCVII (August 14, 1913), 136; "Wilson and the Presidency," *ibid.*, CII (June 22, 1916), 661; "Mr. Wilson's Congress," *ibid.*, CIII (September 14, 1916), 251-252; Edward Porritt, "President Wilson's First Lap," London *Westminster Gazette*, September 1, 1913; London *Morning Post*, September 23, 1913; Oswald G. Villard, "The Mystery of Woodrow Wilson," *North American Review*, CCIV (September 1916), 368-369; "The Burden of Presidential Office," *New Republic*, III (June 19, 1915), 162-163; editorial in *ibid.*, V (January 15, 1916), 268; Herbert Croly, "Unregenerate Democracy," *ibid.*, VI (February 5, 1916), 17-19.

[21] *New York Times*, January 14, 1913.

cratic philosophy with a certain dynamic quality and a willingness to experiment. When Wilson, for example, talked about progressives, he meant the host of men and women all over the country who had been fighting to destroy political machines allied with corrupt businessmen. He meant men like Robert M. La Follette in Wisconsin and Newton D. Baker in Ohio, who stood for integrity and decency in politics and social and economic justice. He meant, in so far as his own party was concerned, the men who had fought for his nomination in 1912 and were willing to follow his leadership in the New Freedom. Circumstances, however, made it extraordinarily difficult for him to follow a policy dictated by principle alone.

To begin with, although Wilson gave an astonishing amount of attention to the minutiae of patronage and made perhaps several hundred personal appointments, the task of dispensing tens of thousands of jobs was simply more than he could comprehend or control. In one of his first statements after the inauguration, he announced his method: he would see no applicant except by invitation and would make appointments only through the Cabinet members. He then proceeded to lay down the general rules, to give each Cabinet member a list of Wilsonian progressives prepared by McCombs and the National Committee, and to trust his Cabinet members and his unofficial advisers, House and Tumulty, to attend to the details. It was the only workable method, but he often did not know what his subordinates were doing; and as time passed he tended to care less and less.

The chief obstacles to the fulfillment of Wilson's intention to strengthen the progressive element, however, were the realities and necessities of practical politics. There were progressive and conservative Democratic factions battling for control in virtually every state in 1913. By and large, the progressives had supported Wilson in 1911 and 1912; in fact, many of them had risked their political careers by opposing the conservative cliques in the preconvention battles. On the other hand, the so-called conservatives were firmly entrenched in many states and constituted a sizable minority of the Democratic congressmen and senators. A bold frontal assault by Wilson through patronage channels might, therefore, disrupt the party and ensure the defeat of his legislative program.

Even so, Wilson was apparently willing at the outset of his administration to run that risk. Soon after the inauguration, perhaps in mid-March 1913, he called Burleson to the White House to discuss basic policy to govern the appointment of postmasters. "Now, Burleson," the President began, "I want to say to you that my administration is going to be a progressive administration. I am not going to advise with reactionary or standpat Senators or Representatives in making these appointments. I am going to appoint forward-looking men, and I am going to satisfy myself that they are honest and capable." Then he repeated, with emphasis: "I am not going to consult the old stand-patters in our party."

Burleson was aghast. "Mr. President," he protested, "if you pursue this policy, it means that your administration is going to be a failure. It means the defeat of the measures of reform that you have next to your heart. These little offices don't amount to anything. They are inconsequential. It doesn't amount to a damn who is postmaster at Paducah, Kentucky. But these little offices mean a great deal to the Senators and Representatives in Congress. If it goes out that the President has turned down Representative So and So and Senator So and So, it means that that member has got bitter trouble at home. If you pursue the right policy, you can make the Democratic Party progressive. . . ."

"As your Postmaster General," Burleson continued, "I am going to make 56,000 appointments. I will see honest and capable men in every office. But I will consult with the men on the 'Hill.' I have been here a long time. I know these Congressmen and Senators. If they are turned down, they will hate you and will not vote for anything you want. It is human nature. On the other hand, if we work with them, and they recommend unsuitable men for the offices, I will keep on asking for other suggestions, until I get a good one. In the end we shall get as able men as we would in any other way, and we will keep the leaders of the party with us."

Burleson left the White House not knowing what impression he had made. A week later Wilson called him to his study to discuss a mammoth list of names for postmasterships. Burleson began with a candidate hotly opposed by Wilson's friends in Tennessee. The President leaned back, threw up his arms, and exclaimed, "Burleson, I can't appoint a man like that!" The Postmaster General then explained why the appointment had been made and how important it was to a key Tennessee representative. "Well, I will appoint him," Wilson said.[22]

It was one of the early decisive turning points in Wilson's presidential career. Burleson's account is somewhat exaggerated, especially when he goes on to relate how Wilson gave him complete control over

[22] R. S. Baker, interview with A. S. Burleson, March 17-19, 1927, Baker Collection.

all the postmasterships; but it is essentially correct. What the President did was to give to Burleson, Tumulty, and Thomas J. Pence, secretary of the National Committee, virtually complete control of the mass of petty jobs, reserving for himself and for Colonel House the right to advise and veto.

As Burleson and Tumulty preferred to control the Democratic party rather than to reform it, the result of Wilson's decision was the triumph of the professional politician over the idealist in the administration. Burleson and the professionals well knew that it made a tremendous difference to the rival factions in Kentucky who was postmaster in Paducah and a hundred other towns in that state. Imbued with the professional politician's conviction that control of the state organizations, party harmony, and support in Congress for administration measures were more to be desired than warfare and a risky regeneration of the Democracy, they used the patronage almost cynically for practical ends. "I had the bait gourd," Burleson afterward boasted. "They had to come to me."

Generally speaking, the effect of Burleson's policy was to strengthen the factions already in control of the city and state organizations or, when the factions were evenly divided, to draw the rivals together in an agreement to cooperate and share the patronage. Thus Burleson and Tumulty tended to favor the Democratic organizations in New York, Boston, Chicago, and other large cities, although these so-called machines were often corrupt and had been among Wilson's most virulent enemies before the Baltimore convention. In many non-southern states, where progressive Democrats were dominant, Burleson's policy operated to strengthen Wilson's friends. In many states where conservatives prevailed, on the other hand, it worked to discourage and weaken the progressive factions.

This was particularly true in the South, where rising groups of anti-machine Democrats in nearly every state had joined the Wilson movement in 1911 and 1912 and launched a powerful campaign to destroy the old cliques allied with the railroads and corrupt courthouse rings. They were minorities in most of the southern states, but they were well organized and growing in strength; and they looked to their leader in Washington for the assistance they were sure would turn the tide of battle. They often looked in vain. The progressive minorities in the South found in Washington, not the sustenance and recognition as the leaders of Wilsonian progressivism that they had confidently expected, but aloofness and rejection.

In Kentucky, for example, Burleson gave control of the federal patronage to Senator Ollie M. James and the Democratic congressmen, most of whom were allied with the railroad and liquor interests and had bitterly fought Wilson's nomination. By the end of Wilson's first year as President, only one Wilson man had been named to federal office in the state. "The most vicious element in Kentucky politics has controlled the patronage. The men who fought for Wilson, not because of his personality only or chiefly, but because he stood for what they believed in, have been ostracized by him," the leader of the Wilson movement in Kentucky wrote in protest.[23] "There has never been, in the history of any state, a more glaring illustration of the use of patronage to build up a political machine to be used by a faction of the party; nor, in our judgment, a more deplorable illustration of the President permitting another to dictate his patronage so as to punish those who fought for, and reward those who fought against the President's nomination."[24]

Virginia was another testing ground of the administration's patronage policy. A large group of insurgents, led by Henry St. George Tucker, John Garland Pollard, and Allan D. Jones, had been fighting since the early 1900's to wrest control of the state Democratic organization from Senator Thomas S. Martin, Representative Henry D. Flood, and the machine closely identified with the railroad and business interests. They had fought hard to swing Virginia into the Wilson column in 1912, had nominated and elected a progressive governor in the same year, and had gone on to capture control in Norfolk, Roanoke, Petersburg, and other cities. Thus it seemed that the progressive movement in the Old Dominion was on the verge of victory when Wilson, in his speech at Staunton on December 28, 1912, attacked the Martin machine and inferentially promised to support the progressives.[25]

And yet it did not work out that way. Tucker had a conference with the President on August 25, 1913. "I am much concerned about his attitude in Virginia affairs," Tucker wrote soon afterward. "He has a decided leaning to the recognition of the Senators with a view of

[23] Desha Breckinridge to W. F. McCombs, March 7, 1914, Wilson Papers.

[24] Desha Breckinridge, editorial in the *Lexington* (Kentucky) *Herald*, March 7, 1914. See also W. G. McAdoo to W. W., September 29, 1913, Wilson Papers, enclosing a letter from Leigh Harris, editor of the *Henderson* (Kentucky) *Daily Journal*.

[25] See above, pp. 25-26.

holding them in line for the tariff and currency measures."[26] When Wilson justified these fears by giving practically all the important Virginia appointments to the Martin organization, the insurgents met in Richmond on January 5, 1914, and addressed a moving protest to the White House. By appointing only reactionaries in Virginia, they wrote, the President had violated his own principles and disheartened his friends in the state. "Can being proscribed because of their very allegiance to those principles have any other effect?"[27] It was a futile gesture.

There was, to cite a final example, the way in which the Wilson administration ignored the progressive minority and gave control of the patronage in Alabama to Senator John H. Bankhead, Representative Oscar W. Underwood, and the other politicians who had fought to prevent Wilson's nomination in 1912.[28]

The issue arose in crucial form when Underwood asked the President to appoint Edward K. Campbell, a railroad and corporation lawyer of Birmingham, to the United States Court of Claims. "His appointment," a former governor and the Alabama member of the National Committee warned Wilson, "would put the teeth of your largest supporters in this state on edge."[29] "Please allow me to say that the appointment of this man would be the coldest chill you could give to your friends in this State," Wilson's most intimate friend in Alabama told him. "No man was more extreme or resourceful in his opposition to any sort of recognition of the will of a large majority of the Democrats of this State. His promotion would be construed by all of your friends as a triumph of the active influence of your opponents in the State congressional delegation."[30] All that the President could say in reply was that he realized what Campbell's appointment would mean, but that it was "inevitable in the circumstances."[31] He meant that he could not risk alienating Underwood, who had charge of the tariff bill then pending in the House.

It was embarrassing, this having to turn one's back on faithful

[26] H. St.G. Tucker to Carter Glass, August 27, 1913, the Papers of Carter Glass, University of Virginia Library; hereinafter cited as the Glass Papers.

[27] J. G. Pollard, *et al.*, to W. W., January 5, 1914, Wilson Papers.

[28] For a general protest, see Horace Hood, editor of the *Montgomery Journal* and a leader of the progressive wing, to W. J. Bryan, October 11, 1913, Bryan Papers, National Archives.

[29] W. D. Jelks to W. W., March 19, 1913, Wilson Papers.

[30] Frank P. Glass to W. W., March 20, 1913, *ibid.*

[31] W. W. to F. P. Glass, April 16, 1913, *ibid.*

friends; and time and again Wilson confessed his helplessness and chagrin. "As for the postmasterships you speak of," he wrote to Bryan in explanation of his policy, "it is extremely difficult, when we are convinced that the Congressmen in the several districts offer us good men, to turn away from their choice and take the choice of someone else."[32] "I am very much distressed that the friends in North Carolina, with whom you spoke, should have got the impression they have got," he explained again. "I do not blame them in the least, but there are many circumstances upon which I do not think they reflect. In the first place, I am bound by the old practice and expectation of everybody as opinion is organized here in Washington to respect and accept the recommendations of Congressmen and Senators, if they recommend men unobjectionable in character and ability. . . . It is a thorny and difficult matter altogether in which I have not satisfied myself and in which I am grieved to learn I have not satisfied my friends."[33] He felt, he wrote to a friend, like putting up the sign that was nailed on the organ loft of a country church for the defense of the organist. It read, Wilson said, "Don't shoot. He is doing his damnedest."

There were, besides, a thousand minor vexations, most of which Burleson, Tumulty, and the Cabinet members absorbed but some of which found their way to the President. Whom could the administration trust in Wooster, Ohio, or Vermont, or Washington State?[34] Why had Burleson appointed Thomas Fox, a known lobbyist for the Southern Pacific Railroad, as postmaster at Sacramento?[35] Did Burleson know that he had appointed an alleged drunkard in Michigan; could he not grant some favor to Representative "Alfalfa Bill" Murray of Oklahoma, "a very faithful and militant friend"; would Burleson please remember not to dismiss General Longstreet's widow, a Republican, as postmistress at Gainesville, Georgia?[36]

Or, again, there were embarrassments like the one Wilson related:

[32] W. W. to W. J. Bryan, June 25, 1913, *ibid.*
[33] W. W. to S. S. Wise, June 4, 1914, *ibid.*
[34] W. W. to A. S. Burleson, April 4, June 2, and July 28, 1913, *ibid.*
[35] This appointment, incidentally, created controversy all over the West and drew protests from Thomas J. Pence, secretary of the National Committee, Senator Key Pittman of Nevada, and many Californians. See T. J. Pence to W. W., May 29, 1913, Burleson Papers; W. W. to A. S. Burleson, May 29 and June 2, 1913, Wilson Papers. Burleson wrote at the bottom of the original of Wilson's letter of June 2, 1913, in the Burleson Papers, the following: "Stood by Fox and put him over. Sacramento went for Wilson in 1916 election and saved the state for Wilson."
[36] W. W. to A. S. Burleson, October 7, September 26, and March 30, 1913, Wilson Papers.

"The Junior Senator from New York was in to see me yesterday and had this to say about the post office appointment at Buffalo: It seems that he recommended a German Lutheran and that upon some impression he gained at your office he permitted it to be announced in Buffalo that his candidate would be appointed, whereupon the said candidate was serenaded, etc., by various Lutheran societies and his not being appointed has caused him considerable mortification. I mean the candidate."[37]

The foregoing general discussion ignores some important areas where the political situation was too complicated to accommodate itself to any pattern. In Massachusetts, for example, where the Democrats were divided into several fiercely warring factions, House, McAdoo, and Tumulty supported the progressives headed by David I. Walsh and Josiah Quincy against the conservatives and the Boston city machine controlled by Mayor John F. Fitzgerald.[38] In Illinois, Tumulty executed a plan for division of the patronage equally among Roger Sullivan, head of the state machine, and Sullivan's rivals, Senator James Hamilton Lewis, Governor Edward F. Dunne, and Mayor Carter Harrison of Chicago.[39]

These problems, however, were simple as compared with the difficulties of working out a purposeful patronage plan for New York. The party in that state, the cornerstone of the Democracy in the Northeast, was virtually torn apart from 1912 to 1914 by struggles between the Tammany organization headed by Charles F. Murphy and an unstable anti-Tammany coalition of upstate progressives and good government reformers in New York City.

The problem confronting administration leaders in Washington was, essentially, to find a formula for reconstructing the party in New York that would give leadership to the anti-Tammany element without driving the rank and file of the Tammany organization into rebellion. Difficult at best, the task was complicated by an intense struggle within the Wilson circle for control of the New York appointments, the richest patronage prize of all, and by the fact that New York's Democratic senator, James A. O'Gorman, allegedly an independent progressive, was on friendly terms with Tammany and soon became personally antagonistic to the President.

[37] W. W. to A. S. Burleson, November 25, 1913, *ibid.*
[38] J. M. Blum, *Joe Tumulty and the Wilson Era*, pp. 81-82.
[39] *ibid.*, p. 82.

In the beginning, however, the reformation of New York seemed an easy task as Colonel House and McAdoo met in House's apartment in March 1913 to map plans. "We both have a keen desire to revamp New York City and State, and to give them efficient government," House recorded in his Diary. "We will try to nominate a proper man for Governor two years from now, and in the meantime to get a Mayor for New York City who will cleanse it. Our first move will be to get a proper man for Collector of the Port [of New York]."[40] For House the objective of the proposed campaign was the destruction of Tammany influence, which he bitterly detested; for McAdoo the chief objective was control of the New York Democracy as the springboard to the presidency.

Moving as quickly as circumstances would permit, House and McAdoo first persuaded the President to name McAdoo's intimate friend, Frank L. Polk, former chairman of the New York Civil Service Commission and a leader of the anti-Tammanyites, as Collector of the Port of New York, the most powerful federal post in the state;[41] and a few days later, on April 15, 1913, to name H. Snowden Marshall, another anti-Tammany leader, as United States attorney for the southern district of New York, perhaps the second most powerful federal position in the state.

House's and McAdoo's plans went momentarily awry, however, because in their haste to gain control of New York they had failed to consult Senator O'Gorman. Sulking because the President had ignored him and suspecting that McAdoo meant to seize control of the party in the Empire State, the senator was in an angry mood. He could not object to Marshall's appointment, although he had suggested other candidates, because Marshall was one of his law partners. But he warned the President that he would prevent Polk's confirmation even if he had to invoke his personal privilege as a senator; and he coun-

[40] House Diary, March 9, 1913.
[41] Wilson had earlier offered the collectorship to George Foster Peabody, a banker, philanthropist, and leader of the progressive wing in New York, and Peabody had declined on the ground that he could better serve the administration as a liaison with Wall Street. See G. F. Peabody to W. W., March 20, 1913, Wilson Papers.

After Peabody's declination, Franklin D. Roosevelt, Assistant Secretary of the Navy, and McAdoo suggested the appointment of John K. Sague, Mayor of Poughkeepsie, as Collector, but O'Gorman and the Tammany organization objected strenuously. It was at this point that McAdoo brought Polk forward as a "compromise" candidate. See Frank Freidel, *Franklin D. Roosevelt: The Apprenticeship*, p. 176.

tered with a list of six men, most of them independents, who would be acceptable to him as Collector.[42]

For several weeks Wilson tried to break the impasse. Determined to control the vast patronage of the Collector's office, McAdoo was adamant and threatened to resign if the President surrendered to O'Gorman.[43] Fearful that an open break would drive the senator to vote against tariff reform, Wilson pleaded with O'Gorman to yield. "I regard the Collectorship as in many ways as central and as intimately connected with my personal success as a place in the Cabinet," Wilson wrote, telling O'Gorman that he had to name Polk.[44] The senator was unmoved. "O'Gorman is always smiling and Jesuitical," Wilson said some time later. "He sat in this very chair some weeks ago and talked with me for an hour, and I made about as much impression upon *him* as I did upon the chair."[45]

McAdoo, moreover, was equally adamant in support of Polk and balked when the President suggested naming one of O'Gorman's nominees, Lawson Purdy, president of the Tax Board of New York City and an anti-Tammany Democrat. Colonel House agreed with McAdoo. "If I were you I would name Polk," he advised Wilson on May 4, 1913. "I believe that to do less would be construed as an unwillingness to confront the issue which the Senator from New York has raised. Your mastery of Congress depends largely upon your maintaining that unflinching courage which our people rightly appreciate and which has made you the dominating figure upon this Continent."[46]

Unmoved by McAdoo's demands or House's flattery, Wilson decided not to force an open fight with O'Gorman. Instead, he agreed to drop Polk's name from consideration and promised to appoint no Collector whom McAdoo and the New York senator could not both approve.[47] "We will work it out as friends should," he reassured O'Gorman, "and [as] those who cordially and as a matter of course understand one another."[48]

By this time, however, Wilson was sick of the quarrel and had made up his mind to impose his own solution. On May 5, 1913—the same

[42] *New York Times*, April 18, 1913; New York *World*, April 22, 1913.

[43] House Diary, May 4, 1913.

[44] W. W. to J. A. O'Gorman, April 20, 1913, Wilson Papers.

[45] Mrs. Crawford H. Toy, "Second Visit to the White House," diary entry dated January 3, 1915, MS. in the Baker Collection.

[46] E. M. House to W. W., May 4, 1913, Wilson Papers.

[47] House Diary, May 6, 1913, relating a conversation with McAdoo.

[48] W. W. to J. A. O'Gorman, May 5, 1913, Wilson Papers.

day on which he promised O'Gorman to solve the matter of the collectorship "as friends should," and a day before he promised McAdoo
to appoint a Collector agreeable to him—the President called his old
friend, James Kerney, publisher of the *Trenton Evening Times,* to the
White House. "He told me," Kerney relates, "that it was not his desire
that either Tammany or McAdoo should have any political control
over the custom-house." He had therefore decided, Wilson went on,
to appoint John Purroy Mitchel, president of the Board of Aldermen
of New York City and a prospective candidate for mayor on a bipartisan fusion anti-Tammany ticket. Wilson then drafted a letter to
Mitchel, telling him of his appointment, and sent Kerney to New
York with written instructions and full authority to speak.[49]

Assured of Wilson's support in the impending mayoralty campaign,
Mitchel accepted the appointment, and the President sent his nomination to the Senate shortly before six o'clock on May 7, 1913. O'Gorman
and McAdoo had meanwhile learned of the appointment, probably
through Tumulty, earlier the same day. McAdoo quietly acquiesced,
although the President's action was a crushing blow to his political ambitions. O'Gorman, on the other hand, was seemingly delighted; he
hastened to suggest Mitchel's name before the appointment was announced and publicly claimed credit for it.[50] The anti-Tammany press
was of course elated.[51]

During the six months following Mitchel's appointment the Washington administration waited to see what new alignments political
events in New York would form before implementing any general
patronage plan. Boss Murphy and his lieutenants in the state legislature
made the opening move, by impeaching the anti-Tammany governor,
William Sulzer, and removing him from office on October 17, 1913,
for dishonestly reporting campaign contributions and receiving large
sums of money from Wall Street promoters for gambling in the stock
market. A pompous and corrupt demagogue, Sulzer was undoubtedly
guilty as charged. But Tammany spokesmen left no doubt that he
had been punished, not for corruption, but for daring to affront their
organization. In the meantime, Mitchel had resigned as Collector to
run for Mayor of New York. Supported by the good government elements and Wilson's friends, Mitchel and his Fusion ticket swept to

[49] W. W. to J. P. Mitchel, May 5, 1913, *ibid.*; James Kerney, *The Political Education
of Woodrow Wilson,* pp. 320-321.
[50] *New York Times,* May 8 and 9, 1913.
[51] e.g., New York *World,* May 9, 1913.

victory in the New York City elections on November 4, 1913, on the crest of a wave of popular revulsion against the Sulzer impeachment.

Now the time seemed ripe for the thoroughgoing reorganization of the party in New York that Wilson, House, and most Democratic leaders desired. The President's first move was to give leadership and control of some important patronage to House and McAdoo and to support them in a broad campaign to purge the Tammany element.

As the first step, Wilson appointed Dudley Field Malone, an intimate friend of House, McAdoo, Mitchel, and the reform leaders, as Collector of the Port of New York to succeed Mitchel. It was a clever way of circumventing O'Gorman, for Malone was the senator's son-in-law, and O'Gorman could not object to the appointment. Next, during December 1913 and January 1914, House, Malone, McAdoo, and McAdoo's former law partner, Stuart G. Gibboney, made plans to form a new Democratic organization to be called, at Wilson's suggestion, "The New Democracy," based upon upstate progressives, the Mitchel administration in New York City, and as many Brooklyn regulars as would cooperate.[52]

It was the beginning of what might have developed into a consistent administration policy had the President been willing to forfeit an immediate advantage for the long-term goal of a rejuvenated and reformed New York Democracy. The trouble was that such a plan as House and Malone proposed was bound to disrupt the party and alienate O'Gorman and the large bloc of Democratic congressmen from New York and Brooklyn, and yet it might still fail to build a new organization with a broad mass support.

Fearful that a continued anti-Tammany policy would lead to overwhelming Democratic defeat in the state and congressional elections in the autumn of 1914, Tumulty, McCombs, and Martin H. Glynn, an independent who had succeeded Sulzer as Governor of New York, countered with a new program for reorganization in February 1914. As Glynn and McCombs described it to the President on February 9, the plan envisaged a thorough purging of the Tammany group and the Wilson administration's recognition of Glynn's and McCombs' leadership in New York State.[53] They set to work with the President's bless-

[52] D. F. Malone to W. W., January 26, 1914, Wilson Papers; House Diary, December 3, 1913, January 16, 1914; Louis M. Antisdale to Montgomery Hare, December 20, 1913, copy in the House Papers; M. Hare to E. M. House, February 14, 16, and 24, 1914, *ibid.*

[53] *New York Times*, February 10, 1914; New York *World*, February 10, 1914.

ing and effected their "reorganization" on March 2, 1914, when the Democratic state committee met in New York City and elected William Church Osborn, an anti-Tammany independent, as the new state chairman.[54]

Actually, the so-called "reorganization" was a sham. Acting through McCombs, Wilson had in effect agreed to call off his war against Tammany in return for promises of good behavior and support of national Democratic policies from Murphy and his allies. Malone and the anti-Tammanyites were heartsick, although they did not yet realize the extent to which the President had abandoned them. "There is no newspaper office, no intelligent political reporter, and there are very few people in the State of New York who seem to have the slightest confidence in the reorganization scheme which Glynn adopted, by the public acquiescence and approval of Murphy, and which merely means a change from one set of officers to another set of officers for the State Committee, all the while the majority of the State Committee remaining in Murphy's control . . . ," Malone wrote in distress to Colonel House. "Murphy's hand is clearly seen in the entire proceedings. He publicly congratulated Osborn. He sat in at the proceedings which effected the change, and McCombs was seen . . . sitting in conference in Governor Glynn's suite with [the Tammany leaders] Bob Wagner, Jim Frawley and Al Smith. . . . It is needless to say that I am deeply disappointed, and that I feel that all our labors for months past in New York State and City are not meeting with the support which is their due."[55]

The New York Democracy was again disrupted during the spring and summer of 1914 as the anti-Tammanyites and the regulars fought for the gubernatorial and senatorial nominations in the Democratic primary election in September. Glynn was the organization's candidate for governor; James W. Gerard, Ambassador to Germany, was its candidate for United States senator. Having earlier publicly repudiated the Glynn-McCombs leadership as a front for Tammany, the Malone-McAdoo faction entered the primary contest by running John A. Hennessy, a flamboyant anti-Tammany leader from New York City, for governor and Franklin D. Roosevelt, Assistant Secretary of the Navy, for the senatorship.

Each faction turned to Washington for patronage and moral support, and Wilson found himself caught in one of the most embarrassing

[54] New York *World*, March 3, 1914.
[55] D. F. Malone to E. M. House, March 7, 1914, House Papers.

personal dilemmas of his political career. His practical instincts told him he must support Glynn and McCombs in the hope that they would give acceptable leadership to a united party. Thus he allowed Tumulty to award some choice appointments to the Tammany machine and its Brooklyn ally, the McCooey organization. The President, moreover, advised administration spokesmen to say as little as possible about the New York situation and to avoid attacking Tammany directly.[56] But how could he support the regulars without seeming to condone the Tammany element and to repudiate his best friends and most loyal supporters in the state?

He managed to avoid making a firm commitment to either faction during the first months of the primary campaign. But the pressures multiplied. On July 21, 1914, for example, Malone, Polk, and Mitchel went directly to the White House to beg the President to come out squarely behind the reform group.[57] In reiteration, Malone ten days later argued that only Hennessy, Roosevelt, or McAdoo could carry the state in the general election and implored Wilson to strengthen the insurgents by appointing only anti-Tammany men to the important federal offices in New York.[58]

It was obviously what the President personally wanted to do. "You may be sure that I will seek to act along the lines you indicate," he assured Malone. "It has been in my mind all along."[59] And yet when the New York congressmen, led by Representative John J. Fitzgerald of Brooklyn and affiliated for the most part with Tammany, went en masse to the White House on July 29, 1914, to protest against Malone's alleged control of the patronage in the city, Wilson replied reassuringly. Tammany congressmen who supported his policies, he said, had nothing to fear from him.[60]

Finally, when Malone informed the President that he was about to begin a speaking tour on behalf of Hennessy and Roosevelt, Wilson could no longer avoid taking a stand. He silenced his friend as gently as he knew how: "I feel extremely reluctant to have the administration as such constructively associated with the primary campaign because that would be so glaringly inconsistent with position taken in other states. Hope you will think it best not to take part as campaigner.

[56] W. W. to W. J. Bryan, April 2, 1914, Wilson Papers; W. W. to F. D. Roosevelt, April 1, 1914, *ibid.*
[57] *New York Times*, July 22, 1914.
[58] D. F. Malone to W. W., August 1, 1914, Wilson Papers.
[59] W. W. to D. F. Malone, August 4, 1914, *ibid.*
[60] *New York Times*, July 23 and 30, 1914; New York *World*, July 28 and 30, 1914.

You will inevitably be considered my spokesman because of our close personal relationship which I so much prize."[61]

Hennessy and Roosevelt campaigned hard, mainly in the upstate counties; claimed they were the true Wilson candidates; attacked Glynn and Gerard as pawns of Tammany;[62] and were supplied with money by Stuart Gibboney, McAdoo's spokesman.[63] But without the Washington administration's open support they waged a hopeless fight. The Democratic voters gave Glynn and Gerard the crucial nominations by large majorities on September 28, 1914, although the reform faction won about one third of the members of the state Democratic committee and carried thirty-three out of the sixty-two counties of the state.

Nothing now remained for the President and his friends to do but to give wholehearted support to Glynn, Gerard, and the Democratic congressional slate. Hennessy bolted to the Republican gubernatorial candidate, but all the other New York Democratic insurgents fell quickly into line. Colonel House, for example, brought Glynn and Mitchel together at his apartment on October 13, 1914, and won a promise of hearty support for the state ticket from Mitchel in return for a promise from Glynn to consult with the Mayor upon all measures and appointments in New York City.[64] McAdoo repudiated Hennessy and came out strongly behind the regulars,[65] although privately he had little enthusiasm for the ticket.[66] Finally, Wilson sent Bryan, Lane,

[61] D. F. Malone to W. W., September 3 and 8, 1914; and W. W. to D. F. Malone, September 8, 1914, all in Wilson Papers.

[62] e.g., see the statement issued by the Hennessy-Roosevelt headquarters and printed in the New York *World*, September 20, 1914; and the account in Frank Freidel, *Franklin D. Roosevelt: The Apprenticeship*, pp. 184-188.

[63] S. Gibboney to F. R. Coudert, December 13, 1915, the Papers of Frank L. Polk, Yale University Library (hereinafter cited as the Polk Papers), tells how Gibboney financed the Hennessy-Roosevelt campaign.

[64] House Diary, October 13, 1914; E. M. House to W. W., October 14, 1914, Wilson Papers.

[65] e.g., W. G. McAdoo to M. H. Glynn, October 23, 1914; W. G. McAdoo to L. M. Antisdale, October 25, 1914; W. G. McAdoo to W. C. Osborn, October 27, 1914, all copies in the House Papers.

[66] "To those of us in New York," McAdoo wrote frankly to the President on October 29, 1914 (Wilson Papers), "who know only too well the meaning and the effect of the activities of the Murphyized New York 'machine' and its affiliated selfish interests, and who, before the [Baltimore] Convention and since have been your strongest friends and supporters in the face of every kind of difficulty, it has been discouraging that a consistent policy in opposition to the 'machine' in New York has not been pursued from the beginning of your administration. My own efforts, my dear Governor, have been constantly back-capped and thwarted. I feel that I ought to tell you this because I have felt keenly the mistakes that were being made in New

and a number of other leaders to speak for the administration in New York and addressed strong personal appeals to the voters on Glynn's and Gerard's behalf.

These measures were not enough, however, to overcome the obstacles confronting the Democratic nominees. Defection of the independent voters, popular resentment against alleged Tammany control of the New York Democracy, and a virulent anti-Catholicism directed at Glynn all combined to generate a Republican landslide in the general election on November 3, 1914. Charles S. Whitman won the governorship by a plurality of more than 136,000 votes; James W. Wadsworth defeated Gerard for the senatorship by nearly 55,000 votes; and the Republicans won the legislature and all state offices.

In the future, the administration tried no more forays against Tammany but rather worked to effect a healing of the wounds inflicted during the bitter intra-party battles of 1913 and 1914. Eventually, with the retirement of Murphy in 1917 and the rise of a new leadership in Tammany headed by Alfred E. Smith, the Wilson administration, reformers, and organization men could unite in a solid phalanx and restore the Democracy to power in the Empire State in 1918. This was possible, however, only because the President and his friends had meanwhile come to terms with the realities of political life and had accepted the Tammany organization as the cornerstone of Democratic power in New York.

There was nothing unique about the vexations and embarrassments that plagued Wilson in dispensing patronage. Like virtually every other President, he discovered that the party leader's power was circumscribed by the Senate's veto over appointments and by the necessity of winning the support of congressmen and senators for domestic and foreign policies. By accepting the realities of political life and by working through the existing party hierarchy, however, he yielded the lesser goal of party reform and won the larger goal of mastery over the Democratic forces in Congress and in the nation. "What you told me about the old standpatters is true," the President admitted to Burleson in

---

York. As a result, the nominees of the party on the state ticket whom we are obliged to support, and whom I am supporting with all my might and main, have decided elements of weakness, which all of us in New York have known from the beginning might prove fatal to Democratic success. If the administration's policy since March 1913 had been one of consistent opposition to the 'machine,' unmistakably manifested through its appointments to office, and in other ways, I am sure that the nominees of the party today would be of such a character that Democratic success in the state would not be the least in doubt."

the summer of 1914. "They at least will stand by the party and the administration. I can rely on them better than I can on some of my own crowd."[67]

The problem of pleasing diverse elements was difficult enough, but even more vexing was the task of reconciling the party workers' natural lust for office with Wilson's oft-expressed allegiance to the principles of civil service reform.

The clamor for jobs during the first months of the New Freedom was incredible; it built such pressures against the Democratic congressmen and senators that the very existence of a trained federal bureaucracy was endangered. "Our Texas Democracy," one faithful party worker wrote, "is in thorough accord with the reform ideas of Mr. Wilson but I have not yet come across any sort of a Texas Democrat who favors letting the Republicans continue to hold the offices."[68] And during the week following the inauguration it seemed that every deserving Democrat in the country had descended upon Washington, as mobs of office seekers crowded the anterooms of the Capitol and the executive departments. "It reminds me of the scriptural quotation: 'The wild asses of the desert are athirst and hungry; they have broken into the green corn,'" exclaimed the aged spoilsman from South Carolina, Senator "Pitchfork" Ben Tillman. "God only knows what the result will be."[69]

Much, of course, would depend upon Wilson's intentions and skill as a herdsman. By and large, he believed in civil service principles, in basing appointment and promotion in the federal service on merit rather than on partisan activity. Moreover, he recognized the danger of affronting the civil service sentiment among the independent voters outside the South. At the same time, he was so much a partisan as to be at times a spoilsman himself; and certainly he would not endanger the success of his legislative program by austere devotion to the civil service principle.

The idealist and the practical politician in Wilson pulled both ways from the beginning. On the one hand, he fought hard and successfully to protect certain notable professionals from the spoilsmen. There were, for example, the early cases of Miss Julia Lathrop, head of the Children's Bureau in the Department of Labor, and of Charles P. Neill,

[67] R. S. Baker, interview with A. S. Burleson, March 17-19, 1927, Baker Collection.
[68] F. H. Bushick to E. M. House, February 5, 1913, House Papers.
[69] *New York Times*, March 11, 1913.

Commissioner of Labor Statistics in the same department, who were bitterly attacked by the senators from the southeastern textile states for their opposition to child labor. The President stood by Miss Lathrop, not only because he admired her but also because he knew that it would be politically fatal if he allowed "anybody to push her out";[70] and he reappointed Neill in spite of the threat of Senator Lee S. Overman of North Carolina to fight the matter out on the floor of the Senate.[71]

Yet Wilson also knew how to act like a professional politician. He dismissed two of the three members of the United States Civil Service Commission, allegedly for thinking that Republicans were better qualified for office than Democrats.[72] He fired E. Dana Durand, Director of the Census, who had earned a distinguished record in the federal service since 1900, and appointed in his stead William J. Harris, chairman of the Democratic state committee of Georgia, who had rendered the President "exceptional service" during the preconvention campaign.[73] He amended executive orders issued by Roosevelt and Taft putting fourth-class postmasters under civil service regulations, by requiring all incumbents to take examinations—a subtle way of opening some 37,000 jobs to Democrats.[74] Finally, he did not object when the Democrats in Congress attached riders to the Underwood tariff and the urgent deficiency bills of 1913 that permitted the appointment of some 3,607 deputy collectors of internal revenue and deputy marshals without regard to the provisions of the Civil Service Act.

Public opinion outside the South, however, reacted violently, especially against Wilson's approval of the riders, which Senator Robert M. La Follette of Wisconsin called "the most serious attack made upon the merit system since its establishment in 1883."[75] "There is no dan-

[70] W. W. to F. K. Lane, March 27, 1913, Wilson Papers.

[71] L. S. Overman to D. A. Tompkins, March 12, 1913, the Papers of Daniel A. Tompkins, University of North Carolina Library; hereinafter cited as the Tompkins Papers.

[72] *New York Times*, May 23, 1913.

[73] W. W. to W. C. Redfield, March 13, 1913, Wilson Papers. For comment, see the New York *Nation*, xcvi (April 24, 1913), 403; and R. M. La Follette, "Bad Straw—Bad Bricks," *La Follette's Weekly*, v (May 3, 1913), 1, 3.

[74] New York *World*, May 8, 1913.

[75] R. M. La Follette, "A Raid on the Merit System," *La Follette's Weekly*, v (October 25, 1913), 1, 3. See also the New York *Nation*, xcvii (October 30, 1913), 399; Charles W. Eliot to W. W., September 10 and October 20, 1913, Wilson Papers; Robert W. Belcher, secretary of the National Civil Service Reform League, to W. W., September 18, 1913, *ibid.*; Robert D. Jenks, chairman of the council, and R. W. Belcher,

ger," the President declared, in a virtual public apology for signing the urgent deficiency bill, "that the spoils principle will creep in with my approval or connivance"; and he went on to reaffirm his "warm advocacy and support both of the principle and of the bona-fide practice of civil-service reform."[76] "The single and most threatening danger to our party just at this moment," he admitted privately, "is that it will yield to the 'spoils' impulse and make a partisan use of the power of appointments to office and of promotion and demotion in the departments."[77]

Although Wilson could not prevent congressional leaders from exempting employees of the Federal Reserve Board from civil service requirements when Congress approved the Federal Reserve bill in December 1913, he was able to force a showdown on the issue soon afterward. In January 1914 the House post office committee reported an appropriation bill for the Post Office Department with a rider that deprived some 2,400 assistant postmasters of civil service standing. Acting through Burleson, the President demanded that the House rules committee refuse clearance for the rider and won speedy compliance. The chairman of the post office committee, Representative John A. Moon of Tennessee, averred that "no domination by the Postmaster General nor threat of veto from the President" would swerve him and his Democratic colleagues from a general assault upon the merit system, but Wilson held firm and won an easy and significant victory.[78]

From this time forward, with a few minor exceptions, Wilson thwarted further raids with even greater ease, as partisan pressures normally decreased after the first great drive for spoils. Even so, one critic could write with some justification in early 1916, "Mr. Wilson is the only President, Democratic or Republican, since the original civil service law was passed, who has not only done nothing to raise the standards of administration but who has actually lowered them."[79]

---

secretary, National Civil Service Reform League, to W. W., October 2, 1913, *ibid.*; "The Merit System Attacked," *The Independent*, lxxvi (October 16, 1913), 106-107.

[76] New York *Nation*, xcvii (October 30, 1913), 399.

[77] W. W. to J. P. Tumulty, January 4, 1914, Wilson Papers.

[78] *The Independent*, lxxvii (January 26, 1914), 116-118.

[79] Herbert Croly, in the *New Republic*, vi (February 5, 1916), 18.

CHAPTER VI

The Battle for Tariff Reform

THE crucial test of Wilson's leadership came during the early months of the New Freedom, when the new President led the Democrats in Congress in the first thoroughgoing downward revision of the tariff laws since 1846. So largely has the tariff been eliminated from present-day partisan debates that it would be easy for the reader to fail to understand the significance of the issue in Wilson's day.

No public question was so perpetually discussed or so potentially dangerous after the Civil War as that of a tariff policy for the United States. By 1900 the Republicans had erected an elaborate structure of high protection for American manufacturers, farmers, and producers of raw materials. Yet even at the high tide of the protectionist policy there were powerful forces at work to generate what would soon become an irresistible movement for lower tariff rates.

To begin with, between 1897 and 1907 American industry reached such a high level of efficiency that manufacturers in many important fields could not only hold their own against foreign competitors in the domestic market but could also compete successfully abroad. This meant, in turn, a progressive slackening of the pressure for a high protective policy. Moreover, popular opinion, which was fairly evenly divided on the tariff issue in 1896, turned increasingly in favor of drastic downward revision during the following decade. This change came about, first, because the adoption of the Dingley Act in 1897, the highest tariff measure in American history to that time, coincided with the onset of a frenzied movement toward consolidation in industry that lasted until about 1902 and resulted in the concentration of productive facilities in many fields in the hands of a few giant corporations. Although there was little if any causal relationship, Democrats argued that the protective tariff was the "mother of the trusts"; and probably a majority of the voters agreed with them by 1908. In the second place, the cost of living in the United States increased nearly one fourth between 1897 and 1907, and Democrats asserted, and most Americans agreed, that high tariffs were largely responsible, even though tariff rates often had little or no effect on domestic prices.

As the protective tariff system was thus connected with the so-called trusts and the high cost of living, sentiment for tariff reform increased in a spectacular way during the early 1900's, especially in the Middle West, where it became a main issue among progressive Republicans after 1902. President Theodore Roosevelt managed to evade the issue, but his successor, William Howard Taft, yielded to the popular demand and called Congress into special session in March 1909 to provide relief. The result was the Payne-Aldrich Act of 1909, which left the protective structure undamaged but nearly wrecked the Republican party because it set off the rebellion of the midwestern insurgents against the Old Guard of the G.O.P. and lent seeming proof to the Democratic charge that the Republicans were the representatives of entrenched special interests.

The American people had their revenge a year later, on November 8, 1910, when they elected Democratic governors in many normally Republican states, gave the Democrats control of the House of Representatives for the first time since 1892, and strengthened the Democratic minority in the Senate. During the next two years the Democratic leaders made the promise of honest tariff revision a prime argument for a Democratic clean sweep in 1912. To prove the party's good faith, the Democratic majority in the House approved three bills for tariff reduction in 1911 and 1912; the Democratic national convention at Baltimore in the latter year promised drastic general reductions; and Wilson made tariff reform secondary only to the issue of the regulation of big business during the ensuing presidential campaign. Never, therefore, had a political party and its leaders been more thoroughly committed to a course of action than were the Democrats after the election of 1912; never had public opinion seemed more emphatic in demanding fulfillment of campaign pledges.

Yet Wilson could read many signs of danger ahead as he began to plan for his first conferences with party leaders after the election. To be sure, all Democrats publicly favored honest revision. But the Democratic congressmen-elect from Massachusetts announced that they would vote against removing the duties on shoes; Senator Charles S. Thomas and Senator-elect John F. Shafroth of Colorado declared that they would have to oppose any sizable reduction in the sugar rates; Senators Furnifold M. Simmons and Lee S. Overman of North Carolina warned that they would not consent to see the cotton textile industry of their state "unduly threatened by low tariff duties."[1] And thus it went all

[1] *New York Times*, November 30, 1912.

over the country, until it was clear that a critical challenge to Democratic unity and Wilson's leadership impended.

Moving confidently, as if there were no obstacles to tariff reform, the President-elect called Representative Oscar W. Underwood of Alabama, chairman of the House ways and means committee, which would have charge of tariff legislation, to Trenton on December 31, 1912. Underwood was reassuring; his committee, he said, was already at work on a general tariff bill, would hold new hearings in January, and should be able to complete its work by March 15, 1913.[2]

The Alabaman was as good as his word. By February 19, 1913, he and his Democratic colleagues had completed hearings and a tentative draft of the new tariff bill; the House Democratic caucus met on March 5, 1913, to confirm the new appointments to the ways and means committee for the impending Sixty-third Congress; and the reorganized committee at once set to work on the final draft. They finished on March 17 and sent a copy of the revised bill to the White House. On the same day, the President called Congress into special session for April 7, 1913, and on March 24, in a four-hour conference at the White House, he and Underwood reviewed all the important provisions of the measure known by this time as the Underwood bill.

Having thus waited to see what the ways and means committee would do, Wilson now began to assert leadership in a decisive way. The bill that he studied after March 24 revealed a genuine determination to accomplish drastic reductions in rates on manufactured products. But the committee, in response to pressure from farm, livestock, and sugar spokesmen in the South and West, had reversed its earlier action and voted to impose duties on all farm products, to retain protection for leather boots and shoes and sugar, and to impose a 15 per cent duty on raw wool.

During the tariff debates in Congress two years before, Underwood had insisted upon moderate protection for sugar and wool, and Wilson had supported him then in a controversy with Bryan. In 1913, as in 1911, disagreement over these products of Democratic southern and western states threatened to disrupt the party and prevent any tariff legislation. Such a measure as the ways and means committee proposed would have mollified the western Democratic senators and assured the approval of the upper house. But it would have belied the party's promise of thoroughgoing reform and, more important, might have opened the door to the logrolling—that is, the trading of votes between rep-

[2] *ibid.*, January 1 and 2, 1913.

resentatives of agrarian and industrial interests—that had wrecked all efforts at tariff reform since the Civil War.

This was the great danger, and Wilson resolved to act boldly. Calling Underwood to the White House on April 1, 1913, he announced that the committee's bill must be rewritten to provide for free food, sugar, leather, and wool. The most he would yield, the President added, was a compromise: the sugar duty to be reduced from 1.9 cents to one cent a pound for three years and then be abolished entirely, and the Louisiana representatives, the chief sugar spokesmen, to agree to support the entire tariff bill. If the House Democrats ignored his advice and adopted the Underwood bill as it then stood, Wilson warned that he would veto the measure, and there would be no tariff legislation at all.[3]

The President's ultimatum brought speedy results. The ways and means committee revised the tariff bill in submission to Wilson's demands after a brief skirmish on April 5; and when the Louisiana sugar interests refused to accept the President's compromise, the committee voted to put sugar on the free list immediately, although it soon reverted to the compromise plan.[4]

The elaborate partisan and congressional machinery began to operate when Congress met in special session two days later, on April 7, 1913. Underwood introduced his measure for technical referral to the full ways and means committee. The following day Wilson appeared in person before a joint session to chart the course in tariff revision. "We must abolish everything that bears even the semblance of privilege or of any kind of artificial advantage," he said, "and put our business men and producers under the stimulation of a constant necessity to be efficient, economical, and enterprising, masters of competitive supremacy, better workers and merchants than any in the world. . . . The object of the tariff duties henceforth laid must be effective competition, the whetting of American wits by contest with the wits of the rest of the world."[5]

Then followed the only critical stage in the House discussions, the Democratic caucus debate on every schedule of the Underwood bill from April 9 through April 19, 1913. There was a threatened revolt on April 11, when seven Ohio representatives urged members to join

[3] *ibid.*, April 2, 1913; New York *World*, April 2 and 3, 1913; the Diary of Josephus Daniels, April 4, 1913, Library of Congress; hereinafter cited as the Daniels Diary.
[4] *New York Times*, April 6, 1913.
[5] R. S. Baker and W. E. Dodd (eds.), *The New Democracy*, I, 33-34.

them in opposing free wool. It fizzled out five days later, however, when the caucus voted 190 to forty-two against a resolution to restore the 15 per cent duty. On April 12 the Louisiana representatives fought to break the sugar schedule, but Underwood held his ranks. And when the caucus had completed its work, only thirteen Democrats signified that they would not be bound by a caucus rule commanding all members to support the Underwood bill in its entirety; they were excused because they had given pledges to their constituents.[6]

From this time forward, Underwood ran the legislative steamroller through the House with unfeigned pleasure. The ways and means committee reported the Underwood bill to the House on April 22, 1913, by a strict party vote, and the Alabaman opened debate the following day with a two-hour speech that summarized the Democratic arguments. "The Democratic Party," he said, "stands for a tariff for revenue only, with the emphasis upon the word 'only.' We do not propose to tax one man for the benefit of another, except for the necessary revenue that we must raise to administer this Government economically. Then how do we arrive at a basis in writing a revenue tariff bill? We adopt the competitive theory. We say that no revenue can be produced at the customhouse unless there is some competition between the products of foreign countries and domestic products . . . , and that if you want to raise revenue at the customhouse you must admit some importations."[7]

Representative Augustus P. Gardner of Massachusetts replied for the Republicans, and then the debate proceeded under a strict rule until May 8, 1913, when the House approved the Underwood bill on schedule by a vote of 281 to 139. Only five Democrats, four of them from Louisiana, voted against the measure; their defection was more than offset by the two Republicans, four Progressives, and one independent who voted with the majority.

Practically all observers agreed that the Underwood bill was the most honest effort at downward revision since the Civil War. In contrast to the Payne-Aldrich Act, for example, Underwood's bill established only open ad valorem rates and contained no hidden jokers to protect special interests and confuse importers. "It is an intelligent measure," declared the New York *World* on April 8, 1913, in a typical comment. "It is a progressive measure. It is not the product of intrigue

---

[6] *New York Times*, April 12, 13, 17, 20, and 22, 1913; New York *World*, April 12, 1913; *Boston Globe*, April 13, 1913.

[7] *Congressional Record*, 63d Cong., 1st sess., p. 330.

and log-rolling. It was bought with no corrupt contributions to a campaign fund. It was framed by the representatives of the people and not by the representatives of privileged interests."[8] As one London editor observed, it was also "the heaviest blow that has been aimed at the Protective system since the British legislation of Sir Robert Peel between 1842 and 1846."[9]

On the other hand, the objective of the Underwood bill was not free trade but rather the destruction of the special privileges and the undue advantage that Republican protectionist policy had conferred upon American producers; relief for the mass of consumers in such basic items as food and clothing; and the placing of American producers in a genuinely competitive position with regard to European manufacturers. The average ad valorem rate of the Payne-Aldrich Act was between 37 and 40 per cent; the average of the Underwood bill, about 29 per cent. But even this comparison does not indicate the full measure of the reduction that the Underwood bill accomplished, because it does not take account of that measure's vast expansion of the free list.

In addition, in order to offset an anticipated decrease in customs receipts when it went into effect, the Underwood bill provided for an income tax to yield about $100,000,000 in revenue, under terms drawn up by Representative Cordell Hull of Tennessee. It was the first income tax under the Sixteenth Amendment, which had been ratified only two months earlier. In spite of Hull's assertion that it represented an important attempt to shift some of the tax burden from the lower and middle classes to the rich,[10] the income tax provision of the Underwood bill was hardly a major threat to privileged wealth in the United States. It imposed a so-called normal tax of 1 per cent on personal and corporate incomes over $4,000 and an additional surtax of 1 per cent on incomes between $20,000 and $50,000, 2 per cent on incomes between $50,000 and $100,000, and 3 per cent on incomes over $100,000.

Easy victory in this first round only pointed up the dangers that now confronted the President. Twice before, during the debates over tariff reform measures in 1893 and 1894 and in 1909, the Senate had

---

[8] See also *Harper's Weekly*, LVII (April 19, 1913), 4; London *Nation*, XIII (April 12, 1913), 43-44; London *Statist*, LXXVI (April 19, 1913), 259-262; *World's Work*, XXVI (June 1913), 137-138; George Harvey, "The House Has Done Its Part," *Harper's Weekly*, LVII (May 17, 1913), 4.

[9] London *Economist*, LXXVI (April 12, 1913), 867.

[10] See Hull's speech explaining the income tax provision, *Congressional Record*, 63d Cong., 1st sess., pp. 503-515.

wrecked not only promising efforts at tariff reform but the administrations in power. The situation in the Senate seemed equally foreboding in March and April of 1913. The Democrats had a majority of six in the upper house, but a change of four votes would turn that majority into a minority; and there were many signs that Wilson's insistence upon sweeping reductions and free sugar and free wool had ruined the chances of retaining solid Democratic support in the Senate for the Underwood bill.

To begin with, there was the danger that the chairman of the Senate finance committee, Furnifold M. Simmons of North Carolina, would become another Aldrich and organize the protectionist senators to defeat tariff reform. Simmons had voted for the Aldrich amendments to the Payne bill in 1909, in return for increased protection for North Carolina lumber and textiles; and Wilson and the progressive Democrats had reluctantly permitted him to become chairman of the finance committee only after he had promised to lead the fight for drastic tariff reductions aggressively in the Senate.[11] Even so, the pressure from North Carolina for continued high protection for cotton textiles was enormous,[12] and there was a rumor early in March 1913 that Simmons and his Tar Heel colleague, Lee S. Overman, were at work to rally southern senators in defense of the cotton textile, tobacco, and lumber interests.[13]

A greater danger to Democratic unity—for Simmons was faithful to his promise to follow the President's leadership—was the threat that

[11] Josephus Daniels, *The Wilson Era, Years of Peace—1910-1917*, pp. 221-222.

[12] The following letter from Daniel A. Tompkins, publisher of the Charlotte *Daily Observer*, the leading editorial spokesman of the textile interests of the Carolinas, to his lobbyist in Washington is revealing. "I seriously apprehend such radical cuts as are proposed in wool, sugar, and cotton. . . . We are already importing a tremendous lot of cotton goods, even with the present high tariffs. The radical reduction proposed will slump the markets of this country from England and Germany. . . . We all like and admire Mr. Wilson very much, but if he is going to be a radical free trade president, there is going to be a lot of trouble in the camp. During the campaign in which he was elected, it was generally understood that he promised to be conservative about the tariff. There are plenty of tariffs that ought to be cut off entirely, like steel rails, but the tariff on cotton goods ought not to be radically changed. . . . In talking to Senators and Representatives, I think it would be well to put forward these views." D. A. Tompkins to W. H. Harris, April 8, 1913, Tompkins Papers.

[13] Charlotte *Daily Observer*, March 11, 1913. Simmons and Overman denied this report in a joint letter to the editor, dated March 12, 1913, and printed in *ibid.*, March 13, 1913. For an excellent survey of southern protectionist sentiment, see John W. Davidson, "The Response of the South to Woodrow Wilson's New Freedom, 1912-1914," unpublished Ph.D. dissertation in the Yale University Library, pp. 49-53, 105-135.

senators from the so-called sugar and wool states would bolt. Canvassing the Democrats on April 6, 1913, Simmons found five senators—the two senators from Louisiana, Henry F. Ashurst of Arizona, Francis G. Newlands of Nevada, and Thomas J. Walsh of Montana—and perhaps a sixth, John F. Shafroth of Colorado, who said they would vote against a tariff bill that included free wool and free sugar.[14] The fol-

The Panhandlers

Macauley in the New York *World*

lowing day, in a conference at the White House, Simmons and the Democratic members of the finance committee warned the President that his entire tariff program might be wrecked unless he agreed to separate the wool and sugar schedules from the Underwood bill.[15] Such action, however, would mean the inevitable defeat of free wool and free sugar in the Senate; moreover, it might open the door to logrolling that could kill the Underwood bill entirely.

Wilson moved quickly to avert such a catastrophe. Going to the President's Room in the Capitol on April 9, he conferred with Democratic senators for an hour and a half. "I hope the Senators will let me come and consult them frequently," he declared afterward. "The net result of this meeting is that we don't see any sort of difficulty about

[14] *New York Times,* April 7, 1913.   [15] *ibid.,* April 8, 1913.

standing firmly on our party programme."[16] Moreover, by conference and correspondence the President heartened senators who were under heaviest pressure from their constituents to protect local interests. "May I not express my warm admiration of the course you have taken?" he wrote, for example, to Senator Ashurst. "I congratulate the party and the country upon having a man to serve them who sees so clearly and does his duty so fearlessly," he wrote to Senator Nathan P. Bryan of Florida.[17]

By May 1, 1913, it seemed that the President's personal campaign was succeeding. On that day he conferred for two hours and a half with six western Democratic senators,[18] heard their arguments against free wool and free sugar, and pleaded eloquently for a full redemption of Democratic pledges. The newspapers reported that the Westerners had made it known that they would vote for the Underwood bill in its entirety.[19] When the press, some two weeks later, reported that Wilson was searching for a compromise on sugar and wool, he promptly scotched the rumor. "When you get a chance," he told reporters on May 15, "just say that I am not the kind that considers compromises when I once take my position. Just note that down so that there will be nothing more of that sort transmitted to the press."[20] A day later, on May 16, the President won his first victory in the Senate, when the Democrats held firm and rejected a resolution offered by Boies Penrose of Pennsylvania to instruct the finance committee to hold hearings on the Underwood bill.[21]

Yet, as Wilson knew, the situation in the Senate was still full of danger. To begin with, the President had alienated progressive Republicans by making the Underwood bill a strict party measure and by excluding them from any participation in the work of the finance committee.[22] Secondly, the two Democratic senators from Louisiana were pledged

[16] New York *World*, April 10, 1913.

[17] W. W. to H. F. Ashurst, April 24, 1913, and W. W. to N. P. Bryan, May 12, 1913, both in Wilson Papers; also W. W. to Morris Sheppard, May 20, 1913; W. W. to J. T. Robinson, May 20, 1913; and W. W. to Key Pittman, May 28, 1913, all in *ibid.*

[18] They were Newlands of Nevada, Shafroth of Colorado, Walsh of Montana, George E. Chamberlain and Harry Lane of Oregon, and William H. Thompson of Kansas.

[19] New York *World*, May 2, 1913.

[20] *New York Times*, May 16, 1913.

[21] *ibid.*, May 17, 1913. For comment on the significance of Penrose's resolution and its defeat, see the *New York Evening Post*, May 19, 1913, and "The Tariff in the Senate," New York *Nation*, xcvi (May 22, 1913), 514.

[22] See, e.g., Senator La Follette's protest, "Tariff Making in the Dark," *La Follette's Weekly*, v (May 24, 1913), 1, 3.

to vote against any measure that provided for free sugar. Hence the Democratic majority in the Senate might at best be one vote, and a further shift of two Democrats would suffice to defeat tariff reform altogether.

The danger became real indeed when Senator Walsh, who had voted with his party against the Penrose resolution, announced on May 19, 1913, that he would be compelled to vote against free sugar and free wool.[23] Actually, as his correspondence shows, Walsh had no intention of bolting in the showdown but was saving face with his constituents and bluffing in the hope that the President would concede moderate duties on sugar and wool.[24] But that important fact was not publicly known, and Democratic leaders in the Senate began to talk of compromise.[25]

The greatest danger, however, came from the horde of lobbyists who had descended upon Washington and were hard at work upon the doubtful Democratic senators from the South and West. The owners and managers of industries that produced the great bulk of American industrial products were unconcerned and took no part in the lobbying. But the spokesmen of the cane sugar planters, beet sugar growers and refiners, cotton textile manufacturers, citrus fruit growers, sheep ranchers, shoe manufacturers, and a hundred other special interests were profoundly alarmed by the Underwood bill's alleged threat to their prosperity and very existence.[26]

"The Senate is the target for the attacks of the accredited and adequately equipped agents of the interests that have decreed the humiliation of the party in control of the Upper House . . . ," one reporter wrote in a general review of the situation in Washington in the spring of 1913. "Every skilful trick known to the underground workers in the lobby has been brought into play; every influence that can be commanded by the combination of interests and trained by them upon the ninety-six Senators has been called into action. Coercion, denuncia-

[23] *New York Times*, May 20, 1913.
[24] See T. J. Walsh to B. K. Wheeler, April 23, 1913; T. J. Walsh to C. A. Drinkard, April 23, 1913; and T. J. Walsh to C. B. Nolan, May 20, 1913, all in the Walsh Papers.
[25] New York *World*, May 23, 1913; *New York Times*, May 24, 1913.
[26] For typical propaganda, see the letters and petitions from various spokesmen of the sugar growers and beet sugar refiners in the Wilson Papers, Series VI, Boxes 167, 168, 171, and 182; the letters and petitions from the wool growers, in *ibid.*, Series VI, Boxes 167 and 168; John J. Fitzgerald, Mayor of Boston, to J. P. Tumulty, March 28, 1913, Wilson Papers, protesting free boots and shoes; Edward F. Green, president of the National Association of Cotton Manufacturers, to D. A. Tompkins, April 30, 1913, Tompkins Papers.

tion, threats of future punishment and promises baited with cajolery of prospective political advancement have been covertly held out to secure enough Democratic votes to obstruct the reduction of the tariff on fostered industries."[27]

Wilson was angry and disturbed. Washington was so full of lobbyists, he told reporters at his semiweekly news conference on May 26, 1913, that "a brick couldn't be thrown without hitting one of them." Then, in a public statement he appealed to the country:

"I think that the public ought to know the extraordinary exertions being made by the lobby in Washington to gain recognition for certain alterations of the tariff bill. Washington has seldom seen so numerous, so industrious, or so insidious a lobby. The newspapers are being filled with paid advertisements calculated to mislead the judgment of public men not only, but also the public opinion of the country itself. There is every evidence that money without limit is being spent to sustain this lobby, and to create an appearance of a pressure of public opinion antagonistic to some of the chief items of the tariff bill.

"It is of serious interest to the country that the people at large should have no lobby and be voiceless in these matters, while great bodies of astute men seek to create an artificial opinion and to overcome the interests of the public for their private profit. It is thoroughly worth the while of the people of this country to take knowledge of this matter. Only public opinion can check and destroy it.

"The Government in all its branches ought to be relieved from this intolerable burden and this constant interruption to the calm progress of debate. I know that in this I am speaking for the members of the two houses, who would rejoice as much as I would, to be released from this unbearable situation."[28]

It was a bold indictment, but much of the public reaction was unfavorable. "Is it possible that the President has mistaken for lobbying the ordinary, usual, and perfectly legitimate measures taken by protected interests to present their case to Congress?" one editor asked in astonishment.[29] "I quite agree with you that his complaint . . . was a threat to arouse the popular indignation, without any substantial foundation. . . . It would seem as if the Administration and Members of Congress were engaged in an effort to create a public opinion which

[27] Louis Seibold, in the New York *World*, May 18, 1913. For additional information, see *ibid.*, April 10, 22, and 23, May 1, 5, 7, and 27, 1913.
[28] *New York Times*, May 27, 1913.
[29] *ibid.*, May 27, 1913.

should be inimical to all business interests," former President Taft wrote.[30] Democrats in Congress were caught unprepared and were a bit bewildered; the most they would say the day after Wilson issued

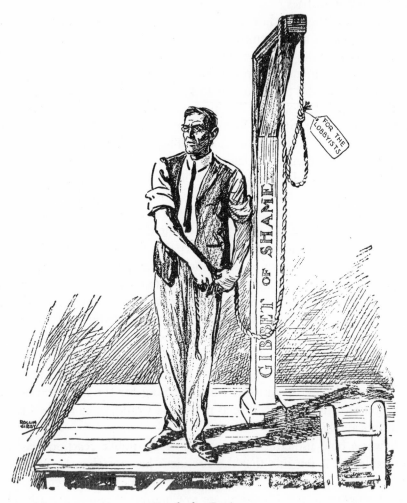

Ready for Business
Kirby in the New York *World*

his statement was that they knew of no lobbyists, at least in the offensive meaning of the word.

The Republican leaders, on the other hand, were elated by what they thought was the President's first blunder. Shortly after the Senate

[30] W. H. Taft to T. W. Loyless, June 5, 1913, Taft Papers.

convened on May 27, 1913, Albert B. Cummins of Iowa introduced a resolution providing that a select committee of five senators investigate the alleged lobby and receive testimony from senators and the President. "I think the country has a right to know what is now surrounding the Senate of the United States," Cummins said. "I think it has a right to know whether Senators are being influenced by improper representations."[31]

This was, actually, a move to embarrass the Democrats by forcing them either to block the investigation or to allow it to proceed and prove that Wilson's charges were groundless. The plot unfolded when the minority leader, Jacob H. Gallinger of New Hampshire, objected to immediate consideration of the resolution. Then Senator Joseph H. Bristow of Kansas explained the plan to Senator Elihu Root of New York; Root hurriedly relayed the message to Gallinger; and the minority leader withdrew his objection, saying that he agreed that the Senate owed the country an explanation and that he personally had nothing to conceal.[32]

The Democrats maneuvered in confusion until they learned the following day that the President was delighted at the prospect of a sweeping investigation. Thus when Cummins offered his resolution again on May 29, 1913, the Democratic majority approved, insisting only upon changing the wording of the provision requesting information from the President and upon giving control of the inquiry to the judiciary committee. Moreover, when Senator James A. Reed of Missouri suggested that all senators disclose their property holdings or financial interests that might be affected by tariff legislation, no one dared publicly to protest. What had begun in part as a political maneuver, therefore, had turned into a plan to investigate not only the lobby but the Senate itself.

Headed by Senator Overman, a subcommittee of the judiciary committee set to work on June 2, 1913. They began with the senators, in alphabetical order; and the country was treated to the spectacle of each senator coming dutifully before the committee and telling how many shares of cotton mill stock or how many acres of grazing or sugar land he owned and how many lobbyists he had talked with or heard from. Senator Nathan P. Bryan of Florida, for example, testified that he had some interests in an orange grove and gave the committee his corre-

---

[31] *Congressional Record*, 63d Cong., 1st sess., p. 1758.
[32] *ibid.*, pp. 1758-1759; *New York Times*, May 28, 1913.

spondence with the Florida Citrus Exchange. Senator William P. Jackson of Maryland revealed that he was part-owner of a lumber mill and owned besides 1,000 shares of the preferred stock of the United States Steel Corporation. Senator Henry F. Lippitt of Rhode Island admitted that he had large holdings in cotton mills and had lobbied in behalf of the textile interests during the discussions over the Payne-Aldrich bill. Senator Albert B. Fall of New Mexico said that he was a large owner of cattle, horses, and sheep. And thus it went, until the property interests of the members of the upper house were laid bare for all to see.

Its inquisition of the senators completed on June 9, 1913, the lobby committee turned the spotlight first upon an assortment of lobbyists representing minor special interests, who admitted working industriously but not insidiously in behalf of tariff increases. Then, when it seemed the committee had failed to uncover any evidence to prove the President's charges, it came upon the trail of the most powerful lobby of all. It was one organized by the beet sugar manufacturers which, the committee discovered, had spent some $5,000,000 during the past twenty years in a far-flung campaign to enlist newspapers, politicians, businessmen, bankers, and railroad executives in the fight against free sugar. Before the reverberations from these disclosures had ended, moreover, the committee exposed a second lobby financed by the Federal Sugar Refining Company, which had worked for years in behalf of free sugar and in close association with Democratic leaders during the campaign of 1912.[33]

The results of the investigation, therefore, must have exceeded Wilson's expectations. The committee had found little actual wrongdoing, to be sure, and no evidence of lobbying by the great industrial interests that had led the fight for high tariffs twenty years before. On the other hand, the committee had found enough industrious lobbies to prove the President's charge. "The country is indebted to President Wilson for exploding the bomb that blew the lid off the congressional lobby," Senator La Follette wrote, speaking for much of the country. "He hurled his short-fuse missile directly at the insidious interference with tariff legislation. . . . Congress sneered. The interests cried demagogue. The public believed. The case is proved."[34]

[33] Senate Judiciary Committee, *Maintenance of Lobby to Influence Legislation, Hearings* . . . , 63d Cong., 1st sess. (4 vols.), *passim*.

[34] *La Follette's Weekly*, v (July 12, 1913), 1.

More important than the committee's actual disclosures was the fact that the investigation had focused public attention on the Senate at the very moment when the crucial stage in the battle for tariff reform was about to begin. For while the lobby investigation proceeded, the Senate finance committee was completing work on the Underwood bill. It not only approved the sugar and wool schedules but effected numerous reductions in other rates as well. Then followed debates by the Senate Democratic caucus, from June 20 through July 7, 1913. The crises came on June 25, when the caucus voted thirty-nine to six in favor of free wool and forty-three to two in favor of free sugar after 1916, and on July 7, when the Democrats voted to make the bill a party measure and forty-seven of the forty-nine senators present pledged their votes for unequivocal tariff reform.[35]

It was, therefore, something of an anticlimax when the Senate began formal debate on the amended Underwood bill on July 19, 1913. The Democrats would have passed the measure within a week except for the fact that the Republicans were determined to consume as much time as possible in order to delay consideration of the banking and currency measure which the administration was then pressing in the House. As an insurgent senator from Minnesota put it, "We begin the tariff debate today. Brother Simmons is going to open it and then there will be three or four weeks and the country will witness and history record the farce of the question of whether the duty on an article should be seven mills or eight and a half mills regarded as a fundamental line of difference between great political parties."[36]

But the Republican senators droned on during the hot July and August weeks, undisturbed by the futility of their outpourings. Then a major controversy developed without warning when the Senate began consideration of the income tax provision of the Underwood bill on August 26, 1913. That measure's provision for a normal tax of 1 per cent on net personal and corporate incomes above $4,000 and an additional surtax rising from 1 to 3 per cent had satisfied progressives in the House and the members of the finance committee, but to a large group of insurgent Republicans in the Senate it seemed a lame beginning for a new democratic tax policy.

All during the debates they had attacked the Underwood bill, charging that the very concept of a revenue tariff was retrogressive, because

[35] *New York Times*, June 26 and July 8, 1913; New York *World*, July 8, 1913.
[36] Moses E. Clapp to A. J. Beveridge, July 19, 1913, the Papers of Albert J. Beveridge, Library of Congress; hereinafter cited as the Beveridge Papers.

it meant a fiscal policy that threw the heaviest tax burden on the lower and middle classes, and arguing that the graduated income tax was the only democratic instrument of taxation. As Senator Cummins said: "With regard to a tariff for revenue . . . , I believe it is obsolete, unjust, and intolerable. . . . Duties imposed for the purpose of raising a revenue are taxes upon consumption. . . . We have reached a stage in our development when the great majority of the humane students of public affairs believe that taxpayers should contribute to the expenses of the Government according to their ability to bear the burden rather than according to their necessities. Or, in other words, they should pay in proportion to their accumulation and not in proportion to their consumption."[37]

William E. Borah of Idaho opened the insurgent attack on the income tax provision on August 26, 1913; Joseph H. Bristow of Kansas pointed the issue the following day by offering an amendment to increase the combined income tax to a maximum of 10 per cent on all net incomes exceeding $90,000. The conservative Democratic spokesman of the finance committee, John Sharp Williams of Mississippi, retorted savagely: "The motive behind the amendment offered by the Senator from Kansas is not revenue. . . . It is to punish and take from those who have large incomes, not because the Government needs the money, but because the Government has the power to do it."[38] Bristow, Borah, Moses E. Clapp of Minnesota, and George W. Norris of Nebraska, all of them insurgents, replied with classic defenses of the income tax; but the Senate defeated the Bristow amendment forty-six to sixteen, with thirty-three senators not voting.

However, this was only the beginning and not the end of the controversy. Just before the Senate adjourned on August 27, 1913, La Follette of Wisconsin struck back with an amendment to increase the maximum income tax to 10 per cent on net incomes above $100,000. The following day the Democratic leaders held their ranks and defeated the La Follette amendment by a vote of forty-three to seventeen. But a few hours later, during the evening of August 28, four so-called radical Democratic senators—James K. Vardaman of Mississippi, Ashurst of Arizona, Thompson of Kansas, and Reed of Missouri—rebelled and demanded that the Democratic caucus meet in special session to consider the La Follette amendment. Claiming the support of a majority of the Democratic senators, the radical leaders threatened to rewrite the income tax

[37] *Congressional Record*, 63d Cong., 1st sess., p. 2557.   [38] *ibid.*, p. 3806.

provision if the finance committee did not approve the amendment.[39]
The radicals had such strong support when the Democratic caucus met on August 29, 1913, that Chairman Simmons and the finance committee offered the following day to compromise by raising the combined income tax to a maximum of 7 per cent. Confident that they could control the caucus, the radical leaders insisted upon the 10 per cent maximum.[40] Simmons then appealed to the Secretary of State to bring his rebellious friends into line. Bryan was willing to endorse the compromise, provided the President, who was then on vacation in New Hampshire, also approved.[41] Wilson quickly settled the controversy by joining the Nebraskan in supporting the finance committee's plan. "My own opinion in the matter is that it is much safer to begin upon somewhat moderate lines," he advised Simmons on September 4, "and I think the proposals of the Committee are reasonable and well considered."[42] On September 5, the day following the receipt of the President's message in the capital, the caucus approved the compromise, which eventually became the income tax provision of the Underwood Act.[43]

The Senate reached the climax of its long debate on September 8, 1913. Senator Norris introduced an amendment to impose an inheritance tax ranging from 1 to 75 per cent. It was defeated after a lengthy discussion by a vote of fifty-eight to twelve. Then Senator La Follette and the Republicans made a supreme effort to break the wool schedule, by proposing a plan to reduce rates on raw wool gradually to a 15 per cent level after January 1, 1916. But the Democratic leaders kept their fellow Democrats in line and rejected the amendment by a vote of thirty-nine to twenty-nine. Senator Joseph E. Ransdell of Louisiana consumed most of the evening in a futile last stand against free sugar.

The debate continued during the following morning and afternoon of September 9, until the exhausted senators agreed to vote. There was an air of tension and expectancy in the crowded chamber when the roll call began at five-thirty o'clock. The roll clerk proceeded deliberately until La Follette's name was called. The Wisconsin senator hesi-

[39] *New York Times,* August 29, 1913.
[40] *ibid.,* September 2, 1913.
[41] J. P. Tumulty to W. W., September 2, 1913, Wilson Papers.
[42] W. W. to F. M. Simmons, September 4, 1913, *ibid.*
[43] It imposed a normal tax of 1 per cent and a surtax of 1 per cent on incomes from $20,000 to $50,000, 2 per cent from $50,000 to $75,000, 3 per cent from $75,000 to $100,000, 4 per cent from $100,000 to $250,000, 5 per cent from $250,000 to $500,000, and 6 per cent on incomes over $500,000.

tated a moment, raised his head, and then shouted "Aye"; and there followed a scene of near-disorder as the galleries cheered and Democratic senators rushed to congratulate the insurgent leader. The final vote was forty-four to thirty-seven, with only two Democrats, Ransdell and John R. Thornton of Louisiana, bolting in the showdown.[44]

News of the victory was telephoned at once to the White House. "A fight for the people and for free business, which has lasted a long generation through, has at last been won, handsomely and completely," Wilson exulted. "A leadership and a steadfastness in council have been shown in both houses of which the Democratic Party has reason to be very proud. There has been no weakness or confusion or drawing back. I am happy to have been connected with the Government of the nation at a time when such things could happen and to have worked in association with men who could do them."[45]

The President did not exaggerate the meaning of the event. Instead of wrecking tariff reform, the Senate had effected an average reduction of some 4 per cent in the Underwood rates and had brought the measure's general ad valorem rates to a level of approximately 26 per cent. It was almost more than many observers could believe. "Think of it—" wrote Secretary Houston in surprised delight, "a tariff revision downwards at all—not dictated by the mfgs; lower in the Senate than in the House—one which will not be made in the Conference Committee room!! A progressive income tax!! I did not much think we should live to see these things." "For the first time since public plunderers sought refuge in the United States Senate," a Democratic editor exclaimed, "a tariff measure emerged from that body fairer and wiser and lower than it was received from the House."[46]

The conference committee appointed to reconcile the differences between the House and Senate bills finished its work on September 29, 1913. The House conferees accepted 427 of the 674 Senate amendments without verbal alterations, compromised on ninety-seven, rejected one

[44] *New York Times*, September 10, 1913; New York *World*, September 10, 1913; *Congressional Record*, 63d Cong., 1st sess., p. 4617.

[45] *New York Times*, September 10, 1913.

[46] D. F. Houston to W. H. Page, c. September 12, 1913, the Papers of Walter H. Page, the Library of Harvard University; hereinafter cited as the Page Papers; New York *World*, September 30, 1913. For additional comment, see the New York *Nation*, xcvii (September 18, 1913), 254; London *Times*, September 13, 1913; London *Economist*, lxxvii (September 20, 1913), 541; London *Spectator*, cxi (September 20, 1913), 410.

hundred fifty-one, and disagreed on one amendment.[47] A day later, on September 30, the House approved the conference report by a vote of 254 to 103, with only four Democrats in opposition. Then, after a perfunctory debate, the Senate adopted the revised Underwood bill by a vote of thirty-six to seventeen on October 2, 1913.

For the President, the first great legislative battle was over, and he gathered some fifty happy Democratic leaders, newspapermen, and friends in his Executive Office for the final ceremony of signing at nine o'clock on the evening of October 3, 1913. After engaging in a few pleasantries he signed the measure with two gold pens, which he handed to Underwood and Simmons. Finally, he tried to express his feelings on the momentous occasion in a moving little speech.

"Gentlemen," he began, "I feel a very peculiar pleasure in what I have just done by way of taking part in the completion of a great piece of business. . . . It is hard to speak of these things without seeming to go off into campaign eloquence, but that is not my feeling. It is one very profound, a feeling of profound gratitude that, working with the splendid men who have carried this thing through with studious attention and doing justice all round, I should have had part in serving the people of this country as we have been striving to serve them ever since I can remember. . . .

"I was quoting the other day to some of my colleagues in the Senate those lines from Shakespeare's 'Henry V,' which have always appealed to me: 'If it be a sin to covet honor, then am I the most offending soul alive.' And I am happy to say that I do not covet it for myself alone. I covet it with equal ardor for the men who are associated with me, . . . and I covet it for the great party of which I am a member, because that party is not honorable unless it redeem its name and serve the people of the United States.

"So I feel to-night like a man who is lodging happily in the inn which lies half way along the journey, and that in the morning, with a fresh impulse, we shall go the rest of the journey, and sleep at the journey's end like men with a quiet conscience, knowing that we have served our fellowmen, and have thereby tried to serve God."[48]

In the long run, because it marked the beginning of a new era in federal fiscal policy and heralded the coming of the day when the mid-

---

[47] For a thorough analysis of the Underwood Act as it was finally approved, see the *New York Times*, September 30, 1913; and F. W. Taussig, *The Tariff History of the United States* (8th edn., 1931), pp. 409-446.

[48] *New York Times*, October 4, 1913.

western insurgents' demand for a progressive tax policy would be fulfilled, the income tax provision was the most important feature of the Underwood Act. The new tariff rates never had a chance to prove the Democratic promise of lower living costs or to justify the Republican

The Funeral Oration

Morgan in the Philadelphia *Inquirer*

prophecy of inevitable disaster. No sooner had the Underwood Act gone into effect than it was rendered virtually inoperative by the disorganization of normal world trade that followed the outbreak of the First World War. Then came a Republican victory after the war and substantial upward tariff revision in 1922. The Underwood duties were of minor consequence for the future, therefore, except in so far as they reflected a lessening of the pressure from the large industrial interests for a McKinley type of protection.

Of great immediate importance, however, were the political consequences of the President's victory in the battle for tariff reform. To begin with, by vanquishing the lobby and resisting the special-interest spokesmen in their own ranks, the Democrats had proved that responsible representative government was possible on the federal level. For, however men might disagree about the wisdom of the Underwood rates, no one could deny that they honored past Democratic promises. All observers agreed, moreover, that the chief significance of the adoption of the Underwood Act was the fact that it confirmed Wilson's supremacy as the spokesman of his party and the leader of Congress. The forces arrayed against tariff reform had been powerful and entrenched, and a weaker President might easily have failed in 1913 and thereby have lost his position of control. But Wilson succeeded where weaker Presidents had failed precisely because he was determined, resourceful, and, above all, bold in leadership.

In conclusion, we can agree with the summary of the London editor who wrote: "This is Dr. Wilson's tariff in no conventional sense. He called the Special Session, himself framed the Bill, co-operated directly with the legislators of his party in the House and Senate, routed and exposed the audacity of the lobbyists who sought even this year to renew their customary attacks upon the virtue of Congress, and carried the measure to a triumphant issue without mutilation or considerable concession. It has raised him at a single stage from the man of promise to the man of achievement."[49]

[49] London *Nation*, xiv (October 11, 1913), 89. For selected additional comment, see the *New York Times*, October 4, 1913; New York *World*, October 4, 1913; New York *Nation*, xcvii (October 9, 1913), 326; *The Independent*, lxxvi (October 9, 1913), 62-63; W. J. Bryan, in *The Commoner*, xiii (October 1913), 1; Mark Sullivan, in *Collier's*, lii (October 18, 1913), 9; George Harvey, "Six Months of Wilson," *North American Review*, cxcviii (November 1913); and *World's Work*, xxvii (November 1913), 3, 9-10.

CHAPTER VII

The Federal Reserve Act

Wilson's triumph in the tariff fight came none too soon or completely, for by the time he signed the Underwood Act he was already deeply engaged in a more ambitious and difficult undertaking. It was his struggle to lead the Democratic party in the great enterprise of reconstructing the nation's banking and currency systems—the second step in the New Freedom's campaign to destroy monopoly and unleash the potential economic energies of the American people. The fight for the Underwood bill was a minor skirmish compared to the controversy that raged over currency and banking legislation; and by the time the latter was over, Wilson had demonstrated more fully than before the qualities that made him a leader.

Men might disagree over method, but no one denied the urgent need for reform of the nation's antiquated banking and currency systems. Established in 1863 and 1864 and altered slightly in 1900, the national banking structure was about as badly adapted to the financial needs of a great industrial and commercial nation as any system could be. By 1913 it comprised some 7,000 individual banks operating under the general supervision of the Comptroller of the Currency, but without any real coordination or effective method of mobilizing reserves in times of crisis. Its chief weakness, therefore, was the absence of any central banking agency. An eminent authority explained this deficiency in 1912:

"The fundamental defect of the national banking system is to be sought in the fact that it is not in any proper sense a 'system' of banking at all, but a series of banks artificially grouped. Because of the lack of cooperative or fundamental relationships between the institutions, it is not possible for them to exercise any general policy with reference to the control of reserves, the fixing of rates of discount [interest], or the granting of loans. They can only act independently of one another, and the well-conducted institutions must, therefore, suffer from the mistakes of others whose conduct tends to arouse suspicion or alarm in the mind of the public. Because of this situation . . . , the national banking system as at present conducted is in a sense a breeder of panics, while it fails entirely to grant any adequate relief from these commercial convulsions."[1]

The monetary system of the United States in 1913 was, if anything, even more badly suited to the country's needs than the national banking structure. Consisting of a miscellany of gold coin and gold certificates, silver coin and silver certificates, so-called greenbacks, and national bank notes issued against government bonds, the money supply totaled some $3,777,000,000 in 1913. It was a supply generally adequate for ordinary needs. The chief trouble was the lack of any power, either public or private, to expand the currency to meet the seasonal needs of industry or agriculture or to prevent financial panics. Consequently, bankers usually had either a surplus or a shortage of money.[2]

Time and again since the 1860's the country had been rocked by a series of financial convulsions that demonstrated the dangers of attempting to get along with a system of immobile reserves and an inelastic money supply. There had been deflation in the 1870's and 1880's and a prolonged depression in the 1890's, which in turn gave rise to agrarian demands for inflation through the free coinage of silver and to the first organized banker agitation for currency reform.[3] Deeply rooted partisan differences over the control of the money supply and the return of prosperity after 1897 prevented any solution by Congress. But a sharp bankers' panic in 1907 again pointed up the dangers of the situation and renewed discussions of a remedy on a large scale.

Congress responded by adopting the Aldrich-Vreeland Act of 1908, which provided for a cumbersome system of emergency currency and, more important, for the appointment of a National Monetary Commission to study the problem and report to Congress. Headed by Senator Nelson W. Aldrich of Rhode Island, the Commission conducted sporadic investigations from 1908 until 1912, sponsored the writing of some twenty-three monographs on all phases of the banking problem, and presented its final report and recommendations to Congress in 1912. Embodied in that report was a plan for the reorganization of the national banking system that set off one of the liveliest controversies of the time.

[1] J. Laurence Laughlin (ed.), *Banking Reform*, p. 12.

[2] See the criticism prepared by the currency commission of the American Bankers' Association, printed in the *New York Times*, June 22, 1913.

[3] This was the so-called Indianapolis Movement, growing out of the Indianapolis Currency Convention of 1897 and the work of its Monetary Commission, which recommended provision for the issuance of currency based upon commercial assets.

Drafted largely by Paul M. Warburg, a partner in the investment firm of Kuhn, Loeb & Company and one of the few American experts on central banking, the Aldrich plan represented the ideal of virtually the entire banking community. It provided for the establishment of one great central bank, the National Reserve Association, with a capital of at least $100,000,000 and with fifteen branches, controlled by member banks, in various sections of the country. The National Reserve Association would carry a portion of member banks' reserves, determine discount rates, buy and sell on the open market, receive the deposits of the federal government, and, most important, issue currency based upon gold and commercial paper, currency that would be the liability of the Reserve Association and not of the government. The National Reserve Association, finally, would be managed by a governing board consisting of governmental officials and private members and controlled by a board of directors composed chiefly of bankers and businessmen.[4]

As they favored private control of banking and the money supply, most of the leaders in the banking and business communities of course approved the Aldrich plan. Moreover, they launched the National Citizens' League for the Promotion of a Sound Banking System in 1910 to awaken the country to the need for immediate legislation and began an intensive propaganda campaign to sell the Aldrich plan to the people at large.

The reaction of the progressive majority, however, was overwhelmingly hostile. To Bryan Democrats, the adoption of the Aldrich plan could only mean the perpetuation of Wall Street control of the credit resources and money supply and the repudiation of everything for which progressive Democrats had stood since 1896. Thus the Democrats at the Baltimore convention in 1912 promised financial reform and opposed the establishment of any kind of central bank. Insurgent Republicans, moreover, were even more explicit in their condemnation of the Aldrich plan. The Progressive platform of 1912 not only denounced the plan but went on to say, in words that Bryan could have approved: "The issue of currency is fundamentally a government function. . . . The control should be lodged with the government and should be protected from domination or manipulation by Wall Street or any special interests." Even the Republicans, many of whom privately fa-

---

[4] H. Parker Willis, *The Federal Reserve System, Legislation, Organization and Operation*, pp. 79-83.

vored the Aldrich plan, did not dare give public sanction in their platform to a proposal so overwhelmingly condemned.

The pressures for thoroughgoing reform continued to mount during the late months of 1912 and the early months of 1913. Stimulated by the propaganda of the National Citizens' League, leaders in the business world were by now thoroughly aroused; literally thousands of them begged Wilson and the Democrats on the House and Senate banking committees to lead the way in meeting the country's most pressing economic need. Even stronger pressure for reform came from a different direction—from a public opinion shocked by the revelations of the so-called Pujo committee during 1912 and early 1913. With Samuel Untermyer, a New York lawyer, as its counsel, this subcommittee of the House banking committee probed all the ramifications of the alleged "Money Trust" and found an astounding concentration of control over the credit resources of the country among J. P. Morgan & Company and allied investment firms in Wall Street.[5]

The President-elect and his colleagues were obliged to formulate an alternative to the Aldrich plan, one that would avoid the danger of Wall Street control and also satisfy moderate opinion that it was not a Bryanistic cheap money scheme. For a time after the election it seemed that the challenge would be too great. Wilson had not yet gone beyond general objectives in his own thinking and was ignorant of the details of the issue. Worse still, there was no agreement or even understanding among the Democratic leaders as to what kind of banking and currency systems should be established. A strong minority favored glossing the Aldrich plan in order to make it palatable to the progressive majority.[6] Carter Glass of Virginia, who would be chairman of the House banking committee in the next Congress, was an ardent foe of a central bank; but he was thoroughly conservative in his belief in private control of the banking system and the money supply. At the other extreme were Bryan and a large group of so-called radical

[5] *Report of Committee Appointed Pursuant to H.R. 429 and 504 . . .* , 62d Cong., 3d sess. For an able summary, see Louis D. Brandeis, *Other People's Money and How the Bankers Use It.*

[6] Colonel House, for example, was conferring discreetly with Paul M. Warburg and other bankers and trying unobtrusively to convert Wilson and Democratic leaders in Congress to a central bank plan. See, e.g., E. M. House to T. C. Dunn, November 29, 1912, House Papers; W. G. Brown to E. M. House, December 10, 1912, *ibid.*; House Diary, January 8, 1913.

Democrats, who were frightening conservatives by their demands for strong federal control.[7]

And yet an effort had to be made. During the spring of 1912 Glass and the House banking committee's expert adviser, H. Parker Willis,[8] had begun preliminary discussions of proposed banking legislation, and Willis had completed a tentative draft of a bill by the end of October 1912. Providing for a decentralized, privately controlled reserve system, with twenty or more independent reserve banks, its chief objective was to destroy the concentration of credit in Wall Street by building rival aggregations of financial power.[9] Glass was eager to begin discussions with the President-elect, but the trip to Bermuda intervened,[10] and it was not until December 26, 1912, that Glass and Willis went to Princeton for the first full-dress conference with Wilson.

It was a memorable meeting. Princeton was blanketed in snow, and Glass and Willis found their host at home on Cleveland Lane, in bed from a severe cold that he had caught while driving from Princeton to Trenton in an open car on Christmas Eve. With great enthusiasm, Glass described the Willis draft, explaining how important he thought it was to create a decentralized system and break Wall Street's control.[11] Wilson tentatively agreed, but he wondered whether Willis' plan to give the Comptroller of the Currency general supervision over the reserve system would provide sufficient coordination and control. What he would like to see, the President-elect continued, was the addition of a "capstone to be placed upon the structure"—a central board to

[7] New York *Journal of Commerce*, November 26, 1912; *New York Times*, November 26 and December 4, 1912; "American Banking Reform and the President-Elect," London *Economist*, LXXVI (January 18, 1913), 111.

[8] Formerly professor of economics at Washington and Lee University in Virginia and in 1912 an associate editor of the New York *Journal of Commerce*.

[9] H. P. Willis, *The Federal Reserve System*, pp. 142-143.

[10] C. Glass to W. W., November 7, 1912, Glass Papers; W. W. to C. Glass, November 14, 1912, printed in Carter Glass, *An Adventure in Constructive Finance*, p. 75.

[11] It is impossible to say who first conceived the idea of a decentralized reserve system, for it was a fairly obvious alternative to the Aldrich plan, and many economists and public leaders favored decentralization. One of the first serious suggestions of a regional reserve plan that this writer has seen was the one proposed by the economist, Victor Morawetz, nebulously in his *The Banking and Currency Problem in the United States* (1909) and more specifically in an address before the Academy of Political Science at Columbia University in November 1910, later published as "The Banking and Currency Problem and Its Solution," *Proceedings of the Academy of Political Science*, I (1910-1911), 343-357. The impact of Morawetz' proposal can be clearly seen in the correspondence of public leaders and bankers outside Wall Street. See, e.g., T. C. Dunn to E. M. House, December 4, 1912; and W. R. Hamby to E. M. House, c. December 5, 1912, both in the House Papers.

control and coordinate and perform the functions of a central bank. A true central bank was probably the best solution, he added; but he "recognized the fact that such an organization was politically impossible even if economically desirable, and that what was to be sought was the provision of those central banking powers which were unmistakably desirable and the elimination of those central banking powers which had caused danger in the past."[12]

The Princeton conference was the first important milestone along the tortuous road to the Federal Reserve Act, for Wilson, apparently by a stroke of sheer genius, had found the only way of reconciling the progressive demand for decentralization with the practical necessity for centralized control. Glass promised to find a way to create a central board, if it could be constituted without "the practical attributes of a central bank." But privately he was aghast at the President-elect's proposal. "It is clear to me," he wrote to Willis three days after the conference at Princeton, "that Mr. Wilson has been written to and talked to by those who are seeking to mask the Aldrich plan and give us dangerous centralization; but we shall have to keep quiet on this point for the present."[13]

Knowing he might have to yield if Wilson insisted upon having his "capstone," Glass set to work with Willis to draft provisions for a central mechanism.[14] Glass next held hearings before his subcommittee from January 7 to February 17, 1913, in response to Wilson's suggestion that the subcommittee merely probe banking and business opinion without committing the incoming administration to any definite plan.[15] At the same time, the Virginian moved to bring leading bankers into the discussions and, if possible, to win the support of the American Bankers' Association for his regional reserve project. "What I most earnestly desire to do," he wrote, for example, to Festus J. Wade, president of the Mercantile Trust Company of St. Louis and a member of the currency commission of the Bankers' Association, "is to aid in the construction of a measure of reform that will commend itself for soundness to the bankers of the country and, at the same time, secure the support of the business community for its fairness and sufficiency."[16]

[12] H. P. Willis, *The Federal Reserve System*, p. 146.
[13] C. Glass to H. P. Willis, December 29, 1912, Glass Papers.
[14] C. Glass to H. P. Willis, January 3, 1913, *ibid.*
[15] The hearings are printed in House Banking and Currency Committee, *Banking and Currency Reform. Hearings before Subcommittee . . . , 62d Cong., 3d sess. (13 parts).
[16] C. Glass to F. J. Wade, January 24, 1913, Glass Papers.

The results of the hearings and of Glass's appeals were unexpectedly gratifying. "After being courteously, but firmly, informed that the committee felt precluded from consideration of the Aldrich scheme or a central bank plan," Glass informed the President-elect on January 27, 1913, "these gentlemen, as I am privately told, concluded that they could not carry out Mr. Warburg's purpose of 'battering the committee into a repudiation of the Democratic platform,' and they are now writing me, after conference among themselves, that they are willing to cooperate with the committee in trying to secure the best remedial legislation that it is possible to obtain. They are expressing a good deal of anxiety for immediate action, and men like Hepburn,[17] of New York, Forgan[18] and Reynolds,[19] of Chicago, and Wade, of St. Louis, have written that they will be glad, at the word from me, to assemble the currency commission of the American Bankers' Association for the purpose of getting behind any sound measure that our committee may construct."[20]

Meanwhile, by the end of January 1913 Glass and Willis had revised their Federal Reserve bill to meet Wilson's suggestions, and Glass went to Trenton on January 30 to explain the new draft to the President-elect. It established a reserve system of fifteen or more regional banks, owned and controlled by member banks, which would hold a portion of member banks' reserves, perform other central banking functions, and issue currency against commercial assets and gold. Controlling the entire system was a powerful Federal Reserve Board composed of six public members and three bankers chosen indirectly by the directors of the regional banks.[21] Wilson was delighted. As Glass afterward wrote, "This conference at Trenton seemed to settle two things: it attached the President-elect to the regional bank system explicitly and, tentatively, to the provisions of the measure as far as drafted. . . . I left Trenton with the leader's cheering word to 'Go ahead!'"[22]

With the promise of administration support, Glass and Willis wound up the subcommittee's hearings and went carefully through the draft

[17] A. Barton Hepburn, chairman of the board of directors of the Chase National Bank of New York City.

[18] David R. Forgan, president of the National City Bank of Chicago.

[19] George M. Reynolds, president of the Continental and Commercial National Bank of Chicago.

[20] C. Glass to W. W., January 27, 1913, Wilson Papers.

[21] "First Complete Draft of Glass Bill," printed in H. P. Willis, *The Federal Reserve System*, pp. 1531-1553.

[22] *An Adventure in Constructive Finance*, pp. 91-92; copyright 1927 by Doubleday & Company, Inc.

bill, revising and strengthening its technical provisions. Working in almost complete secrecy, they completed what they thought would be the administration's bill on about May 1, 1913,[23] and circulated it quietly among the Wilson circle during the next week or ten days. Within a short time there had developed a controversy within the inner circle so serious that it threatened for a time to disrupt the Democratic party and to destroy all hopes for currency reform.

The issue at stake was nothing less than the fundamental character of the new banking system and money supply. What Glass and Willis had constructed and Wilson had tentatively approved was virtually a decentralized version of the Aldrich plan; in it control was balanced in favor of the private bankers, and the regional banks, not the government, were to issue Federal Reserve currency and be liable for it. In contrast, the Democratic progressives and so-called radicals demanded exclusive public control of the reserve system, governmental issue of and liability for the currency, and a relentless campaign to destroy the Wall Street oligarchy of financial and industrial directorates.

Bryan, for example, had not read the Glass bill by the time discussions in the inner administration circle began in early May, but he was profoundly disturbed by reports that it permitted banker representation on the Federal Reserve Board and made Federal Reserve notes the liability of the regional banks.[24] Without his active support the currency measure might never pass; and his open opposition, as Wilson admitted, would mean the disruption of the party and the almost certain defeat of the bill.

The Secretary of State was adamant in his opposition, even after the President called him into private conference on May 19, 1913, explained the Glass plan, and pleaded for his support. "I called his attention to the fact that our party had been committed by Jefferson and Jackson and by recent platforms to the doctrine that the issue of money is a function of government and should not be surrendered to banks," Bryan afterward remembered telling Wilson, "and that I was so committed to the doctrine that I could not consistently indorse the authorization of more bank notes and that to do so would forfeit the confidence of those who trusted me—this confidence being my only politi-

[23] It is printed as "Revised Draft of Glass Bill," in H. P. Willis, *The Federal Reserve System*, pp. 1554-1573.

[24] House Diary, May 11 and 15, 1913; E. M. House to W. W., May 15, 1913, Wilson Papers.

cal asset, the loss of which would deprive me of any power to assist him." Moreover, Bryan warned, he would have to insist upon exclusive public control of the proposed Federal Reserve Board. "I assured him that if I felt compelled to dissent from any part of the plan," the Nebraskan concluded, "I would accompany the dissent with an explicit statement of confidence in the disinterestedness of his intention and make my dissent as mild as conditions would permit."[25] It was a friendly warning, but Wilson caught its ominous undertones. "It begins to look as if W.J.B. . . . and I have come to the parting of the ways on the Currency Bill," the President told Tumulty a short while later.[26]

At the same time, there was the danger that Senator Robert L. Owen of Oklahoma, chairman of the Senate banking committee and a Bryan Democrat, would join the Secretary of State in rebellion against the Glass bill. Willis conferred with Owen on May 21, 1913, and read the draft measure to him. Obviously resentful over the way in which he had been excluded from the early discussions, Owen made it clear that he meant to have a hand in preparing the currency legislation. He objected to the large measure of banker control in the proposed Federal Reserve Board and warned that he would insist upon making Federal Reserve notes obligations of the United States.[27] Moreover,

[25] W. J. and M. B. Bryan, *The Memoirs of William Jennings Bryan*, pp. 370-371; quoted by permission of the John C. Winston Company, publishers; House Diary, May 19, 1913.

[26] Joseph P. Tumulty, *Woodrow Wilson As I Know Him*, p. 178.

In conferences with McAdoo and Tumulty, moreover, Bryan was even more emphatic in criticism. The Glass bill, he declared, for example, "would divide our party and make any currency reform impossible." "Who from Wall Street has been discussing this bill with the President?" he asked Tumulty, voicing perhaps a personal resentment. "I am afraid that some of the President's friends have been emphasizing too much the view of Wall Street in their conferences with the President on this bill." W. J. and M. B. Bryan, *The Memoirs of William Jennings Bryan*, p. 371; and J. P. Tumulty, *Woodrow Wilson As I Know Him*, p. 179, copyright 1921 by Doubleday & Company, Inc.

Samuel Untermyer, who was active in the discussions at the time, tells of a much stormier interview between Wilson and Bryan on May 19, 1913, than Bryan describes. Bryan, Untermyer writes, "warned President Wilson that if the features of the bill drafted by Mr. Willis for . . . Glass, and urged upon the President, . . . were introduced, he would use all his influence . . . with the members of Congress and throughout the country to accomplish its defeat. This is not conjecture or hearsay. *I know it*, for it was upon my urgent request that he went with me to the White House, as the result of a special 'hurry-call' visit made by me to Washington for the purpose." S. Untermyer to R. L. Owen, May 19, 1927, printed in S. Untermyer, *Who Is Entitled to the Credit for the Federal Reserve Act? An Answer to Senator Carter Glass*, pamphlet dated June 18, 1927, copy in the Glass Papers.

[27] R. L. Owen to S. Untermyer, May 14, 1927, printed in *ibid*.

Owen informed Willis that he had drawn up a banking and currency measure of his own, one which Bryan and Samuel Untermyer had approved in principle.[28]

Obviously, a dangerous situation existed when the leaders of the administration could not even agree on the fundamentals of a banking bill. Fearing that the Glass measure would fall between the cross fire of the progressives and the banking spokesmen, McAdoo resolved to find a solution of his own. Between May 15 and May 20, 1913, he conferred with Bryan, Owen, Untermyer, and a few bankers; and with the help of John Skelton Williams, Comptroller of the Currency, and perhaps of Owen and Untermyer also, he prepared the outline of a new currency and banking bill. Based in part upon the Owen bill, McAdoo's plan called for the establishment of a National Reserve, or central bank, in the Treasury Department, with some fifteen branches, the entire system to be administered by a National Reserve Board composed exclusively of political appointees. It provided, moreover, for the issuance of the entire paper money supply, upon a basis of gold and commercial assets, by a National Currency Commission also functioning in the Treasury.[29]

In his memoirs McAdoo relates an interesting tale about the National Reserve plan. Someone in the Treasury, whose name he could not remember, brought him a sketch of the plan, and a grand strategy began to unfold in his mind. The bankers demanded a privately owned central bank and were vehemently opposed to a regional reserve system. "If they want a central bank, I reflected," McAdoo continues, "we'll give them one—or make them think so, at any rate, but it will be a government bank. I felt convinced that when the large banking interests saw a plan sponsored by me for turning the Treasury into a rediscount bank for commercial paper they would be genuinely alarmed. I hoped that their concern would temper their opposition to the regional bank system. . . . I explained to the President the strategy I had in mind. . . . Of course, neither I nor President Wilson had any idea of transforming the Treasury into a bank, but I felt sure that this reserve plan, coming from me, would start something—and it did."[30]

[28] It provided for a regional reserve system to be controlled by a National Currency Board composed entirely of public members. H. P. Willis reprints the Owen bill in *The Federal Reserve System*, pp. 1697-1706.

[29] W. G. McAdoo, *Crowded Years*, p. 242; H. P. Willis, *The Federal Reserve System*, pp. 194-206.

[30] W. G. McAdoo, *Crowded Years*, pp. 242-243; quoted by permission of the Houghton Mifflin Company, publishers.

There is not a shred of fact to substantiate this story, however, while a mass of evidence indicates that McAdoo brought the National Reserve plan forward as a genuine alternative.[31] "I have had to dictate the enclosed memorandum very hurriedly and amid many interruptions," he explained as he sent a copy of his proposal to Colonel House on May 20, 1913, "but I hope it will give you the gist of my thoughts on the subject. Since my talk yesterday with the Secretary [Bryan], I am more than ever convinced that we shall have to come to something along these lines if we are going to succeed, and, for my part, I believe that it is far preferable to anything that has yet been considered. . . . We shall, I think, have to cut away entirely from all the mazes and hazes of previous discussions and bring out something new and simple and direct."[32] At the same time, McAdoo gave a copy of the plan to the President and called Glass to the Treasury building to explain the proposal and tell him that Senator Owen thoroughly approved. "I had not gotten far in my examination of the proposal," Glass has written, "before I looked up from the paper and asked the Secretary if he was 'serious about it.' With characteristic point and punch he exclaimed: 'Hell, yes!' "[33]

Glass left the Treasury building heartsick and fearful that the President might endorse the National Reserve plan in order to win Bryan's and Owen's support. "It seemed an end of currency reform for the time —a nullification of fourteen months of hard work and inconceivable nervous strain," he afterward recalled.[34] "We have simply been brought to a standstill by the new scheme. I am all in the air and do not know

[31] Carter Glass was convinced that Samuel Untermyer, Senator Owen, and John Skelton Williams were the principal authors of the National Reserve plan and that Untermyer used McAdoo in an attempt to sidetrack the Federal Reserve bill and gain the credit for currency legislation.

There is considerable evidence to confirm Glass's view. The President, for example, referred to the National Reserve plan as "Untermyer's paper"; McAdoo, in a letter to Glass, later called it "the Untermyer-Owen scheme." C. Glass to R. S. Baker, February 3, 1927, Baker Collection. But the most convincing substantiation of Glass's accusation comes from a letter that Colonel House wrote to the President on May 20, 1913—the same day on which McAdoo presented the National Reserve plan—supplementing his and Wilson's telephone conversation of the night before. House wrote that he believed a sound currency bill, which Bryan and Owen would probably accept, could be worked out along the lines suggested by Untermyer, and that he had discussed the matter with McAdoo, who agreed. E. M. House to W. W., May 20, 1913, Wilson Papers.

[32] W. G. McAdoo to E. M. House, May 20, 1913, House Papers.

[33] Carter Glass, *An Adventure in Constructive Finance*, pp. 100-101; copyright 1927 by Doubleday & Company, Inc.

[34] *ibid.*, p. 101; copyright 1927 by Doubleday & Company, Inc.

what to say to members of my committee," he wrote during the first week in June 1913, when the issue seemed in doubt.[35] McAdoo had thrown the entire discussion out of joint, Willis agreed. "Up to the time that he interposed, everything was progressing very well, and I think that there was a feeling of confidence that we were going to get out a good bill. I think now that a feeling of doubt, uncertainty and apprehension has succeeded."[36]

But the doughty Virginian counterattacked quickly and hard. First, he appealed to A. Barton Hepburn, chairman of the board of directors of the Chase National Bank of New York, asking him to rally his colleagues in the currency commission of the American Bankers' Association in opposition to McAdoo's plan. "To me the proposition seems amazing," Glass wrote. "It also seems to me an utter perversion of the true function of government. Besides, it is unique and untried, at least in its magnitude."[37] Next, Glass's spokesman, Willis, pleaded with McAdoo, while Glass warned Senator Owen that the National Reserve plan would create "a political revolution."[38] Finally, on June 7, 1913, Glass had a showdown conference with the President. Armed with a memorandum prepared by Willis, denouncing the National Reserve plan as "undesirable financially, hazardous and politically disastrous,"[39] and with a sheaf of letters from Hepburn and other leading bankers, who called the plan "impracticable, inadvisable and unworthy of serious consideration,"[40] Glass pleaded vehemently with Wilson to disavow McAdoo's plan. "I fear Mac is deceived," the President replied, "but fortunately the thing has not gone so far it cannot be stopped."[41] Two days later, on June 9, 1913, McAdoo surrendered and promised to withdraw the National Reserve plan and to support the Glass bill.

One crisis was over, but another impended as the administration leaders began final conferences to resolve their remaining differences over the character of the proposed banking and money systems. How fundamental those differences were became acutely evident during a long and heated conference among Wilson, Glass, McAdoo, and Owen at the White House during the evening of June 17, 1913. Glass still in-

[35] C. Glass to H. P. Willis, June 6, 1913, Glass Papers.

[36] H. P. Willis to C. Glass, June 7, 1913, *ibid.*

[37] C. Glass to A. B. Hepburn, May 30, 1913, *ibid.*

[38] H. P. Willis to C. Glass, June 5, 1913; C. Glass to H. P. Willis, June 7, 1913, both in *ibid.*

[39] H. P. Willis to C. Glass, June 3, 1913, *ibid.*

[40] A. B. Hepburn to C. Glass, June 5, 1913; and G. M. Reynolds to C. Glass, June 3, 1913, both in *ibid.*

[41] Carter Glass, *An Adventure in Constructive Finance*, p. 108.

sisted upon banker representation on the Federal Reserve Board and upon giving the regional reserve banks clear control over the money supply. Echoing Bryan's views, Owen retorted that the Federal Reserve Board must be exclusively a political agency and that he would never approve Glass's currency plan. McAdoo agreed. "The more I have studied this question the more I have become convinced that the right measure is the one which puts the Government in the saddle," he declared.[42]

Profoundly disturbed by the dimensions of the disagreements, Wilson adjourned the conference and asked for a few days' respite. The time had now come when he had to make the decision and break the impasse or else abandon his role as leader and his hopes for currency legislation. Fortunately, we have some indication of his thoughts on the fundamental principles at stake during these crucial days.

Since 1910 Wilson had been slowly evolving in his own mind two basic assumptions that he felt should govern banking and currency reform. The first was that the concentration of credit and money in Wall Street had reached the proportions of monopoly, and that economic freedom could not exist so long as a "Money Trust" had the power to "chill and check and destroy genuine economic freedom."

Thus in 1913 the President supported the regional reserve concept as a means of destroying the "Money Trust," in spite of all the pressure that men like House and Warburg could bring to bear in behalf of a central bank. "Through the measure proposed," he told a reporter in explaining the Glass bill, "I believe we will correct the evil we are most bent upon correcting—that of the present concentration of reserve and control at the discretion of a single group of bankers or by a locality of banking interests. . . . This will be a great advance, because it will make more and more difficult such arbitrary control of great amounts of money by a few banks upon which other and weaker banks of necessity have to depend for any needed accommodations."

Wilson's second basic assumption had also apparently taken firm shape in his mind by the time the discussions over the Glass bill had reached their climax in June 1913. It was that banking was so much a public business that the government must share with private bankers in making fundamental financial decisions. He supported the Federal Reserve bill, he told a reporter, because "it provides . . . for public instead of private control, thus making the banks what they should be

[42] *New York Times*, June 18, 1913; New York *World*, June 18, 1913; W. G. McAdoo to E. M. House, June 18, 1913, House Papers.

—the servants and not the masters of business. . . . With government control, there is created a force which, while it will not attempt to run the business of the banks, will be clothed with some authority to prevent injustice from the banks to the general public. Under the proposed plan, recognition is given to the interests of the people, and there is established the principle of some other control of credit than arbitrary control by the banks. . . . This is a great principle. So long as it is observed, the details themselves are matters of relatively minor importance."[43]

These were important convictions, and we may be sure they helped to form Wilson's decision on the two most controversial points at issue in the administration discussions—banker representation on the Federal Reserve Board and liability for Federal Reserve currency. But he would not make a final decision until he had consulted Louis D. Brandeis, whose opinions on economic matters he respected above all others. Brandeis came to the White House on June 11, 1913, and the President laid the problems squarely before him.

"The power to issue currency should be vested exclusively in Government officials, even when the currency is issued against commercial paper," Brandeis replied. "The American people will not be content to have the discretion necessarily involved vested in a Board composed wholly or in part of bankers; for their judgment may be biased by private interests or affiliation. . . . The conflict between the policies of the Administration and the desires of the financiers and of big business, is an irreconcilable one. Concessions to the big business interests must in the end prove futile."[44]

Fortified by Brandeis' advice, Wilson must have already made up his mind that the progressives were right and Glass was wrong by the time the White House conference of June 17, 1913, occurred. At that meeting he indicated that he favored excluding bankers from the Federal Reserve Board, for we find Glass begging him the following day to reconsider the decision. "The matter has given me much concern," Glass added, "and more than ever I am convinced that it will be a grave mistake to alter so radically the feature of the bill indicated."[45]

---

[43] Interview given by the President to J. C. O'Laughlin of the Chicago *Tribune* about June 20, 1913, and enclosed in J. C. O'Laughlin to J. P. Tumulty, June 26, 1913, Wilson Papers. This interview was apparently never published. I have transposed certain sentences for the sake of clarity.

[44] L. D. Brandeis to W. W., June 14, 1913, *ibid.*, embodying the substance of what Brandeis had told the President on June 11, 1913.

[45] C. Glass to W. W., June 18, 1913, *ibid.*

In any event, the President called Glass, McAdoo, and Owen to the White House on June 18 and told them that he would insist upon exclusive governmental control of the Federal Reserve Board and upon making Federal Reserve notes the obligation of the United States. It was the absolute minimum that would satisfy Bryan and his friends, and Glass had no recourse but to yield and change his measure as Wilson had directed.[46]

Thus was the first great crisis resolved, and the administration, united in a solid phalanx that never broke during all the ensuing controversies, could present the revised Federal Reserve bill to Congress and the country. Glass gave the text of the measure to the newspapers, which published it on June 19, 1913, and the President presented it to the Democratic members of the House banking and currency committee during a two-and-a-half hours' conference at the White House on June 20. Wilson left no doubt that he would insist upon action by the special session and take personal leadership of the fight for banking reform.[47] As he wrote two days later, "Now it is the currency I have

[46] *New York Times*, June 19, 1913. H. P. Willis, *The Federal Reserve System*, pp. 1577-1594, reprints the Federal Reserve bill as it was modified after the White House conference of June 18, 1913.

Wilson's decision on the membership of the Federal Reserve Board was a clear-cut victory for Bryan, McAdoo, and Owen. On the other hand, they won a doubtful victory in the dispute over the character and control of the Federal Reserve currency. What Bryan and his followers really wanted was the retirement of the national bank notes and the issuance, within the exclusive discretion of public officials, of a supply of paper money backed only by the government's promise to pay. In contrast, what they approved was a provision in the revised Glass bill that made Federal Reserve notes obligations of the United States and gave the Federal Reserve Board general control over their issue, without, however, actually changing the character of the Federal Reserve notes. For in spite of the progressives' seeming victory, Federal Reserve notes remained bank money—that is, money issued by the Federal Reserve Board for the regional banks against commercial assets and a 33 1/3 per cent gold reserve, and money which the regional banks had to redeem, although the United States guaranteed such redemption in gold. In brief, under this system initiative in determining the supply of Federal Reserve currency rested with the regional reserve banks and their member banks, and not with a public agency.

The President understood this fact. When Glass argued that it would be meaningless to make Federal Reserve notes "obligations of the United States," since those notes were backed by commercial assets, gold, and the combined resources of the banks in the Federal Reserve districts, Wilson replied, "Exactly so, Glass. Every word you say is true; the government liability *is* a mere thought. And so, if we can hold to the substance of the thing and give the other fellow the shadow, why not do it, if thereby we may save our bill?" Carter Glass, *An Adventure in Constructive Finance*, pp. 124-125; copyright 1927 by Doubleday & Company, Inc.

[47] *New York Times*, June 21, 1913.

tackled. Not an hour can I let it out of my mind. Everybody must be seen; every right means must be used to direct the thought and purpose of those who are to deal with it and of those who, outside of Washington, are to criticise it and form public opinion about it. It is not like the tariff, about which opinion has been definitely forming long years through."[48]

In sweltering heat on June 23, 1913, Wilson went a second time before a joint session to open the administration's campaign for currency and banking legislation. "It is absolutely imperative that we should give the business men of this country a banking and currency system by means of which they can make use of the freedom of enterprise and of individual initiative which we are about to bestow upon them," he began, in answer to friends and critics who had begged him to let Congress go home after completing work on the tariff bill. He snapped his jaws when he added, "We must act now, at whatever sacrifice to ourselves." Then, concluding, he pointed up the issues and explained his general objectives:

"The principles upon which we should act are also clear. . . . We must have a currency, not rigid as now, but readily, elastically responsive to sound credit, the expanding and contracting credits of everyday transactions, the normal ebb and flow of personal and corporate dealings. Our banking laws must mobilize reserves; must not permit the concentration anywhere in a few hands of the monetary resources of the country or their use for speculative purposes in such volume as to hinder or impede or stand in the way of other more legitimate, more fruitful uses. And the control of the system of banking and of issue which our new laws are to set up must be public, not private, must be vested in the Government itself, so that the banks may be the instruments, not the masters, of business and of individual enterprise and initiative. . . . I have come to you, as the head of the Government and the responsible leader of the party in power, to urge action, now while there is time to serve the country deliberately and as we should, in a clear air of common counsel."[49]

It required a certain audacity for the President thus calmly to outline the task ahead, for the spokesmen of conservative opinion and of the banking community had already begun a campaign of violent proportions against the Federal Reserve bill by the time he spoke. It is difficult

[48] W. W. to Mary A. Hulbert, June 22, 1913, printed in R. S. Baker, *Woodrow Wilson*, IV, 170.
[49] R. S. Baker and W. E. Dodd (eds.), *The New Democracy*, I, 37-40.

for Americans of a later generation, accustomed to virtually total public control over banks, the security markets, and the money supply, to understand the causes of the conservative alarm. Much of the fear arose from sheer panic or fancied shortcomings of the measure, to be sure; but it was inevitable that a large body of Americans, reared as they had been on classical economic assumptions, should have reacted as they did.

Reforming Our Currency
Ireland in the Columbus *Dispatch*

The root of the conservative fear was the conviction that the Federal Reserve bill did in fact represent a radical break in federal economic policy—in brief, a partial abandonment of *laissez faire* in the field of banking and the beginning, at least, of a new policy of governmental intervention in the most sensitive area of the capitalistic economy. Thus most conservative criticism ignored the measure's technical imperfections and went straight to the issue of control of the new banking system.

"The scheme of the so-called Glass-Owen currency bill," declared one banking journal in an editorial that summarized the bankers' fears, "is now fully exposed to public view, as a party measure, to establish, under the guise of a central control, a plan for the operation of regional banks, to be absolutely controlled by political appointees of Federal executive power. . . . It is a proposal for the creation of a vast engine of political domination over the great forces of profitable American industry and internal commerce of the country with the richest markets known in the world. . . . The fight is now for the protection of private rights and to be successful it must be waged to enlist public opinion against unwise legislation with tendencies to financial disaster to all the people."[50]

The conservative nonbanking press was, if anything, even more perturbed than were the editorial spokesmen of the banking community. "Bankers and business men will soon understand, even if they do not now understand, that a new idea underlies this banking and currency bill, the Oklahoma idea, the Nebraska idea," exclaimed the *New York Times*, manifesting a typical reaction. "It reflects the rooted dislike and distrust of banks and bankers that has been for many years a great moving force in the Democratic Party, notably in the Western and Far Western States. The measure goes to the very extreme in establishing absolute political control over the business of banking."[51]

However, it remained for the chief spokesman of Wall Street and special privilege to utter the most vituperative comment: "It is difficult to discuss with any degree of patience this preposterous offspring of ignorance and unreason, but it cannot be passed over with the contempt it deserves. . . . This provision for a Government currency and an official board to exercise absolute control over the most important of banking functions is covered all over with the slime of Bryanism."[52]

[50] *Banking Law Journal*, cited in the Minneapolis *Commercial West*, xxiv (September 27, 1913), 38. For other significant comments from banking journals, see Elmer H. Youngman, "Centralized Credit Control or Real Freedom of Credit—Which Shall We Have?" *Bankers Magazine*, lxxxvii (August 1913), 138-142; *Financial Age*, xxvii (June 28, 1913), 1197-1198; *ibid.*, xxviii (July 5, 12, and 26, August 2, September 13, 1913), 17, 56-57, 138, 177, 424; *Bankers Magazine*, lxxxvii (August and October 1913), 135, 370, 371-372, 388; *Financial World*, xxi (August 16, 1913), 1-2; *ibid.*, September 13, 1913, pp. 1, 3; San Francisco *Coast Banker*, cited in *Commercial West*, xxiv (September 6, 1913), 31.
[51] *New York Times*, June 21, 1913.   [52] New York *Sun*, June 21, 1913.

In spite of this furor, Wilson, Glass, and Owen worked confidently during late June of 1913 to prepare the Federal Reserve bill for introduction in the two houses. Wilson, for example, conferred with Speaker Champ Clark on June 24 about strategy in the House and with the members of the Senate banking committee on the following day. But the most important step was a last-minute conference at the White House on June 25 between Wilson, Glass, McAdoo, and Owen, on the one hand, and George M. Reynolds of Chicago, Festus J. Wade of St. Louis, Sol Wexler of New Orleans, and John Perrin of Los Angeles, representing the currency commission of the American Bankers' Association, on the other.

In response to the bankers' suggestions, the administration leaders made several vital changes in the Federal Reserve bill. One provided for a gradual retirement of the national bank notes in such a manner as to protect the banks' large investment in the 2 per cent bonds that supported the national bank currency. Another altered in an important way the Federal Reserve Board's control over the discount rates to be set by the regional reserve banks.[53] Finally, near the end of the meeting the bankers made their most urgent suggestion—a plea for official banker representation on the Federal Reserve Board. When they had finished, Wilson turned and said, "Will one of you gentlemen tell me in what civilized country of the earth there are important government boards of control on which private interests are represented? Which of you gentlemen thinks the railroads should select members of the Interstate Commerce Commission?"[54] There was a "painful silence," perhaps because the bankers knew that it was safer not to give an honest answer. The largest concession Wilson would make was a promise to approve the establishment of a Federal Advisory Council, consisting of representatives of the several regional banks, which should serve as a liaison between the reserve banks and the Federal Reserve Board.[55]

[53] The original Glass bill gave the Federal Reserve Board power "to establish each week, or as much oftener as required, a rate of discount which shall be mandatory upon each Federal reserve bank and for each class of paper." As introduced in the House after the conference of June 25, the Glass bill gave control over discount rates to the reserve banks, "subject to review and determination of the Federal Reserve Board." Carter Glass to Sol Wexler, July 3, 1913, Glass Papers, tells how Glass made this change.

[54] Carter Glass, *An Adventure in Constructive Finance*, p. 116; copyright 1927 by Doubleday & Company, Inc.

[55] This change was effected by an amendment adopted by the House banking committee on July 31, 1913.

Glass and Owen introduced the revised Federal Reserve bill simultaneously in the House and Senate on June 26, 1913.[56] In spite of the force of the conservative criticism, samples of which we have seen, and of signs of an organized banker opposition,[57] the administration could launch its campaign in Congress from a position of considerable strength. The administration leaders, including Bryan and McAdoo, had closed ranks, while the President seemingly had absolute control over the Democrats in Congress. Best of all, there were many signs that the majority, progressive opinion of the country was forming in strong support of the measure.[58]

At the very time that Wilson, Glass, and Owen were preparing the Federal Reserve bill for introduction, however, an entirely unexpected revolt was brewing behind the scenes. It was a rebellion by the leaders of the large southern and western agrarian faction in the House of Representatives—Robert L. Henry and Joe H. Eagle of Texas, Otis T. Wingo of Arkansas, J. Willard Ragsdale of South Carolina, and George H. Neeley of Kansas—who were up in arms against various aspects of the Federal Reserve bill.[59]

Inheritors of the Populistic hatred of Wall Street and old followers of Bryan, these agrarian radicals demanded that the administration first destroy the vast complex of interlocking financial and corporate directorates, popularly known as the "Money Trust," before it set out to reform and strengthen the banking system. To give point to this demand, Representative Henry, leader of the agrarian group,[60] intro-

[56] H. P. Willis, *The Federal Reserve System*, pp. 1595-1613, reprints this version of the bill. The *New York Times*, June 27, 1913, gives a detailed analysis and points up the changes made during the conferences that preceded the introduction of the measure.

[57] The bankers who had conferred with Wilson and Glass on June 25, 1913, for example, gave notice soon after the meeting that they were not satisfied with the concessions that the administration leaders had made. See Sol Wexler and G. M. Reynolds to C. Glass, June 30, 1913, Glass Papers.

[58] e.g., *Harper's Weekly*, LVII (June 28, 1913), 3; the organ of the National Citizens' League, *Banking Reform*, II (July 1, 1913), 1-6; Springfield (Massachusetts) *Republican*, July 3, 1913; *Denver News, Philadelphia Public Ledger*, and New Orleans *Times-Democrat*, cited in *The Commoner*, XIII (July 4, 1913), 4; *The Outlook*, CIV (July 5, 1913), 490-491.

[59] For an extended discussion of this group, see Arthur S. Link, "The South and the New Freedom: An Interpretation," *American Scholar*, XX (Summer 1951), 314-324.

[60] "The Texan," Glass afterward wrote in describing Henry, "was an engaging talker and an exceedingly likable fellow; but he knew as much about banking and currency questions as a child about astronomy. He was not a vicious demagogue;

duced a bill on June 13, 1913, which, if enacted, would have postponed action on the Federal Reserve bill and launched a new investigation looking toward destruction of the "Money Trust."[61] He had, incidentally, strong support from Untermyer and Brandeis. "The beneficent effect of the best conceivable currency bill will be relatively slight," Brandeis warned, for example, "unless we are able to curb the money trust, and to remove the uneasiness among business men due to its power."[62]

The agrarians, moreover, denounced the basic objectives of the Federal Reserve bill. Because that measure provided for private control of the regional banks, they charged that it would create "an oligarchy of boundless wealth forced into controlling the politics of the Nation in order to protect its own proper interests as well also as to govern the financial destiny of the Nation"[63]—a "perfectly organized Financial Trust" operating under governmental protection.[64] Imbued with the Jacksonian hostility to any form of bank-made money, they further charged that the Federal Reserve bill's provision for asset currency betrayed the Democratic demand for a money supply controlled exclusively by Congress. "The supply of money in the United States," one radical declared, "should, at any given time, be a fixed and suitable supply, so that each citizen in the Nation, whether debtor or creditor and whatever his business, may have equal knowledge as to the outstanding volume and quality of money with every other citizen of the Nation."[65]

The agrarians complained most bitterly, however, because the Glass bill made no explicit provision for agricultural credit and, they charged, was designed for the exclusive benefit of moneylenders and businessmen. In voicing this grievance they spoke for the great majority of southern and western farmers, whose chief objective since the days of the agrarian revolt had been to find a way to strike off the shackles of debt and near-peonage. One agrarian spokesman observed, while

---

but a very insinuating one." *An Adventure in Constructive Finance*, pp. 133-134; copyright 1927 by Doubleday & Company, Inc.

[61] *New York Times*, June 15, 1913.

[62] L. D. Brandeis to W. W., June 14, 1913, Wilson Papers.

[63] "Congressman Eagle Analyzes and Opposes the Glass Banking and Currency Bill," MS. news release dated July 31, 1913, copy in the Glass Papers.

[64] Harry B. Fish, secretary-treasurer of the People's Money League, to C. Glass, June 22, 1913, *ibid.*

[65] "Congressman Eagle Analyzes and Opposes the Glass Banking and Currency Bill," Glass Papers.

lamenting the absence in the Federal Reserve bill of any provision for agricultural credit, "To me it is astounding that, in preparing and presenting such a legislative act, its patrons, as well as the public, should have apparently overlooked the vital fact that the banking necessities of one-third of our population have been disregarded and that no provision has been made . . . for the peculiar class of banking needed by the agricultural classes."[66]

The serious dimensions of the radical revolt became apparent soon after the Democratic members of the House banking and currency committee began consideration of the Federal Reserve bill on July 8, 1913. The leaders of the administration and radical factions maneuvered for position amid rumors of a bolt by the agrarian members. Then, on July 23, 1913, the radical majority took control by adopting, over Glass's angry protests, an amendment offered by Representative Wingo to prohibit interlocking directorates among member banks in the Federal Reserve System.[67]

The really dangerous threat to the administration's control came the following day, when Representative Ragsdale offered a series of amendments drawn by Representative Henry. "The bill as now written," Henry explained, "is wholly in the interest of the creditor classes, the banking fraternity, and the commercial world, without proper provision for the debtor classes and those who toil, produce, and sustain the country." In order "to break the Wall Street control of money," the Henry amendments provided, first, for a broadening of the membership of the Federal Reserve Board to include representatives of agriculture and "industrial labor" and former Presidents of the United States, and, second, for the issuance by the Federal Reserve Board of some $700,000,000 in "United States notes" to various classes of borrowers, but particularly to the states for public works and to the farmers, in order to support agricultural prices at a certain level.[68]

[66] Charles Hall Davis, address before the South Carolina Bankers' Association, July 12, 1913, printed in *Report of the Proceedings of the Thirteenth Annual Convention of the South Carolina Bankers' Association*, p. 114.

[67] *New York Times*, July 24, 1913.

[68] The Henry amendments provided that this currency, which, incidentally, would take the place of Federal Reserve notes, should be divided into three classes, as follows: Class A, consisting of $300,000,000 of "commercial currency," to be issued by the Federal Reserve Board for the use of the business world; Class B, consisting of $200,000,000 of "industrial currency," to be issued by the Board to "States and Territories upon legally authorized State or Territorial bonds and county and municipal bonds when legally executed and indorsed by the State or Territory"; and Class C, consisting of $200,000,000 of "agricultural currency," to be issued by the Board to the reserve

At this point, it was evident that Glass had momentarily lost control of the Democrats on the banking committee and that the prospects for the Federal Reserve bill were growing dimmer every day. It was obvious, furthermore, that the committee's approval of such a measure as the radicals desired could only mean the complete wrecking of all hopes for banking legislation of any kind, for the great mass of conservative and middle-class opinion regarded the Henry plan as being little better than the product of the wildest kind of Populism. "The Wingo-Ragsdale-Henry-Pujo notions about currency are quite beyond the pale of discussion," the *New York Times* observed, for example. ". . . But it is just as well that these uncouth ideas should come to the surface. They are like the impurities in the blood—the cutaneous eruption may be unsightly, but the patient is the better for getting rid of his peccant humors."[69]

It was a perilous situation, but the President moved quickly to regain control. He called Henry and Wingo to the White House on July 24 and 25, 1913, and conceded one of their demands, by promising to include a provision forbidding interlocking bank directorates in the administration's forthcoming antitrust bill.[70] He appealed to his friend, Newton D. Baker, to bring pressure to bear upon Representative Robert J. Bulkley of Cleveland, who had been voting with the radicals in the committee, "to support the administration heartily in its present bill."[71] By thus pleading, promising, and perhaps also threatening, Wilson cleared the air and restored a measure of unity. On July 28, 1913, the Democratic members of the banking committee agreed to report the Glass bill to the House Democratic caucus on August 11; four days later they rejected Wingo's amendment to forbid interlocking directorates and Henry's plan for "agricultural currency"; finally, on August 5, 1913, they approved the Federal Reserve bill by a vote of eleven to three.[72]

---

banks for direct lending to cotton, corn, and wheat farmers, who might borrow one half the value of their staple (at a guaranteed price of at least 15 cents a pound for cotton, 60 cents a bushel for corn, and $1 a bushel for wheat) against warehouse receipts. For an analysis of the Henry amendments, see the *New York Times*, July 25, 1913; New York *World*, July 25, 1913; and Carter Glass, *An Adventure in Constructive Finance*, pp. 134-136.

[69] *New York Times*, July 26, 1913. For additional comment, see the *Springfield* (Massachusetts) *Republican*, August 19, 1913; *Financial Age*, xxviii (August 23, 1913), 297; and *Bankers' Magazine*, lxxxvii (September 1913), 234.

[70] New York *World*, July 25 and 26, 1913.

[71] W. W. to N. D. Baker, July 24, 1913, Wilson Papers.

[72] *New York Times*, July 29, August 2 and 6, 1913.

Therefore, the radicals were apparently thoroughly beaten by the time the House Democratic caucus met on August 11, 1913, to consider the Federal Reserve bill. But there were many signs of agrarian discontent as general debate proceeded in the caucus; and on August 14 Glass and the Democratic majority leader, Underwood, accepted a compromise offered by Ragsdale and approved by Bryan. Endorsed officially by the caucus on August 25, it made agricultural paper, that is, bills of exchange based on warehouse receipts, specifically eligible for rediscount by the Federal Reserve banks.[73]

Even this important concession failed to appease the radicals. Henry renewed his attack on August 16 and 17, 1913, charging that the Federal Reserve bill fastened a "huge asset [currency] system upon the country" and therefore violated past Democratic platforms and Bryan's clear position on the money question.[74] Henry was joined by stanch regulars like Representatives Thomas W. Hardwick and Charles L. Barrett of Georgia and Thetus W. Sims of Tennessee, until it seemed that the caucus was on the verge of a general rebellion. At this critical point, Bryan intervened to save the bill. He issued a fervent defense of the measure on August 22, promising that the administration would deal with the problem of interlocking directorates in antitrust legislation, and calling upon his friends to "stand by the President and assist in securing the passage of this measure at the earliest possible moment."[75]

Bryan's stroke shattered the radical opposition, and the caucus debate proceeded smoothly until August 28, 1913, when the House Democrats, by a vote of 116 to nine, approved the Federal Reserve bill and made it a party measure, binding upon all Democrats. "I am proud, as every Democrat must be," the President declared, "of the way in which the committee and the caucus have accomplished a consistent piece of constructive work. . . . It must stimulate the country to see such evidences of harmony along with constructive purpose in a work of no small complexity and difficulty."[76]

[73] ibid., August 15 and 26, 1913. Representatives Henry and Claude Kitchin of North Carolina described the complicated maneuvers that preceded the adoption of this compromise amendment in R. L. Henry to C. Kitchin, August 21, 1915; and C. Kitchin to R. L. Henry, September 6, 1915, both in the Papers of Claude Kitchin, University of North Carolina Library; hereinafter cited as the Kitchin Papers.

[74] New York Times, August 18, 1913.

[75] W. J. Bryan to C. Glass, August 22, 1913, printed in the Boston Journal, August 23, 1913. Glass describes the scene in the caucus after he had finished reading Bryan's letter in An Adventure in Constructive Finance, pp. 139-140.

[76] ibid., p. 141.

Meanwhile, discussions among bankers, businessmen, and public leaders in all sections had begun in earnest during late June and were nearing their first climax by the time the House caucus completed debate on the Federal Reserve bill.

There were many signs of developing support among the mass of businessmen in the country at large. A survey of business opinion in eleven states west of the Missouri River, conducted by the Chamber of Commerce of the United States from July 5 to July 27, 1913, for example, revealed an overwhelming approval of the banking bill, especially among the small businessmen.[77] A typical southern business opinion was expressed by the publisher of the Charlotte, North Carolina, *Daily Observer*, the leading organ of the manufacturing interests of the Carolinas. "I regard the proposed new banking bill with the utmost favor," he wrote. "If it is enacted, I think it will distribute the money over the whole United States much more equally than it has ever been before. . . . Heretofore when times got a little tight, every banker and every cotton mill man would start to New York to arrange to borrow money or rediscount paper. They were never fully accommodated, and the tightness was doubled by the failure. Under the new system no banker will need to go to New York for rediscounting. The member banks in the reserve district all join together to issue asset money and the bankers will do their own rediscounting on the basis of credits and assets."[78]

In general, moreover, progressive opinion had approved the changes effected during the summer's deliberations to strengthen the Federal Reserve bill and was united in demanding speedy approval by the House and Senate. "There is not the slightest probability that the Democratic party could enact a better, sounder currency law next winter and spring, or a year from next winter and spring, than it could this autumn," declared a leading eastern editor.[79] "The issue," the spokesman of Roosevelt's Progressive party agreed, "is between private regulation

[77] Harry A. Wheeler, president of the Chamber of Commerce of the United States, to C. Glass, August 8, 1913, Glass Papers. "The more I go about the country and discuss the administration bill with merchants and bankers," Wheeler wrote soon afterward, "the more thoroughly convinced I am that the merchants of the country deeply desire the legislation." H. A. Wheeler to J. L. Laughlin, August 19, 1913, original in the Wilson Papers.

[78] D. A. Tompkins to J. P. Lucas, July 7, 1913, Tompkins Papers. Indeed, Tompkins was willing to condone governmental control in order to obtain the benefits of a regional reserve system. See D. A. Tompkins to T. F. Kluttz, Jr., June 26, 1913, *ibid.*; and D. A. Tompkins to W. H. Wood, June 30, 1913, *ibid.*

[79] *Springfield* (Massachusetts) *Republican*, August 7, 1913.

by a group of men elected in a directors' room, and public regulation by a group of men in regard to whose choice the entire country has a voice after the fullest publicity and discussion."[80]

Even more significant, however, was the way in which banking opinion had matured during a frenzy of discussions by state, regional, and national banking groups between June and September of 1913. By the end of August the lines were already clearly drawn. A minority of bankers, mainly in the South and Middle West, favored the Federal Reserve bill either outright or with minor amendments. Several leading bankers of Chicago, including David R. Forgan and E. D. Hulbert, emphatically endorsed the measure on June 21, 1913.[81] On June 24 the officers of the banks in the Atlanta Clearing House Association approved the "spirit and purpose" of the banking bill;[82] and during the next two and a half months there were many evidences of undercurrents of support among the so-called country bankers. "I believe the country bankers regard the bill as sound as it stands and that they want this too long delayed reform accomplished at the special session," wrote the secretary of the Alabama Bankers' Association, for example.[83] "A majority of the bankers, business men and citizens of Kansas are well pleased with the manner in which you and Congress are handling the Currency Bill," the president of the Kansas State Bankers' Association assured the President.[84]

[80] *The Outlook*, CIV (August 9, 1913), 796. See also the New York *Nation*, XCVII (August 14 and September 4, 1913), 136-137, 202; and *Harper's Weekly*, LVIII (August 16, 1913), 4.

[81] *New York Times*, June 22, 1913; and *Commercial West*, XXIII (June 28, 1913), 12-13.

[82] *New York Times*, June 25, 1913.

[83] McLane Tilton, Jr., to C. Glass, September 3, 1913, Glass Papers.

[84] William MacFerran to W. W., September 4, 1913, Wilson Papers. For other evidences of southern and midwestern support of the Federal Reserve bill, see David R. Francis of St. Louis to W. W., June 24, 1913; F. W. Foote of Hattiesburg, Mississippi, to W. W., June 26, 1913; and Hugh MacRae of Wilmington, North Carolina, to W. W., June 30, 1913, all in *ibid.*; W. G. McAdoo to W. W., July 2, 1913, *ibid.*; John Skelton Williams to W. W., August 23, 1913, *ibid.*, relating opinions of bankers in North Carolina, Maryland, and Tennessee; and T. C. Dunn to E. M. House, September 18, 1913, House Papers.

It was significant, also, that several regional and state associations of bankers revealed their approval of the basic features of the Federal Reserve bill by suggesting only minor technical amendments. See the reports of the deliberations of a committee representing the state bankers' associations of Minnesota, North Dakota, Montana, Iowa, and Wisconsin, which met in Minneapolis on August 8, 1913, in *Commercial West*, XXIV (August 16, 1913), 11; of the conference of the country national bankers of Wisconsin, which met at Milwaukee on September 3, 1913, in *ibid.*, September 13,

And yet the evidence was overwhelming that the great majority of bankers, whether from Wall Street or Main Street or from the North or the South, regarded the Federal Reserve bill with repugnance ranging from merely strong to violent hostility.[85] From bankers all over the country came denunciations and cries that calamity impended. "The bill makes a political bank as dangerous as the old United States Bank of Jackson's time," protested an Atlanta banker.[86] "It is one of the traditions of the Anglo-Saxon race and in accordance with the spirit of true Americanism that capital must be managed by those who supply it, and furthermore, that the investor must be free to decide whether or not he shall make investments," George M. Reynolds, president of the Continental Commercial National Bank of Chicago proclaimed before the Minnesota Bankers' Association.[87] "It is a communistic idea that is sought to be written into the financial statutes of the country," snorted a banker in San Antonio.[88] "I need not tell you how mortified I am," Paul M. Warburg said, in a letter to Colonel House, "that after all your and my trouble there are still in the Glass-Owen bill issue of notes by the government, *12* reserve banks, and practically management by the government. If such a bill passes, history will write President Wilson as a complete failure and Bryan will once more have ruined the chances of the Democratic party."[89] And thus it went all over the country during the summer of 1913, as the protests swelled into a mighty chorus.[90]

1913, p. 18; of the Kentucky Bankers' Association, which met at Louisville on September 18 and 19, 1913, in *Financial Age*, xxvii (September 27, 1913), 517; of the poll of the country bankers of Missouri, in *ibid.*, p. 510; and of a conference of Illinois country bankers, which met in Springfield on September 20, 1913, in *Commercial West*, xxiv (September 27, 1913), 33.

[85] On this point, see especially "American Banking and Currency Policy," London *Economist*, lxxvii (August 30, 1913), 422-423.

[86] *Commercial West*, xxiii (June 28, 1913), 11.

[87] *ibid.*, xxiv (July 19, 1913), 48.

[88] *Texas Bankers Record*, iii (September 1913), 18.

[89] P. M. Warburg to E. M. House, July 22, 1913, House Papers. Warburg contributed two significant items to the propaganda against the Federal Reserve bill: first, a lengthy pamphlet, *The Owen-Glass Bill, Some Criticisms and Suggestions*, and, second, a widely read article, "The Owen-Glass Bill as Submitted to the Democratic Caucus," *North American Review*, cxcviii (October 1913), 527-555.

[90] For additional evidence of opposition from bankers, see the *New York Times*, June 21 and 28 and July 19, 1913; T. W. McCoy of Vicksburg, Mississippi, to C. Glass, August 13, 1913, Glass Papers; James B. Forgan, president of the First National Bank of Chicago, cited in the *New York Times*, June 24, 1913; report of a conference of western bankers at Omaha, July 17 and 18, 1913, in *Commercial West*, xxiv (August 2,

The bankers' opposition came to a clear focus just at the time that the House Democratic caucus was nearing the completion of its consideration of the Federal Reserve bill. Meeting in Chicago with the currency commission of the American Bankers' Association on August 22 and 23, 1913, the presidents of forty-seven state bankers' associations and the heads of the 191 clearinghouse associations of the country outlined what were virtually the entire banking community's demands and the price of its support for the glass bill. They suggested a number of technical changes, as if to prove what they said about wanting to meet the administration halfway. But their important recommendations revealed their utter refusal to accept any legislation that did not involve the administration's unconditional surrender and a return to the Aldrich plan, slightly amended.[91]

The Chicago conference marked a decisive turning point in the history of the Federal Reserve bill. Up to this time, Wilson, McAdoo, and Glass had believed that most of the bankers' opposition was a play for position and that the leaders of the banking community would, in the showdown, abandon their extreme stand and work responsibly for the administration's plan. The Chicago resolutions, on the other hand, revealed the wide gulf separating the demands of the bankers and the purposes of the Democratic leaders. In fact, the President and his ad-

---

1913), 20-21, and *New York Times*, July 19, 1913; report of a conference of Ohio bankers at Columbus, July 23, 1913, in *Rand-McNally's Bankers' Monthly*, xxx (October 1913), 56; Charles G. Dawes, president of the Central Trust Company of Chicago, statement printed in *Financial Age*, xxviii (August 2, 1913), 180-181; report of resolutions adopted by the Washington State Bankers' Association, *Journal of the American Bankers Association*, vi (September 1913), 199, and *Commercial West*, xxiv (August 23, 1913), 36; statement prepared by a committee of the St. Louis Clearing House Association, in *Financial Age*, xxviii (August 9, 1913), 227; and a report of a meeting of the Illinois Bankers' Association, in *ibid.*, October 4, 1913, pp. 565-566.

[91] The Chicago conference urged, among other things, the establishment of one central federal reserve bank and, if that were not possible, limiting the number of regional reserve banks to five; that membership in the Federal Reserve System be made voluntary for national banks; that the membership of the Federal Reserve Board include three representatives elected by member banks; that the Federal Reserve Board be deprived of authority to compel one Federal Reserve bank to rediscount the paper of another Federal Reserve bank; and that the Federal Reserve banks, not the United States Treasury, issue Federal Reserve currency and be exclusively liable for its redemption.

There is a full report of the Chicago conference in the *Journal of the American Bankers Association*, vi (September 1913), 133-144; but see also the New York *World*, August 23, 1913; *New York Times*, August 24, 1913; and New York *Nation*, xcvii (August 28, 1913), 180.

visers regarded the Chicago manifesto as nothing less than a patent effort by the great banking interests to intimidate the mass of bankers and threaten the government.[92] Speaking to reporters on August 25, 1913, Wilson declared that the Chicago conference did not speak for the rank and file of bankers and that he wanted no help from the large bankers on hostile terms.[93]

Nothing now remained for the administration to do but to proceed in the face of the bankers' opposition and to hope that the weight of public opinion would neutralize it. Glass set the formal legislative machinery in motion, by referring the banking bill to the full membership of the House banking and currency committee in late August 1913. Now in undisputed control of the Democratic steamroller, he won formal committee approval on September 4, 1913,[94] reported the revised banking bill to the House on September 9,[95] and opened general debate the following day.[96]

The House proceeded rapidly under a strict rule that denied the Republicans any opportunity for obstruction. Near the end of the debates, however, the Republican managers tried to kindle old Democratic intraparty antagonisms by proposing an amendment specifically endorsing the gold standard. But Bryan wanted no revival of the free silver issue and advised his followers to vote for the amendment. It passed on September 18, 1913, by a vote of 299 to sixty-eight. A few hours later the House approved the Federal Reserve bill by a vote of 287 to eighty-five. Only three Democrats, all of them southern radicals, opposed the measure, while twenty-three Republicans and ten Progressives, mainly from the Middle West and the Plains states, supported it. It was an emphatic mandate for prompt approval by the upper house.[97]

By mid-September, however, the situation in the Senate was so con-

[92] W. G. McAdoo to E. M. House, August 27, 1913, House Papers.

[93] *New York Times*, August 26, 1913. For the bankers' replies, see *Financial Age*, xxvIII (August 30, 1913), 344; and *New York Times*, August 30 and September 1, 1913.

[94] By a vote of eleven to one. The one negative vote was cast by James F. Burke, Republican, of Pennsylvania. The other six Republican members of the committee were evenly divided and agreed to refrain from voting.

[95] The committee's report, *House Report 69*, 63d Cong., 1st sess., which explains the Federal Reserve bill as it was reported to the lower house, is printed in H. P. Willis, *The Federal Reserve System*, pp. 305-358.

[96] For Glass's speech, see *Congressional Record*, 63d Cong., 1st sess., pp. 4642-4651.

[97] *ibid.*, p. 5129. H. P. Willis, *The Federal Reserve System*, pp. 1614-1637, prints the Federal Reserve bill as it passed the House.

fused that it was impossible to predict the outcome of the battle. That most of the Senate Democrats were eager to close ranks behind the President was revealed when the Senate Democratic caucus, on August 14, 1913, voted to proceed with banking reform after the enactment of the tariff bill.[98] The trouble was that the President's influence was weakest where he needed support most vitally—in the Senate banking and currency committee. Only four of the seven Democratic members—Chairman Owen, Atlee Pomerene of Ohio, John F. Shafroth of Colorado, and Henry F. Hollis of New Hampshire—could be called administration men. For varying reasons, the other three Democratic members—Gilbert M. Hitchcock of Nebraska, James A. O'Gorman of New York, and James A. Reed of Missouri—might welcome an opportunity to delay or prevent altogether favorable committee action on the Federal Reserve bill. It was ironical that seniority and fortuitous organization had given the power of life or death over the administration's most important measure to the President's bitterest antagonists among the Democratic senators.[99]

The strategy of the three insurgents became clear when they combined with the Republican minority on the banking committee to conduct a series of leisurely hearings on the Glass bill and virtually encouraged the leading bankers to renew their assaults against the measure. As the hearings ground on through September and most of October and Hitchcock, O'Gorman, and Reed grew openly boastful in their

[98] *New York Times*, August 15, 1913.

[99] Publisher of the *Omaha World-Herald*, Senator Hitchcock was the leader of the conservative, wet, anti-Bryan faction in Nebraska. The fact that Bryan supported the Federal Reserve bill would have been sufficient reason for Hitchcock to oppose it. In addition, he had apparently sincere reservations about the measure and was at odds with the President, because Wilson had insisted that he share the Nebraska patronage with Bryan.

Senator O'Gorman was sulking during this period for a number of reasons. He had a strong sense of senatorial prerogative, bitterly resented Wilson's highhanded manner with Congress, and was probably eager to teach the President a lesson in the separation of powers. More important, O'Gorman was friendly with the Tammany organization and resented the President's support of the anti-Tammany Democrats in their campaign to drive the machine from power in New York City.

Senator Reed was a congenital maverick and a cunning demagogue who enjoyed irresponsible opposition. Moreover, he was at odds with the administration because the President had refused to appoint his candidates as postmasters in St. Louis and Kansas City.

For an explanation of Hitchcock's, O'Gorman's, and Reed's opposition, see Charles Willis Thompson, in the *New York Times Magazine*, November 16, 1913; and George Creel, "Four-Flush Radicals. I. Reed of Missouri," *Harper's Weekly*, LIX (August 8, 1914), 124-126.

obstruction, the leading bankers intensified their own campaign against the Federal Reserve bill. It culminated in early October, when some 2,000 delegates to the annual convention of the American Bankers' Association met in Boston and adopted resolutions approving the Chicago manifesto and denouncing the banking measure as socialistic and confiscatory. "We are facing," declared Arthur M. Reynolds of Des Moines, acting president of the Association, "proposed legislation which I can hardly regard as less than an invasion of the liberty of the citizen in the control of his own property by putting under Government management enormous individual investments and a branch of the country's business which should be left to individual effort. . . . It is unjust and un-American."[100]

To Wilson, the situation was intolerable, and there must have been many times when he had to restrain the impulse to denounce the great bankers publicly for what he called their conspiracy to "poison the public mind against the currency bill";[101] Hitchcock, O'Gorman, and Reed, for their obstruction; and the Senate as well, for not forcing the banking committee to bring in some report on the Glass bill.

"The struggle goes on down here without intermission," he wrote in frustration, for example, one day in late September. "Why it should *be* a struggle, it is hard (cynicism put on one side) to say. Why *should* public men, senators of the United States, have to be led and stimulated to what all the country knows to be their duty! Why should they see less clearly, apparently, than anyone else what the straight path of service is! To whom are they listening? Certainly not to the voice of the people, when they quibble and twist and hesitate. . . . Therefore it *is* a struggle and must be accepted as such. A man of my temperament and my limitations will certainly wear himself out in it; but that is a small matter; the danger is that he may lose his patience and suffer the weakness of exasperation."[102]

He "suffered" that weakness many times in private during the next three months. To cite one example out of many, there was the time when the senators postponed the final vote on the Federal Reserve bill for a few hours. "It irritated him to think they would postpone it so long when there was no need for it," House recorded. "He spoke of

[100] *New York Times*, October 9, 1913; also the *Journal of the American Bankers Association*, VI (November 1913), 327-328.

[101] W. W. to D. V. Stephens, October 3, 1913, Wilson Papers.

[102] W. W. to Mary A. Hulbert, September 28, 1913, printed in R. S. Baker, *Woodrow Wilson*, IV, 184.

them as being a lot of old women, and one of them was so feminine he considered it immodest for him to wear trousers."[103]

For a short time the President acted with unaccustomed restraint in his relentless drive to force the insurgents into line and to break the impasse in the Senate banking committee. Unable to control the committee, he called the members of the Senate Democratic steering committee to the White House on September 10, 1913, and pleaded for prompt action.[104] Three weeks later he hinted that he would stump the country, and particularly New York, Missouri, and Nebraska, if the three Democratic rebels did not cooperate.[105] "For what do we wait?" he cried out on October 3, 1913. "Why should we wait to crown ourselves with consummate honor? Are we so self-denying that we do not wish to complete our success?"[106]

But the insurgents refused to yield, and Wilson's patience was worn dangerously thin. Calling Senate Democratic leaders to the White House on October 7, 1913, he intimated that he planned to denounce the banking lobby, which he said was trying to split the Democratic party and planned to precipitate a panic, if that were necessary to defeat the Federal Reserve bill.[107] Moreover, he demanded that the Senate Democratic caucus discipline the rebels on the banking committee, reaffirmed his personal leadership of the party, and allegedly added, "The Democrat who will not support me is not a Democrat. He is a rebel."[108] Two days later he told reporters that the American Bankers'

[103] House Diary, December 22, 1913. Unfortunately, House did not identify the senator who should have worn a dress. Perhaps Wilson meant J. Hamilton Lewis of Illinois, who enjoyed a wide reputation for sartorial fastidiousness.

[104] *New York Times*, September 11, 1913; New York *World*, September 11, 1913.

[105] *New York Times*, October 3, 1913.

[106] *ibid.*, October 4, 1913.

[107] By this time Wilson was convinced that the leading bankers had conspired in a sinister way to accomplish the defeat of banking reform. "I think that if you saw as clearly as I do the dangers which we are running in the delay," he wrote to one senator, for example, "you would share some of my eager desire to have the bill pressed forward to report and passage. Things are going on in the banking world which are evidently based upon a desire to make the members of the two houses uneasy in the presence of the bankers' power, and it is possible that with expanding business and contracting credits a panic may be brought on while we wait." W. W. to John Sharp Williams, October 11, 1913, Wilson Papers; also W. W. to Ralph Pulitzer, October 9, 1913, *ibid.*

[108] New York *World*, October 8, 1913; *Washington Post*, October 8, 1913. Following this conference, a number of Democratic senators affirmed support of the banking bill and seconded Wilson's demand for caucus action. The three rebels, however, were so obviously angered by Wilson's alleged charge of party disloyalty that Wilson issued a hasty denial. "I am quoted in your issue of this morning," he wrote to the editor of the *Washington Post* on October 8, 1913, "as saying that any one who does

Association would not dominate the Government of the United States while he was the President![109]

When Hitchcock, O'Gorman, and Reed still persisted in preventing a favorable report on the Federal Reserve bill by the banking committee, Wilson suddenly shifted tactics. Swallowing his pride, he invited the three rebels to the White House on October 16, 1913. The President must have exercised considerable restraint, for the newspapers told of pleasant conferences in which Wilson had agreed that the banking bill might have to be amended.[110]

A few days later, moreover, he continued his little campaign of conciliation by making a public gesture. "Last week you called upon me and . . . asked me what I thought the prospects were with regard to the banking and currency bill in the Senate," Wilson wrote to the House majority leader, Underwood, in a letter intended for publication. "As I then promised you, I have had conferences with members of the Senate Committee on Banking and Currency, both Democrats and Republicans. As a result of those conferences, I feel confident that a report on the bill may be expected not later than the first week in November. Most of the members of the committee with whom I have conferred have shown themselves keenly aware of the disadvantage to the country of any unnecessary delay. . . . I do not believe that there will be any attempt to delay its passage by dilatory tactics. Senators on both sides realize that the business of the country awaits this legislation, impatient of being kept in suspense, and display a most public spirited desire to dispose of it promptly. The passage of the bill is assured."[111]

Just when it seemed that the President might come to terms with O'Gorman and Reed and persuade some of the Republican members to join the Democrats on the Senate banking committee in approving the Federal Reserve bill,[112] there occurred a startling new development,

---

not support me is no Democrat, but a rebel. Of course I never said any such thing. It is contrary both to my thought and to my character, and I must ask that you give a very prominent place in your issue of to-morrow to this denial." Letter published in the *New York Times*, October 9, 1913.

[109] New York *World*, October 10, 1913.

[110] *New York Times*, October 17, 1913.

[111] W. W. to O. W. Underwood, October 20, 1913, Wilson Papers, printed in the *New York Times*, October 21, 1913.

[112] See H. F. Hollis to W. W., two letters, October 17, 1913; W. W. to B. F. Shively, October 20, 1913; W. W. to J. A. O'Gorman, October 21, 1913; and W. W. to W. G. McAdoo, October 21, 1913, all in the Wilson Papers.

Whipt

Tuthill in the St. Louis *Star*

one that threatened to wreck all hopes for banking legislation. On October 23, 1913, Frank A. Vanderlip, president of the National City Bank of New York, appeared before the committee and presented a banking and currency plan, which he had prepared at the request of Senators Hitchcock, O'Gorman, Reed, and Joseph H. Bristow of Kansas, following his first appearance before the committee on October 8 and 9.

The Vanderlip plan provided for the establishment of a Federal Reserve Bank of the United States with a capital of $100,000,000—subscribed by the public, the government, and the national banks—and twelve branches, which would hold the member banks' reserves, perform central banking functions, and issue currency against commercial assets and a 50 per cent gold reserve. Control of the central bank and its branches would be vested exclusively in the hands of the federal government.[113]

Almost immediately the opponents of the Federal Reserve bill in the Senate combined in support of the Vanderlip plan. So-called radicals like Reed and Bristow and nearly all the insurgent Republican senators liked the thoroughgoing measure of public control that it provided. Conservatives like Hitchcock and Senator John W. Weeks of Massachusetts approved because it provided for the creation of a central bank and required national banks to subscribe only to that portion of the Reserve Bank's capital stock not taken by the public or by the government. Within twenty-four hours after Vanderlip proposed his plan, eight of the twelve members of the banking committee had come out in support of it; and one of the President's loyal friends on the committee, Pomerene of Ohio, was reported ready to join the majority.[114]

To make the situation even more discouraging for the President, Senator Reed issued a further blast at the Federal Reserve bill, charging that it was written by a representative of Wall Street, H. Parker Willis, in order to give control of the country's banking resources to the great bankers,[115] while Senator Bristow threatened to fight all winter to prevent the consummation of such designs. Told that Wilson still supported the Federal Reserve bill, Bristow replied, "Does that mean that the President favors a privately owned and privately controlled bank rather than one owned by the people? I know that whatever anybody else's attitude may be, I am for the principles detailed on our suggestion by Mr. Vanderlip. This plan is much more to be desired than the pending bill, which is only the Aldrich bill in disguise. I am in favor of a people's bank rather than the privately owned regional banks of the bill passed by the House."[116]

Convinced that Vanderlip had meant to divert attention from the Federal Reserve bill and to prevent any banking legislation at all,[117]

[113] For details of the Vanderlip plan, see the *New York Times*, October 24, 1913; and F. A. Vanderlip, "How to Amend the Currency Bill," *North American Review*, cxcviii (November 1913), 698-707.

[114] *New York Times*, October 24 and 25, 1913.

[115] *New York World*, October 26, 1913. For Glass's reply, see the *New York Times*, November 10, 1913.

[116] *New York World*, October 25, 1913.

[117] Carter Glass voiced this conviction in a public statement on October 24, 1913, but there is no evidence to controvert Vanderlip's own explanation, namely, that he had prepared his plan because Hitchcock, Reed, O'Gorman, and Bristow asked him

Wilson reacted with undisguised asperity to this new turn of events. "When inquiries were made at the White House as to what the President's attitude was toward the proposals made by Mr. Vanderlip . . . ," he declared in a formal statement on October 24, 1913, "it was stated with the expected emphasis, that of course the President would not recede in any respect from the position he had already so clearly taken and which the whole country understands. He has warmly and unqualifiedly indorsed all the main features of the Glass-Owen bill."[118]

When Vanderlip and two other New York bankers, Henry P. Davison and Benjamin Strong, asked for an opportunity to come to the White House to explain the Vanderlip plan, moreover, Wilson did not attempt to conceal his anger. "I am at a loss to understand how you can have come to think of the bank plan which you proposed to the Senate Committee on Banking and Currency yesterday as 'being along the lines of my own thought,'" he wrote to Vanderlip. "It is so far from being along the lines of my thought in this matter that it would be quite useless for me to discuss it with you and Mr. Davison and Mr. Strong. I could in no circumstances accept or recommend it."[119] Finally, the President called the Senate Democratic leaders to the White House on October 24, 1913, and told them testily that he did not propose to have the national monetary and banking systems dictated by any bankers.[120]

Wilson's sharp warning prevented the banking committee from favorably reporting a bill embodying the Vanderlip plan after it completed hearings and began detailed consideration of the Federal Reserve bill in late October 1913. Meanwhile, under the threat of Senate caucus action and administration retaliation, O'Gorman and Reed had gradually weakened in their opposition. Finally, on November 7, 1913, they joined the President's friends in clear-cut support of the main features of the Glass bill. Now the banking committee was evenly divided, and the six Democrats on the one side and Hitchcock and the five Republican senators on the other wrangled for another two weeks in a vain attempt to find an acceptable compromise. The upshot was an agreement to report two different bills to the Senate—first, an amended

to do so. For Glass's charge, see the New York *World*, October 25, 1913. For Vanderlip's reply and a further explanation, see the *New York Times*, October 28, 1913; and the House Diary, November 9, 1913.

[118] *New York Times*, October 25, 1913.

[119] W. W. to F. A. Vanderlip, October 24, 1913, Wilson Papers.

[120] New York *World*, October 25, 1913.

Federal Reserve bill, supported by the Democratic members, and, second, a bill embodying a modification of the Vanderlip plan, supported by Hitchcock and the Republicans.

The long impasse was broken, and events now began to move with startling speed. Meeting from November 26 through November 30, 1913, the Senate Democratic caucus adopted a few amendments, one of which provided for the creation of a fund to guarantee bank deposits, approved the Glass-Owen bill as revised by the six Democratic members of the banking committee, and made support of the measure binding upon all Democratic senators.[121] Formal Senate debate began on December 2, 1913, and reached a grueling stage four days later when the Democrats, with the help of the progressive Republicans, forced adoption of a rule requiring the Senate to meet thirteen hours a day until a final vote was taken.

The drive for Senate action gained its greatest momentum from public opinion, which by now demanded an end to the haggling. Progressive journals had kept up a steady supporting fire all during the autumn; more encouraging to the President was the growth of strong support for the Federal Reserve bill among organized business opinion and a growing minority of bankers.[122] The Republican leaders in the Senate, therefore, did not attempt to delay passage of the measure but rather sought to prove, as Taft later put it, "that everything that is good in the Currency Legislation came from the Aldrich Bill, and that which is wrong is due to a mixture of Bryanism."[123]

No longer in the Senate, but still the pre-eminent Old Guard spokesman on financial matters, Nelson W. Aldrich opened the conservative

[121] *New York Times*, November 27 and 29, December 1, 1913.

[122] The Merchants Association of New York, for example, endorsed the Glass-Owen bill with suggested amendments on October 9, 1913. *ibid.*, October 10, 1913. The Chamber of Commerce of the United States, representing 125,000 business firms, approved the measure by a vote of 306 to seventeen on October 14, 1913. New York *Journal of Commerce*, October 15, 1913. See Samuel Untermyer to J. P. Tumulty, November 16, 1913, Wilson Papers, for a report on midwestern business opinion.

For evidence of increasing banker support, see E. M. House to W. G. McAdoo, October 25, 1913, House Papers, and House Diary, November 7 and 9, 1913, reporting the opinions of the New York bankers, Otto Kahn, A. Barton Hepburn, and James Speyer. See also the statement of Jacob H. Schiff, head of Kuhn, Loeb & Company, in the *New York Times*, October 27, 1913; Julian S. Carr to W. W., November 15, 1913, Wilson Papers; Sol Wexler to C. Glass, December 12, 1913, Glass Papers, reporting that southern banking opinion was nearly unanimous in support of the Federal Reserve bill; and some one hundred telegrams from bankers in the Middle and Far West to C. Glass, dated December 13-18, 1913, *ibid.*, approving the measure.

[123] W. H. Taft to C. D. Hilles, February 25, 1914, Taft Papers.

Republican attack along these lines in an address before the Academy of Political Science in New York on October 15, 1913. He admitted that many provisions of the Federal Reserve bill were based upon "sound economic principles," but he then went on to charge that Bryan had ruined the measure by insisting upon governmental issue of Federal Reserve notes and public control of the Federal Reserve Board. "If the House bill should be enacted into law," Aldrich exclaimed, "Mr. Bryan will have achieved the purpose for which he has been contending for a decade. It would be difficult to find in history an occasion where a political dogma which had never found a permanent place in the tenets of the dominant [Democratic] party and which had been rejected by unanimous verdict of the civilized world could be successfully injected into a great legislative measure as a price for the support of a faction."[124]

Conservatives echoed Aldrich's animadversions many times during the course of the Senate debate, but the climax came on December 13, 1913, with a long and impassioned address by the old Roman of the G.O.P., Senator Elihu Root of New York. Speaking in behalf of his amendments to eliminate the provision for insurance of bank deposits, increase reserve requirements, and limit the issue of Federal Reserve notes, Root forecast unlimited inflation and ultimate national ruin if the Glass-Owen bill were adopted. "I say that this bill presents the financial heresy twice repudiated by the people of the United States," he declared with unaccustomed vehemence. "I say that the central reserve board appointed under this bill will have to represent that very heresy. . . . Ah, Mr. President, we are turning our faces away from the fundamental principle upon which we have come to our high estate. We are turning them weakly toward practices which history shows have invariably led to decadence, to degradation, and the downfall of nations. We are setting our steps now in the pathway which through the protection of a paternal government brought the mighty power of Rome to its fall; and we are doing it here without a mandate from the people of the United States."[125]

The Senate Democrats heeded Root's warning by adopting an amendment increasing the gold reserve behind Federal Reserve cur-

---

[124] *Proceedings of the Academy of Political Science*, IV (October 1913), 55. For the entire speech, see pp. 31-91.

[125] *Congressional Record*, 63d Cong., 2d sess., pp. 835-836; *New York Times*, December 14, 1913. For a perceptive comment, see the New York *Nation*, XCVII (December 18, 1913), 582-583.

rency from 33 1/3 per cent to 40 per cent.[126] Otherwise, however, they ignored his prophecy of perdition and drove steadily toward final approval of the revised Glass-Owen bill. The final critical test occurred on December 19, 1913, when a solid Democratic bloc, except for Senator Hitchcock, defeated Hitchcock's substitute, which embodied a modified version of the Vanderlip plan, by a vote of forty-four to forty-one.[127] A short time later, on the same day, the senators approved the Federal Reserve bill by a vote of fifty-four to thirty-four. No Democrat, not even Hitchcock, voted against the measure in the showdown, while two regular Republicans, three progressive Republicans, and one Progressive joined the majority on the final roll call.[128]

There now remained only the task of reconciling the differences between the House and Senate bills. Meeting on December 20, 1913, the Democrats on the conference committee excluded the Republicans and finished their work during the early morning hours of December 22. In its main features the measure they reported was the bill adopted by the House, with numerous minor and a few important alterations.[129] The House acted at once, approving the conference report by a vote of 298 to sixty on December 22, with only two Democrats voting against it and forty-nine Republicans and Progressives swelling the majority. The Senate acted the following afternoon, approving the report by a vote of forty-three to twenty-five.

Surrounded by members of his family and Cabinet, Democratic leaders in both houses, and newspapermen, the President signed the Fed-

---

[126] This was done by action of the Senate Democratic caucus on December 17, 1913.

[127] *Congressional Record*, 63d Cong., 2d sess., p. 1225.

[128] They were, in order, John W. Weeks of Massachusetts and George C. Perkins of California; Thomas Sterling of South Dakota, George W. Norris of Nebraska, and Wesley L. Jones of Washington; and Miles Poindexter of Washington, *ibid.*, p. 1230. H. P. Willis, *The Federal Reserve System*, pp. 1637-1666, reprints the measure that the Senate adopted.

[129] The House conferees accepted Senate amendments fixing the number of Federal Reserve banks at between eight and twelve, instead of at least twelve, as the House bill provided; extending the maturity time of agricultural paper admitted to discount by the Federal Reserve Board from three to six months; removing the Secretary of Agriculture from the Board, as the House bill provided; increasing the gold backing of Federal Reserve notes from 33 1/3 per cent to 40 per cent; making redemption of such currency in gold absolutely obligatory; and increasing the salary of members of the Board from $10,000 to $12,000 a year and lengthening their terms from six to ten years. For an analysis of the changes effected, see *Speech of Hon. Carter Glass of Virginia in the House of Representatives December 22, 1913* (pamphlet). This "speech" is not printed in the *Congressional Record*. H. P. Willis, *The Federal Reserve System*, pp. 1667-1696, prints the Federal Reserve Act as it was finally approved.

eral Reserve bill a few hours later, at 6:02 p.m., in a festive ceremony in his Executive Office. The signing completed, Wilson handed the gold pens he had used to McAdoo, Glass, and Owen. Then, turning to the men and women grouped around him, he began to speak in a conversational tone.

"Gentlemen," he began, "I need not tell you that I feel a very deep gratification at being able to sign this bill." He went on to recount Glass's and Owen's special contributions and how members of both parties had strengthened the bill; he spoke of the way in which the new banking system would benefit the entire country. "I cannot say with what deep emotions of gratitude . . . I feel," he concluded, "that I have had a part in completing a work which I think will be of lasting benefit to the business of the country."[130]

Thus ended the long struggle for the greatest single piece of constructive legislation of the Wilson era and one of the most important domestic Acts in the nation's history. Almost exactly one year had passed since that bleak afternoon in Princeton when Glass and Willis had first discussed banking legislation with the President-elect. What changes had been wrought as a result of the fierce controversies that followed! Beginning as a measure designed to strengthen private control over the reserve system and money supply and to serve only the needs of the business classes, the Federal Reserve bill had metamorphosed under progressive pressure into a measure that afforded substantial benefits to farmers and attempted, in the spirit of the New Freedom, to create a fine balance between private management and public supervision.

Eschewing utopian ambitions, the framers of the Federal Reserve Act had not attempted to reconstruct the American economy, banish poverty, redistribute wealth, or even prevent industrial depressions. They had sought merely to establish a workable reserve system, destroy the concentration of credit in Wall Street, and give the country an elastic currency suited to expanding business needs. Their measure was, therefore, a compromise between what the bankers wanted and what the most advanced progressives said the country needed.

Most bankers had grave reservations but were willing to cooperate in good faith to try to make the new system succeed.[131] On the other

[130] *New York Times*, December 24, 1913.

[131] See, e.g., the *Texas Bankers Record*, III (January 1914), 52-53; *Bankers Magazine*, LXXXVIII (February 1914), 136-137; *Proceedings of the 28th Annual Convention of the Iowa Bankers Association*, p. 68; S. R. Bertron to W. W., December 20, 1913; J. H.

side were the group of so-called radicals, who persevered in the belief that the Federal Reserve Act legalized the "Money Trust," as Senator La Follette put it, because the private bankers would own and control the regional reserve banks.[132] "The Senator from Oklahoma," cried Bristow of Kansas, after Owen had presented the conference report to the Senate, ". . . who has denounced the Aldrich bill, has accepted its most offensive provisions and covered them with a mask to deceive the American people."[133] "When the President signs this act," Representative Charles A. Lindbergh of Minnesota added, "the invisible government by the money power, proven to exist by the Money Trust investigation, will be legalized."[134]

Experience was to prove that many of the contemporary criticisms of the new banking and currency law were sound. As conservatives like Paul M. Warburg pointed out, the measure gave the Federal Reserve Board insufficient authority to enable it to assume the necessary functions of a central bank. This weakness was not comprehensively remedied until the adoption of the Banking Act of 1935. As the radicals complained, the Federal Reserve Act did in large measure leave control of the money supply in the hands of private bankers; moreover, by tying the money supply to gold and commercial paper, the Act deprived the government of the power to prevent severe deflation during periods of depression. This defect was remedied by a series of measures between 1932 and 1934 that made government bonds acceptable as collateral for Federal Reserve notes and took the country off the gold standard at home. In other words, the Federal Reserve System was not perfect in the beginning but would change as circumstances and shifting political opinions demanded.

Looking back in December 1913 over the long struggle for banking and currency reform, however, contemporary observers marveled at how much, not how little, Wilson had been able to accomplish. Without derogating the contributions of the National Monetary Commission and of Glass, Willis, Owen, Bryan, and all the other leaders in the administration and in Congress, most observers agreed that Wilson

Schiff to W. W., December 23, 1913; William Huttig to W. W., December 24, 1913; J. L. McCulloch to W. W., December 24, 1913; W. A. Gaston to W. W., December 24, 1913; and Josiah Quincy to W. W., December 26, 1913, all in the Wilson Papers, for representative banking opinion.

[132] R. M. La Follette, "Legalizing the 'Money Power,'" *La Follette's Weekly*, v (December 27, 1913), 1.

[133] *Congressional Record*, 63d Cong., 2d sess., p. 1472.

[134] *ibid.*, p. 1446.

was chiefly responsible for this crowning achievement. Not only had he courageously risked disrupting his party, mediated among the rival factions, and imposed a solution that satisfied both Democratic conservatives and Bryanites; he had also withstood the powerful assaults of private bankers, and had maintained unrelenting pressure upon both houses of Congress until the final victory was achieved. He had given the American people perhaps their best example of responsible leadership in action.

CHAPTER VIII

Reformers, Radicals, and The New Freedom

IN SPITE of Wilson's victories on behalf of tariff and banking reform, there were already signs by the end of 1913 that the New Freedom was nearing the limits of achievement within its ideological boundaries, and that the President faced the prospect of having to confront many of his progressive friends in future battles over legislative policies. This anomaly of a progressive in conflict with reformers and radicals, this contradiction of the New Freedom in tension with the progressive movement, becomes less puzzling when we understand how diverse were the numerous groups that called themselves progressive in Wilson's day. There was a large but probably a minority element in the Democratic party who wanted clean government, destruction of so-called industrial and financial monopolies, and abolition of special interest legislation. To the extent that they championed popular democracy and rebelled against a *status quo* that favored the wealthy, they were progressives. Actually, however, they were so strongly imbued with *laissez-faire* concepts that they were, strictly speaking, liberals in the nineteenth-century English tradition instead of twentieth-century progressives. They wanted impartial government with a modicum of federal regulation, rather than dynamic, positive federal intervention and participation in economic and social affairs. With their state-rights view of the Constitution, these liberal Democrats tended to suspect any attempts to commit the federal government to projects of social amelioration, because such intervention implied an invasion of the police power heretofore exercised almost exclusively by the states.

In 1913 Wilson was the chief leader of the liberal Democrats and the prime articulator of their *laissez-faire*, state-rights philosophy. On coming to the presidency he thought he saw clearly the path of duty. The Democrats, he thought, should wipe out the vestiges of special privilege in tariff legislation, liberate credit from Wall Street control, and rewrite antitrust legislation in order to restore the reign of competition in the business world. This, not the uplift of depressed groups by ambitious projects of federal intervention, was the mission of the New Freedom as he perceived it.

At the other end of the political spectrum stood a large number of advanced progressives, perpetuators of various post-Civil War movements for social and economic reform. Diverse in membership and objectives though they were, they all shared a common faith in the efficacy of legislation and in the superiority of collective over individual remedies. There were the Socialists, who had an influence disproportionate to their numbers. There were the pioneers in many movements for social justice and so-called moral reform, organized in the Anti-Saloon League, the American Association for Labor Legislation, the National Consumers' League, the National Child Labor Committee, the National Association for the Advancement of Colored People, leagues for woman suffrage, and dozens of similar groups. There were the leaders of organized labor, who often worked in conflict with the professional students of the labor problem but who spoke for a large disadvantaged element. There were, finally, the farm organizations and their political spokesmen, who demanded a comprehensive program of federal aid to agriculture, especially the furnishing of credit to farmers.

Large numbers of these reformers and radicals had combined in the Progressive party in 1912 under Theodore Roosevelt's leadership. Adopting a platform that foreshadowed the New Deal program of the 1930's, they fought for an expansion of federal and state power, a democratization of federal fiscal policy, and an enlargement of popular democracy. Defeated in the presidential election and failing to establish a permanent party, they were none the less still strong and vocal in 1913 and 1914.

How wide an ideological gulf separated Wilson and his followers from the advanced progressives first came out clearly during the campaign of 1912, when Wilson gave voice to his most eloquent and coherent expression of the *laissez-faire* ideal.[1] As Herbert Croly, the chief philosopher of the progressive movement, later wrote, "A formula [the New Freedom] was unearthed from the Democratic scriptures which would prove not merely an antidote to the Progressive heresies but an infallible clue to the solution of contemporary social problems. The new nationalism of the Progressives, with its emphasis upon purposive social and political reconstruction, was opposed by the New

[1] See especially *The New Freedom*, a volume of Wilson's campaign speeches arranged and edited by William Bayard Hale and published in 1913.

Freedom—a doctrine which proclaimed substantially that if the system of letting things alone was properly regulated and its abuses eliminated, a permanent peace would be restored to the distracted American nation."[2]

Another perceptive contemporary progressive stated the causes of the tension between Wilson and advanced reformers in another way. Wilson, he wrote, "speaks . . . for the smaller business men and manufacturers of the country . . . , the men who ask only that they shall be given equal business opportunities with the big trusts. . . . He cannot hope to take over the Progressive leadership so long as he holds to his present conception of State rights, and so long as he believes the restoration of regulated competition can solve the problems connected with big business and the fair distribution of wealth. The President must accept the Progressive ideal that the big work of government is not simply the emancipation of business, but, in the words of Colonel Roosevelt, 'that the Government should concern itself chiefly with the matters that are of most importance to the average man and average woman, and that it should be its special province to aid in making the conditions of life easier for these ordinary men and women, who compose the great bulk of our people.' "[3]

These criticisms were somewhat overdrawn, for, as we have seen, even at the flood tide of the New Freedom, Wilson was willing to concede some advanced progressive demands. Even so, there were many indications by the end of 1913 that future inflexible adherence to New Freedom dogmas by the President might bring him into open collision with reformers and radicals. Indeed, before the year had ended Wilson had already fought one battle and several skirmishes, and other conflicts clearly impended.

The one battle—over the segregation of Negroes in the federal civil service—found the President openly arrayed against a host of humanitarians and revealed better than any other episode of the time the dearth in administration circles of any overriding passion for social justice, or, perhaps we should say, the difficulty of reconciling the demands of social justice with the necessities of practical politics. The affair was in a sense supremely ironic. Wilson had appealed openly for Negro support during the campaign of 1912, and a number of Negro leaders and

---

[2] H. Croly, "Unregenerate Democracy," *New Republic*, vi (February 5, 1916), 17.
[3] R. M. McClintock, "What Does President Wilson Mean?" *Collier's*, lii (November 22, 1913), 23.

white spokesmen of their cause had worked hard for his election and helped him win the largest number of Negro votes ever given a Democratic presidential candidate to that time. And Negroes everywhere had hailed the New Freedom as the dawn of a new era for their race. One Washington Negro leader wrote in February 1913, "From the training, high character and Christian sentiment expressed by President-elect Wilson, before and since his election, I see an OPEN DOOR OF HOPE for the negro."[4] And Booker T. Washington, the chief spokesman of American Negroes, said, "Mr. Wilson is in favor of the things which tend toward the uplift, improvement, and advancement of my people, and at his hands we have nothing to fear."[5]

Consequently, at the time of Wilson's inauguration, various Negro leaders and champions of racial democracy had ambitious plans on foot. A host of Negro Democratic politicians looked forward to the speedy removal of Negro Republican officeholders and to their own appointment and recognition as the leaders of a growing Negro Democracy.[6] More important, however, was a project taking shape in the mind of Oswald Garrison Villard, a leader in the N.A.A.C.P., publisher of the *Nation* and the *New York Evening Post*, and a grandson of the abolitionist, William Lloyd Garrison. It envisaged the appointment by the President of a privately financed National Race Commission, composed of fifteen prominent whites and Negroes from the North and South, to conduct "a non-partisan, scientific study of the status of the Negro in the life of the nation."[7]

Villard explained his plan to Wilson at Trenton soon after the election and again at the White House on May 14, 1913. "He is wholly sympathetic," Villard reported the day after the second conference, "and was glad to grant the only request I made of him—that he con-

[4] William P. Morton, "The Future of the Negro in Politics," MS. dated February 13, 1913, in the Wilson Papers.
[5] *New York Times*, March 2, 1913.
[6] Bishop Alexander Walters, president of the National Colored Democratic League, to W. W., December 17, 1912, and March 10, 1913, Wilson Papers; William Monroe Trotter, president of the New England Suffrage League, to W. W., March 11, 1913, *ibid.*; Lester A. Walton, managing editor of the New York *Age*, to J. P. Tumulty, March 25, 1913, *ibid.*; New York *World*, March 13, 1913; Kelly Miller, "The Political Plight of the Negro," *Kelly Miller's Monographic Magazine*, 1 (May 1913), 3-21; and especially Robert S. Hudspeth to J. P. Tumulty, May 6, 1913, Wilson Papers, which describes the work of the Democratic National Committee among Negroes and enumerates the Negroes active in the Democratic party.
[7] *A Proposal for a National Race Commission to be appointed by the President of the United States, Suggested by the National Association for the Advancement of Colored People*, brochure in the Villard Papers.

sider the matter with care until my return on July first. By that time he will be able to judge better his relations with the Senate and Congress, and what it will mean to him to antagonize the reactionary southern politicians. As to the necessity of some such inquiry he was quite clear; it was not necessary to convince him on that point."[8]

In the mid-summer of 1913, after his return from a trip to Europe, Villard sought his promised interview with the President, but Wilson had decided that it would be unwise to appoint the Race Commission and was now too embarrassed to meet Villard face to face.[9]

Then, after Villard renewed his suggestion in a formal memorandum, the President had to give a definite answer. "It would be hard to make any one understand the delicacy and difficulty of the situation I find existing here with regard to the colored people," he explained on August 21, 1913. "You know my own disposition in the matter, I am sure, but I find myself absolutely blocked by the sentiment of Senators; not alone Senators from the South, by any means, but Senators from various parts of the country. . . . Just because the situation is extremely delicate and because I know the feeling of irritation that comes with every effort at systematic inquiry into conditions—because of the feeling that there is some sort of indictment involved in the very inquiry itself—I think that it would be a blunder on my part to consent to name the commission you speak of and which we discussed at our conference in Trenton."[10]

Villard's disappointment over Wilson's abandonment of the Race Commission project was great,[11] but it was small as compared to the bitterness he felt at the way in which southern race concepts and practices had gained ascendancy in Washington, in Congress, and in the

[8] O. G. Villard to R. H. Leavell, May 15, 1913, *ibid.*

[9] As Wilson admitted to John Palmer Gavit. See J. P. Gavit to O. G. Villard, October 1, 1913, *ibid.*

[10] W. W. to O. G. Villard, August 21, 1913, *ibid.*

[11] "Frankly," Villard replied on August 27, 1913, "I feel very sorry that you find yourself 'absolutely blocked by the sentiment of senators.' I believe that like most of your immediate predecessors, the time will come when you will find it necessary to go ahead and do what is right without considering their feelings, and I find it the more difficult to understand this decision because of your promise [given during the campaign of 1912] to stand 'for everything by which I could assist in advancing the interest of their race in the United States,' since, as I explained to you, it involves no appeal to all-powerful senators, no asking for financial aid from them, and left you free to lay the report before Congress or not as you saw fit. How do senators enter into this? If it is true that inquiry sometimes means indictment, should we who search for the truth only hold off, particularly when, as you yourself told me, you felt it was needed and the right thing to do?" O. G. Villard to W. W., August 27, 1913, *ibid.*

administration itself during the months following Wilson's inauguration. To state the matter bluntly, the return of the Democrats to power
had meant precisely what Negroes feared most—control of the federal
government by a party dominated by men determined to impose the
caste system in the nation's capital.

Southerners were strident in the spring of 1913, demanding segregation in Washington streetcars,[12] the dismissal of prominent Negro officeholders, especially those in a position "to boss white girls," as a
southern Negrophobe put it,[13] and the dismissal or downgrading of all
Negro civil servants. "There are no Government positions for negroes
in the South," the newly appointed federal collector of internal revenue
in Atlanta asserted. "A negro's place is in the cornfield."[14]

Most important, some Southerners in Congress and an organization
known as the National Democratic Fair Play Association were promoting a violent campaign, by means of mass meetings and printed
propaganda, for the immediate segregation of Negro workers in the
federal bureaus and agencies. "Deserving white girls in this City . . . ,"
one broadside read, "have appealed to us from nearly every Government Department where they are compelled to work alongside of a
greasy, ill-smelling negro man or woman; that sometimes, where a
negro is in charge or control of that Bureau, Division, or Office, those
poor girls are forced to take dictation from, be subservient to, bear the
ignominy and carry the disgrace of the taunts, sneers or insults of such
negroes."[15]

Although Wilson resented the demagoguery of the more rabid white
supremacists and resisted their extreme demands throughout his presidency, he and probably all his Cabinet members shared the southern
view of race relations. The question of segregation in the federal departments first arose at a Cabinet meeting on April 11, 1913, when

[12] During the special session of the Sixty-third Congress, for example, four bills
were introduced to establish segregation in Washington streetcars. The House committee on the District of Columbia reported a "Jim Crow" bill on February 1, 1915,
but it subsequently died in the House. On the other hand, the House approved a
measure forbidding the marriage of white persons and persons with one eighth or
more of "Negro blood" on January 11, 1915. It was never considered by the Senate.

[13] Thomas Dixon to W. W., July 27, 1913, Wilson Papers.

[14] *Atlanta Georgian and News*, October 7, 1913.

[15] National Democratic Fair Play Association to "Dear Madam," May 9, 1913, copy
of a form letter, Wilson Papers. See also the account of a mass meeting held by this
organization in Washington on May 1, 1913, in the New York *World*, May 2, 1913;
and the call for another such meeting, reproduced in Belle C. La Follette, "The
Color Line," *La Follette's Weekly*, v (August 23, 1913), 6.

Postmaster General Burleson, complaining of the friction that allegedly occurred when white and Negro railway mail clerks worked in the same car, proposed the institution of segregation in all departments.

Burleson "had talked with Bishop Walters[16] and other prominent negroes," Josephus Daniels recorded in his Diary, "and most of them thought it would be a great thing to do. Mr. Burleson thought the segregation would be a great thing as he had the highest regard for the negro and wished to help him in every way possible, but that he believed segregation was best for the negro and best for the Service."

If there were any opponents of segregation in the Cabinet, they did not then or afterward raise their voices. "The President said he made no promises in particular to negroes, except to do them justice, and he did not wish to see them have less positions than they now have, but he wished the [segregation] matter adjusted in a way to make the least friction."[17]

With the President's approval thus clearly given, Burleson and McAdoo, who had charge of the only departments with any significant number of Negro employees, soon afterward began quietly to segregate workers in offices, shops, rest rooms, and lunch rooms in the Post Office Department, the Treasury Department, and the Bureau of Printing and Engraving. Moreover, McAdoo planned, with Wilson's approval, to make the Registry Division of the Treasury Department an all-Negro bureau; the project fell through only because the Senate refused to confirm the appointment of Adam E. Patterson, a Negro Democrat from Oklahoma, as Register.[18]

"The past few months of Democratic party control," an investigator for the N.A.A.C.P. reported in September 1913, "have ... given segregation a tremendous impetus, and have marked its systematic enforcement. It is becoming known as a policy of the present government."[19] "Beyond a question," another careful observer wrote at about the same time, "the *spirit*, the desire, the intention [of a segregation policy], is present in varying degree. No policy has been adopted in any formal sense; no Cabinet officer has issued any instructions. . . . Much of what

[16] Alexander Walters, bishop of the African Methodist Episcopal Zion Church, president of the National Colored Democratic League, and one of Wilson's leading Negro supporters in 1912.
[17] Daniels Diary, April 11, 1913.
[18] W. G. McAdoo to O. G. Villard, October 27, 1913, Villard Papers.
[19] May Childs Nerney to O. G. Villard, September 30, 1913, Wilson Papers.

has been done has been on the initiative of subordinate chiefs who would like to have done it long ago but dared not, or who, mostly newly-appointed Southerners, took the first opportunity."[20]

In addition, Burleson and McAdoo made a clean sweep of Negro political appointees in the South and allowed local postmasters and collectors of internal revenue either to downgrade or to dismiss Negro workers with civil service status. For example, McAdoo dismissed Robert Smalls, the leading Negro citizen of South Carolina, who had been collector of the Port of Beaufort for twenty years, and appointed a white Democrat in his place.[21] A Negro mail clerk on a train that ran between Norfolk and Raleigh, to cite another example, was demoted from clerk to helper because he had formerly exercised authority over white men.[22] And thus it went throughout the South.

The spread of segregation in the Washington bureaus and the obvious anti-Negro bias of the administration's patronage policy came as a crushing blow to Negroes and whites active in the cause of racial democracy, especially to those among them who had hailed Wilson as a deliverer and worked for him during the campaign of 1912.

"When the Wilson Administration came into power, six months ago, it promised a 'new freedom' to all people, avowing the spirit of Christian Democracy," one Negro editor lamented. "But on the contrary we are given a stone instead of a loaf of bread; we are given a hissing serpent rather than a fish."[23] "We had hoped in your election as the President of our common country that a new era in our history would be open to us," another Negro leader wrote in protest, ". . . but the cold facts presented to us show that these cherished hopes are to be dashed to the ground and that for a while longer we must continue to drink from this bitter cup."[24] And from Booker T. Washington came the most telling comment of all: "I have recently spent several

---

[20] J. P. Gavit to O. G. Villard, October 1, 1913, Villard Papers. For additional reports on the extent of segregation, see J. P. Gavit, in the *New York Evening Post*, October 21, 1913; O. G. Villard to W. W., July 21 and September 29, 1913, Villard Papers; O. G. Villard to W. G. McAdoo, October 28, 1913, *ibid.*; William Monroe Trotter, "Federal Segregation Under Pres. Wilson," Boston *Guardian*, November 1, 1913; O. G. Villard, "The President and the Segregation at Washington," *North American Review*, cxcviii (December 1913), 800-807; Belle C. La Follette, "Color Line to Date," *La Follette's Weekly*, vi (January 24, 1914), 6-7; and McGregor (A. J. McKelway), "Segregation in the Departments," *Harper's Weekly*, lix (December 26, 1914), 620-621.

[21] *New York Times*, April 13, 1913.

[22] New York *Nation*, xcvii (September 4, 1913), 199-200.

[23] New York *Amsterdam News*, October 3, 1913.

[24] W. F. Powell to W. W., August 25, 1913, Wilson Papers.

days in Washington, and I have never seen the colored people so discouraged and bitter as they are at the present time."[25]

To Negro Democratic politicians who were hard at work to win northern Negro voters from their traditional allegiance to the G.O.P., the administration's segregation policy and refusal to appoint Negroes to office[26] meant the blasting of their hopes and political careers. They raised a chorus of reproach at Wilson's alleged betrayal of campaign promises, saying: "We are publicly and frequently charged with having sold the Race into slavery and told that we ought to be beaten to death with clubs and forever despised by the colored people,"[27] or "We find ourselves in a political wilderness of despair. . . . Saddened in heart and sick in spirit, . . . I plead with you, as Paul did with Philemon for Onesimus, to receive us unto your graces and let us not perish politically."[28]

[25] B. T. Washington to O. G. Villard, August 10, 1913, *ibid.* For other representative Negro comments, reports of mass meetings of protest, and so on, see Ralph W. Tyler to W. W., May 12, 1913, *ibid.*; W. Calvin Chase to W. W., August 2, 1913, *ibid.*; I. H. Riddick to W. W., August 24, 1913, *ibid.*; William M. Trotter to J. M. Curley, August 11, 1913, *ibid.*; Clifford H. Plummer to W. G. McAdoo, August 14, 1913, *ibid.*; Horace Bumstead to W. W., August 16, 1913, *ibid.*; S. S. Jones to W. W., August 29, 1913, *ibid.*; National Independent Political League to W. W., August 25, 1913, *ibid.*; Columbus Avenue A.M.E. Zion Church Sunday School of Boston to W. W., October 5, 1913, *ibid.*; National Negro Press Association to W. W., October 13, 1913, *ibid.*; Indianapolis Branch, N.A.A.C.P., to W. W., October 19, 1913, *ibid.*; Francis J. Grimke, *Excerpts from a Thanksgiving Sermon* (pamphlet); and especially the Boston *Guardian*, November 1, 1913, for a nation-wide survey of Negro sentiment.

[26] In all fairness, it should be said that Wilson wanted to appoint a few prominent Negro Democrats to offices traditionally held by Negroes but was prevented from so doing by threats from southern senators that they would block confirmation. After the Senate refused to confirm the appointment of Adam E. Patterson as Register of the Treasury, which was mentioned above, the President made no more Negro appointments until March 1914, when he reappointed Robert H. Terrell to the Municipal Court of the District of Columbia. When this appointment stirred Southerners to violent protest—"Your own best friends in the Southern States have been slapped in the face by the reappointment of the negro Terrell," Senator John Sharp Williams of Mississippi wrote to Wilson on March 31, 1914, for example—Wilson replied that he felt morally bound, in view of his campaign promises, to see that Negroes "were not put to any greater political disadvantage than they had suffered under previous Democratic administrations." W. W. to J. S. Williams, April 2, 1914, Wilson Papers. Soon afterward, the President announced that he would appoint a Negro Democrat as Recorder of Deeds in the District of Columbia; he retreated, however, in the face of strong southern opposition and made no other important Negro appointments.

[27] Peter J. Smith to J. P. Tumulty, June 1, 1913, Wilson Papers.

[28] Rufus L. Perry to W. W., July 21, 1913, *ibid.* See also Robert N. Wood, president of the United Colored Democracy of New York, to W. W., August 5, 1913, May 28, 1914, and June 16, 1914, *ibid.*; and Alfred B. Cosey, president of the United Negro Democracy of New Jersey, to J. P. Tumulty, August 22, 1913, *ibid.*

Even more significant a revelation of advanced progressive opinion of Wilson and his policies was the way in which non-southern white progressives and humanitarians rose in bitter protest at what one Boston mass meeting called the "new oppression in Washington."[29] Villard and his *Nation* and *New York Evening Post* and the N.A.-A.C.P., which was controlled by northern social justice leaders, sounded the first alarm in August 1913. "Never before has the Federal Government discriminated against its civilian employees on the ground of color," the N.A.A.C.P. said in a public letter to the President. ". . . For the lowly of all classes you have lifted up your voice and not in vain. Shall ten millions of our citizens say that their civic liberties and rights are not safe in your hands? To ask the question is to answer it. They desire a 'New Freedom,' too."[30]

Almost with one voice humanitarians, social workers, clergymen, church groups, Jewish spokesmen, liberal editors, and progressive political leaders outside the South replied to the N.A.A.C.P.'s call, denouncing the administration's segregation policy as "vicious and offensive," "cruel, unjust and contrary to the spirit and the institutions of this country," "a lamentable betrayal of democratic principles by a democratic administration," and the like.[31]

The strongest condemnation of all, however, came from the President's most loyal friend among the Fourth Estate. "The President

[29] "Resolutions at Faneuil Hall Meeting, Sunday, November Thirtieth, 1913," MS. in *ibid.*

[30] Moorfield Storey, *et al.*, to W. W., August 15, 1913, *New York Times*, August 18, 1913.

[31] See, e.g., the following letters of protest, all in the Wilson Papers: J. H. Schiff to W. W., August 20, 1913; Walter Stern to W. W., August 25, 1913; Jane Addams, *et al.*, to W. W., August 26, 1913; Julius Rosenwald to W. W., September 4, 1913; Henry C. King to W. W., September 5, 1913; Minneapolis Sunday Forum to W. W., September 7, 1913; James Schouler to W. W., September 8, 1913; Wesley P. Jones to W. W., September 29, 1913; Edward Waldo Emerson to W. W., October 14, 1913; Methodist Ministers' Alliance of Kansas City, Missouri, to W. W., November 24, 1914; Eugene N. Foss to W. W., October 20, 1913; William E. Chandler to W. W., November 3, 1913; David I. Walsh to W. W., October 26, 1914.

For representative comment from the secular and religious press, see "The President and the Negro," New York *Nation*, xcvii (August 7, 1913), 114; *ibid.*, November 13, 1913, pp. 447-448; "A Righteous Protest," *The Independent*, lxxv (September 4, 1913), 533-534; "Race Discrimination at Washington," *ibid.*, lxxvi (November 20, 1913), 330; "Segregation and Democracy," Chicago *Public*, xvi (September 5, 1913), 845; *New York Evening Post*, October 21, 1913; *Boston Advertiser*, October 21, 1913; "Turning the Negro Back," *Congregationalist and Christian World*, xcviii (September 18, 1913), 357, 359; "Color Caste at Washington," *ibid.*, xcix (November 19, 1914), 682; Chicago (Baptist) *Standard*, lxi (November 29, 1913), 356; *Lutheran Observer*, lxxxiii (March 5, 1915), 296-297.

thinks that this is not a political question, but he is wrong," Frank Cobb of the New York *World* declared. "Anything that is unjust, discriminating and un-American in government is certain to be a political question. . . . Whether the President thinks so or not, the segregation rule was promulgated as a deliberate discrimination against negro employees. Worse still, it is a small, mean, petty discrimination, and Mr. Wilson ought to have set his heel upon this presumptuous Jim-Crow government the moment it was established. He ought to set his heel upon it now. It is a reproach to his Administration and to the great political principles which he represents."[32]

Wilson was greatly disturbed by the bitterness of the controversy and obviously surprised. At first he tried to calm his northern friends by assuring them that segregation had been instituted only in the interest of the Negro workers, by implying that he did not personally approve of segregation, and by appealing for "a just and cool equipoise" instead of "a bitter agitation."[33] "It is true that the segregation of the colored employees in the several departments was begun upon the initiative and at the suggestion of several of the heads of departments," he wrote at the beginning of the controversy, for example, "but as much in the interest of the negroes as for any other reason, with the approval of some of the most influential negroes I know, and with the idea that the friction, or rather the discontent and uneasiness, which has prevailed in many of the departments would thereby be removed. It is as far as possible from being a movement *against* the negroes. I sincerely believe it to be in their interest."[34]

When his friends demanded that he say whether he personally approved of segregation, however, Wilson had to reply frankly. "I would say that I do approve of the segregation that is being attempted in several of the departments," he wrote in reply to a query from the editor of the *Congregationalist and Christian World*. "I have not always approved of the way in which the thing was done and have tried to change that in some instances for the better, but I think if you were here on the ground you would see, as I seem to see, that it is distinctly to the advantage of the colored people themselves."[35]

Although the forthright protest of the liberal North had considerable effect—the movement toward segregation in all departments was not

[32] New York *World*, November 13, 1914.
[33] W. W. to O. G. Villard, September 22, 1913, Wilson Papers.
[34] W. W. to O. G. Villard, July 23, 1913, *ibid.*
[35] W. W. to H. A. Bridgman, September 8, 1913, *ibid.*

only checked but was in part reversed in the Treasury Department[36]—
the tension between the President and the reformers on the race issue
remained a source of friction for years afterward. It came out especially
clearly in two episodes in 1914 and 1915.

The first was what might be called the Trotter affair. The Boston
Negro editor and leader, William Monroe Trotter, led a delegation
from his National Independent Political League to the White House
on November 12, 1914, to protest the continuation of segregation in
Washington. There was a sharp interchange between Wilson and
Trotter, which ended with the President accusing Trotter of trying to
blackmail him and virtually ordering him from his office. But the significant aspect of the episode was the fact that Wilson publicly affirmed
his belief that the total separation of the races was the policy that would
bring greatest benefit to the Negroes.[37]

The meaning of Wilson's pronouncement was not lost upon humanitarians in the North. The fact that Trotter lost his temper, the President's leading editorial spokesman in New England observed, "should
not obscure the painful fact that Mr. Wilson has fully accepted the
principle and practice of the segregation of the white and black employees in certain administrative departments of the Government. . . .
The President, who a year ago took the question of segregation under
advisement, now unqualifiedly justifies the separation of Government
employees on the basis of color. It is a distressing and sinister development."[38]

The second episode found the President an unwitting accomplice in
the success of one of the most violent pieces of anti-Negro propaganda
in modern American history. In 1915 Thomas Dixon and David W.
Griffith produced a motion picture, "The Birth of a Nation," based
upon Dixon's *The Clansman* (1905), a violently anti-Negro account
of life in the South during Reconstruction.[39] Foreseeing that the N.A.-

[36] *Boston Advertiser*, December 10, 1913, March 7, 1914; Moorfield Storey, *et al.*,
from the N.A.A.C.P. to W. W., January 6, 1914, Wilson Papers.

[37] *New York Times*, November 13, 1914; New York *World*, November 13, 1914.

[38] *Springfield* (Massachusetts) *Republican*, cited in the *New York Evening Post*,
November 18, 1914. For similar comment, see the *New York Evening Post*, November 13, 1914; New York *Nation*, xcix (November 19, 1914), 595; *The Independent*,
lxxx (November 23, 1914), 269; *New Republic*, i (November 21, 1914), 5; *Presbyterian Banner*, ci (November 26, 1914), 812-813; *Boston Traveler*, November 16, 1914;
Des Moines Register and Leader and *Indianapolis News*, cited in the *New York Evening Post*, November 18, 1914.

[39] A Baptist minister in North Carolina with a literary flair, Dixon had written a
series of historical novels aimed at building anti-Negro, pro-southern sentiment in the

A.C.P. and church groups would attempt to prevent the showing of "The Birth of a Nation," on the ground that it was "the pernicious propaganda of race prejudice and injustice" and constantly portrayed the Negro as "ignorant, degraded and lustful,"[40] Dixon conceived a bold scheme—to arrange a private showing of the film at the White House and thereby to obtain the President's implied endorsement.[41]

Wilson fell into Dixon's trap, as, indeed, did also members of the Supreme Court and both houses of Congress. Then, when the N.A.-A.C.P. sought to prevent the showing of "The Birth of a Nation" in New York, Boston, and other cities, Dixon's lawyers countered successfully by declaring that Chief Justice Edward D. White and the President had seen the movie and liked it immensely.[42]

The Chief Justice, a Confederate veteran from Louisiana, put an end to the use of his name by threatening to denounce "The Birth of a Nation" publicly if Dixon did not stop saying that he had endorsed it.[43] Perceiving the political dangers in the situation, Tumulty suggested that Wilson write "some sort of a letter showing that he did not approve the 'Birth of a Nation.' "[44] "I would like to do this," the President replied, "if there were some way in which I could do it without seeming to be trying to meet the agitation . . . stirred up by that unspeakable fellow Tucker [Trotter]."[45] He did, however, let

---

North. He explained his purpose in producing "The Birth of a Nation" in a letter to Joseph P. Tumulty on May 1, 1915 (Wilson Papers) as follows: "Of course, I didn't dare allow the President to know the *real big purpose back of my film—which was to revolutionize Northern sentiments by a presentation of history that would transform every man in my audience into a good Democrat!* And make no mistake about it— we are doing just that thing. . . . Every man who comes out of one of our theatres is a Southern partisan for life—except the members of Villard's Inter-Marriage Society who go there to knock." "This play," Dixon later boasted to Wilson, "is transforming the entire population of the North and West into sympathetic Southern voters. There will never be an issue of your segregation policy." T. Dixon to W. W., September 5, 1915, *ibid.*

[40] As the *Congregationalist and Christian World*, c (September 2 and December 16, 1915), 304, 880, put it.

[41] Dixon tells the story in "Southern Horizons: An Autobiography," unpublished MS. in the possession of Mrs. Thomas Dixon, Raleigh, North Carolina, pp. 423-424.

[42] For accounts of the hearings in New York and Boston, see Mrs. Walter Damrosch to J. P. Tumulty, March 27, 1915, Wilson Papers; Mrs. Harriet B. Beale to J. P. Tumulty, March 29, 1915, *ibid.*; Representative Thomas C. Thacher of Massachusetts to J. P. Tumulty, April 17, 1915, *ibid.*, enclosing letters and documents relating to the hearing in Boston; and Thomas Dixon, "Southern Horizons," pp. 425-441.

[43] E. D. White to J. P. Tumulty, April 5, 1915, Wilson Papers.

[44] J. P. Tumulty to W. W., April 24, 1915, *ibid.*

[45] W. W. to J. P. Tumulty, c. April 25, 1915, *ibid.*

Tumulty say that he had at no time approved the film; and three years later, when the nation was at war, he strongly disapproved the showing of this "unfortunate production."[46]

It was all a tragic business, for Negroes faced even greater travail during the war and postwar periods, as fear of Negro resurgence and the sudden movement of hundreds of thousands of black workers to the North after 1915 stimulated a wave of lynching and race riots unprecedented in American history. Would historians say that "there was much talk in those days of a 'New Freedom,' but it was exclusively for white men?" one reporter asked in 1913.[47] To ask the question in this latter day is to answer it. And yet, given the racial attitudes of Wilson, his circle, and his party, and the political circumstances of the time, this introduction of the caste system into the federal government was perhaps inevitable. As the same reporter wrote, it was "a meeting of the irresistible and the impenetrable; a tragic situation culminating the crimes and hypocrisies of three centuries."[48]

Further insight can be gained into the causes of the tension between the President and advanced reformers by noting the ambiguity of his relation, and sometimes his outright hostility, to the several movements on foot in 1913 and 1914 to commit the federal government to programs of social amelioration—prohibition of child labor, minimum wages for women workers, federal health and educational programs, woman suffrage, prohibition of the manufacture of alcoholic beverages, and the like.

Having supported Theodore Roosevelt and lost in 1912, the unchastened social justice reformers simply redoubled their efforts and propaganda in the hope of winning the incoming President to their side. His first introduction to the leaders of the social reform movement in the East was an interesting experience. During a visit at the home of his old friend, Mrs. Caroline B. Alexander,[49] in Hoboken over the week-end of January 25-26, 1913, he went on an expedition to Ellis

---

[46] J. P. Tumulty to T. C. Thacher, April 28, 1915, *ibid.*; W. W. to J. P. Tumulty, c. April 22, 1918, *ibid.*

[47] J. P. Gavit, in the *New York Evening Post*, October 21, 1913.

[48] J. P. Gavit to O. G. Villard, October 1, 1913, Villard Papers.

[49] Head of the New Jersey State Board of Children's Guardians and chairman of the commission that controlled the State Reformatory for Women, Mrs. Alexander was a sister of Edwin A. Stevens, state highway commissioner of New Jersey and a classmate of Wilson at Princeton.

Island[50] and afterward heard a number of social workers—among them, A. J. McKelway, Josephine Goldmark, Lillian D. Wald, and Mrs. Florence Kelley—tell of their hopes for a large extension of federal activities into new social frontiers.

Wilson was obviously deeply moved. "I want, above all things, to enjoy the confidence of, and to have at my service the information and counsel of, those who are engaged in these fundamental things," he replied. ". . . You are all to regard yourselves as forces playing upon the government, and I hope that during the next four years you will find a sensitive part of the government at the top."[51]

And yet Wilson was never keenly interested in the several movements for federal social legislation before 1916. Congress approved three significant measures of social and labor reform during the period 1913-1915—the labor provisions of the Clayton Antitrust Act and the La Follette-Peters Eight-Hour Act in 1914 and the Seamen's Act in 1915[52]—but Wilson had no part either in their formulation or in their passage. In fact, as we will see, he nearly vetoed the Seamen's bill, and he approved the labor provisions of the Clayton Act only because they denied to organized labor its most important demands. Finally, on two of the most significant measures of social legislation, a federal child labor law and woman suffrage, he was so much out of step with advanced reformers that he refused to give them the support indispensable to the success of their causes.

The pioneer reformers organized in the National Child Labor Committee had been pressing child labor reform on the state level since 1904, and their accomplishments constituted perhaps the greatest

[50] For the best account of this episode, see the New York *World*, January 26, 1913.

[51] *The Survey*, xxix (February 8, 1913), 639-640, gives a full account of the conference and a verbatim print of Wilson's speech; but see also the account in the *New York Times*, January 27, 1913.

Lest there be any doubt in Wilson's mind as to their program, practically the entire body of social justice leaders met in New York City in late March 1913 and addressed a letter to the President, urging him to support a series of reform measures. See Caroline B. Alexander, *et al.*, to W. W., March 31, 1913, Wilson Papers; printed in *The Survey*, xxx (April 5, 1913), 3-4.

[52] See below, pp. 427-433 and 269-274, for a discussion of the labor provisions of the Clayton Act and the struggle for the Seamen's bill. The Eight-Hour Act, which established the eight-hour day for most women workers in the District of Columbia and prohibited the employment of women under eighteen at night, was introduced by Senator La Follette at the request of the National Consumers' League. The President signed the measure on February 24, 1914. See R. M. La Follette, "The Eight Hour Day Will Come," *La Follette's Weekly*, v (July 19, 1913), 1; and *The Survey*, xxxi (December 13, 1913, and March 7, 1914), 289, 689.

single triumph of the social justice movement before the First World War. In 1900 twenty-four states and the District of Columbia made no provision for a minimum age for workers; by 1914, on the other hand, every state but one had established a minimum age, usually fourteen. Convinced that conditions were ripe for action on the federal level, the National Child Labor Committee prepared a model bill, which was introduced in the House of Representatives by A. Mitchell Palmer on January 26, 1914. It prohibited the shipment in interstate commerce of goods manufactured in whole or in part by children under fourteen, of the products of mines or quarries where children under sixteen were employed, or of any goods manufactured by children under sixteen working more than eight hours a day.[53]

In retrospect, it can be seen that the Palmer bill was the most momentous measure of the progressive era, for its adoption marked a turning point in American constitutional history—the use of the commerce power to justify almost any form of federal control over working conditions and wages, questions hitherto regarded as being within the exclusive jurisdiction of the states. If the federal commerce power included the right to control the conditions under which goods were manufactured, articles were sold, or farm products were grown, then there were virtually no limits to national regulation of economic activity. The champions and opponents of the Palmer bill, consequently, recognized the measure for what it actually was—the first step toward a potentially comprehensive national social and economic regulation under the commerce power. "So we shall begin the *standardization of industry itself*, whose products enter into interstate commerce, by the enactment of the Palmer bill," the secretary of the National Child Labor Committee for the southern states boasted.[54]

It was too bold a constitutional doctrine for the Woodrow Wilson of 1914, for the man who still believed in limited government and was imbued with the old state-rights heritage. "My own party in some of its elements represents a very strong state's rights feeling," he warned the social workers early in 1913. "It is very plain that you would have to go much further than most interpretations of the Constitution would allow if you were to give to the government general control over child labor throughout the country."[55] And when A. J. McKelway, Felix Adler, Edward T. Devine, and Owen R. Lovejoy, representing the National

[53] *The Survey*, XXXI (February 7, 1914), 539.
[54] A. J. McKelway to W. W., February 6, 1914, Wilson Papers.
[55] *The Survey*, XXIX (February 8, 1913), 640.

Child Labor Committee, came to the White House in February 1914 to plead for support of the Palmer bill, the President had to reply that he believed that the measure was unconstitutional and would open the door to virtually unlimited national economic regulation.[56] Thus, although the bill passed the House by a vote of 233 to forty-three on February 15, 1915, Wilson said not a word in its support when it ran afoul of the opposition of conservative Republicans and southern Democrats in the Senate. In the circumstances, his refusal to support the measure was the same as opposition.

Resisting the demands of the suffragettes was for Wilson even more embarrassing than having to withhold support from the child labor bill, if for no other reason than because the President was a southern gentleman and had to say "no" to a group of women who were determined to get what they wanted. Actually, in 1913 and 1914 Wilson believed that the world would be a better place if women stayed in the home. But he could not say this openly without appearing reactionary; and he put his refusal to support woman suffrage on other grounds.

"I want you ladies, if I can make it clear to you, to realize just what my present situation is," he told a delegation of suffragettes headed by Anna Howard Shaw at the White House on December 8, 1913. "Whenever I walk abroad I realize that I am not a free man; I am under arrest. . . . I set myself this very strict rule when I was Governor of New Jersey, and have followed it as President, and shall follow it as President —that I am not at liberty to urge upon Congress in messages policies which have not had the organic consideration of those for whom I am spokesman. In other words, I have not yet presented to any Legislature my private views on any subject, and I never shall, because I conceive it to be part of the whole process of government that I shall be spokesman for somebody, not for myself. . . . For that reason, you see, I am by my own principles shut out, in the language of the street, from 'starting anything.' I have to confine myself to those things which have been embodied as promises to the people at an election. . . . I wanted to tell you that to show that I am strictly living up to my principles. When my private opinion is asked by those who are cooperating with me, I am most glad to give it, but I am not at liberty, until I speak for somebody besides myself, to urge legislation upon the Congress."[57]

[56] Wilson's notation on J. P. Tumulty to W. W., January 24, 1914, Wilson Papers, expressing the view that the Palmer bill was unconstitutional; and A. J. McKelway to W. W., February 6, 1914, *ibid.*, paraphrasing what Wilson told the delegation from the National Child Labor Committee.

[57] *New York Times*, December 9, 1913.

But still the suffrage delegations kept coming, and each meeting was more embarrassing than the last. On February 2, 1914, Mrs. Elizabeth Glendower Evans of Boston led a delegation of some four hundred working women, who stormed the White House with a band playing the "Marseillaise" to urge the President to support a national suffrage amendment. One by one they spoke, these representatives of women workers in the sweated industries of the East. "I need not tell you," Wilson replied with obvious embarrassment, "that a group of women like this appeals to me very deeply indeed. I do not have to tell you what my feelings are. But until the party as such has considered a matter of this very supreme importance, and taken its position, I am not at liberty to speak as an individual." Mrs. Evans broke in to say that in 1912 Wilson had led her to believe that he would support woman suffrage. "But, you see," the President replied, "I was speaking as an individual then, and now I am speaking as a representative of the party to which I belong." "Of course," the Boston suffragette shot back, "You were gunning for votes then." Wilson blushed but managed a weak smile.[58]

When a third large delegation of suffrage leaders invaded the White House on June 30, 1914, and demanded that Wilson state his personal views on a national suffrage amendment, he could no longer hide behind the Democratic platform. "I can only say that since you turned away from me as a leader of a party and asked me my position as a man, I am obliged to state it very frankly," he replied. His "passion," he continued, was for local self-government "and the determination by the great communities into which this nation is organized of their own policy and life." He believed, therefore, that the states should determine the suffrage qualifications.[59]

The President never openly avowed opposition to the principle of woman suffrage; and when a suffrage amendment came before the voters of New Jersey in the autumn of 1915 he approved the principle publicly for the first time. "I intend to vote for woman suffrage in New Jersey," he explained in a statement on October 6, 1915, "because I believe that the time has come to extend that privilege and responsibility to the women of the State, but I shall vote, not as the leader of my party in the nation, but only upon my private conviction as a citi-

[58] Elizabeth G. Evans, "An Audience at the White House," *La Follette's Weekly*, VI (February 14, 1914), 5; New York *World*, February 3, 1914.
[59] *New York Times*, July 1, 1914.

zen of New Jersey."[60] It was an important concession, but Wilson tried to hold the line at state enfranchisement before 1916.[61] Eventually, of course, he and his party would be overwhelmed by the increasing demands for the so-called political emancipation of women.

Potentially the most disruptive social issue of the years before the First World War was the question of the prohibition of the manufacture and sale of alcoholic beverages. Beginning in the 1870's as a temperance crusade, the post-Civil War campaign against the Demon Rum had gained powerful new allies among the Protestant churches in the 1880's, had become nationally organized in the Anti-Saloon League in the 1890's, and by 1913 had changed its objective from local option and state-wide prohibition to a national amendment outlawing the liquor traffic. Even more than the movement for woman suffrage, the anti-liquor crusade threatened to engulf any politician who dared resist it.

Experience and conviction told Wilson that the ingrained social habits of millions of Americans could not be changed by legislative fiat, and it is safe to say that at least before 1917 he was opposed to state-wide prohibition. But in his eagerness to please friends in both camps during the preconvention campaign of 1911 and 1912, he had written letters approving both local option, which the liquor forces usually supported as an alternative to prohibition, and state-wide prohibition, which the Anti-Saloon leaders were demanding in almost every state. Trouble arose during several state campaigns in 1913 and 1914 because the wets used Wilson's letter, written to the Reverend Thomas B. Shannon, favoring local option, and the drys made even more extensive use of Wilson's letter to E. W. Grogan of Texas, endorsing state-wide prohibition in certain circumstances.

Wilson wanted only to stay clear of the controversy, but the opposing factions kept pressing for some commitment. No prohibitionist himself, Tumulty tried to deny that the President had written the Grogan letter; but he failed because his falsehood was too obvious.[62] The matter came to a head in the spring of 1915, when the prohibition leaders in Kentucky used the Grogan letter in their campaign for an amendment to outlaw liquor in the Bourbon state. At Tumulty's suggestion, Arthur B. Krock, reporter for the anti-prohibition Louisville

[60] *ibid.*, October 7, 1915.

[61] As late as December 1915, for example, he refused to support a national suffrage amendment. New York *World*, December 7, 1915.

[62] W. E. Johnson to J. P. Tumulty, January 30, 1915; and J. P. Tumulty to W. E. Johnson, February 4, 1915, both in the Wilson Papers.

Courier-Journal and *Louisville Times*, went to the White House on April 30, 1915, and confronted Wilson with the Shannon and Grogan letters.

"How did you come to write that, Governor?" Tumulty asked, pointing to the Grogan letter. "I don't know," Wilson replied wearily. "Were you crazy when you wrote it?" Tumulty asked gently. "I declare I don't know. Have you got it there? . . . I hate to look at it," Wilson said. "Oh, I can explain this, all right," he added after reading the Grogan letter. "You know," Tumulty remarked to Krock, "there's very little the Governor can't do with the English language!" The upshot of the conference was an agreement that some Kentuckian would write the President about the Grogan letter and that Wilson would reply, affirming his support of local option in all conceivable circumstances. "In the meantime," Tumulty told Krock, "stand pat on Shannon and say nothing about Grogan."[63]

On May 5, 1915, therefore, W. B. Haldeman, editor of the *Louisville Times* and a leader of the wets in Kentucky, wrote the promised letter, asking the President to clarify his position in view of the seeming inconsistency of the Shannon and Grogan pronouncements. "The reply to your letter is very simple," Wilson answered on May 14, 1915, in a letter intended for publication. "My so-called Shannon letter precisely defines my position with regard to the liquor issue, not only as it was when I wrote the letter, but as it is now, and the letter to Mr. Grogan is, or was, at any rate, intended to be entirely consistent with it. What I intended to say to Mr. Grogan and think that I said with sufficient clearness was that, while the position I had taken in the Shannon letter expressed my fixed conviction in the matter, I was not self-confident or self-opinionated enough to say what the proper course of action was either in Texas or in any other state where I was not personally in touch with the conditions obtaining. I felt that it would be arrogant on my part to state that there were in my opinion no circumstances which justified an agitation for state-wide prohibition."[64] It was not a precise paraphrase of the Grogan letter,[65] but it sufficed at least to make Wilson's position in support of local option clear.

[63] A. B. Krock, memorandum of an interview at the White House, April 30, 1915, MS. in the Watterson Papers.

[64] W. B. Haldeman to W. W., May 5, 1915; and W. W. to W. B. Haldeman, May 14, 1915, both in the Wilson Papers and printed in the *New York Times*, May 19, 1915.

[65] Compare what Wilson wrote to Haldeman with what he had written to Grogan: "I believe that for some states, state wide prohibition is possible and desirable, because of their relative homogeneity, while for others, I think that state wide prohibition is

Revealing also of the tension between Wilson and advanced progressives was the way in which New Freedom principles collided with the demands of agrarian leaders that a rural credits system be established and operated by the federal government. Superficially, the road seemed clear ahead for rural credits legislation at the beginning of the Wilson administration. The question had been under discussion for many years, and the three major parties had promised some form of federal aid in their platforms in 1912. Then, in the spring of 1913 Congress authorized the President to appoint a Rural Credits Commission to investigate and recommend.[66] The Commission soon discovered the obvious fact that farmers in the South and West paid usurious rates for long-term loans.[67] It undertook a study of rural credits systems in Europe, and then set to work on a measure which its chairman, Senator Duncan U. Fletcher of Florida, introduced on August 9, 1913.[68] The measure provided for the establishment of a nation-wide system of privately owned and controlled land banks operating under federal supervision.[69]

Because the Fletcher bill offered a solution in perfect harmony with the New Freedom concepts of limited federal participation, the President and Secretary of Agriculture warmly urged congressional leaders to approve it.[70] Conflict between the President and the farm spokesmen in Congress, on the other hand, occurred precisely because agrarian leaders wanted, not a New Freedom solution, but a progressive

---

not practicable. I have no reason to doubt from what I know of circumstances, that state wide prohibition is both practicable and desirable in Texas." W. W. to E. W. Grogan, June 6, 1911, printed in *ibid.*, January 8, 1912.

[66] For an excellent note on the composition and plans of the Commission, see *The Survey*, xxx (May 17, 1913), 239-240.

[67] According to a reliable survey made in 1916, the average annual interest rates on farm mortgages ran, for example, 10 per cent in Montana and Wyoming, 9.6 per cent in Arkansas and Florida, 9 per cent in Utah and Texas, 8.9 per cent in Colorado and Idaho, 8.7 per cent in Georgia, North Dakota, and Washington, and from 8 to 8.6 per cent in Louisiana, Mississippi, Oklahoma, South Carolina, South Dakota, and Oregon. Herbert Quick, "The Rural Credit Firing Squad," *Saturday Evening Post*, CLXXXVIII (April 15, 1916), 30.

[68] The Commission submitted two reports, as follows: *Agricultural Cooperation and Rural Credit in Europe* . . . , Senate Document 261, 63d Cong., 2d sess., and *Agricultural Credit* . . . , Senate Document 380, 63d Cong., 2d sess., which contained a draft of the Fletcher bill.

[69] *New York Times*, August 10, 1913; *The Independent*, LXXVII (February 9, 1914), 185-186.

[70] D. F. Houston to W. W., December 23, 1913, Wilson Papers; W. W. to D. U. Fletcher, January 9, 1914, *ibid.*

solution of their most pressing need. In brief, they wanted to enjoy the low interest rates that would come only by decisive federal intervention in the farm mortgage market through a rural credits system owned, operated, and subsidized by the United States.

Secretary Houston pointed up the ideological issues frankly in an address before the annual meeting of the National Grange in Manchester, New Hampshire, in November 1913. "I am not impressed," he said, "with the wisdom and the justice of proposals that would take the money of all the people, through bonds or other devices, and lend it to the farmers or to any other class at a rate of interest lower than the economic conditions would normally require and lower than that at which other classes are securing their capital. This would be special legislation of a particularly odious type, and no new excursions in this direction would be palatable when we are engaged in the gigantic task of restoring the simple rule of equity. . . . One thing is clear, the schemes that conceive the farmer to be a subject for unique and special legislation may at once be condemned."[71] In other words, supplying credits to farmers was no proper business for an administration determined to destroy special privileges and class legislation!

The differences between the administration and the agrarian leaders in Congress came out in a fairly spectacular way when a joint subcommittee of the House and Senate banking committees, headed by Representative Robert J. Bulkley of Ohio and Senator Henry F. Hollis of New Hampshire, set to work on rural credits legislation in the late winter and spring of 1914. In spite of warnings from the White House that the government should not directly enter the rural credits field, the joint subcommittee proceeded to draft a bill that adopted more or less the framework of the system proposed in the Fletcher plan but added a provision requiring the government to furnish capital of at least $500,000 for each of twelve federal land banks and to purchase their bonds, up to an amount of $50,000,000 annually, if private investors did not.[72]

Sentiment in both houses was overwhelmingly favorable to the Hollis-Bulkley bill; ten of the twelve members of the joint subcommittee supported it, for example, and no congressman dared take responsibility for defeating the measure. Only the President himself could prevent quick approval by Congress. The House Democratic leaders,

[71] Quoted in *Commercial West*, xxiv (November 22, 1913), 7-8.
[72] For the details of this, the so-called Hollis-Bulkley bill, see the *New York Times*, May 13, 1914.

Underwood and Glass, explained the situation to Wilson and with his approval convened the House Democratic caucus on May 12, 1914, for a showdown on the issue. Then Glass read the following letter from the President to the assembled Democrats:

"After our conference of this morning, I feel that it is really my duty to tell you how deeply and sincerely I feel that the Government should not itself be drawn into the legislation for credits based on farm mortgages. I think that the bill as it has been outlined would be very serviceable indeed without this feature and that the drawing of the Government into the purchase of land mortgages would launch us upon a course of experimentation in which we should have no guidance from experience either in this country or elsewhere because of the fundamental dissimilarity of conditions here and abroad. Moreover, I have a very deep conviction that it is unwise and unjustifiable to extend the credit of the Government to a single class of the community.

"Since I have learned that my convictions in this matter are not shared by a considerable number of the gentlemen who have given some attention to this matter in the House and in the Senate, I have felt it my duty to consider the matter very deliberately and very carefully and you can rest assured that I would not express to you the conviction I have just avowed if I did not feel it my conscientious duty to do so and if I did not feel privileged to do so because of a study of the conditions and consequences of such legislation. You can see, moreover, how the very fact that this conviction has come to me, as it were, out of fire fixes it clearly and permanently."[73]

The agrarian leaders were angered but helpless, as Wilson's letter clearly foreshadowed a veto of the Hollis-Bulkley bill. Swearing that there would be no rural credits legislation except on their own terms, they appealed unsuccessfully in person to the President soon after the adjournment of the caucus and then agreed to eliminate the rural credits bill from the immediate Democratic program.[74] "We cleaned them up nearly four to one in the caucus tonight," Glass boasted to Burleson. "Only Ragsdale of the Sub-Committee voted with Bulkley for legislation at this session."[75]

The caustic Virginian exaggerated the dimensions of the administration's victory. Hollis and Bulkley introduced their measure im-

---

[73] W. W. to C. Glass, May 12, 1914, Wilson Papers.
[74] *New York Times*, May 13, 1914.
[75] C. Glass to A. S. Burleson, May 12, 1914, Burleson Papers.

mediately after the meeting of the Democratic caucus on May 12, 1914; two agrarian radicals, Otis T. Wingo of Arkansas and Joseph B. Thompson of Oklahoma, organized an unsuccessful filibuster in mid-May, to force the House to vote upon the bill; and spokesmen of the farm organizations applied heavy pressure upon congressional leaders and the President all during the spring of 1914.

They redoubled their pressure, moreover, when Congress reconvened in December 1914. Senator Hollis, for example, warned the President that he and Bulkley planned to renew their campaign, even though Wilson's Annual Message had relegated rural credits legislation to the scrap heap during the lame duck session.[76] Pressure from the rural sections mounted during the following months, and the Senate, without warning, adopted an amendment to the agricultural appropriation bill on February 25, 1915, providing for the creation of a federal rural credits system in the Treasury Department.[77] The House approved the Hollis-Bulkley bill a few days later, but the session expired before the conference committee could submit a report; and the President was spared the embarrassment of having to veto a measure that had overwhelming support in Congress and among farmers in all sections.[78] It was, however, only the beginning of the controversy. Wilson would not adhere forever to New Freedom doctrines that denied the demands of the organized farmers, politically the most powerful pressure group in the United States.

The tension between the New Freedom and advanced progressives was revealed perhaps most clearly when Wilson found himself in conflict with organized labor and its allies on certain critical issues from 1913 through 1915. It was an unexpected development, for the Democratic party had given full endorsement to labor's most important demands since 1908, and Wilson was not unsympathetic to labor's needs and striving.

By the time Wilson entered the White House, Samuel Gompers and his American Federation of Labor were pressing hard for the enactment by Congress of an elaborate program that included federal aid

[76] H. F. Hollis to W. W., December 11, 1914, Wilson Papers. See also J. W. Madden to W. W., December 10, 1914, *ibid.*; C. J. Owens to W. W., December 18, 1914, *ibid.*; and J. D. Brown to W. W., December 19, 1914, *ibid.* For Wilson's reference to rural credits legislation in his Annual Message of December 8, 1914, see R. S. Baker and W. E. Dodd (eds.), *The New Democracy*, I, 220.

[77] *New York Times*, January 19 and February 26, 1915.

[78] *ibid.*, February 27 and March 1, 2, and 3, 1915.

to industrial education, a measure to liberate seamen in American ports from the bondage of their labor contracts, and the restriction of immigration. But for the leaders of the A.F. of L. the overshadowing objective was the winning of immunity from prosecution for acts which the Supreme Court had said violated the Sherman Antitrust Act of 1890. Indeed, Gompers and his friends were convinced that the life or death of the labor movement depended upon the outcome of their battle for such immunity.

The struggle began in 1894, when the Attorney General of the United States obtained an injunction against Eugene V. Debs and other officers of the American Railway Union for conspiring, in violation of the Sherman Act, to obstruct commerce during the Pullman strike in Chicago. The Supreme Court, in 1895, affirmed that the Sherman Act's prohibitions against restraint of trade applied as much to labor unions as to corporations. During the following two decades the Supreme Court sharpened its interdiction against allegedly illegal union activities, particularly in the so-called Danbury Hatters' decision of 1908 and the Buck's Stove and Range Company decision of 1914, which outlawed secondary boycotts and the black-listing of nonunion products by the A.F. of L. The effect of these and other such decisions was to establish the doctrine that all of labor's industrial and economic warfare fell within the purview of the federal courts and that union leaders risked jail terms and loss of property if they defied injunctions.[79]

Obviously, the A.F. of L.'s surest means of protection was to obtain an amendment of the Sherman Act that would give organized labor specific immunity from its prohibitions. After struggling unsuccessfully in the early 1900's for this objective, the leaders of the A.F. of L. presented a Bill of Grievances to Congress and the President in 1906, supported Bryan and the Democratic candidates in 1908, after the Democratic platform of that year had promised immunity, and waged an increasingly aggressive campaign during the next four years. It came to seeming fruition in 1912, with the election of a President and a Congress committed to the passage of a measure to give organized labor and farm unions their long-sought immunity from prosecution under the Sherman law.

The issue of labor exemption arose during the first months of the Wilson administration. Failing to get their immunity measure, the

[79] For a fuller explanation, see Arthur S. Link, *American Epoch, A History of the United States Since the 1890's,* pp. 65-66.

so-called Bacon-Bartlett bill, past the Republican opposition in the Sixty-second Congress, the Democratic leaders had attached a rider to the Sundry Civil appropriation bill of 1913, known as the Hughes-Hamill amendment, which prohibited the Justice Department from using any funds therein appropriated for the prosecution of labor unions or farm organizations for violating the Sherman Act. President Taft had vetoed the bill in one of his last official acts, declaring that the rider was "class legislation of the most vicious sort." Democratic leaders thereupon reintroduced the Sundry Civil bill, with the rider attached, in the special session in April 1913 and unwittingly set the stage for the first testing of the New Freedom's labor policy. "Unless the Hughes-Hamill amendment is made a part of the appropriation bill," Gompers warned, "it will unquestionably justify every one in stigmatizing the Democrats as insincere and simply playing politics when they proposed the amendment, and when they made the declaration they did in the platforms of 1908 and 1912, that it was mere shallow vote-catching devices, that pledges have been broken and trust betrayed."[80]

What organized labor demanded was in fact nothing less than progressive, or "class," legislation to help redress the balance in the unequal struggle between labor and capital.[81] But the future dimensions of the controversy, or the way in which labor's demand violated the New Freedom tenets, were not apparent to Wilson at the outset, and he acted hastily, without thought of the consequences. In a conference with congressional leaders and Attorney General McReynolds at the White House on April 12, 1913, the President declared that he did not regard the controverted rider as "class" legislation and implied that he would sign the Sundry Civil bill with the rider attached, mainly in order to avoid any sign of Democratic dissension during a critical period in the congressional debates over the Underwood bill.[82] Indeed,

[80] S. Gompers to Frank Morrison, April 13, 1913, the Letterbooks of Samuel Gompers, American Federation of Labor Building, Washington, D.C.; hereinafter cited as the Gompers Letterbooks.

[81] As Gompers frankly admitted in a thirty-two-page letter to the President on April 30, 1913, a copy of which was sent to each senator. "I must ask for your patience and forbearance in addressing such a lengthy letter to you," Gompers concluded. ". . . But I can only plead my deep concern for this legislation, a matter that lies very close to my heart and vitally affects the interests of those whom I officially represent and to whose welfare I have long devoted my thought and efforts. We represent great human interests, human lives and hearts that are seeking a better, higher life." S. Gompers to W. W., April 30, 1913, *ibid.*

[82] *New York Times*, April 13 and May 21, 1913.

some newspapers reported that he had asked the congressional leaders to pass the bill and rider as an administration measure.[83]

The enormous violence of the public reaction to these and subsequent reports was all the more impressive in view of Wilson's casual attitude at the outset of the controversy. From personal friends came an inundation of appeals to the President to remember his principles and stand firm against such invidious discrimination as the rider implied.[84] From the National Association of Manufacturers, the United States Chamber of Commerce, and other employer and business groups came warnings that, as former President Taft put it, the conservative classes would make Wilson's action on the Sundry Civil bill "the standard by which to judge him."[85] And from a nearly unanimous body of editors, conservative and progressive, came a chorus of protests against "an attempted discrimination and exemption which no ingenuity of sophistry can make anything else than the hideous un-American thing it really is."[86]

Stunned by this virtually nation-wide outpouring, Wilson thrashed about in an attempt to find a way to mollify conservatives without alienating the leaders of organized labor. Having encouraged Democratic leaders in Congress to reintroduce the Sundry Civil bill with the exemption rider, he could not protest when the House and Senate

[83] George Harvey, "Six Months of Wilson," *North American Review*, cxcviii (November 1913), 581-582.

[84] "The most vicious bill ever enacted by a Congress of the United States now awaits your approval or your dissent," George Harvey wrote, for example. ". . . It divides the American people into two great classes. It provides the means for the prosecution of one set of citizens who may violate the law. It explicitly withholds means for prosecuting another set of citizens for breaking the same law." G. Harvey, "An Appeal to the President," *Harper's Weekly*, lvii (May 17, 1913), 3. See also Samuel Rea to W. W., April 17 and 24, 1913, Wilson Papers; Robert U. Johnson to W. W., May 9, 1913, *ibid.*; Andrew Carnegie to W. W., May 23, 1913, *ibid.*; H. B. Thompson to W. W., May 26, 1913, the Thompson-Wilson Correspondence, Princeton University Library.

[85] W. H. Taft to W. M. Crane, May 21, 1913, Taft Papers. See also Board of Directors of the United States Chamber of Commerce to W. W., April 29, 1913, Wilson Papers; the National Association of Manufacturers, *Bulletin of the National Council for Industrial Defense, 1st Session, 63rd Congress*, No. 10; Elliot H. Goodwin, secretary, United States Chamber of Commerce, to W. W., June 9, 16, and 23, 1913, Wilson Papers; Frank S. Gardner, secretary, New York Board of Trade, to W. W., April 19, 1913, *ibid.*; and *New York Times*, May 13 and 20, 1913, for accounts of the campaign to force the President to veto the Sundry Civil bill.

[86] *New York Sun*, May 15, 1913. See also *New York Nation*, xcvi (April 17, 1913), 377; *New York Evening Post*, May 8, 1913; *Springfield* (Massachusetts) *Republican*, May 9, 1913; *New York Journal of Commerce*, May 9, 1913; and the *Hartford Times* and *Philadelphia Public Ledger*, cited in *Harper's Weekly*, lvii (May 31, 1913), 29.

approved the measure on April 22 and May 7, 1913. Yet how could he sign a bill that members of his class and his own conscience told him violated all his principles of equity and fair play?

He found a way out in casuistry. "I have signed this bill," he explained in a public statement on June 23, 1913, "because I can do so without in fact limiting the opportunity or the power of the Department of Justice to prosecute violations of the law, by whomsoever committed. If I could have separated from the rest of the bill the item which authorized the expenditure by the Department of Justice of a special sum of $300,000 for the prosecution of violations of the anti-trust law, I would have vetoed that item, because it places upon the expenditure a limitation which is, in my opinion, unjustifiable in character and principle. But I could not separate it. I do not understand that the limitation was intended as either an amendment or interpretation of the anti-trust law, but merely as an expression of the opinion of Congress. . . . I can assure the country that this item will neither limit nor in any way embarrass the actions of the Department of Justice. Other appropriations supply the department with abundant funds to enforce the law. The law will be interpreted, in the determination of what the department should do, by independent, and I hope impartial, judgments as to the true and just meaning of substantive statutes of the United States."[87]

It was an unconvincing explanation that pleased neither the leaders of organized labor nor the outraged conservatives. Reminding the President of Democratic platform pledges, Gompers warned that the A.F. of L. still expected outright statutory exemption and would be satisfied "only when the Sherman Anti-trust law is amended in a satisfactory manner or repealed."[88] Conservative spokesmen, on the other hand, were shocked by Wilson's attempt to escape responsibility for the rider. "When during the [preconvention] campaign Mr. Wilson publicly accepted and preached doctrines condemned in his earlier teaching," the *New York Times* declared, "it was hard to maintain belief in his sincerity. By signing this vicious bill he has made it still harder. The President has disappointed the country."[89] "He attempts to retain the support of those who insist upon this special privilege . . . by signing the bill," Taft observed with some relish, "and at the same

[87] *New York Times*, June 24, 1913.

[88] S. Gompers, "The Significance of That 'Rider,'" *American Federationist*, xx (August 1913), 621-622.

[89] *New York Times*, June 25, 1913; also the *Boston Transcript*, June 24, 1913; and *Harper's Weekly*, LVII (July 4, 1913), 3.

time to mitigate the indignation of those who have regarded this as a test of his political character by condemning the rider in a memorandum and excusing his signature."[90] "The signing of the Sundry Civil Appropriation bill by Wilson was *damnable* to my mind and ought to kill him politically," a North Carolina banker maintained. ". . . I may be wrong but I think I see the 'beginning of the end' of Wilson and probably the Democratic party."[91]

But it was, obviously, the end neither of Wilson nor of the controversy over labor exemption, for the issue arose again in a more decisive way a year later, during the discussion over amendment of the Sherman Act.[92] In the meantime, by pressing for the adoption of two other items in the A.F. of L.'s program—a seamen's bill and legislation to limit immigration to the United States—labor leaders and their friends in Congress created new perplexities for the President.

Any discussion of the seamen's bill should begin with some account of its author, Andrew Furuseth, president of the International Seamen's Union. "One of the heroes of the world, who has forfeited money, position, comfort and everything else to fight the battle of the common sailor," as William Kent described him, Furuseth had moved from San Francisco to Washington, "where he lived for fifteen years in shacks and sailors' boardinghouses, refusing to accept more than a seaman's pay,"[93] and worked to free American sailors from the bondage of their contracts and to strengthen maritime safety requirements.

Furuseth won his first victories in 1895 and 1898, with the passage by Congress of legislation to improve the conditions of American seamen. He then began work on a comprehensive seamen's bill, for which he finally found sponsors, Representative William B. Wilson and Senator La Follette, in the Sixty-second Congress. In addition to imposing severe safety requirements on all ships sailing to American ports, it established careful standards to regulate the hours and protect the living conditions of American sailors and abolished imprisonment for all seamen, foreign as well as domestic, who violated their labor contracts while in American ports. The House approved the measure in the wake of the *Titanic* disaster in the spring of 1912; the Senate approved a revised bill on March 2, 1913; and President Taft gave it a

[90] W. H. Taft to G. J. Karger, June 25, 1913, Taft Papers.
[91] W. H. Wood to D. A. Tompkins, June 28, 1913, Tompkins Papers.
[92] See below, pp. 427-433.
[93] The quotations are from William Kent to Norman Hapgood, June 16, 1914, Kent Papers; and Belle C. and Fola La Follette, *Robert M. La Follette*, I, 522.

pocket veto, on the ground that he had no time properly to consider the measure.[94]

Circumstances at the beginning of the Wilson administration, however, augured well for the fulfillment of Furuseth's dreams. The Democratic platform of 1912 promised speedy enactment of the seamen's bill. Even more important, President Wilson cordially approved its objective of giving seamen the same freedom that other American workers enjoyed. "It seems to me of capital consequence," he wrote on March 15, 1913, after a conference with La Follette.[95] And when Furuseth addressed to Wilson a moving plea for his support a few months later,[96] the President replied assuringly and a short time later moved to obtain speedy approval of the seamen's bill by the Senate labor committee.[97] Under this pressure and the spur of a new marine disaster—the burning of the liner *Volturno* off the coast of Newfoundland on October 9, 1913, with heavy loss of life—the Senate approved the measure sponsored by La Follette on October 23, 1913.[98]

The seamen's bill would probably have been promptly approved by the House and the President had it been only a matter of domestic concern. Complications arose, however, because the measure in effect abrogated the contractural obligations of alien seamen on foreign vessels in American ports, thus violating treaties, which promised the arrest and return of deserting seamen, between the United States and the maritime powers. In addition, the Washington government had agreed to participate in an international conference on safety at sea in London in November 1913; and it seemed hardly courteous for the government that had taken leadership in calling the conference to set its own new safety requirements before the conference could assemble.

[94] For the legislative history of the seamen's bill in the Sixty-second Congress, see "Shall 'Involuntary Servitude' Continue Under Our Laws?" *La Follette's Weekly*, v (March 29, 1913), 4.

[95] W. W. to Rudolph Spreckels, March 15, 1913, Wilson Papers.

[96] "We have sought this legislation in vain for nearly twenty years," Furuseth wrote. "We are poor, we are lowly, we have nothing, with which to quicken sympathy and action, except our loyalty and our plainly told tale, therefore, have we been without success and we now come to you." A. Furuseth to W. W., June 26, 1913, *ibid.*

[97] W. W. to A. Furuseth, June 30, 1913, *ibid.*; W. W. to Senator William Hughes, August 22, 1913, *ibid.*

[98] For the impact of the *Volturno* disaster and accounts of the Senate's action, see the Chicago *Public*, xvi (October 17 and 24, 1913), 985-986, 1011-1012; New York *Outlook*, cv (November 8, 1913), 503-504; *The Survey*, xxi (November 8, 1913), 164; *La Follette's Weekly*, v (November 1, 1913), 1, 3, 9; *Harper's Weekly*, lviii (November 15, 1913), 4; and Belle C. and Fola La Follette, *Robert M. La Follette*, i, 524-531.

The envoys of the great maritime powers voiced these objections to the Secretary of State during the early months of 1913,[99] but Wilson was unaware of the international ramifications of the seamen's bill until John Bassett Moore, Counselor of the State Department, called his attention to them on October 16, 1913.[100] It was now too late to prevent action by the Senate; but the administration moved quickly to forestall House approval of the seamen's bill, and the American delegates went to the London Conference, which opened on November 12, 1913, unembarrassed by any unilateral action by their government. In an unusual display of harmony, the conferees drafted a treaty, known as the Convention on Safety at Sea, that imposed uniform and generally rigid safety requirements on the vessels of all maritime nations. The one recalcitrant was Furuseth, who resigned as a member of the American delegation and returned to the United States to work against the treaty, because it established safety standards that fell below the requirements of his own seamen's bill.[101]

Thus it came about that the Washington administration now had to choose between ratifying the Convention on Safety at Sea unconditionally, which would mean abandoning the seamen's bill and disappointing labor and its friends, and ratifying the Convention with a reservation that would permit the adoption of the seamen's bill. After months of spirited controversy, Wilson yielded to the advice of the State and Commerce departments and supported unconditional ratification. In response, the Senate foreign relations committee reported the Convention without amendment in December 1914.[102]

[99] Johann von Bernstorff to the Secretary of State, January 16, 1913, Wilson Papers; J. Loudon to C. P. Anderson, January 21, 1913, *ibid.*; Cecil Spring Rice to the Secretary of State, July 25, 1913, *ibid.*; Thomas Spring Rice to the Secretary of State, October 15, 1913, *ibid.*; E. M. House to W. H. Page, October 22, 1913, House Papers.

[100] J. B. Moore to W. W., October 16, 1913, Wilson Papers.

[101] A. Furuseth to W. W., December 23, 1913, *ibid.*; A. Furuseth, "Report to the President of the United States . . . ," MS. in *ibid.*, dated January 12, 1914.

[102] For documentation to illustrate the above summary, see J. W. Alexander to W. C. Redfield, April 14, 1914, copy in the Daniels Papers; John Sharp Williams to W. W., April 24, 1914, Wilson Papers; W. W. to W. C. Redfield, June 8, 1914, *ibid.*; W. W. to W. J. Bryan, July 13, 1914, *ibid.*; W. W. to J. Hamilton Lewis, July 15, 1914, *ibid.*; S. Gompers to W. W., October 16, 1914, *ibid.*; E. T. Chamberlain to W. H. Page, June 10, 1914, Page Papers; W. J. Bryan to W. W., December 19, 1914, Wilson Papers; *La Follette's Weekly*, v (November 15, 1913), 4; *ibid.*, December 13, 1913, p. 3; resolution of the executive council of the A. F. of L., denouncing the Convention on Safety at Sea and demanding passage of the seamen's bill, in *American Federationist*, xxi (July 1914), 585; *The Survey*, xxxiii (December 19, 1914), 307-308.

But the forces in Congress behind the seamen's bill were too strong and determined to be easily thwarted. The Senate ratified the Convention on Safety at Sea on December 16, 1914. At the same time, it adopted a proviso offered by John Sharp Williams of Mississippi reserving to the United States the right to abrogate treaties providing for the arrest of deserting seamen and to "impose upon all vessels in the waters of the United States, such higher standards of safety and such provisions for the health and comfort of passengers and immigrants as the United States shall enact for vessels of the United States."[103] Then on February 27, 1915, the upper house approved the conference committee's report of the seamen's bill—the House had approved the measure on August 27, 1913—and sent it to the President.[104]

Events now moved swiftly to a final crisis. Following the advice of Counselor Robert Lansing, Bryan urged the President to give the seamen's bill a pocket veto;[105] and the newspapers reported on March 1, 1915, that Wilson would heed the Secretary's advice. On the same day Furuseth appealed in a moving letter, begging the President to approve the bill for which he, Furuseth, had fought so long.[106] Wilson's reply revealed that he was deeply troubled and almost prepared to veto the seamen's bill. "My interest in the relief and protection sought to be afforded in the seamen's bill is no less deep than it was," he wrote to Furuseth on March 2, "and some of my apprehensions with regard to the bill that has just been passed have been removed. But what is troubling me just at this moment is that it demands of the Government what seems a truly impossible thing, namely, the denunciation of some twenty-two commercial treaties. . . . To throw the commercial relations of the country into disorder and doubt just at this juncture might lead to the most serious consequences, and upon that ground I am debating very seriously whether it is possible for me to sign the bill or not."[107]

In a last-ditch effort, Furuseth and La Follette, accompanied by Senator Robert L. Owen of Oklahoma, called on Bryan at the State Department on the afternoon of March 2, 1915. Bryan had apparently

[103] *The Survey*, xxxiii (December 19 and 26, 1914), 307-308, 332.

[104] *New York Times*, February 28, 1915.

[105] On the grounds that the seamen's bill would require the renegotiation of twenty-two treaties with the maritime powers, cause endless confusion, and provoke serious trouble because of its provision for the abolition of imprisonment for desertion. See R. Lansing to W. J. Bryan, March 1, 1915, Wilson Papers; and W. J. Bryan to W. W., March 1, 1915, *ibid.*

[106] A. Furuseth to W. W., March 1, 1915, *ibid.*

[107] W. W. to A. Furuseth, March 2, 1915, *ibid.*

never heard of Furuseth, whom he referred to as "a Mr. Foruseth"; but the Nebraskan was so stirred by the old sailor's plea that he immediately reversed his position and urged the President to approve the seamen's bill if its advocates would concede an amendment giving the State Department ample time in which to abrogate the commercial treaties.[108]

Finally, during the evening of March 2 La Follette took Furuseth to the White House for a personal appeal to the President. "Tumulty, I have just experienced a great half-hour, the tensest since I came to the White House," Wilson told his secretary soon afterward. "That man La Follette pushed me over tonight on the Seamen's bill."[109] The following day La Follette reiterated his personal pledge that Congress would give the State Department all the time it needed to iron out the ensuing international complications,[110] and Wilson signed the seamen's bill on March 4, 1915. "I debated the matter of signing the bill very earnestly indeed, weighing the arguments on both sides with a good deal of anxiety," he wrote on March 5, "and finally determined to sign it because it seemed the only chance to get something like justice done to a class of workmen who have been too much neglected by our laws."[111]

"The Seamen's Act," Gompers rejoiced, "has a rightful place among those really important legislative acts that dedicated our soil to freedom."[112] "In signing the Seamen's Bill," Furuseth said in a personal note to the President, "you gave back to the seamen, so far as the United States can do it, the ownership of their bodies, and thus wiped out the last bondage existing under the American flag. The soil of the United States will be holy ground henceforth to the world's seamen."[113] It was, indeed, a great victory for organized labor but a narrow one; and the defenders of the Seamen's Act would have to fight many hard

[108] W. J. Bryan to W. W., March 2, 1915, *ibid.*
[109] Belle C. and Fola La Follette, *Robert M. La Follette*, I, 535-536.
[110] R. M. La Follette to W. W., March 3, 1915, Wilson Papers.
[111] W. W. to N. D. Baker, March 5, 1915, *ibid.*
[112] *American Federationist*, xxii (April 1915), 274.
[113] A. Furuseth to W. W., March 6, 1915, Wilson Papers. For similar comment, see R. M. La Follette, "The American Sailor a Free Man," *La Follette's Magazine*, vii (March 1915), 1-2; R. M. La Follette, "Andrew Furuseth and His Great Work," *ibid.*, April 1915, p. 2; "Passing the Seamen's Bill," Chicago *Public*, xviii (March 5, 1915), 225-227; Raymond W. Pullman, "The Seamen's Bill a Law After Twenty Years' Fight," *The Survey*, xxxiii (March 13, 1915), 645-646; Andrew Furuseth, "The Dawn of Another Day," *American Federationist*, xxii (September 1915), 717-722; and William B. Wilson, "The Seamen's Act," *Harper's Weekly*, lxii (April 22, 1916), 426-427.

battles with the powerful American shipping interests in the future to save their measure.[114]

The final important item in the A.F. of L.'s legislative program during the New Freedom period was to impose some restriction on the enormous numbers of immigrants coming to American shores. Claiming that unlimited immigration depressed wages at home and multiplied the difficulties of unionizing the basic industries, spokesmen of organized labor had long been the chief advocates of restriction or outright exclusion.[115] By 1913, however, they had been joined by a number of leading sociologists, who were appalled by what they thought were the dire social consequences of unrestrained immigration,[116] and by a large nativistic element who feared a Catholic and Jewish inundation.[117]

The instrument favored by restrictionists before 1917, a literacy test for immigrants, had been embodied in legislation successfully vetoed by Cleveland in March 1897 and by Taft in February 1913 and was the most important feature of the general immigration bill introduced in the House in June 1913 by Representative John L. Burnett of Alabama. Except for voicing his opposition to the literacy test,[118] Wilson did not attempt openly to interfere when the lower house approved the Burnett bill on February 4, 1914. But he did prevent prompt approval by the Senate by warning leaders in that body that he could not approve the measure so long as it contained the literacy qualification.[119] The pressures for restriction mounted so enormously during the summer and autumn of 1914, however, that the Senate ignored the President's warn-

[114] For significant comment on the Seamen's Act and its impact upon the maritime labor market, see Elmo P. Hohman, "Maritime Labour in the United States: The Seamen's Act and Its Historical Background," *International Labour Review*, xxviii (August 1938), 190-218; and E. P. Hohman, "Maritime Labour in the United States: Since the Seamen's Act," *ibid.*, September 1938, pp. 376-403.

[115] For a review of the A.F. of L.'s campaign for immigration restriction and a reiteration of labor's arguments, see Samuel Gompers, "Immigration Legislation Effected," *American Federationist*, xxiv (March 1917), 189-195; and S. Gompers to Senator E. D. Smith, May 1, 1914, Gompers Letterbooks.

[116] They included Henry P. Fairchild of Yale, Edward A. Ross of the University of Wisconsin, Jeremiah W. Jenks of New York University, Leon C. Marshall of the University of Chicago, Thomas N. Carver of Harvard, and Robert A. Woods of South End House, Boston.

[117] See, e.g., *The Menace*, February 20, 1915; C. G. Nelson to W. W., February 18, 1914, Wilson Papers; and W. J. Carpenter to W. W., February 17, 1914, *ibid.*, for expressions of the anti-Catholic point of view.

[118] *New York Times*, February 3, 1914.

[119] New York *World*, February 10, 1914; W. W. to E. D. Smith, March 5, 1914, Wilson Papers.

ings and adopted the Burnett bill by a vote of fifty to seven on January 2, 1915.

Their action represented a turning point in federal policy, and during the weeks following the Senate's approval of the Burnett bill it seemed that almost every champion and opponent of immigration restriction appealed to the White House. Gompers and the entire executive council of the A.F. of L. came first, on January 16, 1915, to plead for approval of the Burnett bill.[120] Then, when Wilson held a public hearing at the White House on January 22, the labor leaders returned, accompanied by spokesmen of farm organizations, the railroad brotherhoods, patriotic societies, and students of the immigration problem. "Protests against the literacy test," J. H. Patten of the Farmers' National Congress argued, "come from those who want to Russianize the laboring world here." The increase of illiterate immigrants, added Professor E. A. Ross of the University of Wisconsin, compounded the difficulties confronting social and political reformers.[121]

Well-organized, vocal, and politically formidable, the opponents of immigration restriction included railroad managers and employers in the mass industries who used large numbers of unskilled immigrants; spokesmen of various Italian-, Polish-, Hungarian-, and Russian-American societies; the entire leadership of the Jewish community in the United States; and, most important, Roman Catholic leaders, who viewed the Burnett bill as a frankly anti-Catholic measure. By mass meetings, petitions, and personal appeals, they made it plain that they would consider the President's action on the controverted measure as a test of his good will.[122]

[120] *New York Times*, January 17, 1915.

[121] *ibid.*, January 23, 1915.

[122] See, e.g., *ibid.*, February 17, 1914, for evidence of the Vatican's opposition; and the New York *World*, January 25, 1915, for the opinion of James Cardinal Gibbons, the leader of the Roman Catholic Church in the United States. For reports of mass meetings and letters and petitions from employers, Jewish leaders, and spokesmen of foreign-born groups, see the *New York Times*, January 23, 25, 26, 1915; New York *World*, January 25, 1915; Jacob H. Schiff to W. W., January 15, 1915, Wilson Papers; Louis Marshall, president of the American Jewish Committee, to W. W., January 17, 1915, *ibid.*; resolution adopted by the New York Assembly, January 26, 1915, *New York Times*, January 27, 1915; and letters of thanks to Wilson for vetoing the Burnett bill, all in the Wilson Papers and dated January 28-30, 1915, from the *Jewish Daily News*, the Hebrew Sheltering and Immigrant Aid Society, Louis N. Hammerling, president of the American Association of Foreign Language Newspapers, the Harrison Hungarian Club of Chicago, Frank Trumbull of the Chesapeake & Ohio Railroad, Rabbi Stephen S. Wise, the Toledo Polish Commercial Club, and K. Zychlinski, president of the National Polish Alliance.

It was a harrowing cross fire, especially since Wilson had no deep convictions one way or the other. "I find myself in a very embarrassing situation about that bill," he confessed to Senator John Sharp Williams, who had urged him to approve the Burnett bill. "Nothing is more distasteful to me than to set my judgment against so many of my friends and associates in public life, but frankly stated the situation is this: I myself personally made the most explicit statements at the time of the presidential election about this subject to groups of our fellow-citizens of foreign extraction whom I wished to treat with perfect frankness and for whom I had entire respect. In view of what I said to them, I do not see how it will be possible for me to give my assent to the bill. I know that you will appreciate the scruple upon which I act."[123]

In the end, therefore, the President vetoed the Burnett bill on January 28, 1915, although he gave other reasons for his decision than considerations of political expediency. The American people, he declared in his veto message, had a clear right to institute a policy of immigration restriction. But he could not approve such a "radical change in the policy of the Nation" without some clear mandate from the people. "Let the platforms of parties speak out upon this policy and the people pronounce their wish," he concluded. "The matter is too fundamental to be settled otherwise."[124]

The veto held in the House on February 4, 1915, in spite of a desperate counterattack by Burnett and a bipartisan coalition. But the proponents of restriction renewed their campaign in the following Congress and re-enacted the Burnett bill over the President's second veto on February 1 and 5, 1917. It was, incidentally, merely another in the series of victories that led to the adoption of a policy of nearly complete exclusion in the 1920's.

[123] W. W. to J. S. Williams, January 7, 1915, Wilson Papers.
[124] *Congressional Record*, 63d Cong., 3d sess., p. 2482.

CHAPTER IX

The Beginnings of New Freedom Diplomacy, 1913-1914

"IT WOULD be the irony of fate if my administration had to deal chiefly with foreign affairs," Wilson remarked to an old Princeton friend a few days before he went to Washington.[1] Unfortunately, fate was not only ironical but in a sense also cruel, for the new President had to confront foreign problems of such magnitude as had not challenged the United States since the early nineteenth century.

The years of the two Wilson administrations were a time of cataclysmic war and world-wide social upheaval, when the American government played an unwilling but decisive role in determining the future of mankind. The burden of decision that would come after 1914 was often more than the American people and their leaders would know how to bear wisely, but even during the months of relative quietude in world affairs before the outbreak of the First World War, the President and his advisers were beset by one crisis after another. It might be well, therefore, by way of introduction, to give some account of the objectives, capacities, and methods of the new makers of American foreign policy.

Whatever their detractors might say, there could be no doubt that Wilson and Bryan entered office determined to inaugurate a new era in American foreign relations. In contrast to Roosevelt's policy of "realism" and Taft's use of "dollar diplomacy" in the Caribbean and the Far East, Wilson and Bryan promised a New Freedom abroad as well as at home—a foreign policy of friendship based upon altruism rather than upon sheer considerations of national and material interests.

To a remarkable degree, both Democratic leaders shared the assumptions and ideals that provided the dynamic for New Freedom diplomacy. Both were men of good will and noble intentions. Both were at heart moralists, who viewed international relations and America's role in world affairs in terms of immutable principles, not in terms of expediency. Both were dedicated to the democratic ideal, at least theo-

---

[1] To E. G. Conklin, quoted in R. S. Baker, *Woodrow Wilson*, IV, 55.

retically, and were imbued with a passion for liberty and self-government, which they were confident would spread inevitably throughout the world. Both were convinced that America had a unique mission, as one writer has said, "to realize an ideal of liberty, provide a model of democracy, vindicate moral principles, give examples of action and ideals of government and righteousness to an interdependent world, uphold the rights of man, work for humanity and the happiness of men everywhere, lead the thinking of the world, promote peace,—in sum, to serve mankind and progress."[2]

In addition, Bryan and Wilson were both fundamentally missionaries of democracy, driven by inner compulsions to give other peoples the blessings of democracy and inspired by the confidence that they knew better how to promote the peace and well-being of other countries than did the leaders of those countries themselves. Even when their motivation was mundane, even when they acted to acquire new naval bases or to protect American economic interests abroad, even when they used force to ram democracy down the throats of foreign peoples, they rationalized their actions in terms of doing good for others.

But good intentions alone do not suffice for the construction and execution of a foreign policy. In spite of a few successes, events soon proved that New Freedom diplomacy was often either inadequate to cope with the realities of international life or else was only a glimmering illusion of policies that ought to be. In brief, the record of the New Freedom in foreign affairs from 1913 to the autumn of 1914 was marked more by contradiction and failure than by consistency and success. Why was this so? Why was it that a President and Secretary of State so obviously well-intentioned failed so often to meet their own criteria? The answer to this question is complex and will emerge perhaps most clearly as we discuss specific episodes; but we might attempt some general explanation at this point.

To begin with, Wilson and Bryan, like most Presidents and Secretaries of State, were poorly equipped in background and training to manage the foreign relations of a great power. They knew next to nothing about the administration of foreign affairs and were equally ignorant of the foreign policies of the other powers and of the tensions that imperiled the peace of the world in 1913 and 1914. Bryan had traveled through Europe and the Far East and had come into touch with some leaders abroad through his activity in the international peace

[2] Harley Notter, *The Origins of the Foreign Policy of Woodrow Wilson*, p. 653; quoted by permission of the Johns Hopkins Press, publishers.

movement, but Wilson knew western Europe only through books and as a casual tourist.

The seriousness of Wilson's and Bryan's ignorance of the techniques and issues of foreign affairs was heightened by the absence, a few months after Wilson's inauguration, of a strong bureaucracy capable of formulating and guiding foreign policy in an orderly way. The professionals in the State Department were understaffed and overworked; and the advantages that had accrued from the reorganization effected during the Taft administration[3] were in part nullified by the resignation, dismissal, or demotion of some of the key staff members to make way for political appointees in the early months of the Democratic regime.[4]

An additional impediment to the formulation and execution of a consistent foreign policy at any time during the Wilson era was the President's own methods of doing business in the international field. His methods stemmed in part from his egotism, secretiveness, and urge for dominance, in part from his deep suspicion of and contempt for the ordinary processes of diplomacy and of the diplomatic profession, and in part from a well-matured conviction that the President alone must make and control foreign policy, governed only by public opinion and his conception of what was the right thing to do. We could digress endlessly here. It must suffice at this point to say that Wilson paid scant attention to expert advice when it challenged his own intuitive conclusions, and he revealed his contempt for the usual diplomatic methods and diplomats themselves by conducting critical negotiations through special envoys whom he thought he could trust.

The most important weakness of New Freedom diplomacy, however, was the naïveté of its underlying assumptions. Wilson and Bryan assumed that moral force controlled the relations of powers, that reason would prevail over ignorance and passion in the formation of public opinion, and that men and nations everywhere were automatically progressing toward an orderly and righteous international society. If these assumptions were true, then a combination of Christian love and moral suasion *would* suffice to solve all international problems.

For the most part, Wilson assumed that they were valid, although he did not go as far as Bryan, who was prepared to renounce the use of force altogether in international relations. "I believe that this nation

---

[3] For this reorganization, which established the bureaucratic structure in effect during the first Wilson administration, see Graham H. Stuart, *The Department of State, A History of Its Organization, Procedure, and Personnel*, pp. 212-220.

[4] See above, pp. 97-98.

could stand before the world today," Bryan declared in 1910, "and tell the world that it did not believe in war, that it did not believe that it was the right way to settle disputes, that it had no disputes that it was not willing to submit to the judgment of the world. If this nation did that, it not only would not be attacked by any other nation on earth, but it would become the supreme power in the world. I have no doubt of it, and I believe that the whole tendency is toward that policy."[5]

It is one thing to hold such a vision for the future and another to try to implement it before the coming of the Kingdom of Heaven. The fact was, as Theodore Roosevelt and a few "realists" argued at the time, that men were motivated more often by greed and ambition than by Christian love, that nations inherently acted in self-interest instead of in a spirit of altruism, and that physical force governed international relations as much as it controlled the relations of communities and states.

New Freedom diplomacy failed in part, therefore, not because it was ignobly conceived, but because it ignored some basic facts of life. The truth was that not even idealists like Wilson and Bryan or the allegedly idealistic American people could live up to the New Freedom ideals, and crises and contradictions arose one after another when apparent altruism had failed. Unhappily, this failure was often due to the fact that American policy in the first instance had been based upon the assumption that altruism was enough.

One of the first and most typical manifestations of New Freedom diplomacy was Bryan's great campaign in 1913 and 1914 to exorcise war. Long active in the international peace movement, the Nebraskan had first conceived a peace plan early in 1905 and had been pressing for its adoption since that time.[6] In its practical aspects, Bryan's solution was based upon the experience of his predecessors in trying to steer arbitration treaties through a Senate jealous of its partial control over foreign relations.[7] Bryan's plan provided, not for arbitration, but simply for

---

[5] Quoted in Merle E. Curti, "Bryan and World Peace," *Smith College Studies in History*, xvi (April-July 1931), 138-139.

[6] Bryan tells the history of his peace plan in a letter to Harry Walker, January 20, 1915, Bryan Papers, Library of Congress. For a full discussion of the background, see M. E. Curti, "Bryan and World Peace," *loc.cit.*, pp. 143-149.

[7] Secretary of State John Hay negotiated a series of arbitration treaties in 1904 and 1905 that excluded all disputes involving vital interest and national honor, but President Roosevelt withdrew the treaties after the Senate amended them to make its consent to each arbitration necessary. In 1908, however, Secretary of State Elihu Root persuaded Roosevelt to surrender to the Senate's terms and negotiated twenty-five limited

agreement that the signatories would submit all disputes to permanent commissions for investigation for a period of six months or one year. During this interval of investigation and "cooling off," neither party

Busy Days for the Handy Man
Sykes in the Philadelphia *Public Ledger*

would resort to war or increase its armaments. And the signatories were free to accept or reject the commission's findings, even to go to

arbitration agreements in 1908 and 1909. In 1911, moreover, Secretary of State Philander C. Knox signed treaties with Great Britain and France providing for the arbitration of all so-called justiciable questions, including disputes affecting national interest and honor. But in approving the treaties in 1912 the Senate exempted all important questions from possible arbitration, and President Taft refused to promulgate the amended treaties.

war, after the investigation and the "cooling off" period had ended. Bryan was of course confident that in such circumstances war could not occur. "When men are mad," he explained, "they talk about what they can do. When they are calm they talk about what they ought to do. And it is the purpose of this plan to provide a time for passion to subside, for reason to regain its throne."[8]

Bryan won Wilson's approval of his project at their conference at Trenton on December 21, 1912, and official Cabinet and presidential endorsement on April 8 and 15, 1913. At Wilson's suggestion, he next explained it to the Senate foreign relations committee on April 23. The senators were encouraging and insisted only that the Secretary omit the provision forbidding signatories to increase their armaments during the period in which a dispute was being investigated. The following day, April 24, 1913, Bryan invited the entire diplomatic corps to the State Department and informed them that the United States was now prepared to negotiate conciliation treaties with all the nations of the world. Finally, he explained his project to the American people in a stirring address on May 9, 1913. "The world is advancing in morals," he exulted. ". . . There is a greater sense of kinship among men than there ever was before. There is more altruism on this earth than this earth has previously known. . . . No nation shall go beyond us in its advocacy of peace or in its work for peace."[9]

Bryan signed the first "cooling off" treaty with El Salvador on August 7, 1913. Then, during the following year, he negotiated similar treaties with twenty-nine other nations, including Great Britain, France, and Italy, twenty of which were eventually ratified and promulgated.[10]

Nor was this the full record of the Nebraskan's contributions to the cause of peace. In the first place, he obtained the Senate's consent in 1914 to the renewal of Root's limited arbitration treaties with some twenty-four nations. In the second, he won clear title as leader of the international peace movement by his ardent good will, which he expressed by word and deed at every opportunity. Once he presented paperweights to the diplomats representing governments that had agreed to sign conciliation treaties—they were miniature plowshares which had been beaten out of an old army sword. On another occasion, he proposed a toast that glorified the friendship binding nations to-

[8] *New York Times,* May 10, 1913.

[9] The above paragraph is based upon accounts in the Daniels Diary, April 8 and 15, 1913; and the *New York Times,* April 23, 24, and 25 and May 10, 1913.

[10] M. E. Curti, "Bryan and World Peace," *loc.cit.,* pp. 151, 157-161.

gether: "Here's to the greatest of ships. Its compass is the human heart. Its shells are bursting with good-will. Love is the smokeless powder that impels the projectiles which it sends forth. The Prince of Peace is its captain. I propose as the consummation of our desire the enduring, the indestructible battleship, whose armor nothing can pierce—FRIENDSHIP."[11]

To the end of his life, Bryan was prouder of his achievements in the field of peace, particularly of his conciliation treaties, than of anything else he accomplished during his long career. "I came into the office of Secretary of State," he wrote in 1915, "just when the time was ripe and the world ready and the honor of signing the treaties has fallen to me and, as they will in all probability continue indefinitely, my name will be found in the chancelleries of the world attached to living treaties that it is hoped will formulate the basis of an enduring peace."[12] It required some optimism to be able to write this way when most of the world was at war. Actually, however, Bryan had helped construct machinery that peace-loving nations could use to avert fighting during momentary but dangerous crises; and he had helped lay the groundwork for a new peace crusade in the 1920's that would culminate in the signing of the Pact of Paris in 1928.

And yet it must be said that, for all its virtues, Bryan's conciliation project also pointed up the general inadequacy of New Freedom diplomacy. What the American people needed in the prewar years was not only good will but also a realistic understanding of the international society in which they lived and a determination to protect their international ideals. By assuming that friendship and conciliation alone would suffice for the settlement of international disputes, Bryan's plan offered an illusory security, increased the reluctance of the American people to assume international responsibilities that carried commitments of force, and compounded the obstacles to the building of military and naval strength commensurate with America's position in the world.

If Bryan's conciliation plan illustrated the naïveté of New Freedom diplomacy, then the erratic way in which the President and Secretary of State dealt with the problem of China in 1913 illustrated their self-esteem and reliance upon unconventional procedures.

[11] Given on May 13, 1913, before the commissioners from Great Britain and Canada assembled to formulate plans for the celebration of a century of peace between Great Britain and the United States, printed in *The Commoner*, XIII (May 23, 1913), 3.

[12] W. J. Bryan to Harry Walker, January 20, 1915, Bryan Papers, Library of Congress.

In 1909 a consortium of British, French, and German bankers signed a contract with the Chinese government to build a network of railways in central and southern China and to furnish funds to stabilize Chinese finances. Arguing that American participation in the consortium was essential to the defense of the Open Door and the territorial integrity of China, a clique in the State Department, who had been working for a more aggressive policy in the Far East, persuaded Secretary of State Philander C. Knox to demand that American bankers be admitted to the consortium. Accordingly, in 1911 an American banking syndicate headed by J. P. Morgan & Company were admitted to a reorganized Six-Power Consortium, which now also included Russian and Japanese bankers. For various reasons the project did not prosper, and there is strong evidence that the European and American bankers were eager to wash their hands of the affair by early 1913.[13]

Writing on behalf of the American syndicate on the day after Wilson's inauguration, Willard Straight pointedly inquired about the new administration's attitude toward continued American participation in the consortium.[14] On March 10, 1913, moreover, Straight and Henry P. Davison of Morgan & Company and Paul M. Warburg of Kuhn, Loeb & Company went to the State Department for a long conference with Bryan and the departmental officials who had helped to formulate the Chinese loan policy.[15]

Bryan could give no immediate answer to the bankers, but he raised the question at a Cabinet meeting on March 12, 1913. There was a long discussion but apparently no serious consideration of the important economic and strategic interests involved. Bryan objected to American participation in the consortium because he thought the arrangements for the six-power loan conferred monopolistic privileges on a few American bankers, gave international bankers a control over China's financial affairs that might lead to the impairment of Chinese sovereignty, and deprived the American government of any independence in dealing with China. The President agreed, adding, "We ought to help China in some better way."[16]

[13] This summary is based upon Tien-yi Li, *Woodrow Wilson's China Policy, 1913-1917*, pp. 24-33; and Max Warburg to Under Secretary of State Zimmermann, March 20, 1913, in *Die Grosse Politik der Europäischen Kabinette, 1871-1914* (40 vols. in 54), XXXII, 380-382; hereinafter cited as *Die Grosse Politik*.

[14] W. Straight to the Secretary of State, March 5, 1913, *Papers Relating to the Foreign Relations of the United States, 1913*, pp. 167-168; hereinafter cited as *Foreign Relations, 1913*.

[15] *New York Times*, March 11, 1913.

[16] Daniels Diary, March 12, 1913; W. J. and Mary B. Bryan, *The Memoirs of William*

Having made his decision, Wilson acted quickly. Without consulting or informing the State Department staff members who had worked so long on behalf of the six-power loan, he issued a statement to the press on March 18, 1913, repudiating American participation in the consortium. "The conditions of the loan," the President declared, "seem to us to touch very nearly the administrative independence of China itself, and this administration does not feel that it ought, even by implication, to be a party to those conditions." The United States, he went on, earnestly desired to aid "the great Chinese people" in every way "consistent with their untrammeled development and its own immemorial principles." But American interests were "those of the open door—a door of friendship and mutual advantage"; and this was the only door the American government cared to enter.[17]

It was, to say the least, a novel way of doing important international business. Wilson had not only implicitly condemned the other powers supporting the loan agreement and credited the American government with superior virtue; he had also denounced an agreement to which the United States was a party without either consulting or informing the associate governments.

The President's action was more than Assistant Secretary of State Huntington Wilson could stomach. "When I consented . . . to continue in the office of Assistant Secretary of State for these few weeks longer . . . ," he wrote in an angry letter of resignation to the President on March 19, 1913, "I had no reason to suppose that the officials on duty in the Department of State would learn first from the newspapers of a declaration of policy which, I think, shows on its face the inadequacy of consideration given to the facts and theories involved. . . . I had no reason to suppose that the fate of negotiations which had so long had the studious attention of the Foreign Offices of six great powers would be abruptly determined with such quite unnecessary haste and in so unusual a manner."[18] "As you know," wrote the German Ambassador in Washington, in a dispatch to the Foreign Office in Berlin, "they have little understanding in America of the formalities of international diplomatic exchanges, and we must constantly remember that the only consistency

---

Jennings Bryan, pp. 362-363; Josephus Daniels, *The Wilson Era, Years of Peace*—1910-1917, pp. 158-159.

[17] *Foreign Relations, 1913*, pp. 170-171. The American syndicate withdrew from the consortium on March 19, 1913.

[18] Printed in the *New York Times*, March 21, 1913. "The principles involved," Bryan retorted on March 20, 1913, "were such that it did not require any great length of time for the President to understand and act upon them." *ibid.*, March 21, 1913.

in the diplomacy of the United States lies in its surprises, which it always offers to the world."[19]

Cynical diplomatists thought they saw some Machiavellian purpose in Wilson's action, but such suspicions credited the President with a diplomatic sophistication that he did not yet possess. There is no reason to doubt that he thought he was acting in a moral capacity to save China from the designs of scheming European and American imperialists. As he put it ten days after issuing his declaration of withdrawal, "I feel so keenly the desire to help China that I prefer to err in the line of helping that country than otherwise. If we had entered into the loan with other powers we would have got nothing but mere influence in China and lost the proud position which America secured when Secretary Hay stood for the open door in China after the Boxer Uprising."[20] "I believe you have won the lasting gratitude of China," Bryan concurred. "With this nation setting such an example no other nation can force her into unfair terms. They will now become rivals for her friendship."[21]

The vast majority of Americans agreed and enthusiastically approved. "The first important act of the Department of State under Secretary Bryan," Senator La Follette declared in a typical progressive comment, "is the rejection of the Dollar Diplomacy policy of Taft and Knox. Humanity is to be placed higher than Property in our international affairs. Patriotism is to be given precedence over Profits. National honor is to count for more than trust aggrandizement."[22] Anti-imperialists, missionaries, and the religious press boasted, moreover, that the American government had again taken moral leadership in the Far East against imperialism,[23] while the Chinese people seemed exhilarated and grateful.[24]

[19] Von Bernstorff to Chancellor von Bethmann Hollweg, March 30, 1913, *Die Grosse Politik,* xxxii, 387-388.
[20] Daniels Diary, March 28, 1913.
[21] W. J. Bryan to W. W., March 23, 1913, Wilson Papers.
[22] R. M. La Follette, "Dollar Diplomacy," *La Follette's Weekly,* v (March 29, 1913), 1.
[23] See, e.g., David Starr Jordan to W. W., March 19, 1913, Wilson Papers; Erving Winslow, secretary of the Anti-Imperialist League, to W. W., March 19, 1913, *ibid.*; Arthur J. Brown, secretary of the Board of Foreign Missions of the northern Presbyterian Church, to W. W., March 20, 1913, *ibid.*; James Sadler, London Missionary Society, to W. W., March 21, 1913, *ibid.; The Presbyterian,* lxxxiii (April 2, 1913), 6; *The Independent,* lxxiv (March 27, 1913), 671-672.
[24] The Chinese leaders, the secretary of the American Presbyterian Mission at Tsingtao reported to the President, were "gratified beyond measure that your administration has broken with the 'dollar diplomacy'—which policy (as we at close range see it applied, 'screwed on,' out here) is disgraceful to the nations practicing it, and which

Sentiments of international friendship further motivated Wilson and Bryan in their handling of a second important Far Eastern problem— the recognition of the so-called Republic of China—in the spring of 1913. A group of southern Chinese revolutionaries under the leadership of Sun Yat-sen had rebelled against the tottering Manchu dynasty in 1911 and established a provisional Republic of China at Nanking. Then, early in 1912, most of the northern Chinese leaders joined the rebels; the Emperor abdicated on February 12; and Sun resigned the provisional presidency of the new republic in favor of Yüan Shih-k'ai, former commander in chief of the imperial army.

In response to these events, a growing body of opinion in America demanded that the Taft administration extend formal recognition to the new "democracy" of the Far East. Predisposed toward recognition, the Washington government agreed to cooperate with the other powers in deciding upon the proper time for recognition, provided such a policy entailed no undue delay. But innumerable delays occurred in 1912 and early 1913, because Japan and the European powers insisted on withholding recognition until the new Chinese government had specifically confirmed their concessions, special privileges, and immunities in China. At the same time, the demands for independent action grew by leaps and bounds in the United States and were reinforced by advice from the American legation in Peking.[25] This, in brief, was the situation when Wilson entered the White House.

As early as March 18, 1913, when he issued his announcement of the American withdrawal from the Six-Power Consortium, Wilson had apparently decided to cut loose from the powers, to extend recognition, and to launch an independent policy in China.[26] The United States, he explained to the Cabinet on March 28, 1913, could best help the Chinese by standing alone and by being able to say to Russia, Japan,

---

the Chinese look upon as brutal & iniquitous. Since we have pulled out of the deal America & Americans have gone up above par with the Chinese. They feel that Americans are their only friends." Charles E. Scott to W. W., May 31, 1913, Wilson Papers. This judgment was confirmed by the German Minister in Peking, who reported: "The entire Chinese press . . . sees in the words of the President with great satisfaction a new proof of the friendship of the great sister republic, which did not want to tolerate that China should be financially and politically oppressed [or raped] by the European powers." Von Haxthausen to Chancellor von Bethmann Hollweg, March 27, 1913, *Die Grosse Politik*, xxxii, 385. On this point, see also Tien-yi Li, *Woodrow Wilson's China Policy*, pp. 45-46.

[25] Tien-yi Li, *Woodrow Wilson's China Policy*, pp. 57-66; E. T. Williams, Chargé d'Affaires, to the Secretary of State, March 18, 1913, *Foreign Relations, 1913*, pp. 96-98.

[26] So the newspapers reported in considerable detail. See the *New York Times*, March 20, 1913.

England, and Germany, "What are your wishes on this part of China?" and "What are your designs?"[27] Three days later, on April 1, he told the Cabinet that he had decided to recognize the Republic of China. He was willing, in response to a suggestion from Bryan, to inform the powers of his plans and to invite their cooperation; but he declared that he would not make American recognition in any way contingent upon the action of other governments.[28]

Bryan informed the foreign envoys of the President's decision on the following day, April 2, 1913. There followed a month of waiting, until the Chinese National Assembly had organized. Then, on May 2, 1913, the American Chargé in Peking went to the President's Palace and delivered a message of recognition to Yüan and his government from the President of the United States. "I extend, in the name of my Government and of my countrymen," it read, "a greeting of welcome to the new China thus entering into the family of nations. In taking this step I entertain the confident hope and expectation that in perfecting a republican form of government the Chinese nation will attain to the highest degree of development and well being."[29]

It was sincerely meant, and during the next four years Wilson persevered in his New Freedom policy of nonintervention and moral support of Yüan's government. Even so, New Freedom diplomacy toward China was not only obviously bankrupt by 1917 but had also worked to the positive detriment of the Chinese people. As one authority friendly to Wilson has concluded, "In the long run it was China who suffered the consequences of Wilson's apparently wise and morally unblemished action."[30] This was true principally because China needed not merely friendship and moral exhortation but aggressive American economic assistance as well. By withdrawing support from the Six-Power Consortium and by afterward failing to give adequate encouragement to Americans interested in investing money in China, the President surrendered leadership in that ancient land to the Japanese, who were less concerned with "moral" principles than he. In 1917 the President abandoned the New Freedom policy, reverted to "dollar diplomacy" by attempting to reorganize the defunct consortium, and adopted a firmer policy of resistance to further Japanese expansion. In subsequent volumes we will tell how this was done, and with what effect.

[27] Daniels Diary, March 28, 1913.   [28] *ibid.*, April 1, 1913.
[29] *Foreign Relations, 1913*, pp. 109-110, 116-119.
[30] Tien-yi Li, *Woodrow Wilson's China Policy*, p. 212.

Further evidence of the inadequacy of New Freedom diplomacy came with the outbreak of a controversy with Japan in the spring of 1913 over the enactment by the California legislature of a measure designed to prevent the ownership of land by Japanese subjects residing in that state. No minor episode, it raised the threat of war and marked the beginning of a long period of acute tension between the United States and Japan. The failure of New Freedom diplomacy in this crisis was, therefore, all the more significant.

The controversy grew immediately out of the efforts of Democratic and Progressive politicians in California to curry favor with the labor and farm vote during the campaign of 1912 by demanding legislation to prohibit Japanese ownership of land. Indeed, the Democrats had outdone their rivals in this agitation.[31]

The fundamental cause, however, was the Californians' fear of a Japanese inundation during the years following the end of the Russo-Japanese War in 1905, and of eventual Japanese economic penetration and what Californians called the "mongrelization" of their state. In 1913 there were actually only about 50,000 Japanese in California, owning 17,000 acres of farm land and leasing another 150,000 acres; and Japanese immigration into the state had been virtually ended by the so-called Gentlemen's Agreement of 1907 and 1908 between the Japanese and American governments. Fanned by racial prejudice, however, the Californians' fear of Japanese competition had grown into a neurosis.

"I beg to inform you that the problem is fundamental and most serious," a Democratic leader wrote in a typical analysis of the question. "It is this: a non-assimilable people, clever and industrious agriculturists working for themselves as owners and lessees, takes farms from [the] hands of white men in destructive competition. The tide must be checked, otherwise California will become a Japanese plantation and republican institutions [will] perish."[32] "The whole question is a social and not an economic one," another Californian explained frankly. "If we permit them to do so, the Japanese can displace white people, as they are doing to a small extent in California and a large extent in the Hawaiian Islands, and the clash of race antipathy which is very real

[31] See J. O. Davis, chairman of the Democratic state central committee of California, to J. P. Tumulty, January 4, 1913, State Department Papers; James D. Phelan to F. K. Lane, April 6, 1913, Wilson Papers; and Anthony Caminetti to W. J. Bryan, received April 8, 1913, State Department Papers.

[32] J. D. Phelan to W. W., April 7, 1913, Wilson Papers.

and very essential will lead to war and not to peace and will prevent democratic development, just as it has done in the South."[33]

Feeling was running high in California when the legislature met in Sacramento in March 1913 to deal with the alleged Japanese menace. Wilson and Bryan were fully informed of the progress of events, but they did not take the affair seriously in its early stages or realize its potential dangers. On the contrary, they sympathized with the Californians' fears and actually encouraged the anti-Japanese leaders in their designs. "I think I understand the gravity of the situation in California," Wilson wrote, for example, to a Democratic leader in the state, "and I have never been inclined to criticize. I have only hoped that the doing of the thing might be so modulated and managed as to offend the susceptibilities of a friendly nation as little as possible."[34]

Indeed, on his own initiative the President volunteered a method whereby California might exclude Japanese subjects from land ownership without violating the Japanese-American treaties of 1894 and 1911, which guaranteed most favored nation treatment to the citizens of both countries. This he did in an interview with Representative William Kent, a California Progressive, whom he called to the White House on April 7, 1913. The President "suggested the extremely irritated state of affairs with Japan, admitted and endorsed the state's right to handle its own land questions, but deferentially submitted the fact that it might be framed in less offensive form [than by singling out the Japanese in an open discrimination, by forbidding aliens 'ineligible to citizenship' to own land, as the bills before the California legislature at the time provided]." Would not Kent suggest to Governor Hiram Johnson of California, Wilson went on, that a bill might be drawn along the lines of the Alien Ownership Act of the District of Columbia of 1887, which excluded from land ownership those persons who had not made application for American citizenship? Such a law, the President explained, would leave "the way open for bona fide prospec-

[33] William Kent to Ida M. Tarbell, May 8, 1913, Kent Papers. See also James D. Phelan, "The Japanese Question from a Californian Standpoint," *The Independent*, LXXIV (June 26, 1913), 1439-1440; Edward Hungerford, "California's Side of It," *Harper's Weekly*, LVII (June 7, 1913), 13; Chester H. Rowell, "The Japanese in California," *World's Work*, XXVI (June 1913), 195-201; John T. Bramhall, "California and the Japanese: I—An Existing Menace," New York *Outlook*, CV (November 1, 1913), 477-478.

[34] W. W. to J. D. Phelan, April 9, 1913, Wilson Papers. It might be added that during the campaign of 1912 Wilson had supported the exclusion of Oriental immigrants because of their alleged nonassimilability and low standard of living. See W. W. to J. D. Phelan, n.d., but printed in *The Independent*, LXXIII (October 10, 1912), 863.

tive citizens to participate in the privilege of owning California land" and would exclude "those who had no such intent, necessarily including the Japanese whose first papers would not be accepted."[35] It was a transparent ruse, but, as future events were to prove, it would have been enough to satisfy the Japanese government.[36]

Kent at once relayed the President's suggestion to Governor Johnson,[37] who replied testily that the Washington government should communicate with Sacramento if it had anything to say to the California authorities.[38] Bryan, therefore, appealed directly,[39] and Wilson was publicly conciliatory, declaring that California was acting within its constitutional rights and that the federal government was really helpless in the matter.[40] Johnson and the California legislators responded with apparent good will and readiness to cooperate, and for a time it seemed that a crisis would be averted.[41]

The truth was, however, that the leaders of California were determined to deal once for all with the issue of land ownership, even if that meant insulting the Japanese people and involving their country in a serious dispute with Japan. On April 15, 1913, therefore, the California Assembly adopted an alien land bill which barred persons "ineligible to citizenship" from land ownership.[42] This was the kind of invidious discrimination that the President had been trying to avoid,

[35] William Kent, "Some Reminiscences of Hiram Johnson," MS. in the Kent Papers.

[36] "In a number of States," the Japanese Ambassador later admitted, "the right of aliens to hold real estate has been made to depend upon actual filing of declarations of intention to become citizens. That requirement, as a condition precedent to the exercise of the right in question, can not be said to be unreasonable or illogical." "*Aide-mémoire . . . ,*" *Foreign Relations, 1913,* p. 639.

[37] William Kent to Hiram Johnson, April 7, 1913, Wilson Papers.

[38] H. Johnson to W. Kent, April 8, 1913, *ibid.*

[39] W. J. Bryan to H. Johnson, April 10, 12, 15, and 16, 1913; and H. Johnson to W. J. Bryan, April 11, 14, 15, and 17, 1913, all in the State Department Papers.

[40] *New York Times,* April 12 and 15, 1913. Wilson engaged in an interesting exchange on this point. "I am sorry that you haven't taken the opportunity offered by the California land bill to knock in the head the silly idea that the police powers of the states comprise an independent limitation on the treaty power of the United States," Edward S. Corwin of Princeton wrote on April 13, 1913. "I do not feel by any means as confident as you do," Wilson replied on April 19, 1913, "as to the power of the Federal Government in the matter of overriding the constitutional powers of the states through the instrumentality of treaties." Both letters are in the Wilson Papers. For further discussion of this point, see below, pp. 293-295, 300.

[41] H. Johnson to W. J. Bryan, April 11, 14, and 15, 1913, State Department Papers; A. Caminetti to W. J. Bryan, April 16, 1913, *ibid.*

[42] H. Johnson to W. J. Bryan, April 16, 1913, Wilson Papers, gives the text of the Assembly bill.

and he was finally spurred on to belated action to head off a controversy that now seemed to threaten a break with Japan.

Since early March 1913 the Japanese envoys in Washington and the American Chargé in Tokyo had repeatedly warned the State Department of the dangers that the passage of a discriminatory alien land bill would raise. "Japan watches with grave concern the progress of the Alien Land Bill in California," the Chargé in Tokyo cabled, for example, on April 12, 1913, paraphrasing the words of the Japanese Foreign Minister, Baron Nobuaki Makino. "She earnestly hopes it may not pass. . . . The Japanese Government, feeling its great responsibility for the preservation of the traditional relations of the two countries, have at this turn of events no recourse but to make a solemn appeal to the American Government to take suitable steps after *further* consideration to prevent such a development of affairs as might lead to very serious misunderstanding between the two peoples."[43] The Foreign Minister's conversation, the Chargé reported two days later, "was characterized by the deepest emotion and, actuated by an apparent feeling that developments might lead to serious misunderstanding, virtually took the form of an appeal to the sympathy of the American Government."[44]

If anything, the Foreign Minister underestimated the growing violence of the reaction of the Japanese public and press to events on the other side of the Pacific. At first Japanese editors commented moderately, while various public spokesmen, Christian leaders, and public groups appealed for fair play and friendship from the United States. "It is a matter of great regret," one newspaper declared in a typical early editorial, "that at the outset of the administration of Mr. Wilson, . . . who is himself regarded as a sort of incarnation of justice, . . . there should occur an event which may easily injure this friendship between the two countries."[45]

[43] A. Bailly-Blanchard to the Secretary of State, April 12, 1913, State Department Papers.

[44] A. Bailly-Blanchard to the Secretary of State, April 14, 1913, *ibid.*

[45] Tokyo *Kokumin Shimbun*, April 10, 1913. See also the Tokyo *Asahi Shimbun*, March 30, 1913; Tokyo *Nichi Nichi Shimbun*, April 8, 1913; Tokyo *Chuo Shimbun*, April 10, 1913; Tokyo *Yorozu Choho*, April 9, 1913; Tokyo *Jiji Shimbo*, April 9, 1913; Tokyo *Japan Times*, April 8, 10, 13, 1913; Tokyo *Japan Advertiser*, April 9, 10, 13, 1913. For protests from Japanese leaders and groups, see A. Bailly-Blanchard to the Secretary of State, April 9, 11, 1913, State Department Papers; K. Okura to W. J. Bryan, April 14, 1913, *ibid.*; Christian Endeavorers of Kyoto to W. J. Bryan, April 27, 1913, *ibid.*; Baron Shibusaw to W. J. Bryan, April 30, 1913, *ibid.*; Viscount Kaneko to W. J. Bryan, received April 24, 1913, *ibid.; New York Times*, April 12 and 13, 1913.

On the other hand, excitement, anger, and war fever among extremist groups began to mount dangerously in Japan after the passage of the discriminatory alien land bill by the California Assembly in mid-April. On April 17, 1913, to cite one example, a crowd of some 20,000 Japanese in Tokyo cheered wildly as a member of the Diet demanded the sending of the Imperial fleet to California to protect Japanese subjects and maintain the nation's dignity.[46] There were other such mass meetings throughout the Empire; anonymous writers in the newspapers told of plans for the seizure of the Philippines and Hawaii; the Japanese press united in condemning the California Assembly bill as "hostile" and an "outrageous insult"; and a flood of protests poured in upon the American Embassy in Tokyo.[47]

In an earlier crisis with Japan in 1906, provoked by the attempted segregation of Oriental school children in San Francisco, Theodore Roosevelt had publicly threatened to use "all the forces of the United States, both civil and military," to enforce respect for the treaty rights of Japanese subjects in the United States.[48] Wilson and Bryan could not refuse to act in the crisis of 1913 after the warnings from the Imperial Foreign Office and the outbursts in Tokyo portended a possible break in relations. But neither Wilson nor Bryan wished to brandish a big stick before the California legislature like Roosevelt to assert the national government's sovereignty. Believing as they did in state rights, they could not conceive of using federal power to coerce a state. Furthermore, they were confident that a display of friendship toward both California and Japan would be enough to prevent a crisis.

Thus on April 18, 1913, three days after the California Assembly had approved the discriminatory alien land bill, Wilson told newspapermen that he could not interfere while legislation was in progress in Sacramento.[49] On the same day, however, he appealed through Bryan to Governor Johnson. "The President directs me to say that while he fully recognizes the right of the people of California to legislate *ac-*

---

[46] Tokyo *Japan Times*, April 18, 1913.

[47] *Boston Herald*, April 19, 1913; *New York Times*, April 19, 1913; *Boston Globe*, April 20, 1913; Tokyo *Japan Times*, April 17 and 25, 1913; Tokyo *Japan Advertiser*, April 16, 17, 18 and 20, 1913; Tokyo *Nichi Nichi Shimbun*, April 15, 1913; Tokyo *Kokumin Shimbun*, April 17, 1913; A. Bailly-Blanchard to the Secretary of State, April 21 and 23, 1913, State Department Papers, enclosing various resolutions and petitions from Japanese leaders and organizations.

[48] Message to Congress of December 18, 1906, quoted in Elting E. Morison (ed.), *The Letters of Theodore Roosevelt* (8 vols.), v, 532. In the same crisis, incidentally, Bryan defended the right of Californians to control "matters purely local."

[49] *New York Times*, April 19, 1913.

cording to their judgment on the subject of land tenure," the message read, "he feels it his duty to urge a recognition of the international character of such legislation. Being anxious to preserve and strengthen the long-standing friendly relation existing between this country and the nations of the Orient, he very respectfully, but most earnestly, *advises* against the use of the words 'ineligible to citizenship.' He asks that you bring this view to the attention of the legislators. He believes the Senate bill as telegraphed to the Department of State is greatly to be preferred. That bill limited ownership to citizens and to those who had declared their intention of becoming citizens."[50]

It was wise advice, but the California leaders did not miss the point that Wilson had in effect surrendered any right to interfere. On April 21, 1913, therefore, the Progressive leaders in the California Senate agreed to suppress the Thompson-Birdsall bill, which had been drawn in accordance with the State Department's advice, and to support a frankly discriminatory land bill, that is, one that denied the right of land ownership to persons "ineligible to citizenship" and to corporations, the majority stockholders of which were aliens "ineligible to citizenship."[51] And when the President urged the Californians to reconsider,[52] Governor Johnson replied that the legislature was acting within its admitted constitutional rights and would not violate any treaty obligations of the United States.[53]

A serious impasse had been reached. Wilson told reporters on April 23, 1913, that he suspected Governor Johnson was playing politics.[54] But what could the federal government do? The President explained his dilemma in a Cabinet meeting on April 22. "He said that it had never been determined by the courts whether a state was bound by

[50] Printed in *ibid.*, April 20, 1913. Italics added.

[51] *ibid.*, April 22, 1913.

[52] "Invidious discrimination," Wilson wrote, "will inevitably draw in question the treaty obligations of the Government of the United States. I register my very earnest and respectful protest against discrimination in this case, not only because I deem it my duty to do so as the Chief Executive of the Nation, but also, and the more readily, because I believe that the people and the legislative authorities of California will generously respond the moment the matter is frankly presented to them as a question of national policy and of national honor." W. W. to the Governor, the President of the Senate, and the Speaker of the House of the State of California, April 22, 1913, Wilson Papers; also printed in the *New York Times*, April 23, 1913.

[53] H. Johnson to W. W., April 22, 1913, Wilson Papers and *New York Times*, April 23, 1913.

[54] New York *World*, April 24, 1913. For a discussion of Johnson's motives, see *ibid.*, April 24, 1913.

any treaty stipulations and this was a matter still to be decided."[55] He wanted, not to do anything to limit the rights of the states, but to point out that a state *ought not* to violate the treaties of the United States. Therefore, he told his Cabinet members, he had decided to send Bryan to California to plead with the Governor and legislators.[56]

The arrangements were quickly made, and Bryan arrived in Sacramento on April 28, 1913, only to find Progressive leaders in the state Senate more determined than before to enact a discriminatory alien land bill. Speaking before an executive session of the legislature, he assured the Californians that the President was eager to reach "that solution of the question" which accomplished their objective "with the least hardship to anyone." But he went on to plead for either a delay in legislation or the enactment of a measure that would not offend the Japanese. "Who is able to look into the future," he asked, "and tell us what it may mean to do that which may be regarded as a declaration to the world of inferiority, that which cannot but wound the pride of a nation that has made wonderful progress, a nation that stands among the powers of the world, a nation which is our friend and ought to remain our friend?"[57]

On the very next day the California Senate responded by approving unanimously a measure drawn by U. S. Webb, Attorney General of the state. It provided that all aliens "eligible to citizenship" might own land in California on the same terms as American citizens and that other aliens might hold land "in the manner and to the extent and for the purposes prescribed by any treaty now existing between the Government of the United States and the nation or country of which such alien is a citizen or subject."[58]

[55] Specialists in American constitutional history will at once recognize the inaccuracy of this statement. In a long series of cases from 1796 to 1890, the Supreme Court had established the doctrine that the federal treaty-making power overrode the police power of the states, particularly in the matter of state legislation relating to the ownership and disposition of real property. For a comprehensive review, see Edward S. Corwin (ed.), *The Constitution of the United States, Analysis and Interpretation*, pp. 415-417.

[56] Daniels Diary, April 22, 1913. Italics added.

[57] From a transcript of Bryan's speech, enclosed in W. J. Bryan to W. W., April 29, 1913, Wilson Papers.

[58] *New York Times*, April 30, 1913; New York *World*, April 30, 1913. Article I of the Japanese-American Commercial Treaty of 1911 stipulated: "The citizens or subjects of each of the High Contracting Parties shall have liberty to enter, travel and reside in the territories of the other to carry on trade, wholesale and retail, to own or lease and occupy houses, manufactories, warehouses and shops, to employ agents of their choice, to lease land for residential and commercial purposes, and generally to do anything incident to or necessary for trade upon the same terms as native citizens and subjects."

Bryan came back before the legislature, begging that he be given an opportunity to try to settle the question by diplomacy and warning that the phrase "eligible to citizenship" was as offensive to the Japanese as the hated words "ineligible to citizenship."[59] The California law-makers, however, were deaf to such entreaties. On May 3, 1913, the state Senate and Assembly almost unanimously approved the Webb bill, amended only to permit aliens ineligible to citizenship to lease agricultural land for a period no longer than three years.[60] "We have accomplished the big thing," Governor Johnson said with satisfaction. "We have prevented the Japanese from driving the root of their civilization deep into California soil."[61] After a final futile appeal from the Secretary of State,[62] the Governor issued a lengthy defense of the Webb bill on May 14, 1913, and signed it five days later.[63]

Meanwhile, the apprehension of the Imperial government and the Japanese people had increased as events in Sacramento progressively demonstrated the futility of Bryan's mission. When the Japanese Ambassador in Washington, Viscount S. Chinda, called at the State Department on May 1, 1913, to warn that his government could not accept the Webb bill, he took the unusual step of intimating that the Wilson administration "had perhaps not gone so far as President Roosevelt did at the time [of] the school question to prevent undesirable action in California."[64]

Moreover, the Japanese government lodged an "urgent and explicit" formal protest on May 9, 1913, ten days before Governor Johnson signed the Webb bill. It used terms as strong as peaceful diplomacy would allow: "In the opinion of the Imperial Government, the act in question is essentially unfair and discriminatory, and it is impossible to ignore the fact that it was primarily directed against my countrymen. Accordingly, this protest is based upon the proposition that the measure is unjust and inequitable, and that it is not only prejudicial to the existing rights of Japanese subjects, but is inconsistent with the provisions of the treaty actually in force between Japan and the United States, and is also opposed to the spirit and fundamental principles of

[59] W. J. Bryan to W. W., May 1 and 2, 1913, State Department Papers; W. J. Bryan to W. W., May 3, 1913, Wilson Papers; *New York Times,* May 4 and 5, 1913.

[60] For a print of the bill as approved, see *Foreign Relations, 1913,* pp. 627-628.

[61] *New York Times,* May 5, 1913.

[62] W. J. Bryan to H. Johnson, May 11, 1913, State Department Papers.

[63] H. Johnson to W. J. Bryan, May 14, 1913, *ibid.; New York Times,* May 20, 1913.

[64] J. B. Moore to W. W., May 1, 1913, Wilson Papers.

amity and good understanding upon which the conventional relations of the two countries depend."[65]

There now followed a week of growing alarm and controversy in Washington, as the civilian and military leaders pondered a course of action. After reading Chinda's note to the Cabinet on May 13, 1913, the President observed that its language was "very strong"; but he agreed with Bryan that it gave no evidence of hostile intentions.[66] The military and naval leaders, on the other hand, were by now acutely disturbed by the possibility of war and alarmed by the knowledge that American defenses in the Pacific were fearfully weak. First, they warned all naval and army commanders in the United States, the Philippines, and Hawaii to stand by for further orders.[67] Next, the Joint Board of the Army and Navy, the over-all planning agency for the two services, met in night session on May 14, 1914, and urgently recommended that three American gunboats in the Yangtze River be ordered to sail at once to Manila to assist in the possible defense of Fort Corregidor.[68] In support, Admiral Bradley A. Fiske, Aid for Operations, addressed an alarming letter to the Secretary of the Navy. The Japanese, Fiske warned, coveted the Philippines and Hawaii, had been deeply offended by the California land bill, and would make war without warning. "Considering these facts," he concluded, "I believe . . . that war is not only possible, but even probable."[69]

The decision on the transfer of the gunboats was made during the following hectic two days. Much excited by the Joint Board's recommendation, Secretary of War Garrison on May 15, 1913, urged Secretary Daniels to join him in endorsing it. Daniels refused, arguing that the transfer would inflame Japanese opinion and provoke a war crisis without adding effectively to the defense of the Philippines. "Even if we were expecting it . . . ," Daniels added, "we could not prevent the Japanese Navy from taking the Philippines if they decided to concentrate their forces on those possessions." Garrison retorted that it was "nobody's business" where the United States sent its warships and that it would be a great mistake for persons who knew so little about military matters to ignore the Joint Board's advice. Failing to agree, the two secretaries went at once to the White House and presented their argu-

---

[65] The Japanese Ambassador to the Secretary of State, May 9, 1913, *Foreign Relations, 1913*, p. 629.

[66] Daniels Diary, May 13, 1913.

[67] New York *World*, May 16, 1913.

[68] Daniels Diary, May 15, 1913.

[69] B. A. Fiske to J. Daniels, May 14, 1913, Daniels Papers.

ments to the President and to John Bassett Moore, Acting Secretary of State in Bryan's temporary absence. It was a matter of such importance, Wilson replied, that the Cabinet would discuss it the following day. Meanwhile, however, he would not consent to the transfer of any ship in the Pacific Ocean.[70]

Tempers were short by the time the Cabinet met the next day, May 16, 1913, for the newspapers had told of a secret meeting at the White House and had provoked a minor war scare by reports of frantic army and naval preparations.[71] Garrison presented the Joint Board's views in strong language and intimated that the opinions of Cabinet members on military questions were not particularly valuable. "At this, Bryan flared up for the first time. He got red in the face and . . . thundered out that army and navy officers could not be trusted to say what we should or should not do, till we actually got into war; that we were discussing not how to wage war, but how not to get into war, and that, if ships were moved about in the East, it would incite to war."[72] In the subsequent discussion, Daniels, William B. Wilson, Lane, and Houston agreed with Bryan, while Redfield, McAdoo,[73] and McReynolds supported Garrison.

It was now the President's duty to make the decision. He had not "seriously entertained the thought of such a criminal possibility as war," he said, "till Thursday, the 15th, when he noticed the extreme perturbation of the Japanese ambassador."[74] "The Joint Board," he continued, "of course has presented the military aspect of the situation as it sees it and it may be right, but we are considering this matter with another light, on the diplomatic side, and must determine the policy. I do not think any movement should be made at this time in the Pacific Ocean and I will, therefore, take the responsibility of holding the ships where they are at present." "I think we did right today," Wilson told Daniels later in the afternoon. ". . . We must not have war except in an honorable way and I fear the Joint Board made a mistake."[75]

[70] Daniels Diary, May 16, 1913.

[71] e.g., New York *World*, May 16, 1913; and *New York Times*, May 16, 1913.

[72] D. F. Houston, *Eight Years with Wilson's Cabinet* (2 vols.), I, 66; copyright 1926, Doubleday & Company, Inc.

[73] For an elaboration of McAdoo's fears, see the House Diary, May 18, 1913.

[74] D. F. Houston, *Eight Years with Wilson's Cabinet*, I, 66. Bryan confirmed this impression after Chinda called at the State Department on May 15, 1913. "He seemed to be personally more disturbed than he has appeared to be at any previous time," Bryan reported. W. J. Bryan to W. W., May 15, 1913, Wilson Papers.

[75] Daniels Diary, May 16, 1913.

There was an interesting sequel to the affair. On May 17, 1913, the Joint Board presented a memorandum to Daniels emphatically protesting the President's decision and recommending that all torpedo-boat destroyers and torpedo boats on the California coast be sent at once to Hawaii. Admiral Fiske urged the Secretary to present the memorandum to the President, even after Daniels told him that the President had made his decision. Daniels relayed the message to the President in the afternoon.

Wilson was astonished by the Joint Board's presumption. "After we talked this matter over in Cabinet Friday [May 16, 1913] and you and the Secretary of War informed these Navy and Army gentlemen that there was to be no movement now," he told Daniels, "they had no right to hold a meeting at all and discuss these matters. When a policy has been settled by the Administration and when it is communicated to the Joint Board, they have no right to be trying to force a different course and I wish you would say to them that if this should occur again, there will be no General or Joint Boards. They will be abolished."[76]

The war scare in the United States vanished almost at once when the President told reporters that the idea of war with Japan was preposterous and made it plain that reports of preparations were false.[77] There now remained, however, the difficult task of finding a solution that would justify California's action—for the President and State Department had concluded that the alien land act did not violate treaty obligations—and at the same time mollify the Japanese government.

Bryan began by using the diplomacy of friendship. In a long conference with Chinda on May 18, 1913, for example, he could give no assurances of any positive remedial action by the United States. But when Chinda asked if the American reply would be final, the Secretary replied that nothing was final between friends and that the American government would be happy to consider any proposition that the Imperial Cabinet might wish to make.[78] "In conversation with Japanese Government," he cabled to the Chargé in Tokyo, "emphasize the extraordinary efforts made by the Washington Government to prevent passage of law. Explain freedom of action allowed states under our constitution; advise restraint and calmness. Suggest that nothing is

---

[76] *ibid.*, May 17, 1913. It might be added that Wilson ordered the Joint Board not to meet again without his permission; that permission was not given until October 1915. Josephus Daniels, *The Wilson Era, Years of Peace—1910-1917*, p. 167.

[77] *New York Times*, May 17, 1913.

[78] W. J. Bryan to W. W., May 18, 1913, Wilson Papers.

final between friends and express confidence that a satisfactory solution can be found for all questions if the parties approach the subject with patience and in the right spirit."[79] A week later, moreover, Bryan instructed the Chargé to assure the Japanese government that the United States had not taken steps to increase its armed forces in the Pacific and did not contemplate taking such action.[80]

Meanwhile, Counselor John Bassett Moore, Bryan, and Wilson had been preparing a reply to the Japanese note of May 9, 1913.[81] Presented to Chinda on May 19, the day on which Governor Johnson signed the alien land bill, the American note was gracious and replete with professions of friendship. It emphasized the efforts that the American government had taken to prevent the passage of the Webb Act, suggested that Japanese subjects adversely affected might appeal for redress to the federal courts, and assured the Imperial authorities that the United States would "safeguard the rights of trade and intercourse between the two peoples now secured by treaty."[82]

The Japanese leaders were grateful for Bryan's expressions of friendship,[83] but unconvinced by his arguments. "That reply did not, I regret to say," the Japanese Ambassador answered officially on June 4, 1913, "have the effect of lessening the sense of disappointment and grave concern experienced by the Imperial Government in consequence of the legislation to which it had reference. . . . The Imperial Government are unable to escape the conclusion that the measure is unfair and intentionally racially discriminatory, and, looking at the terms of the

[79] W. J. Bryan to A. Bailly-Blanchard, May 18, 1913, State Department Papers.

[80] W. J. Bryan to A. Bailly-Blanchard, May 26, 1913, *ibid.*

[81] Moore prepared the note soon after May 9, 1913; Wilson read it to the Cabinet on May 16; and Wilson and Bryan revised it soon afterward.

Wilson's most important change concerned the treaty-making power of the United States. Moore had written that Japanese subjects could appeal to the federal government if they believed the California alien land act contravened the Japanese-American Treaty of 1911, because "by the Constitution of the United States the stipulations of treaties are superior to state legislation." Wilson struck out the words "are superior to state legislation" and made the phrase read: "by the Constitution of the United States the stipulations of treaties made in pursuance thereof are the supreme law of the land." Moore, who was perhaps the leading authority on international law in the United States, protested vigorously after reading a copy of the revised note. "By design and in fact," he wrote to the President, "the treaty-making power is not subject to the Constitutional limitations imposed on the law-making power. The maintenance of this distinction is vital to the preservation of the constitutional supremacy of the Govt. of the U. S. in foreign affairs." J. B. Moore to W. W., June 29, 1913, Wilson Papers.

[82] The Secretary of State to the Japanese Ambassador, May 19, 1913, *Foreign Relations, 1913*, pp. 631-632.

[83] A. Bailly-Blanchard to W. J. Bryan, May 20, 1913, State Department Papers.

treaty between our two countries, they are equally well convinced that the act in question is contrary to the letter and spirit of that compact and they moreover believe that the enactment is at variance with the accepted principles of just and equal treatment upon which good relations between friendly nations must, in the final analysis, so largely depend. . . . I beg to assure you that the Imperial Government have too high an opinion of the sense of right and justice of the American Government to believe for a moment that that Government will permit a State to set aside the stipulations of the treaty or to impair the obligations of reciprocal friendly intercourse and good neighborhood."[84]

Moore prepared the American government's reply, assisted by suggestions from Bryan.[85] Presented to the Japanese Ambassador on July 16, 1913, it denied that the California alien land law was an expression of "any national discriminatory policy," attempted to answer the Imperial government's contention that the measure violated the Japanese-American Treaty of 1911,[86] and offered to compensate any Japanese subject for any loss he might sustain by operation of the California statute.[87]

In reply, Foreign Minister Makino did not ignore Moore's careful legal arguments. The main burden of his protest, however, was the obviously discriminatory character of the Webb Act, which he said was "unjust and obnoxious," "discriminatory against this Empire as compared with other states," and "mortifying to the nation and disregardful of the national susceptibilities of the Japanese people." The Imperial government, he warned, could not consider the question set-

[84] The note, moreover, brushed aside Bryan's suggestion that Japanese subjects in California could appeal for redress to the federal courts by pointing out that "the wrong complained of is directed against my countrymen as a nation" and that Japan had diplomatic relations with the United States, not with the State of California. Japanese Ambassador to the Secretary of State, June 4, 1913, *Foreign Relations, 1913*, pp. 632-635. Chinda afterward submitted an *aide-mémoire*, dated July 3, 1913, which elaborated the legal aspects of the Imperial government's argument. *ibid.*, pp. 635-640.

[85] For Bryan's suggestions and Wilson's comments, see W. J. Bryan to W. W., June 19 and July 1, 1913; and W. W. to W. J. Bryan, July 3, 1913, all in the Wilson Papers.

[86] Moore pointed out that the Treaty was deliberately silent on the question of ownership of agricultural land and cited a note from the Japanese Ambassador to Secretary Knox, dated February 21, 1911, in which the Japanese government promised that it would grant the right of land ownership to American citizens, "reserving for the future, however, the right of maintaining the condition of reciprocity with respect to the separate states."

[87] The Secretary of State to the Japanese Ambassador, July 16, 1913, *Foreign Relations, 1913*, pp. 641-645. For an elaboration of the legal details, see the *aide-mémoire* submitted in conjunction with this note, *ibid.*, pp. 645-650.

tled "so long as the existing state of things is permitted to continue."[88]

The incident had passed out of sight in the United States long before this correspondence ended, but deep popular resentment remained in Japan; and the Imperial Cabinet's determination to obtain redress was spurred by the fear that the opposition would drive it from power if it failed.[89] On August 19, 1913, therefore, the Tokyo Foreign Office proposed a settlement—the negotiation of a treaty conferring the mutual right of land ownership in the future but validating existing legislation in both countries relating to alien land tenure, except to confirm the titles of property acquired by aliens in both countries before the ratification of the treaty. In other words, the Japanese were willing to accept the California statute if the American government would only give lip service to the most favored nation principle in dealing with Japanese subjects and would nullify the California law to the extent of confirming land titles acquired by Japanese subjects in the state before its enactment.[90]

This was the least the United States could do to preserve the dignity and retain the friendship of a great power, but Bryan was forced to tell Chinda informally, first, that the President did not feel justified in presenting a treaty to the Senate that denied to the states the right to make racial and national distinctions in legislation, and, second, that ratification of such a treaty as the Japanese desired was in any event politically impossible at the time.[91]

Presented with further urgent appeals from Tokyo and assurances that Japan did not wish to raise the issues of immigration or naturalization,[92] Wilson finally agreed that the United States could no longer

[88] The Japanese Minister for Foreign Affairs to the Japanese Ambassador, received at the State Department August 26, 1913, *ibid.*, pp. 651-653.

[89] Ambassador Guthrie to the Secretary of State, August 19, 1913, State Department Papers; "Telegram from the Minister for Foreign Affairs, Tokio, Received August 19, 1913," given to Bryan by Chinda, Wilson Papers; and J. B. Moore, memorandum of a conversation with the Japanese Ambassador, dated August 29, 1913, State Department Papers.

[90] Ambassador Guthrie to the Secretary of State, August 19, 1913, *ibid.*, conveys a preliminary draft of the proposed treaty; the Japanese Ambassador to the Secretary of State, December 13, 1913, *ibid.*, conveys a revised version.

[91] W. J. Bryan to W. W., September 17, 1913, Wilson Papers. It should be added, however, that Bryan personally approved the proposed treaty. "If alien land laws are desired," he added in the letter just cited, "they should be made to apply to all aliens alike. It is not fair for a state to endanger international peace by acting independently of the rest of the states on a matter that concerns other nations."

[92] Ambassador Guthrie to the Secretary of State, September 25, October 13, and November 20, 1913, State Department Papers; Chinda to the Secretary of State, December 13, 1913, *ibid.*, transmitting a revised draft of the proposed treaty.

refuse to yield the one concession that the Japanese most desired—American affirmation of the most favored nation status for Japanese subjects in the United States in the future. "The more I consider the suggestions of the Ambassador from Japan," he wrote to Bryan early in 1914, "the more I feel convinced that the chief part of what he suggests is entirely reasonable. When you have an interview with the Committee of Foreign Relations of the Senate, I would be obliged to you if you would say that in my judgment it would be right, as it is desirable, to enter into a treaty with Japan which would assure her that her citizens would receive the same treatment as the citizens of other foreign countries, so far as their personal rights and privileges in the United States might be concerned."[93]

Bryan, therefore, soon afterward discussed the proposed treaty anew with Chinda and the Imperial Foreign Office. Pathetically eager for some settlement that would save their face, the Japanese agreed to waive the most controversial article in the proposed treaty, the one confirming the land titles acquired by Japanese subjects in California before the passage of the Webb Act. It was an important concession, and Bryan reciprocated with entire good will. He could not speak with certainty until he had consulted the Senate, he told Ambassador Chinda on January 23, 1914, but he thought that the waiving of the article in question had made it possible to obtain ratification of the proposed treaty. In any event, he continued, the President approved the purpose of the treaty and he, Bryan, would "proceed to consult the Counselor as to phraseology."[94] The Japanese were delighted. "Baron Makino," Tokyo replied, "accepts the terms and while desirous for consummation is content to trust to the President to decide when to act in order to secure confirmation by the Senate."[95]

The Japanese Cabinet would have been satisfied by almost any positive action by the Washington government, even if the Senate had afterward refused to approve the proposed treaty. But the time for action never seemed to come during the late winter and spring of 1914; and while the President delayed, the Yamamoto Cabinet fell on April 16, 1914, technically because the Diet rejected its naval budget, and a ministry dedicated to a more aggressive foreign policy came into power. One of the first acts of the new Imperial Foreign Minister, Baron Kato,

[93] W. W. to W. J. Bryan, January 15, 1914, Wilson Papers.
[94] W. J. Bryan, memorandum of a conversation with the Japanese Ambassador, January 23, 1914, State Department Papers.
[95] Ambassador Guthrie to the Secretary of State, January 29, 1914. *ibid.*

was to terminate the negotiations looking toward the proposed treaty, on the ground that it would not satisfy Japanese opinion, and to request an answer to the Japanese government's note of August 26, 1913.[96] There then followed a final exchange that only pointed up the hopelessness of a diplomatic settlement.[97]

We do not have to look far to discover the causes for this important failure of New Freedom diplomacy. There was Wilson's curiously narrow view of the federal government's authority, which prevented him from taking firm control of the controversy. There was Wilson's and Bryan's assumption that the California leaders would prove cooperative and that, in any event, professions of friendship would assuage the Japanese. There was Wilson's well-founded fear of violent controversy and defeat if he pressed for the ratification of a new treaty with Japan, which kept him from attempting to satisfy the reasonable wishes of the Imperial government. Above all, there was Wilson's own basic agreement, shared probably by a majority of Americans, with the anti-Japanese prejudices of the people of California, which led him and the State Department to try to evade the burden of Japan's protest by resorting to legalistic arguments. Whatever the causes of the failure, the consequences embittered Japanese-American relations for years to come.

The New Freedom had one clear-cut diplomatic triumph during the period before the outbreak of the First World War—Wilson's effective settlement of a troublesome dispute over Panama Canal tolls that threatened to endanger good relations between the United States and Great Britain. The controversy began in the summer of 1912, when Congress, in writing a measure to establish a schedule of tolls for the use of the Panama Canal, exempted American ships in the coastwise trade from the payment of tolls and authorized the President to charge lower tolls for American than for foreign ships in the foreign trade, and when President Taft justified this action by the strident boast that the United States owned the Canal and could charge what rates it pleased for American vessels.

[96] The Japanese Minister for Foreign Affairs to the Japanese Ambassador, June 9, 1914, *Papers Relating to the Foreign Relations of the United States, 1914*, pp. 426-427; hereinafter cited as *Foreign Relations, 1914*. Also Ambassador Guthrie to the Secretary of State, June 15, 1914, State Department Papers, relating a conversation with Kato.

[97] The Secretary of State to the Japanese Ambassador, June 23, 1914; the Japanese Ambassador to the Secretary of State, November 25, 1914, *Foreign Relations, 1914*, pp. 427-434.

Trouble with the British government arose at once; even before Taft signed the Panama Canal Act on August 24, 1912, the British Foreign Minister, Sir Edward Grey, protested the exemption of coastwise shipping and the potentially lower tolls for American ships in the foreign trade.[98] Grey elaborated his protest in a long and gravely worded note that the British Ambassador handed to the State Department on December 9, 1912. In brief, the Foreign Secretary contended that the Panama Canal Act's discrimination in favor of American shipping violated the Hay-Pauncefote Treaty of 1901, by which Britain had given the United States a free hand in building an isthmian canal and the American government had promised that the canal would be open on "terms of entire equality" to the ships of "all nations." Grey suggested, however, that the British government stood ready to submit the issue to arbitration if the Washington administration could not agree with his interpretation of the Treaty.[99]

Secretary of State Knox replied on January 17, 1913, brushing aside Grey's protest against lower tolls for American ships in the foreign trade—on the ground that the President had in fact already established equal tolls for American and foreign vessels of this class—and declaring that there was nothing left to arbitrate, inasmuch as Grey had earlier conceded that tolls exemption for American coastwise shipping would not necessarily violate the Hay-Pauncefote Treaty.[100]

This, in brief, was the status of the controversy when Wilson entered office in 1913. The issue did not affect the vital interests of either country, to be sure, but to many Americans and to practically all Englishmen it involved the good faith and honor of the United States. "Sir Edward Grey's argument," one New York editor declared, for example, "has both dignity and solemnity, but more important than either, it has

[98] The American Ambassador to the Secretary of State, July 15, 1912, *Papers Relating to the Foreign Relations of the United States, 1912*, pp. 470-471; hereinafter cited as *Foreign Relations, 1912*.

[99] The Secretary of State for Foreign Affairs of Great Britain to the British Ambassador, November 14, 1912, *ibid.*, pp. 481-489.

[100] The Secretary of State to the American Chargé d'Affaires, January 17, 1913, *Foreign Relations, 1913*, pp. 540-547.
It should be added that Knox considerably exaggerated the British government's alleged concession on the matter of exempting American coastwise shipping from the payment of tolls. Grey had conceded that the exemption of bona fide coastwise ships in such a way as not to increase the tolls on foreign shipping might not violate the Hay-Pauncefote Treaty; but he had then proceeded to argue that it was virtually impossible to give tolls exemption to coastwise shipping without also giving a substantial advantage to American foreign shipping.

truth. Never before was a nation more easily or more conclusively proved to be in the wrong. It is a humiliation to reflect that that nation is our own."[101] "Everywhere—in circles the most friendly to us and the best-informed,—I receive commiseration because of the dishonourable attitude of our Government about the Canal Tolls," Ambassador Page reported from London. ". . . All British opinion, so far as I can find out, has the same sort of suspicion of a treaty with the United States that men-of-affairs have of one of our States that repudiated its bonds. And this Canal Tolls matter stands in the way of everything. It is in their minds all the time—the minds of all parties and all sections of opinion. . . . They hold our Government in shame so long as this thing stands."[102]

Wilson had hastily approved the tolls exemption during the campaign of 1912, but sober reflection soon convinced him that national honor required the repeal of the disputed provision. He first revealed his change of mind in a conversation with Colonel House on January 24, 1913.[103] A week later he attended a meeting of the Round Table Dining Club in New York and listened while Joseph H. Choate, who had helped negotiate the Hay-Pauncefote Treaty while Ambassador to England, and Senator Elihu Root confirmed in detail that the British were right. "This has been an illuminating discussion," the President-elect commented. "I knew very little about this subject. I think I now understand it and the principles that are involved. When the time comes for me to act, you may count upon my taking the right stand."[104]

Soon after Wilson's inauguration, the British Ambassador in Washington, James Bryce, pressed hard for a settlement, intimating that his government might not be willing to renew the Anglo-American arbitration treaty, which would expire in June 1913, if the United States continued to refuse to submit the tolls dispute to arbitration.[105] In response, Wilson made it plain that he agreed with the British contention but would not be pressed into hasty action that might risk disrupting

[101] New York *World*, December 11, 1912. For similar expressions of American opinion, see the New York *Nation*, xcvi (January 9, 1913), 26; W. B. Howland, publisher of the New York *Outlook*, to W. W., March 4, 1913, Wilson Papers; and Robert Underwood Johnson, *The Exemption of Coastwise Shipping. Why It Should Be Repealed* (pamphlet).

[102] W. H. Page to W. W., September 10, 1913, Page Papers.

[103] House Diary, January 24, 1913.

[104] Henry White, *The Roster of the Round Table Dining Club*, pp. 21-25.

[105] Daniels Diary, April 18, 1913, relating Bryan's account of a conversation with Bryce.

his party while the tariff and currency bills were before Congress.[106]
Sir Edward Grey was satisfied, especially after his secretary, Sir William
Tyrrell, came to Washington in November 1913 to discuss the Mexican
situation and the tolls dispute and received the President's personal
assurances that the United States would, in good time, live up to its
treaty obligations, "both in the letter and in the spirit."[107]

Wilson moved quickly, therefore, once the Underwood and Federal
Reserve Acts had been passed and discussions looking toward antitrust
legislation had been launched. "You may be sure I will strive to the
utmost to obtain both a repeal of the discrimination in the matter of
the tolls and a renewal of the arbitration treaties, and I am not without
hope that I can accomplish both at this session," he wrote to Page early
in January 1914. "Indeed this is the session in which these things must
be done if they are to be done at all."[108]

Opening his campaign on January 26, 1914, Wilson called the members of the Senate foreign relations committee to the White House for
a three-hour conference. Reviewing the unsatisfactory condition of
America's foreign relations, he pointed to the growth of anti-American
sentiment in Japan, to the dangerous state of Mexican-American relations, and to a general accumulation of grievances against the United
States throughout the world. It was difficult, almost impossible, he said,
to conduct normal diplomacy in such an atmosphere of tension and
distrust. Repeal of the tolls exemption, Wilson continued, might clear
the air of all serious European hostility, but his supreme objective was
to retain the friendship of the British government and its cooperation
in American policy in Mexico. He explained how the Washington and
London governments had recently gone through a sharp crisis over
Mexican policy and how the British had yielded in the dispute. The
next move, he declared, was now up to the United States.[109]

---

[106] *ibid.*, in which the President relates what he told Bryce on March 24, 1913;
House Diary, July 3, 1913.

[107] E. M. House to W. H. Page, November 14, 1913, House Papers, relating the
details of this conference.

[108] W. W. to W. H. Page, January 6, 1914, Page Papers.

[109] *New York Times*, January 27 and 28, 1914; New York *World*, January 27 and 30,
1914.

The President summarized his talk before the foreign relations committee in a
"BRIEF for conference with Foreign Relations Committee of the Senate" (MS. in the
Wilson Papers), as follows:
"*Difficulties* now facing us: Mexico
                                    Japan.
"*What I want to do in Mexico*. Condition precedent, to hold off all foreign assistance
or even countenance [of the Huerta regime].

"I took the position I did on the tolls question because I am convinced after a very careful study of the question that the exemption is in direct contravention of the Hay-Pauncefote treaty," the President again explained confidentially a short time later. "This opinion is held in every capital in Europe and as a consequence embarrasses me every day of my administration in handling foreign affairs; indeed, it is likely, if the situation is not corrected, to make it impossible for me to handle those affairs successfully in the many difficult matters we are now dealing with."[110] "The tolls matter is a very deep one," he said a few weeks later. "The truth is, just between you and me, until we straighten this matter out we shall not enjoy for a moment the confidence of foreign governments in our promises, for they all interpret the treaty one way. It is not merely England that I am thinking of. The distrust runs all through Europe and all through Central and South America."[111]

During the month following the conference with the foreign relations committee, moreover, the President moved systematically to build public support and to marshal his forces in Congress behind repeal of the exemption provision.

To begin with, he came out publicly for repeal for the first time in a ringing letter on February 5, 1914. "The exemption," he wrote, ". . . seems to me in clear violation of the terms of the Hay-Pauncefote treaty. There is, of course, much honest difference of opinion as to . . . [this] point, as there is, no doubt, as to others; but it is at least debatable, and if the promises we make in such matters are debatable, I for one do not care to debate them. I think the country would prefer to let no question arise as to its whole-hearted purpose to redeem its promises in the light of any reasonable construction of them rather than debate a point of honor."[112]

At the same time, Wilson conferred frequently with Representative William C. Adamson of Georgia, chairman of the House commerce

---

"*The central qn.*, therefore, the friendship and at least negative cooperation of Great Britain.

"*Growth of English perception* and change of attitude and even point of view as reported by Page.

"*Next move with us.*

"*Necessary, therefore*, (a) to repeal tolls exemption (perhaps as Judge Adamson suggests) and (b) to ratify arbitration treaties (all of them depending)."

[110] W. W. to J. P. Tumulty, February 19, 1914, Wilson Papers.

[111] W. W. to Albert Shaw, March 17, 1914, *ibid.*

[112] W. W. to William L. Marbury, February 5, 1914, *New York Times*, February 7, 1914.

committee, and with other Democratic leaders to clear the road for legislation repealing the exemption provision.[113] Under tremendous administration pressure, especially from the Postmaster General, most of the House Democrats fell reluctantly into line;[114] and by the end

Ripping It Out
Kirby in the New York *World*

of February 1914 the President was so confident of an easy victory that he announced that he would not send a special message on tolls repeal to Congress. He changed his mind abruptly on March 3, 1914, however, when House Majority Leader Underwood announced that he would

[113] *ibid.*, February 17 and 20, 1914.
[114] W. C. Adamson to W. W., February 23, 1914, Wilson Papers; T. W. Sims to W. W., February 28, 1914, *ibid.*; New York *World*, February 26, 1914.

not only refuse to vote for repeal of the tolls exemption but also lead the opposition to what he called a violation of the solemn pledge given in the Democratic platform of 1912 in behalf of tolls exemption for American coastwise shipping.[115]

Wilson replied to this threatened rebellion by going before a joint session of Congress on March 5, 1914, and virtually demanding repeal of the exemption provision. "We ought to reverse our action," he declared, "without raising the question whether we were right or wrong, and so once more deserve our reputation for generosity and for the redemption of every obligation without quibble or hesitation." He then concluded cryptically: "I ask this of you in support of the foreign policy of the administration. I shall not know how to deal with other matters of even greater delicacy and nearer consequence if you do not grant it to me in ungrudging measure."[116] He could not have taken higher ground or employed a stronger imperative, and reaction throughout the United States and Britain was overwhelmingly favorable.[117]

[115] *New York Times*, March 4, 1914; New York *World*, March 4, 1914.

[116] *Foreign Relations, 1914*, p. 317. Wilson explained to reporters on March 26, 1914, that he had meant nothing mysterious by this concluding sentence. "What I mean by correcting an international situation," he said, "is this: The South American Republics, if their editors speak for them, have voted in the matter, so to speak; and the opinion is unanimous in the world against us. There is a unanimous belief that the exemption clause is a violation of the treaty. So long as that is the case, of course, they are not very enthusiastic about entering into new agreements with us. You can see how that fact embarrasses us in making new treaties. Let us suppose that we were in the habit of entering into very handsome arrangements which we said were for the benefit of the whole world and of which we wished to take no selfish advantage, and then Congress were to take any advantage that it pleased, whether it was contrary to the agreement or not. What impression do you think it would make on the rest of the world? You now see what I really meant by 'questions of nearer consequence and greater delicacy'—a phrase that seems to have puzzled many people. I said that in my opinion the thing was a plain violation of our agreement with Great Britain, but that I was not seeking to impose upon Congress my opinions. I was explaining a situation which was to this effect—that however we might differ in this country there was no difference of opinion anywhere else in the world as to its being a breach of contract and that we couldn't afford to be regarded by all the rest of the world as not living up to our contractual agreements, particularly when we profess to make those contractual agreements in the interest of the whole world. It is very awkward to deal with foreign nations no one of which believes that you will keep your promises and thinks that it has proof that you will not. This is the situation in a nutshell. There is a general impression on the other side that we sail as close to the wind as we choose in interpreting our promises, and, of course, that embarrasses the Administration at every turn. There is no pressure of any government or anything specific." These remarks were summarized in the *New York Times*, March 27, 1914, and printed verbatim in "President Wilson on His Foreign Policy," *World's Work*, xxviii (October 1914), 492-493.

[117] For typical American reactions, most of which were favorable, see *The Inde-*

A leadership less bold might well have failed, for the subsequent battle in the House of Representatives came dangerously near to disrupting the Democratic ranks, and for a time observers wondered whether the President had lost control. Lobbyists for the coastwise shipping interests descended upon Washington and began nation-wide propaganda against repeal.[118] Hundreds of petitions protesting the proposed "cowardly surrender" to England poured in upon Congress from Irish-American societies throughout the country.[119] The far-flung Hearst press was up in arms, denouncing the President, demanding vindication of the national sovereignty, and stirring deeply rooted anti-British feelings. The Anglophobia was aggravated, moreover, when Republicans charged that Wilson had made some deal with Sir Edward Grey at the time of Tyrrell's visit to Washington, by which Britain would support American policy in Mexico in return for repeal of the exemption provision.[120] But the most dangerous development occurred on March 26, 1914, when Speaker Champ Clark joined Underwood in opposition to the administration and implied that he would take personal command of the anti-repeal forces.[121]

Wilson met the challenge with one of the most extraordinary displays of leadership of his entire career. He not only worked closely

---

pendent, lxxvii (March 16, 1914), 364-365; *Chicago Daily Tribune*, March 6, 1914; New York *Outlook*, cvi (March 14, 1914), 576-577; *Commercial West*, xxv (March 14, 1914), 7-8; Dallas *Baptist Standard*, xxvi (April 2, 1914), 9.

British editors and public leaders were profoundly moved and grateful. Sir Edward Grey told Ambassador Page on April 1, 1914, that he had waited for the President to deal with the tolls dispute at his own convenience and that "When he took it up at his own time, to suit his own plans, he took it up in the most admirable way possible." Page Diary, April 1, 1914. "Sir Edward asked me to tell you," Sir William Tyrrell wrote to Colonel House, "that whatever its [the tolls fight's] issue might be he was of opinion that the President's message . . . lifted politics from a dead level to a higher plane from which it would be difficult to descend." W. Tyrrell to E. M. House, April 3, 1914, House Papers. "The striking Message which President Wilson read to Congress yesterday . . . ," declared the London *Times* on March 6, 1914, in a typical British editorial reaction, "will win for him the approbation and respect of all that is best amongst the English-speaking nations of the globe. Mr. Wilson has often shown courage; he has seldom shown more than in this personal appeal to the Legislature." See also the London *Pall Mall Gazette*, March 6, 1914; Birmingham *Daily Post*, March 6, 1914; London *Observer*, March 8, 1914; London *Statist*, lxxix (March 7, 1914), 482; and London *Nation*, xiv (March 14, 1914), 991-992.

[118] New York *World*, March 9, 1914.

[119] *New York Times*, March 9 and 23, 1914.

[120] Wilson replied by virtually accusing his opponents of lying, while Grey also denied the charge. New York *World*, March 20, 1914; *New York Times*, March 31, 1914.

[121] *ibid.*, March 27, 1914; New York *World*, March 27, 1914.

with loyal Democrats in the House[122] but also gave Burleson free rein in using the patronage stick on wavering congressmen.[123] He appealed personally to editors for support.[124] He countered suggestions of compromise by declaring: "Nor should the question be compromised, as some have suggested. In fact, it will not be compromised; it will be repealed."[125] Finally, he answered the charge that he was guilty of bad faith—because he had taken a position contrary to the Democratic platform of 1912—by saying frankly that platform promises on foreign policy could not always be fully honored. As he explained at the beginning of the controversy, "I feel that no promise made in a platform with regard to foreign affairs is more than half a promise. It cannot mean that if the foreign elements in the situation are beyond our control we will undertake to control them."[126]

Actually, the Democratic rupture never occurred, and the President had his way with unexpected ease on March 31, 1914, when the House approved the Sims bill repealing the exemption clause by a vote of 247 to 162. Among the Democrats, only Clark, Underwood, Irish-American representatives from New York, Boston, and Chicago, and a few others voted against the President. "It will always be deeply gratifying to me," Wilson wrote in appreciation soon afterward, "to remember how large a number of the members of our party were willing even to change their former votes in this matter in order to support the administration in a matter which had come to wear a new aspect and in which the welfare and honor of the country were involved."[127]

In the Senate the opponents of repeal were no less determined in their opposition than were those in the House. Unfortunately for the administration, moreover, the leader of the anti-repeal senators, O'Gorman of New York, was also chairman of the committee on inter-oceanic

[122] For evidence on this point, see the *New York Times*, March 23, 1914; and New York *World*, March 28, 1914.

[123] "Burleson, it was a great fight," Wilson told the Postmaster General after the House had voted to repeal the exemption clause. "It was a great victory for you," Burleson replied. "No," said the President, "it was a great victory for you!" R. S. Baker, interview with A. S. Burleson, March 17-19, 1927, Baker Collection. See also W. C. Adamson to A. S. Burleson, April 7, 1914, Burleson Papers, for similar testimony to the effectiveness of Burleson's work.

[124] e.g., W. W. to Charles H. Grasty, editor of the Baltimore *Sun*, March 5, 1914, Wilson Papers.

[125] "President Wilson on His Foreign Policy," *World's Work*, xxviii (October 1914), 493; summarized in the *New York Times*, March 27, 1914.

[126] W. W. to J. P. Tumulty, February 19, 1914, Wilson Papers. He reiterated this opinion to the reporters on March 26, 1914.

[127] W. W. to Representative Thomas M. Bell, April 5, 1914, *ibid*.

canals, which would have charge of the Sims bill. O'Gorman's first move was to persuade his committee to hold hearings for fifteen days; his second, to suggest an amendment to the repeal bill reserving to the United States all rights under the Hay-Pauncefote Treaty.[128]

And yet it was clear throughout the two months' struggle in the upper house that the Sims bill would inevitably pass. The administration could count upon an overwhelming majority of the Democratic votes from the outset, in spite of the defection of a few regulars like Walsh of Montana and Newlands of Nevada, and considerable support from the anti-exemption Republicans led by Root of New York and Lodge of Massachusetts, who did not hesitate to repudiate the record of the Taft administration in this controversy.[129] Moreover, O'Gorman was good-natured in opposition and made it plain that he wanted to avoid a party split; and the majority of the committee on inter-oceanic canals, who were opposed to the repeal bill, made no effort to obstruct its passage once the hearings had ended. Indeed, the committee majority did the unusual thing of reporting the Sims bill to the Senate on April 29, 1914, without an adverse report.[130]

In these circumstances Wilson moved cautiously to avoid even the appearance of coercion. In private correspondence he heartened senators who needed support and pleaded with others to give him a free hand in foreign policy.[131] But he did not threaten when senators disagreed;[132] he publicly disavowed Senator Robert L. Owen, leader of the repeal forces in the Senate, when Owen recommended disciplinary action against the dissenting Democrats on the inter-oceanic canals committee;[133] and as a final gesture he withdrew his opposition to the

[128] W. J. Bryan to W. W., April 11, 1914, *ibid.*

[129] For a discussion of Root's and Lodge's significant contributions to the President's victory in the tolls fight in the Senate, see Philip C. Jessup, *Elihu Root* (2 vols.), II, 262-270; and John A. Garraty, *Henry Cabot Lodge*, p. 299. See also E. Root to George Gilbert, June 6, 1914, the Papers of Elihu Root, Library of Congress; hereinafter cited as the Root Papers.

Needless to say, Taft and former Secretary Knox did not enjoy being portrayed as willful treaty-breakers and bunglers by two leading Republican senators. The laws of good taste forbid the reprinting of their comments, but they may be read in W. H. Taft to P. C. Knox, April 12 and 30, 1914; and P. C. Knox to W. H. Taft, April 28, 1914, all in the Papers of Philander C. Knox, Library of Congress; hereinafter cited as the Knox Papers.

[130] *New York Times*, April 28 and 30, 1914.

[131] e.g., W. W. to J. R. Thornton, February 23, 1914, Wilson Papers; and W. W. to Mark A. Smith, April 6, 1914, *ibid.*

[132] e.g., T. J. Walsh to C. B. Nolan, March 25, 1914, Walsh Papers, relating an account of an interview with the President.

[133] *New York Times*, April 3, 1914.

amendment reserving all American rights under the Hay-Pauncefote Treaty.[134] As a result of these tactics there was not even the threat of a party quarrel, and the President's supporters won an easy victory when the Senate approved the amended Sims bill by a vote of fifty to thirty-five on June 11, 1914.[135]

"I do not know of anything I ever undertook with more willingness or zest and I think that we have reason to be proud of the way in which public opinion of the United States responded to the challenge," Wilson wrote gratefully a short time later. "My own feeling is that the whole country is heartened and reassured by the repeal. I am not so much proud of it as deeply grateful that the country I love should be set in the right light, in the light of its real principles and opinion."[136]

What the President's victory signified was not lost upon the country or upon the rest of the world. It represented both a striking proof of Wilson's continued political control and a vindication of the national honor and the standards of fair dealing among nations. As one of the leaders in the repeal movement wrote to the President, "When I think of the obstacles you have encountered and overcome in this conflict for the national honor, the victory seems colossal. . . . To have held your straight course through such a confusion of duty is to have raised a standard for our people for all time."[137]

But the most important effect of the President's victory was its profound impact upon Anglo-American relations. The British government ratified an agreement to extend the Anglo-American arbitration treaty of 1908 on March 11, 1914, a few days after Wilson spoke before the joint session. And a few months after the end of the tolls fight, on September 15, 1914, the British Ambassador in Washington gave new evidence of his government's friendship by joining the Secretary of State in signing a conciliation treaty. Ratified by the two governments in November 1914, it gave proof that the two democracies were determined to live at peace in a world already at war.

The boldest stroke of New Freedom diplomacy was a quiet diplomatic campaign, inaugurated and executed by Colonel House with Wilson's approval, to draw the United States, Great Britain, France,

[134] *ibid.*, June 7, 1914.
[135] The House accepted the Senate amendment the following day, and Wilson signed the Sims bill on June 15, 1914.
[136] W. W. to James Bryce, July 6, 1914, Wilson Papers.
[137] Robert Underwood Johnson to W. W., June 16, 1914, *ibid.*

and Germany into an informal entente to preserve the peace of the world.

Unlike Wilson and most other American leaders, who paid scant attention to European questions, Colonel House was profoundly alarmed by the growth of tension abroad and convinced that it would be virtually impossible for the United States to remain isolated if a general war occurred. He discussed the causes of the tension with various Europeans during 1913; and on December 2, 1913, he outlined to Sir William Tyrrell a plan that had taken shape in his mind. "I told him," House recorded in his Diary, "the next thing I wished to do was to bring about an understanding between France, Germany, England, and the United States, regarding a reduction of armaments, both military and naval."[138] The Colonel explained his plan to the President ten days later. Wilson warmly approved, promised that the United States would cooperate, and agreed that House should go to Berlin and London for direct conversations during the following summer.[139]

House made plans for what he called his "Great Adventure" during the following winter and spring. His way carefully prepared by Count von Bernstorff, the German Ambassador in Washington,[140] House arrived in Berlin on May 26, 1914. He knew he must act quickly. "The situation is extraordinary. It is jingoism run stark mad,"[141] he warned the President on May 29. "Unless some one acting for you can bring about a different understanding, there is some day to be an awful cataclysm. No one in Europe can do it. There is too much hatred, too many jealousies."[142]

In long talks with the Foreign Secretary, the Minister of Marine, and other German civilian and military leaders, House pointed out

[138] House Diary, December 2, 1913. See Charles Seymour (ed.), *The Intimate Papers of Colonel House*, I, 235-275, for a full account of this episode.

[139] *ibid.*, p. 243; House Diary, December 12, 1913.

[140] See J. von Bernstorff to the Foreign Office, May 6, 1914, and Bernstorff to Count von Montgelas, May 5, 1914, in *Die Grosse Politik*, xxxix, 110-111. Bernstorff requested "the friendliest possible treatment of House, whom one can perhaps characterize as the only personal friend of Wilson."

[141] Mr. Seymour prints this sentence in *The Intimate Papers of Colonel House*, I, 249, as follows: "It is militarism run stark mad." House changed the word "militarism" to "jingoism" in the original of the letter, which he sent to the President, without changing the letter-press copy, which was the only one available to Mr. Seymour when he edited House's papers. It should be added, moreover, that House was referring to the situation in Europe in general, not in Germany alone, when he wrote this prophetic letter. For an interesting discussion of this point, see *Die Grosse Politik*, xxxix, 110-111.

[142] E. M. House to W. W., May 29, 1914, Wilson Papers.

the perils ahead and described his mission—first, to help ease the tension between England and Germany, and, second, to draw Germany, France, Britain, and the United States together in a disarmament plan. But the Texan was most explicit in a private conference with the German Emperor at Potsdam on June 1, 1914. The interview is best described in House's own words:

"We now got to the interesting part and began to discuss the European situation as it affected the Anglo Saxon race. He spoke of the folly of England forming an alliance with the Latins and Slavs, who had no sympathy with our ideals and purposes and who were vacillating and unreliable as allies. . . . His idea was that in the first place the Anglo Saxons should stand together as against the Latins and Slavs in Europe, but all western civilization should stand together as against Oriental races. . . .

"I thought Russia was the greatest menace to England and it was to England's advantage that Germany was in a position to hold Russia in check, and that Germany was the barrier between Europe and the Slavs. I found no difficulty in getting him to admit this. . . . I told him that the English were very much concerned over his ever growing navy, which taken together with his enormous army constituted a menace and there might come a time when they would have to decide whether they ran more danger from him and his people making a successful invasion than they did from Russia, and the possibility of losing their Asiatic colonies. I thought when that point was reached, the decision would be against Germany.

"I spoke of the community of interests between England, Germany and the United States and thought if they stood together, the peace of the world could be maintained. He assented to this quite readily. However, in my opinion, there could be no understanding between Germany and England so long as he continued to increase his navy. He replied that he must have a large navy in order to protect Germany's commerce in an adequate way, and commensurate with her growing power and importance. He also said it was necessary to have a navy large enough to be able to defend themselves against the combined efforts of Russia and France.

"I asked when he would reach the end of his naval program. He said this was well known since they had formulated a policy for building and when that was completed there would be an end; that Great Britain had nothing to fear from Germany and that he, personally, was a friend of England and was doing her incalculable service in holding the balance of power against Russia.

"I told him that the President and I had thought perhaps an American might be able to compose the difficulties here and bring about a better understanding with a view to peace than any European, because of their distrust and dislike of one another. He agreed to this suggestion. I had undertaken this work and that was my reason for coming to Germany as I wanted to see him first. After leaving Germany, it was my purpose to go directly to England where I should take the matter up with that Government as I had done with him.

"I explained that I expected to feel my way cautiously and see what could be accomplished, and if he wished it, I would keep him informed. He asked me to do this and said letters would reach him 'through our friend Zimmermann here in the Foreign Office.' "[143]

Full of hopes and bold plans, House left Berlin for London on June 2, 1914. "I am glad to tell you that I have been as successful as anticipated," he reported to the President, "and have ample material to open negociations at London."[144] The "negociations" proceeded smoothly in the British capital; and in all his conversations with Grey, Prime Minister Herbert Asquith, and other British leaders, House found an evident desire to cooperate in any plan that would ease the European tension and put Anglo-German relations on a better footing.[145]

"Tyrrell brought word to me to-day," the Colonel wrote Wilson on July 3, 1914, "that Sir Edward Grey would like me to convey to the Kaiser the impressions I have obtained from my several discussions with this Government, in regard to a better understanding between the Nations of Europe, and to try and get a reply before I leave. Sir Edward said he did not wish to send anything official or in writing, for fear of offending French and Russian sensibilities in the event it should become known. He thought it was one of those things that had best be done informally and unofficially. He also told Page that he had a long talk with the German Ambassador here in regard to the matter and that he had sent messages by him directly to the Kaiser."[146]

It was all more encouraging than House had thought was possible, and he could send an almost exuberant message to the Kaiser. "I have

[143] House Diary, June 1, 1914.
[144] E. M. House to W. W., June 3, 1914, Wilson Papers.
[145] House Diary, June 17, 1914; E. M. House to W. W., June 26, 1914, Wilson Papers.
[146] E. M. House to W. W., July 3, 1914, *ibid.*

met the Prime Minister and practically every important member of the British Government," the Colonel wrote on July 7, 1914, "and I am convinced that they desire such an understanding as will lay the foundation for permanent peace and security. . . . While this communication is, as Your Majesty knows, quite unofficial, yet it is written in sympathy with the well-known views of the President, and, I am given to understand, with the hope from His Britannic Majesty's Government that it may bring a response from Your Majesty which may permit another step forward."[147]

House left for home soon afterward, confident that the seed he had planted would soon bear good fruit. As Walter Page explained, "His most excellent work leaves the situation the best possible in this way: the future negotiations of almost every sort whatsoever between Germany and England and between our country and either of them or both can proceed on the very friendly understanding that has been reached. . . . An enormous amount of constructive work can be done along the way that he has opened."[148]

Of course, it did not turn out that way, for while House was talking peace in London, a Serbian nationalist murdered the heir to the Austrian and Hungarian thrones in the Austrian province of Bosnia on June 28, 1914, and set in motion a chain of events that led to a general war in Europe and the Far East. It was a tragic climax to House's efforts, but it did not mean that the "Great Adventure" was quixotic. On the contrary, it might conceivably have saved the peace of the world, to the eternal credit of New Freedom diplomacy, if it had come a year before instead upon the eve of Armageddon.

[147] E. M. House to William II, July 7, 1914, House Papers.
[148] W. H. Page to W. W., July 5, 1914, Wilson Papers.

CHAPTER X

First Stages of a Latin American Policy: Promises and Realities

IN THEORY and practice, Europe and the Far East were of peripheral interest to the people of the United States during the years before the First World War. Ever since 1815 American foreign policy had been aimed at the protection of the western hemisphere from European encroachment, and after the Spanish-American war and the adoption of plans to build an isthmian canal the demands of national security had compelled a sharp focusing of this hemispheric defense policy. In consequence, the chief labor of the McKinley, Roosevelt, and Taft administrations in the field of foreign affairs had been to establish the absolute supremacy of the United States in the Caribbean and Central American areas in order to protect the security of the Panama Canal.

Progressives and anti-imperialists in the United States, and Latin Americans generally, expected that the coming to power of the Democrats in 1913 would mean a radical shift in the Latin American policies of the Washington government. Since 1898 the Democratic party and particularly Bryan, its chief spokesman before 1912, had forthrightly opposed the building of an American imperium in the Caribbean, whether by annexation of territory, military intervention, protectorates, "dollar diplomacy," or the accretion of large naval power, without which a strong policy would not be possible. As late as May 8, 1912, for example, the Democrats had combined with anti-imperialists in the Senate to defeat ratification of a treaty providing for the establishment of American control of Nicaraguan financial affairs.

It seemed that these hopes for a drastic reversal of policy would soon be realized, as the new President repudiated "dollar diplomacy" and proclaimed a new program of helpfulness within a week after he was inaugurated. There were good reasons for his haste. The State Department had received warnings that certain revolutionary groups in Central America planned to open hostilities soon after the change of government in Washington; the constitutional President of Mexico had recently been deposed and murdered by a military usurper; and Wilson was eager to help avert other such outbreaks, as well as to announce his new policy.[1]

"One of the chief objects of my Administration," the President declared in a statement given to the press on March 11, 1913, "will be to cultivate the friendship and deserve the confidence of our sister republics of Central and South America and to promote in every proper and honorable way the interests which are common to the peoples of the two continents." But, he continued in a pointed warning to would-be revolutionists, "We can have no sympathy with those who seek to seize the power of government to advance their own personal interests or ambition. . . . As friends, therefore, we shall prefer those who act in the interest of peace and honor, who protect private rights and respect the restraints of constitutional provision. Mutual respect seems to us the indispensable foundation of friendship between States as between individuals.

"The United States has nothing to seek in Central and South America except the lasting interests of the people of the two continents, the security of governments, intended for the people, and for no special group or interest, and the development of personal and trade relationships between the two continents, which shall redound to the profit and advantage of both and interfere with the rights and liberties of neither."[2]

It was a bold beginning, and the President amplified his promise of a new policy toward the southern republics in a speech before the Southern Commercial Congress at Mobile on October 27, 1913. "We must prove ourselves their friends, and champions upon terms of equality and honor," he declared. "You cannot be friends upon any other terms than upon the terms of equality. You cannot be friends at all except upon the terms of honor." He went on, moreover, to prophesy the freeing of Latin America from the stranglehold of foreign concessionaires and to promise the assistance of the United States in that emancipation.[3]

Aside from Wilson's firm stand against the new Mexican government headed by the usurper, Victoriano Huerta—a matter that will be discussed in the following chapters—the first practical manifestation of New Freedom diplomacy in Latin America was the negotia-

[1] See the Daniels Diary, March 11, 1913, relating the Cabinet discussions of these matters.
[2] *New York Times*, March 12, 1913.
[3] R. S. Baker and W. E. Dodd (eds.), *The New Democracy*, I, 67-68.

tion of a treaty with Colombia to repair the moral damage caused by the Roosevelt administration's support of the so-called revolution of 1903, which had torn the province of Panama from the mother country, Colombia.[4] Indeed, Colombia's grievances against the United States were so well founded that both the Roosevelt and Taft administrations had conducted negotiations in Bogotá in 1909 and early 1913 looking toward some settlement of the troublesome dispute.

The Colombian Minister in Washington renewed the negotiations with Bryan on May 3, 1913, by suggesting that the United States agree to submit the dispute to the Hague Tribunal for arbitration. At Wilson's direction, Bryan countered with a proposal that the two governments try to reach an understanding by direct negotiations. The Colombians responded favorably, and the Secretary of State opened discussions on September 29, 1913, by sending a handsome note of instructions, drafted personally by Wilson, to the new American Minister at Bogotá. "The Government and people of the United States," it read, "sincerely desire that everything that may have marred or seemed to interrupt the close and long established friendship between the United States and the Republic of Colombia should be cleared away and forgotten." Therefore, the note continued, the United States was willing to pay $20,000,000 "in full settlement of all claims and differences now pending between the Government of Colombia and the Government of the United States and between the Government of Colombia and the Government of the Republic of Panama."[5]

This display of friendship virtually assured the success of the negotiations. After some hard bargaining, the two governments compromised upon $25,000,000 as the sum of the indemnity, and the American Minister and the Colombian Minister for Foreign Affairs signed the treaty in Bogotá on April 6, 1914. "The Government of the United States of America," the first article read, "wishing to put at rest all controversies and differences with the Republic of Colombia arising out of the events from which the present situation on the Isthmus of Panama resulted, expresses, in its own name and in the name of the people of the United States, sincere regret that anything should have occurred

[4] After Colombia's refusal to ratify a treaty authorizing the United States to build a canal through Panama, the American government had openly assisted a group of revolutionists in the province and had quickly recognized a new Panamanian government in 1903.

[5] W. W. to W. J. Bryan, September 29, 1913, Wilson Papers, enclosing the instructions; the Secretary of State to Minister Thaddeus A. Thompson, September 29, 1913, *Foreign Relations, 1913*, p. 321.

to interrupt or to mar the relations of cordial friendship that had so long subsisted between the two nations."[6]

This act of humble statesmanship was convincing evidence of Wilson's and Bryan's determination to behave honorably in foreign affairs even when it hurt.[7] The sight of the great and powerful government of the United States virtually apologizing to the helpless government of Colombia evoked a warm response throughout all of Latin America. More than any other act of the Wilson administration, the Colombian treaty helped to restore the moral prestige of the United States in the eyes of Latin America.

However, as Wilson and Bryan soon discovered, even "moral diplomacy" has its pitfalls when it is practiced by imperfect human beings. Having made the apology, Wilson tried first to forestall the inevitable Republican reaction by denying as "pure guff" the rumor that the treaty contained an apology or even an expression of regret to Colombia.[8] But the secret came out when *Le Temps* of Paris published a copy of the treaty on April 17, 1914, and the Bogotá *Diario Oficial* printed the Spanish text a week later.

The result was the outbreak of a violent controversy even before Bryan presented the treaty to the Senate foreign relations committee on June 17, 1914. The acrimonious fight continued for weeks afterward. Roosevelt attacked the administration in a two-thousand word blast in the press on June 25, 1914, and an apoplectic letter to the chairman of the foreign relations committee on July 11, in which he characterized the treaty as "a crime against the United States, an attack upon the honor of the United States, which, if true, would convict the United States of infamy, and [be] a serious menace to the future well-being of our people."[9] In defense of the administration, the New York *World* ran a series of articles from July 5 through July 12, 1914, attempting

[6] The text of the treaty is printed in *Foreign Relations, 1914*, pp. 163-164.

[7] There is no evidence in the discussions between Wilson and Bryan of any desire to embarrass Theodore Roosevelt or the Republican party. On the contrary, there is every reason to believe that Wilson was sincere when he wrote: "My personal interest in that treaty has been of the deepest and most sincere sort. I believe that it constitutes a just and honorable understanding between two friendly peoples. . . . The more the matter is studied the more evident it becomes that such a treaty is based upon equity and is the natural outcome of genuine friendship between the two countries." W. W. to T. A. Thompson, February 18, 1915, Wilson Papers.

[8] *New York Times*, April 10, 1914.

[9] For Roosevelt's statement, see the *New York Times*, June 25, 1914; for his letter to the chairman of the foreign relations committee, see E. E. Morison (ed.), *The Letters of Theodore Roosevelt*, VII, 777-779.

to prove that the United States had shamefully wronged Colombia; and Democratic leaders agreed that Roosevelt's alleged aggression had been "the blackest page in the history of American diplomacy."[10]

Bryan tried to end the recrimination by an eloquent appeal on July 12, 1914, saying that it did not matter who had been at fault. "If cordial relations are to be restored with Colombia," he declared, "they must be restored on a basis that is satisfactory to Colombia. Friendships cannot rest upon force; neither can they rest upon acquiescence in the power of might."[11]

But all of Bryan's pleading failed either to assuage the anger of the Republican senators or to persuade the foreign relations committee to report the Colombian treaty to the Senate during 1914 and 1915.[12] The committee finally reported the treaty favorably to the Senate on February 2, 1916, but with amendments mutualizing the expression of regret and reducing the amount of the indemnity to $15,000,000.[13] However, the upper house refused even to consider it during the following year.

After it had become apparent that the United States was heading toward war with Germany during the early months of 1917, the administration made a last desperate effort to obtain ratification of the treaty, as one means of countering alleged German influence in Colombia. Wilson opened the campaign with an urgent appeal to the foreign relations committee on February 17, 1917.[14] Secretary of State Robert Lansing moved into action a short time later, warning the committee that ratification was vital to the national security[15] and using intimate friends of Senator Lodge, the leading opponent of the treaty, in an unsuccessful effort to persuade him to yield.[16] In response, the

[10] See the opinions quoted in the New York *World*, July 6, 1914.

[11] *New York Times*, July 13, 1914.

[12] Actually, Senator William J. Stone of Missouri, chairman of the foreign relations committee, made no serious effort to obtain a report until February 1915. He then gave up the attempt because of the violence of the Republican opposition. See Henry Cabot Lodge to Theodore Roosevelt, March 1, 1915, the Papers of Theodore Roosevelt, Library of Congress; hereinafter cited as the Roosevelt Papers; and W. J. Stone to Robert Lansing, August 8, 1915, the Papers of Robert Lansing, Library of Congress; hereinafter cited as the Lansing Papers.

[13] *New York Times*, February 3, 1916.

[14] W. W. to W. J. Stone, February 17, 1917, Wilson Papers. This letter was published in the newspapers five days later.

[15] H. C. Lodge to T. Roosevelt, March 2, 1917, Roosevelt Papers.

[16] The Desk Diary of Robert Lansing (MS. in the Lansing Papers), March 7, 8, 9, and 13, 1917; also H. C. Lodge to T. Roosevelt, February 22, March 2, 12, 16, and 19, 1917, Roosevelt Papers, for a running account.

foreign relations committee reported an amended treaty[17] on March 13, 1917; but after a day of debate it became obvious that a two-thirds majority could not be obtained, and the Senate adjourned on March 16, 1917, after sending the treaty back to the committee.[18]

Final success in the fight for justice to Colombia would not come until Roosevelt was dead, Wilson had left the White House, and the old passions had subsided.[19] The Wilson administration's attempt to deal honorably here was not fruitless, however, for it gave proof of its belief in the ideal of one rule of conduct toward nations great and small.

The New Freedom's most exalted vision for the New World was a plan to unite the American republics in a Pan-American alliance of nonaggression and mutual cooperation. Coming immediately after the negotiation of the Colombian treaty, the proposal of this alliance offered seemingly final proof that the Wilson administration meant to abandon the Roosevelt-Taft policies of intervention through force and "dollar diplomacy."

Men had long dreamed of a hemispheric peace alliance, but the idea that was translated into the Pan-American pact of the Wilson era grew more immediately out of a continued effort from about 1910 to 1916 to revise the Monroe Doctrine in order to find an alternative to the policy of intervention. Such an alternative, many contemporaries suggested, might be found by transforming the Monroe Doctrine from a unilateral American defense policy, which was inherently selfish, into a hemispheric alliance for common defense built upon the cornerstones of equality and mutual respect.[20]

Such a pact had in fact been suggested in 1910 and 1911 by Representative James L. Slayden of Texas, one of the leaders in the peace

---

[17] One amendment mutualized the expression of regret; another affirmed the title of the United States to the Panama Canal. On this occasion, however, the committee let the amount of the indemnity stand at $25,000,000.

[18] *New York Times*, March 16 and 17, 1917.

[19] In 1921, when a Republican Secretary of State, Charles Evans Hughes, negotiated a new treaty that awarded $25,000,000 to Colombia but omitted any mention of "sincere regret."

[20] For examples of such thought, see Hiram Bingham, *The Monroe Doctrine, An Obsolete Shibboleth* (1913); George H. Blakeslee (ed.), *Latin America* (1914); Roland G. Usher, *Pan-Americanism* (1915); Charles H. Sherrill, *Modernizing the Monroe Doctrine* (1916); G. H. Blakeslee, "A New Basis Needed for the Monroe Doctrine," *North American Review*, cxcviii (December 1913), 779-789; John Barrett, "A Pan-American Policy: The Monroe Doctrine Modernized," *The Annals of the American Academy*, liv (July 1914), 1-4; Richard Olney to Lyman Abbott, January 11, 1915, Olney Papers; Henry White to R. Olney, February 8 and 20, 1916, *ibid.*

movement, and formally proposed by the Colombian government in 1912. The Taft administration had instructed its diplomatic representatives in Latin America to "belittle" the Colombian proposal; but Slayden and the Colombian Minister in Washington renewed their campaign for a nonaggression treaty soon after Wilson was inaugurated.[21]

It was the kind of plan that Bryan might have thought of, but he was engrossed in more pressing diplomatic problems and confident that his own conciliation treaties provided an adequate peace structure for the New World. Initiative in the administration's campaign for a Pan-American pact fell instead to Colonel House, who had caught the dream of hemispheric cooperation from Representative Slayden and other leaders in the peace cause.

House first broached the subject to Wilson in a conference at the White House on November 25, 1914, and amplified his plan at a second meeting on December 16. The President, House suggested, "might or might not have an opportunity to play a great and beneficent part in the European tragedy; but there was one thing he could do at once, and that was to inaugurate a policy that would weld the Western Hemisphere together." It was his idea, House went on, "to formulate a plan, to be agreed upon by the republics of the two continents, which in itself would serve as a model for the European nations when peace is at last brought about."[22] Excited by the prospect, Wilson immediately wrote out the first draft of the Pan-American pact. In its final form the treaty bound the signatories to "a common and mutual guaranty of territorial integrity and of political independence under republican forms of government," to settle all disputes by peaceful means, and to refrain from furnishing assistance to the enemies of any signatory government.[23]

House proceeded with Wilson's blessing to sound out the Argentine,

[21] W. J. Bryan to W. W., November 5, 1913, Wilson Papers, enclosing a letter from J. L. Slayden; W. J. Bryan to W. W., January 24, 1914, *ibid.*; Samuel F. Bemis, *The Latin American Policy of the United States*, pp. 194-196.

[22] House Diary, December 16, 1914.

[23] The Pan-American pact went through several revisions before the final text was written. There was the first rough draft, which Wilson prepared on December 16, 1914, and which is printed in Charles Seymour (ed.), *The Intimate Papers of Colonel House*, I, 209-210. There was, secondly, the first complete draft, which Wilson wrote and sent to Bryan on January 29, 1915. It is printed in *Papers Relating to the Foreign Relations of the United States, The Lansing Papers, 1914-1920* (2 vols.), II, 472-473; hereinafter cited as *The Lansing Papers*. Then there was the final draft, which Wilson, Lansing, and House prepared in October and November 1915. It is printed in *ibid.*, II, 495-496, and in *The Intimate Papers of Colonel House*, I, 233-234.

Brazilian, and Chilean Ambassadors in Washington, and to draw the Secretary of State into the incipient negotiations.[24] Then, while House was in Europe during the late winter and spring of 1915, Bryan opened formal discussions about the proposed treaty with the three leading South American powers, declaring in specific terms that the United States stood ready to join her sister republics in helping to prevent aggression from within as well as from without the hemisphere, and inviting the Latin American countries to join the Washington government in defense of the Monroe Doctrine. "While the United States has, for a century, borne alone the responsibility involved in preventing aggression from countries in the eastern hemisphere," he wrote, for example, to the Chilean government, "and while the purpose of this Government in proposing this treaty is not to secure relief from these responsibilities, still it will be gratifying to this country to have the republics of Latin-America join in the upholding of what is known as the Monroe Doctrine."[25]

The Argentine and Brazilian governments replied enthusiastically, but Chile was opposed to any guarantee of territorial integrity, because of a long-standing boundary dispute with Peru.[26] Interrupted by Bryan's resignation in June 1915, the negotiations were taken up anew in the following September by House and the new Secretary of State, Robert Lansing, and were broadened to include the smaller republics as well as the A.B.C. powers. The results were so encouraging—even Chile seemed willing to cooperate—that Wilson, in his Annual Message of December 7, 1915, and in an address before the Pan-American Scientific Congress in Washington on January 6, 1916, confidently announced the Pan-American treaty project and proclaimed, more eloquently than before, the New Freedom vision of the republics of the New World living in peace and unity.

In his Annual Message of 1915, the President talked of a hemispheric "moral partnership in affairs," in which there would be "no claim of guardianship or thought of wards, but, instead, a full and honorable association . . . between ourselves and our neighbors." All the governments of America, he continued, "stand, so far as we are concerned, upon a footing of genuine equality and unquestioned independence. . . . This is Pan-Americanism. It has none of the spirit of empire in it.

[24] House Diary, December 17, 19, and 29, 1914, January 13, 1915.
[25] W. J. Bryan to the Chilean Ambassador, April 29, 1915, *The Lansing Papers*, II, 484.
[26] W. J. Bryan to W. W., March 8 and April 21, 1915, *ibid.*, pp. 473-474, 476-479.

It is the embodiment, the effectual embodiment, of the spirit of law and independence and liberty and mutual service."[27]

The peace and friendship of the New World, Wilson added in his address before the Pan-American Scientific Congress, "are based, in the first place, so far as the stronger States are concerned, upon the handsome principle of self-restraint and respect for the rights of everybody. They are based upon the principles of absolute political equality among the States, equality of right, not equality of indulgence. They are based, in short, upon the solid eternal foundations of justice and humanity. . . . God grant that it may be granted to America to lift this light on high for the illumination of the world."[28]

Despite these high hopes, the Pan-American treaty foundered during the following months upon the rocks of new Chilean opposition and, even more important, of Latin American fears of American aggression in Mexico and the Caribbean.[29] Even so, Wilson's vision lived on to be later reincarnated on a world scale in the Covenant of the League of Nations and, in the western hemisphere, in the Good Neighbor policy of Franklin D. Roosevelt and Cordell Hull.

Such was the New Freedom's promise of a new hemispheric policy. What does the record say about the performance? The answer is not simple. The promise was manifested, if unfulfilled, in the signing of the Colombian treaty and the attempted negotiation of the Pan-American pact. In dealing with the stable governments of South America, moreover, the Washington leaders not only treated them with the respect due sovereign neighbors but gave frequent evidence of a desire to draw them into a working partnership with the United States.

And yet these manifestations constituted more the appearance than the reality of a new Latin American policy. In contrast to Wilson's fair promises stands the record of American interference in Mexico, Central America, and the Caribbean region from 1913 to 1917, unparalleled before or since in the history of the western hemisphere. In addition, the Wilson administration adopted in several instances the

[27] R. S. Baker and W. E. Dodd (eds.), *The New Democracy*, I, 407-409.
[28] *ibid.*, pp. 444-445.
[29] For the story of these futile negotiations, see H. P. Fletcher to R. Lansing, January 21, 1916, Wilson Papers; F. L. Polk to W. W., March 17, 1916, Polk Papers; House Diary, March 29, 1916; H. P. Fletcher to E. M. House, April 18 and 20, May 4 and 27, June 15 and 24, July 10 and 14, 1916, House Papers; H. P. Fletcher to R. Lansing, June 16, 1916, Lansing Papers; H. P. Fletcher to R. Lansing, August 9, 1916, copy in the House Papers; and Rómulo S. Naón to H. P. Fletcher, June 27, 1916, copy in *ibid.*

very same "dollar diplomacy" that it had earlier roundly condemned.

In this and the next two chapters we will attempt to show how this record unfolded, first in Nicaragua and Central America from 1913 to 1916, next in Mexico during Wilson's war against Huerta in 1913 and 1914. In the following volumes we will describe how the President's policies culminated in virtual war with Mexico, the forceful occupation of Haiti and the Dominican Republic, and the purchase of new naval bases in the Caribbean. Before we proceed to the details, it might be well to examine some of the underlying reasons for the apparent contradiction between New Freedom profession and practice in Latin American policy. This effort requires us to set the New Freedom promises aside momentarily and to analyze the assumptions, motivations, and historical realities that governed the men who made these policies.

The most important cause of the disparity between Wilsonian promise and practice was the fact that New Freedom diplomacy was inadequate to ensure the security of the United States in the western hemisphere. Even more than during the Roosevelt and Taft administrations, the compelling necessity of American foreign policy in 1913 and afterward was the maintenance of an absolute supremacy in the Central American and Caribbean regions in order to protect the Panamanian lifeline. Wilson and Bryan accepted this assumption unconsciously, perhaps, but it governed all their calculations and actions in Latin American policy. They might talk about Pan-Americanism and the absolute equality of states, but they never seriously meant to apply such doctrines to the Caribbean area.[30] One can only wonder, therefore, what they had in mind when they proposed the Pan-American treaty. Cer-

---

[30] Lansing, who was never deceived by fine theories, pointed out the danger of too much talk about Pan-Americanism so long as the United States was determined to maintain supremacy in the western hemisphere. "The Monroe Doctrine," he asserted in a memorandum written in June 1914, ". . . should not be confused with Pan-Americanism. It is purely a national policy of the United States, while Pan-Americanism is the joint policy of the American group of nations. . . . In its advocacy of the Monroe Doctrine the United States considers its own interests. The integrity of other American nations is an incident, not an end. . . . The primacy of one nation, though possessing the superior physical might to maintain it, is out of harmony with the principle of the equality of nations which underlies Pan-Americanism, however just or altruistic the primate may be. . . . [When,] therefore, the Monroe Doctrine and Pan-Americanism may come into conflict, the Monroe Doctrine will in case of conflict prevail so long as the United States maintains the Doctrine and is the dominant power among the American nations. The equality of American republics and, in a measure, their independence are legal rather than actual." "Memorandum by the Counselor for the Department of State," dated June 11, 1914, *The Lansing Papers*, II, 461-462. I have transposed some of these sentences.

tainly, they were unwilling to do more than pay lip service to the Pan-American ideal; and just as certainly, they were not prepared to re-nounce the alleged right of intervention, in spite of the solemn pledges given in the proposed covenant.

Wilson, Bryan, and Lansing never thought of choosing between per-petuating or ending American supremacy in the approaches to the Panama Canal. They thought only of choosing the most effective meth-ods and instruments to maintain the basic American foreign policy. Bryan soon discovered that it was difficult to escape using protectorates and military force in dealing with the Central American and Carib-bean states. However, he begged the President to implement his re-pudiation of "dollar diplomacy" by inaugurating a bold new policy of economic assistance through the direct extension of the credit of the United States to the Latin American countries. In brief, he proposed a loan system which would work in the following manner: The United States government would raise money by selling its own 3 per cent bonds. It would then lend this money at $4\frac{1}{2}$ per cent to needy Latin American republics and use the profits from the transaction to speed the payment of the debt.[31]

"The right of American republics to work out their own destiny along lines consistent with popular government," the Secretary of State wrote, echoing what the President had said at the Southern Commercial Congress in Mobile, "is just as much menaced today by foreign financial interests as it was a century ago by the political aspirations of foreign governments. . . . We must protect the people of these republics in their right to attend to their own business, free from external coercion, no matter what form that external coercion may take. . . . If our coun-try, openly claiming a paramount influence in the Western Hemi-sphere, will go to the rescue of these countries and enable them to se-cure the money they need for education, sanitation and internal de-velopment, there will be no excuse for their putting themselves under obligations to financiers in other lands."[32]

If Wilson had meant what he said at Mobile about freeing Latin America from the grip of concessionaires, he would have at least given serious thought to Bryan's suggestion. But he rejected it on the ground that it "would strike the whole country . . . as a novel and radical pro-posal."[33] The consequence was that Bryan had no alternative but to

[31] W. J. Bryan to W. W., July 20 and August 6, 1913, Wilson Papers.
[32] W. J. Bryan to W. W., October 28, 1913, Bryan Papers, Library of Congress.
[33] W. W. to W. J. Bryan, March 20, 1914, Wilson Papers.

continue to use private bankers to help maintain American political influence in the sensitive areas, and he soon became reluctantly adept in the practice of "dollar diplomacy."

Yet the necessity of using traditional instruments to maintain American supremacy in the approaches to the Panama Canal only partially explains the disparity between New Freedom profession and practice in Latin America, for security considerations actually played a secondary role in the Wilson administration's most ambitious projects of intervention and control. An often more important factor was the way in which Wilson and Bryan were entangled by their own good intentions and inadequacies.

The desire to lead so-called backward peoples toward stability and democratic institutions was a basic motivation of New Freedom diplomacy in Latin America. Wilson and Bryan accepted as axiomatic the assumptions that the extension of American influence meant the advancement of the welfare of native peoples and that American statesmen like themselves were in a better position to advance that welfare than were the native leaders. Intervention, therefore, could always be rationalized in terms of the good Samaritan rescuing helpless neighbors from foreign dangers or internal chaos. Because he thought so much in these terms, it did not occur to Bryan that he was acting in a conventionally imperialistic manner when he projected bold schemes to establish new American naval bases or to fasten American control over the internal affairs of the Caribbean and Central American countries.[34]

A program of helpfulness would have been difficult in the most favorable circumstances. Wilson and Bryan, however, were neither experienced in diplomacy nor wise in the ways of Latin America. As evangels of democracy, they thought they could teach the Mexican, Central American, and Caribbean peoples how to elect good rulers,

[34] This was true also perhaps of Wilson, but not of Lansing, who proposed the frank adoption of a comprehensive policy of intervention aimed at establishing stable governments under American control in Central America and the Caribbean region in order to end forever the threat of European intervention. "I make no argument on the ground of the benefit which would result to the peoples of these republics by the adoption of this policy," he added. "That they would be the chief beneficiaries in that their public and private rights would be respected, and their prosperity and intellectual development insured, is manifest. Nevertheless the argument based on humanitarian purpose does not appeal to me, even though it might be justly urged, because too many international crimes have been committed in the name of Humanity. It seems to me that the ground of national safety, the conservation of national interests, is the one which should be advanced in support of this policy. It is reasonable, practical, and in full accord with the principle of the Monroe Doctrine." R. Lansing to W. W., November 24, 1915, *The Lansing Papers*, ii, 467.

establish democratic institutions, and maintain peace. They thought they could impose moral and democratic criteria upon a region where revolution was an integral part of the political process and democracy was a sham.

At first they believed they could further their aims simply by being helpful, without the use of force. But inevitably a policy of helpfulness led first to intervention in internal affairs, next to occupation or control through other means, and finally, in the case of Mexico, which was strong enough to resist, to war. As one authority has put it, the New Freedom became "paternal despotism" for northern Latin America. "In the eyes of the idealist," he continues, "this paternal despotism was no less than a great and holy cause adopted on behalf of unfortunate humanity; in the eyes of cynical critics it was the hypocritical disguise assumed by the wolf of imperialism when he disposed of Little Red Riding-hood's grandmother and took her place in bed to deceive the next trusting and hoped-for victim."[35]

The formation of the Wilson administration's Nicaraguan policy reveals the way in which a complex of factors utterly frustrated Bryan's good intentions and perpetuated a policy of intervention and "dollar diplomacy." In 1909 President Taft had sent marines to Nicaragua when an American-inspired revolution broke out there against the government of the Central American troublemaker, José Santos Zelaya. With American support the revolutionists drove Zelaya from power and established a government in Managua headed first by Juan J. Estrada and afterward by Adolfo Díaz, leader of the pro-American Conservative party.

From 1909 to 1913 the State Department intervened frequently in Nicaraguan affairs but succeeded in bringing neither political peace nor financial stability to the distressed republic. In 1911 Secretary Knox concluded a treaty that provided, first, for the refunding of the English-held Nicaraguan foreign debt by the American banking houses of Brown Brothers and J. and W. Seligman and, second, for the establishment of an American receivership of the Nicaraguan customs. The American Senate, however, refused to approve the treaty, on the ground that it permitted intervention in Nicaraguan affairs![36]

[35] Wilfrid H. Callcott, *The Caribbean Policy of the United States, 1890-1920*, p. 430.
[36] The State Department none the less put the receivership arrangement into effect by informal agreement, while the American bankers extended a loan of $1,500,000 in return for majority control of the Nicaraguan National Bank and an option on 51 per cent of the stock of the state-owned railroads.

At the same time, political unrest against the minority Díaz government became so strong that the Zelaya forces, known as the Liberal party, began a revolution in 1911 that would have succeeded had not President Taft sent some 2,700 marines to Nicaragua. Finally, in order to succor the ailing Díaz regime, Knox concluded a new treaty with Nicaragua in early 1913. It provided for the payment by the United States to Nicaragua of $3,000,000 in return for an exclusive option on the Nicaraguan canal route, the right to build a naval base in the Gulf of Fonseca on the Pacific side, and a ninety-nine year lease on the Great Corn and Little Corn Islands in the Caribbean. The Wilson administration came to power, however, before the Senate could consider the treaty.[37]

Conditions in Nicaragua were nearing the crisis stage by the spring of 1913. The national treasury was empty—it had been looted by President Díaz and his friends; the American bankers refused to lend more money; and a revolt against the Díaz regime and American control was brewing among the people.[38] The Nicaraguan government, therefore, appealed in desperation for speedy approval of Knox's second treaty soon after Wilson and Bryan came into office.[39] Nicaraguan representatives in Washington warned the Secretary of State that collapse and revolution in their country would inevitably ensue if the United States now withdrew support. Officials in the Latin American Affairs Division of the State Department agreed, advising, "What Nicaragua needs and wants is peace. It seems doubtful whether she can secure it without some support and cooperation on the part of the United States."[40]

If he had ever had any doubts about the necessity of continued American intervention in Nicaragua, Bryan dismissed them in the face of such warnings and quickly decided to support ratification of the canal treaty as the first step toward the rehabilitation of Nicaraguan finances. "I am inclined to think," he wrote to Wilson on May 24, 1913,

[37] This summary is based upon S. F. Bemis, *The Latin American Policy of the United States,* pp. 162-164.

[38] W. A. Deverall to C. C. Eberhardt, Consul-General at Large, May 1, 1913, enclosed in C. C. Eberhardt to the State Department, May 2, 1913, State Department Papers.

[39] Adolfo Díaz to W. W., April 12, 1913, Wilson Papers.

[40] "Memorandum of the Latin-American Division . . . ," dated May 22, 1913, *Foreign Relations, 1913,* p. 1042. For comprehensive reviews of the Nicaraguan debt and financial situation in the spring and summer of 1913, see this memorandum and the Legation of Nicaragua to the Department of State, July 15, 1913, in *ibid.,* pp. 1043-1045.

"that the purchase of the Canal option might give sufficient encouragement to the bankers to loan without the conditions which were, at their
request, put into the other treaty in regard to a loan."[41]

With the President's approval, Bryan began discussions with Nicaraguan officials, particularly with Charles A. Douglas, counsel for the
Díaz government in Washington, in late May of 1913. Warned by the
chairman of the Senate foreign relations committee that the Democrats would never approve the second Nicaraguan treaty, because it
permitted too much interference in Nicaraguan affairs, Bryan and
Douglas agreed to negotiate a new treaty, one untainted by "dollar diplomacy."

The turning point in the discussions came on June 9 and 11, 1913,
when Douglas submitted the draft of a treaty to the Secretary of State.
It included the provisions of the discarded treaty relating to the option
on the Nicaraguan canal route, the lease on the Great Corn and Little
Corn Islands, the naval base on Fonseca Bay, and American payment
of $3,000,000 to Nicaragua.

More important, however, were two new articles, which Douglas
had included at the instruction of the Nicaraguan government. The
first, Article IV, stipulated that Nicaragua should never conclude "any
treaty or other compact with any foreign power or powers which will
impair or tend to impair the independence of Nicaragua, nor in any
manner authorize or permit any foreign power or powers to obtain by
colonization or for military or naval purposes, or otherwise, lodgment
in or control over any portion of said Republic." The second, Article
VI, was modeled after the Platt Amendment, which the United States
had earlier imposed upon the Cuban government. "The Government
of Nicaragua," the article read, "consents that the United States may
exercise the right to intervene for the preservation of Nicaraguan independence, the maintenance of a government adequate for the protection of life, property, and individual liberty and for discharging any
obligations which it may assume or contract in accordance with the
provisions of Article IV above."[42]

"The Republic of Nicaragua," Douglas warned, "is in such a condition financially that law and order cannot be maintained and the
functions of the Government cannot be exercised unless financial relief can be obtained, and that this relief cannot be obtained unless some

[41] W. J. Bryan to W. W., May 24, 1913, Wilson Papers.
[42] Draft of a Nicaraguan treaty, sent to Bryan on June 11, 1913, by C. A. Douglas,
MS. in the State Department Papers.

such power as that suggested is vested in and accepted by the United States."[48]

As he explained to the President, Bryan had certain reservations about the proposed treaty. He was worried, for example, because it provided that the $3,000,000 to be paid for the canal option should be used for the current expenses of the Nicaraguan government and the payment of claims growing out of the revolutions of 1909 and 1911-1912. "My own preference," the Secretary wrote, "would be to have the money used for education or permanent public works," as Knox's second treaty had provided. But this, Bryan thought, was a minor objection. "As I am more interested in the securing of the option and the naval base than I am in the manner in which the money is spent, I would not regard the change as vital."[44] Wilson agreed without qualification. "The proposed Nicaraguan treaty has my entire approval," he replied on June 19, 1913, "and I sincerely hope that the Senate may approve it, as well as our friends, the Nicaraguan government."[45]

How did it happen that Bryan, the great opponent of imperialism, became overnight the leading defender of a treaty, the chief objectives of which were to enrich the Díaz clique, maintain an unpopular regime in Managua, and fasten American control on Nicaragua? Fortunately, we need not speculate, for Bryan explained his motivation many times during the ensuing violent controversy over the Nicaraguan treaty. And in so doing he revealed the forces that propelled him and the administration away from New Freedom principles toward a policy that he and the Democratic party had consistently opposed since 1898.

To begin with, as Bryan explained to the Senate foreign relations committee and the President, he had inherited and had not made the Nicaraguan policy of the United States. The Taft administration had helped to establish and had maintained the Conservative government in Managua. The alternative to continuing the Taft policy was to withdraw support from Díaz, and this would mean inviting an insurrection and the probable overthrow of the government. It was all very well to talk about withdrawing the marines and letting the Nicaraguans decide their own fate, Bryan continued, "but whatever may have been the fault of those who helped to inaugurate this government four years

[43] C. A. Douglas to W. J. Bryan, June 9, 1913, *ibid.*
[44] W. J. Bryan to W. W., June 16, 1913, Wilson Papers.
[45] W. W. to W. J. Bryan, June 19, 1913, *ibid.*

ago, nothing is to be gained by throwing the country into chaos merely to see which faction can win in the fight that would ensue. Zelaya was a despot of the worst kind and those who went out with him would be ready to champion his cause again."[46]

Under these circumstances, the United States could not in Christian conscience refuse to discharge its duties as a good neighbor toward Nicaragua. "Nicaragua has seen what the Platt Amendment has done for Cuba, and has become convinced of the disinterestedness of the United States, in our dealings with Latin America," Bryan explained to the foreign relations committee. "It is a compliment to us that we should be asked, and our government can hardly discharge its neighborly obligations without acceding to the request."[47] "Those Latin republics are our political children, so to speak," he declared on another occasion. ". . . They not only look to us but pattern after us. It is written that much is required of them to whom much is given, and this country will fall short of its duty if it does not do more than any other country in the work of fellowship and brotherhood. The commandment is to 'Love thy neighbor as thyself.' It is the only precept on which we can safely build, so we want to be friends with those countries and help them."[48]

Finally, security considerations weighed heavily in Bryan's mind. "As long as the canal route is upon the market for sale," he warned the foreign relations committee in July 1914, "we shall be continually disturbed by the reports, even if they be without foundation, that other governments are trying to secure the right to build a canal along the Nicaraguan route. We have recently learned of [German] efforts being made to dissuade the Nicaraguan Government from selling to the United States, on the ground that the option would bring a higher price in Europe than we have offered to pay." In the same memorandum, moreover, the Secretary of State defended plans for a large American naval base in Fonseca Bay by including testimony from Admiral George Dewey and the General Board of the navy to the effect that such a naval base would greatly enhance the security of the Panama Canal.[49]

[46] See Bryan's defense before the foreign relations committee, reported in the *New York Times*, June 19, 1914; W. J. Bryan to W. W., July 8, 1914, Wilson Papers; and W. J. Bryan to W. W., January 22, 1915, Bryan Papers, National Archives.

[47] W. J. Bryan to W. J. Stone, July 2, 1914, enclosing "Memorandum. Presented by Mr. Bryan before the Foreign Relations Committee of the Senate," State Department Papers.

[48] Speech before the Nebraska State Association, quoted in the New York *World*, August 3, 1913.

[49] W. J. Bryan to W. J. Stone, July 2, 1914, enclosing "Memorandum. Presented by

Bryan knew there were troubles ahead in the fight for the ratification of the proposed treaty, in spite of his eloquent efforts to put the best face possible on his Nicaraguan policy. On July 19 and 26, 1913, therefore, he took the unusual step of seeking the advice and approval of the Senate foreign relations committee before he signed the treaty.[50] He accompanied his explanations with an announcement that the United States was also prepared to make special treaties in order to protect the rights of Costa Rica and Honduras in the Nicaraguan canal route and Fonseca Bay; and Senator A. O. Bacon, chairman of the foreign relations committee, further explained that of course the proposed Nicaraguan treaty would "inaugurate a policy which doubtless will be extended to other Central American States when the necessity for the same shall arise in the future."[51]

These pronouncements fell like a thunderbolt upon an astonished country and world. Republican defenders of the policy of intervention, Senators Lodge, Root, George Sutherland of Utah, and Theodore E. Burton of Ohio, could hardly believe their ears, but they were effusive in commendation.[52] "The treaty with Nicaragua, which Mr. Bryan hopes to get ratified," an incredulous London editor remarked, "means that the Democrats have adopted bodily the foreign policy of the Republicans. It seemed unlikely that such a thing could ever happen, but the character of the Nicaraguan Treaty leaves us in no doubt."[53] "If all goes well," the *New York Times* agreed, "we shall soon see the dawn of a new era in our Latin American relations, but it will be due to a cheerful acceptance and amplification by President Wilson's Administration of the much-condemned dollar diplomacy of his predecessors."[54]

On the other hand, Bryan's policy was more than most Democrats and progressives could accept. "This means the going up of the American flag all the way to the Panama Canal, so surely as time goes on," Senator William E. Borah, the Idaho anti-imperialist exclaimed. "It is the beginning of that policy whose irrefutable logic is complete domi-

---

Mr. Bryan before the Foreign Relations Committee of the Senate," State Department Papers. The opinion of the General Board to which Bryan referred was dated January 27, 1914, and may be found, along with a second and more elaborate opinion, enclosed in Josephus Daniels to the Secretary of State, November 18, 1915, *ibid.*

[50] New York *World*, July 20 and 27, 1913.   [51] *Boston Transcript*, July 21, 1913.
[52] *New York Times*, July 22, 1913.
[53] *The Spectator*, cxi (September 20, 1913), 410.
[54] *New York Times*, July 21, 1913; also the New York *Outlook*, civ (August 2, 1913), 738-739.

nance and control."[55] " 'Dollar diplomacy,' which was so strenuously denounced by Secretary Bryan," protested Senator George W. Norris of
Nebraska, "looks like the proverbial 30 cents alongside of the proposed treaty with Nicaragua."[56]

The majority of the Democratic members of the foreign relations
committee did not attack the administration publicly,[57] but they joined
Borah in the showdown vote on August 2, 1913, refusing, by a vote of
eight to four, to approve the proposed Nicaraguan protectorate. At the
same time, they made it clear that they would approve a treaty providing simply for the purchase of an option on the canal route and
leases for naval bases in Fonseca Bay and the Corn Islands.[58]

But while Americans denounced or defended the policy of protectorates, affairs in Nicaragua worsened. Bankrupt and unable to pay its
creditors and employees, or to meet the payment on its loan from
Brown Brothers and J. and W. Seligman which would fall due on
October 15, 1913, the Managua government frankly warned the Washington authorities that national collapse impended.[59]

It was during this crisis that Bryan first conceived his Latin American
loan plan. He discussed the idea with the President on about July 20,
1913,[60] and came back a month later with a detailed description of
Nicaragua's financial troubles and a solution. "My recommendation,"
he wrote, "is that we propose to the Nicaraguan Government that we
loan them a million and a half or two million—whatever sum to you
may seem proper—on the basis that I outlined a few weeks ago, namely,
that we take from them 4½% bonds for the amount and hold them as
security for 3% bonds of our own, with the understanding that, if their
bonds are paid, principal and interest, as due, 1½% of the interest will
be used as a sinking fund to retire the principal."[61]

When the President rejected the proposal, Bryan had no alternative
but to get the best possible terms for Nicaragua from private bankers.
The upshot was the conclusion of a new loan agreement between the
Nicaraguan government and Brown Brothers and J. and W. Seligman

[55] *New York Times*, July 22, 1913.   [56] New York *World*, August 3, 1913.
[57] For an explanation of their position, see John Sharp Williams to Henry Watterson,
August 9, 1913, Watterson Papers.
[58] New York *World*, August 3, 1913; *New York Times*, August 3, 1913.
[59] The Legation of Nicaragua to the Department of State, July 15, 1913, *Foreign
Relations, 1913*, pp. 1043-1045; Pedro Rafael Cuadra, Minister of the Treasury, to the
Secretary of State, August 30, 1913, *ibid.*, pp. 1047-1049.
[60] W. J. Bryan to W. W., enclosing a memorandum of their discussion, received at
the White House July 20, 1913, Wilson Papers.
[61] W. J. Bryan to W. W., August 16, 1913, *ibid.*

in October 1913. It afforded the financial relief that Managua so desperately needed; but it also fastened the control of these banking houses over the Nicaraguan economy more firmly than before.[62] Bryan endorsed the agreement reluctantly but warned that the State Department would "be free to act according to its judgment and with the light that it then has upon any request that may be made thereafter in connection with the carrying out of the terms of these contracts."[63] This was "dollar diplomacy," but it was the best the Nebraskan could do in the circumstances.

The financial crisis momentarily averted, the Nicaraguan government now increased its pressure upon the State Department for the speedy conclusion and approval of the treaty. Bryan would have preferred to omit the controversial provisions establishing an American protectorate.[64] The Nicaraguans, however, insisted that they remain, and the President and Secretary of State finally yielded on the condition that the Nicaraguan President made it clear to the rest of Central America that the protectorate provisions had been included in the treaty at his request.[65]

The matter was quickly arranged by an exchange between Díaz and Wilson,[66] and yet the weeks passed without any action because the Washington administration was deeply involved in the tolls exemption fight. Once again the State Department was deluged with warnings of impending catastrophe from Managua.[67] And when these failed to stir the Washington authorities, there came a more ominous warning— that the German Chargé d'Affaires in Managua had visited President Díaz and intimated that his government might be willing to pay considerably more than $3,000,000 for the option on the canal route.[68] In

[62] For the terms of the loan contracts, see Brown Brothers and J. and W. Seligman to the Secretary of State, October 2, 1913, *Foreign Relations, 1913*, p. 1055; and "Statement of the features of the loan contracts of October 8, 1913 . . . ," *ibid.*, pp. 1061-1063.

[63] W. J. Bryan to Brown Brothers and J. and W. Seligman, October 6, 1913, *ibid.*, p. 1057.

[64] As he told the President, in W. J. Bryan to W. W., July 31, 1913, Wilson Papers.

[65] W. J. Bryan to W. W., January 15, 1914, *ibid.*; W. W. to W. J. Bryan, January 20, 1914, *ibid.*; and W. J. Bryan to W. W., January 23, 1914, with Wilson's marginal comments, in Bryan Papers, National Archives.

[66] Adolfo Díaz to W. W. February 3, 1914, Wilson Papers; W. W. to A. Díaz, February 20, 1914, State Department Papers.

[67] E. Chamorro to C. A. Douglas, March 25, 1914, *ibid.*; C. A. Douglas to W. J. Bryan, March 26, 1914, *ibid.*; A. Díaz to W. W., May 19, 1914, *ibid.*

[68] A. Díaz to E. Chamorro, May 27, 1914, *ibid.*; Minister Jefferson to the Secretary of State, May 27, 1914, *ibid.*

response, Bryan and Wilson agreed to push the treaty, Platt Amendment and all, as soon as the Senate had passed the bill repealing the tolls exemption.[69]

They could not, however, have foreseen the violent storm ahead. Going before the foreign relations committee on June 18, 1914, to appeal for prior approval of the treaty, Bryan was hectored by Senator William Alden Smith, Republican from Michigan, for approving the recent loan agreement.[70] Four days later, moreover, the committee voted to conduct an investigation of Nicaraguan financial affairs; it was a prolonged embarrassment to both the Washington and Managua governments.[71] "I believe," Senator Borah declared midway through the hearings, "that the Nicaraguan treaty is based upon deception, misrepresentation, fraud, tyranny and corruption, and I am prepared to show it."[72] At the same time, the administration's leading editorial spokesman, the New York *World*, began a devastating attack upon the Wall Street bankers and the Nicaraguan politicians who had used their alleged dupe, Bryan, to foist an iniquitous treaty upon the Nicaraguan people.[73]

In the face of such overwhelming opposition, Bryan yielded quickly and signed a revised treaty with the Nicaraguan Minister in Washington, Emiliano Chamorro, on August 5, 1914. Omitting the protectorate provisions, it provided only for payment by the United States of $3,-000,000 in return for a perpetual option on the Nicaraguan canal route, renewable ninety-nine year leases on the Great Corn and Little Corn Islands, and a site for a naval base in the Gulf of Fonseca.[74]

Weeks passed, and still the foreign relations committee refused to act upon the Bryan-Chamorro Treaty. "The situation in Nicaragua is perilous," Bryan reported to the President in late September 1914. "I have been trying to get a report on the Nicaragua Treaty but I have found it impossible to secure a quorum and they cannot make a report without a quorum. . . . The Senators seem to be so tired and worn that they will not come together."[75] At Bryan's suggestion, the Presi-

---

[69] W. J. Bryan to W. W., June 12, 1914, Wilson Papers; W. W. to W. J. Bryan, June 13, 1914, *ibid*.

[70] *New York Times*, June 19, 1914.

[71] *ibid*., June 23 and 26, 1914; New York *World*, July 15 and 18, 1914.

[72] New York *World*, July 7, 1914.

[73] *ibid*., July 8, 9, 10, 11, 12, 13, and 15, 1914.

[74] The text of the treaty is printed in *Papers Relating to the Foreign Relations of the United States, 1916*, pp. 849-851; hereinafter cited as *Foreign Relations, 1916*.

[75] W. J. Bryan to W. W., September 30, 1914, Wilson Papers.

dent warned the chairman of the foreign relations committee that serious consequences would ensue if the Senate failed to act quickly.[76] Even so, the committee did not make a favorable report until December 16, 1914; and threats of a filibuster by Senator Borah and other opponents of the treaty prevented Senate consideration during the closing days of the lame duck session of the Sixty-third Congress.[77]

Victory in the long fight came a year later, during a time of renewed tension between the United States and Germany over the submarine issue, after the American people had been alarmed by the threat of war with Germany and the fear of German intrigues in the Caribbean and Central American regions. Confronted with new testimony from the General Board that the construction of a naval base in the Gulf of Fonseca would greatly enhance American security[78] and with rumors that Germany was still trying to obtain an option on the Nicaraguan canal route,[79] the opponents of the Bryan-Chamorro Treaty relented, and the Senate gave its approval by a vote of fifty-five to eighteen on February 18, 1916. The Nicaraguan government reciprocated on April 13, and ratifications were exchanged at Washington on June 22, 1916.

For the State Department there now remained the more important tasks of helping to form a relatively honest government in Nicaragua and putting the republic's financial affairs in order. The opportunity for a political reorganization came soon after the ratification of the treaty, as the Nicaraguans prepared to elect a President to succeed Adolfo Díaz, whose term would expire in 1917. In order to perpetuate their control and to get their hands on the $3,000,000 purchase money for the option on the canal route, the Díaz faction nominated their own candidate, Carlos Cuadra Pasos. The State Department, however, was determined to be rid once and for all of the corrupt Díaz clique and to install an honest, pro-American government in Managua. To achieve these objectives, it supported the candidacy of the Nicaraguan Minister in Washington, Emiliano Chamorro, who had impressed both Bryan and Lansing by his integrity. When Díaz and his friends threatened to defy the United States and throw the election to Cuadra, Lansing replied by having Secretary Daniels send warships to both coasts of Nicaragua, by strengthening the marine guard at Managua, and by

[76] W. W. to W. J. Stone, October 1, 1914, *ibid.*

[77] W. J. Stone to W. W., February 24, 1915, *ibid.*; *New York Times*, February 25, 1915.

[78] R. Lansing to W. J. Stone, February 3, 1916, State Department Papers.

[79] New York *World*, February 15, 1916.

warning Díaz that he would not recognize or support or pay the option purchase money to any government "illegally" elected.

As it was obvious that Washington would tolerate no defiance, Cuadra withdrew in return for a promise of the Ministership to the United States. Under similar threats from the American Minister in Managua, the Liberal candidate, Julian Irías, withdrew and called upon his followers to boycott the election. Thus Chamorro was duly elected President under the cover of American guns in a "peaceful" canvass on October 2 and 3, 1916.[80]

The reform of Nicaraguan financial affairs proceeded as successfully as political rehabilitation, if more slowly. The gradual payment of the $3,000,000 by the United States ensured the solvency of the Nicaraguan government while the State Department and Nicaraguan officials worked out a comprehensive plan of financial reform in 1917. Approved by the bankers and by Nicaragua's other creditors at the State Department's insistence, the plan provided an orderly schedule for the payment of all foreign debts and vested control of Nicaraguan finances in a Joint High Financial Commission and a Public Debt Commission. In short, as one authority has concluded, "Under this Plan . . . Nicaraguan finances prospered, and the state was able to purchase back from the bankers the National Bank in 1920 and the Pacific Railroad in 1924. Thus did the republic free itself, with the aid of American di-

---

[80] The above summary is based upon an article in the *New York Times*, September 17, 1916, and upon manuscript materials in the State Department Papers, the Lansing Papers, and the Polk Papers. (Frank L. Polk was at the time Counselor of the State Department.)

The documents from the State Department Papers are listed in order, as follows: Secretary of State to Minister Jefferson, April 14, 1916; Jefferson to the Secretary of State, May 29, June 17 and 19, July 18, 1916; F. L. Polk to Jefferson, July 22, 1916; F. L. Polk to the Secretary of the Navy, August 3, 1916; F. L. Polk to Jefferson, July 27, 1916; Jefferson to the Secretary of State, August 10, 1916; Secretary of State to Minister Jefferson, August 14, 1916; Jefferson to the Secretary of State, August 15 and 20, 1916; J. B. Stabler to R. Lansing, August 22, 1916; Secretary of State to Jefferson, August 25, 1916; Jefferson to the Secretary of State, September 6, 1916; J. B. Stabler to R. Lansing, September 7, 1916; Secretary of State to Minister Jefferson, September 7, 1916; Jefferson to the Secretary of State, September 10, 1916; Secretary of State. to Jefferson, September 12, 1916; Jefferson to the Secretary of State, September 15, 17, 21, 26, and October 2 and 3, 1916.

For the documents from the Lansing Papers, see J. B. Wright to F. L. Polk, August 2, 1916, and the Lansing Desk Diary, August 16 and 24, 1916.

The documents from the Polk Papers are listed in order, as follows: J. B. Wright, memorandum of a conversation with General Chamorro, dated December 15, 1915; A. Díaz to the Chargé d'Affaires, July 26, 1916, together with comment by J. B. Wright, dated July 28, 1916; F. L. Polk, memorandum of a conversation with the Nicaraguan Chargé, dated July 27, 1916; John Foster Dulles to the Secretary of State, July 28, 1916.

plomacy, from the control which the bankers had installed in 1912 when the Senate rejected the Knox-Castrillo treaty."[81]

Meanwhile, Bryan's Nicaraguan policy had raised new fears in Central America of Yankee imperialism, provoked a sharp diplomatic crisis between Nicaragua and her neighbors, and culminated in an ambitious but ill-fated effort by the State Department to bring the Central American states within the orbit of the United States.

The basic cause of Central American resentment was the fact that American policy in Nicaragua after 1909 had upset the delicate balance of power in the area and destroyed the promising beginnings of a movement toward a form of union. In 1907 the Central American states had devised an elaborate structure for peace and cooperation, capped by a Central American Court of Justice for the compulsory settlement of all disputes. This auspicious beginning was gravely weakened by Secretary Knox's intervention in Nicaragua and his "dollar diplomacy" in Honduras; it was completely destroyed by events at the time of and after the negotiation of Bryan's treaty with Nicaragua.

Tension between the United States, on the one hand, and Costa Rica, Honduras, and Salvador, on the other, developed rapidly as a consequence of the negotiation of the Bryan-Chamorro Treaty during 1913 and 1914. Costa Rica alleged that the treaty violated her important interests in the Nicaraguan canal route;[82] Honduras and Salvador protested that the treaty's provisions relating to the construction of an American naval base in Fonseca Bay impaired their neutrality and rights, since the waters of the bay washed their shores as well as Nicaragua's. The main cause of the Central American resentment, however, was the so-called Platt Amendment provisions of the proposed treaty. As the Costa Rican Minister in Washington explained in July 1914, "My Government believes that any weakening of the autonomy of the Republic of Nicaragua would seriously affect the autonomy of the Republic of Costa Rica, considering the special nature of the relations between the States of Central America since the beginning of their existence."[83]

[81] S. F. Bemis, *The Latin American Policy of the United States*, p. 187; quoted by permission of Harcourt, Brace and Company, publishers.

[82] On the grounds that she shared control of the San Juan River, which would constitute part of the canal's channel, with Nicaragua, and that Nicaragua was bound by a treaty with Costa Rica not to dispose of her rights in the canal route without first consulting the government of Costa Rica.

[83] The Minister of Costa Rica to the Secretary of State, July 7, 1914, *Foreign Rela-*

Bryan answered these protests, not merely with friendly legal arguments, but also by offering to compensate Costa Rica, Honduras, and Salvador for their rights in the Nicaraguan canal route and Fonseca Bay.[84] Soon after Bryan held forth these olive branches, however, the American press ran sensational stories to the effect that the Secretary planned to impose protectorates upon all the Central American republics.[85] Wilson and Bryan tried to explain that the newspapers had gravely distorted their intentions, but the damage was done. There were heated anti-American demonstrations and outbursts in the press in Costa Rica, Honduras, and Salvador, and the government of the last-named country issued a call for a Central American conference to consider means of mutual defense against Yankee imperialism.

Bryan replied in good temper, with earnest assurances that the United States had no desire to impose its authority upon any Central American state. In consequence, the anti-American sentiment diminished perceptibly, especially after the Secretary of State withdrew the protectorate provisions from the Nicaraguan treaty. Indeed, relations with the disgruntled Central American governments were so much improved by the beginning of 1915 that Bryan set out anew to negotiate treaties to obtain Costa Rica's, Honduras', and Salvador's approval for the American option on the Nicaraguan canal route and a naval base in the Gulf of Fonseca.[86]

Discussions proceeded uneventfully and for the most part unsuccessfully until President Carlos Melendez of Salvador called the American Minister, Boaz Long, to his office in mid-March of 1915. What he would like to see, the President told Long, was a working partnership between the Central American countries and the United States, under which the United States would build its naval base in the Gulf of Fonseca and would then go on to help stabilize Central American finances, develop

---

tions, 1914, p. 959. The Central American protests against Knox's Nicaraguan treaty of 1913 and the proposed Bryan-Chamorro Treaty are printed in *Foreign Relations, 1913*, pp. 1022-1031, and *Foreign Relations, 1914*, pp. 956-969.

[84] See "Memorandum by the Secretary," dated June 12, 1913, State Department Papers; F. M. Dearing of the Latin American Affairs Division, "Memorandum for the Secretary," dated June 19, 1913, *ibid.*; the Secretary of State to the Minister of Salvador, February 18, 1914, *Foreign Relations, 1914*, pp. 954-956.

[85] e.g., the *New York Times*, July 21, 1913; *Boston Transcript*, July 21, 1913; New York *World*, July 22, 1913.

[86] e.g., see the Secretary of State to Minister Hale at San José, January 28, 1915, *Papers Relating to the Foreign Relations of the United States, 1915*, p. 1104; hereinafter cited as *Foreign Relations, 1915*; Secretary of State to Minister Long at San Salvador, January 28, 1915, *ibid.*, p. 1105.

railroads and trade, and construct a large school to train Central American youths in agriculture and business. He would sound out the governments of Costa Rica and Guatemala on the idea, Melendez continued, but he hoped that the United States would take leadership in opening formal negotiations.[87]

Fired with enthusiasm,[88] Bryan won the President's approval of the project and instructed Long to conduct personal discussions in all the Central American capitals. On June 8, 1915, at the end of his tour, Long reported that reaction in Nicaragua, Salvador, and Honduras had been favorable and urged the State Department to take quick action. "If skillful management can secure three naval base treaties, one each with Nicaragua, Honduras, and Salvador, and a general Central American approval of the idea," he added, "it would stand as a proof of the Department's wisdom and disinterested regard, and as a silent rebuke to those who have attacked the Administration in this matter."[89]

The discussions over the proposed Central American treaties, however, were interrupted by Bryan's resignation in June 1915 and the subsequent sharp crisis with Germany. The project was then virtually forgotten until Long returned to Washington in November 1915 and conducted a spirited campaign in the State Department for a consummation of the plan.[90] The new Secretary of State, Lansing, enthusiastically approved[91] and permitted Long to draft instructions and treaties to be sent to the American Ministers in Guatemala, Salvador, Costa Rica, and Nicaragua.[92]

[87] Minister Long to the Secretary of State, March 26, 1915, State Department Papers.
[88] See W. J. Bryan to W. W., March 27, 1915, Bryan Papers, National Archives.
[89] B. W. Long to the Secretary of State, June 5, 1915, enclosing two memoranda, State Department Papers.
[90] See B. W. Long to R. Lansing, November 30 and December 8, 1915, enclosing memoranda and documents relating to the proposed Central American treaties, *ibid.*
[91] In fact, Lansing proposed amending the Nicaraguan treaty to remove the provisions relating to the naval base in Fonseca Bay, in order that the United States might obtain the right to build such a base through the new series of Central American treaties. See R. Lansing to W. W., December 11, 1915, Wilson Papers.
[92] The proposed treaties with Guatemala, Salvador, and Nicaragua were identical. They granted the United States permission to construct and operate a naval base in the Gulf of Fonseca; in return, the United States promised to use its good offices to improve the transportation and finances of these countries and to give $500,000 for each of the signatories to help establish and maintain a Central American training school. Under the terms of the proposed treaty with Costa Rica, the United States promised to set aside $500,000 for the Central American school, which would be used for the benefit of Costa Rican students; in return, Costa Rica gave the United States an option on the Nicaraguan canal route and the right to build a naval base in the Gulf

Yet Lansing never sent the instructions or presented the proposed treaties to the Central American governments.[93] Instead, the American Senate proceeded to ratify the Bryan-Chamorro Treaty on February 18, 1916. The upper house added an amendment to protect the rights of Costa Rica, Honduras, and Salvador, but it was not enough to repair the damage caused by the unilateral action of the United States. Near-panic and a wave of anger swept over Central America. "The traditional sentiment of a disunited but integral Central America is gone," was the bitter comment of one Honduran editor. "Nicaragua has chained herself, her life, her destiny, her aspirations to a foreign people. . . . Unscrupulous men . . . have sold their fatherland into blind servitude, solely because of the diabolical passion for gold, for ambition, for power."[94] The governments of Costa Rica and Salvador protested in notes that accused the United States of a "contemptuous slight" and of flagrant violation of international law.[95]

Central American resentment culminated on March 24, 1916, when the Costa Rican government arraigned Nicaragua before the Central American Court of Justice for violating its rights in the canal route by concluding a separate treaty with the United States.[96] Nicaragua refused to appear, arguing that the Court lacked jurisdiction. And when the tribunal ruled in favor of Costa Rica on September 30, 1916,[97] Nicaragua withdrew its member from the tribunal, and the whole Central American peace structure soon came tumbling down. Thus events turned out as one member of the Court had predicted at the beginning of Costa Rica's case:

---

of Nicoya. The draft instructions and treaties are enclosed in B. W. Long to R. Lansing, December 10, 1915, State Department Papers.

[93] Mainly because of the continued crisis with Germany, the threat of war with Mexico, domestic contention over measures of military and naval preparedness, and the impending presidential election.

[94] Ceiba, Honduras, *Pabellon Latino*, March 15, 1916.

[95] The Minister of Costa Rica to the Secretary of State, February 21, 1916, *Foreign Relations, 1916*, pp. 818-819; the Foreign Minister of Salvador to the American Chargé, March 3, 1916, *ibid.*, pp. 827-831.

[96] *Demanda de la República de Costa Rica contra la de Nicaragua, ante la Corte de Justicia Centroamericana, con motivo de una Convención firmada par la segunda con la República de los Estados Unidos de América, para la venta del río San Juan, y otros objetos* and *Anexos de la Demanda de la República de Costa Rica . . .* (San José, Costa Rica, 1916).

[97] For the Court's analysis and decision, see *Foreign Relations, 1916*, pp. 862-886. It should be added that Salvador also brought suit against Nicaragua in the Central American Court on about August 29, 1916, for violating her rights in the Gulf of Fonseca by concluding a separate treaty with the United States. The Court rendered judgment in favor of Salvador on March 9, 1917.

"The affair promises to be noisy and will attract seriously the attention of the world, in the first place, for the character and time of the [Costa Rican] demand, in the second place, for the jurisdiction which the Central American Court of Justice will take upon this international litigation, and from which, undoubtedly, the right of force will triumph and the force of right will be laughed at. The Court, according to this criterion, will cease to be what it has pretended to be—that which decided international questions, giving to each one that which belonged to it, but in the case which we are considering it will not be so, and the Court will have to disappear *ipso facto*. And forever."[98]

[98] Manuel Castro Ramirez, in *La Prensa* of San Salvador, March 27, 1916.

CHAPTER XI

Mexico: The Background of Wilsonian Interference

For nearly two years Mexico was the major cause of perplexity, in both domestic and foreign affairs, for the Wilson administration. The desire to help the Mexican people overthrow a military dictator and establish a constitutional government first prompted Wilson and Bryan to interfere in a developing Mexican civil war. This interference led in turn to unforeseen entanglements, the outgrowth of which was an attempt by the Washington leaders to impose their own control upon what was one of the most important revolutions of the twentieth century. The story of these events reveals the full danger inherent in the motives and methods of New Freedom diplomacy. Its consequences were almost catastrophic for both Mexico and the United States.

As with Nicaragua, Wilson and Bryan inherited a troubling problem in Mexico. In 1910 and 1911 an incongruous coalition of revolutionaries and reformers under the leadership of Francisco I. Madero had overthrown the old regime headed by the senile dictator, Porfirio Díaz, and had installed Madero in the National Palace in Mexico City. Madero's regime was short-lived. His attempts to reconstruct Mexican society on a democratic basis provoked the inevitable counterrevolutions that weakened his power, and because he did not move fast and drastically enough, he incurred the hostility of the radicals, especially of the agrarian reformer of the State of Morelos, Emiliano Zapata. To the world at large, he seemed an idealist and a dreamer who was leading Mexico into chaos because of his incompetence and bungling.[1]

Madero's downfall resulted, however, not from any general uprising, but from one of the most treacherous betrayals in modern history. Felix Díaz, a nephew of the deposed dictator, led part of the army in a revolt in the Mexican capital on February 9, 1913. The *coup d'état*, however, soon turned into a fiasco, and Díaz and his men sought refuge in the

---

[1] The recent work, Charles C. Cumberland, *The Mexican Revolution, Genesis Under Madero*, has done much to correct this inaccurate judgment.

Ciudadela, the military prison. Madero then brought in General Victoriano Huerta and additional federal troops to subdue the rebels. Instead of suppressing the rebellion, Huerta concluded a secret agreement with Díaz, the *Pacto de la Ciudadela*, on February 17, 1913; deposed Madero the following day and allowed him to be murdered soon afterward; had himself elected provisional President; and sent the following message to President Taft on February 18: "I have the honor to inform you that I have overthrown this Government. The forces are with me, and from now on peace and prosperity will reign."[2]

These events of what Mexicans call the "Tragic Ten Days" set forces in motion that were soon to shake the western hemisphere. That fact, however, was not apparent when the Taft administration pondered the adoption of a policy toward the Huerta regime. The American Ambassador in Mexico City, Henry Lane Wilson, who had harried Madero throughout his administration and had indirectly assisted Huerta and Díaz in their coup,[3] pleaded for immediate *de jure* recognition of the provisional government. The State Department, however, hesitated, not because of any revulsion it felt against the means that Huerta had used to seize power, but because it desired to use recognition as a lever to obtain prompt settlement of a number of disputes outstanding with Mexico. Until those issues were settled, Secretary Knox declared, the United States would maintain *de facto* relations with Huerta's government without extending formal recognition.[4] On the other hand, Britain, France, Germany, Japan, and many of the other governments with envoys in Mexico City soon afterward recognized the Huerta regime, on the ground that it was in fact the constitutional government of Mexico.

Such was the state of affairs when Wilson and Bryan took control of foreign policy in March 1913. From Mexico City, Ambassador Wilson intensified his appeals for recognition and began a campaign to convince his superiors that Huerta had saved Mexico from debauchery and national ruin.[5] Specialists in the State Department supported the

[2] General Huerta to the President, February 18, 1913, *Foreign Relations, 1913*, p. 721.
[3] For a further discussion of this matter, see below, p. 353.
[4] Secretary of State to the American Ambassador, February 21 and 28, 1913, *Foreign Relations, 1913*, pp. 728-729, 747-748. Knox and Taft afterward declared that they would have given formal recognition if they had known that President Wilson would not recognize the Huerta government. See the Diary of Chandler P. Anderson, Library of Congress, March 15, 1915; and W. H. Taft to W. V. Backus, July 10, 1916, Taft Papers.
[5] e.g., the American Ambassador to the Secretary of State, March 12 and May 15, 1913, *Foreign Relations, 1913*, pp. 772-773, 801-804; and H. L. Wilson to W. W., July 1, 1913, Wilson Papers.

Ambassador's plea with learned arguments to the effect that Huerta's government was in fact the only government in Mexico and that the refusal of recognition by the United States would encourage revolutionary elements and make it difficult for Huerta to protect foreign lives and property.[6] "The Government of the United States having originally set itself up by revolution," Counselor John Bassett Moore added in an invocation of the principles of diplomatic intercourse, "has always acted [in the matter of recognition] upon the de facto principle. We regard governments as existing or not existing. We do not require them to be chosen by popular vote. . . . Our deprecation of the political methods which may prevail in certain countries can not relieve us of the necessity of dealing with the governments of those countries. . . . We look simply to the fact of the existence of the government and to its ability and inclination to discharge the national obligations."[7]

Finally, the large American colony in Mexico City, most of the members of which had feared and hated Madero and expected Huerta to restore the old order, joined Americans with financial and railroad interests in Mexico to demand recognition and support of the provisional government. Only Huerta, they argued, could maintain order and protect the 40,000 Americans living in Mexico and an American property investment in that country totaling nearly $1,000,000,000.[8]

The President was neither moved nor convinced by these appeals and arguments. He announced through the newspapers that he would deal with the Huerta government on a *de facto* basis and would settle the issue of formal recognition only after waiting to see what future developments would bring[9]; otherwise, he said little about the Mexican situation during the first two months of his administration. At the same time, certain attitudes and judgments, which would later help to shape his policy, were forming in his mind.

The first was a feeling of deep revulsion against Huerta and what

[6] e.g., F. M. Dearing, "Considerations on According Recognition to the Present De Facto Government of Mexico," memorandum dated April 16, 1913, State Department Papers.

[7] J. B. Moore, "The Mexican Situation," memorandum dated May 14, 1913, *ibid.* I have transposed some of these sentences. See also J. B. Moore, "CONFIDENTIAL. For the Secretary," memorandum dated August 22, 1913, *ibid.*

[8] House Diary, March 27, 1913, relating a conversation with E. N. Brown, president of the National Railways of Mexico; W. A. Tucker to E. M. House, April 17, 1913, House Papers; James Speyer to J. B. Moore, May 1, 1913, State Department Papers; J. Speyer, "MEMORANDUM AS TO MEXICO," dated May 5, 1913, Wilson Papers; J. Speyer to J. B. Moore, May 31, 1913, State Department Papers.

[9] New York *World*, March 13, 1913; *New York Times*, May 9 and 17, 1913.

Wilson once called Huerta's "government of butchers."[10] As the President pondered the situation in Mexico, the issue crystallized: a popular, constitutional government had been overthrown and the rightful rulers of Mexico had been murdered by a treacherous usurper. How could he recognize and support such a man in a country as important as Mexico without encouraging government by assassination throughout the western hemisphere? To Wilson, the answer was clear. As he declared in a public statement on March 11, 1913, "We can have no sympathy with those who seek to seize the power of government to advance their own personal interests or ambition."[11]

This same feeling of moral outrage led Wilson to repudiate the historic American practice of extending recognition to all governments in power and to improvise for Mexico a radical new test for recognition. It was a test, as Wilson afterward put it, of "constitutional legitimacy," which, as one authority has explained, "implied the right of the United States to inquire fully into whether the new government was complying with its own national constitution and even to go behind its existence to scrutinize whether it had come to power because its leaders were motivated by personal interests and ambitions."[12] And he adopted this new policy, not blindly, but in the face of clear warnings from Counselor Moore that it was historically and legally unsound and could lead only to immeasurable interference in Mexican affairs.

During these early months before the formation of a firm Mexican policy, the President was also crystallizing his thoughts on the nature of the revolutionary upheaval in Mexico. He sensed intuitively that it had underlying economic causes, but for the most part he conceived of the Revolution in sheerly political terms, that is, in terms of the Mexican masses struggling for constitutional government and political democracy. Almost inevitably, therefore, he thought in terms of a political solution: the restoration of constitutional government through free elections. Events would later prove how romantic and superficial this approach was, but it governed all of Wilson's early Mexican policy.

There was one development during this early period that strengthened Wilson's determination not to accord a hasty recognition to the provisional regime in Mexico City and confirmed his judgment about the political character of the Revolution. Almost immediately after Huerta's coup, the *Maderista* leaders in the northern Mexican states

[10] Charles Willis Thompson to "Rube" Bull, May 22, 1913, Thompson Papers.
[11] *New York Times,* March 12, 1913.
[12] Howard F. Cline, *The United States and Mexico,* p. 142.

raised the standards of rebellion against Mexico City. Calling themselves Constitutionalists, the anti-*Huertistas* met at Guadalupe on March 26, 1913, and adopted a platform demanding the restoration of constitutional government and appointing Venustiano Carranza, Governor of the State of Coahuila, as "First Chief," or leader, of the movement to overthrow the tyrant in Mexico City. On March 30, 1913, moreover, Carranza proclaimed himself provisional President of Mexico. It was impossible at this time to predict the future of the Constitutionalist cause; but the widespread proportions of the rebellion in the northern states and the renewal of Zapata's uprising in the State of Morelos belied Huerta's boast that he had pacified his country.

The first sign that the Washington administration might be moving toward a definite Mexican policy came during early May 1913. On May 6, 1913, Julius Kruttschnitt, chairman of the board of directors of the Southern Pacific Railroad, presented to Colonel House a plan prepared by Delbert J. Haff of Kansas City and approved, Kruttschnitt said, by the officers of two copper companies with large interests in Mexico[13] and by Edward L. Doheny of the Mexican Petroleum Company. Haff proposed, first, that the United States recognize Huerta on the condition that he agree to hold an early election in the states which he controlled, and, second, that the Constitutionalists be asked to suspend hostilities, hold elections in the states under their control, and support the President chosen in the election.[14] Haff soon afterward reiterated his suggestions by letter and in person to the President.[15]

Wilson was much impressed by the Haff plan, even though it provided for a momentary recognition of Huerta. It seemed to offer an easy solution; more important, it had the approval of Cleveland H. Dodge, Wilson's intimate friend, who introduced Haff to the President. Perhaps it was at their conference at the White House on about May 12, 1913, that Wilson wrote out in shorthand the first cryptic formulation of what later became his plan of mediation in Mexico.[16] A short time later he elaborated the proposal in the draft of a note to be sent to Mexico City:

> Please represent to Huerta that our understanding was that he was to seek an early constitutional settlement of affairs in Mexico by means of a free popular election, and that our delay and hesitation about recogni-

[13] Phelps, Dodge & Company and the Greene Cananea Copper Company.
[14] J. Kruttschnitt to E. M. House, May 6, 1913, Wilson Papers.
[15] D. J. Haff to W. W., May 12, 1913, *ibid.*
[16] "Mexico. Settlement," transcribed MS. in *ibid.*

tion has been due to the apparent doubt and uncertainty as to what his plans and purposes really were. Our sincere wish is to serve Mexico. We stand ready to assist in any way we can in a speedy and promising settlement which will bring peace and the restoration of order. The further continuation of the present state of affairs will be fatal to Mexico and is likely to disturb most dangerously all her international relations. We are ready to recognize him now on condition that all hostilities cease, that he call an election at an early date, the twenty-sixth of October now mentioned being, in our judgment, too remote, and that he absolutely pledge himself as a condition of our action in his behalf that a free and fair election be secured by all proper machinery and safeguards. Upon this understanding this Government will undertake the friendly office of securing from the officials of the states which are now refusing to acknowledge the authority of Huerta's government an agreement to cease hostilities, maintain the status quo until the election shall have been held, and abide by the result of the election if it be held freely and without arbitrary interference of any kind as we have suggested.[17]

Not long after the President drafted this note, Kruttschnitt came with some friends to the State Department to urge the adoption of a revised plan for the settlement of the Mexican civil war. Omitting any reference to the recognition of Huerta, Kruttschnitt now proposed that the United States simply use its good offices to mediate between the Huerta government and the Constitutionalists, to the end that a fair nation-wide election might be held.[18] "The suggestion they make is a new one, and it strikes me very favorably," Bryan wrote in approval on May 27, 1913. "Instead of asking for the recognition of Huerta, they suggest that Huerta be notified that this Government will recognize a constitutional President, if the Congress will call an election for an early date, and supervise the election so as to give a fair chance for an expression of the opinion of the people. . . . This seems to offer a way out."[19]

Wilson again agreed and two weeks later drafted new instructions to Ambassador Wilson. The American government, the proposed message read, "is convinced that within Mexico itself there is a fundamental lack of confidence in the good faith of those in control at Mexico City and in their intention to safeguard constitutional rights and methods of action." However, the draft continued, the United States would be glad to use its good offices to arrange an armistice and a conference of

[17] Printed in R. S. Baker, *Woodrow Wilson*, IV, 248.
[18] J. Kruttschnitt to W. J. Bryan, May 26, 1913, Wilson Papers.
[19] W. J. Bryan to W. W., May 27, 1913, *ibid.*

all leaders in Mexico if the Huerta government would give "satisfactory assurances that an early election will be held, free from coercion or restraint, that Huerta will observe his original promise and not be a candidate at that election and that an absolute amnesty will follow."[20]

After drafting these notes, however, the President decided not to send them, probably because he felt still too ignorant about conditions in Mexico and was beginning to doubt the credibility and the integrity of Ambassador Wilson and his ability to serve as an impartial mediator in the Mexican struggle. On March 7, 1913, the New York *World* had begun a fierce campaign to discredit the Ambassador and force his recall, by exposing his alleged complicity in the Huerta-Díaz coup.[21] These charges shook Wilson's and Bryan's confidence in the Ambassador, while his obviously inaccurate reports on Huerta's strength must have caused them to discount all reports from the Embassy in Mexico City. Indeed, the Washington leaders would have recalled Ambassador Wilson at once if they could have thought of a way to send a new envoy without thereby automatically extending recognition to the provisional government.

[20] Printed in R. S. Baker, *Woodrow Wilson*, IV, 254.

[21] New York *World*, March 7, 8, and 12, 1913. In view of the doubt which has existed on this important question, an attempt at clarification is pertinent here.

Henry Lane Wilson played an important role in the tragic events in Mexico City that led to Madero's downfall. To begin with, the Ambassador had an unconcealed hatred for Madero and opposed him at every turn throughout his administration, as a reading of Wilson's dispatches from the Mexican capital during 1912 and early 1913 will reveal. Then, after Díaz began his rebellion on February 9, 1913, Ambassador Wilson hounded Madero with impossible demands for the protection of foreign lives and property and persuaded the British, German, and Spanish Ministers to join him in demanding that Madero resign in order to avert further bloodshed. When these efforts failed, the Ambassador entered into communication with Díaz and Huerta, undoubtedly learned of their plan to depose Madero, and probably encouraged them in their conspiracy. Finally, Ambassador Wilson called the two conspirators to the American Embassy on February 18, 1913, and persuaded them to confirm formally the *Pacto de la Ciudadela*, which they had concluded the day before. Known also as the "Pact of the Embassy," this agreement provided for the establishment of a provisional government with Huerta as provisional President and promised that Díaz might be a candidate for the presidency in the next election. The agreement consummated, the Ambassador then presented Huerta to the diplomatic corps and proceeded to bombard the State Department with pleas for the recognition of the provisional government.

The above account is based upon Wilson's own dispatches to the State Department, particularly the American Ambassador to the Secretary of State, March 12, 1913, *Foreign Relations, 1913*, pp. 768-776; Robert H. Murray, "Huerta and the Two Wilsons," *Harper's Weekly*, LXII (March 25-April 29, 1916), 301-303, 341-342, 364-365, 402-404, 434-436, 466-469; William B. Hale to W. J. Bryan, June 18, 1913, State Department Papers; and H. F. Cline, *The United States and Mexico*, pp. 130-132.

Yet the President knew that he could not mediate between Huerta and the Constitutionalists until he had a true estimate of affairs in Mexico. Thus in late May 1913, soon after he had abandoned the Haff plan for mediation through Ambassador Wilson, the President asked his friend and literary collaborator, William Bayard Hale, to go to the Mexican capital to investigate and report. Hale knew next to nothing about Mexican affairs when he undertook his mission, but he was one of the most intelligent reporters of his time, and the President trusted him implicitly.

Hale's dispatches from Mexico City, written from June 3 to about August 24, 1913, confirmed the President's own intuitive judgment of Huerta. "General Huerta," Hale wrote, for example, on July 9, "is an ape-like old man, of almost pure Indian blood. He may almost be said to subsist on alcohol. Drunk or only half-drunk (he is never sober), he never loses a certain shrewdness. He has been life-long a soldier, and one of the best in Mexico, and he knows no methods but those of force. It is now believed by some who come into contact with him that Huerta is finding the presidency a hard and uncongenial task. . . . But he is a hard fighter, glories in the exercise of power, and I see no signs that he will abandon his office, except, as is possible, to take the field for a few months, so as to render himself legally eligible to take the presidency again under the pretence of election."[22]

More important than Hale's devastating reports,[23] were his estimate of political conditions in Mexico and his recommendations for an American policy toward the Huerta regime. Hale portrayed a nation heading toward inevitable bankruptcy and chaos under Huerta's tyrannical and corrupt rule. He sensed that Mexico was in the throes of a "struggle between surviving mediaevalism, with its ideas of aristocracy, exploitation, and peonage, and modern civilization." Nevertheless, because he was so far from the center of the Constitutionalist movement, the major threat to Huerta's power, Hale tended to underestimate both the strength of the Constitutionalist movement and the ability of the Constitutionalist leaders to govern Mexico.

Convinced that Huerta could not survive and that the United States would have to occupy Mexico if the American President permitted

[22] W. B. Hale, "Memoranda on Affairs in Mexico," dated Mexico City, July 9, 1913, State Department Papers.

[23] There was also his characterization of Ambassador Wilson: "Wilson is vain busy-body, highly nervous temperament increased by indulgence, not scandalous, which slight frame is not equal to." W. B. Hale to Ben G. Davis, incomplete telegram, June 3, 1913, *ibid.*

events to run their natural course, Hale went on to urge a bold plan of action. The President, he suggested, should demand the elimination of Huerta, the holding of a free election, and the formation of a new Mexican government, which the United States could recognize and support. At the same time, Hale continued, the President should explain the reasons for his action to the European governments and appeal on high moral grounds for their acquiescence. He was convinced, Hale concluded, that the European governments would cooperate and that Huerta would yield peacefully, provided the American government made it plain that it was prepared to use force to obtain its demands.[24]

Soon after Hale had arrived in Mexico City, Wilson and Bryan sent an obscure friend of Bryan's, one Reginald F. Del Valle, on a secret mission to the northern Mexican states to judge the character and strength of the Constitutionalist movement. Del Valle interviewed most of the rebel leaders, but he completely misjudged or confused everything that he heard and saw. Indeed, the Washington leaders could not have taken the Constitutionalist movement seriously if they had believed Del Valle's reports.[25]

Del Valle went from northern Mexico to Mexico City, preparatory to a tour of inspection in Zapata's stronghold and the surrounding region. In the Mexican capital, however, he boasted to reporters that he was on a secret mission from the President of the United States,[26] and Bryan abruptly called him back to Washington. Del Valle's mission was not merely a fiasco; it was a positive disaster, for his reports on the Constitutionalist movement were gravely misleading at the very time the President most sorely needed accurate information about the possible future rulers of Mexico.

By the middle of July 1913, it appeared that conditions in Mexico would soon force Wilson to move from deliberation to an active Mexican policy. The provisional government was nearly bankrupt, unable to obtain adequate funds in Europe because of American opposition, and obviously incapable of suppressing the growing Constitutionalist

[24] See especially W. B. Hale to B. G. Davis, June 3 and July 17, 1913, *ibid.*; W. B. Hale, "The Mexican Question," undated memorandum in *ibid.*, written probably about August 8, 1913; and W. B. Hale to the Secretary of State, received August 20, 1913, Wilson Papers.

[25] See R. F. Del Valle to B. G. Davis, June 8, 9, 12, 17, and 23, 1913, State Department Papers.

[26] Mexico City *El Diario*, July 7, 1913; W. B. Hale to B. G. Davis, July 8, 1913, State Department Papers.

rebellion. Huerta's collapse seemed daily imminent, and his fall at this time might plunge Mexico into anarchy and lead to the wholesale destruction of foreign lives and property. The European powers, particularly England and Germany, would not stand by if the United States refused to protect their nationals in Mexico; and wholesale killing of Americans and the looting of American property would generate almost irresistible pressures in the United States for intervention. Thus it seemed that failure to take firm action before Mexico drifted into anarchy might in the end compel Wilson and Bryan to take the drastic step of trying to occupy that country, which would surely result in war. These hypotheses were urged upon the President by Huerta's friends and foes alike.

Wilson and Bryan worked out their policy during the last two weeks of July 1913 in response mainly to Hale's reports and recommendations. First, they recalled Henry Lane Wilson from Mexico City on July 16, ostensibly for the purpose of consultation but actually to remove him from his post.[27] Next, on about July 20, Wilson and Bryan agreed that the time had come to offer their good offices of mediation along the lines suggested by Haff, Kruttschnitt, and Hale.[28] Finally, on July 28, they summoned former Governor John Lind of Minnesota to Washington and asked him to go as their confidential agent to Mexico City to present their offer to the provisional government.

Precisely why they chose Lind, who had had no diplomatic experience, could not speak Spanish, was strongly anti-Catholic, and knew nothing about Mexican affairs, remains as much a mystery today as it was to Lind at the time.[29] Perhaps it was enough that Lind was a friend of Bryan, an anti-imperialist, and a progressive Democrat who would presumably have character enough to resist the blandishments of the Mexican politicians and to ignore the suggestions of the leaders of the American colony in Mexico City.

The President explained his plan and purposes in a letter of introduction and instructions that he personally prepared for Lind. The letter read as follows:

[27] Hale's long dispatch describing H. L. Wilson's role in the Huerta-Díaz coup (W. B. Hale to W. J. Bryan, June 18, 1913, State Department Papers) reached Washington around the end of June 1913 and was responsible for the President's decision to remove the Ambassador. See W. W. to W. J. Bryan, July 1 and 3, 1913, Wilson Papers.

[28] For some evidence of their thought, see W. J. Bryan to W. W., received at the White House on July 20, 1913, *ibid.*

[29] George M. Stephenson, *John Lind of Minnesota*, p. 208.

To Whom It May Concern:

This will introduce the Honorable John Lind, who goes to Mexico at my request and as my personal representative, to act as advisor to the American Embassy in the City of Mexico. I bespeak for him the same consideration that would, in other circumstances, be accorded a regularly accredited representative of the Government of the United States.

Instructions (Mexico)

Press very earnestly upon the attention of those who are now exercising authority or wielding influence in Mexico the following considerations and advice:

The Government of the United States does not feel at liberty any longer to stand inactively by while it becomes daily more and more evident that no real progress is being made towards the establishment of a government at the City of Mexico which the country will obey and respect.

The Government of the United States does not stand in the same case with the other great Governments of the world in respect of what is happening or what is likely to happen in Mexico. We offer our good offices, not only because of our genuine desire to play the part of a friend, but also because we are expected by the powers of the world to act as Mexico's nearest friend.

We wish to act in these circumstances in the spirit of the most earnest and disinterested friendship. It is our purpose in whatever we do or propose in this perplexing and distressing situation not only to pay the most scrupulous regard to the sovereignty and independence of Mexico —that we take as a matter of course to which we are bound by every obligation of right and honor—but also to give every possible evidence that we act in the interest of Mexico alone, and not in the interest of any person or body of persons who may have personal or property claims in Mexico which they may feel that they have the right to press. We are seeking to counsel Mexico for her own good and in the interest of her own peace, and not for any other purpose whatever. The Government of the United States would deem itself discredited if it had any selfish or ulterior purpose in transactions where the peace, happiness and prosperity of a whole people are involved. It is acting as its friendship for Mexico, not as any selfish interest, dictates.

The present situation in Mexico is incompatible with the fulfillment of international obligations on the part of Mexico, with the civilized development of Mexico herself, and with the maintenance of tolerable political and economic conditions in Central America. It is upon no common occasion, therefore, that the United States offers her counsel and assistance. All America cries out for a settlement.

A satisfactory settlement seems to us to be conditioned on—

(a) An immediate cessation of fighting throughout Mexico, a definite armistice solemnly entered into and scrupulously observed;

(b) Security given for an early and free election in which all will agree to take part;

(c) The consent of General Huerta to bind himself not to be a candidate for election as President of the Republic at this election; and

(d) The agreement of all parties to abide by the results of the election and cooperate in the most loyal way in organizing and supporting the new administration.

The Government of the United States will be glad to play any part in this settlement or in its carrying out which it can play honorably and consistently with international right. It pledges itself to recognize and in every way possible and proper to assist the administration chosen and set up in Mexico in the way and on the conditions suggested.

Taking all the existing conditions into consideration, the Government of the United States can conceive of no reasons sufficient to justify those who are now attempting to shape the policy or exercise the authority of Mexico in declining the offices of friendship thus offered. Can Mexico give the civilized world a satisfactory reason for rejecting our good offices? If Mexico can suggest any better way in which to show our friendship, serve the people of Mexico, and meet our international obligations, we are more than willing to consider the suggestion.[30]

Thus armed with Wilsonian rhetoric, Lind left Washington for Mexico City on the afternoon of August 4, 1913. Few envoys in history have ever undertaken a more quixotic mission or one more surely doomed to failure. Blithely assuming that the Mexicans would welcome his assistance, the President had not only failed to consult with the American Embassy in Mexico City, the provisional government, or the Constitutionalist leaders; he had also let them all learn the news of Lind's mission from the newspapers, which printed a summary of Lind's instructions on August 5, 1913.[31] "I will resist with arms any attempt by the United States to interfere in the affairs of Mexico," Huerta retorted on August 8. "The limit of patience has been reached over the policy of non-recognition made by the United States. I intend

[30] From the original text in the Wilson Papers and as reprinted in _Foreign Relations, 1913_, pp. 821-822.

[31] Actually, this report came out as the result of a bad leak in the State Department. Wilson tried to repair the damage caused by its publication by telling reporters on August 9 that he planned to make no "proposals" to the Huerta government through Lind. _New York Times_, August 10, 1913.

to absolutely ignore Lind's presence unless he bears official credentials as Ambassador."[32]

Actually, of course, Huerta's warlike threats were not seriously meant. Lind arrived safely in Mexico City on August 11, 1913, and was graciously received the following day by the Foreign Minister of the *de facto* government, Federico Gamboa.[33] Two days later Lind returned to the Foreign Office, delivered the President's proposals, and added verbally a message from Wilson to the effect that he would never recognize Huerta. Gamboa replied bitterly in a long formal note to Lind on August 26, 1913. After reviewing and answering Wilson's message point by point, he concluded:

"The Confidential Agent may believe that solely because of the sincere esteem in which the people and Government of the United States of America are held by the people and Government of Mexico . . . , my Government consented to take into consideration, and to answer as briefly as the matter permits, the representations of which you are the bearer. Otherwise, it would have rejected them immediately because of their humiliating and unusual character, hardly admissible even in a treaty of peace after a victory. . . . With reference to the final part of the instructions of President Wilson, . . . [I] propose the following equally decorous arrangement: One, that our Ambassador be received in Washington; two, that the United States of America send us a new ambassador without previous conditions."[34]

Undaunted, Lind increased his pressure as the parleys proceeded, by warning that the President might take the Mexican affair before Congress, was contemplating permitting the Constitutionalists to purchase arms in the United States, and might be willing as a last resort to use military force against the provisional regime.[35] When Gamboa still refused to yield or even to compromise, Lind went his limit on August 22 and 25, 1913, by promising that the State Department would immediately approve a large American loan to the *de facto* government if Huerta would only agree to hold a fair election and give assurances that he would not be a candidate for the presidency.[36]

In a blistering reply on August 26, 1913, Gamboa bluntly repudiated Wilson's right to interfere in Mexican affairs and put an end to the

[32] *ibid.*, August 9, 1913.
[33] J. Lind to the Secretary of State, August 12, 1913, State Department Papers.
[34] F. Gamboa to J. Lind, August 16, 1913, *Foreign Relations, 1913*, p. 827.
[35] J. Lind to the Secretary of State, August 18, 1913, Wilson Papers.
[36] J. Lind to the Secretary of State, August 22 and 25, 1913, State Department Papers and Wilson Papers.

negotiations. After a long sarcastic introduction, the Foreign Minister went to the root of the Mexican resentment. "If even once we were to permit the counsels and advice (let us call them thus) of the United States of America," he exclaimed, "not only would we . . . forego our sovereignty but we would as well compromise for an indefinite future our destinies as a sovereign entity, and all the future elections for president would be submitted to the veto of any President of the United States of America. And such an enormity, Mr. Confidential Agent, no government will ever attempt to perpetrate; and this I am sure of unless some monstrous and almost impossible cataclysm should occur in the conscience of the Mexican people." In conclusion, Gamboa rejected almost contemptuously Lind's offer of an American loan in return for Huerta's compliance with Wilson's demands. "When the dignity of the nation is at stake," he wrote, "I believe that there are not loans enough to induce those charged by the law to maintain it to permit it to be lessened."[37]

In Washington, meanwhile, the President had informed the members of the Senate foreign relations committee and the Cabinet of the failure of the Lind mission and had been pondering a future course. "Our friend Huerta is a diverting brute!" he wrote on August 24, 1913. "He is always so perfectly in character: so false, so sly, so full of bravado (the bravado of ignorance, chiefly), and yet so courageous, too, and determined,—such a mixture of weak and strong, of ridiculous and respectable! One moment you long for his blood, out of mere justice for what he has done, and the next you find yourself entertaining a sneaking admiration for his nerve. He will not let go till he pulls the whole house down with him. He loves only those who advise him to do what he wants to do. He has cold lead for those who tell him the truth. He is seldom sober and always impossible, and yet what an indomitable fighter he is for his own hand! Every day the news from Mexico City unsettles the news of the day before. . . . Any hour of the day or night I may have to revise my judgment as to what it is best to do."[38]

On August 27, 1913, the day after Lind left Mexico City for Veracruz and before Gamboa's final note arrived in Washington, Wilson went before a joint session to explain his Mexican policy to the Amer-

[37] F. Gamboa to J. Lind, August 26, 1913, quoted in the Chargé to the Secretary of State, August 27, 1913, Wilson Papers.
[38] W. W. to Mary A. Hulbert, August 24, 1913, printed in R. S. Baker, *Woodrow Wilson*, IV, 273.

ican people. The United States, he declared, desired only to help the Mexican people to find peace and establish an "honest constitutional government." But the Huerta regime had proved its incapacity, and "war and disorder, devastation and confusion" seemed the inevitable outcome of letting events in Mexico run a natural course. "It was our duty at least to volunteer our good offices—to offer to assist, if we might, in effecting some arrangement which would bring relief and peace and set up a universally acknowledged political authority there."

The President then gave a full account of Lind's mission and its failure. The United States, he continued, could not thrust its good offices upon Mexico; it could now only wait patiently and watch developments as the two sides fought it out in bloody civil war. Meanwhile, however, the American government would urge its citizens to leave Mexico and would "follow the best practice of nations in the matter of neutrality" by forbidding the export of munitions to any part of Mexico.[39]

The month following Wilson's announcement of what the newspapers promptly called a policy of "watchful waiting" saw a marked lessening of the acute tension between Washington and Mexico City. To begin with, congressional leaders, the newspapers, and other public spokesmen so overwhelmingly approved the President's new policy of nonintervention in Mexican affairs that there could be no doubt of the peaceful intentions of the American people. "I cannot allow this hour to pass without telling you how gratified I am with your message on Mexico and its reception by Congress," Bryan wrote happily. "If I am competent to judge of merit in the domain of morals and statesmanship you have set a record in both. . . . I have heard nothing but praise from those with whom I have spoken."[40]

The leaders of the provisional government and the *Huertista* editors were as nearly delighted as the great apostle of peace. They had feared that the President would either give open support to the Constitutionalists or else use direct measures against the provisional government as a consequence of the failure of the Lind mission. Instead, Wilson had promised a policy of complete abstention and true neutrality. And such a policy, the *Huertistas* realized, could only work to their benefit, because, in contrast to the landlocked Constitutionalists, they controlled the seaports of Mexico and could import munitions from Europe and

---

[39] Wilson's address is printed in *Foreign Relations, 1913,* pp. 820-823.
[40] W. J. Bryan to W. W., August 27, 1913, Bryan Papers, Library of Congress.

Japan. "That is substantially what I expected. We never had any reason to doubt the United States' friendship and disinterested motives," Huerta replied gratefully after a reporter read to him a summary of Wilson's address.[41]

The most important cause of the lessening of the tension, however, were numerous signs that the Lind mission had succeeded in spite of its apparent failure—that Huerta would actually withdraw and permit the election of a so-called constitutional President during the election scheduled to be held on October 26, 1913. Indeed, for all its sarcasm, Gamboa's final note of August 26, 1913, had in a sense conceded Wilson's demand that Huerta eliminate himself from the presidency at an early date, by pointing out that the Mexican constitution forbade a provisional President to succeed to the constitutional presidency. On August 28, 1913, moreover, the Foreign Minister assured the American Chargé in Mexico City, Nelson O'Shaughnessy, that Huerta could not resign in order to enter the next presidential election.[42]

"Every point contended for in the last note is accepted in fact, though not in form," Lind rejoiced. "From a diplomatic standpoint the mission is a success." "Accept my hearty congratulations," Bryan replied. "Huerta's announcement that he will not be a candidate is the one thing necessary to the restoration of peace."[43] "Now that the crisis is passed," the Secretary added the following day, "there will be time for deliberation and consultation as to the various steps to be pursued."[44]

"Deliberation and consultation" began anew on September 1, 1913, when the provisional government proposed to send a confidential agent, Manuel de Zamacona, former Mexican Ambassador to the United States, to Washington for secret talks. "I am of the opinion," O'Shaughnessy remarked in transmitting the suggestion, "that both he and the provisional President are desirous of coming to an understanding with our Government."[45] Bryan replied encouragingly, suggesting that Zamacona first confer with Lind in Veracruz "in regard to the carrying out of the proposals of the President looking for the restoration of permanent peace."[46]

[41] New York *World*, August 28, 1913.
[42] N. O'Shaughnessy to the Secretary of State, August 28, 1913, State Department Papers.
[43] J. Lind to the Secretary of State, August 27, 1913, Wilson Papers; W. J. Bryan to J. Lind, August 27, 1913, State Department Papers.
[44] W. J. Bryan to J. Lind, August 28, 1913, *ibid.*
[45] N. O'Shaughnessy to the Secretary of State, September 1, 1913, *ibid.*
[46] W. J. Bryan to J. Lind, September 8, 1913, *ibid.*

Nothing came of Huerta's effort to establish intimate relations with the Wilson administration, but developments in Washington and Mexico City during September 1913 seemed to promise the establishment of a constitutional Mexican government that the United States would recognize. On September 12 the American newspapers announced, upon the obvious authority of the White House, that President Wilson had decided to recognize the President chosen in the Mexican elections scheduled for October 26, 1913, even though the Constitutionalists refused to participate and the authorities in Mexico City refused to agree to an armistice.[47] Huerta replied on September 16, 1913, in an address to the Mexican Congress. "I will spare no effort and no sacrifice to obtain the coveted peace and to guarantee fully in the coming election the free casting of the ballot," he declared. "You may be sure it will constitute the greatest possible triumph for the interim Government to surrender office to its successor if the latter, as is to be expected, enters upon its functions with public peace and order an accomplished fact."[48]

The most encouraging news from Mexico City, however, came on September 24, 1913, when the Catholic party held its convention in the capital and nominated Federico Gamboa and Ugenio Rascon, two distinguished leaders untainted by any association with the Huerta-Díaz coup, for the presidency and vice presidency. "Huerta has agreed to this move and given his promise for uninfluenced elections," O'Shaughnessy wrote from the Embassy in Mexico City. ". . . He gives me to understand that he has made but two political promises: to pacify the country and to enforce the laws; he states that he has no political favorites; that Felix Díaz will go to Japan and will not be a candidate."[49]

To the leaders in Washington, it was a thoroughly acceptable solution. "I feel that we have nearly reached the end of our trouble," Bryan wrote with satisfaction to the White House. "This eliminates Huerta, which is the first thing that we desired. I know of no objections that can be raised to Gamboa personally and we have, therefore, only to await the election to see whether it is fairly conducted."[50] Bryan went

[47] *New York Times*, September 12, 1913.
[48] *ibid.*, September 17, 1913. For Lind's and Bryan's reaction, see J. Lind to W. J. Bryan, September 16, 1913, State Department Papers; W. J. Bryan to W. W., September 17, 1913, Wilson Papers; and W. J. Bryan to J. Lind, September 18, 1913, State Department Papers.
[49] N. O'Shaughnessy to W. J. Bryan, two dispatches dated September 24, 1913, Wilson Papers.
[50] W. J. Bryan to W. W., September 25, 1913, *ibid.*; see also W. J. Bryan to J. Lind, September 26, 1913, State Department Papers.

on, moreover, to seal his approval by making a momentous declaration of policy through the newspapers. An officially inspired dispatch from Washington declared that by promising to withdraw and to hold an orderly election on October 26, 1913, Huerta had in fact complied with Wilson's demands. If Gamboa were elected President, the American government would extend prompt recognition and financial support to the new regime, even though the Constitutionalists and the Mexican Liberal party carried out their threat to boycott the election and to maintain the civil war.[51]

It was a simple solution, but a hopelessly unrealistic one—first, because the Catholic party did not speak for a majority of literate Mexicans even in the states under Huerta's control, and above all because it ignored the Constitutionalists, the most dynamic factor in the Mexican situation. To have recognized Gamboa and supported a Catholic government, as Wilson and Bryan were prepared to do, could only have meant an intensification of the civil war and the identification of the United States with a reactionary minority regime.

By the autumn of 1913 the Constitutionalists controlled the broad areas of the northern states except for a few isolated *Huertista* garrisons.[52] Their armies were poorly equipped and included uncontrolled bandit gangs that sacked, looted, and raped; they had not yet formed a government or elaborated a program of social and economic reform. And yet it was evident that they carried the torch of the Madero Revolution and represented the only hope of satisfying the aspirations of the mass of enslaved and landless peons. More important, it was evident that they would accept no superficial solution that merely substituted a respectable reactionary for the usurper Huerta.[53]

And yet Wilson and Bryan proceeded throughout the summer and early autumn of 1913 very much as if the Constitutionalists did not exist. William Bayard Hale, the President's former agent in Mexico City, came to Washington on about September 28, 1913, to emphasize the danger of agreeing to a Mexican settlement that ignored the northern rebels. "So far as I know," he warned the President, "our government has made no approaches to the Revolutionists. Ought we not do

[51] New York *World*, September 26, 1913.

[52] By mid-September 1913 the Constitutionalists controlled the states of Durango, Zacatecas, Coahuila, Sonora, Sinaloa, Tepic, and Chihuahua, and had besieged the *Huertista* garrisons in the cities of Juárez and Chihuahua.

[53] See Carranza's statement printed in the *New York Times*, August 2, 1913.

so?... It would be the greatest blessing to Mexico if the United States could somehow quietly bring the Mexico City government and the Revolutionists into communication with each other."[54]

Hale's suggestion struck Wilson with the force of a revelation. He conferred with Bryan on September 30, 1913, and the following day Bryan instructed Lind to inform the provisional authorities that the American government would not feel that a satisfactory constitutional solution had been achieved unless the provisional government in Mexico City made a sincere effort to persuade the Constitutionalists to participate in the election on October 26, 1913.[55] At the same time, Bryan opened negotiations with Carranza, the First Chief of the Constitutionalists, looking toward his cooperation in an armistice and a general election. The plan collapsed on October 7, 1913, when Carranza informed the Secretary of State that he intended, not to participate in an election controlled by his enemies, but to conquer all Mexico.[56]

A series of catastrophic events in Mexico City soon afterward brought an end to "watchful waiting," set the American government in violent hostility to Huerta, and spared Wilson and Bryan from the consequences of their promise to support a new "constitutional" regime in Mexico City after the impending election.

On October 8, 1913, Torreón, the key to Huerta's defenses in northern Mexico, fell to the Constitutionalists, and near-panic ensued in Mexico City. Two days later, the Chamber of Deputies of the Mexican Congress, which had been a center of *Maderista* opposition to the provisional administration from the beginning, threatened to dissolve the government by moving from the capital to a point perhaps behind the Constitutionalist lines. Moving swiftly to avert open rebellion, Huerta surrounded the Chamber with troops and arrested and imprisoned 110 deputies on October 10, 1913. On the following day he dissolved the Mexican Congress and assumed dictatorial power until a new Congress, which would presumably be elected on October 26, 1913, could meet and form a new constitutional government. Finally, Huerta called the diplomatic corps to the National Palace on October 23 and explained that he had dissolved the Chamber because it was disloyal. He declared,

[54] W. B. Hale to W. W., September 28, 1913, Wilson Papers.
[55] W. W. to W. J. Bryan, September 29, 1913, *ibid.*; W. J. Bryan to J. Lind, October 1, 1913, State Department Papers; J. Lind to W. J. Bryan, October 7, 1913, *ibid.*
[56] Francisco Escudero, "Aide Mémoire" for the Secretary of State, October 7, 1913, Wilson Papers.

moreover, that he was not a candidate for the presidency and would not accept that office even if the people elected him to it.[57]

Meanwhile, a new British Minister, Sir Lionel Carden—"a slow-minded, unimaginative, heavy-footed, commercial Briton, with as much nimbleness as an elephant," as Page once described him[58]—arrived in Mexico City on October 11, 1913, the day following Huerta's arrest of the deputies, and ostentatiously presented his credentials to the dictator. In addition, Carden told reporters on October 21, 1913, that Great Britain had no intention of withdrawing recognition from Huerta, that the Washington leaders did not understand the seriousness of the Mexican crisis, and that Mexico needed a strong man and a drastic purging of dissident elements. It was "ridiculous," he added, to suppose that such a strong man could be "found in a haphazard election under the present circumstances."[59]

There were hurried conferences in Washington following news of Huerta's arrest of the Mexican deputies. Cutting short a vacation in North Carolina, Bryan returned to the State Department on October 12, 1913, in time to dispatch a warning to Huerta that "any violence done to legislators will shock the civilized world and raise serious questions with our own and other Governments."[60] Then, after discussions during the following morning, the President composed and Bryan sent the following note to O'Shaughnessy:

Call upon the Foreign Office at once and deliver the following message:

"The President is shocked at the lawless methods employed by General Huerta and as a sincere friend of Mexico is deeply distressed at the situation which has arisen. He finds it impossible to regard otherwise than as an act of bad faith toward the United States General Huerta's course in dissolving the Congress and arresting deputies. It is not only a violation of constitutional guarantees but it destroys all possibility of a free and fair election. The President believes that an election held at this time and under conditions as they now exist would have none of the sanctions with which the law surrounds the ballot and that its results therefore could not be regarded as representing the will of the people. The President would not feel justified in accepting the result of such an election or in recognizing a President so chosen."[61]

[57] N. O'Shaughnessy to the Secretary of State, October 11, 13, and 23, 1913, *Foreign Relations, 1913*, pp. 836, 838-839, 848-849; *New York Times*, October 12, 1913.

[58] W. H. Page to W. J. Bryan, March 30, 1914, Page Papers.

[59] *New York Times*, October 22, 1913.

[60] W. J. Bryan to the American Chargé, October 12, 1913, *Foreign Relations, 1913*, p. 837.

[61] W. J. Bryan to the American Embassy, October 13, 1913, State Department Papers.

During the week and a half following the dispatch of this note, Wilson and Bryan worked feverishly to forestall European recognition of the new Mexican government scheduled for election on October 26, 1913, and to formulate a policy of direct action against Huerta. As a precaution, Bryan sent a copy of the note to O'Shaughnessy to the governments with representatives in Mexico City on October 14, 1913; and ten days later he asked these governments to withhold recognition until the State Department had had an opportunity to make its views known.[62]

Meanwhile, from about October 22 to October 30, 1913, the President and Secretary of State were at work on the drafts of definitive enunciations of policy, to be sent to Mexico City and to the powers. First, Wilson typed out the following outline, which he sent to the State Department for its guidance in the preparation of a circular note. It read:

This government most interested, most responsible.

The political fortunes and economic development of all Central America involved.

The government of Huerta, based upon usurpation and force, would long ago have broken down but for the encouragement and financial aid derived from its recognition by other nations, without regard to the wishes or purposes of the United States.

The continuance of that government is impossible with the consent of the United States.

Will the other governments cooperate with the United States, or is their policy and intention to antagonize and thwart us and make our task one of domination and force?

No joint intervention will be considered.

W. W.

Note: *As strong and direct as the courtesies and proprieties of pacific diplomacy permit.*

To England: The bottom was about to drop out when Sir Lionel Carden appeared upon the scene and took charge of its rehabilitation.[63]

In response, Bryan, apparently,[64] prepared the draft of a circular note. "You will please lay before the Foreign Office," it began, "the following statement of facts and request:

---

[62] The Secretary of State to certain diplomatic officers, October 14 and 24, 1913, *Foreign Relations, 1913*, pp. 841, 849.

[63] MS. in the State Department Papers.

[64] This is sheer guesswork, as there is no way, either by use of external or internal evidence, to determine the authorship of this draft. It would seem reasonable to assume, however, that both Bryan and Counselor John Bassett Moore had a hand in preparing the draft, although, as will subsequently appear, Moore did not approve of its contents.

"The President directs me to say that the responsibilities of this Government as Mexico's neighbor and as the nation of paramount influence in the western hemisphere, compel him to lay before the various European governments which have recognized the Government of General Huerta the following facts." Here followed an account of Huerta's rise to power "through methods so abhorrent to conscience and so destructive of constitutional government, that the President *of the U.S.* felt that a recognition of his Government would offend the judgment of the civilized world and put a premium upon lawless and despotic methods *throughout Latin America.*" The draft went on to tell of Wilson's offer of mediation. "It is probable," it charged accusingly, "that these good offices would have been accepted and that the differences between the contending factions would have been adjusted but for the encouragement which General Huerta received from European nations. While this nation has larger material interests in Mexico than any other nation, and while more of its citizens are residing there, this Government has steadfastly refused to allow these material interests to control its course and, in company with the governments of nearly all of the Latin American countries, has given paramount consideration to the political and moral questions involved. European financiers, however, apparently in return for commercial concessions and aided by the recognition given by European governments, have supplied means whereby General Huerta has attempted to force himself upon his country *and perpetuate his power.*"

Now Huerta held sway by sheer military force, the draft continued, and planned to have himself elected President in the forthcoming canvass. "It need hardly be pointed out that an election held under such conditions would not be in any sense an election," it concluded, "but merely a farcical attempt to clothe tyranny and despotism in the livery of popular government. Under these circumstances the President feels it his duty to bring to the attention of those governments which have recognized General Huerta the grave consequences which have followed the adoption of that course, and, in the name of the people of the western hemisphere, whose lands have been dedicated to free and constitutional government, ask them to withdraw that recognition which has exerted so baneful an influence, to the end that the people of Mexico may the more quickly put an end to arbitrary power and reestablish a government deriving its just powers from the consent of the governed."[65]

[65] Draft of a note, in the State Department Papers. The words italicized were inserted by Wilson in his own handwriting.

At the same time, Bryan or Wilson, or perhaps both of them, prepared a note to be sent to Mexico City and to accompany the message to the powers. After denouncing Huerta's usurpation in hostile terms, the note continued:

> This Government having, in the announcement and maintenance of the Monroe doctrine, shown its willingness to protect the people of this hemisphere from encroachment at the hands of European powers, . . . is now prepared to assert with equal emphasis its unwillingness to have an American Republic exploited by the commercial interests of our own or any other country through a government resting upon force. If the influences at work in Mexico were entirely domestic this Government would be willing to trust the people to protect themselves against any ambitious leader who might arise. But since such a leader relies for his strength, not upon the sympathy of his own people but upon the influence of foreign people, this Government . . . would be derelict in its duty if by silence or inaction it seemed to sympathize with such an interference in the rights and welfare of Mexico. . . . The President has confidence that the people of Mexico, if free to choose their own rulers, would choose men in sympathy with the nation's highest aspirations—men who would regard it a duty and a pleasure to carry out the will of the people. It will not, therefore, recognize as a legitimate government a government established by force and terrorism, whether the force and terrorism be exercised, as they were, in the establishment of the Huerta regime or are secured through the empty forms of a mock election.[66]

We cannot understand Wilson's extraordinary vehemence and particularly his anger at the British government at this time unless we go back for a moment and review the causes of the development of what was in fact a dangerous state of tension in Anglo-American relations over Mexico.

The British government had recognized Huerta's regime in the spring of 1913 in company with the other European powers. All during the following summer, moreover, Sir Edward Grey, the British Foreign Secretary, had applied gentle pressure upon the State Department either for American recognition of the provisional government or for joint Anglo-American intervention.[67] Even so, no Anglo-American tension developed before October 1913, because Grey repeatedly assured

[66] The Secretary of State to the American Embassy, October 24, 1913, original in the Wilson Papers, copy in the Bryan Papers, Library of Congress.

[67] W. H. Page to the Secretary of State, July 11, 17, and 25, August 20, 1913, State Department Papers; Ambassador Cecil Spring Rice to W. J. Bryan, August 11, 1913, Wilson Papers.

the Washington administration that British recognition of Huerta was only provisional, pending the formation of a constitutional government after the Mexican election on October 26, 1913.[68]

In view of historical British diplomatic practice, the realities of the Mexican situation, and the importance of British interests in Mexico, it would have been impossible for the London government to have followed any other course. "Modern British diplomacy," one member of the British Embassy in Washington in 1913 and 1914 has written, "had been born after the Napoleonic wars, in Castlereagh's and Canning's struggle against the Holy Alliance—*i.e.* against the claim of foreign governments to impose their own principles of morals or political philosophy upon the internal affairs of other nations."[69]

Thus, like the American government before 1913, the British Foreign Office had followed the predictable practice of extending *de facto* recognition to governments in power without asking questions as to origins, morality, or internal politics. "By the standards of Latin America (always excepting the Argentine and Chile)," the same British commentator continues, "there was nothing very novel about the Mexican revolution of 1912-1913, and, by those standards, the problem for foreign governments was simple. They had to await the emergence, from the welter of competing revolutionaries, of a government stable enough to maintain law and order and fulfil its international obligations; and they had to recognise it, at least *de facto*, as soon as possible after it had emerged."[70]

But there were other equally important reasons why the British government had no alternative but to recognize and support Huerta. British subjects had invested several hundred million dollars in Mexican railways, banks, public utilities, and oil wells, all of which had contributed to Mexican prosperity and development. In addition, the British navy had converted from coal burners to oil burners in 1912; and Mexico, with its production of some 25,000,000 barrels in 1912, was virtually the sole source of oil for the British fleet. Huerta promised and did, in fact, give protection to foreign investments and interests. As Grey pointed out time and again, the British government had to

[68] W. H. Page to the Secretary of State, July 11, 1913, State Department Papers.

[69] Lord Percy of Newcastle, "The Mexican Question, 1913-1914, viewed from the British Embassy at Washington," MS. in the possession of A. S. Link; quoted by permission of Lord Percy.

[70] See also Sydney Brooks, "A British View of the Mexican Problem," *North American Review*, cxcviii (October 1913), 444-456, for a superb contemporary exposition of British diplomatic practice and a defense of British policy in Mexico.

support Huerta as the only alternative to chaos and destruction for Mexicans, and great losses for the British. Because of the Monroe Doctrine, Britain could not intervene; it had to look to the established government for the protection of its vital interests.[71]

This, in general, was the background of the divergence of British and American policy in Mexico. That divergence was not important so long as Wilson thought the British were not actively opposing his plans for Huerta's withdrawal and the establishment of a new Mexican constitutional government. Following Carden's arrival in Mexico City after Huerta's dissolution of the Mexican Congress, however, anti-British feeling in Washington grew suddenly to proportions so dangerous as to menace friendly Anglo-American relations.

The reasons for this development are clear. From Lind in Veracruz, who was as anti-British as he was gullible, came almost daily reports and warnings to the State Department and the White House about sinister British machinations in Mexico. He wrote, for example, that Sir Lionel Carden had come to Mexico City to take charge of Huerta's crumbling government and had helped to plan Huerta's assumption of a dictatorship.[72] O'Shaughnessy in Mexico City reported that Carden was violently anti-American and had become Huerta's mainstay.[73] And Page in London frequently complained that the British were blind to moral principles in foreign policy. "I have not seen nor heard even an allusion to any moral principle involved nor a word of concern for the Mexican people," he wrote on October 25, 1913. "It is all about who is the stronger, Huerta or some other bandit, and about the necessity of order for the sake of financial interests. Nobody gives us credit for any moral purpose."[74]

But the most important cause of Wilson's anger was a conviction formed on a basis of newspaper stories, Lind's reports, and information received from Henry C. Pierce, a large American oil operator in Mexico.[75] It was the belief that S. Weetman Pearson, Lord Cowdray,

[71] See, e.g., W. H. Page to the Secretary of State, October 29, 1913, State Department Papers.

[72] J. Lind to the Secretary of State, October 15, 23, and 29, 1913, Wilson Papers and State Department Papers; J. Lind to the Secretary of State, October 27, 1913, State Department Papers.

[73] N. O'Shaughnessy to the Secretary of State, October 14 and 20, 1913, Wilson Papers and State Department Papers.

[74] W. H. Page to W. W., October 25, 1913, Wilson Papers; also W. H. Page to W. W., November 2, 1913, *ibid.*

[75] See B. W. Long to W. J. Bryan, August 26 and November 3, 1913, Wilson Papers and State Department Papers, reporting interviews with Pierce.

who had enormous investments in Mexican railways and oil developments, controlled British policy in Mexico. Cowdray, these reports alleged, was actually the sinister power behind Huerta. Cowdray lent Huerta money and kept him in power in return for new concessions; as a large contributor to the Liberal party, Cowdray dominated the Foreign Office; Carden was merely Cowdray's mouthpiece in Mexico, and so on. As Lind once put it, "After canvassing all the evidence available with the utmost care and reflection I have become convinced that the control and monopoly of the oil fields and oil business in Mexico is not only the aim of the Lord Cowdray interests but also of the English Government. England's Mexican policy for some time past has been shaped and exerted with this sole aim in view."[76]

Actually, these allegations were either grossly exaggerated or else entirely false. Carden obviously believed that Huerta was the only person capable of preserving order in Mexico; but there was no reliable evidence to prove that he was in any way involved in Huerta's plans and actions, or even that he was anti-American in outlook.[77] "I do not think you realize how hard we worked to get from either Lind or O'Shaughnessy definite items of speech or conduct with which we could furnish you as material for what you had to say to the Ministers about Carden," Wilson afterward told Page. "It simply was not obtainable. Everything that we got was at second or third hand."[78]

It turned out also that the stories of Cowdray's influence and activities had been similarly fabricated or magnified by the newspapers, by Lind, and by Henry C. Pierce, who was himself secretly seeking concessions from Carranza at the time that he was acting as the State Department's chief informant on Cowdray. Cowdray's agents dealt with the Huerta government because it controlled the territory in which Cowdray's properties were situated; but there is not a shred of reliable evidence even to suggest that Cowdray either controlled British policy or the British Minister in Mexico, or supported Huerta in order to extend his property holdings in that country.[79]

[76] J. Lind to W. J. Bryan, October 25, 1913, Wilson Papers.

[77] Asked for proof of his charges against Carden, Lind had to reply that he had no evidence that would stand up in a court of law. He could not prove the charges, he continued, but he was morally certain they were well founded. See J. Lind, to the Secretary of State, December 17, 1913, State Department Papers. Moreover, O'Shaughnessy confessed that he had based his reports about Carden on secondhand accounts and could give no concrete proof of the British Minister's alleged machinations. See O'Shaughnessy to the Secretary of State, December 18, 1913, *ibid*.

[78] W. W. to W. H. Page, January 6, 1914, Wilson Papers.

[79] See Lord Cowdray to W. H. Page, November 17, 1913, State Department Papers,

The point, however, is that Wilson believed that these rumors and accusations were true[80] and proceeded to act as if the entire British Cabinet and Foreign Service were both morally obtuse and intent on thwarting his purposes in Mexico. "The President is determined the British public shall know of this alliance between the Mexican Government and oil interests," Colonel House wrote after a conversation at the White House on October 30, 1913, "and he believes British public opinion will be so strong against them that if it does not overthrow the present Ministry it will compel them to recede from their attitude."[81]

Wilson worked out a grand strategy either to force the British Cabinet to give up its alleged Mexican policy or else to blast it from office. His first step was to compose, or to ask Bryan and the State Department to compose, the angry circular note to the powers, printed above, denouncing them, and Britain particularly by implication, for their support of Huerta. He believed, correctly, that it would cause an explosion heard round the world.

At about the same time, on October 23, 1913, he gave, or allowed someone high in the administration to give, a summary or copy of the proposed circular note to the Washington reporters. Thus the following day the newspapers carried sensational stories to the effect that the Washington administration was "seething with indignation" over British policy in Mexico; that the British had intervened and strengthened Huerta when he was about to collapse; that financial and industrial interests controlled British policy in Mexico; and that the President was prepared to warn the British government that it must go no further in its defiance of his wishes.[82]

Finally, in his address at Mobile on October 27, 1913, Wilson prepared the way for his *démarche* by publicly denouncing concessionaires

---

and Cowdray to various editors, November 12 and 17, 1913, in which Cowdray answered his critics. Copies of the last two letters were kindly furnished the author from the Cowdray Papers by the present Viscount Cowdray of London.

[80] In fact, Wilson continued to believe the charges against Carden and to hound the British Minister until he was removed from Mexico City, even after Lind and O'Shaughnessy had failed to adduce any real evidence. After admitting that the American government had no evidence in its case against Carden, Wilson went on to write: "That he was working against us was too plain for denial, and yet he seems to have done it in a very astute way which nobody could take direct hold of." W. W. to W. H. Page, January 6, 1914, Wilson Papers.

[81] House Diary, October 30, 1913.

[82] *New York Times*, October 24, 1913; New York *World*, October 24, 1913. It is remarkable how accurately these reports summarized the draft of the circular note.

and promising American help in freeing Latin America from their alleged stranglehold.

Wilson's projected drive to force the British government to abandon support of Huerta succeeded in a way that he had neither planned nor expected. Instead of a major Anglo-American crisis, there was a sudden reconciliation and almost a joining of hands in a common policy.

This, obviously, would not have happened if Wilson had sent the circular note that the State Department had prepared. He did not send it, in the first instance, because of a stern warning from the Department's learned Counselor, John Bassett Moore. Bryan handed the circular note to Moore for polishing, suggesting that the Counselor add a paragraph invoking the Monroe Doctrine. Moore studied it for several days and prepared a formal draft. Then, on October 28, 1913, he gave the President his opinion of the note without mincing words.

The Monroe Doctrine, Moore began, was in no way involved in the question of the recognition of the Huerta government. The United States did not supervise the foreign relations of the independent states of America, and it had "never been considered necessary for foreign Powers to ask our consent to their recognition of an American government, or to explain to us their reason for such a step." Moreover, Moore continued, it might be well to consider the Mexican issue in all its aspects before accusing the powers of acting in subservience to financial interests by recognizing Huerta. As the provisional government in Mexico was the only government in Mexico, the United States itself had conducted *de facto* diplomatic relations with it. Seventeen powers had recognized the Huerta regime, normally and without any knowledge that the United States disapproved. In considering the effect of imputing improper or sordid motives to Great Britain for its policy in Mexico, he went on, it might be well to remember that the British had certain rankling grievances against the United States—the tolls exemption, the failure of the Senate to renew the arbitration treaty, and others. Therefore, the Counselor concluded, nothing "short of the clearest proof would at this juncture justify us in attributing to other governments, by means of a direct diplomatic communication, motives the imputation of which they would necessarily repel and resent."[83]

As a result, Wilson hesitated before sending the circular note; and, while he waited, the British Cabinet, alarmed by the reports from Washington of the President's resentment, moved quickly to seek a

[83] J. B. Moore to W. W., October 28, 1913, State Department Papers.

rapprochement with the United States. On October 25, 1913, the day after the publication of the newspaper reports of Wilson's determination to deal sternly with the British, Sir William Tyrrell, Sir Edward Grey's private secretary, sailed for America to take charge of the Mexican situation in Washington, in the absence of the ailing British Ambassador, Sir Cecil Spring Rice. At the same time, there came from London inspired reports saying that British recognition of Huerta had ended and that the Foreign Office would consult with Washington before making any further moves.[84] A short time later, moreover, Prime Minister Herbert Asquith declared publicly that the British government would not intervene in Mexico and certainly had no intention of attempting to thwart American policy there.[85]

The extreme anti-British tension in Washington had considerably subsided, therefore, by the time Tyrrell arrived in the capital on November 12, 1913. Colonel House, who had been brought into the discussions by Page and President Wilson, saw Tyrrell at the British Embassy on November 12. "I told him very frankly what our purpose was in Mexico," House wrote soon afterward, "and that we were determined to carry it through if it was within our power to do so. That being so, I suggested that he get his Government to cordially cooperate with ours rather than to accept our policy reluctantly."[86]

House took Tyrrell to the White House the following morning. "The President received him in the Blue Room," House recorded. "He had on a grey sack suit, while Sir William wore a cutaway. They both appeared a little embarrassed. The President opened the conversation by saying I had told him of my conversation with him yesterday; and then outlined the purpose of our Government regarding Mexico, very much as I had done the day before. Sir William replied much as he had to me."[87] Wilson told Tyrrell, in addition, "I am going to teach the South American Republics to elect good men!"[88]

"Sir William was very happy after the interview," House later wrote, "and when the President left us he remained to talk to me and to express his gratification. He cleared up in the President's mind all suspicion, I think, in regard to concessions and as to the intentions and purposes of the British Government. He assured the President that his Government would work cordially with ours and that they would do

[84] New York *World*, October 28, 1913.
[85] *New York Times*, November 11, 1913.
[86] E. M. House to W. H. Page, November 14, 1913, House Papers.
[87] House Diary, November 13, 1913.
[88] Burton J. Hendrick, *The Life and Letters of Walter H. Page* (3 vols.), I, 204.

all that they could to bring about joint pressure through Germany and France for the elimination of Huerta. . . . Sir William said that if foreign diplomats could have heard our conversation they would have fallen in a faint it was so frankly indiscreet and undiplomatic."[89]

The Tyrrell mission, however, had merely cleared the air, and there still remained the task of working out the details of a settlement. Sir Edward Grey had agreed to cooperate in putting pressure on Huerta to retire. But he had done so reluctantly, against his better judgment, only because there was no other way to avoid risking the loss of American friendship, which loss he knew might prove fatal in the event of a general war in Europe. At the same time, Grey was determined to obtain, in exchange for his own concession, a promise that the American government would hereafter protect British interests in Mexico if chaos followed Huerta's fall.

Grey set doggedly to work to obtain this commitment even before Tyrrell arrived in America, voicing his concern in a long conversation with Page on October 29, 1913.[90] On November 8 he again raised the question of what would happen if Huerta were eliminated. Would chaos and destruction of foreign property ensue? Page replied that "the United States accepts the full responsibility of its action in eliminating Huerta," and that the only question was whether Huerta would be eliminated with or without the moral support of the British government. But still Grey was not satisfied. "It is a very grim situation," he replied.[91]

Tyrrell must have discussed American protection of British interests in Mexico in his conversation with the President on November 13, 1913, for he put the question squarely in a letter to Wilson before he left for London. "I am more than willing to comply with Sir Edward Grey's suggestion as conveyed to me in your letter of yesterday, which has just been placed before me," Wilson replied. "My only embarrassment is this, whenever I make any public announcement, it is met by some form of defiance or some indication of irritation on the part either of the Huerta people or the Constitutionalists in Mexico. . . . I beg that you will assure Sir Edward Grey that the United States Government intends not merely to force Huerta from power, but also to exert every influence it can exert to secure Mexico a better government under which all contracts and business and concessions will be safer than they have been. . . . I hope that Sir Edward Grey will feel free to convey the

[89] E. M. House to W. H. Page, November 14, 1913, House Papers.
[90] W. H. Page to the Secretary of State, October 29, 1913, State Department Papers.
[91] W. H. Page to the Secretary of State, November 8, 1913, *ibid.*

contents of this letter to those British and Canadian investors for whom he, naturally, feels a sympathetic anxiety."[92]

In brief, the outcome of the Tyrrell mission and of the subsequent negotiations between Washington and London was the immediate establishment of an Anglo-American accord on Mexico. In effect, Grey subordinated his policy to the personal wishes of the President of the United States. Grey did not withdraw formal recognition from Huerta, but he bridled Carden at once and transferred him from Mexico City soon afterward; and he made it clear that Huerta would receive no support from the London Foreign Office. As the other powers with important interests in Mexico had earlier indicated their willingness to follow the American lead, Wilson's diplomatic isolation of the Mexican dictator was complete. He could now turn with a free hand to the formulation of bold new plans to oust Huerta and take control of the establishment of a new constitutional government in Mexico.

[92] W. W. to Sir William Tyrrell, November 22, 1913, Wilson Papers.

CHAPTER XII

Wilson and the Triumph of the Constitutionalists

WHILE Wilson and Bryan threatened, Huerta went stubbornly on his way. He held the canvass scheduled for October 26, 1913, and managed the election of a subservient Congress in familiar revolutionary fashion. The new legislature, in turn, declared the presidential election null and void, on the ground that not enough votes had been cast for a Chief Executive, and appointed Huerta President *ad interim* until new elections could be held in July 1914.[1]

In the wake of these events, Wilson decided to abandon "watchful waiting" and to take personal charge of a campaign to eliminate the dictator. "Many fateful possibilities are involved in that perplexing situation," he wrote on November 2, 1913. "I lie awake at night praying that the most terrible of them may be averted. No man can tell what will happen while we deal with a desperate brute like that traitor, Huerta. God save us from the worst!"[2]

House's diary provides a further glimpse of some of Wilson's tentative thoughts and plans at this time: "The President has in mind to declare war against Mexico even though actual armed entrance into Mexico is not made. . . . He will first blockade the ports, thereby cutting off all revenue from the Mexican Government which will have a tendency to break down Huerta's resistance. He has in mind also throwing a line across the southern part of Mexico, perhaps another line just south of the Northern States. He plans to send troops to the Northern States, if they consent, in order to protect the lives and property of foreign citizens. . . . It is his purpose to send six battleships at once. A real crisis has arisen and . . . the President seems alert and unafraid."[3]

[1] J. Lind to W. J. Bryan, October 26, 27, and 28, 1913, State Department Papers; N. O'Shaughnessy to W. J. Bryan, November 3, 1913, *ibid.; New York Times*, October 27 and December 10, 1913.

[2] W. W. to Mary A. Hulbert, November 2, 1913, printed in R. S. Baker, *Woodrow Wilson*, IV, 287-288.

[3] House Diary, October 30, 1913.

Wilson preferred, however, to accomplish Huerta's downfall by diplomatic and moral pressure rather than by force. Thus he sent the following pronouncement to O'Shaughnessy in Mexico City on November 1, 1913, and a short time later to the powers:

Convey the following, in confidence, to the minister of foreign affairs, in view of his recent conversations with you, and the impressions you have received from them:

"(1) That the President of the United States feels that the recent coup d'état was in direct contravention of the assurances that had been conveyed to this government by General Huerta;

"(2) That, unless General Huerta now voluntarily and as if of his own motion retires from authority and from all attempt to control the organization of the government and the course of affairs, it will be necessary for the President of the United States to insist upon the terms of an ultimatum, the rejection of which would render it necessary for him to propose very serious practical measures to the Congress of the United States. (Suggest here as if from your own mind the countenance and active assistance of the Constitutionalistas by the United States.)

"(3) That the Government of the United States is anxious to avoid extreme measures, for Mexico's sake no less than for the sake of the peace of America, and is therefore willing to do anything within reason to spare General Huerta's feelings and dignity and afford him personal protection;

"(4) That it, therefore, suggests the following course: The choice of some man or small group of men, as little as possible identified with the recent troubles (elderly men now in retirement, for example, who enjoy the general public confidence) to constitute a provisional government and arrange for early general elections at which both a new congress and a new executive shall be chosen, and the government put upon a constitutional footing;

"(5) That some such course, approved by the Government of the United States, is now absolutely necessary, that government being firmly and irrevocably resolved, by one method or another, to cut the government of Huerta off, if he persists, from all outside aid or countenance, and Huerta will only for a very few days longer be free to act with apparent freedom of choice in the matter. His retirement and an absolutely free field for a constitutional rehabilitation being the least the United States can accept. This Government cannot too earnestly urge him to make the inevitable choice wisely and in full view of the terrible consequences of hesitation or refusal.

"(6) That the attempt to substitute Blanquet or any other representative of Huerta and the Huerta coup would lead to deeper irritation on the part of the United States and the inevitable final rupture, as would also any attempt to carry out the pretended or apparent choices of the recent elections, either as regards the presidency or the congress."[4]

O'Shaughnessy presented Wilson's ultimatum to Huerta's private secretary on November 3, 1913, and used all the pressure he could command during the next few days to force Huerta to yield. At first the dictator seemed ready to retire, and the Washington administration instructed Lind to proceed from Veracruz to Mexico City to take charge of the final negotiations and the establishment of a new government.[5] But Huerta, angered by reports in the American press of a Wilsonian ultimatum, suddenly stiffened. On November 8, 1913, he addressed a circular note to the powers affirming the constitutionality of his regime and his determination to remain in power until he had pacified Mexico.[6]

It was, actually, what Wilson had expected, and he now set in motion the plans that had been forming in his mind. First, on November 8, 1913, he composed and sent to the governments with envoys in Mexico City a preliminary warning of what he meant to do. "Please say to the Minister of Foreign Affairs," it read, "that, while the President does not feel that he can yet announce his policy with regard to Mexico in detail, he feels he should make known to the ------ government confidentially in advance his clear judgment that it is his immediate duty to require Huerta's retirement from the Mexican government and that this government must now proceed to employ such means as may be necessary to secure this result. Also inform the ------ government that this government will not regard as binding upon the people of Mexico anything done by Huerta since the assumption of dictatorial powers or anything that may be done by the fraudulent legislature which he is about to call together. The President hopes that the ------ government will see fit to use its influence to impress upon Huerta the wisdom of retiring in the interest of peace and constitutional government."[7]

[4] W. J. Bryan to the American Embassy, November 1, 1913, State Department Papers. This note was written by Wilson on his own typewriter.

[5] N. O'Shaughnessy to the Secretary of State, November 3 and 5, 1913, *ibid.*; W. J. Bryan to J. Lind, November 5, 1913, *ibid.*

[6] N. O'Shaughnessy to the Secretary of State, November 5, 1913, *ibid.*; N. O'Shaughnessy to the Secretary of State, November 9, 1913, enclosing a circular note by Foreign Minister Querido Moheno, dated November 8, 1913, *ibid.* For the newspaper reports referred to above, see the *New York Times*, November 4, 1913.

[7] Circular note, written by Wilson on his own typewriter, sent November 7-10, 1913, State Department Papers.

The President's next move was to attempt to come to some understanding with the Constitutionalists, whom he hoped to use as the instrument of Huerta's destruction. Toward the end of October 1913 he had sent William Bayard Hale to the border to wait in readiness to negotiate with Carranza and the other Constitutionalist chieftains, who were then assembling in Hermosillo for the purpose of forming a provisional Mexican government.[8] On about November 10, 1913, following the receipt from Mexico City of the news of Huerta's refusal to retire, Wilson instructed Hale to proceed to Nogales, Mexico, to present some proposals to Carranza and his Cabinet, and to obtain certain commitments.

One of Wilson's purposes in seeking a conference was to ascertain whether the Constitutionalists were prepared to accept his cooperation in the formation of a constitutional regime in Mexico City, to which they would submit to the extent of cooperating in plans for a nationwide election. The President's bait was the lifting of the embargo against the export of munitions to revolutionary groups in Mexico that President Taft had imposed in 1912. Another purpose was to warn the Constitutionalist generals that continued depredations against foreign lives and property in northern Mexico would lead to American military intervention and occupation. "Confer with northern leaders and inform them that we contemplate permitting shipments of arms but before doing so desire you to make following statement," the President telegraphed to Hale on about November 11, 1913. "We desire above all things else to avoid intervention. If the lives and property of Americans and all other foreigners are safeguarded we believe intervention may be avoided. If not we foresee we shall be forced to it. We rely upon them to see to it that there is no occasion for it in their territory."[9]

Hale discussed Wilson's suggestions and plans for Mexico with Carranza and his Cabinet in the tiny customhouse at Nogales, Mexico, from November 12 to November 18, 1913. At first the American agent was deeply impressed by the First Chief and his lieutenants. "With few exceptions," he wrote to Washington on November 14, "the leaders are plain men; their speech is remarkable for Quaker-like conscientiousness and precision. Carranza is a positive character, huge, slow-moving of body and mind. He is deferred to absolutely. . . . His capacity for silent

[8] W. J. Bryan to W. W., c. October 30, 1913, Wilson Papers.
[9] W. W. to W. B. Hale, c. November 11, 1913, penciled draft in Wilson's handwriting, *ibid.*

deliberation is remarkable, though when he speaks it is with fluency and appositeness."[10]

But Hale soon discovered that Carranza's benign countenance concealed his stubborn strength and unyielding character, for friction arose as soon as the Constitutionalist leaders perceived the meaning of Wilson's message.

The Constitutionalists, Carranza declared, wanted only the right to purchase arms and munitions in the United States, not American interference or even assistance of any kind. He wanted to take "occasion solemnly to reiterate and emphasize anew," the First Chief declared in a formal reply, "that the Constitutionalists refused to admit the right of any nation on this continent acting alone or in conjunction with European Powers to interfere in the domestic affairs of the Mexican Republic; that they held the idea of armed intervention from outside as unconceivable and inadmissible upon any grounds or upon any pretext. He desired to warn the United States that any attempt in this direction would rekindle old animosities now almost forgotten and be utterly disastrous."[11]

The American President must also understand, Carranza continued, that the Constitutionalists would be satisfied with nothing less than the total destruction of Huerta and the old regime and their own unencumbered triumph. "These men are plainly bent on a complete political and social revolution for Mexico," Hale explained. "They are taciturn of speech but their moral enthusiasm is evident. They describe themselves as citizens in arms and declare their abhorrence of militarism. . . . They say they have resorted to arms as a result of intolerable conditions. Having done so they propose to stop at nothing short of possession of Mexico City and the Government. They declare they will destroy the taste of [the] military element and landed aristocracy, restore peace, then as soon as possible hold a free, general election and hand over the Government to officials named by the people."[12]

These forthright pronouncements came as a crushing blow to all of Wilson's hopes for leading the Mexican Revolution into democratic and constitutional channels. The President, Bryan replied, was deeply disturbed. "He would not be willing, even indirectly, to assist them if they took so narrow and selfish a view. It would show that they do not understand constitutional processes." Were the Constitutionalists willing to have constitutional government restored by peaceful means,

[10] W. B. Hale to the Secretary of State, November 14, 1913, State Department Papers.
[11] *ibid.*   [12] *ibid.*

Bryan went on, or did they prefer to use force? If assured of a "free and fair" election, would they submit their cause to the ballot, or did they still insist upon the sword as the only available weapon? If the Constitutionalists succeeded in setting up a government by force, did they intend to give the people an early opportunity to elect a President and Congress at a free and fair election?[13]

Hale went back to the conference on November 17, 1913, pleading that the hope of the Constitutionalists lay in their accepting "constitutional processes." Carranza was forthright in his reply. The Constitutionalists, he declared, would accept nothing less than a complete military victory. They would have nothing to do with a provisional government, even one established under Wilsonian auspices. They would stand by the Plan of Guadelupe, institute sweeping social and economic reforms by decree, and then hold a free and fair general election. And they would act in their own way, as befitted the rulers of a sovereign people.[14]

Carranza broke up the negotiations the day following this exchange by telling Hale that hereafter he would have to communicate in writing to the Constitutionalist Minister for Foreign Affairs, Francisco Escudero. Angrily accusing the First Chief of bad faith, Hale returned to Nogales, Arizona, and told reporters: "You know, the world is full of all kinds of people. Some of them are not only impossible, but highly improbable. Please understand that I am not speaking of the gentlemen across the border who are with such admirable skill preventing their friends from helping them."[15]

Deeply wounded by Carranza's rejection of the proferred American assistance, Wilson now thought that he had no alternative but to abandon his plans for lifting the arms embargo and to proceed on his own to eliminate Huerta and establish a provisional government in Mexico City.

In fact, even before Hale went to Nogales, the President had begun a diplomatic campaign through Lind in Mexico City to force Huerta to dissolve the Congress recently elected and to resign in favor of a provisional government of elder statesmen. Huerta at first refused, and Lind broke off the negotiations and returned to Veracruz.[16] But news

---

[13] W. J. Bryan to W. B. Hale, November 16, 1913, *ibid.*

[14] W. B. Hale to the Secretary of State, November 17, 1913, *ibid.*

[15] *New York Times*, November 20, 1913.

[16] J. Lind to W. J. Bryan, November 11, 12, and 13, 1913, State Department Papers; *New York Times*, November 13, 1913.

of the impending American discussions with the Constitutionalists so badly shook the dictator that he reopened the talks on November 13, 1913, by suggesting a compromise. He would cooperate in establishing a provisional government that the United States could support, if only the American President would agree that the new Mexican Congress should convene and provide for new elections before its dissolution.[17]

Wilson replied at once with a statement of the "conditions" upon which negotiations might be resumed:

> I. The explicit agreement of General Huerta, First, that the Congress called tomorrow shall not assemble; and second, that General Huerta will absolutely eliminate himself from the situation immediately upon the constitution of an *ad interim* government acceptable to the United States, the character and personnel of such a government to be agreed upon by negotiation; it being understood that Mr. Lind will return to Mexico City and will in conjunction with our Chargé conduct these negotiations with General Huerta himself or with any one whom General Huerta may fully authorize to represent and speak for him. It being also understood that the Government of the United States will do anything within its right and power to safeguard the personal dignity and safety of General Huerta throughout.
>
> II. Such a provisional government having been agreed upon, we will arrange for its prompt recognition by the Government of the United States and will at once come to an understanding with it with regard to the complete reconstitution of the Government of Mexico under the constitution of 1857 by means of free elections to be held at as early a date as possible.[18]

Under pressure from the British Minister, Carden, who warned the dictator that he could expect no help from London,[19] Huerta virtually surrendered during the morning of November 15, 1913, by promising O'Shaughnessy to submit a list of names for the provisional presidency.[20] By the late afternoon of the same day, when the American Chargé returned to the Foreign Office to receive Huerta's final reply, however, the situation had changed completely. Convinced by reports from Nogales that there was no longer any danger that the United States would lift the arms embargo, Huerta now struck a defiant pos-

[17] N. O'Shaughnessy to the Secretary of State, November 13, 1913, State Department Papers.

[18] W. J. Bryan to N. O'Shaughnessy, November 14, 1913, *ibid.*

[19] *New York Times*, November 15, 1913.

[20] N. O'Shaughnessy to the Secretary of State, November 15, 1913, State Department Papers.

ture. "We cannot accept the intervention of any foreign power," he replied in a formal note to O'Shaughnessy, "no matter how high and respectable it may be in the matter of resolving domestic questions which are solely of the competence of the Mexican people, however just it may be for us to admit friendly suggestions, always provided that these be absolutely disinterested and do not affect the national dignity."[21] "Oh, no, I shall not quit," the dictator told reporters a few hours later. "I shall continue, just as I have been doing, to put forth my best efforts to bring about the pacification of the country, and thus fulfill the promise I made on taking office."[22]

In the circumstances, there was nothing Wilson could do except wait to see whether Huerta would be deposed either by some coup from within his own administration or by the Constitutionalists, for direct military intervention at this time would obviously provoke war with the Constitutionalists as well as with the *Huertistas* and might unite the entire Mexican people under Huerta's leadership. Through the newspapers, on November 20, 1913, the President announced his decision to revert to "watchful waiting."[23] In order to remove any doubt as to his ultimate plans and objectives, however, he composed a circular note and sent it to the powers on November 24, 1913. It was perhaps the clearest and most remarkable enunciation of his Mexican policy:

OUR PURPOSES IN MEXICO:

The purpose of the United States is solely and singly to secure peace and order in Central America by seeing to it that the processes of self-government there are not interrupted or set aside.

Usurpations like that of General Huerta menace the peace and development of America as nothing else could. They not only render the development of ordered self-government impossible; they also tend to set law entirely aside, to put the lives and fortunes of citizens and foreigners alike in constant jeopardy, to invalidate contracts and concessions in any way the usurper may devise for his own profit, and to impair both the national credit and all the foundations of business, domestic or foreign.

It is the purpose of the United States, therefore, to discredit and defeat such usurpations whenever they occur. The present policy of the Government of the United States is to isolate General Huerta entirely; to cut him off from foreign sympathy and aid and from domestic credit, whether moral or material, and so to force him out.

[21] N. O'Shaughnessy to the Secretary of State, November 15, 1913, 11 p.m., *ibid.*
[22] *New York Times*, November 16, 1913.
[23] *ibid.*, November 21, 1913.

It hopes and believes that isolation will accomplish this end, and shall await the results without irritation or impatience. If General Huerta does not retire by force of circumstances, it will become the duty of the United States to use less peaceful means to put him out. It will give other governments notice in advance of each affirmative or aggressive step it has in contemplation, should it unhappily become necessary to move actively against the usurper; but no such step seems immediately necessary.

Its fixed resolve is, that no such interruptions of civil order shall be tolerated so far as it is concerned. Each conspicuous instance in which usurpations of this kind are prevented will render their recurrence less likely, and in the end a state of affairs will be secured in Mexico and elsewhere upon this continent which will assure the peace of America and the untrammeled development of its economic and social relations with the rest of the world.

Beyond this fixed purpose the Government of the United States will not go. It will not permit itself to seek any special or exclusive advantages in Mexico or elsewhere for its own citizens, but will seek, here as elsewhere, to show itself the consistent champion of the open door.

In the meantime it is making every effort that the circumstances permit to safeguard foreign lives and property in Mexico and is making the lives and fortunes of the subjects of other governments as much its concern as the lives and fortunes of its own citizens.[24]

Events during the weeks following this solemn pledge to depose Huerta revealed anew the futility of a policy of pronouncements and threats unaccompanied by measures of force. No uprising against Huerta occurred in Mexico City. On the contrary, the dictator grew stronger. The business and banking interests, the Church, and the large landowners realized that he alone could save them from the fury of the Constitutionalists, and they finally began to support the provisional government in a substantial way.[25]

By mid-December 1913, moreover, the Constitutionalist offensive had ground to a halt on nearly every front. In part, this was a result of the decisive intervention of Admiral Frank F. Fletcher, commander of the large American naval force stationed off the eastern coast of Mexico. Acting under orders from Washington, Fletcher forced the Constitutionalists to abandon their plans to attack Tampico and Tuxpam in

---

[24] The Secretary of State to all embassies except Turkey and Mexico, and to European legations, Belgium, Netherlands, Norway, Sweden, Denmark, and Portugal, November 24, 1913, State Department Papers.

[25] See especially J. Lind to the Secretary of State, January 8, 1914, *ibid.*

the heart of the rich oil region. In larger measure, however, the Constitutionalist decline was a result of Huerta's own aggressive counterattacks, which culminated in his recapture of the important stronghold of Torreón on about December 13, 1913.

For the American President, who had promised the powers to dispose of Huerta, it was a potentially dangerous and embarrassing situation. What could he do in these circumstances short of instituting armed intervention, which would raise more problems than it would solve? As Lind pointed out almost daily in urgent messages from Veracruz, Wilson's only hope lay in lifting the arms embargo against the Constitutionalists and in lending moral and diplomatic support to their cause.[26] This was not the solution that the President preferred, but it seemed the only way to hasten Huerta's downfall without involving the United States in war with the Mexican people.

The first indication that the Washington government might be moving toward open support of the Constitutionalists came on December 12, 1913, in the following message from Bryan to Lind: "President's sympathy entirely with Constitutionalists but their attitude makes it impossible at present to give any open manifestation of that sympathy. . . . No objection to your making confidential communication to Constitutionalist leaders."[27]

On January 2, 1914, moreover, Wilson conferred with Lind aboard the U.S.S. *Chester* off Gulfport, Mississippi. They talked about ways of assisting the Constitutionalists.[28] "I now know how the president feels. I did not before. That is, I wasn't sure," Lind reported to his wife. "I had kept firing in my stuff and made my views clear but I did not know whether he agreed with me. He does."[29] As Wilson explained to Colonel House a few days later, the Constitutionalists had come to a standstill and might not be able to make further progress unless he allowed them to obtain arms in the United States. He thought, therefore, that he had either to do this or else to send the army into Mexico and put Huerta out by force.[30]

The decision to recognize the belligerency of the Constitutionalists was made soon after the President talked to Lind and House, and the

[26] J. Lind to the Secretary of State, December 5, 9, 13, 14, 19, 22, and 27, 1913, January 7, 14, 15, 19, 26, and 30, 1914, *ibid.* and Wilson Papers.

[27] W. J. Bryan to J. Lind, December 12, 1913, State Department Papers.

[28] There is a transcription of Wilson's cryptic stenographic notes taken at the conference in the Wilson Papers.

[29] G. M. Stephenson, *John Lind of Minnesota*, p. 252.

[30] House Diary, January 16, 1914.

State Department opened negotiations with Luis Cabrera, Carranza's agent in Washington, on January 27, 1914. The American government obviously feared that the Constitutionalists would confiscate foreign property, nullify concessions, and refuse to acknowledge foreign claims for damages growing out of the civil war. Cabrera's reply to the Department's pointed inquiries was reassuring. The Constitutionalists, he declared, meant to accomplish radical social and economic reforms; but they would use constitutional and legal methods, respect the rights of property, uphold "just and equitable" concessions, and eschew confiscation and anarchy.[31]

These assurances were all that Wilson needed to find justification for what was, as he admitted, "an inevitable course of action in the circumstances."[32] He was now ready to effect a radical change in his Mexican policy—in brief, to abandon his former plan to establish a provisional government in Mexico City, and to shift to virtually complete support of the Constitutionalists. In a message to the British Foreign Office on January 29, 1914, he explained his new policy:

> The President . . . fears that the revolution in Mexico has reached such a stage that the sort of settlement proposed [by Sir Edward Grey on January 28, 1914], namely the elimination of General Huerta and the substitution of others in authority at Mexico City, would be without the desired effect of bringing peace and order. The men in the north, who are conducting a revolution with a programme which goes to the very root of the causes which have made constitutional government in Mexico impossible, and who are not mere rebels, would still have to be reckoned with. No plan which could be carried out at Mexico City at the present juncture could be made the basis of a satisfactory settlement with them. No plan which could not include them can now result in anything more than a change in personnel of an irrepressible contest. If the European powers would jointly or severally inform General Huerta in plain terms that he could no longer expect countenance or moral support from them, the situation would be immensely simplified and the only possible settlement [i.e., the triumph of the Constitutionalists] brought within sight.[33]

On January 31, 1914, besides, the President addressed a circular note to the powers informing them of his intention, "almost immediately, to

[31] Luis Cabrera to William Phillips, January 27 and 28, 1914, Wilson Papers; W. Phillips to W. W., January 28, 1914, *ibid.*

[32] W. W. to P. J. McCumber, January 29, 1914, *ibid.*

[33] The Secretary of State to Ambassador Page, January 29, 1914, *Foreign Relations, 1914*, p. 445. Wilson wrote this message on his own typewriter.

remove the inhibition on the exportation of arms and ammunition from the United States into Mexico." No one outside Mexico, he explained, could control Mexican affairs. "From many sources which it deems trustworthy," he continued, "the Government of the United States has received information which convinces it that there is a more

In the Interest of Peace

Sykes in the Philadelphia *Public Ledger*

hopeful prospect of peace, of the security of property and of the early payment of foreign obligations if Mexico is left to the forces now reckoning with one another there than there would be if anything by way of a mere change of personnel were effected at Mexico City." Settlement by civil war was a terrible thing, he went on, "but it must come now whether we wish it or not, unless some outside power is to sweep Mexico with its armed forces from end to end; which would be the beginning of a still more difficult problem."[34]

Wilson took the fateful step of revoking the arms embargo on February 3, 1914. The Constitutionalists, of course, were delighted. "The war will soon be over! The war will soon be over!" General Francisco Villa, one of Carranza's chief generals, shouted as he heard the news.[35] Huerta feigned indifference, saying he did not think the President's action would make much difference.[36]

Reaction in the United States was generally favorable, especially among the members of the Senate foreign relations committee, many of whom had long been urging the President to lift the arms embargo.[37] But English commentators, most of whom viewed the Constitutionalists as bandits and rapists, were outraged. "Plainly speaking," one London editor declared in a typical editorial, "there has been nothing so cruelly immoral and so cynically cruel in the history of the world before. No State pretending to civilisation has ever before announced its readiness to supply the anarchical elements in a neighbouring community with the means of rapine and massacre for mere profit. . . . To complete the sinister monstrosity of President Wilson's intervention, the United States are still 'officially at peace' with the unfortunate population of Mexico."[38]

[34] The Secretary of State to all diplomatic missions, January 31, 1914, *ibid.*, pp. 446-447. I have transposed some of these sentences. Wilson also composed this note on his typewriter.

[35] *New York Times*, February 4, 1914.

[36] N. O'Shaughnessy to the Secretary of State, February 3, 1914, State Department Papers. But see *El Pais* (Mexico City), February 4, 1914, and *El Imparcial* (Mexico City), February 4, 1914, for typical *Huertista* reaction, which was generally violent.

[37] *New York Times*, February 4, 1914.

[38] London *Outlook*, xxxiii (February 7, 1914), 163; also London *Financial News*, February 5, 1914; and "Machiavelli in a Mortarboard," London *Spectator*, cxii (February 7, 1914), 215-216.

The English editors were the most incisive critics of Wilson's policy of interference in Mexican affairs. Their comments have such enduring value that the following list of editorials is submitted for the convenience of readers who desire to explore this subject further:

"Mexico and the United States," London *Spectator*, cxi (October 18, 1913), 598-600; "The Mexican Crisis," *ibid.*, November 8, 1913, pp. 745-746; "The Mexican Imbroglio," *ibid.*, November 15, 1913, pp. 808-809; "The Mexican Situation," *ibid.*, cxii (January 3, 1914), 4-5; "The Mexican Crisis," London *Outlook*, xxxii (August 30, 1913), 281-282; "President Wilson and President Huerta," *ibid.*, November 15, 1913, pp. 671-672; "Mexico and the United States," London *Economist*, lxxvii (August 23, 1913), 373; "Mexico and President Wilson's Message," *ibid.*, August 30, 1913, pp. 406-407;

While Wilson waited for the Constitutionalists to sweep into Mexico City following the lifting of the arms embargo, events seemed to conspire to ruin his hopes of deposing Huerta without the active military intervention of the United States. The reasons for this development were complex but not obscure. To begin with, the Constitutionalist ranks were beginning to be torn by a fierce rivalry between Carranza and Villa, who was scheming to seize leadership of the revolutionary forces from the First Chief. As a consequence, the two leaders often seemed more concerned with building their own power in preparation for a final internecine struggle than with fighting Huerta. Many responsible Mexicans, Lind reported, feared that the civil war might continue for years.[39]

A more important cause of the stalemate was the fact that Huerta continued to grow in prestige and power. After the lifting of the American arms embargo, the Church and the propertied classes of Mexico knew that their only hope of survival lay in wholehearted support of Huerta. They responded in early March 1914 with such an enormous domestic loan that the provisional government at last had sufficient funds to stabilize exchange and prosecute the war.[40] For his part, Huerta gave increasing evidence of an ability to govern and pacify the country. He stopped drinking heavily, made an alliance with the Church and the Catholic party, and strengthened his army and his defenses.[41] It is difficult to believe that Wilson had seriously considered the implications of his earlier threats against Huerta, but here he was, trapped by his own essentially reckless promises. As Lind hinted in a staccato of advice from Veracruz, the President had to do something or else stand exposed before the governments of the world as a bluffer.[42]

Wilson must have tried many times during March and early April of 1914 to discover some way to intervene and depose Huerta without risking a general war. And yet there seemed to be no way out. In these circumstances, as the necessity for military action grew increasingly

---

"President Wilson's Mexican Dilemma," London *Saturday Review*, cxvi (August 23, 1913), 226-227; "The Mexican Maze," *ibid.*, November 1, 1913, pp. 547-548; "The Deadlock in Mexico," *ibid.*, cxvii (January 31, 1914), 133-134.

Among American editors of consequence, only George Harvey raised his voice against a policy of endless interference through moralistic diplomacy. See his "The President and Mexico," *North American Review*, cxcviii (December 1913), 737-744.

[39] J. Lind to the Secretary of State, February 24, 1914, State Department Papers.
[40] J. Lind to the Secretary of State, March 8, 1914, *ibid.*
[41] J. Lind to the Secretary of State, March 10, 19, and 22, 1914, *ibid.*
[42] J. Lind to the Secretary of State, March 19, 23, 25, 27, and 28, 1914, *ibid.*

pressing, the President for the first time thought searchingly about the Mexican problem, the meaning of the Revolution, and what he conceived to be his own large opportunities to serve the Mexican people. Actually, he was finding a moral justification for a program of larger participation in Mexican affairs; but with him the process of rationalization was unconscious, automatic, and completely satisfying.

To begin with, he now saw clearly the deep roots and large meaning of the Mexican Revolution. "To some extent," he observed in April 1914, "the situation in Mexico is similar to that in France at the time of the Revolution."[43] The Mexican Revolution was on the whole no mere struggle for personal power and riches. It was a "revolution as profound as that which occurred in France"[44]—a glorious moment in the history of human freedom.

Convinced, besides, that the Constitutionalists intended to effect a genuine economic and social regeneration and to lead the Mexican masses eventually to political democracy, Wilson was willing by the spring of 1914 to accept a revolutionary rather than a "constitutional" solution. He explained these new convictions:

"My ideal," he told a reporter in April 1914, "is an orderly and righteous government in Mexico; but my passion is for the submerged eighty-five per cent of the people of that Republic, who are now struggling toward liberty.

"I challenge you to cite me an instance in all the history of the world where liberty was handed down from above! Liberty always is attained by the forces working below, underneath, by the great movement of the people. That, leavened by the sense of wrong and oppression and injustice, by the ferment of human rights to be attained, brings freedom.

"It is a curious thing that every demand for the establishment of order in Mexico takes into consideration, not order for the benefit of the people of Mexico, the great mass of the population, but order for the benefit of the old-time regime, for the aristocrats, for the vested interests, for the men who are responsible for this very condition of disorder. No one asks for order because order will help the masses of the people to get a portion of their rights and their land; but all demand it so that the great owners of property, the overlords, the hidalgos, the men who have exploited that rich country for their own selfish

[43] Samuel G. Blythe, "Mexico: The Record of a Conversation with President Wilson," *Saturday Evening Post*, CLXXXVI (May 23, 1914), 4.
[44] W. W. to L. M. Garrison, August 8, 1914, Wilson Papers.

purposes, shall be able to continue their processes undisturbed by the protests of the people from whom their wealth and power have been obtained.

"The dangers that beset the Republic are held to be the individual and corporate troubles of these men, not the aggregated injustices that have been heaped on this vastly greater section of the population that is now struggling to recover by force what has always been theirs by right.

"They want order—the old order; but I say to you that the old order is dead. . . .

"They say the Mexicans are not fitted for self-government; and to this I reply that, when properly directed, there is no people not fitted for self-government. The very fact that the extension of the school system by Diaz brought about a certain degree of understanding among some of the people which caused them to awaken to their wrongs and to strive intelligently for their rights, makes that contention absurd. I do not hold that the Mexican peons are at present as capable of self-government as other people—ours, for example; but I do hold that the widespread sentiment that they never will be and never can be made to be capable of self-government is as wickedly false as it is palpably absurd."[45]

It was inevitable that a man of Wilson's active disposition would also believe that the United States could not refuse the opportunity, even the duty, to help the Mexican people. "I hold this to be a wonderful opportunity," he declared, "to prove to the world that the United States of America is not only human but humane; that we are actuated by no other motives than the betterment of the conditions of our unfortunate neighbor, and by the sincere desire to advance the cause of human liberty." The United States, he went on, must lead the Mexicans into the paths of quiet and prosperity, leaving them to work out their own destiny if possible, but always watching and insisting that they accept guidance when they needed it. "It is not my intention," he added, "having begun this enterprise, to turn back—unless I am forced to do so—until I have assurances that the great and crying wrongs the people have endured are in process of satisfactory adjustment."[46]

The immediate excuse for military intervention arose on April 9, 1914, out of what would otherwise have been a minor incident at

---

[45] S. G. Blythe, "Mexico: The Record of a Conversation with President Wilson," *loc.cit.*, pp. 3-4.

[46] *ibid.*, pp. 4, 71.

Tampico, then besieged by the Constitutionalists. The paymaster and crew of the whaleboat of the U.S.S. *Dolphin*, one of the American warships stationed off Tampico, were arrested by a Mexican colonel, one Hinojosa, when they landed without permission behind the federal lines near the Iturbide Bridge for the purpose of purchasing some gasoline. The local *Huertista* commander, General Morelos Zaragoza, "was dumbfounded when he was informed by us of the arrest," the American consul at Tampico afterward reported. "At no time did he raise the point that the boat should have secured a permit. He apologized profusely for the action of his subordinate and in our presence ordered telephone instructions be sent for the release of the Paymaster and his men." Zaragoza also sent an immediate apology to the commander of the American squadron off Tampico, Admiral Henry T. Mayo.[47]

Mayo, however, was in no mood to tolerate the "insult." On his own initiative he replied at once to Zaragoza: "I must require that you send me, by suitable members of your staff, formal disavowal of and apology for the act, together with your assurance that the officer responsible for it will receive severe punishment. Also that you publicly hoist the American flag in a prominent position on shore and salute it with twenty-one guns, which salute will be duly returned by this ship. Your answer to this communication should reach me and the called-for salute be fired within twenty-four hours from 6 p.m. of this date."[48]

The affair would have passed without a crisis, however, had not President Wilson been seeking a pretext at this precise moment for launching large-scale military operations against Huerta. "Really," he afterward said, "it was a psychological moment."[49] We can understand what he meant only by reading his cryptic statement in the context of events during the few days preceding the Tampico affair. The Constitutionalists had recaptured Torreón on April 1 and 2, 1914, in a victory that seemingly opened the road to Mexico City. All that was necessary to assure their speedy triumph, Lind had urged, was American action to cut Huerta off from access to the Gulf ports.[50] Wilson's

---

[47] The above quotation is taken from Clarence A. Miller to the Secretary of State, May 21, 1914, State Department Papers, a superb account of the Tampico affair. For other accounts, both of which agree, see *New York Times*, April 11, 1914, and Morelos Zaragoza, "Truth of the 'Dolphin' Incident at Tampico," Mexico City *El Excelsior*, December 6, 1931.

[48] H. T. Mayo to M. Zaragoza, April 9, 1914, *Foreign Relations, 1914*, pp. 448-449.

[49] S. G. Blythe, "Mexico: The Record of a Conversation with President Wilson," *loc.cit.*, p. 4.

[50] J. Lind to the Secretary of State, April 1, 1914, State Department Papers.

actions in the wake of the Tampico affair leave no doubt that he agreed and resolved to make the most of the opportunity at hand.

In White Sulphur Springs, West Virginia, at the time that the crisis began, the President approved Mayo's ultimatum on April 10, 1914, and warned Mexico City that "the gravest consequences" might follow unless Huerta complied.[51] Huerta had issued a virtual apology a short time before and promised to punish Hinojosa if an investigation proved that he had acted improperly; now, in response to Wilson's demand, the dictator asked for an extension of the time limit in the ultimatum.[52] Saying publicly that he thought Huerta's apology sufficed, Bryan gladly granted the request. Secretary of the Navy Daniels was also satisfied. "I am inclined to believe that Admiral Mayo, who, after all, has this whole matter in his hands," he told reporters, "will regard the apology of Huerta as sufficient. The greater includes the less, and if the Federal commander at Tampico should not actually salute the flag, Admiral Mayo will pass by the matter, satisfied with what Huerta has said of the incident."[53]

Yet while Bryan and Daniels talked of peace, the President was maneuvering to press Huerta as hard as circumstances and American public opinion would permit. After the dictator submitted a formal reply on April 12, 1914, refusing to render the salute,[54] Wilson returned to Washington on the following day to take personal charge of turning the screws on the provisional government in Mexico City. The day after his arrival in the capital he ordered the entire North Atlantic battleship fleet to proceed to Tampico; sent a message to Mexico City warning of the "very serious character of the present situation and the very grave consequences which it may involve";[55] and composed a memorandum for the information of the newspapermen, charging that the Tampico affair had been only one manifestation of Huerta's ap-

[51] The Secretary of State to N. O'Shaughnessy, April 10, 1914, *Foreign Relations, 1914*, p. 450.

[52] N. O'Shaughnessy to the Secretary of State, April 11, 1914, *ibid.*, p. 450; N. O'Shaughnessy to the Secretary of State, April 15, 1914, enclosing the Minister of Foreign Affairs to the Chargé, April 10, 1914, *ibid.*, pp. 462-463; *New York Times*, April 12, 1914.

[53] *New York Times*, April 12, 1914.

[54] On the grounds that the American sailors had had no business entering a fighting zone without permission and that he and General Zaragoza had already exceeded the demands of courtesy by rendering their own apologies. N. O'Shaughnessy to the Secretary of State, April 12, 1914, *Foreign Relations, 1914*, pp. 454-455.

[55] The Secretary of State to N. O'Shaughnessy, April 14, 1914, *ibid.*, p. 459.

parent determination to act contemptuously toward the United States.[56] On April 15, 1914, moreover, the President ordered all warships in the Pacific Fleet to sail at once to the western coast of Mexico.

At the same time, the President set to work with his naval advisers to perfect plans for punitive action and called the senior members of the House and Senate foreign relations committees to the White House on April 15, 1914, for a general review of the Mexican situation. It was evident that he labored under great embarrassment as he began his explanations. He said that his patience was exhausted and that he "could no longer tolerate a strict observance of the pacific policy which he had outlined when he addressed Congress on the subject of relations with Mexico," because Huerta had embarked upon a deliberate policy of insulting the United States and its citizens. Unless Huerta promptly complied with the American demands, Wilson continued, he planned to seize Veracruz and Tampico and blockade both coasts of Mexico. He would take such action without asking for a declaration of war, he concluded, but he would ask Congress to approve before he put his plans into operation.[57]

A series of ridiculous exchanges between Washington and Mexico City ensued during the four days following the White House conference of April 15, 1914. Huerta finally agreed to render the flag salute that Wilson demanded; but he was determined to avoid total humiliation and insisted that an American warship return a simultaneous salute. When Wilson demanded unconditional compliance, Huerta retaliated by suggesting a "reciprocal" salute, "fired first by the Mexican land battery to the American flag to be raised on the *Dolphin* in Tampico harbor, to be answered by guns from the *Dolphin* to the Mexican flag raised on one of our gunboats."[58] Wilson rejected this compromise, saying that of course the *Dolphin* would return the salute but that Huerta must comply without conditions.

On April 19, 1914, Huerta finally refused point-blank to surrender unconditionally, and Wilson broke off the negotiations and went before Congress the following day to explain and ask for approval of punitive action. He described the Tampico affair on the whole so accurately as to make it appear totally insignificant. The incident at Tampico, he explained, was only one of a series that had created the *impression* that

---

[56] "Memorandum on the Mexican Situation, April 14, 1914," MS. in the Wilson Papers; printed verbatim in the *New York Times*, April 16, 1914.

[57] *ibid.*, April 16, 1914; New York *World*, April 16, 1914.

[58] The quotation is from the Mexican Embassy to the Department of State, April 19, 1914, *Foreign Relations, 1914*, p. 472. For the entire exchange, see *ibid.*, pp. 463-473.

"the representatives of General Huerta were willing to go out of their way to show disregard for the dignity and rights of this Government and felt perfectly safe in doing what they pleased, making free to show in many ways their irritation and contempt."[59]

Because such disregard of the rights of the United States might lead to open conflict, Wilson continued, he had supported Admiral Mayo in "the whole of his demand." Huerta had refused to comply, and he, Wilson, had now come to ask Congress for authority to "use the armed forces of the United States in such ways and to such an extent as may be necessary to obtain from General Huerta and his adherents the fullest recognition of the rights and dignity of the United States, even amidst the distressing conditions now unhappily obtaining in Mexico." The United States, he added, had no desire to interfere in Mexican affairs, did not want war with the Mexican people, and sought only to maintain its own dignity and influence unimpaired "for the uses of liberty, both in the United States and wherever else it may be employed for the benefit of mankind."[60]

The House responded during the evening of April 20, 1914, by approving by a vote of 337 to thirty-seven a joint resolution declaring that the President was "justified in the employment of armed forces of

[59] The present writer feels obliged to say that this was a misrepresentation of the facts. Huerta and his subordinates had acted with studied courtesy toward the United States government and its representatives and had shown an extraordinary concern in protecting American citizens and property in Mexico.

Wilson could adduce only two additional incidents to prove that the Huerta government had set out to humiliate the United States and its citizens. The first was the momentary arrest of a mail orderly from an American warship in Veracruz on April 11, 1914. Yet the commander of the American naval forces in Mexican waters had reported on April 16, 1914, that the Mexican responsible had been promptly arrested and properly punished by the Mexican authorities. "The attitude of the Mexican authorities was correct," Fletcher had written; "there is no cause for complaint against them and the incident is without significance." (F. F. Fletcher to the Secretary of the Navy, April 16, 1914, *Foreign Relations, 1914,* p. 465.) The second incident was the momentary withholding of an official dispatch from Washington by the telegraphic service in Mexico City on April 11, 1914. Yet O'Shaughnessy had explained that the telegram had been withheld by an ignorant censor and that the matter was of no significance. (N. O'Shaughnessy to the Secretary of State, April 12, 1914, *ibid.,* pp. 453-454.)

One is tempted to believe that Wilson was not being frank with Congress, just as he had not been frank in his earlier explanations to the House and Senate foreign relations committees, and that he was manufacturing charges against the provisional government in order to justify the use of force, which now seemed necessary if Huerta were to be deposed.

[60] Wilson's address before the joint session is printed in *ibid.,* pp. 474-476.

the United States to enforce demands made on Victoriano Huerta."[61] While the House voted, the President was closeted at the White House with Garrison, Daniels, and high army and naval commanders. By ten o'clock the conferees had agreed upon a comprehensive plan of operations for the seizure of Tampico and Veracruz, the possible dispatch of an expeditionary force from Veracruz to Mexico City, and a complete naval blockade of both coasts of Mexico. This plan was to be put into effect after the main body of the Atlantic Fleet had arrived in Mexican waters.[62]

The operational timetable was upset, however, by the arrival at the State Department, at two-thirty o'clock in the morning of April 21, 1914, of a message from the American consul at Veracruz. The consul warned that the steamer *Ypiranga* of the Hamburg-American Line would deliver a tremendous load of ammunition for Huerta the following morning and that a number of trains stood ready to carry the cargo to Mexico City.[63]

Bryan telephoned the news of the *Ypiranga*'s arrival to the White House, and hasty telephone conversations among Wilson, Bryan, Garrison, and Daniels ensued. The conferees agreed that the United States could not, in the absence of a formal blockade, seize the German vessel or prevent it from landing its cargo. The only way to prevent the ammunition from reaching Mexico City, they concluded, was to seize the customhouse at Veracruz and to impound the ammunition. They were confident that this could be done without actual fighting or without having to capture the entire city. Thus early in the morning Daniels sent the following message by wireless to Admiral Frank F. Fletcher, commander of the naval forces in Mexican waters: "Seize custom house. Do not permit war supplies to be delivered to Huerta government or to any other party."[64]

A few minutes after eleven o'clock in the morning of April 21, 1914,

---

[61] The Senate approved this resolution on April 22, 1914, after an unsuccessful attempt by Senator Lodge to broaden the resolution so as to empower the President to intervene in Mexico generally for the protection of American citizens and property. Lodge thought that there were good reasons for intervening but that the President had not mentioned them.

[62] New York *World*, April 21, 1914.

[63] Consul Canada to the Secretary of State, April 20, 1914, *Foreign Relations, 1914*, p. 477.

[64] *New York Times*, April 22, 1914; Josephus Daniels, *The Wilson Era, Years of Peace—1910-1917*, pp. 192-193. It might be added here that the *Ypiranga* did not unload her cargo at Veracruz but later sailed to Puerto México, discharged her cargo there, and eventually carried Huerta into exile.

about one thousand marines and sailors from the American squadron stationed off Veracruz entered the port unopposed and quickly seized the customhouse and other public buildings in the lower part of the city. At twelve-thirty p.m. the Mexican garrison of some eight hundred men left their barracks and scattered in small detachments through the central part of Veracruz; joined by cadets from the Mexican Naval Academy, they opened fire on the Americans from windows and house-tops. As the fighting grew heavier, the Mexicans opened fire with artillery, and the guns of the U.S.S. *Prairie* replied. The following morning, April 22, Rear Admiral Charles J. Badger arrived off Vera-cruz with five battleships, the main body of the Atlantic Fleet, and sent some three thousand men ashore from his ships before daybreak. By noon the reinforced Americans had completely routed the Mexican defenders. Mexican casualties were 126 dead and 195 wounded; American casualties were nineteen dead and seventy-one wounded.[65]

Wilson had ordered the occupation of Veracruz in the belief that the Mexicans would not resist and that Huerta would soon withdraw after a show of American force. Events following the Veracruz occupation, however, seemed to point inevitably to war with a united Mexican people, with *Huertistas* and Constitutionalists alike.

Huerta broke off diplomatic relations with the United States on April 22, 1914, and sent all the troops he could muster to the Veracruz area. Meanwhile, a wave of patriotism and hot anger had swept over Mexico in the wake of the American invasion. In Mexico City, the correspondent for the London *Daily Telegraph* reported, "three years of fratricidal war was forgotten in a day," as thousands of Mexicans volunteered for service.[66] In Saltillo, Manzanillo, Guadalajara, Nuevo Laredo, Monterey, and Mazatlán, mobs and troops looted and de-stroyed American consulates, burned American flags, and imprisoned American consuls and citizens.[67]

Indeed, events seemed out of control. Having taken Veracruz, the President had to hold and defend it and be prepared for general hos-

[65] *New York Times,* April 22 and 23, 1914; J. Daniels, *The Wilson Era, Years of Peace,* p. 197.

[66] Quoted in the New York *World,* April 25, 1914.

[67] J. R. Silliman, "Vice Consul John R. Silliman's narration . . . ," MS. in the Wilson Papers dated June 8, 1914; Richard M. Stadden to the Secretary of State, May 2, 1914, *ibid.*; P. H. Hanna to the Secretary of State, April 26, 1914, *ibid.*; Garrett to the Secretary of State, April 24, 1914, *ibid.*; William E. Alzer to the Secretary of State, April 24, 1914, State Department Papers; *New York Times,* April 25 and 27, May 4 and 13, 1914; New York *World,* April 25, 1914.

tilities. Thus, on April 23, 1914, he ordered the Fifth Brigade under General Frederick N. Funston to sail from Galveston to relieve the marines and bluejackets in the occupied port and sent additional troops to the border; at the same time, the War Department put other forces in readiness and made plans to mobilize the National Guard for service in Mexico.[68] All this, however, seemed only the beginning. Secretary Garrison and his army advisers were also hard at work planning a general campaign that envisaged the capture of Tampico and the sending of an expeditionary force from Veracruz to capture the City of Mexico. At a war conference at the White House during the evening of April 24, 1914, Garrison urged the President to move decisively to prevent a general slaughter of Americans in Mexico. Bryan and Daniels, on the other hand, pleaded as eloquently for limiting operations to Veracruz and its environs.[69]

The President took control of the situation from April 22 to April 25, 1914, and made the decision to cease further offensive operations. First, he abandoned his plan for a general blockade of the Mexican coasts, vetoed the army's plans for an expedition to Mexico City, and gave Funston explicit orders to take no action that would "tend to increase the tension of the situation or embarrass your government in its present relations with Mexico without explicit orders and directions from the Secretary in each case."[70] Second, when the Argentine, Brazilian, and Chilean envoys in Washington offered on April 25, 1914, to mediate the conflict, the President accepted at once.

The reasons for Wilson's sudden abandonment of his earlier plans to give Huerta the *coup de grace* by large-scale operations against his government are fairly clear. In the first place, it is evident that the President had blundered into hostilities on the assumption that the Mexicans would not resist. "Do not get the impression that there is about to be war with the United States and Mexico," he had told reporters before he addressed Congress on April 20, 1914. "That isn't the outlook at present at all. . . . This need not eventuate into war if we handle it with firmness and promptness."[71]

[68] *New York Times,* April 24, 1914; New York *World,* April 24, 1914.

[69] House Diary, April 28, 1914; *New York Times,* April 25, 1914; New York *World,* April 25, 1914.

[70] New York *World,* April 23 and 25, 1914; Chief of Staff, Memorandum for the Adjutant General, April 26, 1914, Wilson Papers, enclosing the President's instructions to Funston.

[71] Stenographic report of Wilson's talk with the correspondents, printed in "President Wilson on His Foreign Policy," *World's Work,* xxviii (October 1914), 489.

The President was, therefore, profoundly unnerved by the news of the sharp fighting at Veracruz. "I remember how preternaturally pale, almost parchmenty, Mr. Wilson looked when he stood up there and answered the questions of the newspaper men," a friend recalled afterward. "The death of American sailors and marines owing to an order of his seemed to affect him like an ailment. He was positively shaken."[72]

Two further important developments reinforced the President's natural revulsion and influenced him in limiting his operations. The first was the violent reaction of the Constitutionalist leaders and masses after the occupation of Veracruz. Wilson had failed to inform the Constitutionalists in advance of his plans to seize Veracruz; but before the fighting in that city had ended he sent a special message to Carranza, assuring him that his sole objective was to force reparation from Huerta.[73] Carranza, however, replied angrily, warning that the American invasion might "indeed drag us into an unequal war . . . which until today we have desired to avoid," and demanding that the American forces evacuate Veracruz immediately.[74] And from consular officials throughout northern Mexico came reports that Carranza spoke for most of his generals and for the rank and file of the people.[75]

Indeed, only by the most unusual circumstances and exertions on both sides were actual hostilities between the Constitutionalists and the American forces along the border averted. Fearing such an outbreak, Wilson immediately imposed an embargo on the shipment of arms and munitions to the Constitutionalists. At the same time, he issued a public reply to the First Chief, again assuring him that the United States had no quarrel with the Mexican people and would "respect in every possible way the sovereignty and independence of the people of Mexico."[76] In addition, Bryan sent even stronger private assurances through two of Carranza's friends and agents in the United States.[77]

[72] H. J. Forman to R. S. Baker, quoted in R. S. Baker, *Woodrow Wilson*, IV, 330.

[73] The Secretary of State to Special Agent G. C. Carothers, April 21, 1914, *Foreign Relations, 1914*, p. 480.

[74] V. Carranza to W. J. Bryan, transmitted in G. C. Carothers to the Secretary of State, April 22, 1914, *ibid.*, pp. 483-484.

[75] G. C. Carothers to the Secretary of State, April 21, 1914, State Department Papers; Edwards to the Secretary of State, April 21 and 23, 1914, *ibid.*; Hostetter to the Secretary of State, April 24, 1914, *ibid.*; Hamm to the Secretary of State, April 24, 1914, *ibid.*; W. P. Blocher to the Secretary of State, April 24, 1914, *ibid.*; Letcher to the Secretary of State, April 24, 1914, *ibid.*

[76] *New York Times*, April 24, 1914.

[77] Charles A. Douglas to Pesquiera, April 23, 1914, copy in the State Department Papers; S. G. Hopkins to V. Carranza, April 24, 1914, Scott Papers.

These professions of friendship helped to relieve the tension, but the event that precluded a conflict was the defection of General Villa from the otherwise solid Constitutionalist ranks. Already scheming to seize control of the revolutionary forces from Carranza, Villa now saw an opportunity to gain American good will in the future. He rushed to Juárez and assured the special agent assigned to deal with him, George C. Carothers, that he approved the American action at Veracruz and would not allow any conflict to develop. "He said that no drunkard, meaning Huerta, was going to draw him into a war with his friend," Carothers reported.[78] Shortly afterward, moreover, Villa sent a confidential message to Wilson, reaffirming his affectionate friendship for the United States and declaring that Carranza did not speak for the Constitutionalists.[79] Although the danger of hostilities with the Constitutionalists quickly passed as a consequence of Villa's stand,[80] the threat had nevertheless been sufficiently acute to cause Wilson to understand the perils of further offensive operations.

The second development that strengthened Wilson's decision against incurring the risk of a general war in Mexico was the way in which American and world opinion recoiled from the Veracruz aggression and demanded a peaceful settlement. In large measure, it must be admitted, the President was himself responsible for the tidal wave of denunciation that engulfed him after the action at Veracruz. Because he had not been frank with Congress and the people, because he had declared that his only purpose in using military force was the vindication of the nation's honor, and not the elimination of Huerta,[81] no one

[78] G. C. Carothers to the Secretary of State, April 23, 1914, *Foreign Relations, 1914*, p. 485.

[79] G. C. Carothers to the Secretary of State, April 25, 1914, transmitting Villa's message, *ibid.*, p. 488.

[80] Villa's action left Carranza no alternative but to withdraw from his high ground. The two leaders met at Chihuahua on April 28, 1914, and agreed that the Constitutionalists would not oppose the Americans unless they actually invaded Constitutionalist territory. On May 4, 1914, moreover, Carranza's representative in Washington gave formal assurances of the friendship of the Mexican people for the United States. See the *New York Times*, April 29, 1914; New York *World*, April 29, 1914; and R. Zubáran Campany to the President and Secretary of State, May 4, 1914, *Foreign Relations, 1914*, pp. 496-497.

[81] Wilson told reporters on April 20, 1914, for example: "What, then, is the purpose of our naval operation in Mexico? It is not, as you gentlemen seem to think—not this act, that is—the elimination of Huerta. Its purpose is to compel the recognition of the dignity of the United States. That is all we want—a full recognition of that dignity and such a recognition as will constitute a guarantee that this sort of thing does not happen any more. As I have said, I have no enthusiasm for war; but I have an

outside high administration circles understood the reasons for his action.

Consequently, in the eyes of most thoughtful Americans, the President appeared willing to make war over an absurd point of honor. "Never again let us treat with contempt the most ridiculous superstitious rite of the most ignorant savage tribe," declared a Chicago editor. ". . . Surely a question of etiquette may no longer be considered justification for an aggressive war."[82] "Such a war as seems pending," Andrew Carnegie wrote in a personal note to the President, "will in after days be held akin to the fabled war of the two kings to decide which end of the egg should first be broken."[83]

Indeed, it was difficult to find a responsible spokesman among any group or class in the United States who thought Wilson had acted wisely. There was no demand for war from the financial leaders who had a large material stake in Mexico.[84] Republican spokesmen, generally, were outraged by what they regarded as Wilson's diplomatic bungling and his desire to make political capital out of the Mexican crisis.[85] Among the leading newspapers and periodicals, only the faithful New York *World*, the Chicago *Tribune*, the Hearst press, and a few others scattered throughout the country had any enthusiasm for war.[86] Moreover, during the week following the Veracruz action, petitions begging the President not to permit the incident to develop into full-scale hostilities poured into the White House from church councils, peace and anti-imperialist societies, labor and socialist groups, and from leaders in all walks of life.[87] As he was always keenly sensitive

---

enthusiasm for the dignity of the United States." Quoted in "President Wilson on His Foreign Policy," *World's Work*, xxviii (October 1914), 489-490.

[82] *The Public*, xvii (April 24, 1914), 381-382.

[83] A. Carnegie to W. W., April 21, 1914, Wilson Papers.

[84] e.g., see the *Financial World*, xxii (April 18, 1914), 2; and *Financial Age*, xxix (April 25, 1914), 673.

[85] See especially W. H. Taft to Mabel T. Boardman, April 19, 1914, Taft Papers; W. H. Taft to P. C. Knox, April 21, 1914, *ibid.*; W. H. Taft to G. W. Wickersham, April 29, 1914, *ibid.*; G. W. Wickersham to W. H. Taft, April 30, 1914, *ibid.*; Frederick W. Kelsey to Elihu Root, April 25, 1914, Root Papers; John W. Foster to E. Root, April 24, 1914, *ibid.*; E. Root to A. T. Mahan, April 27, 1914, *ibid.*

[86] For typical adverse editorial comment, see the *Springfield* (Massachusetts) *Republican*, April 21, 1914; *Chicago Record-Herald*, April 21, 1914; New York *Nation*, xcviii (April 23, 1914), 451; *The Independent*, lxxviii (April 27, 1914), 151-152; *La Follette's Weekly*, vi (May 2, 1914), 1; *The Survey*, xxxii (May 2, 1914), 157.

[87] e.g., Commission on Peace and Arbitration of the Federal Council of Churches of Christ in America to W. W., April 21, 1914, Wilson Papers; Massachusetts Federation of Churches to W. W., April 22, 1914, *ibid.*; Moorfield Storey, president of the

to public opinion, the President could not have failed to be profoundly influenced by this outpouring.

Nor could Wilson have ignored the outburst of opinion abroad, which, if anything, was more condemnatory than opinion at home. There were anti-American riots and demonstrations in San José, Costa Rica; Rodeo, Guatemala; Santiago, Chile; Guayaquil and Quito, Ecuador; and in Montevideo, Uruguay; and riots were prevented in Buenos Aires only by severe police action.[88] There were, besides, angry charges throughout Latin America that the Veracruz action marked the beginning of rapacious Yankee imperialism in Mexico. "We are conscious of the fact that the incident springs from a state of affairs in which the integrity and independence of Mexico are at stake," declared *La Nación* of Buenos Aires. "The memory of this conflict will live in the history of the relations between the United States and Latin America."[89] Throughout Europe, moreover, liberal editors condemned Wilson for making war on "points of punctillio," while the entire reactionary anti-American press had a field day castigating alleged Wilsonian hypocrisy and American imperialism.[90] Altogether, it was an unhappy time for a President and a people who claimed the moral leadership of the world.

In such a hostile climate of opinion at home and abroad, Wilson hastily accepted the mediation that the Argentine, Brazilian, and

Anti-Imperialist League, to W. W., April 25, 1914, *ibid.*; National Executive Committee of the Socialist Party to W. W., April 24, 1914, enclosing "Proclamation on the Mexican War by the Socialist Party of America," *ibid.*; W. R. Thayer to W. W., April 20, 1914, *ibid.*; O. G. Villard to W. W., April 23, 1914, *ibid.*; Oscar Straus to W. W., April 23, 1914, *ibid.*; Washington Gladden to W. W., April 27, 1914, *ibid.*; William Kent to W. W., April 28, 1914, *ibid.*; C. W. Eliot to W. W., April 29, 1914, *ibid.*

[88] Grevstad to the Secretary of State, April 24 and 26, 1914, State Department Papers; Hale to the Secretary of State, April 26, 1914, *ibid.*; Leavell to the Secretary of State, April 27, 1914, *ibid.*; Fletcher to the Secretary of State, April 28, 1914, *ibid.*; Lorillard to the Secretary of State, April 29, 1914, *ibid.*; Hartman to the Secretary of State, May 13, 1914, *ibid.*

[89] Buenos Aires *La Nación*, April 24, 1914; also the Bogotá *El Neuvo Tiempo*, April 22, 1914; Bogotá *La Unidad*, April 27, 1914; Bogotá *La Crónica*, April 29, 1914; Buenos Aires *La Prensa*, April 24, 1914. Brazilian newspapers, on the other hand, were inclined to be more friendly toward the United States. See e.g., Rio de Janeiro *O Paíz*, April 28, 1914; and Rio de Janeiro *Jornál do Commercio*, May 1, 1914.

[90] For examples of European opinion, see the London *Economist*, LXXVIII (April 18 and 25, May 9, 1914), 906-907, 954-955, 1072-1073; London *Outlook*, XXXIII (April 25, 1914), 546; Saloniki *L'Indépendant*, April 23, 1914; *Budapesti Hirlap*, April 24, 1914; Roland de Mares, in *L'Indépendance Belge* of Brussels, April 27, 1914; St. Petersburg *Novoe Vremya*, 9/22 and 15/28 April 1914; St. Petersburg *Retch*, 9/22 April 1914 and 20 April/3 May 1914; Moscow *Russkoe Slovo*, 11/24 April 1914.

A Sort of War

President Wilson—"I hope you are not shooting at my dear friends the Mexicans?"

U.S. Gunner—"Oh, no, sir. We have strict orders only to aim at one Huerta."

Punch (London)

Chilean governments offered on April 25, 1914.[91] Under pressure from the British, French, and German Foreign Offices, Huerta also assented on April 27. There was something absurd about the President agreeing to go to a peace conference with the representatives of a government he had refused to recognize. But the time for logical distinctions had passed; something had to be done quickly to allay Latin American suspicions of Yankee imperialism and to ease the war fear in the United States.

And yet Wilson had no intention of submitting to a genuine mediation. Instead, he had evolved a new plan, as ambitious as any of his earlier ones. In brief, he meant to use the A.B.C. mediation, first, to eliminate Huerta and, second, to establish a new provisional government in Mexico City that he could control.

The President revealed these purposes frankly in a confidential memorandum that accompanied Bryan's eloquent note accepting the A.B.C. mediation. It read:

> In the interest of a lasting settlement which will relieve the anxieties of all America, the Government of the United States feels itself bound in frankness to make the following confidential communication to the representatives of the Republics of Brazil, Argentina, and Chile, who have so generously offered on behalf of their respective governments to attempt a settlement of the difficulties which have for the time interrupted the cordial relations between the United States of America and the acting authorities of the Republic of Mexico:
>
> No settlement could have any prospect of permanence or of proving acceptable to public opinion in the United States or to the practical judgment of the Government of the United States which did not include these features:
>
> First, the entire elimination of General Huerta;
>
> Second, the immediate setting up in Mexico of a single provisional government acceptable to all parties and pledged to proceed at once to the establishment of a permanent government constituted in strict accordance with the Constitution of Mexico and committed to the prosecution of such reforms as will reasonably assure the ultimate removal of the present causes of discontent.
>
> This government ventures to suggest that the essence of any hopeful settlement would of necessity be a concert of the contending elements of the republic and that such a concert can be obtained only upon the

[91] See the Brazilian Ambassador and the Argentine and Chilean Ministers to the Secretary of State, April 25, 1914, and the Secretary of State to the Mediators, April 25, 1914, in *Foreign Relations, 1914*, pp. 488-489.

basis of such reforms as will satisfy the just claims of the people of Mexico to life, liberty and independent self-support.[92]

During early May 1914 the leaders in Washington were hard at work on plans for the coming peace conference and new schemes for reconstruction in Mexico. Completed by May 20, 1914, the President's program envisaged the cessation of hostilities between the *Huertistas* and the Constitutionalists, the resignation of Huerta, and the establishment under A.B.C. and American auspices of a provisional government controlled by the Constitutionalists. Working intimately with the American government, the provisional authorities were expected to effect sweeping land reform and then hold national elections leading to the creation of a permanent government.[93]

From the beginning of the negotiations looking toward the peace conference, Huerta cooperated with the mediators in the hope that he could yet obtain a compromise that would leave the upper classes in control of Mexico. He readily agreed to an armistice with the United States[94] and declared that he was willing to accept any settlement that the mediators might recommend, even one demanding his withdrawal.[95]

But Huerta, now denied the vital revenues from the ports of Veracruz and Tampico[96] and virtually cut off from the rest of the world, was at last doomed. The success of the President's plan would depend, not upon whether Huerta cooperated, but upon whether the Constitutionalists were willing to accept the mediation and cooperate in Wilson's plan for reconstruction. Poised for attacks against Saltillo, Mazatlán, San Luis Potosí, and Zacatecas, preparatory to a final assault upon Mexico City, the Constitutionalists had no intention either of halting on the eve of victory or of permitting their American friends to tell them how to reconstruct Mexico. Carranza accepted "in principle" the

[92] "Confidential Memorandum," MS. in the Wilson Papers.

[93] *New York Times*, May 13 and 18, 1914; New York *World*, May 19, 1914.

[94] Both sides informally accepted the armistice on April 30, 1914. It was seriously threatened afterward on only two occasions—first, when Wilson reinforced the troops at Veracruz in early May, and, second, when the Washington government, around May 8, 1914, contemplated seizing Puerto México in order to stop the continued flow of war matériel to Mexico City. On the first occasion, Huerta accepted Bryan's assurances that the United States had no aggressive intentions; on the second, Wilson and Bryan decided not to take action at Puerto México that would disrupt the peace negotiations before they could be started.

[95] The Foreign Office to Ambassador Spring Rice, c. May 20, 1914, copy in the Wilson Papers.

[96] Constitutionalist forces captured Tampico on May 14, 1914.

A.B.C. mediation of "the pending conflict between the United States and Mexico" on April 29, 1914, but he refused point-blank when the mediators demanded a cessation of hostilities.[97] Moreover, the First Chief made it plain through the American press that the Constitutionalists intended to conquer Mexico and carry out their own reform program without American help, and that they would permit neither the mediators nor the American government to interfere in internal Mexican affairs.[98]

There was, therefore, an air of unreality about the proceedings of the peace conference that opened at Niagara Falls, Canada, on May 20, 1914. For two weeks the delegates and mediators discussed plans for pacification and a comprehensive settlement of the Mexican civil war. The mediators and the Mexican delegates were willing to concede Huerta's retirement and the appointment of a man of Constitutionalist principles to head a new provisional government. Yet it became progressively apparent that their objective was the creation of a provisional government in fact controlled by conservatives, which, with American support, would be strong enough to compel the Constitutionalists to agree to an armistice and the holding of nation-wide elections for a new constitutional government.[99]

Directing the American negotiations firmly from Washington, Wilson and Bryan refused to be drawn into this trap. To all proposals for compromise they replied frankly and unequivocally that there was now only one acceptable solution—acknowledgment of the triumph of the Constitutionalists and the establishment of a government under their control. The President explained his views in a personal dispatch to the American delegates on May 27, 1914:

> The most serious and pressing question with regard to any plan, the question by which it must, whatever our preference, be tested, is this: Who would put it into operation if the victorious party refused to accept it? We are of necessity seeking a solution which is practicable as well as just, and likely to yield the results we have all along had in mind. Our

[97] The Mediators to V. Carranza, April 29 and 30, May 2 and 3, 1914; and V. Carranza to the Mediators, April 29 and May 3, 1914, all in *Foreign Relations, 1914*, pp. 517-519.

[98] *New York Times*, May 20, 1914.

[99] e.g., see the Special Commissioners to the Secretary of State, May 20, 23, 26, 28, and 31, 1914, *Foreign Relations, 1914*, pp. 501-502, 504-505, 507-509, 510-512, 514-516; Secretary Dodge to the Secretary of State, June 9, 1914, *ibid.*, pp. 525-526; Special Commissioner Lamar to the Secretary of State, June 12, 1914, *ibid.*, pp. 527-529; Special Commissioner Lehmann to the Secretary of State, June 13, 1914, *ibid.*, pp. 530-533.

object is the pacification of Mexico by reforms and changes instituted by her own leaders and accepted by her own people. A provisional arrangement established by force, especially if established by the force of the United States, would inevitably be temporary and the prelude to other revolutions. Certain things are clearly inevitable in Mexico, as things now stand, whether we act or not. One of these is the elimination of Huerta. Another is resistance, and successful resistance, to any arrangement which can be made to seem to be a continuation of the Huerta régime.

It would, in our judgment, be futile to set up a provisional authority which would be neutral. It must, to be successful, be actually, avowedly and sincerely in favor of the necessary agrarian and political reforms, and it must be pledged to their immediate formulation, not merely "requested to devote special attention" to them.

And it will be impossible for the United States to withdraw her hand until this Government is finally and fully satisfied that the programme contemplated will be carried out in all respects. . . .

The case lies in our mind thus: the success of the Constitutionalists is now inevitable. The only question we can now answer without armed intervention on the part of the United States is this: Can the result be moderated; how can it be brought about without further bloodshed; what provisional arrangement can be made which will temper the whole process and lead to the elections in a way that will be hopeful of peace and permanent accommodation? If we do not successfully answer these questions, then the settlement must come by arms, either ours or those of the Constitutionalists.

Every plan suggested must, therefore, of necessity be subjected to the test of these questions. We will not make war on the Mexican people to force upon them a plan of our own based upon a futile effort to give a defeated party equality with a victorious party. The whole present hopeful effort for peace would fall to pieces were we to attempt it.[100]

In a second personal message to the American delegates on June 3, 1914, the President was more specific about the kind of settlement he would approve:

We feel obliged to say that we could not consider the recognition of a provisional government made up in any part of neutrals. There can be no such persons in Mexico among men of force and character. All men of real stuff must have taken sides in one way or another and those who call themselves neutrals are quite certainly partisans of the kind of order and supremacy which Huerta tried to establish, whether they adhere to Huerta personally or not. We are convinced that peace can be secured

[100] The Secretary of State to the Special Commissioners, May 27, 1914, *ibid.*, pp. 509-510.

only by facing the inevitable and facing it promptly and with the utmost frankness.

The plan, therefore, should be of this sort: an avowed Constitutionalist of undoubted character and ability, other than Carranza or Villa, should be made provisional president and should be personally charged with the formulation and promulgation of the necessary and inevitable reforms as a duty to which he would be definitely pledged beforehand; and a board of three persons acceptable to the revolutionists, but one of whom should be a conservative not actively identified with the revolution, should be associated with him to arrange for and have complete charge of the conduct and oversight of the elections which should be planned for to occur not immediately but at a definite future date to be proclaimed by them in consultation with the provisional president.

We should in no circumstances outline or even suggest the detail of the reforms. The provisional president would of course consult with whom he pleased in formulating them, and their success is entirely dependent upon their being of domestic origin and in no respect dictated by the United States or any outside Government.[101]

Actually, Wilson's arguments were grounded upon the realities of the situation in Mexico, for while the conferees talked at Niagara Falls the Constitutionalists continued their inexorable advance toward the outpost cities guarding the Mexican capital. Even so, in spite of the President's eloquent denials of any desire to interfere in internal Mexican affairs, it is plain that he still hoped to play a strong and active role in the final settlement.

A showdown on the question of what role the United States should play occurred on June 16, 1914, at a meeting in Buffalo between the First Chief's representatives, Rafael Zubáran Campany and Luis Cabrera, and the American delegates to the peace conference. Under American pressure, Carranza had sent Zubáran and Cabrera as delegates to Niagara Falls, but the mediators had refused to admit them to the peace table because they would neither approve an armistice nor acknowledge the mediators' right to discuss internal Mexican affairs.

---

[101] The Secretary of State to the Special Commissioners, June 3, 1914, *ibid.*, pp. 523-524. In the balance of this dispatch, which is not printed in *Foreign Relations, 1914,* but may be seen in the copy in the State Department Papers, Wilson went on to specify in more elaborate detail the plan that he outlined in the portions printed above. "It ought to be conclusive even with the Mexican representatives," he ended in a final warning, "that unless the United States is to intervene with arms and practically conquer Mexico, which nobody desires, the only alternative to such a plan as we propose is the armed entrance of Carranza into Mexico City and the assumption of the provisional presidency by Carranza himself."

Wilson and Bryan had consequently asked the American commissioners to meet the Constitutionalists in Buffalo in order to find out whether any hope for their cooperation existed.

Zubáran and Cabrera made it clear in the course of a four-hour conference that the Mexican Revolution was still out of American control. Speaking for Carranza, they declared that the Constitutionalists would not admit the right of the mediators to interfere; more important, they would not accept the President's help in establishing a provisional government. "They say," the commissioners reported, "that . . . they are entitled to fight out their own fight in their own way, just as the United States in 1860 and 1864 was entitled to settle the questions of slavery without the intervention of foreign powers. . . . They insisted that they might be willing to take up the question of surrender with some one outside of the mediation with which the United States had nothing to do, but that so far as mediation was concerned, they would absolutely decline to receive anything from the mediators or through the mediation—not in effect, but in words saying—that they would not accept as a gift anything which the mediators could give them, even though it was what they were otherwise seeking; that they would not take it 'on a silver platter.'"[102]

Carranza's refusal to cooperate revealed once more the futility of the President's plans for Mexican reconstruction but gave him a new excuse for prolonging the negotiations at Niagara Falls and continuing the occupation of Veracruz in order to speed Huerta's downfall. For a week following the Buffalo conference the delegates at Niagara Falls wrangled over a plan to establish a provisional government in Mexico City, a proposition rendered daily more meaningless by the Constitutionalist advances. Finally, the delegates signed an agreement on June 24, 1914. Omitting any reference to the Tampico affair or the occupation of Veracruz, it simply provided that the United States would recognize whatever provisional government might be established as a result of the civil war, that the United States would not demand an indemnity or "other internal satisfaction" as reparation for the Tampico affair, and that the provisional government would proclaim a political amnesty and agree to compensate foreigners for their losses in Mexico during the civil war.[103] Then, after trying vainly to persuade Carranza

[102] The Commissioners to the Secretary of State, June 17, 1914, State Department Papers.

[103] Secretary Dodge to the Secretary of State, June 25, 1914, *Foreign Relations, 1914,* pp. 547-549; *New York Times,* June 25, 1914.

to enter negotiations for the creation of a provisional government, the conferees exchanged final notes and adjourned on July 2, 1914.[104]

Events in Mexico moved rapidly toward a climax after the breakup of the Niagara Falls conference. On July 10, 1914, Huerta appointed Chief Justice Francisco Carbajal, who was known as a Constitutionalist sympathizer, as Minister for Foreign Affairs—the first step in the organization of a new provisional government. Then, on July 15, 1914, Huerta resigned, yielded the provisional presidency to Carbajal, and left the capital for Puerto México, whence the steamer *Ypiranga* carried him into European exile. "I will say that I abandon the Presidency of the republic, carrying with me the highest sum of human wealth," he asserted in a valedictory to the Mexican Congress, "for I declare that I have arraigned at the bar of universal conscience the honor of a Puritan, whom I, as a gentleman, challenge to wrest from me that possession."[105]

There was joy in Washington at Huerta's going; congratulations poured in upon the White House; and the American press thanked God that the long struggle in Mexico was nearly over.[106] Yet Wilson could not pause to celebrate his triumph, for new perils threatened the peace of Mexico on the eve of the Constitutionalist triumph.

To begin with, the quarrel between Carranza and Villa had erupted into an open break in June 1914 and threatened the success of the revolutionary movement a month before Huerta resigned.[107] American consular officials and special agents in the field had patched up the quarrel,[108] but the fear that Villa would try to seize control of the

[104] Secretary Dodge to the Secretary of State, July 3, 1914, *Foreign Relations, 1914,* pp. 554-556; *New York Times,* July 3, 1914.

[105] *New York Times,* July 16, 1914.

[106] e.g., see W. C. Adamson to W. W., July 16, 1914, Wilson Papers; W. H. Page to W. W., July 19, 1914, *ibid.*; New York *World,* July 16, 1914; New York *Christian Advocate,* LXXXIX (July 23, 1914), 1017; Dallas *Baptist Standard,* XXVI (July 23, 1914), 4; Chicago *Public,* XVII (July 24, 1914), 693-694; New York *Nation,* XCIX (July 23, 1914), 91.

[107] Letcher to the Secretary of State, June 4, 1914, State Department Papers; Z. L. Cobb to W. J. Bryan, June 12, 1914, transmitting G. C. Carothers to Z. L. Cobb, June 10, 1914, *ibid.*; Z. L. Cobb to the Secretary of State, June 16 and 17, 1914, *ibid.; New York Times,* June 17, 1914.

[108] Edwards to the Secretary of State, June 18, 1914, State Department Papers; G. C. Carothers to the Secretary of State, June 18, 1914, *ibid.*; Z. L. Cobb to the Secretary of State, June 29, 1914, *ibid.*; L. J. Canova to the Secretary of State, July 2, 1914, *ibid.*; Z. L. Cobb to the Secretary of State, July 5, 1914, *ibid.*; G. C. Carothers to Z. L. Cobb, July 8, 1914, *ibid.*; L. J. Canova to the Secretary of State, July 14, 1914, *ibid.*

Constitutionalist forces as soon as they had entered Mexico City hung like a cloud over the Washington government in July and August of 1914.

More immediately urgent, however, was the fear that Carranza would refuse to accept a peaceful transfer of power and would permit his troops to sack Mexico City and loot foreign property in the capital and its environs. Wilson could not now stand by and tolerate such a catastrophe. He had not only made the victory of the Constitutionalists possible; he also stood committed in the eyes of the world as their champion and friend. Yet what could he do? The Revolution was out of his control at the very time that he wanted most to guide it.

The President resorted first to advice and hints of stern punishment by the United States if the Constitutionalists failed to behave responsibly. On July 23, 1914, he wrote the following warning to be delivered personally to Carranza by Consul John R. Silliman, who was attached to the First Chief's headquarters:

> Not only the United States, but all the world, will watch with the greatest interest and concern the course now to be pursued by the leaders of the Constitutionalist cause in effecting a transfer of power at Mexico City. This Government feels that the critical time has come when the choice which is now to be made by the Constitutionalist leaders will practically determine the success or failure of the government they mean to set up and the reforms they hope to effect.
>
> We venture to say this because of our earnest sympathy with the main purposes of the Constitutionalists and our desire to be of permanent service to them in bringing Mexico out of her troubles. We have been forced by circumstances into a position in which we must practically speak for the rest of the world. It is evident that the United States is the only first-class power that can be expected to take the initiative in recognizing the new government. It will in effect act as the representative of the other powers of the world in this matter and will unquestionably be held responsible by them for the consequences. Every step taken by the Constitutionalist leaders from this moment on and everything which indicates the spirit in which they mean to proceed and to consummate their triumph must of necessity, therefore, play a very important part in determining whether it will be possible for the United States to recognize the government now being planned for.
>
> In the most earnest spirit of friendship, therefore, this Government wishes to call attention to the following matters of critical consequence:
>
> First, the treatment of foreigners, foreign lives, foreign property, foreign rights, and particularly the delicate matter of the financial obliga-

tions, the legitimate financial obligations, of the government now super-seded. Unless the utmost care, fairness and liberality are shown in these matters the most dangerous complications may arise.

Second, the treatment of political and military opponents. Unless there is to be a most generous amnesty it is certain that the sympathy of the whole world, including the people of the United States, now the real friends of the Constitutionalists, will be hopelessly alienated and the situation become impossible.

Third, the treatment of the Roman Catholic Church and of those who represent it. Nothing will shock the civilized world more than punitive or vindictive action toward priests or ministers of any church, whether Catholic or Protestant; and the Government of the United States ventures most respectfully but most earnestly to caution the leaders of the Mexican people on this delicate and vital matter. The treatment already said to have been accorded priests has had a most unfortunate effect upon opinion outside of Mexico.

You can not too earnestly urge these matters upon the attention of those now in the counsels of the Constitutionalists. . . . Nothing ought to be overlooked or dealt with hastily which may result in our being obliged to withhold the recognition of this Government from the new government to be created at Mexico City as we withheld it from General Huerta. Our ability or inability to serve them they must now determine.[109]

When Carranza replied that his government would protect foreign lives and property and respect all legitimate contracts and obligations, but would use its own judgment in dealing with *Huertistas* and the Church,[110] Wilson came back with an even sterner warning "Our advice offered, and everything stated in our telegram of the 23d," he wrote, "cannot be modified nor can we recede from it in the least without deep and perhaps fatal consequences to the cause of the present revolution which, if that advice is accepted in the spirit in which it is given, may now be made completely and gloriously successful. This Government is reluctant to contemplate the possible consequences to Mexico if it should be forced to withhold recognition from those who are now to succeed General Huerta. It is our plain duty as friends,

[109] The Secretary of State to Vice Consul Silliman, July 23, 1914, *Foreign Relations, 1914*, pp. 568-569.

[110] Isidro Fabela to J. R. Silliman, July 27, 1914, *ibid.*, p. 575; but see especially J. R. Silliman to the Secretary of State, July 26, 1914, State Department Papers, explaining the Constitutionalists' determination to destroy the aristocracy and punish the Church for having allegedly propagated error, corrupted the people, and connived to perpetuate the old regime.

therefore, to reiterate with deep earnestness all that we have said. Our recent messages have been most deliberately conceived, with a full consciousness of all they implied, and were sent with a very suggestive feeling of our responsibility to Mexico, to ourselves and to the world."[111]

Carranza could not have missed the meaning of Wilson's words, but he proceeded serenely to effect a transfer of power in his own way. Receiving commissioners from the Carbajal government who came to his headquarters at Saltillo on August 2, 1914, to discuss terms and guarantees, the First Chief declared that he would accept nothing less than the unconditional surrender of Mexico City.[112] The Washington government protested strongly, but Carranza had his way. On August 13, 1914, Carbajal's representatives signed an agreement with Álvaro Obregón, one of Carranza's generals, providing for Carbajal's withdrawal, the dissolution of the federal army, and the peaceful occupation of Mexico City by Obregón's division on August 15.[113]

Carranza waited in Tlalnepantla, seven miles north of the capital, until Obregón had completed the occupation. Then, surrounded by his generals—except Villa and his coterie—the First Chief entered the City of Mexico on August 20, 1914. An impressive figure, tall and erect astride a superb horse, he rode through streets lined with cheering crowds and a double rank of Constitutionalist soldiers. When he reached the front of the National Palace at 12:40 p.m., the multitudes broke down the barriers and surged around him, while cannon fired the presidential salute, massed bands played the Mexican national anthem, and the buglers of all regiments kept up an incessant fanfare. Going to the balcony of the Palace, Carranza acknowledged the cheers of his countrymen and asked for their support in the days ahead.[114]

One phase of the Revolution was over, but new and more terrible travail awaited the Mexican people in their bloody progress toward peace and democratic institutions. For while the crowds cheered in Mexico City, Villa was plotting Carranza's downfall, and the stubborn man in the White House was making incredible new plans to gain control of the Mexican situation. But this is part of a later story.

[111] The Secretary of State to J. R. Silliman, July 31, 1914, *Foreign Relations, 1914*, p. 577.
[112] J. R. Silliman to the Secretary of State, August 3, 1914, *ibid.*, p. 580.
[113] J. R. Silliman to the Secretary of State, August 13, 1914, *ibid.*, pp. 586-587.
[114] *New York Times*, August 21, 1914.

CHAPTER XIII

Antitrust Legislation: The Final Surge of New Freedom Reform

Absorbing and important though they were, the Mexican troubles in no way diminished the energies of New Freedom reform at home. Although the President gave priority to the adoption of tariff and banking measures, the question of an antitrust program to fulfill the promises of the Democratic platform of 1912 arose during the early months of the new administration and remained persistently important until the program was completed in the autumn of 1914.

The first test of the New Freedom's attitude toward big business arose as a consequence of Attorney General James C. McReynolds' desire for belated vengeance against the reorganized components of the "Tobacco Trust,"[1] or the American Tobacco Company, which had been dissolved by the Supreme Court in 1911. As one of the government's attorneys in the case, McReynolds had been outraged by the plan of dissolution approved by Attorney General George W. Wickersham. That plan, McReynolds alleged, was a sham because it left control of the tobacco industry after dissolution in the hands of the men who had controlled the old "Tobacco Trust." Admitting that there were no grounds for reopening the case, McReynolds proposed an indirect attack—the imposition of a graduated internal revenue tax so high in its upper limit that it would seriously weaken the former members of the "Tobacco Trust" and stimulate the growth of small competitors.[2] The Attorney General presented his plan to the Cabinet on June 3, 1913, and the President authorized him to begin discussions with the members of the Senate finance committee.

McReynolds conferred on June 4, 1913, with Senator Furnifold M. Simmons of North Carolina, chairman of the finance committee, and with Senator Gilbert M. Hitchcock of Nebraska, an old foe of the "Tobacco Trust." As a result, Hitchcock introduced an amendment to

---

[1] They were the American Tobacco Company, Liggett & Myers, Lorillard & Company, the American Snuff Company, G. W. Helme Company, and Weyman & Bruton Company.

[2] *New York Times,* June 5, 1913.

the Underwood bill on June 5 embodying McReynolds' plan for a graduated tax. His purpose, the Nebraskan frankly averred, was to weaken the big tobacco companies and benefit the independents; moreover, he added, the plan might well be used to encourage small producers in many branches of manufacturing.[3]

It was a new and simple method, one that could be used to cripple big business if it were seriously applied. Although small manufacturers and radical progressives applauded, the large industrial and financial interests, their editorial spokesmen, and even most moderate progressives were horrified by the thought of a determined effort to atomize the industrial complex. "The fact that a measure, so monstrous and oppressive and so shocking to the public sense of justice and fair play as that which Senator Hitchcock of Nebraska introduced following the announcement of the Attorney General's proposal, was allowed to be embodied in the pending tariff bill," protested one editor, in a typical conservative reaction, "cannot but be regarded as a reflection of the Administration's attitude toward the larger business interests of the country."[4]

The response of the President and of Democratic leaders in Congress to this outburst of criticism revealed that they did not contemplate adopting any serious plan for the destruction of big business. Wilson evaded all responsibility for McReynolds' proposal by saying that he had not discussed it with the Attorney General and had only read about it in the newspapers,[5] while a White House correspondent reported on June 6 that the President had not authorized McReynolds to apply his plan to the steel, oil, and other industries, as some correspondents had implied.[6] A subcommittee of the Senate finance committee quietly pigeonholed the Hitchcock amendment, and it passed out of sight when the Senate Democratic caucus rejected it on July 2, 1913, by a vote of twenty-three to eighteen.[7]

McReynolds, meanwhile, had turned with determination to the unfinished business before his department—the settlement of pending antitrust proceedings. There was first the task of working out a plan to end the Union Pacific Railroad's control of its competitor, the South-

[3] *ibid.*, June 6, 1913.
[4] *Financial Age*, xxvii (June 14, 1913), 1016. For similar comment, see the *New York Times*, June 5, 1913; New York *Nation*, xcvi (June 12 and 19, 1913), 588-589, 609; *The Independent* lxxiv (June 12, 1913), 1318.
[5] New York *World*, June 6, 1913.
[6] *New York Times*, June 7, 1913.
[7] *ibid.*, July 3, 1913.

ern Pacific, in response to a Supreme Court decision of December 2, 1912. With the help of a special assistant, Thomas W. Gregory of Texas, McReynolds obtained a dissolution decree on June 30, 1913, that avoided "the fundamental defect in the plans adopted in the Standard Oil and Tobacco cases, where the separate parts into which the business was divided were left under the control of the same stockholders."[8] "In my judgment," Gregory wrote soon after the dissolution decree had been approved, "it is the first decree based on violations of the Sherman Act which has really accomplished anything in the way of a remedy."[9]

Among the dozens of antitrust cases awaiting trial,[10] none was so important politically and economically as the pending suit for the dissolution of the United States Steel Corporation. Begun by the Taft administration in 1911, this case involved not the question of outright monopoly but rather the more important issues of the use of subtle means of suppressing competition and the alleged control of a basic industry by its greatest single producer and its financial ally, J. P. Morgan & Company.

Fearing an adverse decision, the president of the steel corporation, Henry C. Frick, appealed directly to the President through Colonel House on March 22, 1913, for a settlement that would leave the corporation intact but also guarantee its future good behavior.[11] Wilson replied coldly, saying that the steel corporation would receive no special favors from him and that Frick would have to discuss the matter of a settlement out of court with the Attorney General.[12] Frick thereupon appealed to McReynolds, but the Attorney General would accept nothing less than a thoroughgoing dissolution. "He sees no hope of such a settlement," House wrote after a conversation with McReynolds in September 1913, "for both he and the President are determined that real competition shall be had, and that is far from the notion of the Steel Trust people."[13] Thus the case went forward to eventual decision.[14]

[8] *Annual Report of the Attorney General of the United States for the Year 1913*, p. 7. McReynolds explains the dissolution plan on pp. 7-8 of this volume.

[9] T. W. Gregory to E. M. House, July 2, 1913, House Papers.

[10] For a list of them, see *Annual Report of the Attorney General, 1913*, pp. 10-16.

[11] House Diary, March 22, 1913.   [12] *ibid.*, March 24 and 26, 1913.

[13] *ibid.*, September 30, 1913.

[14] The proceedings were begun in federal district court in October 1914. The case moved from one court to another, was suspended during 1917 and 1918, and finally reached the Supreme Court after the First World War. In 1920 the Court ruled in favor of the corporation, on the grounds chiefly that mere bigness was no violation of the antitrust law and that the government had not proved its charges that the corporation had used illegal methods to suppress competition.

McReynolds also manifested the New Freedom's antitrust ardor by beginning a series of prosecutions of his own against alleged combinations and restraints of trade. Few of these cases engaged the public attention, for the Roosevelt and Taft administrations had commenced proceedings against virtually all the obvious monopolies. There were, however, two new cases of major importance.

The first was McReynolds' suit, begun in July 1913, to prevent the great Bell telephone system, the American Telephone & Telegraph Company, from acquiring a monopoly of telephone services in Oregon, Washington, and Idaho. There was more involved in this case than met the eye. The directors of A.T.&T. had frankly avowed their intention to gain control of all telephone and telegraph systems in the

It Looks Like a Revival

Ireland in the Columbus *Dispatch*

United States. McReynolds was equally determined that the progress of combination in the communications field must not merely stop but must be rolled back. In the face of the Attorney General's warning that A.T.&T. would either have to accept terms of surrender or else face dissolution proceedings, the company's directors accepted the consent decree drawn by McReynolds. It provided that the company would divest itself of the ownership and control of the Western Union Telegraph Company, make no further acquisitions of competing telephone systems, and open its long-distance lines to the independent companies. In addition, A.T.&T. agreed to restore certain telephone systems in the Pacific Northwest to independent ownership.[15]

The second new antitrust proceeding of the Wilson administration stirred up a violent controversy with repercussions that were heard for years to come. It was a double-barreled attack on the New York, New Haven, & Hartford Railroad's monopoly of the transportation facilities of New England and on that railroad's directors for criminally conspiring to violate the Sherman Act.

The background of this story can be briefly told. In 1903, J. P. Morgan acquired control of the New Haven, which was then a prosperous, well-managed railroad. During the next ten years Morgan and his agent, Charles S. Mellen, chairman of the board of directors, pursued a wild campaign to monopolize virtually every form of public transportation in the New England states, buying control not merely of competing railroad lines like the Boston & Maine but of interurban trolley systems and the Long Island Sound steamship lines as well. In the process they also bribed editors, debauched local and state politicians, and virtually bankrupted the New Haven in their reckless drive for power. In fact, the great system was tottering on the brink of ruin when Woodrow Wilson was inaugurated.[16]

Determined to destroy Morgan's New England empire, McReynolds appointed Thomas W. Gregory as special attorney on May 20, 1913, to manage the New Haven case. Gregory worked all through the summer and autumn preparing civil and criminal suits. The government's case was so airtight that the New Haven directors decided to surrender rather than risk a fight in the courts. As a result of protracted negotiations, therefore, the New Haven directors promised McReynolds and

[15] *New York Times*, December 20, 1913; *Annual Report of the Attorney General of the United States for the Year 1914*, pp. 13-15.

[16] For an excellent general account, see Henry L. Staples and Alpheus T. Mason, *The Fall of a Railroad Empire, Brandeis and the New Haven Merger Battle*.

Gregory that they would dispose of the company's holdings in the Boston & Maine, various trolley systems, and certain Long Island Sound steamship lines.[17]

Actually, the New Haven directors were maneuvering in the hope that they could prolong the discussions and frighten the Washington government into accepting a compromise that would leave their transportation monopoly intact. Thus they balked at disposing of the Boston & Maine within the time limit set by the Attorney General and refused to sell water terminals in the Sound ports; at the same time, they warned that dissolution proceedings by the Justice Department would force the New Haven into receivership and precipitate a catastrophic panic in New England.[18]

McReynolds struck back by accusing the New Haven directors of bad faith and by explaining the issues in the controversy in a public letter to the President on July 21, 1914.[19] "I . . . request and direct," Wilson replied at once, "that a proceeding in equity be filed, seeking the dissolution of the unlawful monopoly of transportation facilities in New England now sought to be maintained by the New York, New Haven & Hartford Railroad Company, and that the criminal aspects of the case be laid before a Grand Jury."[20]

The dissolution proceedings were begun in the New York federal district court on July 23, 1914, but the case never came off because the administration leaders had no desire to force proceedings that might bankrupt the New Haven if they could win their objectives by a peaceful settlement. Secret negotiations among Colonel House and McReynolds on the one side and Richard Olney and former Senator W. Murray Crane of Massachusetts on the other yielded an agreement on August 11, 1914; and the Attorney General withdrew the dissolution suit and accepted a consent decree on October 17, 1914.[21] The Justice Department went on with its plans to prosecute the New Haven directors for criminal violations of the Sherman Act; but it failed to win convictions because the chief culprit, Charles S. Mellen, former chair-

[17] *New York Times,* January 11, 1914.

[18] *ibid.,* March 14, 15, and 17, 1914; Henry L. Higginson to W. W., March 21, 1914, Wilson Papers; Richard Olney to W. W., May 26, 1914, Olney Papers.

[19] J. C. McReynolds to J. H. Hustis, July 9, 1914; and J. C. McReynolds to W. W., July 21, 1914, both printed in the *New York Times,* July 22, 1914.

[20] W. W. to J. C. McReynolds, July 21, 1914, *ibid.*

[21] E. M. House to R. Olney, August 3, 1914, Olney Papers; W. M. Crane to R. Olney, August 6, 1914, *ibid.*; E. M. House to R. Olney, August 11, 1914, *ibid.*; W. M. Crane to R. Olney, August 12, 1914, *ibid.; New York Times,* August 12 and October 18, 1914.

man of the board of directors, had obtained immunity by confessing his sins before the Interstate Commerce Commission during a searching investigation into the New Haven's affairs conducted by former Governor Joseph W. Folk of Missouri in the spring of 1914.

Meanwhile, a long debate over federal antitrust policy was nearing its climax as Wilson and the Democratic leaders in Congress were at work enacting the Underwood tariff and Federal Reserve bills. The debate was set off by the Supreme Court's promulgation of the rule of reason—the doctrine that the Sherman Antitrust Act of 1890 had forbidden only unreasonable, or direct, restraint of trade—in the Standard Oil decision in May 1911. It was stimulated from 1911 to 1913 by a thoroughgoing House investigation of the United States Steel Corporation, by a thoughtful Senate inquiry into every aspect of the question of maintaining competition, and by a flood of bills in Congress and of articles in the periodical press. It was clarified by Wilson's and Roosevelt's masterful analyses of the problem during the campaign of 1912.

By the time of Wilson's inauguration, the lines had been fairly clearly drawn. There was no important argument over the virtues or dangers of industrial monopoly and the restraint of competition by private groups; all major spokesmen agreed that competition in industry must be preserved when possible. However, there was a significant disagreement in 1913 over the means of achieving and maintaining economic freedom. One group, representing the large business interests and conservative opinion, argued that the Sherman Act and the Supreme Court's elucidation of that measure provided sufficient remedies to preserve competition. A second, representing Theodore Roosevelt and advanced progressive opinion, proposed combining the acceptance of the big-business structure with a large degree of federal control. A third group, speaking for moderate progressives and agrarians, demanded thoroughgoing amendment of the Sherman Act in order to destroy or hamper the super-corporations and interlocking directorates and to establish and maintain competition.

Wilson had ranged himself squarely on the side of the advocates of revision of the Sherman Act during the presidential campaign of 1912. Under the tutelage of Louis D. Brandeis, the intellectual leader of this group, Wilson had grounded his New Freedom program mainly upon the concept of re-establishing and maintaining competition and had savagely rejected Roosevelt's plan to accept big business and regulate it by a strong federal trade commission. Not until the Underwood bill was enacted and the Federal Reserve bill was safely on its way to passage, however, could the President give serious thought to the details of antitrust legislation.

He began to study various proposals and held preliminary conferences with House and Senate leaders during the last two weeks of November 1913. Then, following the convening of the regular session in early December, came a flood of new bills and proposals.[22] Some of them were general revisions like the measure written by Senator La Follette in cooperation with Brandeis; others were more limited and specific, like the bill introduced by Representative Robert L. Henry of Texas to provide prison terms for violators of the Sherman law, or like several bills establishing strict federal control of the issuance of railroad securities and of the stock exchanges. But the sheer range and diversity of the proposals gave convincing evidence of the overwhelming congressional determination to deal decisively with the so-called trust issue. The main task ahead of the President in these circumstances would be to guide congressional energies into orderly and constructive channels.

Wilson pondered the question and laid his plans during his vacation in Pass Christian, Mississippi, in late December 1913 and early January 1914. If any doubts existed in his mind, they were quickly dispelled during this brief period of rest and meditation. He decided that he would press ahead for legislation along the lines he had demanded in 1912, in spite of warnings from certain friends that a business depression was developing and that antitrust legislation would only disturb the business community, and in spite of the seeming surrender of the House of Morgan, which on January 2, 1914, announced its withdrawal from the directorates of thirty banks, railroads, and industrial corporations and its intention to withdraw from other directorships in the future.[23]

Returning to Washington on January 13, 1914, Wilson set to the task of getting the legislative machinery into gear. He read the draft of a special message to Congress that he had prepared at Pass Christian to his Cabinet on the morning of his arrival in the capital. During a

[22] See the *New York Times*, December 2, 1913; A. O. Stanley to W. W., December 9, 1913, Wilson Papers; and especially Joseph E. Davies, "MEMORANDUM OF RECOMMENDATIONS AS TO TRUST LEGISLATION BY JOSEPH E. DAVIES, COMMISSIONER OF CORPORATIONS," sent to Wilson on December 27, 1913, *ibid.*, for a detailed analysis of various proposals.

[23] *New York Times*, January 3, 1914.

four-hour conference with members of the House judiciary committee and the Senate interstate commerce committee at the White House on the following day, January 14, he outlined the legislative program that had taken shape in his mind.[24] Then, on January 20, 1914, he appeared before a joint session to explain his broad purposes to the country. The antagonism between government and business was over, he declared, and the administration and Congress could now proceed "in quiet moderation, without revolution of any untoward kind," to write "the additional articles of our constitution of peace, the peace that is honor and freedom and prosperity."[25]

Wilson spoke with honeyed words, but the program that he and the Democratic leaders in Congress formulated during the week following the address before the joint session was sweeping and severe enough to win the approval even of the ardent opponents of big business.

There was, first of all, the measure drawn by Henry D. Clayton of Alabama, chairman of the House judiciary committee, which was known as the Clayton bill and was introduced in the House on April 14, 1914. It enumerated and outlawed a number of unfair trade practices, such as price-cutting to destroy competition, refusal to sell to responsible persons and firms, and so-called tying contracts; made owners and directors of businesses and corporations criminally responsible for civil violations of the antitrust laws; forbade corporations to acquire or hold the stock of other corporations, when the effect of such action was to lessen competition; forbade interlocking directorates among the great banks in large cities, competing railroads, and banks, corporations, and railroads doing business among themselves; and gave the benefit of judgments rendered in antitrust suits begun by the government to private parties suing for damages under the Sherman law.[26]

There was, in the second place, an interstate trade commission bill, prepared by Representatives William C. Adamson of Georgia and James H. Covington of Maryland, Senator Francis G. Newlands of Nevada, Attorney General McReynolds, and others in response to the President's directive and introduced in the House in revised form on

[24] *ibid.*, January 15, 1914; New York *World*, January 15, 1914.
[25] R. S. Baker and W. E. Dodd (eds.), *The New Democracy*, I, 81-88.
[26] This last provision meant that when the government won an antitrust suit, private parties which had suffered injuries from the convicted corporation might obtain the threefold damages allowed by the Sherman Act by simply establishing the extent to which they had been damaged, without having to institute a private suit to prove that the convicted corporation was a monopoly or had acted illegally.

March 16, 1914. Known as the Covington bill, it created an independent bipartisan Interstate Trade Commission, which was empowered to investigate all business and corporate activities, to determine whether corporations had violated the antitrust laws, and to recommend procedures to enable erring corporations to comply with the laws. But it was no such powerful administrative agency, able to take direct control of business affairs, as Roosevelt and many advanced progressives demanded. On the contrary, it was the old Bureau of Corporations, which it supplanted, under a new name and with broader investigative authority—as Wilson said, no "dangerous experiment," but a "safe and sensible" agency that all Democrats could approve.[27]

Rounding out the President's antitrust program was a measure prepared by Representatives Adamson and Sam Rayburn of Texas and by Louis D. Brandeis, introduced in the House on May 7, 1914, and known as the Rayburn bill, which gave the Interstate Commerce Commission authority over the issuance of new securities by the railroads. An outgrowth of the New Haven scandal, the Rayburn bill passed the House on June 5, 1914, but later died in the Senate. It was a casualty, in the first place, of the panic that disorganized the American security markets following the outbreak of the World War and, secondly, of the opposition of many railroad presidents, state-rights Southerners, and extreme progressives like La Follette, who charged that the measure would result in governmental approval for railroad financing.[28] A companion measure to establish federal control of the stock exchanges, prepared by Samuel Untermyer and Senator Robert L. Owen of Oklahoma, never won the administration's support and died in the Senate.[29]

The outbreak of a controversy in mid-April 1914 occasioned by the A.F. of L.'s demand for an amendment granting labor unions complete immunity from prosecution under the antitrust laws delayed the progress of the Clayton, Covington, and Rayburn bills. But the congressional machinery moved into high gear after the resolution of this conflict. Meeting in caucus session on May 12, 1914, the House Democrats

[27] W. W. to John Sharp Williams, January 27, 1914, Wilson Papers.

[28] On the opposition to the Rayburn bill, see R. M. La Follette, "'Let Us Reason Together,'" *La Follette's Weekly*, VI (January 31, 1914), 1-3; New York *World*, June 4 and 5, 1914; *New York Times*, June 12, July 12, August 28, 1914; and especially B. H. Innes Brown to E. M. House, August 7 and 24, 1914, House Papers.

[29] In its provisions requiring full publicity of all facts relating to the value of securities and to all stock transactions, the Owen bill was almost identical to the Truth-in-Securities Act of 1933. See the New York *World*, January 11, 1914; *New York Times*, January 23, February 6, and June 26, 1914.

yielded to the President's demand and adopted a rule binding Democratic members to support the administration's program. Then, after a hurried and uncritical debate, most of which was devoted to discussing various new labor amendments, the House approved the Clayton, Covington, and Rayburn bills on June 5, 1914, the first by a vote of 275 to fifty-four, the second by a voice vote, and the third by a vote of 325 to twelve.

This, therefore, was the original New Freedom antitrust program in its entirety and essential simplicity—an attempt to rewrite the rules of the business game in order to restore and maintain competition, without, however, trying to destroy big business *per se* or launching the government upon a bold program of administrative control. It manifested almost perfectly the New Freedom faith in competition and free enterprise and its original abhorrence of direct governmental participation in economic affairs.

The first important modification of the administration's antitrust program came as a result of a controversy that threatened to wreck the Clayton bill before it was seriously debated by the House of Representatives. That controversy erupted when the leaders of the A.F. of L. and their friends in Congress read the revised Clayton bill in mid-April 1914 and discovered that the measure included no provisions exempting labor unions from the application of the antitrust laws.

Earlier in this volume we have described the beginning of the A.F. of L.'s campaign for immunity from prosecution and judicial interference for using methods of industrial warfare that the Supreme Court had defined as restraints of trade outlawed by the Sherman Act. We have also seen how the Democratic party endorsed labor's demand in 1908 and 1912, and how Wilson met the issue when it first arose in his administration, by signing an appropriation bill in 1913 that included a rider forbidding the Justice Department to use any of the funds appropriated for the prosecution of labor and farm organizations and by promising at the same time to enforce the law impartially against all violators.[30]

Yet Samuel Gompers, president of the A.F. of L., and the heads of several powerful farm organizations still demanded nothing less than a full immunity written permanently into the federal statutes. Throughout most of 1913 and the early weeks of 1914 Gompers pressed hard for the approval of a specific immunity measure known as the Bacon-

[30] Above, pp. 264-269.

Bartlett bill. "The proposed legislation contained in the Bartlett-Bacon bills," Gompers wrote, for example, early in 1914, "is the paramount issue before the working people of our land."[31] "Viewing the whole field of human activity," he said in another letter in support of the proposed legislation, "I know of no one thing that impresses itself so much upon my mind as one of immediate importance and necessity as to secure the enactment of the legislation which shall restore to the toilers of our country the right of the exercise of their normal activities."[32]

Unable to obtain committee approval for the Bacon-Bartlett bill, Gompers and his friends shifted their strategy during the period when Wilson and the Democratic leaders in Congress were formulating the antitrust program. In brief, the labor spokesmen and their farm allies, who were eager to obtain immunity from antitrust prosecution for agricultural organizations, decided to demand the incorporation of the Bacon-Bartlett provisions as amendments to the new general antitrust legislation. This, they declared bluntly, was their price for the support of a large labor bloc in Congress and for the A.F. of L.'s and the farm organizations' support of the Democratic ticket in the congressional elections of 1914. "Without further delay," Gompers warned the Democratic leaders at the outset of the antitrust discussions, "the citizens of the United States must decide whether they wish to outlaw organized labor. . . . Those of that party whom the people elected to office are in honor bound to redeem that pledge that they gave to those who elected them."[33] "Organized labor," he stated two months later, "will be satisfied with nothing but full recognition of the principle for which it has been contending. It now appeals to the hearts, minds, and sense of justice of the law-makers."[34]

Thus again, as during the conflict over the rider to the Sundry Civil bill in 1913, was the President confronted squarely with a demand for alleged class privileges that violated an essential article of the historic Democratic doctrine of equal rights for all, special privileges for none. There was no doubt where Wilson stood personally on the issue of

[31] S. Gompers to C. M. Fisher and H. X. Phillips, February 11, 1914, Gompers Letterbooks.

[32] S. Gompers to Matthew Woll, February 27, 1914, *ibid.*; see also S. Gompers to Champ Clark, January 24, 1914, *ibid.*; S. Gompers to Perl D. Decker, January 24, 1914, *ibid.*; S. Gompers to Oscar W. Underwood, January 24, 1914, *ibid.*

[33] S. Gompers, "Antitrust Law and Labor," *American Federationist,* xxi (January 1914), 35, 37.

[34] S. Gompers, "Antitrust Law Enmeshes Labor," *ibid.,* March 1914, p. 228.

labor exemption. "I appreciate fully the importance of what you urge," he wrote in reply to F. N. Doubleday, the anti-union publisher, who had begged him to stand fast in opposition to labor's demand, "and you may be sure that my own conviction is that which you express, that there must be an absolutely impartial enforcement of the law."[35] There was considerable doubt, however, whether Wilson could personally resist the combined pressure of the A.F. of L. and the farm organizations or, in any event, whether he could prevent the Democrats in Congress from honoring their party's platform promises.

Sometime between about the first of March 1914, when Gompers and the executive committee of the A.F. of L. began their intensive campaign for the amendment of the Clayton bill, and the middle of April, Wilson must have determined to stand firm, regardless of the political risks, against labor's demand for exemption. Conferring for the first time about the matter with the members of the House judiciary committee on April 13, 1914, he declared that he was willing to grant some of labor's moderate demands, that is, amendments providing for jury trials in cases of criminal contempt and circumscribing the issuance of injunctions in industrial disputes.[36] He was willing also, he indicated, to approve an amendment affirming that labor unions and farm organizations were not, *per se*, conspiracies in restraint of trade.[37] But this was as far as he would go.[38]

For the leaders of the A.F. of L. and their allies it was not enough. Gompers appealed over Wilson's head to Democratic leaders in Congress, warning that the labor and farm allies were "totally unsatisfied and dissatisfied" with the President's concessions,[39] and called the labor bloc in Congress into frequent conferences with officials of the A.F. of L., the railroad brotherhoods, and the National Farmers' Union to

[35] W. W. to F. N. Doubleday, February 16, 1914, Wilson Papers.

[36] These provisions had been embodied in a bill written and sponsored by Representative Clayton in the Sixty-second Congress. This measure had passed the House on May 14, 1912, and had been pigeonholed by a subcommittee of the Senate judiciary committee. It might be added that criminal contempt consists of a violation of an injunction or court order committed outside the courtroom, for example, the violation of an injunction forbidding mass picketing. Civil contempt, on the other hand, consists of violations of the dignity and decorum of the court itself in session.

[37] This concession, it should be emphasized, did nothing more than reaffirm a doctrine that had long been enunciated by the American courts. It added nothing new to labor's rights and immunities.

[38] New York *World*, April 14, 1914; *New York Times*, April 15, 1914.

[39] S. Gompers to Senator F. G. Newlands, April 27, 1914, Gompers Letterbooks; also S. Gompers to H. D. Clayton, April 22, 1914, *ibid.*; S. Gompers to R. L. Henry, April 22, 1914, *ibid.*; and S. Gompers to J. A. Reed, April 27, 1914, *ibid.*

plan strategy for the fight ahead.[40] Spokesmen for the labor group in Congress went to the White House on April 30, 1914, and angrily told the President that they would launch an all-out attack against the Clayton bill unless he conceded the demand for complete immunity for labor from prosecution and injunctions under the Sherman Act.[41] Finally, on May 18, 1914, David J. Lewis of Maryland, leader of the labor congressmen, and Frank Morrison, secretary of the A.F. of L., appeared before the House judiciary committee to warn that the labor bloc would join the Republicans to defeat the antitrust program and that the A.F. of L. would oppose Democratic congressional candidates in the coming campaign unless the administration surrendered.[42]

Yet Wilson stood immovable in the face of these threats. He told reporters on April 30, 1914, that he was ready to take the issue to the floor of the House and to the people, if that were necessary.[43] Two weeks later, on May 16, he warned congressional leaders that he would not sign the Clayton bill if they surrendered to labor's demands for complete exemption.[44]

Washington correspondents predicted the outbreak of a fight that would disrupt the Democratic party when the House began general debate on the Clayton bill on May 23, 1914. But the administration forces held firm, and Gompers and his allies gave in on May 26 and accepted the compromise that the President had offered earlier.[45]

Thus without any outward controversy the House approved amendments to the Clayton bill on June 1 and 2, 1914, declaring that labor, farm, fraternal, and cooperative organizations should not be "construed to be illegal combinations in restraint of trade under the antitrust laws"; approving peaceful strikes, lawful boycotts, and lawful picketing; giving workers the right to a jury trial in cases of criminal contempt; and forbidding the issuance of injunctions in labor disputes

[40] See the form letter that Gompers sent to officials of the A.F. of L., the railroad brotherhoods, and the National Farmers' Union, and to the so-called labor representatives and senators on April 27, 1914, *ibid.*

[41] New York *World*, May 1, 1914.

[42] *ibid.*, May 19, 1914. See also Gompers' demand that the Clayton bill be so amended "that it will definitely and clearly exempt the organizations of workers from the civil as well as the criminal sections of the Sherman Anti-Trust law, and by so doing redeem the pledges of the Democratic party." *ibid.*, May 18, 1914.

[43] *ibid.*, May 1, 1914.

[44] New York *Times*, May 17, 1914; New York *World*, May 18 and 19, 1914.

[45] New York *Times*, May 27, 1914; New York *World*, May 28, 1914.

"unless necessary to prevent irreparable injury to property, or to a property right, of the party making the application, for which injury there is no adequate remedy at law."

If any doubts remained as to the meaning of these provisions, the President and congressional leaders soon dispelled them. The labor provisions of the Clayton bill, Wilson told reporters on June 1, 1914, confirmed labor's right to organize without in any way sanctioning conspiracies to injure employers or competitors or methods of industrial warfare like the blacklist and secondary boycott.[46] "The so-called labor exemption," he added a short time later, "does not seem to me to do more than exclude the possibility of labor and similar organizations being dissolved as in themselves combinations in restraint of trade."[47] But the clearest explanation came from Representative Edwin Y. Webb, who had recently succeeded Clayton as chairman of the House judiciary committee:

"The framers of the Sherman law never intended to place labor organizations and farmers' organizations under the ban of that law. The existence of a labor or farmers' union never has been unlawful, and it is not unlawful today, but it was decided to place in the statutory law of the country a recognition of the rights of those organizations to exist and carry out their lawful purposes.

"After the original Section 7 of the Anti-trust bill was drawn, certain representatives of labor contended that the section did not give labor all it was entitled to and demanded that we should make the section provide that the anti-trust laws should not apply to labor organizations. The acceptance of this amendment would have placed labor organizations beyond the pale of the anti-trust law entirely, which neither the President nor the members of the committee would agree to. Finally, after ten days' parleying, we agreed to add . . . that such organizations, orders, or associations and their members should not be held [to be] illegal combinations in restraint of trade under the anti-trust laws. This added nothing material, but seemed a pretty good compromise proposition.

"Considerable furor, as if it were revolutionary and unusual, has been made over this section. There is nothing revolutionary or radical about it. Boycotting is legal today in all the courts. The right to quit work is not denied to any man. The right to peaceably assemble and discuss

[46] *New York Times*, June 2, 1914; New York *World*, June 2, 1914.
[47] W. W. to C. R. Van Hise, July 13, 1914, Wilson Papers.

grievances is a constitutional right. What is known as the secondary boycott is not authorized or legalized."[48]

Undaunted, the labor and farm leaders renewed their campaign when the Senate judiciary committee began consideration of the Clayton bill in July 1914.[49] However, the committee and afterward the Senate itself not only resisted these demands but also added amendments to make doubly clear that the labor sections of the Clayton bill permitted only "lawful" and "peaceful" strike activities and methods of economic warfare. The measure, as revised by the Senate and approved by the conference committee, declared, for example, that nothing contained in the antitrust laws should be construed to prevent members of labor and farm organizations from "*lawfully* carrying out the *legitimate* objects thereof," authorized boycotts "by *peaceful* and *lawful* means," and declared that injunctions should not restrain strikers "from attending at any place where any such person or persons may *lawfully* be."[50]

The Senate made one other change that was to be often quoted in the future but was not legally important. At the suggestion of Albert B. Cummins of Iowa it added the preface, "The labor of a human being is not a commodity or article of commerce," to the provision affirming the legality of labor and farm organizations. Incorporated in the final Clayton Act, it was a pious affirmation of congressional opinion but did not enlarge labor's rights under the law.

The Clayton bill was, apparently, a solution that pleased everyone. Gompers hailed it as labor's "Magna Carta"[51] and afterward tried frantically to convince himself and the country that labor unions were now entirely freed from the inhibitions of the antitrust laws.[52] Administration spokesmen with an eye on the labor vote talked glowingly about labor's emancipation from judicial tyranny.[53] At the other extreme, Daniel Davenport, the general counsel of the American Anti-Boycott

---

[48] *New York Times*, June 14, 1914.

[49] See, e.g., S. Gompers, *et al.*, to Senator L. S. Overman, July 30, 1914, copy in the Walsh Papers.

[50] Italics added.

[51] S. Gompers, "Labor's Magna Carta—Demand It," *American Federationist*, xxi (July 1914), 553-557.

[52] S. Gompers, "The Charter of Industrial Freedom," *ibid.*, November 1914, pp. 957-974; and the symposium on the labor sections of the Clayton Act in *ibid.*, xxii (September 1915), 666-716.

[53] e.g., *The Public*, xvii (June 12, 1914), 549; New York *World*, October 11, 1914; and William B. Wilson, "Labor and the Clayton Act," *Harper's Weekly*, lxii (April 29, 1916), 473-474.

Association, perhaps the most aggressive anti-union organization in the country, was equally satisfied. "The [Clayton] bill," he declared, "makes few changes in existing laws relating to labor unions, injunctions and contempts of court, and those are of slight practical importance."[54]

Davenport's analysis, obviously, was in the main correct. Labor's net gain from all its effort was protection against the indiscriminate and irresponsible issuance of injunctions in labor disputes and the right to a jury trial in criminal contempt cases. Otherwise, the Clayton Act merely confirmed benefits recognized by the American courts if not heretofore embodied in the federal statutes.[55] There was nothing secret or even devious in the motives and purposes of the President and the congressional leaders who framed the labor sections of the Act. They tried neither to deceive the public, nor, as former President Taft alleged, to buy labor's vote with a gold brick.[56] Nor did they try to confuse historians who would later perpetuate Gompers' claim that Wilson and Congress had meant to exempt labor unions from the application of the antitrust laws, only to have their purposes frustrated by a reactionary Supreme Court in the 1920's.

The House of Representatives' approval of the Clayton, Covington, and Rayburn bills on June 5, 1914, marked the high tide of the New Freedom philosophy of antitrust reform, that is, of the idea that all that the circumstances required was clarification and strengthening of the *legislative* prohibitions against restraint of trade. From this time forward, the New Freedom concepts gave way to other and quite different concepts advanced by powerful groups and spokesmen; and in the end the President approved an antitrust program that bore only a family resemblance to his original measure. The story of how this metamorphosis occurred is somewhat involved, but knowledge of it is essential to an understanding of Wilson's effort to deal with the antitrust problem.

The catalyst in the change was the conviction, shared by the vast majority of businessmen, Rooseveltian Progressives, many progressive Republicans and Democrats, and by a large majority of the thoughtful

---

[54] *Springfield* (Massachusetts) *Republican*, October 11, 1914.

[55] On this point, see Edwin Witte, "The Clayton Bill and Organized Labor," *The Survey*, XXXII (July 4, 1914), 360; "The Changed Clayton Bill," New York *Nation*, XCIX (October 15, 1914), 456-457; and " 'Labor Is Not a Commodity,' " *New Republic*, IX (December 2, 1916), 112-114.

[56] W. H. Taft to Jeremiah Smith, December 24, 1914, Taft Papers.

students of the antitrust problem, that the Clayton and Covington bills provided a hopelessly unrealistic, unworkable, and even dangerous solution.

To begin with, the mass of small businessmen were in revolt against the Clayton bill's provisions that provided jail terms for every violation and, as one authority has said, "put every business executive at an indeterminate risk of criminal indictment and punishment."[57] The American business community was at this time in the process of working out radically new concepts for the regulation and, their spokesmen claimed, the preservation of competition—concepts that involved so-called self-regulation of business through trade associations to end cutthroat practices, heretofore employed to destroy competition. As the Clayton bill threatened possible jail terms for the practitioners of the "new cooperation," the protest that arose from businessmen "was neither sectional nor political; it was practically unanimous."[58] It was, moreover, given additional weight by Louis D. Brandeis, who, in his fervent desire to protect and encourage small enterprise, had endorsed the new concepts of controlled competition.[59]

In the second place, there was a widespread conviction, which gained momentum after the presentation of the revised Clayton bill in April 1914, that it was impossible to define in statutory language all the possible forms of restraint of trade. "Surely," Wilson had confidently told Congress, "we are sufficiently familiar with the actual processes and methods of monopoly and of the many hurtful restraints of trade to make definition possible, at any rate up to the limits of what experience has disclosed. These practices, being now abundantly disclosed, can be explicitly and item by item forbidden by statute." Experience soon revealed, however, that the task confronting the framers of the Clayton bill was not an easy one. By attempting to specify the generalizations of the Sherman Act, they inevitably "left open a wide field for the exercise of ingenuity in devising other practices destructive of competition"[60]

[57] Nelson B. Gaskill, *The Regulation of Competition*, p. 43.

[58] *ibid.*

[59] See L. D. Brandeis, "The Solution of the Trust Problem," *Harper's Weekly*, LVIII (November 8, 1913), 18-19; L. D. Brandeis to F. K. Lane, December 12, 1913, Brandeis Papers; L. D. Brandeis to J. C. McReynolds, February 22, 1914, *ibid.*; and Brandeis' speech before the Chamber of Commerce of the United States, February 12, 1914, *New York Times*, February 13, 1914.

[60] George Rublee, "The Original Plan and Early History of the Federal Trade Commission," *Proceedings of the Academy of Political Science*, XI (January 1926), 115.

and, as many contemporaries observed, raised the danger of actually weakening the sweeping prohibitions of the Sherman law.[61]

Virtually all the critics of the President's program agreed that the wise solution of the antitrust problem would be to abandon the effort to define restraints of trade, to outlaw in general terms what the Supreme Court had called "unfair" trade practices, and to establish a federal trade commission with full power to prevent monopoly and unfair competition, through direct supervision of the day-to-day activities of the business world.

Many businessmen supported this proposal in the hope that such a commission would approve trade agreements in advance and in general act as friend, guide, and protector of the business community.[62] On the other hand, the most important support for a strong trade commission came from students of the antitrust problem like Brandeis, from Roosevelt's followers, and from progressive Republicans and Democrats, including Francis G. Newlands and Albert B. Cummins, the senior Democratic and Republican members of the Senate commerce committee. Condemning the Covington bill for establishing a weak commission, they argued that the surest safeguard against monopoly lay in creating an administrative agency popularly controlled and powerful enough to confront the leaders of big business on equal terms.[63]

Wilson was impressed by these criticisms and interested in the proposals for a strong trade commission, but he adhered doggedly to his original program until it had passed the House of Representatives in early June 1914. He acted, at least at the outset of the discussions, in the New Freedom conviction that direct control and supervision of the business world by a freewheeling administrative agency was no proper function of the federal government. "My own judgment," he wrote to President Charles R. Van Hise of the University of Wisconsin, who had urged him to support the strong commission plan, "is that it is not wise to begin, at any rate, by giving the commission the authority

[61] See, e.g., "The New Trust Bills," New York *Nation*, xcviii (January 29, 1914), 100; "The Trust Bills," New York *Outlook*, cvi (March 28, 1914), 663-664; *New York Times*, May 14, 1914; "The Trust Program," *Harper's Weekly*, lviii (June 13, 1914), 4.

[62] See especially Thomas Creigh of the Cudahy Packing Company to J. P. Tumulty, February 13, 1914, Wilson Papers, enclosing "Chicago Plan for Amendment to Sherman Anti-Trust Law," a memorandum of a plan for the creation of a strong trade commission, prepared by a committee of the Chicago Association of Commerce.

[63] See, e.g., *The Independent*, lxxvii (March 30, 1914), 431-432; New York *Outlook*, cvi (March 28, 1914), 663-664; F. G. Newlands to W. W., March 5 and June 6, 1914, Wilson Papers; and C. R. Van Hise to W. W., March 5, 1914, *ibid.*

you suggest. I think that it ought to be a means of systematic information both for Congress and the country, and that it ought to be an instrument of the Department of Justice and the courts in determining the just and wise things to do with regard to the restoration of normal competition, but to allow it to authorize acts and practices seems to me to be taking a dangerous step."[64]

However, reasons of strategy were probably even more important than ideological considerations in Wilson's decision to adhere to the original administration antitrust program until it had passed the House. There was confusion and disagreement enough at this point, Wilson must have thought, without attempting to change the legislation while the lower house was debating it. Even more important was the fact that the southern Democrats who controlled the House interstate commerce committee and had charge of the trade commission bill were violently opposed to all plans for a strong commission. To them it meant the creation of a government of men, not of laws, and the beginning of a movement toward bureaucratic absolutism.[65]

While these southern exponents of New Freedom doctrines were proclaiming their undying hostility to all forms of administrative tyranny, a small group in Washington was laying the plans that would soon culminate in the transformation of the Wilsonian antitrust program. The leader of the group was George Rublee, a New York lawyer of independent means and a member of the Progressive party, who had joined Brandeis in September 1913 in work on financial legislation and had gone to Washington in the following November to serve as Brandeis' liaison with the congressional committees. Rublee has told how he came to write the measure that became the cornerstone of the administration's antitrust program:

"It happened that I was a friend of Congressman Raymond B. Stevens of New Hampshire who was a member of the Committee on Interstate and Foreign Commerce to which the Trade Commission Bill had been referred. I was much interested in the anti-trust legislation and Mr. Stevens and I talked it over together. It seemed to us that enactment of the bills in their then form instead of clarifying the antitrust laws would add to the existing uncertainty and also subject to criminal penalties business activities which in certain circumstances might be quite legitimate.

[64] W. W. to C. R. Van Hise, March 10, 1914, *ibid.*
[65] John W. Davidson, "The Response of the South to Woodrow Wilson's New Freedom, 1912-1914," pp. 200-210; W. C. Adamson to W. W., April 23, 1914, Wilson Papers.

"There were a number of other bills besides the Clayton Bill in which monopolistic practices were defined. I had noticed that in most of these bills at the end of the list of forbidden practices there was a general clause prohibiting all other forms of unfair competition. The same general clause appeared at the end of lists of specific practices enjoined in various decrees of Federal Courts in cases arising under the Sherman Law. . . . It therefore appeared that the phrase 'unfair competition' had a recognized meaning in the terminology of anti-trust law. So I suggested to Mr. Stevens that the right way to legislate would be to strike out of the Clayton Act the objectionable and insufficient definitions and instead to declare unfair competition to be unlawful and give the Trade Commission power to prevent it. I drafted a bill on the general lines of the Committee's bill with the addition of a section declaring unfair competition to be unlawful and authorizing the Commission to issue complaints and make cease and desist orders."[66]

We have another revealing account of Rublee's activities at this time, that is, April 1914, from Norman Hapgood, editor of *Harper's Weekly* and an important liaison between Rublee and Brandeis and the White House.

"Mr. Brandeis," Hapgood wrote the President on April 24, 1914, "has been so tied up with his railroad work that he has given only general thought to the trust situation as it has developed in the bills now before Congress, and as it has been affected by recent decisions of the Supreme Court. The most important part of the really hard work done recently by the little group he represents has been carried on by Mr. George Rublee, a classmate and very intimate friend of mine, who is spending this winter in Washington. He is not only in intimate touch with Mr. Brandeis, Senator La Follette and others but he has one of the best minds for this sort of thinking I ever knew. . . . Mr. Stevens has introduced the bill which was really drawn up by Mr. Rublee. . . . Unlike the Covington Bill, the Stevens Bill is complete in itself. One does not need to look at other statutes to learn what the powers and duties of the Commission are. . . . The Stevens Bill gives broader powers of investigation than the Covington Bill does. The Stevens Bill authorizes the Commission in its discretion to prescribe a uniform method of accounting for any class of corporation. The Stevens Bill declares unfair competition to be unlawful, and empowers the Commission, whenever it has reason to believe that a corporation is using any unfair

[66] George Rublee, "The Original Plan and Early History of the Federal Trade Commission," *loc.cit.*, pp. 115-116.

method of competition, to hold a hearing, and if it is of opinion that the method of competition in question is unfair to restrain the use thereof by injunction."[67]

At some time between late April and early June of 1914 Wilson concluded that the Stevens bill offered a way out of the dilemma created by the failure of the Clayton bill and a perfect answer to the critics of the weak trade commission plan. He afterward described his change of mind to a reporter: "At first I was inclined to think that various . . . practices had become obviously unfair and detrimental and that it would be best to define them as such in the Clayton law. As I talked with business men and students of legislation, however, I came to agree with them that these unfair practices would be reached [best] through the Trade Commission law [i.e., the Rublee plan]."[68]

As we have seen, for good strategic reasons the President refused to interfere while the House was debating the Clayton, Covington, and Rayburn bills. But he had made up his mind and was planning his new strategy even before the House voted on the original program. "I believe that we can by a combination of the measures now pending accomplish what it is necessary to accomplish at this session," he wrote to Senator Henry F. Hollis of New Hampshire, who had urged him to abandon the Clayton bill and support the Stevens plan. "What I have in mind is a little too intricate to be put into a hastily dictated letter, but conference will bring it out as we progress. . . . The men you speak of,—Representative Stevens, Mr. Brandeis, and Mr. Rublee,— have themselves suggested, I hope, a better way of dealing with the only really debatable part of the Clayton Bill [the definitions section]. The rest of it seems to me rather plain sailing."[69]

Wilson moved quickly to put his new plans into effect once the original antitrust program was safely through the House. He called Brandeis, Stevens, Rublee, and Hollis to the White House on June 10, 1914, and told them that he had decided to incorporate the Stevens bill as an amendment to the Covington bill. Moreover, he asked Hollis and Brandeis to convey his plan to the members of the Senate interstate commerce committee who were then considering the Covington bill.[70]

Wilson's conversion to the strong trade commission plan was the

[67] N. Hapgood to W. W., April 21, 1914, Wilson Papers.

[68] A. W. Shaw, memorandum of an interview with Wilson on January 4, 1915, MS. in *ibid.*

[69] W. W. to H. F. Hollis, June 2, 1914, *ibid.*

[70] L. D. Brandeis, telephone message for the President embodied in a memorandum dated June 10, 1914, *ibid.*; New York *World*, June 11, 1914.

decisive event in the history of the antitrust program. Virtually all the members of the Senate interstate commerce committee, Democratic as well as Republicans, were such enthusiastic advocates of a strong trade commission that it is doubtful that they would have approved an unamended Covington bill, even if such refusal had meant the ruin of the administration's antitrust plans. Welcoming the President's change of mind as a surrender to their own demands, the committee members incorporated the heart of the Stevens bill as Section 5 of the Covington bill on June 12, 1914, and reported the amended measure, now known as the Federal Trade Commission bill, favorably to the Senate the following day.[71]

The measure was a compromise, but it bore closer resemblance to the kind of legislation that Roosevelt had proposed in 1912 than to the Covington weak commission bill. It established an independent bipartisan Federal Trade Commission of five members, modeled after the Interstate Commerce Commission, appointed by the President with the consent of the Senate for seven-year terms, and endowed with sweeping powers of investigation. The heart of the new bill was Section 5, which empowered the commission to investigate and prevent unfair competition by the issuance of cease and desist orders, which would be enforced by the federal district courts.[72]

For the President there remained only to win the support of the main body of Senate Democrats and to steer the Federal Trade Commission bill to final passage without crippling amendments. At first these seemed easy tasks,[73] but when the measure reached the floor of the Senate in late July 1914, a strange coalition of conservatives and radicals from both parties, led by Republican Senators Frank Brandegee of Connecticut and George Sutherland of Utah, Charles S. Thomas, a Bryan Democrat from Colorado, and William E. Borah, insurgent Republican from Idaho, launched an attack so powerful that it threatened to wreck the measure altogether.

[71] H. F. Hollis to W. W., June 13, 1914, Wilson Papers; *New York Times*, June 14, 1914.

[72] There is a print of the Federal Trade Commission bill as introduced in the Senate by the commerce committee in *Congressional Record*, 63d Cong., 2d sess., pp. 10377-10378; see also George Rublee, "MEMORANDUM CONCERNING SECTION 5 OF THE BILL TO CREATE A FEDERAL TRADE COMMISSION," enclosed in F. K. Lane to W. W., July 10, 1914, Wilson Papers.

[73] e.g., see W. W. to H. F. Hollis, June 16, 1914, *ibid.*, and the *New York Times*, June 16, 1914, describing Wilson's meeting with the members of the Democratic Senate steering committee and the chairmen of the Senate commerce and judiciary committees on June 15, 1914.

Conservatives charged that the proposed Federal Trade Commission bill would, as Brandegee declared in a scathing attack on July 27, 1914, propel the government upon "a socialistic program" of comprehensive regulation through an irresponsible agency endowed with despotic power, unrestrained by the courts.[74] The radical opponents of the measure objected, not because they opposed severe legislation to restrain monopolistic practices, but because they feared regulation through an administrative agency empowered to make its own rules and definitions. Echoing a point that Wilson had raised repeatedly during the campaign of 1912, they argued that there was a grave danger that a powerful trade commission might become the tool of big business. In any event, they added, the very concept of direct federal control of economic activity was a Rooseveltian heresy utterly repugnant to fundamental democratic doctrines. As Senator Thomas put it on July 28, 1914:

"Is it democratic . . . to create a commission such as is here proposed and clothe it with the vast and inquisitorial powers with which we invest it by this bill? . . . I deny that we should clothe five men with any such authority. I do not care how experienced or how wise they may be, how unimpeachable their integrity and their purposes, it is not democratic to do it, it is not safe to do it."[75]

In the face of this mounting attack, the Democratic managers in the Senate, Newlands and Hollis, wavered; and the newspapers reported that they were prepared to abandon the Stevens amendment or perhaps to emasculate its strong grant of power to the commission, either by denying the commission the right to define unfair trade practices or by stripping it of all power to enforce its rulings.[76] At this critical point, however, the President intervened,[77] and the administration forces held firm. The showdown came a few days later during the final debate on August 5, 1914. With the support of most of the insurgent Republicans, the Democratic leaders beat down all attempts to weaken the bill and pushed it through by a bipartisan vote of fifty-three to sixteen.

On the same day that the Senate voted, Wilson began his final campaign for the Federal Trade Commission bill by politely demanding that the House members of the conference committee accept the Senate measure without important alterations. "I am . . . going to ask you

[74] *Congressional Record*, 63d Cong., 2d sess., pp. 12799-12801.
[75] *ibid.*, p. 12865.
[76] *New York Times*, July 29 and 30, 1914.
[77] W. W. to C. A. Culberson, July 30, 1914, Wilson Papers.

to forgive me," he wrote to Representative Adamson, the leader of the House conferees and an opponent of a strong commission, "if I take the liberty of sending you this note to express my deep interest in the retention in the bill in its integrity of Section V, the section about unfair competition. It seems to me a feasible and very wise means of accomplishing the things that it seems impossible in the complicated circumstances of business to accomplish by any attempted definition. . . . It meets the difficulties of my thought admirably which were largely concerned with the effort to regulate competition without making terms with monopoly."[78]

Actually, there was no danger that the House leaders would defy the President and what was by this time an obviously overwhelming public and business opinion behind the strong trade commission plan. In the conference committee, therefore, the House members accepted Section 5 of the Senate bill virtually *in toto*. "If the bill is wrong," Rublee wrote soon afterward, revealing the part that he played in the final deliberations, "I shall be much to blame. I drafted the conference report which was agreed to. Section 5 is exactly as I wanted it to be."[79]

Having yielded so much, however, the House members, apparently with the help of the President and the approval of Rublee, won one concession that drastically affected the subsequent development of regulation by the Federal Trade Commission. It was a change broadening the power of the courts to review the commission's decrees ordering a corporation to cease and desist from practicing unfair methods of competition.[80] The Senate had adopted an amendment offered by Cummins providing for narrow court review, which denied the courts the right to go behind the rulings of the commission to determine whether they were reasonable on a basis of the evidence.[81] In the conference committee, on the other hand, the House members won an amendment that facilitated appeals from the commission's rulings and

---

[78] W. W. to W. C. Adamson, August 5, 1914, *ibid.*

[79] G. Rublee to L. D. Brandeis, October 6, 1914, Brandeis Papers.

[80] See W. W. to J. H. Covington, August 27, 1914, Wilson Papers, advising the House conferees to stand "stoutly" on "the matter of the scope of the court review" and saying that he, Wilson, thought he had converted Newlands "to that view." See also George Rublee, "MEMORANDUM CONCERNING SECTION 5 . . . ," enclosed in F. K. Lane to W. W., July 10, 1914, *ibid.*, in which Rublee affirms his support of the principle of broad court review; and G. Rublee to L. D. Brandeis, October 6, 1914, Brandeis Papers, telling how hard it had been "to bring Cummins round," apparently to the amendment for broad court review.

[81] For the text of the Cummins amendment, see *Congressional Record*, 63d Cong., 2d sess., p. 13045.

declared that in such cases the findings of the commission were to be conclusive only if supported by testimony and evidence.[82] In other words, the ultimate definition of unfair methods of competition would rest with the courts, not with the Federal Trade Commission.

Thus amended by the conference committee, the Federal Trade Commission bill was approved by the Senate and the House on September 8 and 10, respectively, and was signed by the President on September 26, 1914. Approved by the great majority of small businessmen, it was also hailed by progressives of all political faiths as the beginning of a new era in constructive federal regulation of economic life. Senator Cummins voiced the general feeling in an eloquent speech on September 5, 1914. "I predict that in the days to come," he declared, "the Federal trade commission and its enforcement of the section with regard to unfair competition . . . will be found to be the most efficient protection to the people of the United States that Congress has ever given the people by way of a regulation of commerce, and that it will rank in future years with the antitrust law; and I was about to say that it would be found still more efficient in the creation of a code of business ethics and the establishment of the proper sentiments with regard to business morals. I am not half-hearted in my support of this measure. I believe in it thoroughly. I look forward to its enforcement with a high degree of confidence."[83]

Meanwhile, having espoused the strong trade commission plan, the President had seemed to lose all interest in the Clayton bill, the cornerstone of his original antitrust program. Cut adrift without administration guidance, it emerged from the Senate judiciary committee in mid-August 1914 with amendments that either completely nullified or else gravely weakened many of its important provisions.

This was due, in the first instance, to the fact that the committee members agreed that it was futile to attempt to define all possible forms of restraint of trade. Thus, after the Senate's approval of the Federal Trade Commission bill with its sweeping interdiction, the committee struck out Sections 2 and 4 of the Clayton bill, which had attempted to define certain illegal trade practices. It was due, even more, to the fact that the committee was dominated by conservatives who proceeded in honest conviction to make the Clayton bill less threatening to the business community. For example, the committee removed the criminal penalties in the original measure for civil violations of the antitrust

[82] *ibid.*, p. 14766.   [83] *ibid.*, p. 14770.

laws and made court decrees in antitrust suits initiated by the government prima-facie, instead of "conclusive," evidence in private damage suits against convicted corporations.

Senator James A. Reed of Missouri and a small group of southern and western agrarian radicals protested bitterly and fought hard, not merely to restore the Clayton bill's original provisions, but also to obtain severe new amendments to outlaw all industrial holding companies and to limit the size of industrial corporations. Their attack, however, broke against a solid conservative-administration coalition; and by the time the Senate had approved the revised Clayton bill on September 2, 1914, the radicals had won only the restoration of a provision outlawing so-called tying contracts.

The crucial struggle over the Clayton bill occurred when the House and Senate members of the conference committee worked from September 3 to September 23, 1914, to reconcile the strong House measure with the Senate's numerous crippling amendments. The House members won a seemingly important concession with the restoration of the various prohibitions against restraint of trade. Actually, however, the real victory went to the Senate conferees, who won the elimination of criminal penalties for civil violations of the antitrust laws; the addition of qualifying phrases like "where the effect may be to substantially lessen competition or tend to create a monopoly" to the provisions outlawing unfair trade practices, acquisition of the stock of one corporation by another, and the interlocking of corporate directorates; and the exemption of the directors of banks with resources under $5,000,000 from the provision forbidding the interlocking of bank directorates. In brief, the effect of these qualifications of the main provisions of the Clayton bill was to leave the ultimate amplification of the Sherman Act's generalities to the courts, rather than to define that measure's prohibitions in precise statutory language, as Wilson had originally intended.

During the final debates over the conference report, administration spokesmen in both houses made heroic efforts to prove that the Clayton bill in its final form represented the comprehensive attack on monopolistic big business that the Democratic platform and candidate had promised in 1912. "Mr. President," Senator Reed replied on September 28, 1914, in a devastating analysis of the changes in the measure, "this bill is entitled 'An act to supplement existing laws against unlawful restraints and monopolies, and for other purposes.' I shall endeavor to show that, if it passes in its present form, the title ought to be amended to read: 'An apology to unlawful restraints and monopolies.' . . . This measure has been loudly heralded as the Clayton antitrust bill. . . . Presumably it was brought forward as the legislative crystallization of the years-old Democratic promise that the trusts should be exterminated root and branch. The people were led to believe that the Democratic Party, now in full possession of all branches of the Government, by this bill intended to make private monopoly . . . both unprofitable and dangerous. In its inception this legislation was a challenge to the field of battle. In its finality it is a sort of Hague propaganda promulgated under white flags to the soothing melodies of 'Peace on earth, good will toward the trusts.' "[84]

The Missouri senator made an unsuccessful final assault on October 5, 1914, with a motion to recommit the Clayton bill to the conference committee, with instructions that it add criminal penalties for civil violations. Immediately afterward, the Senate approved the conference report by a vote of thirty-five to twenty-four. Three days later the House approved the Clayton bill by a vote of 245 to fifty-two; and the President, who had taken no part in the final struggle over the weakening of the measure, signed it without ceremony on October 15, 1914.

Engrossed in sensational developments in the European war during the summer and early autumn of 1914, few Americans paused to consider the meaning of the transformation that had occurred in the Wilsonian antitrust program. The President's failure to solve the antitrust problem by doctrinaire remedies had pointed up the essential inadequacy of the New Freedom approach for the solution of the complex economic and social problems that confronted the American people in the twentieth century. By abandoning his original measures and espousing an advanced progressive solution, Wilson and his Democratic leaders in Congress revealed greater ideological flexibility than they had heretofore shown, even during the struggles over the Federal Reserve bill. As Herbert Croly, editor of the *New Republic*, exclaimed in surprise, "In this Trade Commission act is contained the possibility of a radical reversal of many American notions about trusts, legislative power, and legal procedure. It may amount to historic political and constitutional reform. It seems to contradict every principle of the party which enacted it."[85]

[84] *Congressional Record*, 63d Cong., 2d sess., pp. 15818-15819.
[85] *New Republic*, 1 (January 9, 1915), 8.

$$\text{W} \boxed{\text{CHAPTER XIV}} \text{W}$$

The Last Months of the New Freedom

THE various groups in the political field campaigning for new advances along the progressive front—for a national child labor law and a federal rural credits system, for example—were pressing hard all during the months when Congress was debating the antitrust legislation. The movement toward new social and economic frontiers that these progressives demanded did not occur. Instead, a general reaction against further excursions into reform set in around the beginning of 1914, gradually permeated the administration and the majority membership of Congress, and gained momentum during the summer and early autumn as the antitrust discussions progressed in Congress. Indeed, by mid-November 1914 the President had become alienated from many progressive leaders in Congress, had attempted to build new support for his party among conservative and business elements, and had proclaimed the completion of the New Freedom reform program.

The first important cause of this ebbing of the reform impulse in 1914 was a business depression that began during late 1913 and varied in severity until the early months of 1915. It was world-wide in scope, the result of a tightening of credit in Europe because of the Balkan Wars and the fear of a general conflict and of the disorganization of international and domestic markets that followed the outbreak of the First World War.[1] In the United States, business failures increased sharply, and production declined slightly. Unemployment was widespread and especially acute in the metropolitan areas, in part because of a decline in construction, and in the coal and steel producing regions, occasioned in part by a decline in railroad purchases.[2]

---

[1] See the review of financial developments in 1914 by S. S. Fontaine, in the New York *World*, January 3, 1915.

[2] There were no comprehensive surveys of unemployment during this period, but special studies yielded valuable information. Returns received from labor organizations representing 66 per cent of the total trade union membership in Massachusetts revealed that 18.3 per cent of the members were unemployed at the end of December 1914, as compared with an average rate of 6.9 per cent for the period 1909-1914. Bureau of Statistics, Labor Division, Commonwealth of Massachusetts, *Thirtieth Quarterly Report on Unemployment in Massachusetts, Quarter Ending June 30, 1915*. A

Actually, it was no major depression, although it might have become one had not heavy European war purchases turned the tide in the spring of 1915; and it was not nearly as severe as the complaints of businessmen seemed to indicate.[3] The important point, however, is that it was sufficiently frightening to cast a pall over Washington and to have a profound impact upon Wilson and his advisers.

As early as December 1913 and January 1914 appeals begging the President to abandon his antitrust program and to give assurances to the business world began to pour into the White House from frightened businessmen.[4] In the administration circle, McReynolds, Garrison, Burleson, and Tumulty added their voices to these demands; indeed, among the President's official family only Bryan and McAdoo counseled pushing ahead with reform legislation.[5]

Wilson responded almost at once to these pressures by embarking upon a broad campaign calculated to ease the tension that existed between his administration and the business community. He did not give up his antitrust legislation, to be sure; but he accommodated that legislation, or allowed it to be accommodated, to meet the criticism of businessmen. As Representative Covington put it in an address before the Chicago Association of Commerce, "The President told me that he wanted to meet Big Business half way in considering the trust legislation programme, and that he wanted to be fair in every way."[6] Moreover, Wilson worked incessantly from the beginning of the antitrust discussions to the adoption of the final bills to make it clear that he would tolerate no reckless assaults against business and meant only to embody in statutory language the best thought of the business community.

---

survey by the Metropolitan Life Insurance Company of its industrial policy holders showed an unemployment rate of 18 per cent in January 1915. Mayor's Committee on Unemployment, New York City, *Report of the Mayor's Committee on Unemployment*, p. 11.

[3] See, e.g., Lee C. Bradley of Birmingham, Alabama, to W. W., April 9, 1914, Wilson Papers; John F. Fitzgerald of Boston to W. W., June 17, 1914, *ibid.*; Julian S. Carr of Durham, North Carolina, to W. W., July 10, 1914, *ibid.*; and Senator C. W. Watson of West Virginia to J. P. Tumulty, April 14, 1914, *ibid.*

[4] e.g., C. H. Dodge to E. M. House, December 19, 1913, House Papers; New York *World*, January 9 and 12, 1914; and scores of letters to Wilson from manufacturers' associations, chambers of commerce, manufacturers, businessmen's leagues, and the like, in the Wilson Papers, Series VI, Boxes 413, 433, and 435.

[5] House Diary, January 16, March 29, May 7 and 8, 1914.

[6] *New York Times*, July 10, 1914.

"We have had ten or fifteen years of ceaseless agitation about business," he declared, in a typical assurance. "During that length of time we have read stories in the newspapers and the magazines of the extravagantly wrong things that were going on, and an atmosphere of almost universal suspicion has been created; so that if a man became a business man in a big way he had the uncomfortable feeling that his fellow-men probably looked upon him as not coming by his money in the right way. . . . I just want to leave that thought with you—that we are not running amuck; we are trying to close this era of suspicion, of recrimination, by putting in the law what the moral judgment of the community has said ought to be there."[7]

This picture of a new Wilson, of the sober, constructive friend of business, was drawn many times by friendly reporters. "Instead of being a destroyer," one of them wrote, for example, "Mr. Wilson is a harmonizer. . . . [He] is curbing and driving the wild horses in Congress with a skill that does him the highest credit. I doubt if any other man, similarly placed, could hold such radical forces in check. Business has nothing to fear from Mr. Wilson so long as he continues his present course."[8]

Redoubling his efforts to win the confidence of the business and financial communities during the late spring and early summer of 1914, the President declared on numerous occasions that the current depression was "psychological," that the business of the country was fundamentally sound, that a gigantic boom would follow the enactment of the antitrust bills, and that he had only the friendliest feeling for businessmen.[9] "Of course," he wrote, for example, to a Boston banker, "I agree with you that the business men of the country as a body are as 'honest, high-minded, patriotic, and altruistic' as any other body of men in the country. We are settling down and I think that the period of suspicion and accusation will presently be behind us."[10] "I wish you would say," he advised Burleson a short time later, ". . . that I not only never said that 'big business is bad because it is big,'

[7] Speech to a delegation from the National Trade Association of Wholesalers, July 29, 1914, *New York Times*, July 30, 1914.

[8] Isaac F. Marcosson, "Wilson and Wall Street," *Saturday Evening Post*, CLXXXVI (February 21, 1914), 4.

[9] *Financial Age*, XXIX (June 6, 1914), 973-974; *New York Times*, June 16, 21, and 26, 1914. For comment, see the *Financial World*, XXII (June 27, 1914), 2; *The Independent*, LXXVII (June 29, 1914), 544-545; New York *Outlook*, CVII (July 4, 1914), 507-508; W. G. McAdoo to E. M. House, June 28, 1914, House Papers.

[10] W. W. to H. L. Higginson, July 3, 1914, Wilson Papers.

but again and again in my campaign speeches said what was practically the opposite, that neither I nor any thoughtful man was afraid of business because it was big."[11]

During the summer of 1914, furthermore, Wilson began for the first time to welcome leading bankers and businessmen to the White House,

"I wonder how I'd feel if there *was* something the matter with me?"
Sykes in the Philadelphia *Public Ledger*

ostensibly to seek their advice and cooperation. J. P. Morgan, Jr., came for a long and friendly chat on July 2, 1914, and received Wilson's assurances that he desired only to help all legitimate business, big and small.[12] "I am sincerely sorry that you should be so blue about the

[11] W. W. to A. S. Burleson, July 27, 1914, *ibid.*; also W. W. to H. L. Higginson, October 23, 1914, *ibid.*, for an expression of similar sentiments.
[12] *New York Times*, July 3, 1914; New York *World*, July 3, 1914.

situation," the President wrote afterward to cheer the Wall Street banker. "I believe that being blue is just the wrong thing, if you will permit me to say so. It is a situation which requires nothing more, in my judgment, than courage and the kind of intelligence which our bankers and men of affairs have shown themselves equal of applying to any circumstances that have yet arisen."[13] A delegation from the Chicago Association of Commerce called at the White House on July 8, 1914, a group from the Illinois Bankers' Association and Henry Ford, the Detroit automobile manufacturer, the following day. Before all of them the President radiated confidence and good will.[14]

The climax of Wilson's campaign—his appointment of a known conservative to the Interstate Commerce Commission and of a Federal Reserve Board composed in large part of representatives of big business and high finance—provoked a storm of opposition and hot words between the President and progressive leaders in Congress.

To men like La Follette, who had won comprehensive federal regulation of railroad rates only after many hard battles in the past, the perpetuation of progressive control over the Interstate Commerce Commission was a duty even more imperative than the enactment of new antitrust legislation. The issue was especially crucial during late 1913 and early 1914, first, because there were two vacancies on the I.C.C. and, second, because the railroads had petitioned the Commission for a 5 per cent increase in freight rates in May 1913 and had meanwhile launched a gigantic propaganda campaign to stimulate public support for the rate increase.[15] Even one conservative appointment to the I.C.C., progressives feared, might tip the balance in the Commission in favor of the railroads.

In spite of many appeals for relief for the railroads, Wilson stayed clear of the rate controversy until late January 1914, when he submitted to the Senate the nominations of Henry C. Hall of Colorado and Winthrop M. Daniels of New Jersey to the I.C.C. Hall, it turned out, was acceptable to the progressives and was promptly confirmed. Daniels had been a former professor of economics at Princeton and one of Wilson's most loyal supporters among the faculty. Appointed

[13] W. W. to J. P. Morgan, Jr., September 17, 1914, Wilson Papers.

[14] *New York Times*, July 9 and 10, 1914. For comment, see the New York *Nation*, xcix (July 9 and 16, 1914), 32, 61-62; *Chicago Record-Herald*, July 4, 1914; W. H. Taft to G. J. Karger, July 12, 1914, Taft Papers.

[15] For a comprehensive review of the railroad propaganda, see R. M. La Follette, "A Conspiracy Against Justice," *La Follette's Weekly*, vi (May 16, 1914), 1-2.

chairman of the New Jersey Board of Public Utility Commissioners by Governor Wilson in 1911, Daniels had earned a reputation for being perhaps the most "reactionary" public service commissioner in the United States.[16]

Progressive leaders in the Senate, including many of the President's best friends, were stunned when Wilson named Daniels to the I.C.C. Led by La Follette, they fought approval of the nomination by the interstate commerce committee; and, after the committee had acted favorably, they carried the fight to the Senate floor with such vehemence that the administration spokesmen advised the President to withdraw the nomination rather than risk defeat.[17] Wilson refused, and enough administration senators joined a solid conservative Republican bloc to put Daniels across on April 3, 1914.[18] But it was a narrow victory, and it left many progressives wondering whether the President had surrendered to the "interests." "What an inspiring spectacle to the millions who voted for Wilson as a true Progressive," La Follette exclaimed in disgust, "to see him in one short year triumph over progressive Democrats and progressive Republicans by securing the support of about all that remains of the old Aldrich Oligarchy in the United States Senate! It reminds thoughtful men of the beginning of the second year of the reign of one William Howard Taft."[19]

Yet this controversy was a tempest in a teapot as compared to the storm provoked by Wilson's appointment of an obviously conservative Federal Reserve Board in June 1914. McAdoo and House had engaged in an epic battle over the character and personnel of the new agency for several months after the approval of the Federal Reserve Act. Arguing that the Board should work in subordination to the Treasury, McAdoo pleaded frankly for the appointment of men who would work with him to break Wall Street's control over the nation's credit. "Please don't think me unduly fearful of the 'Money Trust,'" he wrote to the

---

[16] Daniels' reputation as a "reactionary" stemmed largely from his conviction that intangible assets and good will should be taken into account in determining rates that public service corporations and railroads should be permitted to charge. In the so-called Passaic gas company case, for example, Daniels voted to allow the company about 17 per cent of its physical valuation for intangible assets and 30 per cent in addition for its value as a going concern. Moreover, he allowed an annual return of 8 per cent upon the gross value of the company's property, including the value allowed for intangible assets and so-called good will.

[17] *New York Times*, April 3 and 4, 1914.

[18] The vote was taken in executive session, but La Follette printed the line-up in *La Follette's Weekly*, VI (April 18, 1914), 9.

[19] "Turning the Corner," *ibid.*, p. 1.

President on May 20, 1914. "I am not. I simply know, after a year's experience in the Treasury, that it is not a fiction, but a real thing and I want to keep the upper hand for the people while we have it."[20] House, on the other hand, fought just as hard for the appointment of a Federal Reserve Board that would win the confidence and cooperation of the banking community.[21]

Wilson not only agreed in principle with House but also suspected that McAdoo was trying to gain personal control of the Board;[22] and this suspicion made the President virtually impervious to the Secretary's advice. Given a free hand by Wilson, House consulted widely among conservative and banking circles during the early months of 1914 and played the dominant role in the selection of the members of the Board, although Wilson made several appointments on his own initiative.[23] The original nominees—excluding Richard Olney, conservative Boston lawyer and former Secretary of State, and Harry A. Wheeler, Chicago businessman and former president of the United States Chamber of Commerce, both of whom refused appointment— were Paul M. Warburg, partner in the Wall Street investment firm of Kuhn, Loeb & Company and recently a foe of the Federal Reserve bill; Charles S. Hamlin, Democrat of Boston; Thomas D. Jones, businessman from Chicago; William P. G. Harding, president of the First National Bank of Birmingham, Alabama; and Adolph C. Miller, a former professor of economics at the University of California.

It was almost more than bankers and business leaders could believe, this delegation of supervision over the nation's banking policies to a group of men so patently representative of the great financial and industrial interests. "To those who realize how important to the success of the new banking and currency system the composition of the Federal Reserve Board is to be," wrote one Wall Street editor in surprise, "the names of the members who will constitute that body, as announced this week by President Wilson,[24] will give general satisfac-

[20] W. G. McAdoo to W. W., May 20, 1914, Wilson Papers; also W. G. McAdoo to W. W., December 20, 1913, *ibid.*

[21] e.g., E. M. House to W. W., February 21, 1914, *ibid.*

[22] House Diary, December 22, 1913.

[23] See C. W. Eliot to E. M. House, December 19, 23, and 29, 1913, January 25 and February 2, 1914, House Papers; S. R. Bertron to E. M. House, March 21 and 30, 1914, *ibid.*; S. R. Bertron to W. W., February 4, 1914, Wilson Papers; W. W. to E. M. House, March 30, 1914, *ibid.*; E. M. House to W. W., March 31, 1914, *ibid.*; W. W. to C. H. McCormick, April 22, 1914, *ibid.*; W. W. to T. D. Jones, April 22, 1914, *ibid.*; W. W. to R. Olney, April 30, 1914, *ibid.*

[24] Wilson announced his first list of nominees, which included Olney and Wheeler, on May 4, 1914. He sent the revised list to the Senate on June 15, 1914.

tion. . . . The men chosen are fairly well known for conservatism and breadth of view, and their selection will go a long way toward restoring confidence among bankers and business men generally in the operation of the new system."[25] Everywhere throughout the country, except among extreme Republican partisans, financial and business spokesmen joined in a chorus of approval.[26]

Progressives, on the other hand, were aghast. "A more reactionary Federal Reserve Board could not have been found with a fine-tooth comb," one midwestern insurgent Republican senator exclaimed, for example, after reading the preliminary list of nominees. "Why, it looks as if Mr. [Frank A.] Vanderlip [president of the National City Bank of New York] has selected them. . . . The selections indeed could not have been worse. The reactionary bankers would be in control."[27]

Withholding comment for the most part until Wilson sent the Federal Reserve Board list to the Senate on June 15, 1914, the insurgents, led by Reed of Missouri, then opened fire on the two most vulnerable nominees, Paul M. Warburg and Thomas D. Jones. To progressives generally, Warburg was suspect because he was a member of a Wall Street firm and one of the leading advocates in the United States of a central bank. But the midwestern progressives had particular reason for opposing Jones, for he was a director in the International Harvester Company, the so-called Harvester Trust, which was almost universally hated by midwestern farmers and was in 1914 under state and federal indictment for being an illegal combination. "Had I nominated a man for an important position like this, who was a defendant in a Government suit under the anti-trust law," Taft observed sardonically, "the condemnation that would have followed it staggers my imagination. This only goes to show one of the great characteristics of the present state of the public mind, as viewed by Roosevelt and Wilson, namely, that reform is entirely personal."[28]

It was all most embarrassing to the President, because Jones was an old friend[29] who had agreed to accept appointment to the Board only

[25] *Financial Age*, xxix (May 9, 1914), 769.

[26] e.g., see the *Financial World*, xxii (May 9, 1914), 2-3; *Commercial West*, xxv (May 9, 1914), 12; New York *Journal of Commerce*, June 17, 1914; *New York Financial Chronicle*, June 20, 1914; *Boston Financial News*, June 18, 1914; *Washington Post*, June 23, 1914; S. R. Bertron to E. M. House, May 5, 1914, House Papers.

[27] *Boston Advertiser*, May 6, 1914.

[28] W. H. Taft to G. J. Karger, July 20, 1914, Taft Papers.

[29] As a member of the board of trustees of Princeton University, Jones had been fiercely loyal to Wilson during the battles over the quadrangle plan and the location

after Wilson had appealed to him in the name of their friendship.[30] After Senator Robert L. Owen warned that a hard battle impended in the banking committee, therefore, the President took personal charge of the campaign for Jones' confirmation. In an extraordinary letter to Owen on June 18, 1914, he made it clear that he was willing to risk his prestige in the fight.

"I am afraid that Mr. Thomas D. Jones is the man about whom the committee will have the least information," he began, "and I venture to write you this letter to tell you what I know, and fortunately I can say that I do really know it.

"I have been associated with Mr. Jones in various ways for more than fifteen years and have seen him tried by fire in causes which were like the very causes we are fighting for now. He has always stood for the rights of the people against the rights of privilege. . . .

"His connection with the Harvester Company is this: He owns one share, and only one share, of stock in the company which he purchased to qualify as a director. He went into the board of the Harvester Company for the purpose of assisting to withdraw it from the control which had led it into the acts and practices which have brought it under the criticism of the law officers of the Government and has been very effective in that capacity. His connection with those acts and practices is absolutely nil. His connection with it was a public service, not a private interest, and he has won additional credit and admiration for his courage in that matter.

". . . My close association with him was in the Board of Trustees of Princeton University, where he stood by me with wonderful address and courage in trying to bring the University to true standards of democracy by which it would serve not special classes but the general body of our youth. . . . He is . . . a man whom I can absolutely guarantee in every respect to the committee. He is the one man of the whole number who was in a peculiar sense my personal choice."[31]

The imperative of this letter was considerably weakened when some member of the banking committee gave a copy to the press, which published it on June 21, 1914, and when George W. Perkins, one of the directors of the Harvester Company, gave out a statement flatly denying that Jones had become a member of the board in order to

---

and control of the graduate college. Jones had also been a heavy contributor to the Wilson preconvention campaign fund in 1911 and 1912.

[30] W. W. to T. D. Jones, June 5, 1914, Baker Collection.
[31] W. W. to R. L. Owen, June 18, 1914, Wilson Papers.

reform the corporation.[32] The Senate banking committee, therefore, voted on July 2, 1914, to call Jones before it for further investigation. He came on July 6, 1914, and, during the course of a long grilling, declared that he had become a member of the Harvester board to oblige Cyrus H. McCormick, the company's chief owner, and that he fully approved of all the company's policies since he had become a director in 1909. He also disclosed that he and his brother, David B. Jones, were among the principal owners of the New Jersey Zinc Company, popularly known as the Zinc Trust.[33]

Meanwhile, the Senate banking committee had also refused to confirm Warburg and had requested him to appear for questioning, but the New York banker's pride was so wounded that he asked the President on July 3, 1914, to withdraw his nomination.[34] Wilson struck back angrily in a statement to the country on July 8:

"It would be particularly unfair to the Democratic Party and the Senate itself to regard it as the enemy of business, big or little. I am sure that it does not regard a man as an object of suspicion merely

[32] *New York Times,* June 21 and 23, 1914.

[33] *ibid.,* July 7, 1914. The question still remains, therefore, where Wilson obtained the information that caused him to inform Senator Owen that Jones had become a director of the Harvester Company in order to help bring it into conformity with the antitrust laws. Through the Justice Department, Wilson obtained a letter from Edwin P. Grosvenor, who had managed the antitrust suit against the Harvester Company in the Taft administration, declaring that Jones had had no connection with the acts and policies that had led to the indictment of the corporation. But nowhere in the Wilson Papers is there any evidence that Jones had become a director of the company, as Wilson said, "for the purpose of assisting to withdraw it from the control which had led it into the acts and practices which have brought it under the criticism of the law officers of the Government." We must conclude, therefore, that Wilson invented his explanation.

This conclusion is supported circumstantially by an exchange between Cyrus H. McCormick, Jr., and Wilson. Young McCormick wrote a warm letter to the President on July 12, 1914, accusing him of unfairly attacking his father in telling the Senate banking committee that Jones had become a director of the Harvester Company in order to help reform it. C. H. McCormick, Jr., to W. W., July 12, 1914, Wilson Papers.

Wilson's reply was ingenious but unconvincing. "I have not at present the text of the letter before me," he wrote, "but I think the quotation you mark . . . about Mr. Jones is correct. But you have put an entirely wrong construction on it. There is no man whom I respect or in whom I have a more complete and unwavering belief, as well as affection, than your father. I knew that Mr. Jones had gone into the directorate of the corporation at your father's request and that every purpose he had was also your father's purpose. I have been most unfortunate if I have conveyed any other implication. I wish now that I had made the statement different. I was making it with all this in mind and I am sure if you will recall the circumstances you will see that what I meant was true." W. W. to C. H. McCormick, Jr., July 23, 1914, *ibid.*

[34] P. M. Warburg to W. W., July 3, 1914, two letters, *ibid.*

because he has been connected with great business enterprises. It knows that the business of the country has been chiefly promoted in recent years by enterprises organized on a great scale and that the vast majority of the men connected with what we have come to call big business are honest, incorruptible and patriotic. . . . It is the obvious business of statesmanship at this turning point in our development to recognize ability and character, wherever it has been displayed, and unite every force for the upbuilding of legitimate business along the new lines which are now clearly indicated for the future."[35]

The Senate banking committee replied the following day, July 9, 1914, by voting, seven to four, to disapprove Jones' nomination and to postpone further action on Warburg until he had appeared in person for questioning. "It was impossible to draw the line between Mr. Jones and any other man who believes in pools, trusts, and combinations," explained Senator Gilbert M. Hitchcock of Nebraska who, together with Reed of Missouri, had joined the insurgent Republicans on the committee to defeat confirmation. "I cannot be sitting in the Senate drawing up anti-Trust bills and at the same time putting into office men who make trusts."[36] Privately most senators agreed.

Infuriated by the committee's defiance, Wilson abandoned caution, announced that he would carry the fight for Jones' confirmation to the Senate floor, and, more audaciously still, hinted that he would excommunicate any rebellious Democrat.[37] The fight broke out during a secret Senate session on July 14, 1914, and raged for several days as a number of senators who were normally aligned with the President joined Reed, the leader of the insurgents.[38] On July 15 the President called some of the waverers to the White House in an attempt to turn the tide; Secretary Bryan, Postmaster General Burleson, the Assistant Postmaster General, and Tumulty applied their heaviest pressure.[39] Then, on July 18, the administration played its last trump, by attempting to persuade the Senate Democratic leaders to call a caucus and make a vote for Jones' confirmation binding.[40] All such desperate measures failed; indeed, the number of insurgent Democratic senators increased as the battle reached its climax.

Privately Wilson conceded defeat—his first, incidentally, at the hands of either house of the Congress—on July 19 and 20, 1914.[41] But

[35] *New York Times,* July 9, 1914.   [36] New York *World,* July 10, 1914.
[37] *ibid.,* July 10 and 11, 1914.   [38] *New York Times,* July 15, 16, and 17, 1914.
[39] New York *World,* July 16, 1914.   [40] *New York Times,* July 19, 1914.
[41] W. W. to C. H. Dodge, July 19, 1914, Baker Collection; W. W. to C. R. Crane, July 20, 1914, Wilson Papers.

he would not surrender publicly and sent Thomas W. Gregory to Chicago to ask Jones to request the withdrawal of his nomination.[42] Jones complied gladly on July 20, 1914.[43] Angrier and more upset than he had been at any time since his defeat in the graduate college controversy at Princeton four years before, the President vented his feelings in a public letter that excoriated the insurgents and called for a new spirit toward big business.

"I believe that the judgment and desire of the country cry out for a new temper in affairs," he wrote to Jones, accepting his withdrawal. "The time has come when discriminations against particular classes of men should be absolutely laid aside and discarded as unworthy of the counsels of a great people. The effort for genuine social justice, for peace which is founded in common understanding and for prosperity, the prosperity of co-operation and mutual trust and confidence, should be a united effort, without partisan prejudice or class antagonism. It is only of such just and noble elements that the welfare of a great country can be compounded. We have breathed already too long the air of suspicion and distrust. The progress of reform is not retarded by generosity and fairness."[44]

The President next went to work to salvage the Warburg appointment. The New York banker was still sulking; but Wilson begged him to reconsider and agree to appear before the banking committee,[45] and Senator Hitchcock assured Warburg that the senators would treat him kindly.[46] Warburg, therefore, appeared for questioning on August 1 and 3 and was promptly approved by the committee and confirmed by the Senate on August 7, 1914. On the same day, the Senate confirmed Frederic A. Delano of Chicago, president of the Monon Railroad, whom Wilson had appointed to the Federal Reserve Board to replace Jones.[47]

Thus ended the Jones-Warburg affair, one of the bitterest and most significant episodes of the first Wilson administration. It revealed Wilson in extreme difficulties for the first time since his inauguration and, some men charged, confirmed his critics' accusations that he was overbearing and lacking in personal scruple in certain circumstances. Politically, the affair was a sign of the growing tension between the Presi-

---

[42] At least, so Gregory told Colonel House. House Diary, August 10, 1914.

[43] T. D. Jones to W. W., July 20, 1914, two letters, Wilson Papers.

[44] W. W. to T. D. Jones, July 23, 1914, *New York Times*, July 24, 1914.

[45] W. W. to P. M. Warburg, July 25, 1914, Wilson Papers.

[46] P. M. Warburg to W. W., July 29, 1914, *ibid*.

[47] *New York Times*, August 8, 1914.

dent and advanced progressives and further evidence of Wilson's intention to make his peace with the financial and business interests and to call for an end to reform and the beginning of a new era of mutual accommodation among all classes.

The country was rocked a few weeks before the outbreak of the Jones-Warburg controversy by the news of massacre and civil war in Colorado—the climax of a bitter struggle for the unionization of the coal miners in that state. One of the great tragedies of American labor history, the Colorado coal strike partially diverted public attention from the Jones-Warburg affair, stimulated an unprecedented public discussion of the root causes of social and economic discontent, and led to the military occupation of a large part of Colorado by the United States.[48]

The Colorado troubles of 1913 and 1914 were the culmination of social and economic tensions, class hatred, and outbreaks of unrestrained violence that had been mounting for thirty years in the coal mining counties in the southeastern part of the state. There had been one notable eruption in 1903 and 1904, when the United Mine Workers of America had led the workers in a strike for the eight-hour day and other demands. During this struggle, the operators—principally the Colorado Fuel & Iron Company, owned by the Rockefeller family—and the state militia had joined forces to suppress the strike and drive the union's leaders from the state.[49]

Conditions for the workers grew worse, not better, during the decade following the strike of 1903. The United Mine Workers came back in force for a second time in the Colorado coal region in early 1913 and, after an intensive organizational campaign had succeeded and peaceful efforts to win recognition had failed, called the miners out of the pits on September 23, 1913. From 80 to 85 per cent of them responded in a mass exodus from the company towns to a number of tent colonies. Tension and violence increased sharply during the next six weeks, as the operators imported several thousand guards and strikebreakers and

[48] The author wishes to acknowledge his indebtedness to the excellent study by his former student, George S. McGovern, "The Colorado Coal Strike, 1913-1914," unpublished Ph.D. dissertation, Northwestern University, 1953. For briefer surveys, see George P. West, *Report on the Colorado Strike* (prepared for the United States Commission on Industrial Relations in 1915); and Eugene Porter, "The Colorado Coal Strike of 1913: An Interpretation," *The Historian*, XII (Autumn 1949), 3-27.

[49] Ray S. Baker, "The Reign of Lawlessness: Anarchy and Despotism in Colorado," *McClure's Magazine*, XXIII (May 1904), 43-57.

huge quantities of arms and ammunition in preparation for general warfare, and state and federal mediators worked vainly to persuade the operators to accept a compromise settlement. Finally, the Governor of Colorado, Elias M. Ammons, yielded to the demands of the operators and the business and financial leaders of the state and sent the Colorado National Guard into the strike zone on October 28, 1913.

Events developed catastrophically from this time forward. Frequent clashes between the strikers and mine guards and national guardsmen compounded the bitterness and suspicion and culminated in a tragedy that plunged a large part of Colorado into virtual anarchy and seared the conscience of the American people. That tragedy was the so-called Ludlow Massacre of April 20, 1914, when state troops under the command of a psychopathic sadist charged and burned a large tent colony at Ludlow. Eight strikers, two young mothers, and eleven children perished in the smoke and flames.

It was more than the embattled strikers could bear. Throughout the strike area they rose in frenzied rebellion, seizing and destroying mining property and killing law officers and mine guards. As a contemporary investigator observed, "This rebellion constituted perhaps one of the nearest approaches to civil war and revolution ever known in this country in connection with an industrial conflict."[50] "The ruthless use of force against the strikers," a recent historian has added, "had finally led to the destruction of the police authority of the state. . . . Anarchy and unrestrained class warfare had this time reached a new peak in the long and bitter history of industrial warfare in Colorado."[51]

At once there poured into the White House pitiful appeals for help from the spokesmen of the miners in Colorado and of labor throughout the country, horrified protests from humanitarians, and a call for federal intervention from Governor Ammons, who warned that Colorado was unable to suppress the miners' insurrection and maintain order in the strike area.[52] Wilson had intervened indirectly earlier, in a futile attempt to persuade the mine owners to accept the mediation of the Labor Department; but he abhorred the thought of the military occupation of the territory of a state by the United States. Instead, he ap-

[50] G. P. West, *Report on the Colorado Strike*, p. 132.

[51] G. S. McGovern, "The Colorado Coal Strike, 1913-1914," p. 307.

[52] e.g., John P. White to W. W., April 21, 1914, Wilson Papers; J. M. Stonesifer to W. W., April 21, 1914, *ibid.*; E. L. Doyle to W. W., April 22, 1914, *ibid.*; *Rocky Mountain News* to W. W., April 25, 1914, *ibid.*; E. M. Ammons to W. W., April 25, 1914, *ibid.*

pealed personally to John D. Rockefeller to accept federal arbitration in order to avert the necessity of sending federal troops. But Rockefeller's son and spokesman, John D., Jr., refused,[53] and the President had no alternative but to order the army to occupy the strike zone on April 28, 1914.[54] Peace returned at once to southeastern Colorado, and Secretary Garrison and his army commanders worked in close association with officials in the Labor Department until the occupation ended in January 1915, earning credit for what one authority has called "the most successful police action by soldiers in American labor history."[55]

In the meantime, however, President Wilson had met one frustration after another in an effort to persuade the spokesman of the operators, John D. Rockefeller, Jr., to accept what Wilson called a "peaceful and humane settlement of the difficulties" in Colorado. The President used almost every conceivable weapon at his command. When the United Mine Workers agreed to abandon their demand for recognition, for example, Wilson sent Dudley Field Malone to plead personally with Rockefeller. But Rockefeller and the operators refused even to meet the union officials who, they said, were alone "responsible for the terrible reign of disorder and bloodshed."[56] Or again, during the summer of 1914, Labor Department mediators prepared a comprehensive plan providing for a three-year truce and the establishment of a federal arbitration board, but Rockefeller and the operators rejected the proposal, in part because the miners had approved it gratefully.[57]

Near the end of his patience, Wilson threatened to close the Colorado mines until the operators accepted the truce plan; and he appointed the arbitration commission in spite of the mine owners' refusal to cooperate.[58] It was a futile gesture, for the United Mine Workers were at the end of their resources and had to call a halt to the strike on December 10, 1914. Soon afterward, the operators proceeded to impose a settlement of their own making.

It almost seemed that fate was conspiring during the spring and summer of 1914 to end the period of grand achievement for the ad-

---

[53] W. W. to J. D. Rockefeller, April 25, 1914, *ibid.*; J. D. Rockefeller, Jr., to W. W., April 27, 1914, *ibid.*

[54] *New York Times*, April 29, 1914.

[55] G. S. McGovern, "The Colorado Coal Strike, 1913-1914," p. 359.

[56] *New York Times*, May 1, 1914.

[57] *ibid.*, September 8, 16, 23, 24, and 28, 1914.

[58] *ibid.*, October 30 and November 30, 1914.

ministration and to create intolerable troubles for Woodrow Wilson. The Jones-Warburg controversy, the civil war in Colorado, and the near-outbreak of general war with Mexico were disturbing enough, but they were merely a prelude to two overwhelming tragedies that engulfed the President in August 1914: the outbreak of war in Europe and the Far East, and the death of his wife Ellen.

There were certain signs during 1913 that Mrs. Wilson was losing strength, but the disease moved so slowly that no one knew that she was ill. The first evidence of the malady came on March 1, 1914, when she fell in her room. Wilson described the "accident" without suspecting its fatal cause. "My dear one two weeks ago had a very bad fall on the polished floor of her bedroom and has been in bed ever since from the effects of it," he wrote on March 15, 1914. "Coming as it did at the end of an exhausting social season of all sorts of functions and exacting duties, when she was fairly well worn out and in sore need of rest, the shock and the effect on her nerves went all the deeper. But there was no deep serious injury, I am thankful to say. At last the effects are wearing off."[59] "Mrs. Wilson is steadily recovering from the effects of her fall," the President wrote reassuringly a week later, "and has at no time been seriously ill. It was just a general jar from top to bottom, and her nerves have needed restoration."[60]

The soreness from the fall was soon gone, and yet Mrs. Wilson seemed unable to gain much strength during the following weeks. "I am sorry to say that Ellen does not make as rapid progress in the recovery of her strength as we had hoped," Wilson wrote to a relative on April 1, 1914. "She is entirely out of the woods, so far as the effects of her fall are concerned, but it has left her very weak indeed and she only sits up for a little while every day and has not yet got back appetite enough to build her up."[61] There were afterwards occasional signs of returning health, as Ellen fought to hide her weakness. She went to the Capitol to hear her husband deliver his Mexican message on April 20, 1914, and she managed to receive the guests at Eleanor's wedding on May 7, but near the end of May she had to give up and remain in her room.

Rallies alternated with declines as the disease—tuberculosis of the kidneys and Bright's disease—ran its course during the next two

[59] W. W. to Mary A. Hulbert, March 15, 1914, printed in R. S. Baker, *Woodrow Wilson*, IV, 473.
[60] W. W. to X, March 21, 1914, Wilson Papers.
[61] W. W. to X, April 1, 1914, *ibid.*

months. Not knowing the truth until near the end, the President was alternately heartened and discouraged. His letters tell the story:

"I am very, very blue and out of heart to-day," he wrote on June 7, 1914. "My dear one absolutely wore herself out last winter and this spring and has not even started to come up hill again. She can eat and retain almost nothing, and grows weaker and weaker, with a pathetic patience and sweetness all the while which make it all the more nearly heart-breaking for those of us who love her. There is nothing at all the matter with her organically: it is altogether functional; and the doctors assure us that all with care will come out right. But a nervous break down is no light matter and my heart is very heavy."[62]

"The dear lady here is at last beginning to come up hill," he wrote on June 21, 1914, after a seeming turn for the better, "and my reassurance lightens my heart immeasurably. For some time I was almost without hope: I thought, with leaden heart, that she was going to be an invalid, another victim of the too great burden that must be carried by the lady of the White House; but that fear, thank God, is past and she is coming along slowly but surely!"[63] Then came new discouragement, as Ellen failed rapidly during July. Still ignorant of the inevitable consequence, Wilson could write on July 28, 1914: "Mrs. Wilson's troubles are constantly taking on new forms and she seems, I must say, at present to be making little progress, and yet it still seems certain that there is nothing organic the matter and we are hoping and believing that it is only the weather that holds her back."[64]

But the end was near. Dr. Cary T. Grayson, the White House physician, moved into the room adjoining Ellen's on July 23, 1914. The President, who had been constant in his devotion, now sat by her bed until early in the mornings, watching vainly for some sign of improvement. On August 4 Dr. Grayson suggested that the President call his absent daughters, Margaret and Jessie, and Wilson understood. Early Thursday morning, August 6, 1914, Ellen told her husband that she had only one wish now—that Congress would enact the alley clearance bill for which she had worked so hard. A few hours later, Dr. Edward P. Davis of Philadelphia, the family's former physician, arrived at the White House. After examining Ellen, he took the President downstairs and told him that she could live only a few hours longer.

[62] W. W. to Mary A. Hulbert, June 7, 1914, printed in R. S. Baker, *Woodrow Wilson*, IV, 475.

[63] W. W. to Mary A. Hulbert, June 21, 1914, *ibid.*, pp. 475-476.

[64] W. W. to X, July 28, 1914, Wilson Papers.

All morning and into the afternoon Wilson and his daughters kept watch at the bedside. Tumulty brought news, before Ellen lost consciousness, that Congress would pass the alley bill. Ellen smiled and, drawing Dr. Grayson to her side, said, "Doctor, if I go away, promise me that you will take good care of my husband." Wilson was holding her hand when she died at five o'clock. He looked up and asked, "Is it all over?" Grayson nodded. Wilson rose quickly and went to a window; looking out over the White House grounds, he cried, "Oh, my God, what am I to do?"[65]

There were brief funeral services in the East Room at two o'clock in the afternoon of August 10, 1914, with only the family, members of the Cabinet and their wives, and delegations from the houses of Congress present. The Reverend J. H. Taylor of Washington read from John 14 and First Corinthians, and the Reverend Sylvester Beach of Princeton offered prayer: "We magnify Thy name for the gift of this precious life, for Thine image graciously reflected in her spirit and her character; for her love so tender, her loyalty so unflinching, her devotion to duty, her Christly unselfishness, her self-forgetfulness, her services for others, her charity. . . ."

Then the President, his daughters, Tumulty, and Ellen's brother, Stockton Axson, accompanied the hearse to Union Station and boarded a special train for Rome, Georgia, Ellen's girlhood home, for the interment. Church bells tolled, and crowds standing silently at railroad stations could see the President sitting beside the coffin as the train sped through the green hills of the Virginia Piedmont.[66]

The funeral train arrived at Rome at two-thirty o'clock the following afternoon, August 11, 1914. Eight of Ellen's cousins carried the coffin to the hearse, and the presidential party drove through black-draped streets to the First Presbyterian Church, where the Reverend G. G. Sydnor conducted a brief service and the choir sang two of Ellen's favorite hymns, "Art Thou Weary, Art Thou Languid" and "For All the Saints Who From Their Labors Rest." On the way to the Myrtle Hill Cemetery the procession passed near the house where Ellen had lived as a girl and the place on the banks of the Etowah River where she and Wilson had become engaged. Torrential rains began to fall as the cortege reached the cemetery. As Doctor Sydnor read the

[65] R. S. Baker, interview with C. T. Grayson, February 18-19, 1926, Baker Collection; *New York Times*, August 6 and 7, 1914.

[66] New York *World*, August 11, 1914; *New York Times*, August 11, 1914.

services at the grave, the President's iron control gave way finally, and he sobbed like a child.[67]

During the ensuing months Wilson passed through the direst emotional crisis of his life. A nation mourned, and the President's friends tried to share his sorrows; but he would not be comforted in his loneliness, and for two weeks he was nearly paralyzed by the pain of grief. Then he poured out his sorrow in a torrent of letters to old friends:

"At last I can speak a little. Until now a sort of dumb spirit seems to have had hold of my heart whenever I tried to speak to those who I knew really cared. To others I could speak, with little effort, and tell them how I appreciated their sympathy. But whenever I tried to speak to those bound to me by affection and intimate sympathy it seemed as if a single word would open the flood-gates and I would be lost to all self-control. . . .

"I never understood before what a broken heart meant, and did for a man. It just means that he lives by the compulsion of necessity and duty only and has no other motive force. Business, the business of a great country that must be done and cannot wait, the problems that it would be deep unfaithfulness not to give my best powers to because a great people has trusted me, have been my salvation; but, oh! how hard, how desperately hard, it has been to face them, and to face them worthily! Every night finds me exhausted,—dead in heart and body, weighed down with a leaden indifference and despair (so far as everything concerning myself is concerned). I am making a brave fight, the best I know how to make, to work out into the light and see my way. And I am not ungrateful; how could I be when I had her so many happy, happy years?"[68]

"For five months, nearly, I saw my dear one go slowly, slowly down the hill, a great fear growing darker and darker in my heart, the burden more and more nearly intolerable to my heart, while I tried to command myself for the great tasks which *had* to be performed. . . . I do not see the light yet; but it is not necessary for me to see it: I know that it shines, and I know where it shines. . . . All that I need do now is to go straight ahead with the near duty, and lean on that to be steadied: for it comes from where the light does."[69]

"Thank you with all my heart for your letter with the reports of conversations with Ellen. The whole thing touched me very deeply,—

[67] *ibid.*, August 12, 1914.   [68] W. W. to X, August 23, 1914.
[69] W. W. to X, September 6, 1914, Baker Collection.

your thoughtfulness and the sweet flavour of my dear one which the quotations so unmistakably carry. How wonderful she was, in her thought, which went to the heart of things, no less than in the whole loveliness of her nature! Every day, it seems to me, I find something new by which to measure my loss, which is yet truly immeasurable, and yet can be in part understood by those who knew her as we did. How empty everything (everything personal to myself) seems without her."[70]

Colonel House visited the President at Cornish, New Hampshire, during this period of deepest gloom. "The second afternoon," House writes, "as we were sitting on the terrace looking out over the broad Valley of the Connecticut, he began to talk of Mrs. Wilson and of what her loss meant to him personally. Tears came into his eyes, and he said he felt like a machine that had run down, and there was nothing left in him worth while. . . . He looked forward to the next two years and a half with dread. He did not see how he could go through with it. I was surprised at his desire to discuss Mrs. Wilson. He showed me photographs of her, read poems written about her, and talked of her as freely as if she were alive."[71]

So heavy was the pall of loneliness that there were times when Wilson lost the will to live. "He said," House recorded on November 6, 1914, "he was broken in spirit by Mrs. Wilson's death, and was not fit to be President because he did not think straight any longer, and had no heart in the things he was doing."[72] A short time later he visited Colonel House in New York City. "When we reached home," House wrote in his Diary, "he began to tell me how lonely and sad his life was since Mrs. Wilson's death, and he could not help wishing when we were out tonight that someone would kill him. He has told me this before. His eyes were moist when he spoke of not wanting to live longer, and of not being fit to do the work he had in hand. He said he had himself so disciplined that he knew perfectly well that unless someone killed him, he would go on to the end doing the best he could."[73]

Gradually the pain subsided and Wilson found salvation in unrelenting work. "You see," he explained, "I am trying just now what I must believe to be the most difficult thing in the world: I am trying to live, and to live without loss of energy and zest for the daily task,

---

[70] W. W. to X, October 2, 1914, Accessions to the Wilson Papers.
[71] House Diary, August 30, 1914.
[72] *ibid.*, November 6, 1914.   [73] *ibid.*, November 14, 1914.

on a broken heart. . . . It is possible; and I think the method is this: not to sit and look on,—especially not to sit and look on at oneself,—but to project oneself as far afield as possible, into fields where one's personal feelings count for nothing, or should count for nothing, except enhanced sympathy and quickened insight."[74]

"It seems, indeed," he wrote again, "as if my individual life were blotted out, or, rather, swallowed up, and consisted only of news upon which action must be taken. . . . How can one live an individual life in the midst of all this? What difference does it make what happens to him, or whether he can find happiness or not? The day's work must be done, and he must play his full part in doing it. It matters little how much life is left in him when the day is over. . . . I write this not to make complaint . . . but only to record a singular thing: how one in such circumstances seems to realize his submergence and to be made to feel that his individual life is suspended and cast out of the reckoning,—even in his own consciousness. He knows that his own happiness and enjoyment are neither here nor there in the place in which he is put, the task which a ruling of Providence has assigned him. . . . I long for the time when I may be released and allowed an individual life and daily fortune again. But here I must stay for a little while; and the less I analyze my feelings the better. They are wholly irrelevant, and only mess and belittle matters when they intrude. Woodrow Wilson does not matter; but the United States does and all that it may accomplish for its own people and the people of the world outside of it."[75]

While Wilson was passing through the dark valley, the party managers had been hard at work in preparation for the congressional campaign and election of 1914, when the voters would render their first verdict on the New Freedom. In the Democratic high command, William F. McCombs, the national chairman, still exercised titular leadership; but power had fallen to Tumulty, Burleson, Thomas J. Pence of North Carolina, and a coterie of other professionals.[76] Controlling most of the patronage, they began in June 1913 to strengthen the state organizations in preparation for the crucial test. Then, during the summer and autumn of 1914, Pence's office in Washington, known as the Permanent Headquarters of the Democratic National Committee, got the campaign into high gear. Working with the congressional cam-

[74] W. W. to X, October 15, 1914, Baker Collection.
[75] W. W. to X, November 22, 1914.
[76] John M. Blum, *Joe Tumulty and the Wilson Era*, p. 72.

paign committee, it sent Cabinet members and Democratic spellbinders into all the doubtful states. More important, it flooded the country with some 9,000,000 copies of a Campaign Text Book, pamphlets, and other propaganda pieces magnifying the accomplishments of the administration and the Democratic party.[77]

On the other side, the Republican leaders entered the campaign with high hopes that popular discontent stemming from the business depression would lead to a mass repudiation of the administration. Republican orators and publicists opened an early attack against the Underwood tariff, which they said had caused the depression. But the outbreak of the war in Europe in early August 1914 wrecked Republican hopes and plans even before the campaign had got seriously under way. The war diverted public attention from the domestic scene and, more important, stimulated a general disposition to stand by the President in this time of world crisis—a disposition which Democratic speakers and newspapers assiduously encouraged.[78] For the most part the Republican managers were forced to concentrate their energies upon rebuilding their shattered state and local organizations and upon winning back the rank and file of the now disintegrating Progressive party.

Engrossed in new complications in Mexico and in trying to define a policy of neutrality vis-à-vis the European belligerents, and weakened by the emotional crisis through which he was passing, the President had neither the heart nor the time to take to the stump. He officially opened the Democratic campaign on September 4, 1914, in a public letter refusing to take an active part. "In view of the unlooked-for international situation," he explained, "our duty has taken on an unexpected aspect. Every patriotic man ought now to 'stay on his job' until the crisis is passed. . . . My job, as I now know, can be done best only if I devote my whole thought and attention to it, and think of nothing but the duties of the hour. I am not at liberty, and shall not be, so far as I can now see, to turn away from those duties to undertake any kind of political canvass."[79]

[77] For a detailed review, see T. J. Pence to the Executive Campaign Committee of the Democratic National Committee, February 13, 1915, copy in the Wilson Papers.

[78] e.g., see George Harvey, "Uphold the President," *North American Review,* cc (October 1914), 481-484; Richard Olney to G. Harvey, October 17, 1914, printed in the *New York Times,* October 29, 1914; New York *World,* October 25, 1914; and the New York *Nation,* xcix (October 29, 1914), 514-515, for comment on the impact of the war on the congressional campaign of 1914.

[79] W. W. to F. E. Doremus, September 4, 1914, *New York Times,* September 7, 1914.

Of course the leader of the Democracy could not remain completely aloof while his cohorts were fighting in the field. Besieged by appeals from Democratic candidates, he replied with letters of endorsement[80] and even tried to persuade the editor of the *St. Louis Post-Dispatch* to support a corrupt Democratic candidate for Congress.[81] He made his most important contribution on October 17, in a long public letter to Representative Underwood reviewing the achievements of the Sixty-third Congress since March 1913 and appealing for a general vote of confidence by the re-election of a Democratic Congress.

"I wish I could speak by name of the many men who have so honorably shared in these distinguished labors," Wilson concluded. ". . . This letter may, I hope, serve in some sort as a substitute for that.

"I look forward with confidence to the elections. The voters of the United States have never failed to reward real service. They have never failed to sustain a Congress and Administration that were seeking, as this Congress and, I believe, this Administration, have sought, to render them a permanent and disinterested benefit in the shape of reformed and rectified laws. They know that, extraordinary as the record is which I have recited, our task is not done. . . . They know, too, that without a Congress in close sympathy with the Administration a whole scheme of peace and honor and disinterested service to the world, of which they have approved, cannot be brought to its full realization. I would like to go into the district of every member of Congress who has sustained and advanced the plans of the party and speak out my advocacy of his claim for re-election. But, of course, I cannot do that; and with so clear a record no member of Congress needs a spokesman. . . .

"The Democratic Party is now, in fact, the only instrument ready to the country's hand by which anything can be accomplished. It is united as the Republican Party is not; it is strong and full of the zest of sober achievement, and has been rendered confident by carrying out a great constructive programme such as no other party has attempted; it is absolutely free from entangling alliances which made the Republican Party, even before its rupture, utterly unserviceable as an instrument of reform; its thought, its ambition, its plans are of the vital present and the hopeful future. A practical nation is not likely to

[80] e.g., W. W. to J. W. Kern, September 29, 1914, *ibid.*, October 2, 1914; W. W. to George White, *ibid.*, October 3, 1914.

[81] W. W. to George S. Johns, September 19 and October 9, 1914; G. S. Johns to W. W., October 6, 1914, all in Wilson Papers.

reject such a team. . . . Every thoughtful man sees that a change of parties made just now would set the clock back, not forward. I have a very complete and very confident belief in the practical sagacity of the American people."[82]

Wilson's confidence was somewhat shaken by the action of the voters in the state and congressional elections on November 3, 1914. The Democratic majority in the House of Representatives was reduced from seventy-three to twenty-five; there was no change of party strength in the Senate; but the Republicans swept back into or stayed impressively in power in the key states of New York, Pennsylvania, Ohio, Illinois, Wisconsin, and Kansas. It was not a landslide, but Republican gains were so great as to point toward a probable Republican victory in 1916, especially if the dissolution of the Progressive party were complete by that time.

Leaders in the reform movement were everywhere discouraged. "The morning news is disappointing to the progressive minded," Brandeis wrote. "We are saddened by many defeats."[83] "Well, the cataclysm was just about what I expected it would be," Roosevelt observed, in what was in effect a requiem for the Progressive organization. "Our cause is exactly as good as ever and in the future some day it will be recognized. . . . But for various causes the time is not ripe now."[84] For Wilson, the election results were a bitter blow. It had not been worth while, he complained to Colonel House, to work so hard for two years and then to have the people virtually repudiate him. "People are not so stupid not to know that to vote against a Democratic ticket is to vote indirectly against me," he said.[85]

Studying the returns during the weeks following the election, analysts agreed that dissatisfaction over the depressed state of business affairs and a general sagging of the popular interest in reform had contributed to the Democratic reversal. They all agreed, however, that the chief cause had been the decline of the Progressive party and the return of many of its members to the G.O.P.[86] This was the most notable event of the campaign and the one with greatest significance for the future, for a return to traditional two-party politics would

[82] W. W. to O. W. Underwood, October 17, 1914, *New York Times*, October 19, 1914.

[83] L. D. Brandeis to Gifford Pinchot, November 4, 1914, Brandeis Papers.

[84] T. Roosevelt to A. B. Roosevelt, November 7, 1914, Roosevelt Papers.

[85] House Diary, November 4, 1914.

[86] *The Independent*, LXXX (November 16, 1914), 221-222; *Harper's Weekly*, LIX (November 21 and 28, 1914), 481, 524-525; *New Republic*, I (November 7, 1914), 3, 8-9.

inevitably mean the early triumph of the Republicans—unless unforeseen developments raised new issues and once again destroyed party lines.

From his lonely outpost during the weeks before and after the election, the President looked back upon the tumultuous course of American political history since the rise of progressivism and reflected in particular upon the significance of events since his own inauguration. What did it all mean, this great national uprising against organized wealth and special privilege that had begun with the Populists and had been carried forward by Bryan, Roosevelt, La Follette, and so many other men? What relation existed between the reforms accomplished since March 1913 and the progressive movement?

The conviction grew in Wilson's mind that the progressive movement had found fulfillment through the New Freedom program for the reorganization of American economic life, and that he had finished the work he set out to do in March 1913. During the campaign he wrote: "The reconstructive legislation which for the last two decades the opinion of the country has demanded. . . has now been enacted. That programme is practically completed. Until the present European war is over and normal conditions have been restored it will not be possible to determine how readily or how completely the business of the country has adjusted itself to the new conditions. . . . Meanwhile, and for a long time to come, legislative questions will be questions of progress, of suiting means to new ends, of facilitating business and using to the utmost the resources of the country in the vast development of our business and our enterprise, which, I think, has but just begun."[87]

"We have only to look back ten years or so," the President said again in a public letter to McAdoo two weeks after the election, "to realize the deep perplexities and dangerous ill-humors out of which we have now at last issued, as if from a bewildering fog, a noxious miasma. Ten or twelve years ago the country was torn and excited by an agitation which shook the very foundations of her political life, brought her business ideals into question, condemned her social standards, denied the honesty of her men of affairs, the integrity of her economic processes, the morality and good faith of many of the things which her law sustained.

"Those who had power, whether in business or in politics, were almost universally looked upon with suspicion, and little attempt was

[87] W. W. to Powell Evans, October 20, 1914, Wilson Papers.

made to distinguish the just from the unjust. They in turn seemed to distrust the people and to wish to limit their control. There was ominous antagonism between classes. Capital and labor were in sharp conflict without prospect of accommodation between them. Interests harshly clashed which should have co-operated.

"This was not merely the work of irresponsible agitators. There were real wrongs which cried out to be righted. . . . We were living under a tariff which had been purposely contrived to confer private favors upon those who were co-operating to keep the party that originated it in power, and in that all too fertile soil all the bad, interlacing growth and jungle of monopoly had sprung up. Credit, the very life of trade, . . . was too largely in the control of the same small groups who had planted and cultivated monopoly. The control of all big business, and by consequence of all little business, too, was for the most part potentially, if not actually, in their hands.

"And the thing stood so until the Democrats came into power last year. The legislation of the past year and a half has in a very large measure done away with these things. With their correction, suspicion and ill-will will pass away. . . . The future is clear and bright with promise of the best things. While there was agitation and suspicion and distrust and bitter complaint of wrong, groups and classes were at war with one another, did not see that their interests were common, and suffered only when separated and brought into conflict. Fundamental wrongs once righted, as they may now easily and quickly be, all differences will clear away. . . . We shall advance, and advance together, with a new spirit, a new enthusiasm, a new cordiality of spirited co-operation. It is an inspiring prospect. Our task is henceforth to work, not for any single interest, but for all the interests of the country as a united whole.

"The future will be very different from the past, which we shall presently look back upon, I venture to say, as if upon a bad dream. The future will be different in action and different in spirit, a time of healing because a time of just dealing and co-operation between men made equal before the law in fact as well as in name."[88]

How should this be interpreted? advanced progressives wondered. Was it a funeral oration for the New Freedom and progressivism as well? Was the Democratic party done with the business of reform? If what the President said were true, then where would the still powerful

[88] W. W. to W. G. McAdoo, November 17, 1914, *New York Times*, November 18, 1914.

forces agitating for advances toward new social and economic frontiers go? And what kind of progressive leader was Wilson to abandon the field after the battle had just begun?

Herbert Croly, the most perceptive philosopher of the advanced groups, tried to answer these questions. "How can a man of his [Wilson's] shrewd and masculine intelligence possibly delude himself into believing the extravagant claims which he makes on behalf of the Democratic legislative achievement. . . ?" Croly began. "How many sincere progressives follow him in believing that this legislation has made the future clear and bright with the promise of best things? Where will such leadership finally land the Democratic party and the progressive movement?

"President Wilson could not have written his letter unless he had utterly misconceived the meaning and the task of American progressivism. After every allowance has been made for his justifiable pride . . . , there remains an ominous residue of sheer misunderstanding. Any man of President Wilson's intellectual equipment who seriously asserts that the fundamental wrongs of a modern society can be easily and quickly righted as a consequence of a few laws passed between the birth and death of a single Congress, casts suspicion either upon his own sincerity or upon his grasp of the realities of modern social and industrial life. Mr. Wilson's sincerity is above suspicion, but he is a dangerous and unsound thinker upon contemporary political and social problems. He has not only, as he himself has said, 'a single-track mind,' but a mind which is fully convinced of the everlasting righteousness of its own performances and which surrounds this conviction with a halo of shimmering rhetoric. He deceives himself with these phrases, but he should not be allowed to deceive progressive popular opinion."[89]

It was Croly, not Wilson, who read correctly the future course of American political history. It was only the New Freedom phase of progressivism that had ended in the autumn of 1914. Wilson, the apostle of *laissez faire* and the opponent of advanced federal social and economic reform, had indeed fulfilled his mission, and with a minimum of concessions to advanced concepts. But the future was still "clear and bright with promise" for the progressive movement. Indeed, in the months to come it was Wilson himself who would lead the American people forward in their progress toward a more democratic economic and social order.

[89] *New Republic,* 1 (November 21, 1914), 7.

Bibliography of Sources and Works Cited[1]

THE author wishes to acknowledge his indebtedness to the following publishers:

To Appleton-Century-Crofts, Inc., for permission to quote from *The Political Education of Woodrow Wilson*, by James Kerney.

To the Bobbs-Merrill Company, for permission to quote from *Presidents I've Known and Two Near Presidents*, by Charles Willis Thompson.

To Doubleday, Inc., for permission to quote from *An Adventure in Constructive Finance*, by Carter Glass; *Eight Years with Wilson's Cabinet*, by David F. Houston; *The True Story of Woodrow Wilson*, by David Lawrence; and *Woodrow Wilson As I Know Him*, by Joseph P. Tumulty.

To Harcourt, Brace, and Company, for permission to quote from *The Latin American Policy of the United States*, by Samuel F. Bemis.

To the Houghton Mifflin Company, for permission to quote from *Joe Tumulty and the Wilson Era*, by John M. Blum; *Forty-two Years in the White House*, by Irwin H. Hoover; and *Crowded Years, the Reminiscences of William Gibbs McAdoo*, by William G. McAdoo.

To the John C. Winston Company, for permission to quote from *The Memoirs of William Jennings Bryan*, by William J. and Mary B. Bryan.

To the Johns Hopkins Press, for permission to quote from *The Origins of the Foreign Policy of Woodrow Wilson*, by Harley Notter.

To the J. B. Lippincott Company, for permission to quote from *The Gentleman and the Tiger, The Autobiography of George B. McClellan, Jr.*, edited by Harold C. Syrett.

To the University of North Carolina Press, for permission to quote from *The Wilson Era, Years of Peace—1910-1917*, by Josephus Daniels.

To the Yale University Press, for permission to quote from *The United States Oil Policy*, by John Ise.

And to the following persons and libraries, for permission to quote from books, letters, and diaries:

Mr. Allen W. Dulles, the Diary of Robert Lansing; Dr. Sherman Kent, letters and other writings of William Kent; Mr. Merritt Lane, Jr., letters of Lindley M. Garrison; Mrs. Eleanor Wilson McAdoo, *The Woodrow Wilsons*; Mr. William F. Schnitzler, Secretary-Treasurer, American Federation of Labor and Congress of Industrial Organizations, letters of Samuel Gompers; Dr. Charles Seymour and the Yale University Library, the Diary of

---

[1] This bibliography includes *only* those works and sources cited in the footnotes in this volume. For a full review and analysis of the sources and literature dealing with the New Freedom period, see Arthur S. Link, *Woodrow Wilson and the Progressive Era* (New York: Harper & Brothers, 1954), pp. 283-313.

Edward M. House, letters of E. M. House, and letters in the Papers of E. M. House; Mrs. Woodrow Wilson, letters of Woodrow Wilson.

MANUSCRIPTS

The Diary of Chandler P. Anderson, Library of Congress.

The Papers of Warren Worth Bailey, Princeton University Library.

The Ray Stannard Baker Collection of Wilsonia, Library of Congress.

The Papers of Albert J. Beveridge, Library of Congress.

The Papers of Louis D. Brandeis, Law Library of the University of Louisville.

The Papers of William E. Brooks, Library of Congress.

The Papers of Albert S. Burleson, Library of Congress.

The Papers of William Jennings Bryan, Library of Congress.

The Papers of William Jennings Bryan, National Archives.

The Papers of S. Weetman Pearson, First Viscount Cowdray, in possession of Viscount Cowdray of London.

The Diary and Papers of Josephus Daniels, Library of Congress.

The Papers of the Department of State, National Archives.

The Papers of Carter Glass, University of Virginia Library.

The Papers of Lindley M. Garrison, Princeton University Library.

The Letterbooks of Samuel Gompers, American Federation of Labor Building, Washington, D.C.

The Papers of Thomas Watt Gregory, Library of Congress.

The Diary and Papers of Edward M. House, Yale University Library.

The Papers of David F. Houston, Harvard University Library.

The Papers of William Kent, Yale University Library.

The Papers of Claude Kitchin, University of North Carolina Library.

The Papers of Philander C. Knox, Library of Congress.

The Diary, Desk Diary, and Papers of Robert Lansing, Library of Congress.

The Papers of Richard Olney, Library of Congress.

The Diary and Papers of Walter H. Page, Harvard University Library.

The Papers of Frank L. Polk, Yale University Library.

The Papers of Theodore Roosevelt, Library of Congress.

The Papers of Elihu Root, Library of Congress.

The Papers of Hugh L. Scott, Library of Congress.

The Papers of William Howard Taft, Library of Congress.

The Papers of Charles Willis Thompson, Princeton University Library.

The Thompson-Wilson Correspondence, Princeton University Library.

The Papers of Daniel A. Tompkins, University of North Carolina Library.

The Papers of George Sylvester Viereck, Yale University Library.

The Papers of Oswald Garrison Villard, Harvard University Library.

The Papers of Thomas J. Walsh, Library of Congress.

The Papers of Henry Watterson, Library of Congress.

The Papers of William B. Wilson, Pennsylvania Historical Society.
The Papers of Woodrow Wilson, Library of Congress.
The Papers of Woodrow Wilson, New Jersey State Library, Trenton.

PUBLIC DOCUMENTS

Publications of the United States Government
Congressional Record, 63d Cong., 1st through the 3d sess. Washington, 1913-1915.
Corwin, Edward S. (ed.) *The Constitution of the United States of America, Analysis and Interpretation.* Document No. 170, 82d Cong., 2d sess., Washington, 1953.
Department of Agriculture. *Electric Power Development in the United States*, 3 v. Senate Document No. 316, 64th Cong., 1st sess. Washington, 1916.
[Department of the Interior] Lane, Franklin K., "Annual Report of the Secretary of the Interior," in *Reports of the Department of the Interior, 1913.* Washington, 1914.
[Department of the Interior] Lane, Franklin K., "Annual Report of the Secretary of the Interior," in *Reports of the Department of the Interior, 1914.* Washington, 1915.
[Department of the Interior] "Report of the Commissioner of the General Land Office," in *Reports of the Department of the Interior, 1917.* Washington, 1918.
Department of Justice. *Annual Report of the Attorney General of the United States for the Year 1913.* Washington, 1913.
Department of Justice. *Annual Report of the Attorney General of the United States for the Year 1914.* Washington, 1914.
Department of State. *Papers Relating to the Foreign Relations of the United States, 1912.* Washington, 1919.
Department of State. *Papers Relating to the Foreign Relations of the United States, 1913.* Washington, 1920.
Department of State. *Papers Relating to the Foreign Relations of the United States, 1914.* Washington, 1922.
Department of State. *Papers Relating to the Foreign Relations of the United States, 1915.* Washington, 1924.
Department of State. *Papers Relating to the Foreign Relations of the United States, 1916.* Washington, 1925.
Department of State. *Papers Relating to the Foreign Relations of the United States, The Lansing Papers, 1914-1920*, 2 v. Washington, 1939-1940.
[House of Representatives] House Banking and Currency Committee, *Banking and Currency Reform. Hearings before Subcommittee . . .* , 13 parts. 62d Cong., 3d sess. Washington, 1913.
[House of Representatives] *Report of the Committee Appointed Pursuant*

to House Resolutions 429 and 504 to Investigate the Concentration of Control of Money and Credit. 62d Cong., 3d sess., Report No. 1593. Washington, 1913.

[Rural Credits Commission] *Agricultural Cooperation and Rural Credit in Europe* ..., 63d Cong., 2d sess., Senate Document 261. Washington, 1914.

[Rural Credits Commission] *Agricultural Credit* ..., 3 parts. 63d Cong., 2d sess., Senate Document 380. Washington, 1914.

[United States Senate] Senate Judiciary Committee. *Maintenance of Lobby to Influence Legislation, Hearings* ..., 4 v. 63d Cong., 1st sess. Washington, 1913.

Publications of American States and Cities

Commonwealth of Massachusetts, Bureau of Statistics, Labor Division. *Thirtieth Quarterly Report on Unemployment in Massachusetts, Quarter Ending June 30, 1915.* Boston, 1915.

State of New Jersey. *Acts of the One Hundred and Thirty-Seventh Legislature of the State of New Jersey.* Union Hill, N.J., 1913.

State of New Jersey. *Journal of the Sixty-Ninth Senate of the State of New Jersey.* Trenton, 1913.

State of New Jersey. *Minutes of Votes and Proceedings of the One Hundred and Thirty-Seventh General Assembly.* Trenton, 1913.

City of New York, Mayor's Committee on Unemployment. *Report of the Mayor's Committee on Unemployment.* New York City, 1916.

Publications of Foreign Governments

Republic of Costa Rica. *Anexos de la Demanda de la República de Costa Rica. . . .* San José, 1916.

Republic of Costa Rica. *Demanda de la República de Costa Rica contra la de Nicaragua, ante la Corte de Justicia Centro-americana, con motivo de una Convención firmada par la segunda con la República de los Estados Unidos de América, para la venta del río San Juan, y otros objetos.* San José, 1916.

Republic of Germany. *Die Grosse Politik der Europäischen Kabinette, 1871-1914,* 40 v. in 54 v. Berlin, 1926.

CORRESPONDENCE AND COLLECTED WORKS

Baker, Ray Stannard. *Woodrow Wilson, Life and Letters,* 8 v. Garden City: Doubleday, Page, and Doubleday, Doran, 1927-1939.

Baker, Ray Stannard and William E. Dodd (eds.). *The Public Papers of Woodrow Wilson,* 6 v. New York: Harper & Brothers, 1925-1927.

Hendrick, Burton J. *The Life and Letters of Walter H. Page,* 3 v. Garden City: Doubleday, Page, 1924-1926.

Lane, Anne W. and Louise H. Wall (eds.). *The Letters of Franklin K. Lane, Personal and Political.* Boston: Houghton Mifflin, 1922.

Morison, Elting E. (ed.). *The Letters of Theodore Roosevelt,* 8 v. Cambridge: Harvard University Press, 1951-1954.

Seymour, Charles (ed.). *The Intimate Papers of Colonel House,* 4 v. Boston: Houghton Mifflin, 1926-1928.

White, Henry. *The Roster of the Round Table Dining Club.* New York: privately printed, 1926.

AUTOBIOGRAPHIES AND MEMOIRS

Bryan, William J. and Mary B. *The Memoirs of William Jennings Bryan.* Philadelphia and Chicago: John C. Winston, 1925.

Daniels, Jonathan. *The End of Innocence.* Philadelphia: J. B. Lippincott, 1954.

Daniels, Josephus. *The Wilson Era, Years of Peace—1910-1917.* Chapel Hill: University of North Carolina Press, 1944.

Dixon, Thomas. "Southern Horizons: An Autobiography." Unpublished MS. in the possession of Mrs. Thomas Dixon, Raleigh, N.C.

Glass, Carter. *An Adventure in Constructive Finance.* Garden City: Doubleday, Page, 1927.

Hoover, Irwin H. *Forty-two Years in the White House.* Boston: Houghton Mifflin, 1934.

Houston, David F. *Eight Years with Wilson's Cabinet, 1913 to 1920,* 2 v. Garden City: Doubleday, Page, 1926.

McAdoo, Eleanor Wilson. *The Woodrow Wilsons.* New York: Macmillan, 1937.

McAdoo, William G. *Crowded Years, the Reminiscences of William G. McAdoo.* Boston: Houghton Mifflin, 1931.

McCombs, William F. *Making Woodrow Wilson President.* New York: Fairview, 1921.

Myers, William S. (ed.). *Woodrow Wilson: Some Princeton Memories.* Princeton: Princeton University Press, 1946.

Rublee, George. "The Original Plan and Early History of the Federal Trade Commission," *Proceedings of the Academy of Political Science,* XI (January 1926), 114-120.

Syrett, Harold C. (ed.). *The Gentleman and the Tiger, The Autobiography of George B. McClellan, Jr.* Philadelphia: Lippincott, 1956.

Thompson, Charles Willis. *Presidents I've Known and Two Near Presidents.* Indianapolis: Bobbs-Merrill, 1929.

Tumulty, Joseph P. *Woodrow Wilson As I Know Him.* Garden City: Doubleday, Page, 1921.

Zaragoza, Morelos, "Truth of the 'Dolphin' Incident at Tampico," Mexico City *El Excelsior,* December 6, 1931.

MISCELLANEOUS CONTEMPORARY WORKS

Bingham, Hiram. *The Monroe Doctrine, An Obsolete Shibboleth*. New Haven: Yale University Press, 1913.

Blakeslee, George H. (ed.). *Latin America*. New York: Stechert and Co., 1914.

Brandeis, Louis D. *Other People's Money and How the Bankers Use It*. New York: Frederick A. Stokes Company, 1914.

Glass, Carter. *Speech of Hon. Carter Glass of Virginia, December 22, 1913*. Washington: Government Printing Office, 1914.

Grimke, Francis J. *Excerpts from a Thanksgiving Sermon*. Washington: privately printed, 1914.

Johnson, Robert Underwood. *The Exemption of Coastwise Shipping. Why It Should Be Repealed*. New York: New York Peace Society, 1913.

Laughlin, J. Laurence (ed.). *Banking Reform*. Chicago: The National Citizens' League for the Promotion of a Sound Banking System, 1912.

Morawetz, Victor. *The Banking and Currency Problem in the United States*. New York: North American Review Publishing Company, 1909.

Sherrill, Charles H. *Modernizing the Monroe Doctrine*. Boston: Houghton Mifflin, 1916.

Untermyer, Samuel. *Who Is Entitled to the Credit for the Federal Reserve Act? An Answer to Senator Carter Glass*. New York: n.p., 1927.

Usher, Roland G. *Pan-Americanism, A Forecast of the Inevitable Clash Between the United States and Europe's Victor*. New York: Century, 1915.

[Villard, Oswald Garrison?] *A Proposal for a National Race Commission to be Appointed by the President of the United States, Suggested by the National Association for the Advancement of Colored People*. New York [?]: n.p., c. 1912.

Warburg, Paul M. *The Owen-Glass Bill, Some Criticisms and Suggestions*. New York: n.p., 1913.

West, George P. *Report on the Colorado Strike*. Washington: United States Commission on Industrial Relations, 1915.

Willis, H. Parker. *The Federal Reserve System, Legislation, Organization and Operation*. New York: Ronald Press, 1923.

Wilson, Woodrow. *Leaders of Men* (T. H. Vail Motter, ed.). Princeton: Princeton University Press, 1952.

Wilson, Woodrow. *The New Freedom, A Call for the Emancipation of the Generous Energies of a People*. New York: Doubleday, Page, 1913.

NEWSPAPERS CITED

Atlanta Georgian and News, 1913.

Birmingham, England, *Daily Post*, 1914.

Bogotá, Colombia, *La Crónica*, 1914.
Bogotá, Colombia, *El Neuvo Tiempo*, 1914.
Bogotá, Colombia, *La Unidad*, 1914.
Boston Advertiser, 1914.
Boston Financial News, 1914.
Boston Globe, 1913.
Boston *Guardian*, 1913.
Boston Journal, 1912.
Boston Post, 1913.
Boston Transcript, 1913.
Boston Traveler, 1914.
Brussels *L'Indépendance Belge*, 1914.
Budapesti Hirlap, 1914.
Buenos Aires *La Nación*, 1914.
Buenos Aires *La Prensa*, 1914.
Charlotte (N.C.) *Daily Observer*, 1913.
Chicago *Daily Tribune*, 1914.
Chicago Record-Herald, 1914.
Jersey City *Jersey Journal*, 1912-1913.
Lexington (Ky.) *Herald*, 1914.
London *Daily Chronicle*, 1913-1914.
London *Financial News*, 1914.
London *Morning Post*, 1913.
London *Observer*, 1914.
London *Pall Mall Gazette*, 1913-1914.
London *Times*, 1913.
Mexico City *El Diario*, 1913.
Mexico City *El Imparcial*, 1914.
Mexico City *El Pais*, 1914.
Moscow *Russkoe Slovo*, 1914.
Newark Evening News, 1912-1913.
Newark Evening Star, 1913.
New York *Amsterdam News*, 1913.
New York Evening Post, 1913.
New York Financial Chronicle, 1914.
New York *Journal of Commerce*, 1912-1914.
New York Press, 1912.
New York Times, 1912-1915.
New York *World*, 1912-1914.
Richmond News Leader, 1912.
Richmond *Times-Dispatch*, 1912.
Rio de Janerio *Jornál do Commercio*, 1914.
Rio de Janerio *O Paíz*, 1914.

Saloniki *L'Indépendant*, 1914.
San Salvador, Costa Rica, *La Prensa*, 1916.
Springfield (Mass.) *Republican*, 1913-1914.
Springfield (Mass.) *Union*, 1913.
St. Petersburg *Novoe Vremya*, 1914.
St. Petersburg *Retch*, 1914.
Tokyo *Asahi Shimbun*, 1913.
Tokyo *Chuo Shimbun*, 1913.
Tokyo *Japan Advertiser*, 1913.
Tokyo *Japan Times*, 1913.
Tokyo *Jiji Shimbo*, 1913.
Tokyo *Kokumin Shimbun*, 1913.
Tokyo *Nichi Nichi Shimbun*, 1913.
Tokyo *Yorozu Choho*, 1913.

PERIODICALS CITED FOR EDITORIAL OPINION

America, 1913.
American Federationist, 1915.
Bankers Magazine, 1913.
Baptist Standard (Dallas), 1914.
Christian Advocate (Nashville), 1913.
Christian Advocate (New York), 1913-1914.
Commercial West (Minneapolis), 1913-1914.
The Commoner (Lincoln, Neb.), 1913.
Congregationalist and Christian World, 1913, 1916.
The Economist (London), 1913-1914.
Everybody's Magazine, 1916.
Financial Age, 1913.
Financial World, 1913.
Harper's Weekly, 1913-1915.
The Independent, 1913-1914.
Journal of the American Bankers Association, 1913.
La Follette's Weekly Magazine (Madison, Wisc.), 1913-1914.
La Follette's Magazine (Madison, Wisc.), 1914.
Literary Digest, 1915.
Lutheran Observer, 1913.
The Menace, 1915.
The Nation (London), 1913-1914.
The Nation (New York), 1913-1914.
New Republic, 1914-1916.
North American Review, 1915.
The Outlook (London), 1914.
The Outlook (New York), 1913-1914.

Pentecostal Herald (Louisville), 1913.
The Presbyterian, 1913.
Presbyterian Banner, 1914.
The Public (Chicago), 1913-1914, 1916.
Rand-McNally's Bankers' Monthly, 1913.
The Spectator (London), 1913.
The Statist (London), 1913-1914.
The Survey, 1913-1914.
Texas Bankers Record, 1913-1914.
World's Work, 1913, 1915.

SIGNED CONTEMPORARY ARTICLES

Abbott, Ernest H., "The New Administration: An Impression," New York *Outlook*, CIII (April 5, 1913), 759-762.

An American Diplomat, "The Diplomatic Service—Its Organization and Demoralization," New York *Outlook*, CVI (March 7, 1914), 533-538.

Atwood, Albert W., "Telephone Securities and Government Ownership," *Harper's Weekly*, LVIII (November 8, 1913), 29-31.

Baker, Ray S., "The Reign of Lawlessness: Anarchy and Despotism in Colorado," *McClure's Magazine*, XXIII (May 1904), 43-57.

Baker, Ray S., "Wilson," *Collier's*, LVIII (October 7, 1916), 5-6.

Barrett, John, "A Pan-American Policy: The Monroe Doctrine Modernized," *The Annals of the American Academy*, LIV (July 1914), 1-4.

Barton, George, "Woodrow Wilson: His Human Side," *Current History*, XXII (April 1925), 1-9.

Bicknell, Mrs. Ernest P., "The Home-Maker of the White House," *The Survey*, XXXIII (October 3, 1914), 19-22.

Blakeslee, George H., "A New Basis Needed for the Monroe Doctrine," *North American Review*, CXCVIII (December 1913), 779-789.

Blythe, Samuel G., "Mexico: The Record of a Conversation with President Wilson," *Saturday Evening Post*, CLXXXVI (May 23, 1914), 3-4, 71.

Blythe, Samuel G., "Our New President," *Saturday Evening Post*, CLXXXV (March 1, 1913), 3-4, 48-49.

Blythe, Samuel G., "A Talk with the President," *Saturday Evening Post*, CLXXXVII (January 9, 1915), 3-4, 37-38.

Blythe, Samuel G., "Wilson in Washington," *Saturday Evening Post*, CLXXXVI (November 8, 1913), 8-9, 44-45.

Bramhall, J. T., "California and the Japanese: I—An Existing Menace," New York *Outlook*, CV (November 1, 1913), 477-478.

Brandeis, Louis D., "The Solution of the Trust Problem," *Harper's Weekly*, LVIII (November 8, 1913), 19.

Brooks, Sydney, "A British View of the Mexican Problem," *North American Review*, CXCVIII (October 1913), 444-456.

Brooks, Sydney, "President Wilson," London *Outlook*, xxxv (March 6, 1915), 299.

Brooks, Sydney (unsigned), "A Premier-President," London *Nation*, xiii (May 17, 1913), 259-260.

Brooks, Sydney (unsigned), "President Wilson's Record," London *Nation*, xvi (March 6, 1915), 709-710.

Brown, L. Ames, "President Wilson and Publicity," *Harper's Weekly*, lviii (November 1, 1913), 19-21.

Creel, George, "Four-Flush Radicals. I. Reed of Missouri," *Harper's Weekly*, lix (August 8, 1914), 124-126.

Croly, Herbert, "Unregenerate Democracy," *New Republic*, vi (February 5, 1916), 17-19.

Daniels, Josephus, "Training Our Bluejackets for Peace," *The Independent*, lxxvi (December 11, 1913), 490-492.

Evans, Elizabeth G., "An Audience at the White House," *La Follette's Weekly*, vi (February 14, 1914), 5.

Furuseth, Andrew, "The Dawn of Another Day," *American Federationist*, xxii (September 1915), 717-722.

Gompers, Samuel, "Antitrust Law and Labor," *American Federationist*, xxi (January 1914), 35, 37.

Gompers, Samuel, "Antitrust Law Enmeshes Labor," *American Federationist*, xxi (March 1914), 228.

Gompers, Samuel, "The Charter of Industrial Freedom," *American Federationist*, xxi (November 1914), 957-974.

Gompers, Samuel, "Immigration Legislation Effected," *American Federationist*, xxiv (March 1917), 189-195.

Gompers, Samuel, "Labor's Magna Carta—Demand It," *American Federationist*, xxi (July 1914), 553-557.

Gompers, Samuel, "The Significance of that 'Rider,'" *American Federationist*, xx (August 1913), 621-622.

Hale, William B., "Watching President Wilson at Work," *World's Work*, xxvi (May 1913), 71-72.

Hapgood, Norman, "The Shields Bill," *Harper's Weekly*, lxii (March 25, 1916), 295.

Hapgood, Norman, "Water Power in Congress," *Harper's Weekly*, lxii (April 15, 1916), 391.

Harding, Gardner, "Congress Quit," *Everybody's Magazine*, xxxiv (April 1916), 405-417.

Harvey, George, "An Appeal to the President," *Harper's Weekly*, lvii (May 17, 1913), 3.

Harvey, George, "The Case of Brother Pindell," *North American Review*, cxcviii (December 1913), 752-759.

Harvey, George, "The Diplomats of Democracy," *North American Review*, cxcix (February 1914), 161-174.

Harvey, George, "The House Has Done Its Part," *Harper's Weekly*, LVII (May 17, 1913), 4.

Harvey, George, "Mr. Bryan Rides Behind," *North American Review*, CXCIX (March 1914), 321-334.

Harvey, George, "Preparedness a Political Issue," *North American Review*, CCIII (April 1916), 481-492.

Harvey, George, "The President and Mexico," *North American Review*, CXCVIII (December 1913), 737-744.

Harvey, George, "Six Months of Wilson," *North American Review*, CXCVIII (November 1913), 577-608.

Harvey, George, "Uphold the President," *North American Review*, CC (October 1914), 481-484.

Hendrick, Burton J., "The Case of Josephus Daniels," *World's Work*, XXXII (July 1916), 281-296.

Hungerford, Edward, "California's Side of It," *Harper's Weekly*, LVII (June 7, 1913), 13.

Kinney, J. Kendrick, "A Scholar's View of Mr. Bryan," *North American Review*, CXCIX (February 1914), 219-227.

La Follette, Belle C., "The Color Line," *La Follette's Weekly*, V (August 23, 1913), 6.

La Follette, Belle C., "Color Line to Date," *La Follette's Weekly*, VI (January 24, 1914), 6-7.

La Follette, Robert M., "The American Sailor a Free Man," *La Follette's Magazine*, VIII (March 1915), 1-2.

La Follette, Robert M., "Andrew Furuseth and His Great Work," *La Follette's Magazine*, VIII (April 1915), 2.

La Follette, Robert M., "Bad Straw—Bad Bricks," *La Follette's Weekly*, V (May 3, 1913), 1, 3.

La Follette, Robert M., "A Conspiracy Against Justice," *La Follette's Weekly*, VI (May 16, 1914), 1-2.

La Follette, Robert M., "Dollar Diplomacy," *La Follette's Weekly*, V (March 29, 1913), 1.

La Follette, Robert M., "The Eight Hour Day Will Come," *La Follette's Weekly*, V (July 19, 1913), 1.

La Follette, Robert M., "Legalizing the 'Money Power,'" *La Follette's Weekly*, V (December 27, 1913), 1.

La Follette, Robert M., "'Let Us Reason Together,'" *La Follette's Weekly*, VI (January 31, 1914), 1-3.

La Follette, Robert M., "The New Cabinet," *La Follette's Weekly*, V (March 15, 1913), 1.

La Follette, Robert M., "A Raid on the Merit System," *La Follette's Weekly*, V (October 25, 1913), 1, 3.

La Follette, Robert M., "Tariff Making in the Dark," *La Follette's Weekly*, V (May 24, 1913), 1, 3.

Leupp, Francis E., "The President—and Mr. Wilson," *The Independent*, LXXVI (November 27, 1913), 392-393.

Low, A. Maurice, " 'The New Bossism,' " *Harper's Weekly*, LVII (April 19, 1913), 8.

McClintock, R. M., "What Does President Wilson Mean?" *Collier's*, LII (November 22, 1913), 23.

McGregor (A. J. McKelway), "The Attorney-General for the United States," *Harper's Weekly*, LVIII (February 7, 1914), 15.

McGregor (A. J. McKelway), "Segregation in the Departments," *Harper's Weekly*, LIX (December 26, 1914), 620-621.

McGregor (A. J. McKelway), "The Social Activities of the White House," *Harper's Weekly*, LVIII (April 25, 1914), 26-27.

Marcosson, Isaac, "Wilson and Wall Street," *Saturday Evening Post*, CLXXXVI (February 21, 1914), 3-5, 65-66.

Miller, Kelly, "The Political Plight of the Negro," *Kelly Miller's Monographic Magazine*, 1 (May 1913), 3-21.

Morawetz, Victor, "The Banking and Currency Problem and Its Solution," *Proceedings of the Academy of Political Science*, 1 (1910-1911), 343-357.

Murray, Robert H., "Huerta and the Two Wilsons," *Harper's Weekly*, LXII (March 25-April 29, 1916), 301-303, 341-342, 364-365, 402-404, 434-436, 466-469.

An Onlooker, "Woodrow Wilson the Man," *Harper's Weekly*, LVIII (January 10, 1914), 25-26.

Pettigrew, R. F., "Congress Should Stop Giving Away the People's Property," *The Public*, XIX (December 8, 1916), 1167-1168.

Phelan, James D., "The Japanese Question from a Californian Standpoint," *The Independent*, LXXIV (June 26, 1913), 1439-1440.

Pinchot, Gifford, "Open Letter to the President," *The Public*, XIX (February 11, 1916), 130-131.

Porritt, Edward, "President Wilson's First Lap," London *Westminster Gazette*, September 1, 1913.

Pullman, Raymond W., "The Seamen's Bill a Law After Twenty Years' Fight," *The Survey*, XXXIII (March 13, 1915), 645-646.

Quick, Herbert, "The Rural Credit Firing Squad," *Saturday Evening Post*, CLXXXVIII (April 15, 1916), 30.

Rowell, Chester H., "The Japanese in California," *World's Work*, XXVI (June 1913), 195-201.

Tarbell, Ida M., "A Talk with the President of the United States," *Collier's*, LVIII (October 28, 1916), 5-6.

Vanderlip, Frank A., "How to Amend the Currency Bill," *North American Review*, CXCVIII (November 1913), 698-707.

Villard, Oswald G., "The Mystery of Woodrow Wilson," *North American Review*, CCIV (September 1916), 362-372.

Villard, Oswald G., "The President and the Segregation at Washington," *North American Review*, cxcviii (December 1913), 800-807.

Warburg, Paul M., "The Owen-Glass Bill as Submitted to the Democratic Caucus, Some Criticisms and Suggestions," *North American Review*, cxcviii (October 1913), 527-555.

Willsie, Honoré, "Mr. Lane and the Public Domain," *Harper's Weekly*, lviii (August 23, 1913), 6-8.

Wilson, William B., "Labor and the Clayton Act," *Harper's Weekly*, lxii (April 29, 1916), 473-474.

Wilson, William B., "The Seamen's Act," *Harper's Weekly*, lxii (April 22, 1916), 426-427.

Witte, Edwin, "The Clayton Bill and Organized Labor," *The Survey*, xxxii (July 4, 1914), 360.

UNSIGNED CONTEMPORARY ARTICLES

"American Banking and Currency Policy," London *Economist*, lxxvii (August 30, 1913), 422-423.

"American Banking Reforms and the President Elect," London *Economist*, lxxvi (January 18, 1913), 111.

"The Bryan Scandal," New York *Nation*, xcvii (September 18, 1913), 256-257.

"The Burden of Presidential Office," *New Republic*, iii (June 19, 1915), 162-163.

"The Changed Clayton Bill," New York *Nation*, xcix (October 15, 1914), 456-457.

"Conservation in Peril," *New Republic*, vii (May 13, 1916), 32-33.

"The Currency Bill and the Banks. I—Why the Bankers Oppose the Bill and Why They Ought to Support It," *Outlook*, civ (August 9, 1913), 796.

"Dangerous Legislation," *Living Church*, liv (March 4, 1916), 624-625.

"The Deadlock in Mexico," London *Saturday Review*, cxvii (January 31, 1914), 133-134.

"The First Year of the Wilson Administration, a Review," New York *Outlook*, cvi (March 7, 1914), 523-529.

"J. C. McReynolds, the New Preceptor of the Trusts," *New York Times Magazine*, March 9, 1913.

"'Labor Is Not a Commodity,'" *New Republic*, ix (December 2, 1916), 112-114.

"Lenroot's Good Work," *La Follette's Weekly*, vi (October 24, 1914), 4.

"Machiavelli in a Mortarboard," London *Spectator*, cxii (February 7, 1914), 215-216.

"The Merit System Attacked," *The Independent*, lxxvi (October 16, 1913), 106-107.

"The Mexican Crisis," London *Outlook*, xxxii (August 30, 1913), 281-282.

"The Mexican Crisis," London *Spectator*, cxi (November 8, 1913), 745-746.

"The Mexican Imbroglio," London *Spectator*, cxi (November 15, 1913), 808-809.

"The Mexican Maze," London *Saturday Review*, cxvi (November 1, 1913), 547-548.

"The Mexican Situation," London *Spectator*, cxii (January 3, 1914), 4-5.

"Mexico and President Wilson's Message," London *Economist*, lxxvii (August 30, 1913), 406-407.

"Mexico and the United States," London *Economist*, lxxvii (August 23, 1913), 373.

"Mexico and the United States," London *Spectator*, cxi (October 18, 1913), 598-600.

"Mr. Wilson's Congress," New York *Nation*, ciii (September 14, 1916), 251-252.

"The New Trust Bills," New York *Nation*, xcviii (January 29, 1914), 100.

"The Other-Worldliness of Wilson," *New Republic*, ii (March 27, 1915), 194-195.

"Passing the Seamen's Bill," *The Public*, xviii (March 5, 1915), 225-227.

"The President and the Department of State," *The Independent*, lxxvii (March 16, 1914), 365.

"The President and Legislation," New York *Nation*, xcvi (April 10, 1913), 350.

"The President and the Negro," New York *Nation*, xcvii (August 7, 1913), 114.

"President Wilson and President Huerta," London *Outlook*, xxxii (November 15, 1913), 671-672.

"President Wilson on His Foreign Policy," *World's Work*, xxviii (October 1914), 489-490, 492-493.

"President Wilson's Mexican Dilemma," London *Saturday Review*, cxvi (August 23, 1913), 226-227.

"Race Discrimination at Washington," *The Independent*, lxxvi (November 20, 1913), 330.

"A Righteous Protest," *The Independent*, lxxv (September 4, 1913), 533-534.

"Santo Domingo and Secretary Bryan, A Poll of the Press," New York *Outlook*, cix (February 3, 1915), 267-270.

"Segregation and Democracy," *The Public*, xvi (September 5, 1913), 845.

"Senator Root on the Banking Bill," New York *Nation*, xcvii (December 18, 1913), 582-583.

"Shall 'Involuntary Servitude' Continue Under Our Laws?" *La Follette's Weekly*, v (March 29, 1913), 4.

"The Tariff in the Senate," New York *Nation*, xcvi (May 22, 1913), 514.

"The Trust Bills," New York *Outlook*, cvi (March 28, 1914), 663-664.
"Turning the Corner," *La Follette's Weekly*, vi (April 18, 1914), 1.
"Wilson and Legislation," New York *Nation*, xcvii (August 14, 1913), 136.
"Wilson and the Presidency," New York *Nation*, cii (June 22, 1916), 661.

SECONDARY WORKS AND ARTICLES

Bemis, Samuel F. *The Latin American Policy of the United States, An Historical Interpretation.* New York: Harcourt, Brace, 1943.

Blum, John M. *Joe Tumulty and the Wilson Era.* Boston: Houghton Mifflin, 1951.

Callcott, Wilfrid H. *The Caribbean Policy of the United States, 1890-1920.* Baltimore: Johns Hopkins Press, 1942.

Cline, Howard F. *The United States and Mexico.* Cambridge: Harvard University Press, 1953.

Cumberland, Charles C. *The Mexican Revolution, Genesis Under Madero.* Austin: University of Texas Press, 1952.

Curti, Merle E. "Bryan and World Peace," *Smith College Studies in History,* xvi (April-July 1931). Northampton, Mass., 1931.

Davidson, John W. "The Response of the South to Woodrow Wilson's New Freedom, 1912-1914." Unpublished Ph.D. dissertation, Yale University Library, 1954.

Faulkner, Harold U. *The Decline of Laissez-Faire, 1897-1917.* New York: Rinehart, 1951.

Freidel, Frank. *Franklin D. Roosevelt: The Apprenticeship.* Boston: Little, Brown, 1952.

Garraty, John A. *Henry Cabot Lodge, A Biography.* New York: Knopf, 1953.

Gaskill, Nelson B. *The Regulation of Competition.* New York: Harper & Brothers, 1936.

Gaus, John M., *et al. Public Administration of the United States Department of Agriculture.* Chicago: Committee on Public Administration of the Social Science Research Council, 1940.

Hohman, Elmo P. "Maritime Labour in the United States: The Seamen's Act and Its Historical Background," *International Labour Review,* xxviii (August 1938), 190-218.

Hohman, Elmo P. "Maritime Labour in the United States: Since the Seamen's Act," *International Labour Review,* xxviii (September 1938), 376-403.

Ise, John. *The United States Oil Policy.* New Haven: Yale University Press, 1926.

Jessup, Philip C. *Elihu Root,* 2 v. New York: Dodd, Mead, 1938.

Kerney, James. *The Political Education of Woodrow Wilson.* New York: Century, 1926.

La Follette, Belle C. and Fola. *Robert M. La Follette,* 2. v. New York: Macmillan, 1953.

Lawrence, David. *The True Story of Woodrow Wilson.* New York: Doran, 1924.

Li, Tien-yi. *Woodrow Wilson's China Policy, 1913-1917.* New York: University of Kansas City Press-Twayne Publishers, 1952.

Link, Arthur S. *American Epoch, A History of the United States Since the 1890's.* New York: Knopf, 1955.

Link, Arthur S. "The South and the New Freedom: An Interpretation," *American Scholar,* xx (Summer 1951), 314-324.

Link, Arthur S. *Wilson: The Road to the White House.* Princeton: Princeton University Press, 1947.

McGovern, George S. "The Colorado Coal Strike, 1913-1914." Unpublished Ph.D. dissertation, Northwestern University Library, 1953.

Notter, Harley. *The Origins of the Foreign Policy of Woodrow Wilson.* Baltimore: Johns Hopkins Press, 1937.

Porter, Eugene. "The Colorado Coal Strike of 1913: An Interpretation," *The Historian,* xii (Autumn 1949), 3-27.

Robbins, Roy M. *Our Landed Heritage: The Public Domain, 1776-1936.* Princeton: Princeton University Press, 1942.

Staples, Henry L., and Alpheus T. Mason. *The Fall of a Railroad Empire, Brandeis and the New Haven Merger Battle.* Syracuse: Syracuse University Press, 1947.

Stephenson, George M. *John Lind of Minnesota.* Minneapolis: University of Minnesota Press, 1935.

Stuart, Graham H. *The Department of State, A History of Its Organization, Procedure, and Personnel.* New York: Macmillan, 1949.

Taussig, Frank W. *The Tariff History of the United States.* New York: Putnam's, eighth edn., 1931.

Willert, Sir Arthur. *The Road to Safety, A Study in Anglo-American Relations.* London: Derek Verschoyle, 1952.

Index